P9-CRN-982

CompTIA Network+ N10-007 Cert Guide

Anthony Sequeira, CCIE No. 15626

Pearson IT Certification
800 East 96th Street
Indianapolis, Indiana 46240 USA

CompTIA Network+ N10-007 Cert Guide

Anthony Sequeira

ISBN-13: 978-0-7897-5981-8

ISBN-10: 0-7897-5981-0

Library of Congress Control Number: 2017957346

Printed in the United States of America

6 2021

Trademarks

All terms mentioned in this book that are known to be trademarks or service marks have been appropriately capitalized. Pearson IT Certification cannot attest to the accuracy of this information. Use of a term in this book should not be regarded as affecting the validity of any trademark or service mark.

Warning and Disclaimer

This book is designed to provide information about IT networking in the scope of the CompTIA Network+ exam. Every effort has been made to make this book as complete and as accurate as possible, but no warranty or fitness is implied.

The information is provided on an "as is" basis. The author shall have neither liability nor responsibility to any person or entity with respect to any loss or damages arising from the information contained in this book or from the use of the discs or programs that may accompany it.

The opinions expressed in this book belong to the author and are not necessarily those of Pearson.

Special Sales

For information about buying this title in bulk quantities, or for special sales opportunities (which may include electronic versions; custom cover designs; and content particular to your business, training goals, marketing focus, or branding interests), please contact our corporate sales department at corpsales@pearsoned.com or (800) 382-3419.

For government sales inquiries, please contact governmentsales@pearsoned.com.

For questions about sales outside the U.S., please contact intlcs@pearson.com.

Editor-in-Chief
Mark Taub

Product Line Manager
Brett Bartow

Managing Editor
Sandra Schroeder

Development Editor
Marianne Bartow

Project Editor
Mandie Frank

Copy Editor
Bart Reed

Technical Editor
Robert Fleming

Editorial Assistant
Vanessa Evans

Designer
Chuti Prasertsith

Composition
Studio Galou

Indexer
Heather McNeill

Proofreader
Paula Lowell

CompTIA.

Becoming a CompTIA Certified IT Professional is Easy

It's also the best way to reach greater professional opportunities and rewards.

Why Get CompTIA Certified?

Growing Demand

Labor estimates predict some technology fields will experience growth of over 20% by the year 2020.* CompTIA certification qualifies the skills required to join this workforce.

Higher Salaries

IT professionals with certifications on their resume command better jobs, earn higher salaries and have more doors open to new multi-industry opportunities.

Verified Strengths

91% of hiring managers indicate CompTIA certifications are valuable in validating IT expertise, making certification the best way to demonstrate your competency and knowledge to employers.**

Universal Skills

CompTIA certifications are vendor neutral—which means that certified professionals can proficiently work with an extensive variety of hardware and software found in most organizations.

Learn more about what the exam covers by reviewing the following:

- Exam objectives for key study points.
- Sample questions for a general overview of what to expect on the exam and examples of question format.
- Visit online forums, like LinkedIn, to see what other IT professionals say about CompTIA exams.

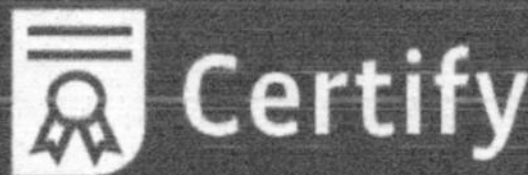

Purchase a voucher at a Pearson VUE testing center or at CompTIAstore.com.

- Register for your exam at a Pearson VUE testing center:
- Visit pearsonvue.com/CompTIA to find the closest testing center to you.
- Schedule the exam online. You will be required to enter your voucher number or provide payment information at registration.
- Take your certification exam.

Congratulations on your CompTIA certification!

- Make sure to add your certification to your resume.
- Check out the CompTIA Certification Roadmap to plan your next career move.

Learn more: **Certification.CompTIA.org/networkplus**

* Source: CompTIA 9th Annual Information Security Trends study: 500 U.S. IT and Business Executives Responsible for Security
** Source: CompTIA Employer Perceptions of IT Training and Certification

Contents at a Glance

Introduction xxviii

CHAPTER 1 Computer Network Fundamentals 3

CHAPTER 2 The OSI Reference Model 31

CHAPTER 3 Network Components 63

CHAPTER 4 Ethernet Technology 117

CHAPTER 5 IPv4 and IPv6 Addresses 153

CHAPTER 6 Routing IP Packets 205

CHAPTER 7 Wide Area Networks (WANs) 239

CHAPTER 8 Wireless Technologies 275

CHAPTER 9 Network Optimization 305

CHAPTER 10 Command-Line Tools 337

CHAPTER 11 Network Management 379

CHAPTER 12 Network Security 409

CHAPTER 13 Network Policies and Best Practices 467

CHAPTER 14 Network Troubleshooting 481

CHAPTER 15 Final Preparation 529

APPENDIX A Answers to Review Questions 537

APPENDIX B CompTIA Network+ N10-07 Cert Guide Exam Updates 547

Glossary 551

Index 585

ONLINE ELEMENTS:

APPENDIX C Memory Tables

APPENDIX D Memory Tables Answer Key

APPENDIX E Study Planner

Exam Essentials Interactive Study Guide

Key Terms Flash Cards Application

Instructional Videos

Performance-Based Exercises

CompTIA Network+ N10-007 Hands-on Lab Simulator Lite Software

Table of Contents

Introduction **xxviii**

Chapter 1 **Computer Network Fundamentals 3**

Foundation Topics 4

Defining a Network 4

The Purpose of Networks 4

Overview of Network Components 5

Networks Defined by Geography 7

LAN 7

WAN 8

WLAN 8

SAN 9

Other Categories of Networks 9

CAN 9

MAN 9

PAN 9

Networks Defined by Topology 10

Physical Versus Logical Topology 10

Bus Topology 11

Ring Topology 13

Star Topology 15

Hub-and-Spoke Topology 16

Full-Mesh Topology 17

Partial-Mesh Topology 18

Wireless Topologies 20

Ad Hoc 20

Infrastructure 20

Mesh 20

Networks Defined by Resource Location 21

Client/Server Networks 21

Peer-to-Peer Networks 22

Real-World Case Study 24

Summary 25

Exam Preparation Tasks 25

Review All the Key Topics 25
Complete Tables and Lists from Memory 26
Define Key Terms 26
Complete Chapter 1 Hands-On Lab in Network+ Simulator Lite 26
Additional Resources 26
Review Questions 26

Chapter 2 The OSI Reference Model 31

Foundation Topics 32
The Purpose of Reference Models 32
The OSI Model 33
Layer 1: The Physical Layer 35
Layer 2: The Data Link Layer 38
Media Access Control 39
Logical Link Control 40
Layer 3: The Network Layer 41
Layer 4: The Transport Layer 44
Layer 5: The Session Layer 46
Layer 6: The Presentation Layer 47
Layer 7: The Application Layer 48
The TCP/IP Stack 49
Layers of the TCP/IP Stack 49
Common Application Protocols in the TCP/IP Stack 53
Real-World Case Study 56
Summary 57
Exam Preparation Tasks 58
Review All the Key Topics 58
Complete Tables and Lists from Memory 59
Define Key Terms 59
Complete Chapter 2 Hands-On Labs in Network+ Simulator Lite 59
Additional Resources 59
Review Questions 60

Chapter 3 Network Components 63

Foundation Topics 64
Media 64

Coaxial Cable 64
Twisted-Pair Cable 66
Shielded Twisted Pair 66
Unshielded Twisted Pair 67
Plenum Versus Nonplenum Cable 70
Fiber-Optic Cable 70
Multimode Fiber 70
Single-Mode Fiber 72
Fiber Connector Polishing Styles 74
Media Converters 75
Cable Distribution 75
Wireless Technologies 77
Technologies for the Internet of Things 78
Network Infrastructure Devices 79
Hubs 80
Bridges 81
Switches 82
Multilayer Switches 89
Routers 90
Infrastructure Device Summary 91
Specialized Network Devices 91
VPN Concentrators 91
Firewalls 92
DNS Servers 93
DHCP Servers 96
Proxy Servers 98
Content Engines 99
Content Switches 100
Other Specialized Devices 101
Virtual Network Devices 101
Virtual Servers 101
Virtual Routers and Firewalls 103
Virtual Switches 103
Virtual Desktops 104

Other Virtualization Solutions 105
Cloud Computing 105
Software-Defined Networking (SDN) 107
Voice over IP Protocols and Components 107
Real-World Case Study 108
Summary 110
Exam Preparation Tasks 110
Review All the Key Topics 110
Complete Tables and Lists from Memory 111
Define Key Terms 112
Complete Chapter 3 Hands-On Labs in Network+ Simulator Lite 112
Additional Resources 112
Review Questions 113
Chapter 4 Ethernet Technology 117
Foundation Topics 118
Principles of Ethernet 118
Ethernet Origins 118
Carrier-Sense Multiple Access/Collision Detect 120
Distance and Speed Limitations 123
Ethernet Switch Features 126
Virtual LANs 126
Switch Configuration for an Access Port 128
Trunks 129
Switch Configuration for a Trunk Port 130
Spanning Tree Protocol 130
Corruption of a Switch's MAC Address Table 131
Broadcast Storms 132
STP Operation 133
Link Aggregation 136
LACP Configuration 137
Power over Ethernet 138
Port Monitoring 139
Port Mirroring Configuration 141
User Authentication 141

Management Access and Authentication 142
First-Hop Redundancy 144
Other Switch Features 145
Real-World Case Study 145
Summary 146
Exam Preparation Tasks 146
Review All the Key Topics 146
Complete Tables and Lists from Memory 147
Define Key Terms 147
Complete Chapter 4 Hands-On Labs in Network+ Simulator Lite 147
Additional Resources 148
Review Questions 148
Chapter 5 IPv4 and IPv6 Addresses 153
Foundation Topics 154
Binary Numbering 154
Principles of Binary Numbering 154
Converting a Binary Number to a Decimal Number 155
Converting a Decimal Number to a Binary Number 155
Binary Numbering Practice 157
Binary Conversion Exercise 1 157
Binary Conversion Exercise 1: Solution 158
Binary Conversion Exercise 2 158
Binary Conversion Exercise 2: Solution 158
Binary Conversion Exercise 3 159
Binary Conversion Exercise 3: Solution 159
Binary Conversion Exercise 4 160
Binary Conversion Exercise 4: Solution 160
IPv4 Addressing 161
IPv4 Address Structure 161
Classes of Addresses 163
Types of Addresses 165
Unicast 165
Broadcast 165
Multicast 166

Assigning IPv4 Addresses 166

IP Addressing Components 167

Static Configuration 168

Dynamic Configuration 172

BOOTP 173

DHCP 173

Automatic Private IP Addressing 174

Subnetting 176

Purpose of Subnetting 176

Subnet Mask Notation 177

Subnet Notation: Practice Exercise 1 178

Subnet Notation: Practice Exercise 1 Solution 178

Subnet Notation: Practice Exercise 2 179

Subnet Notation: Practice Exercise 2 Solution 179

Extending a Classful Mask 179

Borrowed Bits 179

Calculating the Number of Created Subnets 180

Calculating the Number of Available Hosts 180

Basic Subnetting Practice: Exercise 1 181

Basic Subnetting Practice: Exercise 1 Solution 181

Basic Subnetting Practice: Exercise 2 182

Basic Subnetting Practice: Exercise 2 Solution 182

Calculating New IP Address Ranges 183

Advanced Subnetting Practice: Exercise 1 186

Advanced Subnetting Practice: Exercise 1 Solution 186

Advanced Subnetting Practice: Exercise 2 187

Advanced Subnetting Practice: Exercise 2 Solution 188

Additional Practice 189

Classless Interdomain Routing 190

IP Version 6 191

Need for IPv6 191

IPv6 Address Structure 192

IPv6 Address Types 193

IPv6 Data Flows 194

Unicast 194
Multicast 195
Anycast 195
Real-World Case Study 196
Summary 197
Exam Preparation Tasks 197
Review All the Key Topics 197
Complete Tables and Lists from Memory 198
Define Key Terms 199
Complete Chapter 5 Hands-On Labs in Network+ Simulator Lite 199
Additional Resources 199
Review Questions 200
Chapter 6 Routing IP Packets 205
Foundation Topics 206
Basic Routing Processes 206
Sources of Routing Information 209
Directly Connected Routes 209
Static Routes 210
Dynamic Routing Protocols 211
Routing Protocol Characteristics 213
Believability of a Route 214
Metrics 214
Interior Versus Exterior Gateway Protocols 215
Route Advertisement Method 215
Distance Vector 216
Link State 218
Routing Protocol Examples 218
Address Translation 220
NAT 220
PAT 222
Multicast Routing 224
IGMP 224
PIM 226

PIM-DM 227
PIM-SM 229
Real-World Case Study 230
Summary 231
Exam Preparation Tasks 232
Review All the Key Topics 232
Complete Tables and Lists from Memory 233
Define Key Terms 233
Complete Chapter 6 Hands-On Lab in Network+ Simulator Lite 233
Additional Resources 233
Review Questions 234
Chapter 7 Wide Area Networks (WANs) 239
Foundation Topics 240
WAN Properties 240
WAN Connection Types 240
WAN Data Rates 242
WAN Media Types 243
Physical Media 243
Wireless Media 244
WAN Technologies 245
Dedicated Leased Line 246
T1 246
E1 247
T3 247
E3 247
CSU/DSU 248
Metro Ethernet 248
Point-to-Point Protocol 249
Point-to-Point Protocol over Ethernet 250
Microsoft RRAS 251
Digital Subscriber Line 252
Cable Modem 254
Synchronous Optical Network 255

Satellite 257
Plain Old Telephone Service 258
Integrated Services Digital Network 260
Frame Relay 262
SIP Trunk 264
Asynchronous Transfer Mode 264
Multiprotocol Label Switching 266
Overlay Networks 268
Real-World Case Study 268
Summary 269
Exam Preparation Tasks 270
Review All the Key Topics 270
Complete Tables and Lists from Memory 270
Define Key Terms 271
Complete Chapter 7 Hands-On Lab in Network+ Simulator Lite 271
Additional Resources 271
Review Questions 271
Chapter 8 Wireless Technologies 275
Foundation Topics 276
Introducing Wireless LANs 276
WLAN Concepts and Components 276
Wireless Routers 276
Wireless Access Point 277
Antennas 278
Frequencies and Channels 281
CSMA/CA 283
Transmission Methods 284
WLAN Standards 285
802.11a 285
802.11b 285
802.11g 285
802.11n 285
802.11ac 286
802.11x Standard Summary 286

Deploying Wireless LANs 287
Types of WLANs 287
IBSS 287
BSS 288
ESS 288
Mesh Topology 289
Sources of Interference 289
Wireless AP Placement 291
Securing Wireless LANs 292
Security Issues 292
Approaches to WLAN Security 294
Security Standards 295
WEP 296
WPA 296
WPA2 297
Additional Wireless Options 297
Real-World Case Study 298
Summary 298
Exam Preparation Tasks 299
Review All the Key Topics 299
Complete Tables and Lists from Memory 299
Define Key Terms 300
Complete Chapter 8 Hands-On Lab in Network+ Simulator Lite 300
Additional Resources 300
Review Questions 300
Chapter 9 Network Optimization 305
Foundation Topics 306
High Availability 306
High-Availability Measurement 306
Fault-Tolerant Network Design 307
Hardware Redundancy 308
Layer 3 Redundancy 309
Design Considerations for High-Availability Networks 310
High-Availability Best Practices 311

Content Caching 312
Load Balancing 312
Hardware Redundancy 313
QoS Technologies 313
Introduction to QoS 314
QoS Configuration Steps 315
QoS Components 316
QoS Mechanisms 317
Classification 318
Marking 318
Congestion Management 319
Congestion Avoidance 319
Policing and Shaping 320
Link Efficiency 322
Case Study: SOHO Network Design 323
Case Study Scenario 323
Suggested Solution 325
IP Addressing 325
Layer 1 Media 326
Layer 2 Devices 327
Layer 3 Devices 327
Wireless Design 328
Environmental Factors 329
Cost Savings Versus Performance 329
Topology 329
Real-World Case Study 330
Summary 331
Exam Preparation Tasks 331
Review All the Key Topics 331
Complete Tables and Lists from Memory 332
Define Key Terms 332
Complete Chapter 9 Hands-On Lab in Network+ Simulator Lite 332
Additional Resources 333
Review Questions 333

Chapter 10 Command-Line Tools 337

Foundation Topics 338

Windows Commands 338

arp 338

ipconfig 340

nbtstat 343

netstat 346

nslookup 348

ping 350

ping with IPv6 352

route 352

tracert 356

tracert with IPv6 358

PathPing 358

UNIX Commands 358

arp 360

dig and nslookup 362

host 363

ifconfig 363

iptables 364

nmap 365

tcpdump 365

traceroute 365

traceroute for IPv6 366

netstat 366

ping 368

Real-World Case Study 371

Summary 371

Exam Preparation Tasks 371

Review All the Key Topics 371

Complete Tables and Lists from Memory 372

Define Key Terms 373

Complete Chapter 10 Hands-On Lab in Network+ Simulator Lite 373

Additional Resources 373

Review Questions 374

Chapter 11 Network Management 379

Foundation Topics 380

Maintenance Tools 380

Bit-Error Rate Tester 380

Butt Set 381

Cable Certifier 381

Cable Tester 382

Connectivity Software 382

Crimper 383

Electrostatic Discharge Wrist Strap 383

Environmental Monitor 384

Loopback Plug 385

Multimeter 385

Protocol Analyzer 386

Wi-Fi Analyzer 387

Looking-Glass Sites 387

Speed Test Sites 388

Punch-Down Tool 388

Throughput Tester 388

Time Domain Reflectometer and Optical Time Domain Reflectometer 389

Toner Probe 390

Spectrum Analyzer 390

Network Documentation 391

Monitoring Resources and Reports 392

SNMP 392

Syslog 395

Logs 398

Application Logs 398

Security Logs 399

System Logs 399

Remote Access Methods 400

Real-World Case Study 401

Summary 402
Exam Preparation Tasks 402
Review All the Key Topics 402
Complete Tables and Lists from Memory 403
Define Key Terms 403
Complete Chapter 11 Hands-On Lab in Network+ Simulator Lite 403
Additional Resources 404
Review Questions 404
Chapter 12 Network Security 409
Foundation Topics 410
Security Fundamentals 410
Network Security Goals 410
Confidentiality 410
Symmetric Encryption 411
Asymmetric Encryption 412
Integrity 414
Availability 415
Categories of Network Attacks 415
Confidentiality Attacks 415
Integrity Attacks 419
Availability Attacks 422
Logic Bomb 422
Wireless Attacks 422
Denial of Service 422
Distributed Denial of Service 423
TCP SYN Flood 423
Buffer Overflow 424
ICMP Attacks 424
Electrical Disturbances 425
Attacks on a System's Physical Environment 426
Defending Against Attacks 427
User Training 427
Patching 428
Security Policies 429

Governing Policy 430
Technical Policies 431
End-User Policies 431
More Detailed Documents 431
Incident Response 432
Vulnerability Scanners 433
Nessus 434
Nmap 434
Honey Pots and Honey Nets 435
Access Control Lists 436
Physical Security Devices 437
Network Device Hardening 438
Layer 2 Protections 439
Remote-Access Security 439
Firewalls 442
Firewall Types 442
Firewall Inspection Types 443
Packet-Filtering Firewall 443
Stateful Firewall 444
Firewall Zones 445
Unified Threat Management Firewalls 446
Virtual Private Networks 447
Overview of IPSec with IKEv1 449
IKE Modes and Phases 449
Authentication Header and Encapsulating Security Payload 451
The Five Steps in Setting Up and Tearing Down an IPSec Site-to-Site VPN Using IKEv1 452
Other VPN Technologies 454
Intrusion Detection and Prevention 454
IDS Versus IPS 455
IDS and IPS Device Categories 456
Detection Methods 456
Signature-Based Detection 456
Policy-Based Detection 457
Anomaly-Based Detection 457

Deploying Network-Based and Host-Based Solutions 458

Real-World Case Study 459

Summary 460

Exam Preparation Tasks 461

Review All the Key Topics 461

Complete Tables and Lists from Memory 462

Define Key Terms 462

Complete Chapter 12 Hands-On Lab in Network+ Simulator Lite 463

Additional Resources 463

Review Questions 463

Chapter 13 Network Policies and Best Practices 467

Foundation Topics 468

Policies 468

Password Policy 468

Data Loss Prevention 469

Remote-Access Policies 470

Incident Response Policies 470

Bring Your Own Device (BYOD) 471

Acceptable Use Policy (AUP) 471

Safety Procedures 472

Best Practices 472

Privileged User Agreement (PUA) 472

On-boarding/Off-boarding Procedures 473

Licensing Restrictions 473

International Export Controls 474

Non-Disclosure Agreement (NDA) 474

System Life Cycle 474

Real-World Case Study 475

Summary 475

Exam Preparation Tasks 476

Review All the Key Topics 476

Complete Tables and Lists from Memory 476

Define Key Terms 476

Complete Chapter 13 Hands-On Lab in Network+ Simulator Lite 477
Additional Resources 477
Review Questions 477
Chapter 14 Network Troubleshooting 481
Foundation Topics 482
Troubleshooting Basics 482
Troubleshooting Fundamentals 482
Structured Troubleshooting Methodology 484
Physical Layer Troubleshooting 487
Physical Layer Troubleshooting: Scenario 488
Physical Layer Troubleshooting: Solution 489
Data Link Layer Troubleshooting 490
Data Link Layer Troubleshooting: Scenario 491
Data Link Layer Troubleshooting: Solution 491
Network Layer Troubleshooting 492
Layer 3 Data Structures 492
Common Layer 3 Troubleshooting Issues 494
Network Layer Troubleshooting: Scenario 496
Network Layer Troubleshooting: Solution 496
Wireless Troubleshooting 497
Wireless Network Troubleshooting: Scenario 499
Wireless Network Troubleshooting: Solution 500
Specialized Networks 500
Real-World Case Study 501
Troubleshooting Scenarios 501
Summary 522
Exam Preparation Tasks 523
Review All the Key Topics 523
Complete Tables and Lists from Memory 523
Define Key Terms 524
Complete Chapter 14 Hands-On Lab in Network+ Simulator Lite 524
Additional Resources 524
Review Questions 524

Chapter 15 Final Preparation 529

Tools for Final Preparation 529

Video Training 530

Memory Tables 530

Simulations and Performance-Based Exercises 531

End-of-Chapter Review Tools 531

Suggested Plan for Final Review and Study 531

Strategies for Taking the Exam 533

Summary 535

Appendix A Answers to Review Questions 537

Appendix B CompTIA Network+ N10-07 Cert Guide Exam Updates 547

Always Get the Latest at the Book's Product Page 547

Technical Content 548

Glossary 551

Index 585

ONLINE ELEMENTS:

Appendix C Memory Tables

Appendix D Memory Tables Answer Key

Appendix E Study Planner

Exam Essentials Interactive Study Guide

Key Terms Flash Cards Application

Instructional Videos

Performance-Based Exercises

CompTIA Network+ N10-007 Hands-on Lab Simulator Lite Software

About the Author

Anthony Sequeira began his IT career in 1994 with IBM in Tampa, Florida. He quickly formed his own computer consultancy, Computer Solutions, and then discovered his true passion—teaching and writing about networking technologies. Anthony has lectured to massive audiences around the world while working for Mastering Computers. Anthony has never been happier in his career than he is now as a trainer for CBT Nuggets. He is an avid tennis player, a private pilot, a semi-professional poker player, and loves anything at all to do with technology.

About the Technical Reviewers

Rob Fleming is a Cisco Certified Systems Instructor (CCSI #35229) and is a trainer for Boson, Nterone, and other learning partners. He has been an IT enthusiast since the mid-1980s, has more than 10 years of experience as a network administrator, and has a bachelor's degree in Management Information Systems. Rob has worked for all sizes of companies, from small IT startups to Fortune 100 companies. He has written lab guides and built environments for several networking courses, but his true passion is in instruction, where he enjoys transferring knowledge to students. When not training or studying for new certifications in security and wireless, Rob can be found attending IT meet-ups and conferences, programming on Raspberry PIs, or nerding out with fellow IT enthusiasts on a variety of new technologies.

Dedication

This book is dedicated to the amazing Keith Barker. Keith is a true inspiration and an incredible friend.

Acknowledgments

It is rare for it to go well when you work with your friends, especially in what could be a stressful environment of constant deadlines. Fortunately, I work with my friends Brett and Marianne Bartow. Thank you so much for your friendship—and PATIENCE!

Thanks also to my dear friend Kevin Wallace. He is a wonderful friend, and crazy talented.

Check out all of his great training products at https://kwallaceccie.mykajabi.com.

Command Syntax Conventions

The conventions used to present command syntax in this book are the same conventions used in Cisco's Command Reference. The Command Reference describes these conventions as follows:

- **Boldface** indicates commands and keywords that are entered literally as shown. In actual configuration examples and output (not general command syntax), boldface indicates commands that are manually input by the user (such as a **show** command).
- *Italics* indicate arguments for which you supply actual values.
- Vertical bars (|) separate alternative, mutually exclusive elements.
- Square brackets [ ] indicate optional elements.
- Braces { } indicate a required choice.
- Braces within brackets [{ }] indicate a required choice within an optional element.

We Want to Hear from You!

As the reader of this book, *you* are our most important critic and commentator. We value your opinion and want to know what we're doing right, what we could do better, what areas you'd like to see us publish in, and any other words of wisdom you're willing to pass our way.

We welcome your comments. You can email or write to let us know what you did or didn't like about this book—as well as what we can do to make our books better.

Please note that we cannot help you with technical problems related to the topic of this book.

When you write, please be sure to include this book's title and author as well as your name and email address. We will carefully review your comments and share them with the author and editors who worked on the book.

Email: feedback@pearsonitcertification.com

Mail: Pearson IT Certification
ATTN: Reader Feedback
800 East 96th Street
Indianapolis, IN 46240 USA

Reader Services

Register your copy of *CompTIA Network+ N10-007 Cert Guide* at www.pearsonitcertification.com for convenient access to downloads, updates, and corrections as they become available. To start the registration process, go to www.pearsonitcertification.com/register and log in or create an account*. Enter the product ISBN 9780789759818 and click Submit. When the process is complete, you will find any available bonus content under Registered Products.

*Be sure to check the box that you would like to hear from us to receive exclusive discounts on future editions of this product.

Introduction

The CompTIA Network+ certification is a popular certification for those entering the computer networking field. Although many vendor-specific networking certifications are popular in the industry, the CompTIA Network+ certification is unique in that it is vendor neutral. The CompTIA Network+ certification often acts as a stepping-stone to more specialized and vendor-specific certifications, such as those offered by Cisco Systems.

In CompTIA Network+, the topics are mostly generic in that they can apply to networking equipment regardless of vendor. Although the CompTIA Network+ is vendor neutral, network software and systems are implemented by multiple independent vendors. In that light, several of the exercises, examples, and simulations in this book include using a vendor's configuration and technology, such as Microsoft Windows operating systems or Cisco Systems routers and switches. More detailed training for a specific vendor's software and hardware can be found in books and training specific to that vendor.

Who Should Read This Book?

This book was written with two audiences in mind—those who want to learn all they can about networking technology, and those who want to pass the CompTIA Network+ exam. I think that both groups are going to be very impressed with the breadth of technologies this book details. Although it would be impossible to cover every topic found in networking today, this book manages to cover all the massive areas that make networking the exciting field so many want to learn.

Readers will range from people who are attempting to attain a position in the IT field to people who want to keep their skills sharp or perhaps retain their job because of a company policy that mandates they take the new exams. This book is also for the reader who wants to acquire additional certifications beyond the Network+ certification (for example, the Cisco Certified Network Associate [CCNA] certification and beyond). The book is designed in such a way to offer easy transition to future certification studies.

Resources

This book comes with a wealth of digital resources to help you review, practice, and assess your knowledge. The end of each chapter contains a review section that references several of these tools, and you should be sure to use them as you complete each chapter to help reinforce the knowledge you are learning. You can use them again after you finish the book to help you review and make sure you are fully prepared for the exam.

Here's a list of resources available on the companion website:

- Interactive glossary flash card application
- Interactive exam essentials appendix
- Performance-based exercises
- CompTIA Network+ Hands-on Lab Simulator Lite Software for exam N10-007
- The Pearson Test Prep practice test software
- Video training on key exam topics
- Memory Table review exercises and answer keys
- A study planner tool
- Instructions to redeem your Network+ certification exam voucher, providing a 10% discount on the exam

To access the companion website, follow these steps:

Step 1. Go to http://www.pearsonitcertification.com/register.

Step 2. Either log in to your account (if you have an existing account already) or create a new account.

Step 3. Enter the ISBN of your book (9780789759818) and click Submit.

Step 4. Answer the challenge questions to validate your purchase.

Step 5. In your account page, click the **Registered Products** tab and then click the **Access Bonus Content** link.

Pearson Test Prep Practice Test Software

The companion website that accompanies this book includes the Pearson Test Prep practice test engine (software that displays and grades a set of exam-realistic practice test questions). Using the Pearson Test Prep practice test engine, you can either study by going through the questions in study mode or take a simulated CompTIA Network+ exam that mimics real exam conditions. The software also has a flash card mode that allows you to challenge yourself to answer the questions without seeing the multiple-choice answers.

The Pearson Test Prep software is available both online and as a Windows desktop application that you can run offline. The online version can be accessed at www.pearsontestprep.com. This version can be used on any device that has an Internet connection, including desktop computers, laptop computers, tablets, and smartphones. It is optimized for viewing on screens as small as a standard iPhone screen. The desktop application can be downloaded and installed from the companion website.

NOTE The desktop application is a Windows-based application, so it is only designed to run on Windows. Although it can be run on other operating systems using a Windows emulator, other operating systems are not officially supported on the desktop version. If you are using an OS other than Windows, you may want to consider using the online version instead.

Accessing the test engine is a two-step process. The first step is to either install the software on your desktop or access the online version website. However, the practice exam (that is, the database of CompTIA Network+ exam questions) is not available to you until you register the unique access code that accompanies your book.

NOTE The cardboard sleeve in the back of the physical book includes a piece of paper. The paper lists the *access code* for the practice exam associated with this book. Make sure you keep the access code even after you have registered your exam, as you may need to refer to it later. Also, on the opposite side of the paper from the activation code is a unique, one-time-use coupon code for the purchase of the *CompTIA Network+ Cert Guide, Premium Edition eBook and Practice Test* product, a $40 value!

Installing the Pearson Test Prep Software

If you choose to use the Windows desktop version of the practice test software, you will need to download the installers from the companion website.

The software-installation process is similar to other wizard-based installation processes. If you have already installed the Pearson Test Prep practice test software from another Pearson product, you do not need to reinstall the software. Just launch the software on your desktop and proceed to activate the practice exam from this book by using the activation code included in sleeve in the back of the book. The following steps outline the installation process:

Step 1. Download the software to your computer from the companion website.

Step 2. Extract all files from the .zip file you downloaded.

Step 3. Launch the installer from the extracted files folder.

Step 4. Respond to the wizard-based prompts.

The installation process gives you the option to activate your exam with the activation code supplied on the paper in the back of book sleeve. This process requires that you establish a Pearson website login. You need this login to activate the exam, so please register when prompted. If you already have a Pearson website login, you do not need to register again; just use your existing login.

Activating and Downloading the Practice Exam

The second step to accessing your practice exam product is to activate the product using the unique access code found in the back of book sleeve. You must follow this step regardless of which version of the product you are using—the online version or the Windows desktop version. The following steps walk you through how to activate your exam on each platform.

Windows Desktop Version:

1. Start the Pearson Test Prep Practice Test software from the Windows Start menu or from your desktop shortcut icon.
2. To activate and download the exam associated with this book, from the My Products or Tools tab, click the **Activate** button.
3. At the next screen, enter the *access code* from the paper inside the cardboard sleeve in the back of the book. Once this is entered, click the **Activate** button.
4. The activation process will download the practice exam. Click **Next** and then click **Finish**.

Online Version:

1. From a device with an active Internet connection, open your browser of choice and go to the website www.pearsontestprep.com.
2. Select Pearson IT Certification under product group.

3. Enter the email address and password associated with your account and click **Login**.
4. In the middle of the screen, click the **Activate New Product** button.
5. Enter the access code from the paper inside the cardboard sleeve in the back of the book and click the **Activate** button.

After the activation process is complete, the My Products tab should list your new exam. If you do not see the exam, make sure that you selected the My Products tab on the menu. At this point, the software and practice exam are ready to use. Simply select the exam and click the **Exams** button.

To update an exam that you have already activated and downloaded, simply select the **Tools** tab and click the **Update Products** button. Updating your exams ensures that you have the latest changes and updates to the exam data.

If you want to check for updates to the Pearson Cert Practice Test exam engine software, simply select the **Tools** tab and click the **Update Application** button. This ensures that you are running the latest version of the exam engine.

NOTE The online version always contains the latest updates to the exam questions, so there is never a need to update when you're using that version.

Activating Other Exams

The exam-software installation process and the registration process both only occur once. Then, for each new exam, only a few steps are required. For example, if you buy another new Pearson IT Certification Cert Guide, extract the activation code from the sleeve in the back of that book. From there, all you have to do is start the exam engine (if it's not still up and running) and perform the activation steps from the previous list.

Premium Edition

In addition to the free practice exam provided with the book, you can purchase additional exams with expanded functionality directly from Pearson IT Certification. The Premium Edition eBook and Practice Test for this title contains an additional two full practice exams and an eBook (in PDF, EPUB, and Kindle formats). Also, the Premium Edition title has remediation for each question that links to the specific part of the eBook that relates to that question.

For those who purchased the print version of this title, you can purchase the Premium Edition at a deep discount. You'll find a coupon code in the back of book sleeve that contains a one-time-use code and instructions for where you can purchase the Premium Edition.

To view the Premium Edition product page, go to the following website: http://www.pearsonitcertification.com/title/9780134861012.

Goals and Methods

The goal of this book is to assist you in learning and understanding the technologies covered in the Network+ N10-007 blueprint from CompTIA. This also allows you to demonstrate that knowledge by passing the N10-007 version of the CompTIA Network+ exam.

To aid you in mastering and understanding the Network+ certification objectives, this book uses the following methods:

- **Opening topics list:** This defines the topics that are covered in the chapter.
- **Foundation topics:** At the heart of a chapter, this section explains the topics from a hands-on and a theory-based standpoint. This includes in-depth descriptions, tables, and figures that build your knowledge so that you can pass the N10-007 exam. The chapters are each broken into multiple sections.
- **Key topics:** This section indicates important figures, tables, and lists of information that you need to know for the exam. They are sprinkled throughout each chapter and are summarized in table format at the end of each chapter.
- **Memory tables:** You can find these on the book's companion website within Appendixes C and D. Use them to help you memorize important information.
- **Key terms:** Key terms without definitions are listed at the end of each chapter. Write down the definition of each term, and check your work against the complete key terms in the Glossary. On the companion website, you will find a flash card application with all the glossary terms separated by chapter, so feel free to use that to study key terms as well.
- **Exercises:** This book comes with 40 performance-based practice exercises that are designed to help you prepare for the hands-on portion of the Network+ exam. These exercises are available on the companion website. Make sure you do the exercises as you complete each chapter and again when you have completed the book and are doing your final preparation.

- **Hands-on Labs:** These include matching, drag and drop, and simulations. These hands-on exercises are an important part of this book. In addition to reading this book, you should go through all the exercises included with the book. These interactive hands-on exercises provide examples, additional information, and insight about a vendor's implementation of the technologies. To perform the labs, simply install the CompTIA Network+ N10-007 Hands-on Lab Simulator Lite software. This software is a Windows and Mac desktop application. You should be sure to install the software prior to reading the book, as each chapter will indicate what labs you should perform. To install the software, follow these steps:

  Step 1. Go to the companion website for the book (see the "Resources" section for how to access the companion website).

  Step 2. Click the link to download the CompTIA Network+ N10-007 Hands-on Lab Simulator Lite software.

  Step 3. Once you have downloaded the software to your computer, extract all the files from the .zip file.

  Step 4. Launch the installer from the extracted files.

  Step 5. Respond to the wizard-based prompts.

- **Practice Exams:** This book comes complete with several full-length practice exams available to you in the Pearson Test Prep practice test software, which you can download and install from the companion website. The Pearson Test Prep software is also available to you online at www.PearsonTestPrep.com. You can access both the online and desktop versions using the access code printed on the card in the sleeve in the back of this book. Be sure to run through the questions in Exam Bank 1 as you complete each chapter in study mode. When you have completed the book, take a full practice test using Exam Bank 2 questions in practice exam mode to test your exam readiness.

- **Exam Essentials:** This book includes an Exam Essentials appendix that summaries the key points from every chapter. This review tool is available in print and as an interactive PDF on the companion website. Review these essential exam facts after each chapter and again when you have completed the book. This makes a great review summary that you can mark up as you review and master each concept.

For current information about the CompTIA Network+ certification exam, visit https://certification.comptia.org/certifications/network.

Strategies for Exam Preparation

This book comes with a study planner tool on the companion website. This spreadsheet helps you keep track of the activities you need to perform in each chapter and helps you organize your exam preparation tasks. As you read the chapters in this book, jot down notes with key concepts or configurations in the study planner. Each chapter ends with a summary and series of exam preparation tasks to help you reinforce what you learned. These tasks include review exercises such as reviewing key topics, completing memory tables, defining key terms, answering review questions, performing hands-on labs and exercises, and so on. Make sure you perform these tasks as you complete each chapter to improve your retention of the material and record your progress in the study planner.

The book concludes with a "Final Preparation" chapter that offers you guidance on your final exam preparation and provides you with some helpful exam advice. Make sure you read over that chapter to help you assess your exam readiness and identify areas where you need to focus your review.

Make sure you complete all the performance-based question exercises and hands-on labs associated with this book. The exercises and labs are organized by chapter, making it easy to perform them after you complete each section. These exercises will reinforce what you have learned, offer examples of some popular vendors' methods for implementing networking technologies, and provide additional information to assist you in building real-world skills and preparing you for the certification exam.

Download the current exam objectives by submitting a form on the following web page: http://certification.comptia.org/training/testingcenters/examobjectives.aspx.

Use the practice exam, which is included on this book's companion website. As you work through the practice exam, use the practice test software reporting features to note the areas where you lack confidence and then review those concepts. After you review these areas, work through the practice exam a second time and rate your skills. Keep in mind that the more you work through the practice exam, the more familiar the questions become, and the practice exam becomes a less-accurate judge of your skills.

After you work through the practice exam a second time and feel confident with your skills, schedule the real CompTIA Network+ exam (N10-007).

CompTIA Network+ Exam Topics

Table I-1 lists general exam topics (*objectives*) and specific topics under each general topic (*subobjectives*) for the CompTIA Network+ N10-007 exam. This table lists the primary chapter in which each exam topic is covered. Note that many objectives and subobjectives are interrelated and are addressed in multiple chapters within the book itself.

Table I-1 CompTIA Network+ Exam Topics

Chapter	N10-007 Exam Objective	N10-007 Exam Subobjective
1 Computer Network Fundamentals	1.0 Networking Concepts	1.5 Compare and contrast the characteristics of network topologies, types, and technologies
2 The OSI Reference Model	1.0 Networking Concepts	1.1 Explain the purposes and uses of ports and protocols 1.2 Explain devices, applications, protocols, and services at their appropriate OSI layers
3 Network Components	1.0 Networking Concepts 2.0 Infrastructure	1.7 Summarize cloud concepts and their purposes 1.8 Explain the functions of network services 2.1 Given a scenario, deploy the appropriate cabling solution 2.2 Given a scenario, determine the appropriate placement of networking devices on a network and install/configure them 2.3 Explain the purposes and use cases for advanced networking devices 2.4 Explain the purposes of virtualization and network storage technologies
4 Ethernet Technology	1.0 Networking Concepts	1.3 Explain the concepts and characteristics of routing and switching
5 IPv4 and IPv6 Addresses	1.0 Networking Concepts	1.4 Given a scenario, configure the appropriate IP addressing components
6 Routing IP Packets	1.0 Networking Concepts	1.3 Explain the concepts and characteristics of routing and switching
7 Wide Area Networks (WANs)	2.0 Infrastructure	2.5 Compare and contrast WAN technologies

Chapter	N10-007 Exam Objective	N10-007 Exam Subobjective
8 Wireless Technologies	1.0 Networking Concepts	1.6 Given a scenario, implement the appropriate wireless technologies and configurations
	4.0 Network Security	4.3 Given a scenario, secure a basic wireless network
9 Network Optimization	3.0 Network Operations	3.2 Compare and contrast business continuity and disaster recovery concepts
10 Command-Line Tools	5.0 Network Troubleshooting	5.2 Given a scenario, use the appropriate tool
11 Network Management	3.0 Network Operations	3.1 Given a scenario, use appropriate documentation and diagrams to manage the network
		3.3 Explain common scanning, monitoring, and patching processes and summarize their expected outputs
		3.4 Given a scenario, use remote access methods
12 Network Security	4.0 Network Security	4.1 Summarize the purposes of physical security devices
		4.2 Explain authentication and access controls
		4.4 Summarize common networking attacks
		4.5 Given a scenario, implement network device hardening
		4.6 Explain common mitigation techniques and their purposes
13 Network Policies and Best Practices	3.0 Network Operations	3.5 Identify policies and best practices
14 Network Troubleshooting	5.0 Network Troubleshooting and Tools	5.1 Explain the network troubleshooting methodology
		5.3 Given a scenario, troubleshoot common wired connectivity and performance issues
		5.4 Given a scenario, troubleshoot common wireless connectivity and performance issues
		5.5 Given a scenario, troubleshoot common network service issues

How This Book Is Organized

Although this book could be read cover to cover, it is designed to be flexible and allow you to easily move between chapters and sections of chapters to cover just the material that you need more work with. However, if you do intend to read all the chapters, the order in the book is an excellent sequence to use:

- **Chapter 1: Computer Network Fundamentals**—This chapter covers what a network does, what components tend to make up a network, and how we like to define different networks.
- **Chapter 2: The OSI Reference Model**—The OSI model is an extremely powerful guide we can use as we design, implement, and troubleshoot networks.
- **Chapter 3: Network Components**—This chapter drills deep into the different devices we find in the network today as well as the media that connect these devices.
- **Chapter 4: Ethernet Technology**—Speaking of media in the network, this chapter expands on one of the most popular categories of network media—Ethernet.
- **Chapter 5: IPv4 and IPv6 Addresses**—Addressing of systems is critical in networks, and this chapter covers the addressing used in IPv4 and IPv6.
- **Chapter 6: Routing IP Packets**—Moving packets from one network to another is the job of the router. This chapter ensures you are well versed in the many technologies that operate in this category.
- **Chapter 7: Wide Area Networks (WANs)**—Moving packets across large geographic distances is the job of the WAN, and this chapter breaks down the technologies found in this area.
- **Chapter 8: Wireless Technologies**—Wires, who needs wires? Wireless networking is here to stay. This chapter provides you with the details and even includes such important topics as security and emerging technologies.
- **Chapter 9: Network Optimization**—Making the network more reliable is the focus of this chapter.
- **Chapter 10: Command-Line Tools**—Fortunately, a tremendous number of valuable tools can assist you in network troubleshooting. Some of these tools are not graphical in nature and you use them at a command line.
- **Chapter 11: Network Management**—This chapter covers network management in general and includes a look at more valuable tools.

- **Chapter 12: Network Security**—Now more than ever, our networks are under attack. This chapter prepares you for the many challenges ahead in this area.
- **Chapter 13: Network Policies and Best Practices**—Many excellent policies and plenty of best practices can assist you in your networking career. This chapter covers some of the most important ones.
- **Chapter 14: Network Troubleshooting**—Whereas other chapters just touch on network troubleshooting, this chapter makes it the focus. Here, you get a nice overall methodology you can use, as well as specifics on tools and techniques.
- **Chapter 15: Final Preparation**—This chapter provides guidance on how to make sure you are as prepared as possible for the big exam (should you choose to take it on).

After completion of this chapter, you will be able to answer the following questions:

- What is the purpose of a network?
- What are some examples of network components?
- How are networks defined by geography?
- How are networks defined by topology?
- How are networks defined by resource location?

CHAPTER 1

Computer Network Fundamentals

What comes to mind when you think of a computer network? Is it the Internet? Is it email? Is it the wireless connection that lets you print to your printer from your laptop? Is it the smart thermostat and lights of your home?

Whatever your current perception of a computer network, this book helps you gain a deep appreciation and understanding of networked computing. Be aware that although you think of computer networks as interconnecting computers, today's computer networks interconnect a variety of devices in addition to just computers. Examples include game consoles, video-surveillance devices, IP-based telephones, tablets, and smartphones. Therefore, throughout this book, think of the term *computer network* as being synonymous with the more generic term *network*, because these terms are used interchangeably.

In this chapter, the goal is to acquaint you with the purpose of a network and help you categorize a given network based on criteria such as geography, topology, and the location of the network's resources. An implied goal of this and all other chapters in this book is to prepare you to successfully pass the CompTIA Network+ exam, which is a cornerstone exam in the information technology (IT) industry.

Foundation Topics

Defining a Network

In the movie *Field of Dreams*, you heard, "If you build it, they will come." That statement most certainly applies to the evolution of network-based services seen in modern-day networks. Computer networks are no longer relegated to allowing a group of computers to access a common set of files stored on a computer chosen as a *file server*. Instead, with the building of high-speed, highly redundant networks, network architects are seeing the wisdom of placing a variety of traffic types on a single network. Examples include voice and video, in addition to data. As you will learn in this chapter, the Internet of Things (IoT) means that just about everything wants to join your network, from the lights in your home to many of your household appliances!

One could argue that a network is the sum of its parts. So, as you begin your study of networking, you should start to grasp a basic understanding of fundamental networking components. These components include such entities as the client, server, hub, switch, and router, as well as the media used to interconnect these devices.

The Purpose of Networks

At its essence, a network's purpose is to make connections. These connections might be between a PC and a printer or between a laptop and the Internet, as just a couple of examples. However, the true value of a network comes from the traffic flowing over those connections. Consider a sampling of applications that can travel over a network's connections:

- File sharing between two computers
- Video chatting between computers located in different parts of the world
- Surfing the Web (for example, to use social media sites, watch streaming video, listen to an Internet radio station, or do research for a school term paper)
- Instant messaging (IM) between computers with IM software installed
- Email
- Voice over IP (VoIP), to replace traditional telephony systems

A term given to a network transporting multiple types of traffic (for example, voice, video, and data) is *converged network*. A converged network might offer significant cost savings to organizations that previously supported separate network infrastructures for voice, data, and video traffic. This convergence also potentially reduces staffing costs, because only a single network needs to be supported, rather than separate networks for separate traffic types.

Overview of Network Components

Designing, installing, administering, and troubleshooting a network uses your ability to recognize various network components and their functions. Although this is the focus of Chapter 3, "Network Components," before you continue much further, you need a basic working knowledge of how individual components come together to form a functioning network.

The components to consider for now are the client, server, hub, switch, router, media, and wide area network (WAN) link. As a reference for this discussion, consider Figure 1-1.

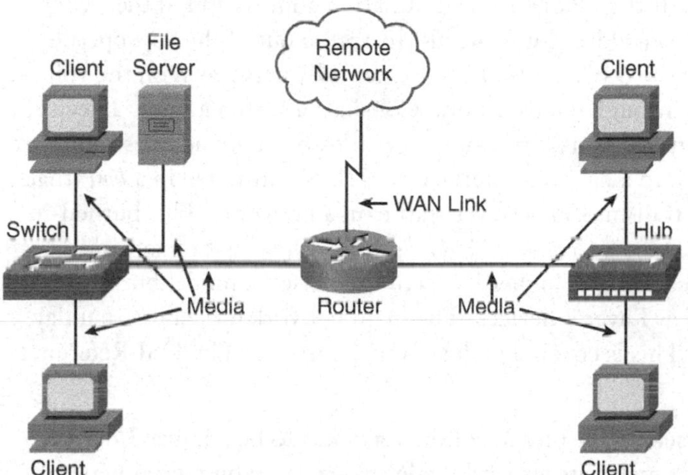

Figure 1-1 Sample Computer Network

The following list describes the network components depicted in Figure 1-1 and the functions they serve:

- **Client:** The term *client* defines the device an end user uses to access a network. This device might be a workstation, laptop, smartphone with wireless capabilities, or a variety of other end-user terminal devices.
- **Server:** A *server*, as the name suggests, serves up resources to a network. These resources might include email access as given by an email server, web pages as offered by a web server, or files available on a file server.

- **Hub:** A *hub* is an older technology that interconnects network components, such as clients and servers. Hubs vary in their number of available ports. However, for scalability, you can interconnect hubs, up to a point. If you chain too many hubs together, network errors can result. As discussed further in Chapter 3, a hub is a Layer 1 device and does not perform any inspection of the traffic it passes. Rather, a hub simply receives traffic in a *port* (that is, a receptacle to which a network cable connects) and repeats that traffic out all the other ports. Remember, for the local area network (LAN), the hub is considered obsolete. This chapter covers it for academic purposes.

- **Switch:** Like a hub, a *switch* interconnects network components, and switches are available with a variety of port densities. However, unlike a hub, a switch does not simply take in traffic on one port and blast that traffic out all other ports. Rather, a switch learns which devices live off of which ports. It does this by inspecting traffic that comes into the port (inbound) and recording the source address. It then looks at the destination address and, if the switch knows the destination address, it forwards the traffic out of the appropriate port, not out of all the other ports. This dramatically cuts down on the volume of traffic coursing through your network. Consider a switch a *Layer 2* device, which means that it makes its forwarding decisions based on addresses that are physically burned into a network interface card (NIC) installed in a *host* (that is, any device that transmits or receives traffic on a network). This burned-in address is a Media Access Control (MAC) address. Note that today's switches are capable of functioning at higher layers of the network model but are still mostly considered as Layer 2 devices. The main network model in use today is the OSI model. This is covered in detail in Chapter 2, "The OSI Reference Model."

- **Router:** As discussed in Chapter 3, consider a *router* to be a Layer 3 device, which means that it makes its forwarding decisions based on logical network addresses. Most modern networks use Internet Protocol (IP) addressing. Therefore, most routers know what logical IP networks live off which router interfaces. Then, when traffic comes into a router, the router examines the destination IP address of the traffic and, based on the router's database of networks (that is, the routing table), it intelligently forwards the traffic out the appropriate interface.

- **Media:** The previously mentioned devices need to be interconnected via some sort of *media*. This media could be copper cabling. It could be a fiber-optic cable. Media might not even be a cable, as is the case with wireless networks, where radio waves travel through the media of air. Chapter 3 expands on this discussion of media. For now, realize that media varies in its cost, bandwidth capacity, and distance limitation. For example, although fiber-optic cabling is more expensive than unshielded twisted-pair cabling, it can typically carry traffic over longer distances and has a greater bandwidth capacity (that is, the capacity to carry a higher data rate).

- **WAN link:** Today, most networks connect to one or more other networks. For example, if your company has two locations, and those two locations are interconnected, via a Multiprotocol Label Switching (MPLS) network, the link that interconnects those networks is typically referred to as a *wide area network* (WAN) link. WANs, and technologies supporting WANs, are covered in Chapter 7, "Wide Area Networks."

Networks Defined by Geography

As you might be sensing at this point, not all networks look the same. They vary in many ways. One criterion by which networks are classified is how geographically dispersed the network's components are. For example, a network might interconnect devices within an office, or a network might interconnect a database at a corporate headquarters location with a remote sales office found on the opposite side of the globe.

Based on the geographic dispersion of network components, you can classify networks into various categories, including the following:

- Local area network (LAN)
- Wide area network (WAN)
- Wireless local area network (WLAN)
- Storage area network (SAN)
- Campus area network (CAN)
- Metropolitan area network (MAN)
- Personal area network (PAN)

The following sections describe these different classifications of networks in more detail.

LAN

A LAN interconnects network components within a local area (for example, within a building). Examples of common LAN technologies you are likely to meet include Ethernet (that is, IEEE 802.3) and wireless networks (that is, IEEE 802.11). Figure 1-2 illustrates an example of a LAN.

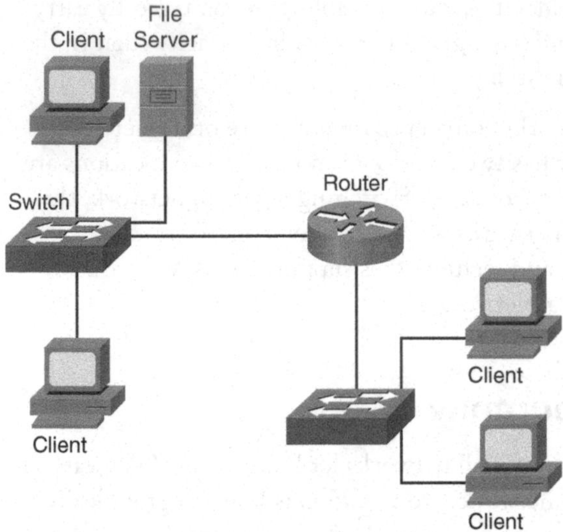

Figure 1-2 Sample LAN Topology

> **NOTE** IEEE stands for the *Institute of Electrical and Electronics Engineers*, and it is an internationally recognized standards body.

WAN

A WAN interconnects network components that are geographically separated. For example, a corporate headquarters might have multiple WAN connections to remote office sites. Multiprotocol Label Switching (MPLS) and Asynchronous Transfer Mode (ATM) are examples of WAN technologies. Figure 1-3 depicts a simple WAN topology, which interconnects two geographically dispersed locations.

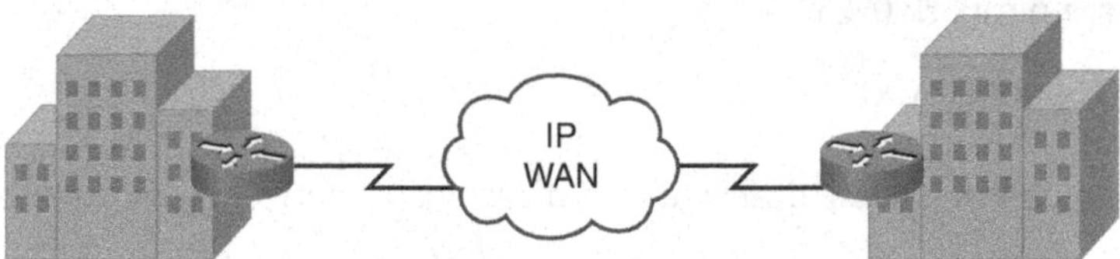

Figure 1-3 Sample WAN Topology

WLAN

A local area network made up of wireless networking devices is a wireless local area network (WLAN). Chapter 8, "Wireless Technologies," deals with this topic in detail.

SAN

You can construct a high-speed, highly reliable network for the express purpose of transmitting stored data. This network is called a storage area network.

Other Categories of Networks

Although LANs and WANs are the most common terms used to categorize computer networks based on geography, other categories include campus area network (CAN), metropolitan area network (MAN), and personal area network (PAN).

CAN

Years ago, I was a network manager for a university. The university covered several square miles and had several dozen buildings. Within many of these buildings was a LAN. However, those building-centric LANs were interconnected. By these LANs being interconnected, another network type was created, a CAN. Besides an actual university campus, you might also find a CAN in an industrial park or business park.

MAN

More widespread than a CAN and less widespread than a WAN, a MAN interconnects locations scattered throughout a metropolitan area. Imagine, for example, that a business in Chicago has a location near O'Hare Airport, another location near the Navy Pier, and another location in the Willis Tower (previously known as the Sears Tower). If a service provider could interconnect those locations using a high-speed network, such as a 10Gbps (that is, 10 billion bits per second) network, the interconnection of those locations would form a MAN. One example of a MAN technology is Metro Ethernet, which features much higher speeds than the traditional WAN technologies that might have been used in the past to connect such locations.

PAN

A PAN is a network whose scale is even smaller than a LAN. For example, a connection between a PC and a digital camera via a universal serial bus (USB) cable could be considered a PAN. Another example is a PC connected to an external hard drive via a FireWire connection. A PAN, however, is not necessarily a wired connection. A Bluetooth connection between your cell phone and your car's audio system is considered a wireless PAN (WPAN). The main distinction of a PAN, however, is that its range is typically limited to just a few meters.

Networks Defined by Topology

In addition to classifying networks based on the geographic placement of their components, another approach to classifying a network is to use the network's topology. Looks can be deceiving, however. You need to be able to distinguish between a physical topology and a logical topology.

Physical Versus Logical Topology

Just because a network appears to be a star topology (that is, where the network components all connect back to a centralized device, such as a switch), the traffic might be flowing in a circular pattern through all the network components attached to the centralized device. The actual traffic flow decides the *logical topology*, whereas the way components are physically interconnected determines the *physical topology*.

For example, consider Figure 1-4, which shows a collection of computers connected to a Token Ring media access unit (MAU). From a quick inspection of Figure 1-4, you can conclude that the devices are physically connected in a star topology, where the connected devices radiate out from a centralized aggregation point (that is, the MAU in this example).

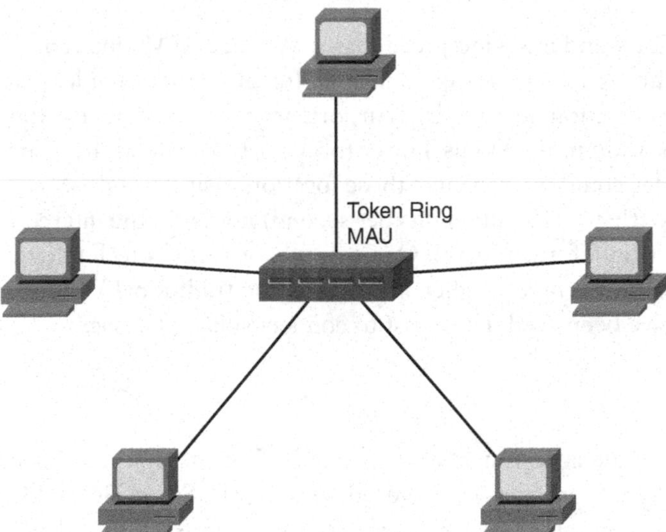

Figure 1-4 Physical Star Topology

Next, contrast the physical topology in Figure 1-4 with the logical topology illustrated in Figure 1-5 and later in Figure 1-8. Although the computers physically connect to a centralized MAU, when you examine the flow of traffic through (or in this case, around) the network, you see that the traffic flow actually loops round-and-round the network. The traffic flow dictates how to classify a network's logical topology. In this instance, the logical topology is a *ring topology* because the traffic circulates around the network as if circulating around a ring.

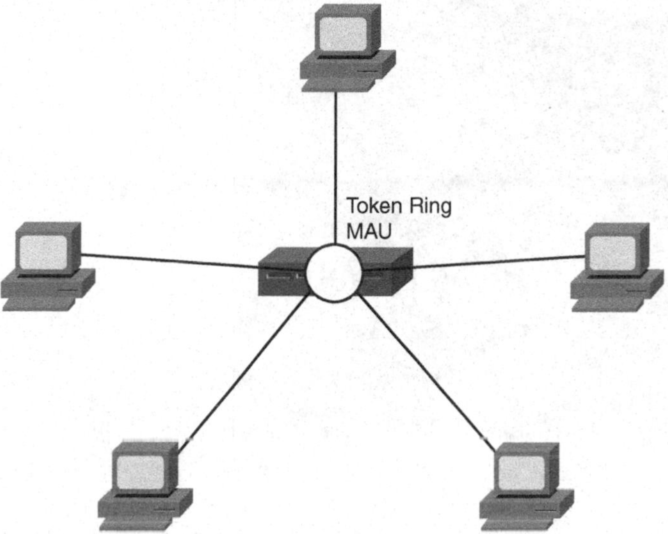

Figure 1-5 Logical Ring Topology

Before you run out and try and purchase a Token Ring network for your LAN, keep in mind you'll only see this technology in networking museums now!

Bus Topology

A bus topology, as depicted in Figure 1-6, typically uses a cable running through the area needing connectivity. Devices that need to connect to the network then tap into this nearby cable. Early Ethernet networks relied on bus topologies.

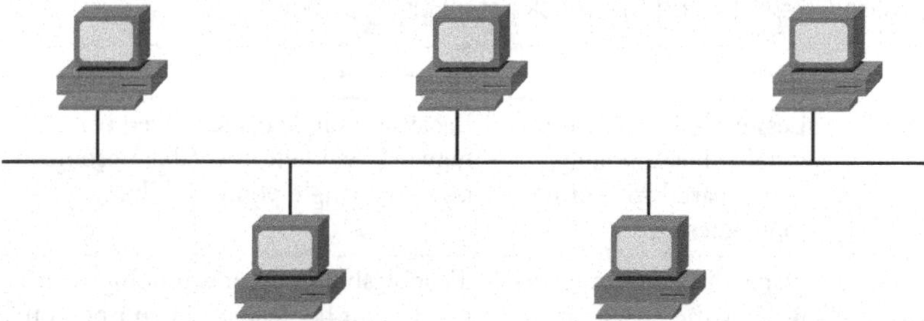

Figure 1-6 Bus Topology

A network tap might be in the form of a T connector (used in older 10BASE2 networks) or a vampire tap (used in older 10BASE5 networks). Figure 1-7 shows an example of a T connector.

Figure 1-7 T Connector

NOTE The Ethernet standards mentioned here (that is, 10BASE2 and 10BASE5), in addition to many other Ethernet standards, are discussed in detail in Chapter 4, "Ethernet Technology."

A bus and all devices connected to that bus make up a *network segment*. As discussed in Chapter 4, a single network segment is a single collision domain, which means that all devices connected to the bus might try to gain access to the bus at the same time, resulting in an error condition known as a *collision*. Table 1-1 shows some of the primary characteristics, benefits, and drawbacks of a bus topology.

Table 1-1 Characteristics, Benefits, and Drawbacks of a Bus Topology

Characteristics	Benefits	Drawbacks
One cable is used per network segment.	Less cable is needed to install a bus topology, as compared with other topologies.	Because a single cable is used per network segment, the cable becomes a potential single point of failure.
To support appropriate electrical characteristics of the cable, the cable requires a terminator (of a specific resistance) at each end of the cable.	Depending on the media used by the bus, a bus topology can be less expensive.	Troubleshooting a bus topology can be difficult because problem isolation might need an inspection of multiple network taps to make sure they either have a device connected or they are properly terminated.

Characteristics	Benefits	Drawbacks
Bus topologies were popular in early Ethernet networks.	Installation of a network based on a bus topology is easier than some other topologies, which might require extra wiring to be installed.	Adding devices to a bus might cause an outage for other users on the bus.
Network components tap directly into the cable via a connector such as a T connector or a vampire tap.		An error condition existing on one device on the bus can affect performance of other devices on the bus.
		A bus topology does not scale well because all devices share the bandwidth available on the bus. Also, if two devices on the bus simultaneously request access to the bus, an error condition results.

Ring Topology

Figure 1-8 offers an example of a ring topology, where traffic flows in a circular fashion around a closed network loop (that is, a ring). Typically, a ring topology sends data, in a single direction, to each connected device in turn, until the intended destination receives the data. Token Ring networks relied on a ring topology.

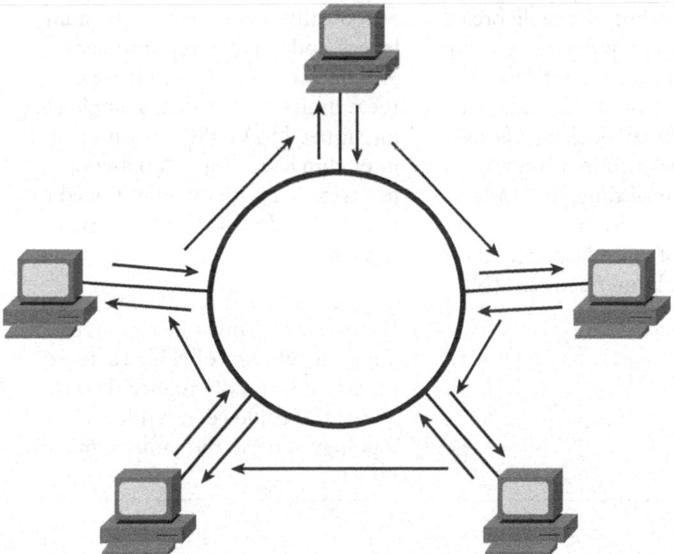

Figure 1-8 Ring Topology

Token Ring, however, was not the only popular ring-based topology popular in networks back in the 1990s. Fiber Distributed Data Interface (FDDI) was another variant of a ring-based topology. Most FDDI networks (which, as the name suggests, have fiber optics as the media) used not just one ring, but two. These two rings sent data in opposite directions, resulting in *counter-rotating rings*. One benefit of counter-rotating rings was that if a fiber broke, the stations on each side of the break could interconnect their two rings, resulting in a single ring capable of reaching all stations on the ring.

Because a ring topology allows devices on the ring to take turns transmitting on the ring, contention for media access was not a problem, as it was for a bus topology. If a network had a single ring, however, the ring became a single point of failure. If the ring were broken at any point, data would stop flowing. Table 1-2 shows some of the primary characteristics, benefits, and drawbacks of a ring topology.

Table 1-2 Characteristics, Benefits, and Drawbacks of a Ring Topology

Characteristics	Benefits	Drawbacks
Devices are interconnected by connecting to a single ring or, in some cases (for example, FDDI), a dual ring.	A dual-ring topology adds a layer of fault tolerance. Therefore, if a cable break occurred, connectivity to all devices could be restored.	A break in a ring when a single ring topology is used results in a network outage for all devices connected to the ring.
Each device on a ring includes both a receiver (for the incoming cable) and a transmitter (for the outgoing cable).	Troubleshooting is simplified in the event of a cable break, because each device on a ring contains a repeater. When the repeater on the far side of a cable break does not receive any data within a certain amount of time, it reports an error condition, typically in the form of an indicator light on a network interface card (NIC).	Rings have scalability limitations. Specifically, a ring has a maximum length and a maximum number of attached stations. Once either of these limits is exceeded, a single ring might need to be divided into two interconnected rings. A network maintenance window might need to be scheduled to perform this ring division.
Each device on the ring repeats the signal it receives.		Because a ring must be a complete loop, the amount of cable required for a ring is usually higher than the amount of cable required for a bus topology serving the same number of devices.

Star Topology

Figure 1-9 shows a sample star topology with a hub at the center of the topology and a collection of clients individually connected to the hub. Notice that a star topology has a central point from which all attached devices radiate. In LANs, that centralized device was typically a hub back in the early 1990s. Modern networks, however, usually have a switch located at the center of the star.

NOTE Chapter 3 discusses UTP and other types of cabling.

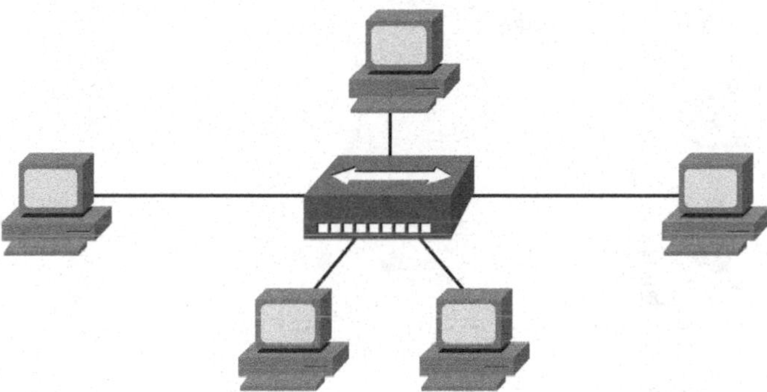

Figure 1-9 Star Topology

The star topology is the most popular physical LAN topology in use today, with an Ethernet switch at the center of the star and unshielded twisted-pair (UTP) cable used to connect from the switch ports to clients.

Table 1-3 identifies some of the primary characteristics, benefits, and drawbacks of a star topology.

Table 1-3 Characteristics, Benefits, and Drawbacks of a Star Topology

Characteristics	Benefits	Drawbacks
Devices have independent connections back to a central device (for example, a hub or a switch).	A cable break only impacts the device connected via the broken cable, and not the entire topology.	More cable is required for a star topology, as opposed to bus or ring topologies because each device requires its own cable to connect back to the central device.
Star topologies are commonly used with Ethernet technologies (described in Chapter 4).	Troubleshooting is relatively simple because a central device in the star topology acts as the aggregation point of all the connected devices.	Installation can take longer for a star topology, as opposed to a bus or ring topology, because more cable runs that must be installed.

Hub-and-Spoke Topology

When interconnecting multiple sites (for example, multiple corporate locations) via WAN links, a hub-and-spoke topology has a WAN link from each remote site (that is, a *spoke site*) to the main site (that is, the *hub site*). This approach, an example of which is shown in Figure 1-10, is similar to the star topology used in LANs.

With WAN links, a service provider is paid a recurring fee for each link. Therefore, a hub-and-spoke topology helps minimize WAN expenses by not directly connecting any two spoke locations. If two spoke locations need to communicate between themselves, their communication is sent via the hub location. Table 1-4 contrasts the benefits and drawbacks of a hub-and-spoke WAN topology.

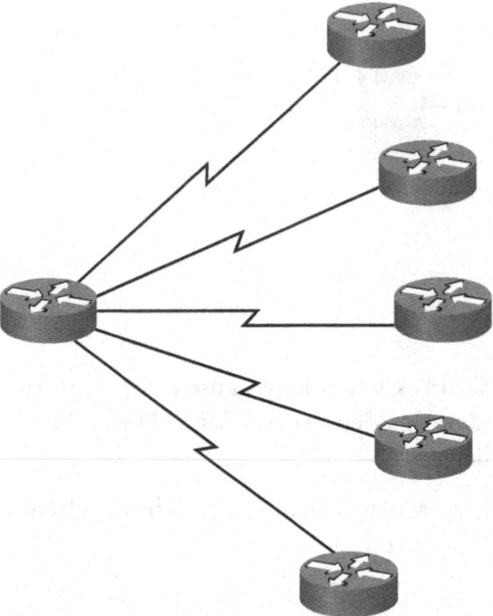

Figure 1-10 Hub-and-Spoke Topology

Table 1-4 Characteristics, Benefits, and Drawbacks of a Hub-and-Spoke WAN Topology

Characteristics	Benefits	Drawbacks
Each remote site (that is, a spoke) connects back to a main site (that is, the hub) via a WAN link.	Costs are reduced (as compared to a full-mesh or partial-mesh topology) because a minimal number of links is used.	Suboptimal routes must be used between remote sites because all intersite communication must travel via the main site.

Characteristics	Benefits	Drawbacks
Communication between two remote sites travels through the hub site.	Adding one or more additional sites is easy (as compared to a full-mesh or partial-mesh topology) because only one link needs to be added per site.	Because all remote sites converge on the main site, this hub site potentially becomes a single point of failure.
		Because each remote site is reachable by only a single WAN link, the hub-and-spoke topology lacks redundancy.

Full-Mesh Topology

Whereas a hub-and-spoke WAN topology lacked redundancy and suffered from suboptimal routes, a full-mesh topology, as shown in Figure 1-11, directly connects every site to every other site.

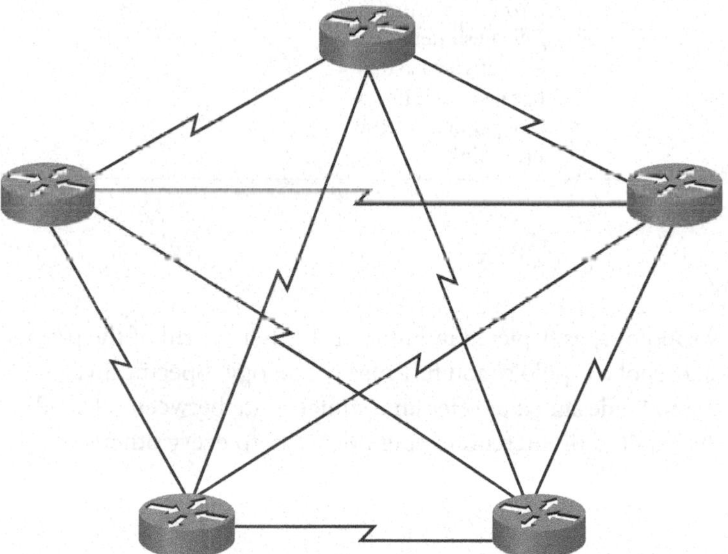

Figure 1-11 Full-Mesh Topology

Because each site connects directly to every other site, an optimal path can be selected, as opposed to relaying traffic via another site. Also, a full-mesh topology is highly fault tolerant. By inspecting Figure 1-11, you can see that multiple links in the topology could be lost, and every site might still be able to connect to every other site. Table 1-5 summarizes the characteristics of a full-mesh topology.

Table 1-5 Characteristics, Benefits, and Drawbacks of a Full-Mesh WAN Topology

Characteristics	Benefits	Drawbacks
Every site has a direct WAN connection to every other site.	An optimal route exists between any two sites.	A full-mesh network can be difficult and expensive to scale, because the addition of one new site requires a new WAN link between the new site and every other existing site.
The number of required WAN connections can be calculated with the formula $w = n * (n - 1) / 2$, where w = the number of WAN links and n = the number of sites. For example, a network with 10 sites would require 45 WAN connections to form a fully meshed network: $45 = 10 * (10 - 1) / 2$.	A full-mesh network is fault tolerant because one or more links can be lost and reachability between all sites might still be maintained.	
	Troubleshooting a full-mesh network is relatively easy because each link is independent of the other links.	

Partial-Mesh Topology

A partial-mesh WAN topology, as depicted in Figure 1-12, is a hybrid of the previously described hub-and-spoke topology and full-mesh topology. Specifically, a partial-mesh topology can be designed to offer an optimal route between selected sites while avoiding the expense of interconnecting every site to every other site.

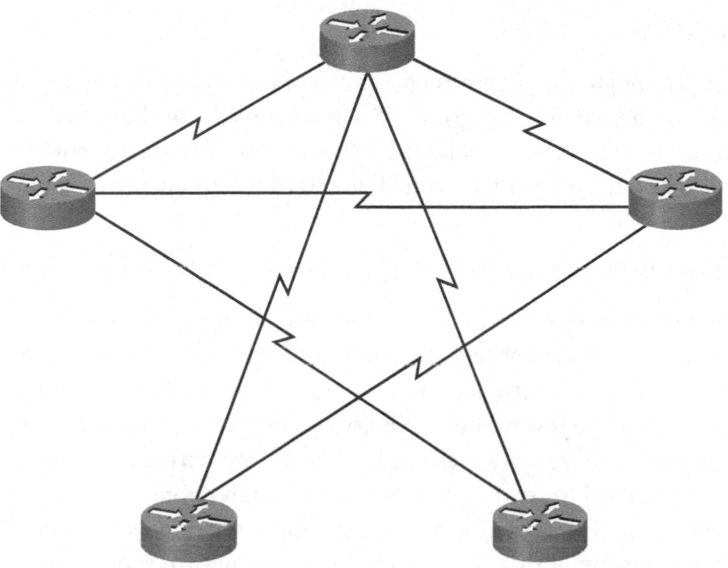

Figure 1-12 Partial-Mesh Topology

When designing a partial-mesh topology, a network designer must consider network traffic patterns and strategically add links interconnecting sites that have higher volumes of traffic between themselves. Table 1-6 highlights the characteristics, benefits, and drawbacks of a partial-mesh topology.

Table 1-6 Characteristics, Benefits, and Drawbacks of a Partial-Mesh Topology

Characteristics	Benefits	Drawbacks
Selected sites (that is, sites with frequent intersite communication) are interconnected via direct links, whereas sites that have less-frequent communication can communicate via another site.	A partial-mesh topology provides optimal routes between selected sites with higher intersite traffic volumes while avoiding the expense of interconnecting every site to every other site.	A partial-mesh topology is less fault tolerant than a full-mesh topology.
A partial-mesh topology uses fewer links than a full-mesh topology and more links than a hub-and-spoke topology for interconnecting the same number of sites.	A partial-mesh topology is more redundant than a hub-and-spoke topology.	A partial-mesh topology is more expensive than a hub-and-spoke topology.

Wireless Topologies

To say that wireless technologies have grown popular as of late would be a huge understatement. As such, three major categories of wireless topologies have been identified. Although this section provides a high-level overview of these network designs, keep in mind that Chapter 8 offers a much greater level of detail.

Ad Hoc

The simplest of wireless topologies is the ad hoc wireless network. This means that the wireless nodes are in charge of sending and receiving traffic to each other, without the assistance of infrastructure devices, such as switches or access points. Some network engineers refer to the ad hoc topology as simply a wireless peer-to-peer (P2P) type of network. One common example of an ad hoc wireless network would be Apple's AirDrop, used to send files between two smartphones. This author prefers the more formal and specific ad hoc terminology. Your Network+ exam does as well! The opposite of this approach is an infrastructure topology, which is discussed next.

Infrastructure

With the infrastructure topology, you have specialized wireless equipment for permitting the wireless communications to take place. Many homes today feature a wireless local area network (WLAN). A wireless access point (WAP) allows the various computers (and other wireless devices) to communicate with each other through the WAP acting like a hub device. This WAP connects to the service provider (SP) of the home user with a wired connection. For example, a coaxial cable could connect to the broadband cable service for high-speed Internet connectivity.

Mesh

A specific type of ad hoc wireless topology is the mesh. This topology is more sophisticated than the ad hoc in that specialized nodes help move the traffic throughout the topology. Note that these devices are not as fancy as the access points found in an infrastructure type of topology. The first wireless mesh topology I ever had the pleasure of working on was one that could adequately provide coverage for a large recreational vehicle (RV) park. Obvious challenges with this design came in the form of interference and the nodes' ability to sustain harsh environmental conditions often found in Florida, USA. Yes, that would be sun and the occasional tropical storm.

Networks Defined by Resource Location

Yet another way to categorize networks is based on where network resources reside. An example of a *client/server network* is a collection of PCs all sharing files found on a centralized server. However, if those PCs had their operating system (for example, Microsoft Windows 10 or Mac OS X) configured for file sharing, they could share files from one another's hard drives. This is referred to as a *peer-to-peer network*, because the peers (the PCs in this example) make resources available to other peers. The following sections describe client/server and peer-to-peer networks in more detail.

Client/Server Networks

Figure 1-13 illustrates an example of a client/server network, where a dedicated file server gives shared access to files, and a networked printer is available as a resource to the network's clients. Client/server networks are commonly used by businesses. Because resources are found on one or more servers, administration is simpler than trying to administer network resources on multiple peer devices.

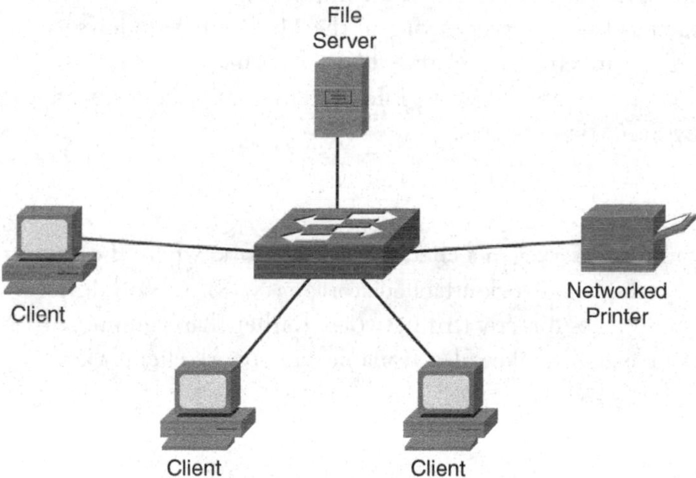

Figure 1-13 Client/Server Network Example

The performance of a client/server network can be better than that of a peer-to-peer network because resources can be located on dedicated servers rather than on a PC running a variety of end-user applications. You can simplify backups because fewer locations must be backed up. However, client/server networks come with the extra expense of dedicated server resources. Table 1-7 contrasts the benefits and drawbacks of client/server networks.

Table 1-7 Characteristics, Benefits, and Drawbacks of a Client/Server Network

Characteristics	Benefits	Drawbacks
Client devices (for example, PCs) share a common set of resources (for example, file or print resources) located on one or more dedicated servers.	Client/server networks can easily scale, which might require the purchase of additional client licenses.	Because multiple clients might rely on a single server for their resources, the single server can become a single point of failure in the network.
Resource sharing is made possible via dedicated server hardware and network operating systems.	Administration is simplified, because parameters, such as file-sharing permissions and other security settings, can be administered on a server as opposed to multiple clients.	Client/server networks can cost more than peer-to-peer networks. For example, client/server networks might need the purchase of dedicated server hardware and a network OS with an appropriate number of licenses.

NOTE A server in a client/server network could be a computer running a network operating system (NOS) such as Linux Server or one of the Microsoft Windows Server operating systems. Alternatively, a server might be a host making its file system available to remote clients via the Network File System (NFS) service, which was originally developed by Sun Microsystems.

NOTE A variant of the traditional server in a client/server network, where the server provides shared file access, is network-attached storage (NAS). A NAS device is a mass storage device that attaches directly to a network. Rather than running an advanced NOS, a NAS device usually makes files available to network clients via a service such as NFS.

Peer-to-Peer Networks

Peer-to-peer networks allow interconnected devices (for example, PCs) to share their resources with one another. Those resources could be, for example, files or printers. As an example of a peer-to-peer network, consider Figure 1-14, where each of the peers can share files on their own hard drives, and one of the peers has a directly attached printer that can be shared with the other peers in the network.

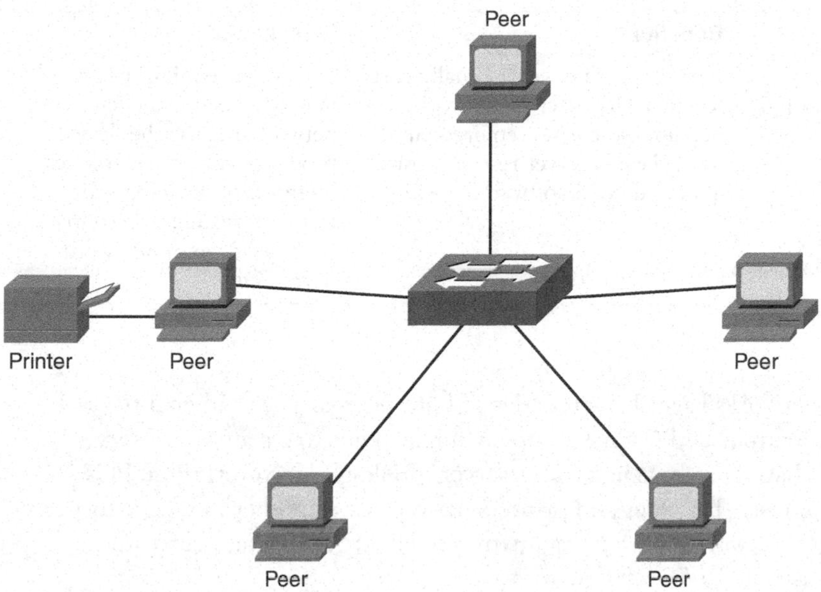

Figure 1-14 Peer-to-Peer Network Example

Peer-to-peer networks are seen in smaller businesses and in homes. The popularity of these peer-to-peer networks is fueled in part by client operating systems that support file and print sharing. Scalability for peer-to-peer networks is a concern, however. Specifically, as the number of devices (that is, peers) increases, the administration burden increases. For example, a network administrator might have to manage file permissions on multiple devices, as opposed to a single server. Consider the characteristics of peer-to-peer networks as presented in Table 1-8.

Table 1-8 Characteristics, Benefits, and Drawbacks of a Peer-to-Peer Network

Characteristics	Benefits	Drawbacks
Client devices (for example, PCs) share their resources (for example, file and printer resources) with other client devices.	Peer-to-peer networks can be installed easily because resource sharing is made possible by the clients' operating systems, and knowledge of advanced NOSs is not required.	Scalability is limited because of the increased administration burden of managing multiple clients.

Characteristics	Benefits	Drawbacks
Resource sharing is made available through the clients' operating systems.	Peer-to-peer networks usually cost less than client/server networks because there is no requirement for dedicated server resources or advanced NOS software.	Performance might be less than that seen in a client/server network because the devices providing network resources might be performing other tasks not related to resource sharing (for example, word processing).

NOTE Some networks have characteristics of both peer-to-peer and client/server networks. For example, all PCs in a company might point to a centralized server for accessing a shared database in a client/server topology. However, these PCs might simultaneously share files and printers between one another in a peer-to-peer topology. Such a network, which has a mixture of client/server and peer-to-peer characteristics, is called a *hybrid* network.

Real-World Case Study

The headquarters for Acme, Inc., is located on a single floor of a downtown building. Acme also has two branch offices, Branch1 and Branch2, that are in remote locations. The company wants to do file sharing, instant messaging, email, and voice on its own private networks when possible. It also wants connectivity to the Internet. At the headquarters location, they set up a LAN with UTP (Cat 5) cabling, with the clients and servers connected to a central switch. This forms a physical star topology. For connectivity between HQ and its two branch offices, the company uses a service provider (SP) for WAN connectivity. The SP provides logical, point-to-point connections between the headquarters office to both of the branch locations. Physically, the path between the headquarters to each branch office is going through several routers in the SP's network. For the time being, Branch1 and Branch2 do not have direct connectivity to each other, so branch-to-branch traffic must pass through the headquarters site (hub and spoke). Next year, as more funds are available, the company can add WAN connectivity directly between Branch1 and Branch2. This will change the WAN topology from hub and spoke to full mesh.

Summary

The main topics covered in this chapter are the following:

- This chapter introduced you to various network components, including the client, server, hub, switch, router, media, and WAN link.
- One way to classify networks is by their geographical dispersion. Specifically, these network types were identified: LAN, WAN, CAN, MAN, PAN, WLAN, and SAN.
- Another approach to classifying networks is based on a network's topology. Examples of network types, based on topology, include bus, ring, star, partial mesh, full mesh, and hub and spoke. This text also provided information on the various wireless topologies available.
- This chapter contrasted client/server and peer-to-peer networks.

Exam Preparation Tasks

Review All the Key Topics

Review the most important topics from inside the chapter, noted with the Key Topic icon in the outer margin of the page. Table 1-9 lists these key topics and the page numbers where each is found.

Table 1-9 Key Topics for Chapter 1

Key Topic Element	Description	Page Number
List	Network types, as defined by geography	7
Table 1-1	Characteristics, benefits, and drawbacks of a bus topology	12
Table 1-2	Characteristics, benefits, and drawbacks of a ring topology	14
Table 1-3	Characteristics, benefits, and drawbacks of a star topology	15
Table 1-4	Characteristics, benefits, and drawbacks of a hub-and-spoke topology	16
Table 1-5	Characteristics, benefits, and drawbacks of a full-mesh topology	18
Table 1-6	Characteristics, benefits, and drawbacks of a partial-mesh topology	19
Table 1-7	Characteristics, benefits, and drawbacks of a client/server network	22
Table 1-8	Characteristics, benefits, and drawbacks of a peer-to-peer network	23

Complete Tables and Lists from Memory

Print a copy of Appendix C, "Memory Tables," or at least the section for this chapter, and complete as many of the tables as possible from memory. Appendix D, "Memory Tables Answer Key," includes the completed tables and lists so you can check your work.

Define Key Terms

Define the following key terms from this chapter, and check your answers in the Glossary:

client, server, hub, switch, router, media, WAN link, local area network (LAN), wide area network (WAN), campus area network (CAN), metropolitan area network (MAN), personal area network (PAN), wireless local area network (WLAN), storage area network (SAN), logical topology, physical topology, bus topology, ring topology, star topology, hub-and-spoke topology, full-mesh topology, partial-mesh topology, ad hoc topology, infrastructure topology, wireless mesh topology, client/server network, peer-to-peer network

Complete Chapter 1 Hands-On Lab in Network+ Simulator Lite

- Network Topologies

Additional Resources

Routers and Switches, Oh My!: http://ajsnetworking.com/intrors

Network Topology: https://en.wikipedia.org/wiki/Network_topology

Review Questions

The answers to these review questions appear in Appendix A, "Answers to Review Questions."

1. Which of the following provides the media (wired or wireless) to facilitate the transfer of data?
   a. Server
   b. LAN
   c. Client
   d. Router

2. Which device makes traffic-forwarding decisions based on MAC addresses?
   a. Hub
   b. Router
   c. Switch
   d. Multiplexer

3. A company has various locations in a city interconnected using Metro Ethernet connections. This is an example of what type of network?
   a. WAN
   b. CAN
   c. PAN
   d. MAN

4. A network formed by interconnecting a PC to a digital camera via a USB cable is considered what type of network?
   a. WAN
   b. CAN
   c. PAN
   d. MAN

5. Which of the following physical LAN topologies requires the most cabling?
   a. Bus
   b. Ring
   c. Star
   d. WLAN

6. Which of the following topologies offers the highest level of redundancy?
   a. Full mesh
   b. Hub and spoke
   c. Bus
   d. Partial mesh

7. How many WAN links are required to create a full mesh of connections between five remote sites?
   a. 5
   b. 10
   c. 15
   d. 20

8. Identify two advantages of a hub-and-spoke WAN topology as compared to a full-mesh WAN topology.
   a. Lower cost
   b. Optimal routes
   c. More scalable
   d. More redundancy

9. Which type of network is based on network clients sharing resources with one another?
   a. Client/server
   b. Client-peer
   c. Peer-to-peer
   d. Peer-to-server

10. Which of the following is an advantage of a peer-to-peer network, as compared with a client/server network?
   a. More scalable
   b. Less expensive
   c. Better performance
   d. Simplified administration

11. What type of wireless topology features the use of access points to facilitate network communications?
   a. Ad hoc
   b. Mesh
   c. Infrastructure
   d. Ring

12. What network type would help facilitate communications when large video or audio files need to be housed and transferred through the network?

    a. WLAN

    b. CAN

    c. PAN

    d. SAN

After completion of this chapter, you will be able to answer the following questions:

- What is the purpose of a network model?
- What are the layers of the OSI model?
- What are the characteristics of each layer of the OSI model?
- How does the TCP/IP stack compare to the OSI model?
- What are the well-known TCP and/or UDP port numbers for a given collection of common applications?

CHAPTER 2

The OSI Reference Model

Way back in 1977, the International Organization for Standardization (ISO) developed a subcommittee to focus on the interoperability of multivendor communications systems. This is fancy language for getting network "thingies" to communicate with each other, even if different companies made those network "thingies." What sprang from this subcommittee was the Open Systems Interconnection (OSI) reference model (referred to as the *OSI model* or the *OSI stack*). With this model, you can talk about any networking technology and categorize that technology as residing at one or more of the seven layers of the model.

This chapter defines those seven layers and offers examples of what you might find at each layer. It also contrasts the OSI model with another model—the TCP/IP stack, also known as the Department of Defense (DoD) model—that focuses on Internet Protocol (IP) communications.

Foundation Topics

The Purpose of Reference Models

Throughout this book, various protocols and devices that play a role in your network (and your networking career) are introduced. To better understand how a technology fits in, it helps to have a common point of reference against which various technologies from different vendors can be compared. Understanding the OSI model is useful in troubleshooting networks.

One of the most common ways of categorizing the function of a network technology is to say at what layer (or layers) of the OSI model that technology runs. Based on how that technology performs a certain function at a certain layer of the OSI model allows you to better decide whether one device is going to be able to communicate with another device, which might or might not be using a similar technology at that layer of the OSI reference model.

For example, when your laptop connects to a web server on the Internet, your service provider assigns your laptop an IP address. Similarly, the web server to which you are communicating has an IP address. As you see in this chapter, an IP address lives at Layer 3 (the network layer) of the OSI model. Because both your laptop and the web server use a common protocol (that is, IP) at Layer 3, they are capable of communicating with one another.

Personally, I have been in the computer-networking industry since 1989, and I have had the OSI model explained in many classes I have attended and books I have read. From this, I have taken away a collection of metaphors to help describe the operation of the different layers of the OSI model. Some of the metaphors involve sending a letter from one location to another or placing a message in a series of envelopes. However, my favorite (and a more correct) way to describe the OSI model is to simply think of it as being analogous to a bookshelf, such as the one shown in Figure 2-1.

Figure 2-1 A Bookshelf Is Analogous to the OSI Model

If you were to look at a bookshelf in my home, you would see that I organized diverse types of books on different shelves. One shelf has my collection of *Star Wars* books, another shelf holds the books I wrote for Pearson, another shelf holds my old-school audio books, and so on. I grouped similar books together on a shelf, just as the OSI model groups similar protocols and functions together in a layer.

A common pitfall my readers meet when studying the OSI model is to try to neatly fit all the devices and protocols in their network into one of the OSI model's seven layers. However, not every technology is a perfect fit into these layers. In fact, some networks might not have any technologies running at one or more of these layers. This reminds me of my favorite statement about the OSI model. It comes from Rich Seifert's book *The Switch Book*. In that book, Rich reminds us that the OSI model is a *reference* model, not a *reverence* model. That is, no cosmic law states that all technologies must cleanly plug into the model. So, as you discover the characteristics of the OSI model layers throughout this chapter, remember that these layers are like shelves for organizing similar protocols and functions, not immutable laws.

The OSI Model

As previously described, the OSI model consists of seven layers:

- **Layer 1:** The physical layer
- **Layer 2:** The data link layer
- **Layer 3:** The network layer
- **Layer 4:** The transport layer

- **Layer 5:** The session layer
- **Layer 6:** The presentation layer
- **Layer 7:** The application layer

Graphically, we depict these layers with Layer 1 at the bottom of the stack, as shown in Figure 2-2.

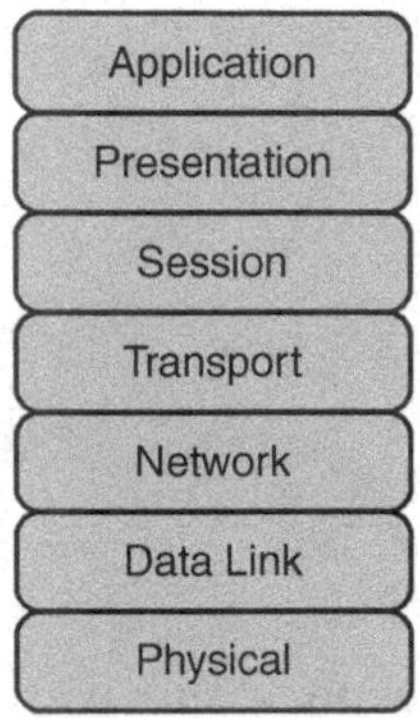

Figure 2-2 OSI "Stack"

Various mnemonics are available to help memorize these layers in their proper order. A top-down (that is, starting at the top of the stack with Layer 7 and working your way down to Layer 1) acrostic is ***All People Seem To Need Data Processing***. As a couple of examples, using this acrostic, the *A* in *A*ll reminds us of the *A* in *A*pplication, and the *P* in *P*eople reminds us of the *P* in *P*resentation. Another common memory aid is ***Please Do Not Throw Sausage Pizza Away***, which begins at Layer 1 and works its way up to Layer 7.

At the physical layer, binary expressions (that is, a series of 1s and 0s) represent data. A binary expression is created using bits, where a bit is a single 1 or a single 0. At upper layers, however, bits are grouped together, into what is known as a *protocol data unit* (PDU) or a *data service unit*.

Engineers tend to use the term *packet* generically to refer to these PDUs. However, PDUs might have an added name, depending on their OSI layer. Figure 2-3 illustrates these PDU names. A common memory aid for these PDUs is ***Some People Fear Birthdays***, where the *S* in *S*ome reminds us of the *S* in *S*egments. The *P* in *P*eople reminds us of the *P* in *P*ackets, and the *F* in *F*ear reflects the *F* in *F*rames. Finally, the *B* in *B*irthdays reminds us of the *B* in *B*its.

Key Topic

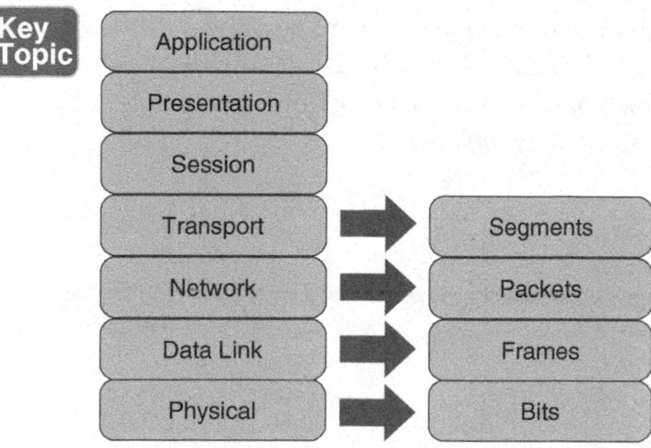

Figure 2-3 PDU Names

Layer 1: The Physical Layer

The concern of the physical layer, as shown in Figure 2-4, is the transmission of bits on the network along with the physical and electrical characteristics of the network.

Key Topic

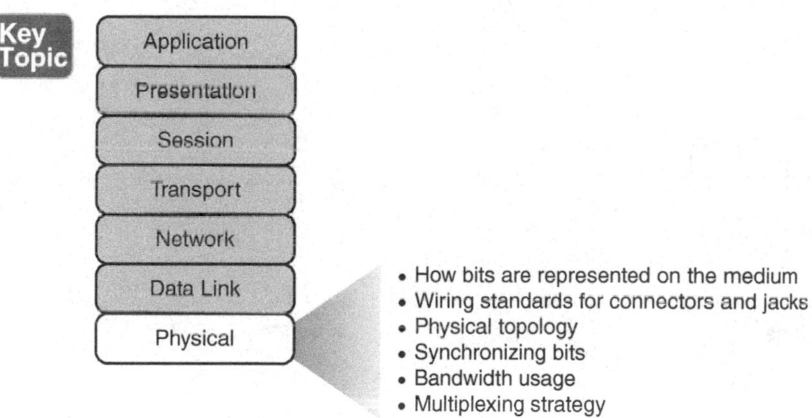

Figure 2-4 Layer 1: The Physical Layer

The physical layer defines the following:

- **How to represent bits on the medium:** Data on a computer network is represented as a binary expression. Chapter 5, "IPv4 and IPv6 Addresses," discusses binary in much more detail. Electrical voltage (on copper wiring) or light (carried via fiber-optic cabling) can represent these 1s and 0s.

For example, the presence or the absence of voltage on a wire portrays a binary 1 or a binary 0, respectively, as illustrated in Figure 2-5. Similarly, the presence or absence of light on a fiber-optic cable renders a 1 or 0 in binary. This type of approach is called *current state modulation*.

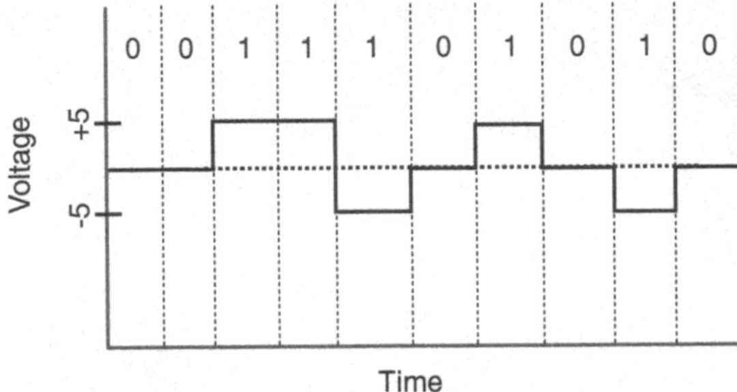

Figure 2-5 Current State Modulation

An alternate approach to portraying binary data is *state transition modulation*, as shown in Figure 2-6, where the transition between voltages or the presence of light shows a binary value.

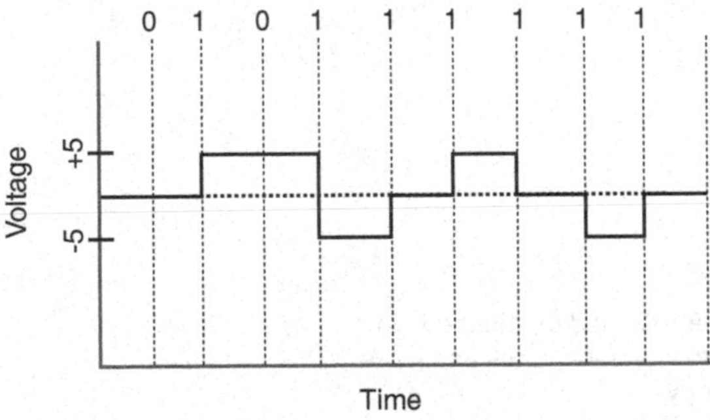

Figure 2-6 Transition Modulation

> **NOTE** Other modulation types you might be familiar with from radio include amplitude modulation (AM) and frequency modulation (FM). AM uses a variation in a waveform's amplitude (that is, signal strength) to portray the original signal. However, FM uses a variation in frequency to stand for the original signal.

- **Wiring standards for connectors and jacks:** Chapter 3, "Network Components," describes several standards for network connectors. For example, the TIA/EIA-568-B standard describes how to wire an RJ-45 connector for use on a 100BASE-TX Ethernet network, as shown in Figure 2-7.

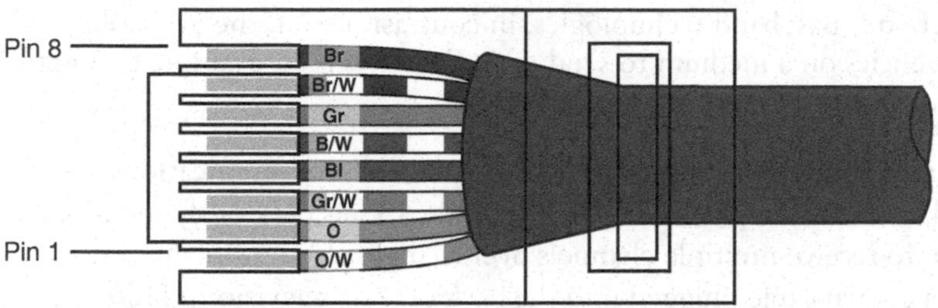

Figure 2-7 TIA/EIA-568-B Wiring Standard for an RJ-45 Connector

- **Physical topology:** Layer 1 devices view a network as a physical topology (as opposed to a logical topology). Examples of a physical topology include bus, ring, and star topologies, as described in Chapter 1, "Computer Network Fundamentals."
- **Synchronizing bits:** For two networked devices to successfully communicate at the physical layer, they must agree on when one bit stops and another bit starts. Specifically, the devices need a method to synchronize the bits. Two basic approaches to bit synchronization include *asynchronous* and *synchronous* synchronization:
  - **Asynchronous:** With this approach, a sender states that it is about to start transmitting by sending a start bit to the receiver. When the receiver sees this, it starts its own internal clock to measure the next bits. After the sender transmits its data, it sends a stop bit to say that it has finished its transmission.
  - **Synchronous:** This approach synchronizes the internal clocks of both the sender and the receiver to ensure that they agree on when bits begin and end. A common approach to make this synchronization happen is to use an external clock (for example, a clock given by a service provider). The sender and receiver then reference this external clock.
- **Bandwidth usage:** The two fundamental approaches to bandwidth usage on a network are *broadband* and *baseband*:
  - **Broadband:** Broadband technologies divide the bandwidth available on a medium (for example, copper or fiber-optic cabling) into different channels. A sender can then transmit different communication streams over the various channels. For example, consider frequency-division multiplexing (FDM) used by a cable modem. Specifically, a cable modem uses certain ranges of frequencies on the cable coming into your home from the local cable company to carry incoming data, another range of frequencies for outgoing data, and several other frequency ranges for various TV stations.

- **Baseband:** Baseband technologies, in contrast, use all the available frequencies on a medium to send data. Ethernet is an example of a networking technology that uses baseband.

- **Multiplexing strategy:** Multiplexing allows multiple communications sessions to share the same physical medium. Cable TV, as previously mentioned, allows you to receive multiple channels over a single physical medium (for example, a coaxial cable plugged into the back of your television). Here are some of the more common approaches to multiplexing:

  - **Time-division multiplexing (TDM):** TDM supports different communication sessions (for example, different telephone conversations in a telephony network) on the same physical medium by causing the sessions to take turns. For a brief period, defined as a *time slot*, data from the first session is sent, followed by data from the second session. This continues until all sessions have had a turn, and the process repeats itself.
  - **Statistical time-division multiplexing (StatTDM):** A downside to TDM is that each communication session receives its own time slot, even if one of the sessions does not have any data to send at the moment. To make a more efficient use of available bandwidth, StatTDM dynamically assigns time slots to communications sessions on an as-needed basis.
  - **Frequency-division multiplexing (FDM):** FDM divides a medium's frequency range into channels, and different communication sessions send their data over different channels. As previously described, this approach to bandwidth usage is called *broadband*.

Examples of devices defined by physical layer standards include hubs, wireless access points, and network cabling.

NOTE A hub interconnects PCs in a LAN. However, it is considered a physical layer device because a hub takes bits coming in on one port and retransmits those bits out all other ports. At no point does the hub interrogate any addressing information in the data.

Layer 2: The Data Link Layer

The data link layer is concerned with the following:

- Packaging data into frames and transmitting those frames on the network
- Performing error detection/correction
- Uniquely finding network devices with an address
- Handling flow control

These processes are referred to collectively as *data link control* (DLC) and are illustrated in Figure 2-8.

Key Topic

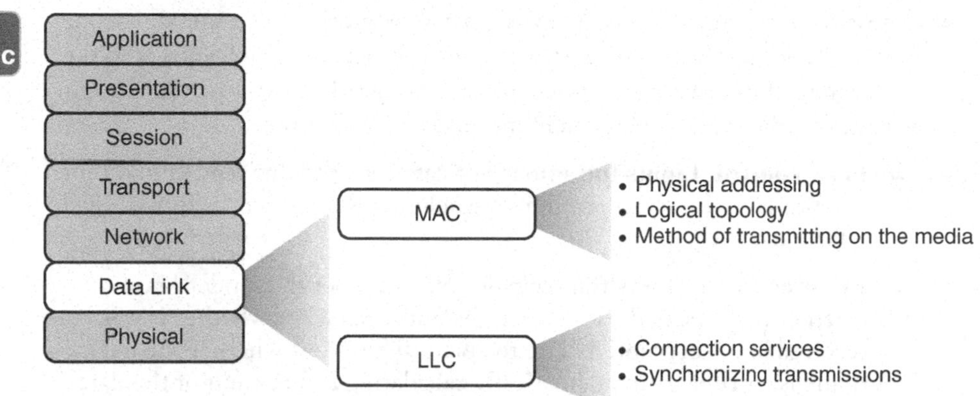

Figure 2-8 Layer 2: The Data Link Layer

In fact, the data link layer is unique from the other layers in that it has two sublayers of its own: MAC and LLC.

Media Access Control

Characteristics of the Media Access Control (MAC) sublayer include the following:

- **Physical addressing:** A common example of a Layer 2 address is a MAC address, which is a 48-bit address assigned to a device's network interface card (NIC). MAC addresses are written in hexadecimal notation (for example, 58:55:ca:eb:27:83). The first 24 bits of the 48-bit address is the *vendor code*. The IEEE Registration Authority assigns a manufacturer one or more unique vendor codes. You can use the list of vendor codes at http://standards.ieee.org/develop/regauth/oui/oui.txt to identify the manufacturer of a networking device, based on the first half of the device's MAC address. The last 24 bits of a MAC address are assigned by the manufacturer, and they act as a serial number for the device. No two MAC addresses in the world should have the same value.
- **Logical topology:** Layer 2 devices view a network as a logical topology. Examples of a logical topology include bus and ring topologies, as described in Chapter 1.
- **Method of transmitting on the media:** With several devices connected to a network, there needs to be some strategy for deciding when a device sends on the media. Otherwise, multiple devices might send at the same time and thus interfere with one another's transmissions.

Logical Link Control

Characteristics of the Logical Link Control (LLC) sublayer include the following:

- **Connection services:** When a device on a network receives a message from another device on the network, that recipient device can give feedback to the sender in the form of an acknowledgment message. The two main functions provided by these acknowledgment messages are as follows:
  - **Flow control:** Limits the amount of data a sender can send at one time; this prevents the sender from overwhelming the receiver with too much information.
  - **Error control:** Allows the recipient of data to let the sender know whether the expected data frame was not received or whether it was received but is corrupted. The recipient figures out whether the data frame is corrupt by mathematically calculating a checksum of the data received. If the calculated checksum does not match the checksum received with the data frame, the recipient of the data draws the conclusion that the data frame is corrupted and can then notify the sender via an acknowledgment message.
- **Synchronizing transmissions:** Senders and receivers of data frames need to coordinate when a data frame is being transmitted and should be received. The three methods of performing this synchronization are detailed here:
  - **Isochronous:** With isochronous transmission, network devices look to a common device in the network as a clock source, which creates fixed-length time slots. Network devices can determine how much free space, if any, is available within a time slot and then insert data into an available time slot. A time slot can accommodate more than one data frame. Isochronous transmission does not need to provide clocking at the beginning of a data string (as does synchronous transmission) or for every data frame (as does asynchronous transmission). As a result, isochronous transmission uses little overhead when compared to asynchronous or synchronous transmission methods.
  - **Asynchronous:** With asynchronous transmission, network devices reference their own internal clocks, and network devices do not need to synchronize their clocks. Instead, the sender places a start bit at the beginning of each data frame and a stop bit at the end of each data frame. These start and stop bits tell the receiver when to monitor the medium for the presence of bits.

An additional bit, called the *parity bit*, might also be added to the end of each byte in a frame to detect an error in the frame. For example, if even parity error detection (as opposed to odd parity error detection) is used, the parity bit (with a value of either 0 or 1) would be added to the end of a byte, causing the total number of 1s in the data frame to be an even number. If the receiver of a byte is configured for even parity error detection and receives a byte where the total number of bits (including the parity bit) is even, the receiver can conclude that the byte was not corrupted during transmission.

NOTE Using a parity bit to detect errors might not be effective if a byte has more than one error (that is, more than one bit that has been changed from its original value).

- **Synchronous:** With synchronous transmission, two network devices that want to communicate between themselves must agree on a clocking method to show the beginning and ending of data frames. One approach to providing this clocking is to use a separate communications channel over which a clock signal is sent. Another approach relies on specific bit combinations or control characters to indicate the beginning of a frame or a byte of data.

  Like asynchronous transmissions, synchronous transmissions can perform error detection. However, rather than using parity bits, synchronous communication runs a mathematical algorithm on the data to create a cyclic redundancy check (CRC). If both the sender and the receiver calculate the same CRC value for the same chunk of data, the receiver can conclude that the data was not corrupted during transmission.

Examples of devices defined by data link layer standards include switches, bridges, and NICs.

NOTE NICs are not entirely defined at the data link layer because they are partially based on physical layer standards, such as a NIC's network connector.

Layer 3: The Network Layer

The network layer, as shown in Figure 2-9, is primarily concerned with forwarding data based on logical addresses.

Key Topic

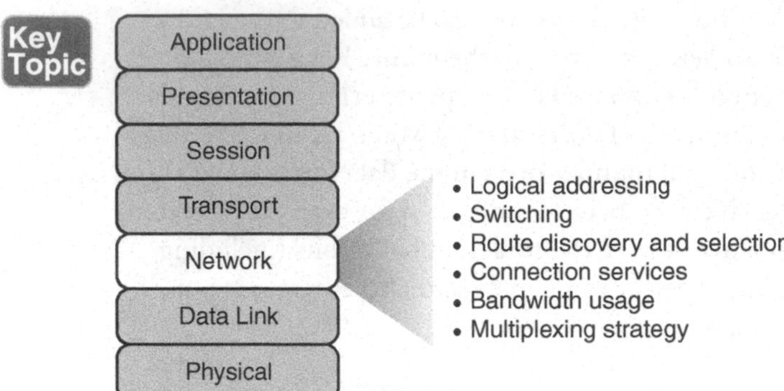

Figure 2-9 Layer 3: The Network Layer

Although many network administrators think of routing and IP addressing when they hear about the network layer, this layer is actually responsible for a variety of tasks:

- **Logical addressing:** Whereas the data link layer uses physical addresses to make forwarding decisions, the network layer uses logical addressing to make forwarding decisions. A variety of routed protocols (for example, AppleTalk and IPX) have their own logical addressing schemes, but by far, the most widely deployed routed protocol is Internet Protocol (IP). Chapter 5 discusses IP addressing in detail.
- **Switching:** Engineers often associate the term *switching* with Layer 2 technologies; however, the concept of switching also exists at Layer 3. Switching, at its essence, is making decisions about how data should be forwarded. At Layer 3, three common switching techniques exist:
  - **Packet switching:** With packet switching, a data stream is divided into packets. Each packet has a Layer 3 header that includes a source and destination Layer 3 address. Another term for packet switching is *routing*, which is discussed in more detail in Chapter 6, "Routing IP Packets."
  - **Circuit switching:** Circuit switching dynamically brings up a dedicated communication link between two parties for those parties to communicate.

    As a simple example of circuit switching, think of making a phone call from your home to a business. Assuming you have a traditional landline servicing your phone, the telephone company's switching equipment interconnects your home phone with the phone system of the business you are calling. This interconnection (that is, *circuit*) only exists for the duration of the phone call.

- **Message switching:** Unlike packet switching and circuit switching technologies, message switching is usually not well suited for real-time applications because of the delay involved. Specifically, with message switching, a data stream is divided into messages. Each message is tagged with a destination address, and the messages travel from one network device to another network device on the way to their destination. Because these devices might briefly store the messages before forwarding them, a network using message switching is sometimes called a *store-and-forward* network. Metaphorically, you could visualize message switching like routing an email message, where the email message might be briefly stored on an email server before being forwarded to the recipient.

- **Route discovery and selection:** Because Layer 3 devices make forwarding decisions based on logical network addresses, a Layer 3 device might need to know how to reach various network addresses. For example, a common Layer 3 device is a router. A router can maintain a routing table indicating how to forward a packet based on the packet's destination network address.

  A router can have its routing table populated via manual configuration (that is, by entering static routes), via a dynamic routing protocol (for example, RIP, OSPF, or EIGRP), or simply by the fact that the router is directly connected to certain networks.

NOTE Routing protocols are discussed in Chapter 6.

- **Connection services:** Just as the data link layer offers connection services for flow control and error control, connection services also exist at the network layer. Connection services at the network layer can improve the communication reliability, if the data link's LLC sublayer is not performing connection services.

The following functions are performed by connection services at the network layer:

- **Flow control (also known as congestion control):** Helps prevent a sender from sending data more rapidly than the receiver is capable of receiving it.

- **Packet reordering:** Allows packets to be placed in the proper sequence as they are sent to the receiver. This might be necessary because some networks support load balancing, where multiple links are used to send packets between two devices. Because multiple links exist, packets might arrive out of order.

Examples of devices found at the network layer include routers and multilayer switches. The most common Layer 3 protocol in use, and the protocol on which the Internet is based, is IPv4. However, IPv6 is beginning to be more common on networks today.

NOTE Routers and multilayer switches are discussed in Chapter 3.

Layer 4: The Transport Layer

The transport layer, as shown in Figure 2-10, acts as a dividing line between the upper layers and lower layers of the OSI model. Specifically, messages are taken from upper layers (Layers 5–7) and are encapsulated into segments for transmission to the lower layers (Layers 1–3). Similarly, data streams coming from lower layers are de-encapsulated and sent to Layer 5 (the session layer), or some other upper layer, depending on the protocol.

Key Topic

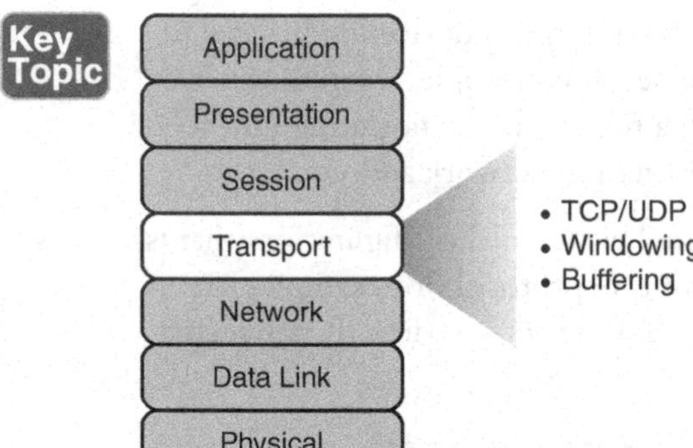

Figure 2-10 Layer 4: The Transport Layer

Two common transport layer protocols are Transmission Control Protocol (TCP) and User Datagram Protocol (UDP):

- **Transmission Control Protocol (TCP):** A connection-oriented transport protocol. Connection-oriented transport protocols offer reliable transport, in that if a segment is dropped, the sender can detect that drop and retransmit the dropped segment. Specifically, a receiver acknowledges segments that it receives. Based on those acknowledgments, a sender can decide which segments were successfully received and which segments need to be transmitted again.
- **User Datagram Protocol (UDP):** A connectionless transport protocol. Connectionless transport protocols offer unreliable transport, in that if a segment is dropped, the sender is unaware of the drop, and no retransmission occurs.

Just as Layer 2 and Layer 3 offer flow control services, flow control services also exist at Layer 4. Two common flow control approaches at Layer 4 are windowing and buffering:

- **Windowing:** TCP communication uses windowing, in that one or more segments are sent at one time, and a receiver can attest to the receipt of all the segments in a window with a single acknowledgment. In some cases, as illustrated in Figure 2-11, TCP uses a sliding window, where the window size begins with one segment. If there is a successful acknowledgment of that one segment (that is, the receiver sends an acknowledgment asking for the next segment), the window size doubles to two segments. Upon successful receipt of those two segments, the next window holds four segments. This exponential increase in window size continues until the receiver does not acknowledge successful receipt of all segments within a certain amount of time—known as the *round-trip time* (RTT), which is sometimes called *real transfer time*—or until a configured maximum window size is reached.

Key Topic

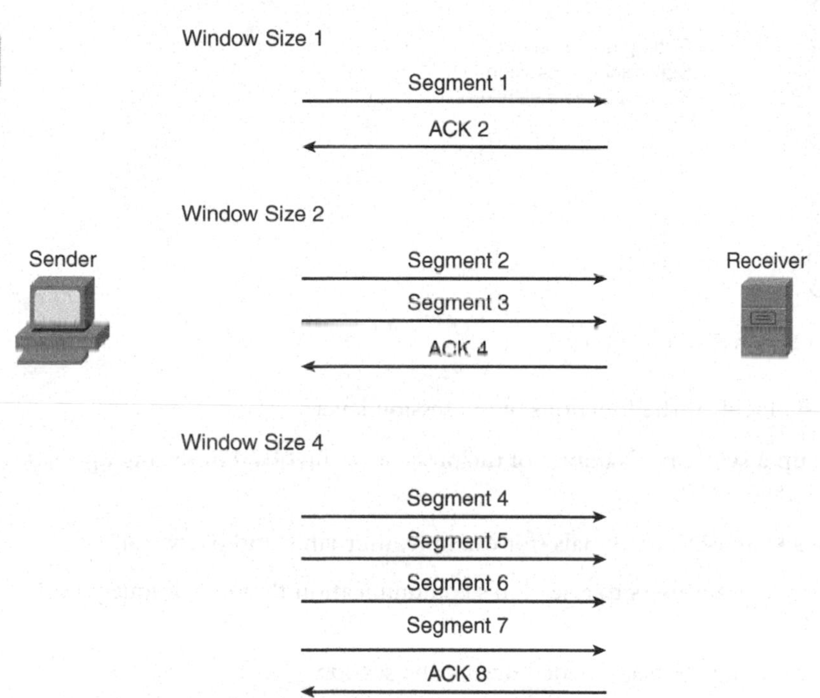

Figure 2-11 TCP Sliding Window

- **Buffering:** With buffering, a device (for example, a router) uses a chunk of memory (sometimes called a *buffer* or a *queue*) to store segments if bandwidth is not available to send those segments. A queue has a finite capacity, however, and can overflow (that is, drop segments) in case of sustained network congestion.

In addition to TCP and UDP, Internet Control Message Protocol (ICMP) is another transport layer protocol you are likely to meet. ICMP is used by utilities such as ping and traceroute, which are discussed in Chapter 10, "Command-Line Tools."

Layer 5: The Session Layer

The session layer, as shown in Figure 2-12, is responsible for setting up, maintaining, and tearing down sessions. You can think of a session as a conversation that needs to be treated separately from other sessions to avoid the intermingling of data from different conversations.

Key Topic

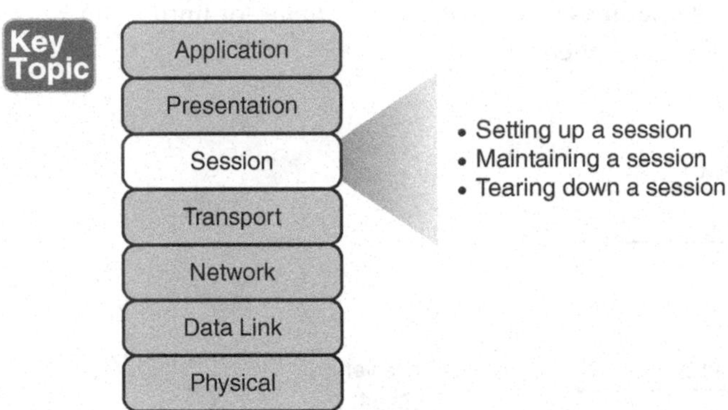

Figure 2-12 Layer 5: The Session Layer

Here is a detailed look at the functions of the session layer:

- **Setting up a session:** Examples of the procedures involved in setting up a session include the following:
  - Checking user credentials (for example, username and password)
  - Assigning numbers to a session's communication flows to uniquely find each one
  - Negotiating services needed during the session
  - Negotiating which device begins sending data
- **Maintaining a session:** Examples of the procedures involved in supporting a session include the following:
  - Transferring data
  - Reestablishing a disconnected session
  - Acknowledging receipt of data

- **Tearing down a session:** A session can be disconnected based on agreement of the devices in the session. Alternatively, a session might be torn down because one party disconnects (either intentionally or because of an error condition). If one party disconnects, the other party can detect a loss of communication with that party and tear down its side of the session.

H.323 is an example of a session layer protocol, which can help set up, support, and tear down a voice or video connection. Keep in mind, however, that not every network application neatly maps directly to all seven layers of the OSI model. The session layer is one of those layers where it might not be possible to name what protocol in each scenario is running in it. Network Basic Input/Output System (NetBIOS) is one example of a session layer protocol.

NOTE NetBIOS is an application programming interface (API) developed in the early 1980s to allow computer-to-computer communication on a small LAN (specifically, PC-Network, which was IBM's LAN technology at the time). Later, IBM needed to support computer-to-computer communication over larger Token Ring networks. As a result, IBM enhanced the scalability and features of NetBIOS with a NetBIOS emulator named NetBIOS Extended User Interface (NetBEUI).

Layer 6: The Presentation Layer

The presentation layer, as shown in Figure 2-13, handles formatting the data being exchanged and securing that data with encryption.

Key Topic

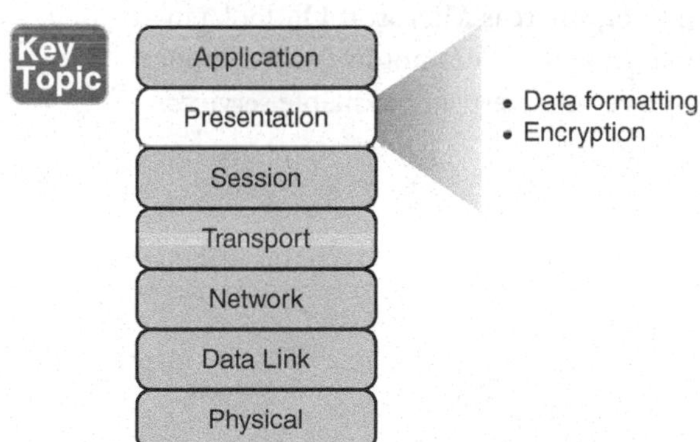

Figure 2-13 Layer 6: The Presentation Layer

The following list describes the function of data formatting and encryption in more detail:

- **Data formatting:** As an example of how the presentation layer handles data formatting, consider how text is formatted. Some applications might format text using American Standard Code for Information Interchange (ASCII), while other applications might format text using Extended Binary Coded Decimal Interchange Code (EBCDIC). The presentation layer handles formatting the text (or other types of data, such as multimedia or graphics files) in a format that allows compatibility between the communicating devices.
- **Encryption:** Imagine that you are sending sensitive information over a network (for example, your credit card number or bank password). If a malicious user were to intercept your transmission, they might be able to obtain this sensitive information. To add a layer of security for such transmissions, encryption can be used to scramble up (encrypt) the data in such a way that if the data were intercepted, a third party would not be able to unscramble it (decrypt). However, the intended recipient would be able to decrypt the transmission.

Encryption is discussed in detail in Chapter 12, "Network Security."

Layer 7: The Application Layer

The application layer, as shown in Figure 2-14, gives application services to a network. An important (and often-misunderstood) concept is that end-user applications (such as Microsoft Word) live at the application layer. Instead, the application layer supports services used by end-user applications. For example, email is an application layer service that does exist at the application layer, whereas Microsoft Outlook (an example of an email client) is an end-user application that does not live at the application layer. Another function of the application layer is advertising available services.

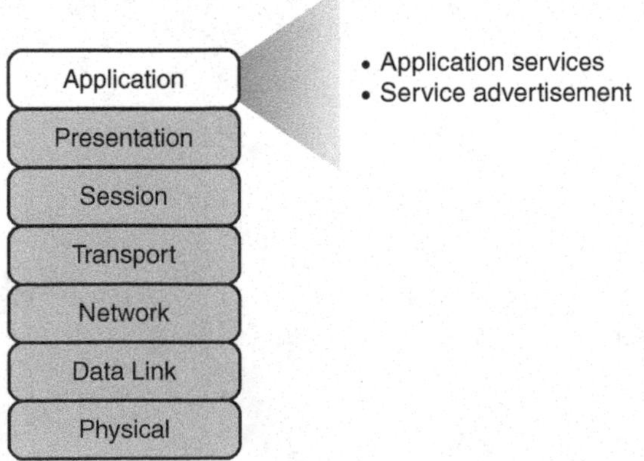

Figure 2-14 Layer 7: The Application Layer

The following describes the functions of the application layer in more detail:

- **Application services:** Examples of the application services living at the application layer include file sharing and email.
- **Service advertisement:** Some applications' services (for example, some networked printers) periodically send out advertisements, making their availability known to other devices on the network. Other services, however, register themselves and their services with a centralized directory (for example, Microsoft Active Directory), which can be queried by other network devices seeking such services.

Recall that even though the application layer is numbered as Layer 7, it is at the top of the OSI stack because its networking functions are closest to the end user.

The TCP/IP Stack

The ISO developed the OSI reference model to be generic, in terms of what protocols and technologies could be categorized by the model. However, most of the traffic on the Internet (and traffic on corporate networks) is based on the TCP/IP protocol suite. Therefore, a more relevant model for many network designers and administrators to reference is a model developed by the United States Department of Defense (DoD). This model is known as the *DoD model* or the *TCP/IP stack*.

NOTE An older protocol known as the Network Control Protocol (NCP) was similar to the TCP/IP protocol. NCP was used on ARPANET (the predecessor to the Internet), and it provided features like those offered by the TCP/IP suite of protocols on the Internet, although they were not as robust.

Layers of the TCP/IP Stack

The TCP/IP stack has only four defined layers, as opposed to the seven layers of the OSI model. Figure 2-15 contrasts these two models for an illustrative understanding.

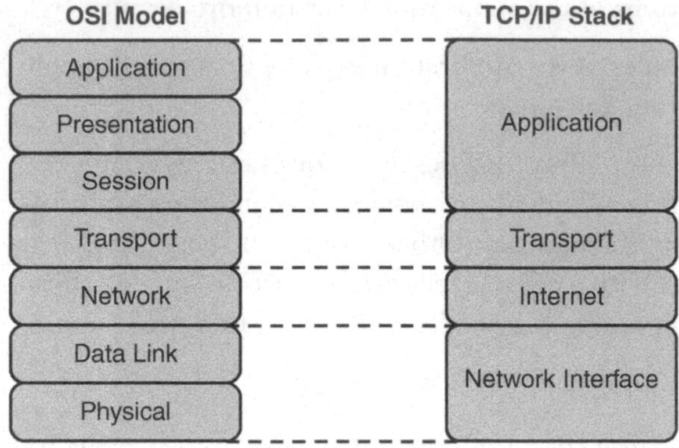

Figure 2-15 TCP/IP Stack

The TCP/IP stack is composed of the following layers:

- **Network interface:** The TCP/IP stack's network interface layer encompasses the technologies offered by Layers 1 and 2 (the physical and data link layers) of the OSI model.

> **NOTE** Some literature refers to the network interface layer as the *network access layer*.

- **Internet:** The Internet layer of the TCP/IP stack maps to Layer 3 (the network layer) of the OSI model. Although multiple routed protocols (for example, IP, IPX, and AppleTalk) live at the OSI model's network layer, the Internet layer of the TCP/IP stack focuses on IP as the protocol to be routed through a network. Figure 2-16 shows the format of an IP Version 4 packet.

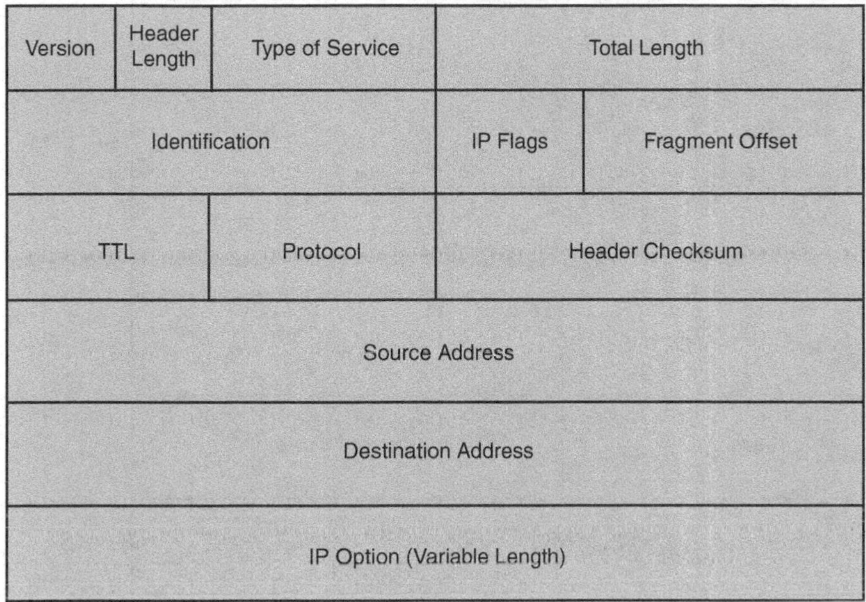

Figure 2-16 IP Version 4 Packet Format

Notice that there are fields in the IP packet header for both a source and a destination IP address. The Protocol field shows the transport layer protocol from which the packet was sent or to which the packet should be sent. Also of note is the Time-to-Live (TTL) field. The value in this field is decremented by 1 every time this packet is routed from one IP network to another (that is, passes through a router). If the TTL value ever reaches 0, the packet is discarded from the network. This behavior helps prevent routing loops. As a common practice, the OSI layer numbers of 1, 2, and 3 are still used when referring to physical, data link, and network layers of the TCP/IP stack, even though the TCP/IP stack does not explicitly separate the physical and data link layers.

- **Transport:** The transport layer of the TCP/IP stack maps to Layer 4 (the transport layer) of the OSI model. The two primary protocols found at the TCP/IP stack's transport layer are TCP and UDP.

  Figure 2-17 details the structure of a TCP segment. Notice the fields for source and destination ports. As described later in this chapter, these ports identify to which upper-layer protocol data should be forwarded, or from which upper-layer protocol the data is being sent.

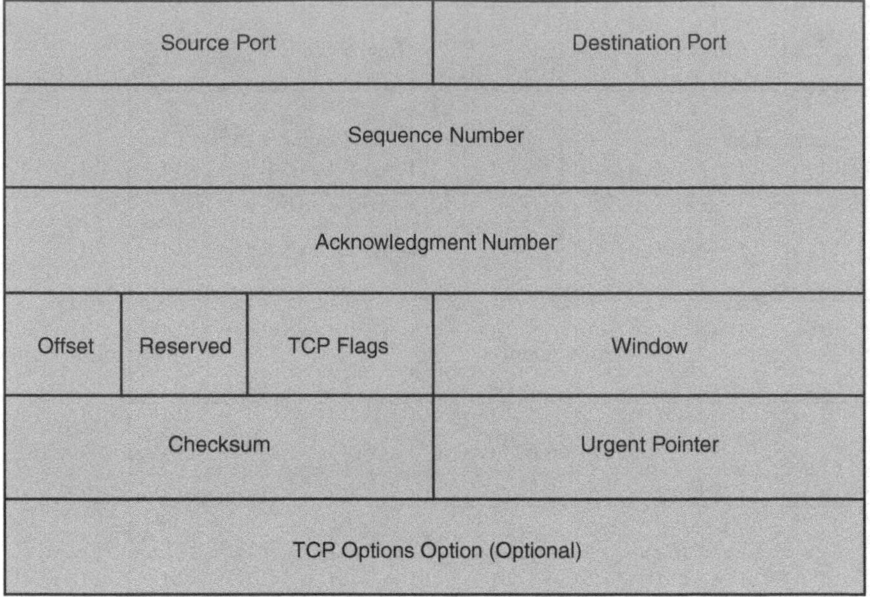

Figure 2-17 TCP Segment Format

Also notice the field for window size. The value in this field determines how many bytes a device can receive before expecting an acknowledgment. As previously described, this feature offers flow control.

The header of a TCP segment also contains sequence numbers for segments. With sequence numbering, if segments arrive out of order, the recipient can put them back in the proper order based on these sequence numbers.

The acknowledgment number in the header shows the next sequence number the receiver expects to receive. This is a way for the receiver to let the sender know that all segments up to and including that point have been received. Due to the sequencing and acknowledgements, TCP is considered to be a *connection-oriented* transport layer protocol.

Figure 2-18 presents the structure of a UDP segment. UDP is a connectionless, unreliable protocol. UDP lacks the sequence numbering, window size, and acknowledgment numbering present in the header of a TCP segment. The UDP segment's header simply contains source and destination port numbers, a UDP checksum (which is an optional field used to detect transmission errors), and the segment length (measured in bytes).

Source Port	Destination Port
UDP Length	UDP Checksum

Figure 2-18 UDP Segment Format

Because a UDP header is so much smaller than a TCP header, UDP becomes a good candidate for the transport layer protocol for applications that need to maximize bandwidth and do not require acknowledgments (for example, audio or video streams).

- **Application:** The biggest difference between the TCP/IP stack and the OSI model is found at the TCP/IP stack's application layer. This layer addresses concepts described by Layers 5, 6, and 7 (the session, presentation, and application layers) of the OSI model.

With the reduced complexity of a four-layer model like the TCP/IP stack, network designers and administrators can more easily categorize a given networking technology into a specific layer. For example, although H.323 was shown earlier as a session layer protocol within the OSI model, you would have to know more about the behavior of H.323 to properly categorize it. However, with the TCP/IP stack, you could quickly figure out that H.323 is a higher-level protocol that gets encapsulated inside of TCP, and thus classify H.323 in the application layer of the TCP/IP stack.

Common Application Protocols in the TCP/IP Stack

Application layer protocols in the TCP/IP stack are identifiable by unique port numbers. For example, when you enter a web address in an Internet browser, you are (by default) communicating with that remote web address using TCP port 80. Specifically, Hypertext Transfer Protocol (HTTP), which is the protocol used by web servers, uses TCP port 80. Therefore, the data you send to that remote web server has a destination port number of 80. That data is then encapsulated into a TCP segment at the transport layer. That segment is then further encapsulated into a packet at the Internet layer and sent out on the network using an underlying network interface layer technology such as Ethernet.

Continuing with the example depicted in Figure 2-19, when you send traffic to that remote website, the packet you send out to the network needs not only the destination IP address (172.16.1.2 in this example) of the web server and the destination port number for HTTP (that is, 80), it also needs the source IP address of your computer (10.1.1.1 in this example). Because your computer is not acting as a web server, its port is not 80. Instead, your computer selects a source port number greater than 1023. In this example, let's imagine that the client PC selects the source port 1248.

Key Topic

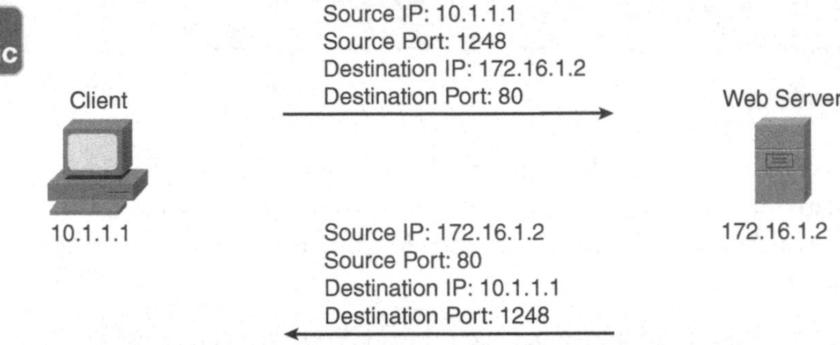

Figure 2-19 Example: Port Numbers and IP Addresses

Notice that when the web server sends content back, the IP addresses and port numbers have now switched, with the web server as the source and your PC as the destination. With both source and destination port numbers, along with source and destination IP addresses, two-way communication becomes possible.

NOTE Ports numbered 1023 and below are called *well-known* ports, and ports numbered above 1023 are called *ephemeral* ports. The maximum value of a port is 65,535. Well-known port number assignments are found at http://www.iana.org/assignments/port-numbers.

Table 2-1 serves as a reference for some of the more popular application layer protocols and applications found in the TCP/IP stack. Some protocols or applications (such as DNS) may use TCP or UDP for their transport protocol, depending on the specific function being performed.

Table 2-1 Application Layer Protocols/Applications

Protocol	Description	TCP Port	UDP Port
DHCP	Dynamic Host Configuration Protocol: Dynamically assigns IP address information (for example, IP address, subnet mask, DNS server's IP address, and default gateway's IP address) to a network device		67, 68
DNS	Domain Name System: Resolves domain names to corresponding IP addresses	53	53

Protocol	Description	TCP Port	UDP Port
FTP	File Transfer Protocol: Transfers files with a remote host (typically requires authentication of user credentials)	20 and 21	
H.323	A signaling protocol that provides multimedia communications over a network	1720	
HTTP	Hypertext Transfer Protocol: Retrieves content from a web server	80	
HTTPS	Hypertext Transfer Protocol Secure: Used to securely retrieve content from a web server	443	
IMAP	Internet Message Access Protocol: Retrieves email from an email server	143	
IMAP4	Internet Message Access Protocol Version 4: Retrieves email from an email server	143	
LDAP	Lightweight Directory Access Protocol: Provides directory services (for example, a user directory that includes username, password, email, and phone number information) to network clients	389	
LDAPS	Lightweight Directory Access Protocol over SSH: A secured version of LDAP	636	
MGCP	Media Gateway Control Protocol: Used as a call control and communication protocol for Voice over IP networks		2427, 2727
NetBIOS	Network Basic Input/Output System: Provides network communication services for LANs that use NetBIOS	139	137, 138
NNTP	Network News Transport Protocol: Supports the posting and reading of articles on Usenet news servers	119	
NTP	Network Time Protocol: Used by a network device to synchronize its clock with a time server (NTP server)		123
POP3	Post Office Protocol Version 3: Retrieves email from an email server	110	
RDP	Remote Desktop Protocol: A Microsoft protocol that allows a user to view and control the desktop of a remote computer	3389	
rsh	Remote Shell: Allows commands to be executed on a computer from a remote user	514	
RTP	Real-time Transport Protocol: Used for delivering media-based data (such as Voice over IP) through the network	5004, 5005	5004, 5005

Protocol	Description	TCP Port	UDP Port
RTSP	Real-Time Streaming Protocol: Communicates with a media server (for example, a video server) and controls the playback of the server's media files	554	554
SCP	Secure Copy: Provides a secure file-transfer service over an SSH connection and offers a file's original date and time information, which is not available with FTP	22	
SFTP	Secure FTP: Provides FTP file-transfer service over an SSH connection	22	
SIP	Session Initiation Protocol: Used to create and end sessions for one or more media connections, including Voice over IP calls	5061	5060
SMB	Server Message Block: Used to share files, printers, and other network resources	445	
SMTP	Simple Mail Transfer Protocol: Used for sending email	25	
SNMP	Simple Network Management Protocol: Used to monitor and manage network devices		161
SNMP Trap	Simple Network Management Protocol Trap: A notification sent from an SNMP agent to an SNMP manager	162	162
SNTP	Simple Network Time Protocol: Supports time synchronization among network devices, similar to Network Time Protocol (NTP), although SNTP uses a less complex algorithm in its calculation and is slightly less accurate than NTP		123
SSH	Secure Shell: Used to securely connect to a remote host (typically via a terminal emulator)	22	
Telnet	Telnet: Used to connect to a remote host (typically via a terminal emulator)	23	
TFTP	Trivial File Transfer Protocol: Transfers files with a remote host (does not require authentication of user credentials)		69

Real-World Case Study

Bob, a manager of the networking team at Acme, Inc., is paying extra attention to the specific words he uses as he talks to his team in preparation for the implementation of the network. When referring to transport protocols such as the connection-oriented TCP and the connectionless UDP, the word Bob uses to describe those protocol data units is *segment*.

In discussing the applications that the company will be using over its network, Bob notes that many of these applications will be using TCP at the transport layer. This includes HTTP for web browsing, HTTPS for secure web traffic, and SMTP and IMAP for email services.

The SSH protocol, which also uses TCP at the transport layer, is a secure method that the company will use to remotely connect to and manage its network devices. A common connectionless UDP protocol is DNS, which will be used thousands of times a day to translate a friendly name like http://www.pearson.com to an IP address that is reachable over the network. Another protocol based on UDP that will be used often is Dynamic Control Host Protocol (DHCP), which assigns client computers on the network an IP address that is required for sending and receiving Layer 3 packets.

For the traffic on the LAN, the Ethernet cables and electronic signals being sent as bits going over those cables represent Layer 1 from an OSI perspective. On the LAN, they will be using Ethernet technology, and as a result the Layer 2 frames that are sent on the LAN will be encapsulated and sent as Ethernet Layer 2 frames.

For datagrams being sent across the serial WAN connections provided by the service provider, it is likely that either PPP or HDLC encapsulation will be used for the Layer 2 frames. On both the LAN and the WAN, at Layer 3 (the network layer), IPv4 will be used for host addressing and defining networks. The same Layer 1, Layer 2, and Layer 3 infrastructure is also capable of transporting IPv6, if desired.

Inside the Layer 3 IP headers, each packet contains the source and destination address, in addition to the information to tell the receiving network device about which Layer 4 transport protocol is encapsulated or carried inside of the Layer 3 packet. When a network device receives the packet and opens it up to look at the contents, this process is called *de-encapsulation*. As the recipient de-encapsulates and looks at the Layer 4 information, it identifies the application layer protocol or service being used. A segment going to a web server is likely to have a TCP destination port of 80 or 443, depending on whether encryption is being used for a secure connection. A DNS request uses a UDP destination port of 53.

Summary

Here are the main topics covered in this chapter:

- The ISO's OSI reference model consists of seven layers: physical (Layer 1), data link (Layer 2), network (Layer 3), transport (Layer 4), session (Layer 5), presentation (Layer 6), and application (Layer 7). The purpose of each layer was presented, along with examples of technologies living at the individual layers, as it pertains to networking.

- The TCP/IP stack was presented as an alternative model to the OSI reference model. The TCP/IP stack consists of four layers: network interface, Internet, transport, and application. These layers were compared with the seven layers of the OSI model.
- This chapter discussed how port numbers are used to associate data at the transport layer with a proper application layer protocol. Examples of common application layer protocols in the TCP/IP suite were presented, along with their port numbers.

Exam Preparation Tasks

Review All the Key Topics

Review the most important topics from inside the chapter, noted with the Key Topic icon in the outer margin of the page. Table 2-2 lists these key topics and the page numbers where each is found.

Table 2-2 Key Topics for Chapter 2

Key Topic Element	Description	Page Number
List	Layers of the OSI model	33
Figure 2-3	Protocol data unit names	35
Figure 2-4	Layer 1: The physical layer	35
Figure 2-8	Layer 2: The data link layer	39
Figure 2-9	Layer 3: The network layer	42
Figure 2-10	Layer 4: The transport layer	44
Figure 2-11	TCP sliding window	45
Figure 2-12	Layer 5: The session layer	46
Figure 2-13	Layer 6: The presentation layer	47
Figure 2-14	Layer 7: The application layer	48
Figure 2-15	TCP/IP stack	50
Figure 2-16	IP Version 4 packet format	51
Figure 2-17	TCP segment format	52
Figure 2-18	UDP segment format	53
Figure 2-19	Example: Port numbers and IP addresses	54
Table 2-1	Application layer protocols/applications	54

Complete Tables and Lists from Memory

Print a copy of Appendix C, "Memory Tables," or at least the section for this chapter, and complete as many of the tables as possible from memory. Appendix D, "Memory Tables Answer Key," includes the completed tables and lists so you can check your work.

Define Key Terms

Define the following key terms from this chapter, and check your answers in the Glossary:

Open Systems Interconnection (OSI) reference model, protocol data unit (PDU), current state modulation, state transition modulation, cyclic redundancy check (CRC), physical layer, data link layer, network layer, transport layer (OSI model), session layer, presentation layer, application layer (OSI model), network interface layer, Internet layer, transport layer (TCP/IP stack), application layer (TCP/IP stack), time-division multiplexing (TDM), Transmission Control Protocol (TCP), User Datagram Protocol (UDP), TCP/IP stack

Complete Chapter 2 Hands-On Labs in Network+ Simulator Lite

- Matching Well-Known Port Numbers
- TCP/IP Protocols and Their Functions
- Network Application Protocols
- OSI Model Layer Functions

Additional Resources

Bring the OSI Model to Life: http://www.ajsnetworking.com/osi-life

The OSI Reference Model: https://youtu.be/OHpzuPvQygU

The OSI Model Challenge: http://ajsnetworking.com/osiquiz1

Review Questions

The answers to these review questions appear in Appendix A, "Answers to Review Questions."

1. Which layer of the OSI reference model contains the MAC and LLC sublayers?
   - a. Network layer
   - b. Transport layer
   - c. Physical layer
   - d. Data link layer

2. Which approach to bandwidth usage consumes all the available frequencies on a medium to transmit data?
   - a. Broadband
   - b. Baseband
   - c. Time-division multiplexing
   - d. Simplex

3. Windowing is provided at what layer of the OSI reference model?
   - a. Data link layer
   - b. Network layer
   - c. Transport layer
   - d. Physical layer

4. IP addresses reside at which layer of the OSI reference model?
   - a. Network layer
   - b. Session layer
   - c. Data link layer
   - d. Transport layer

5. Which of the following is a connectionless transport layer protocol?
   - a. IP
   - b. TCP
   - c. UDP
   - d. H.323

6. Identify the four layers of the TCP/IP stack. (Choose four.)
   a. Session layer
   b. Transport layer
   c. Internet layer
   d. Data link layer
   e. Network layer
   f. Application layer
   g. Network interface layer

7. What is the range of well-known TCP and UDP ports?
   a. Below 2048
   b. Below 1024
   c. 16,384–32,768
   d. Above 8192

8. Which protocol supports a secure connection to a remote host via terminal emulation software?
   a. Telnet
   b. SSH
   c. FTP
   d. SFTP

9. Identify the well-known UDP port number for NTP.
   a. 53
   b. 69
   c. 123
   d. 143

10. Identify three e-mail protocols. (Choose three.)
   a. SNMP
   b. SMTP
   c. POP3
   d. IMAP4

After completion of this chapter, you will be able to answer the following questions:

- What are the characteristics of various media types?
- What is the role of a given network infrastructure component?
- Specialized network devices offer what features?
- How are virtualization technologies changing traditional corporate data center designs?
- What are some of the primary protocols and hardware components found in a Voice over IP (VoIP) network?

CHAPTER 3

Network Components

Many modern networks can have a daunting number of devices, and it is your job to understand the function of each device and how it works with the others. To create a network, these devices need some sort of interconnection. That interconnection uses one of a variety of media types. Therefore, this chapter begins by delving into the characteristics of media types, such as coaxial cable, twisted-pair cable, fiber-optic cable, and wireless technologies.

Next, this chapter covers infrastructure components (for example, hubs, bridges, switches, multilayer switches, and routers), along with their purpose. This book gives special attention to switches, because they make up a significant part of a local area network's (LAN) infrastructure.

Finally, this chapter introduces you to a collection of specialized network devices. These include virtual private network (VPN) concentrators, firewalls, Domain Name System (DNS) servers, Dynamic Host Configuration Protocol (DHCP) servers, proxy servers, caching engines, and content switch, to name just a few!

Foundation Topics

Media

A network is an interconnection of devices. Those interconnections occur over some type of media. The media might be physical, such as a copper or fiber-optic cable. Alternatively, the media might be the air, through which radio waves propagate (as is the case with wireless networking technologies).

This section contrasts various media types, including physical and wireless media. Although some wireless technologies are covered here, be aware that wireless technologies are examined more thoroughly in Chapter 8, "Wireless Technologies."

Coaxial Cable

Coaxial cable (referred to as *coax*) consists of two conductors. As illustrated in Figure 3-1, one of the conductors is an inner insulated conductor. This inner conductor is surrounded by another conductor. This second conductor is sometimes made of a metallic foil or woven wire.

Figure 3-1 Coaxial Cable

Because the inner conductor is shielded by the metallic outer conductor, coaxial cable is resistant to electromagnetic interference (EMI). For example, EMI occurs when an external signal is received on a wire and might result in a corrupted data transmission. As another example, EMI occurs when a wire acts as an antenna and radiates electromagnetic waves, which might interfere with data transmission on another cable. Coaxial cables have an associated characteristic impedance that needs to be balanced with the device (or terminator) with which the cable connects.

> **NOTE** The term *electromagnetic interference* (EMI) is sometimes used interchangeably with the term *radio frequency interference* (RFI).

The following list details three of the most common types of coaxial cables:

- **RG-59:** Typically used for short-distance applications, such as carrying composite video between two nearby devices. This cable type has loss characteristics such that it is not right for long-distance applications. RG-59 cable has a characteristic impedance of 75 Ohms.

- **RG-6:** Used by local cable companies to connect individual homes to the cable company's distribution network. Like RG-59 cable, RG-6 cable has a characteristic impedance of 75 Ohms.
- **RG-58:** Has loss characteristics and distance limitations like those of RG-59. However, the characteristic impedance of RG-58 is 50 ohms, and this type of coax was popular with early 10BASE2 Ethernet networks (which are discussed in Chapter 4, "Ethernet Technology").

Although RG-58 coaxial cable was commonplace in early computer networks (in 10BASE2 networks), coaxial cable's role in modern computer networks is as the media used by cable modems. Cable modems are commonly installed in residences to provide high-speed Internet access over the same connection used to receive multiple television stations.

NOTE The *RG* prefix used in coaxial cable types stands for *radio guide*.

Common connectors used on coaxial cables are as follows:

- **BNC:** A Bayonet Neill-Concelman (BNC) connector (*British Naval-Connector* in some literature) can be used for a variety of applications, including as a connector in a 10BASE2 Ethernet network. A BNC coupler could be used to connect two coaxial cables together back to back.
- **F-connector:** An F-connector is often used for cable TV (including cable modem) connections. Notice that some refer to it is simply as **F-type, including CompTIA.**

Figure 3-2 shows what both of these connectors look like.

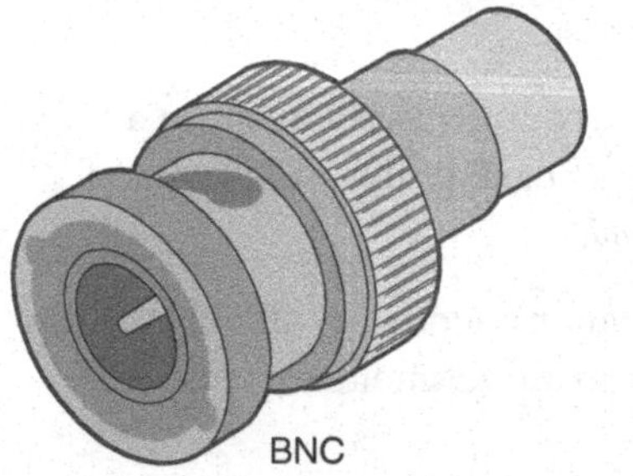

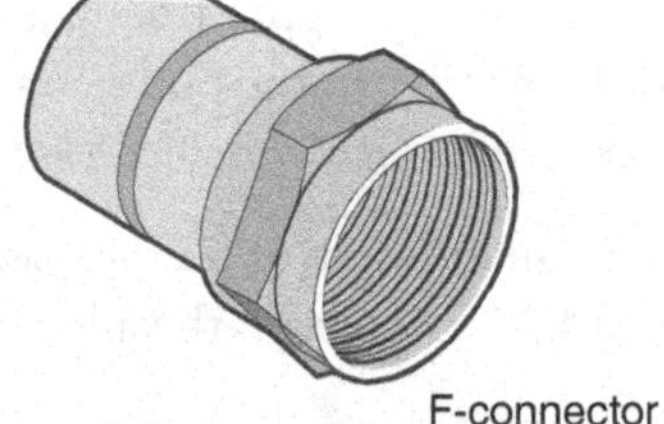

Figure 3-2 Coaxial Cable Connectors

Twisted-Pair Cable

Today's most popular LAN media type is twisted-pair cable, where individually insulated copper strands are intertwined. Two categories of twisted-pair cable include shielded twisted pair (STP) and unshielded twisted pair (UTP). A UTP coupler could be used to connect two UTP cables, back to back. Also, for adherence to fire codes, you might need to select plenum cable versus nonplenum cable.

To define industry-standard pinouts and color coding for twisted-pair cabling, the TIA/EIA-568 standard was developed. The first iteration of the TIA/EIA-568 standard has come to be known as the *TIA/EIA-568-A* standard, which was released in 1991.

NOTE The TIA/EIA acronym comes from Telecommunications Industry Association/Electronic Industries Alliance.

In 2001, an updated standard was released, which became known as *TIA/EIA-568-B*. Interestingly, the pinout of these two standards is the same. However, the color coding of the wiring is different. 568-B is the more commonly used standard in the United States.

Shielded Twisted Pair

If wires in a cable are not twisted or shielded, that cable can act as an antenna, which might receive or transmit EMI. To help prevent this type of behavior, the wires (which are individually insulated) can be twisted together in pairs.

If the distance between the twists is less than a quarter of the wavelength of an electromagnetic waveform, the twisted pair of wires will not radiate that wavelength or receive EMI from that wavelength (in theory, if the wires were perfect conductors). However, as frequencies increase, wavelengths decrease.

One option of supporting higher frequencies is to surround a twisted pair in a metallic shielding, similar to the outer conductor in a coaxial cable. This type of cable is referred to as a *shielded twisted-pair* (STP) *cable*.

Figure 3-3 shows an example of STP cable. These outer conductors shield the copper strands from EMI; however, the addition of the metallic shielding adds to the expense of STP.

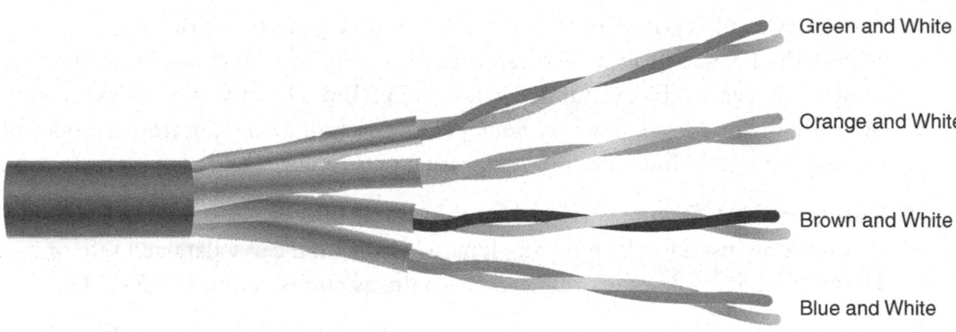

Figure 3-3 Shielded Twisted Pair

Unshielded Twisted Pair

Another way to block EMI from the copper strands making up a twisted-pair cable is to twist the strands more tightly (that is, more twists per centimeter). With these strands wrapped around each other, the wires insulate each other from EMI.

Figure 3-4 illustrates an example of UTP cable. Because UTP is less expensive than STP, it has grown in popularity since the mid-1990s to become the media of choice for most LANs.

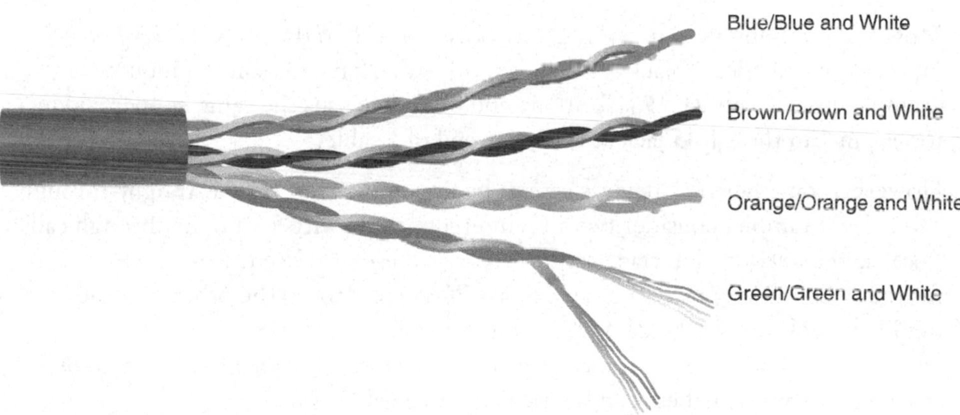

Figure 3-4 Unshielded Twisted Pair

UTP cable types vary in their data carrying capacity. Common categories of UTP cabling include the following:

- **Category 3:** Category 3 (Cat 3) cable was used in older Ethernet 10BASE-T networks, which carried data at a rate of 10Mbps (where Mbps stands for megabits per second, meaning millions of bits per second). However, Cat 3 cable can carry data at a maximum rate of 16Mbps, as seen in some older Token Ring networks.

- **Category 5:** Category 5 (Cat 5) cable is commonly used in Ethernet 100BASE-TX networks, which carry data at a rate of 100 Mbps. However, Cat 5 cable can carry ATM traffic at a rate of 155 Mbps. Most Cat 5 cables consist of four pairs of 24-gauge wires. Each pair is twisted, with a different number of twists per meter. However, on average, one pair of wires has a twist every 5 cm.
- **Category 5e:** Category 5e (Cat 5e) cable is an updated version of Cat 5 and is commonly used for 1000BASE-T networks, which carry data at a rate of 1Gbps. Cat 5e cable offers reduced crosstalk, as compared to Cat 5 cable.
- **Category 6:** Like Cat 5e cable, Category 6 (Cat 6) cable is commonly used for 1000BASE-T Ethernet networks. Some Cat 6 cable is made of thicker conductors (for example, 22-gauge or 23-gauge wire), although some Cat 6 cable is made from the same 24-gauge wire used by Cat 5 and Cat 5e. Cat 6 cable has thicker insulation and offers reduced crosstalk, as compared with Cat 5e.
- **Category 6a:** Category 6a (Cat 6a), or augmented Cat 6, supports twice as many frequencies as Cat 6 and can be used for 10GBASE-T networks, which can transmit data at a rate of 10 billion bits per second (10 Gbps).

Although other wiring categories exist, those presented in the previous list are the categories most commonly seen in modern networks.

Most UTP cabling used in today's networks is considered to be *straight-through*, meaning that the RJ-45 jacks at each end of a cable have matching pinouts. For example, pin 1 in an RJ-45 jack at one end of a cable uses the same copper conductor as pin 1 in the RJ-45 jack at the other end of a cable.

However, some network devices cannot be interconnected with a straight-through cable. For example, consider two PCs interconnected with a straight-through cable. Because the network interface cards (NICs) in these PCs use the same pair of wires for transmission and reception, when one PC sends data to the other PC, the receiving PC would receive the data on its transmission wires, rather than its reception wires. For such a scenario, you can use a crossover cable, which swaps the transmit and receive wire pairs between the two ends of a cable.

NOTE A crossover cable for Ethernet devices is different from a crossover cable used for a digital T1 circuit (as discussed in Chapter 7, "Wide Area Networks (WANs) "). Specifically, an Ethernet crossover cable has a pin mapping of 1 > 3, 2 > 6, 3 > 1, and 6 > 2, whereas a T1 crossover cable has a pin mapping of 1 > 4, 2 > 5, 4 > 1, and 5 > 2. Another type of cable is the rollover cable, which is used to connect to a console port to manage a device such as a router or switch. The pin mapping for a rollover cable is 1 < > 8, 2 < > 7, 3 < > 6, 4 < > 5. The end of the cable looks like an RJ-45 eight-pin connector.

NOTE A traditional port found in a PC's NIC is called a *media-dependent interface* (MDI). If a straight-through cable connects a PC's MDI port to an Ethernet switch port, the Ethernet switch port needs to swap the transmit pair of wires (that is, the wires connected to pins 1 and 2) with the receive pair of wires (that is, the wires connected to pins 3 and 6).

Therefore, a traditional port found on an Ethernet switch is called a *media-dependent interface crossover* (MDIX), which reverses the transmit and receive pairs. However, if you want to interconnect two switches, where both switch ports used for the interconnection were MDIX ports, the cable would need to be a crossover cable.

Fortunately, most modern Ethernet switches have ports that can automatically detect whether they need to act as MDI ports or MDIX ports and make the appropriate adjustments. This eliminates the necessity of using straight-through cables for some Ethernet switch connections and crossover cables for other connections. With this *Auto-MDIX* feature, you can use either straight-through cables or crossover cables.

Common connectors used on twisted-pair cables are as follows:

- **RJ-45:** A type 45 registered jack (RJ-45) is an eight-pin connector found in most Ethernet networks. However, most Ethernet implementations only use four of the eight pins.
- **RJ-11:** A type 11 registered jack (RJ-11) has the capacity to be a six-pin connector. However, most RJ-11 connectors have only two or four conductors. An RJ-11 connector is found in most home telephone networks. However, most home phones only use two of the six pins.
- **DB-9 (RS-232):** A nine-pin D-subminiature (DB-9) connector is an older connector used for low-speed asynchronous serial communications, such as a PC to a serial printer, a PC to a console port of a router or switch, or a PC to an external modem. Do not confuse the DB-9 with a DB-25. The DB-25 connector was also used for the serial or parallel ports of early personal computers.

Figure 3-5 shows what these connectors look like.

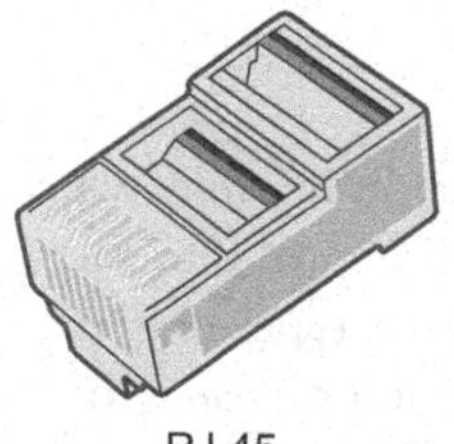

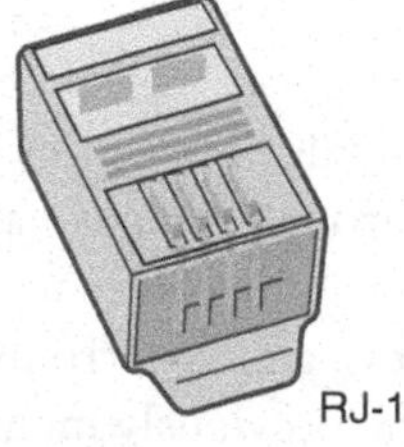

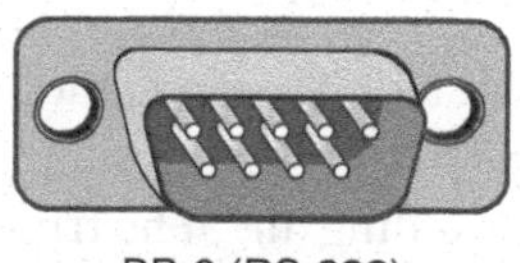

Figure 3-5 Twisted-Pair Cable Connectors

Plenum Versus Nonplenum Cable

If a twisted-pair cable is to be installed under raised flooring or in an open-air return, fire codes must be considered. For example, imagine that there was a fire in a building. If the outer insulation of a twisted-pair cable caught on fire or started to melt, it could release toxic fumes. If those toxic fumes were released in a location such as an open-air return, those fumes could be spread throughout a building, posing a huge health risk.

To mitigate the concern of pumping poisonous gas throughout a building's heating, ventilation, and air conditioning (HVAC) system, *plenum* cabling can be used. The outer insulator of a plenum twisted-pair cable is not only fire retardant; some plenum cabling uses a fluorinated ethylene polymer (FEP) or a low-smoke polyvinyl chloride (PVC) to minimize dangerous fumes.

NOTE Check with your local fire codes before installing network cabling.

Fiber-Optic Cable

An alternative to copper cabling is fiber-optic cabling, which sends light (instead of electricity) through an optical fiber (typically made of glass). Using light instead of electricity makes fiber optics immune to EMI. Also, depending on the Layer 1 technology being used, fiber-optic cables typically have greater range (that is, a greater maximum distance between networked devices) and greater data-carrying capacity.

Lasers are often used to inject light pulses into a fiber-optic cable. However, lower-cost light-emitting diodes (LED) are also on the market. Fiber-optic cables are generally classified according to their diameter and fall into one of two categories: multimode fiber (MMF) and single-mode fiber (SMF).

The wavelengths of light also vary between MMF and SMF cables. Usually, wavelengths of light in a MMF cable are in the range of 850–1300 nm, where nm stands for nanometers. A nanometer is one billionth of a meter. Conversely, the wavelengths of light in a SMF cable use usually in the range of 1310–1550 nm. A fiber coupler could be used to connect two fiber cables, back to back.

Multimode Fiber

When a light source, such as a laser, sends light pulses into a fiber-optic cable, what keeps the light from simply passing through the glass and being dispersed into the surrounding air? The trick is that fiber-optic cables use two different types of glass. There is an inner strand of glass (that is, a *core*) surrounded by an outer *cladding* of glass, similar to the construction of the previously mentioned coaxial cable.

The light injected by a laser (or LED) enters the core, and the light is prevented from leaving that inner strand and going into the outer cladding of glass. Specifically, the indices of refraction of these two different types of glass are so different that if the light attempts to leave the inner strand, it hits the outer cladding and bends back on itself.

To better understand this concept, consider a straw in a glass of water, as shown in Figure 3-6. Because air and water have different indices of refraction (that is, light travels at a slightly different speed in air and water), the light that bounces off of the straw and travels to our eyes is bent by the water's index of refraction. When a fiber-optic cable is manufactured, dopants are injected into the two types of glasses, making up the core and cladding to give them significantly different indices of refraction, thus causing any light attempting to escape to be bent back into the core.

Figure 3-6 Example: Refractive Index

The path that light travels through a fiber-optic cable is called a *mode of propagation*. The diameter of the core in a multimode fiber is large enough to permit light to enter the core at different angles, as depicted in Figure 3-7. If light enters at a steep angle, it bounces back and forth much more frequently on its way to the far end of the cable as opposed to light that enters the cable perpendicularly. If pulses of light representing different bits travel down the cable using different modes of propagation, it is possible that the bits (that is, the pulses of light representing the bits) will arrive out of order at the far end (where the pulses of light, or absence of light, are interpreted as binary data by photoelectronic sensors).

Key Topic

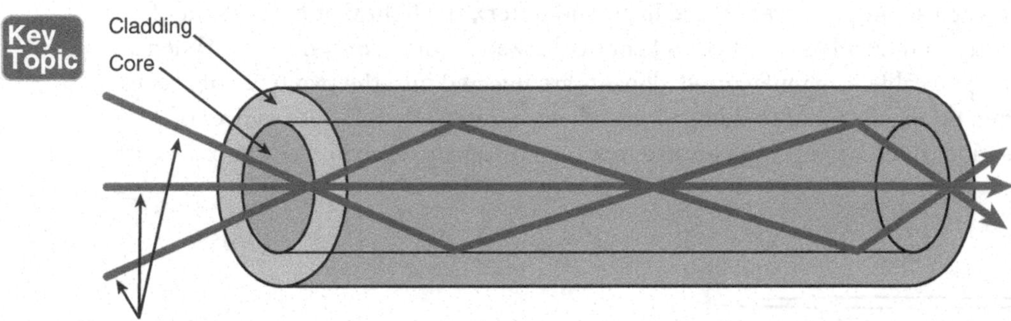

Figure 3-7 Light Propagation in Multimode Fiber

For example, perhaps the pulse of light representing the first bit intersected the core at a steep angle and bounced back and forth many times on its way to the far end of the cable, while the light pulse representing the second bit intersected the core perpendicularly and did not bounce back and forth very much. With all of its bouncing, the first bit has to travel further than the second bit, which might cause the bits to arrive out of order. Such a condition is known as *multimode delay distortion*. To mitigate the issue of multimode delay distortion, MMF typically has shorter distance limitations, as opposed to SMF.

Single-Mode Fiber

SMF eliminates the issue of multimode delay distortion by having a core with a diameter so small that it only permits one mode (that is, one path) of propagation, as shown in Figure 3-8. With the issue of multimode delay distortion mitigated, SMF typically has longer distance limitations than MMF.

Key Topic

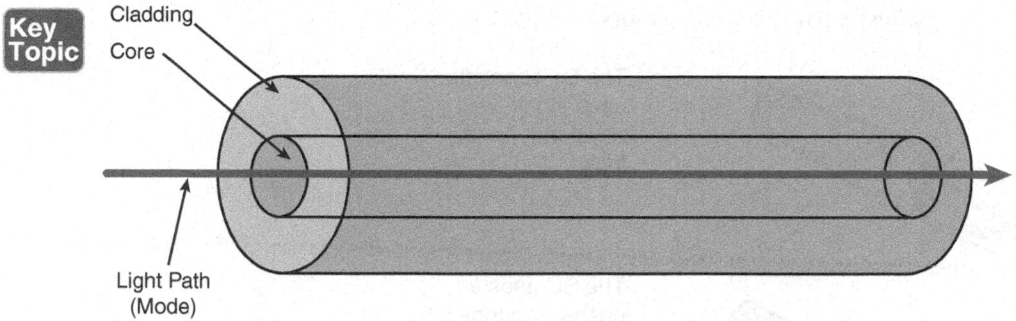

Figure 3-8 Light Propagation in Single-Mode Fiber

A potential downside to SMF, however, is cost. Because SMF has to be manufactured to very exacting tolerances, you usually pay more for a given length of fiber-optic cabling. However, for some implementations, where greater distances are required, the cost is an acceptable trade-off to reach greater distances.

Some common connectors used on fiber-optic cables are as follows:

- **ST:** A *straight tip* (ST) *connector* is sometimes referred to as a *bayonet connector*, because of the long tip extending from the connector. ST connectors are most commonly used with MMF. An ST connector connects to a terminating device by pushing the connector into the terminating equipment and then twisting the connector housing to lock it in place.
- **SC:** Different literature defines an SC connector as *subscriber connector*, *standard connector*, or *square connector*. The SC connector is connected by pushing the connector into the terminating device, and it can be removed by pulling the connector from the terminating device. The connector has slight variants within the industry, with the major types being APC, UPC, and MTRJ. Always consult with the vendor or IT staff member regarding the exact requirements.
- **LC:** A *Lucent connector* (LC) connects to a terminating device by pushing the connector into the terminating device, and it can be removed by pressing the tab on the connector and pulling it out of the terminating device.
- **MTRJ:** The most unique characteristic of a *media termination recommended jack* (MTRJ) connector is that two fiber strands (a transmit strand and a receive strand) are included in a single connector. An MTRJ connector is connected by pushing the connector into the terminating device, and it can be removed by pulling the connector from the terminating device.

Figure 3-9 shows what these connectors look like.

Key Topic

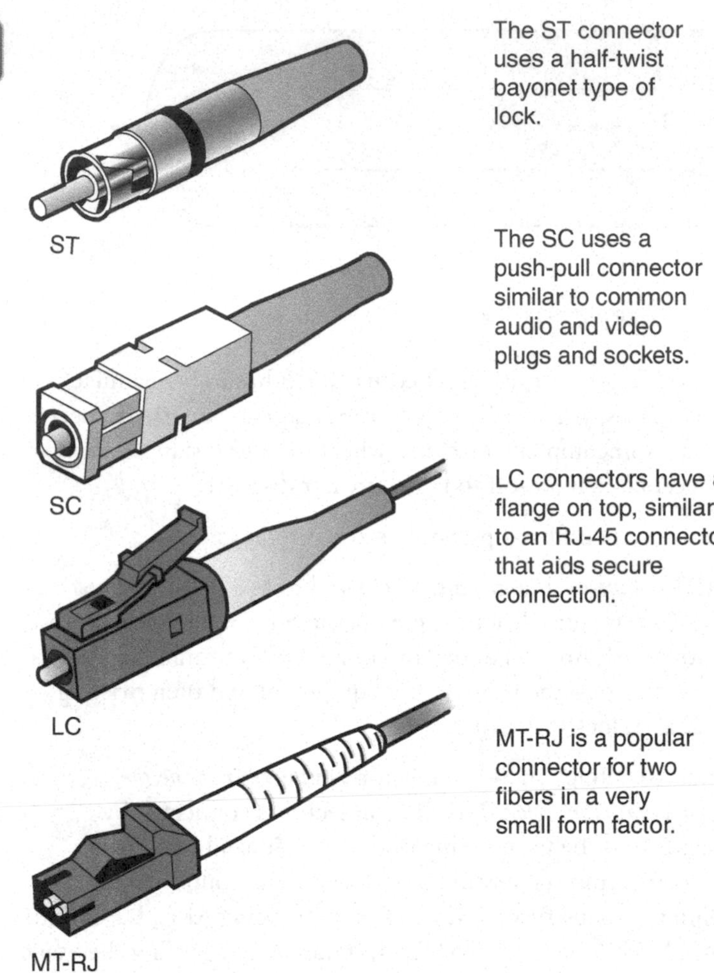

The ST connector uses a half-twist bayonet type of lock.
ST
The SC uses a push-pull connector similar to common audio and video plugs and sockets.
SC
LC connectors have a flange on top, similar to an RJ-45 connector, that aids secure connection.
LC
MT-RJ is a popular connector for two fibers in a very small form factor.
MT-RJ

Figure 3-9 Common Fiber-Optic Connectors

Fiber Connector Polishing Styles

Fiber-optic cables have different types of mechanical connections. The type of connection impacts the quality of the fiber-optic transmission. Listed from basic to better, the options include Physical Contact (PC), Ultra Physical Contact (UPC), and Angled Physical Contact (APC), which refer to the polishing styles of fiber-optic connectors. The different polish of the fiber-optic connectors results in different performance of the connector. The less back reflection, the better the transmission. The PC back reflection is –40 dB, the UPC back reflection is around –55 dB, and the APC back reflection is about –70 dB.

Media Converters

There may be times when the media needs to be converted. To do this, a media converter could be used. Examples may include single-mode fiber to Ethernet, multimode fiber to Ethernet, fiber to coaxial, and single-mode to multimode fiber.

Cable Distribution

After deciding on what type of media you are going to use in your network (for example, UTP, STP, MMF, or SMF), you should install that media as part of an organized cable distribution system. Typically, cable distribution systems are hierarchical in nature.

Consider the example profiled in Figure 3-10. In this example, cable from end-user offices runs back to common locations within the building. These locations are sometimes referred to as *wiring closets*. Cables in these locations might terminate in a *patch panel*. This patch panel might consist of some sort of cross-connect block wired into a series of ports (for example, RJ-45 ports), which can be used to quickly interconnect cables coming from end-user offices with a network device, such as an Ethernet switch. A building might have multiple patch panels (for example, on different floors of a building). These common locations, where cables from nearby offices terminate, are often called *intermediate distribution frames* (IDFs).

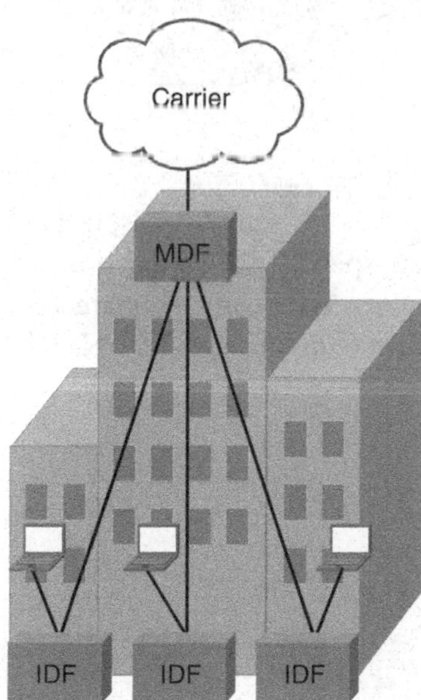

Figure 3-10 Example: Cable Distribution System

The two most popular types of cross-connect blocks found in an IDF are detailed here:

- **66 block:** A 66 block, as shown in Figure 3-11, was traditionally used in corporate environments for cross-connecting phone system cabling. As 10Mbps LANs grew in popularity, in the late 1980s and early 1990s, these termination blocks were used to cross-connect Cat 3 UTP cabling. The electrical characteristics (specifically, crosstalk) of a 66 block, however, do not support higher-speed LAN technologies, such as 100Mbps Ethernet networks.

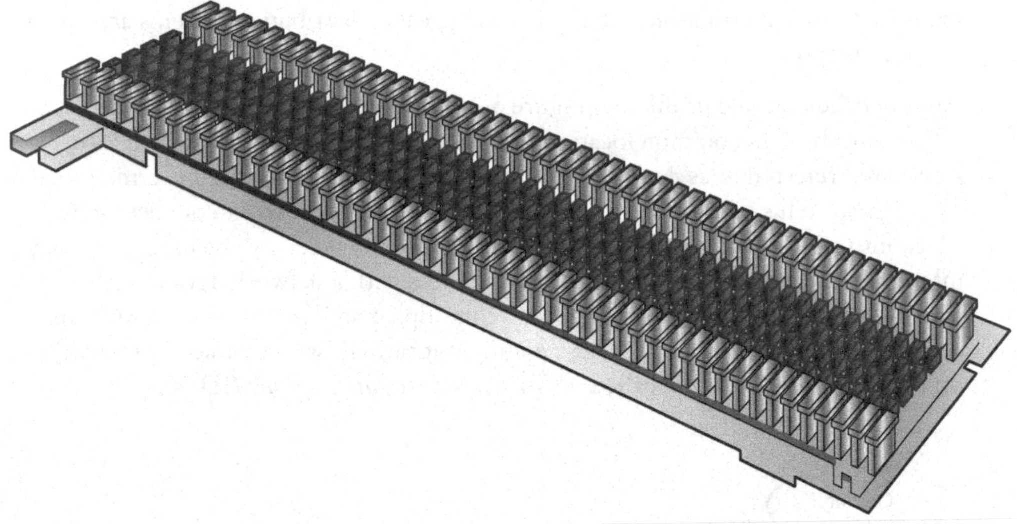

Figure 3-11 66 Block

- **110 block:** Because 66 blocks are subject to too much crosstalk (that is, interference between different pairs of wires) for higher-speed LAN connections, 110 blocks, an example of which is provided in Figure 3-12, can terminate a cable (for example, a Cat 5 cable) being used for those higher-speed LANs.

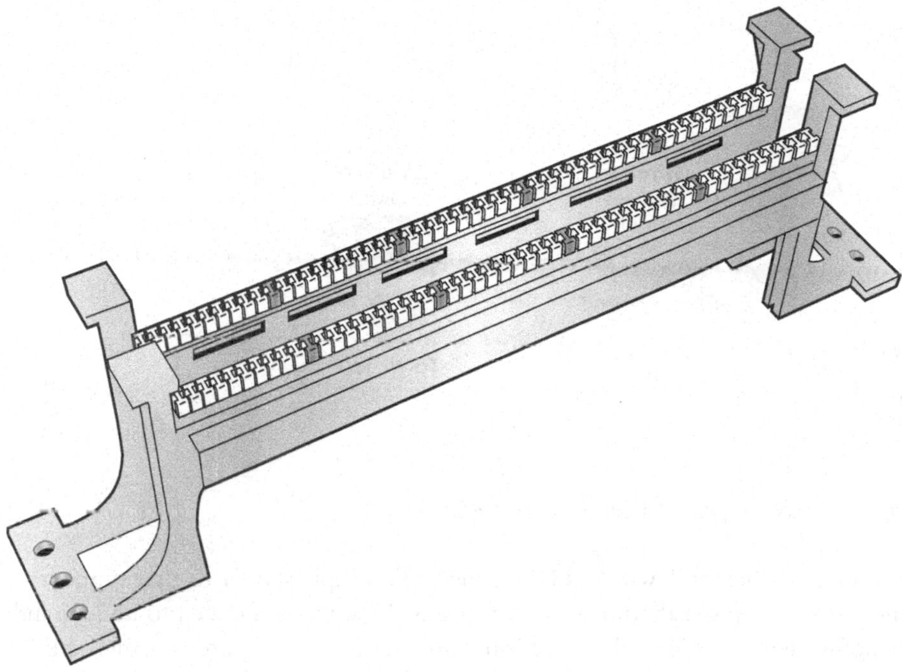

Figure 3-12 110 Block

This centralized distribution frame, which connects out to multiple IDFs, is called the *main distribution frame* (MDF).

Another component you might use is a fiber optic patch panel. This is often termed a fiber distribution panel. You use this to organize and distribute optical cables. It also allows you to terminate cable elements and provides a secure, organized chamber for housing connectors and splice units.

With such a wide variety of copper and fiber cabling used by different network devices, you might need one or more *media converters*. Examples of media converters include the following:

- Fiber (MMF or SMF) to Ethernet
- Fiber to coaxial
- SMF to MMF

Wireless Technologies

Not all media is physical, as is the case of wireless network technologies. This book dedicates Chapter 8 to these technologies. However, for now, you just need to understand the basics.

Consider the sample wireless topology presented in Figure 3-13. Notice that wireless clients gain access to a wired network by communicating via radio waves with a wireless access point (AP). The AP is then hardwired to a LAN.

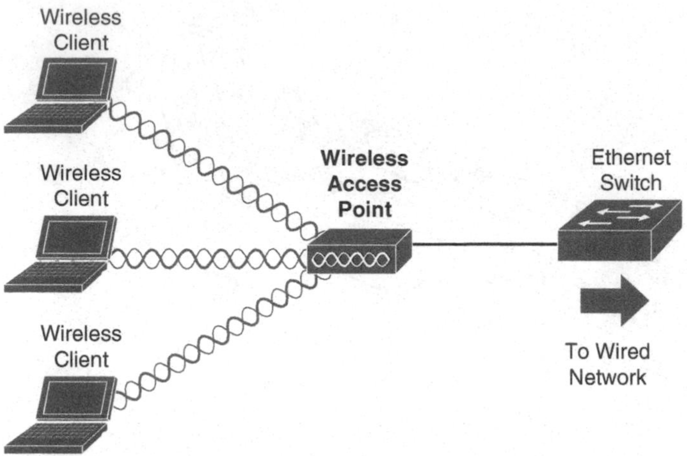

Figure 3-13 Example: Wireless Network Topology

As discussed in Chapter 8, wireless LANs include multiple standards that support various transmission speeds and security features. However, you need to understand, at this point, that all wireless devices connecting to the same AP are considered to be on the same *shared network segment*, which means that only one device can send data to and receive data from an AP at any one time.

Technologies for the Internet of Things

Many wireless technologies (or related to wireless) come in to play to make the Internet of Things (IoT) a reality. IoT refers to the trend today to connect everyday objects to the Internet in order to make them "smart." In my home, I speak to my Amazon Echo speaker in order to have it control the lights, for example. This Internet-connected speaker and the lights are perfect examples of IoT in action.

Here are key technologies you should be aware of that help make the modern IoT a reality:

- **Z-Wave**: A wireless communications protocol used primarily for home automation. It is a mesh network using low-energy radio waves to communicate from appliance to appliance. Z-Wave is found with devices such as lighting control systems, security systems, thermostats, windows, locks, swimming pools, and garage door openers.
- **Ant+**: A wireless protocol for monitoring sensor data such as a person's heart rate or a car's tire pressure, as well as for controlling systems such as indoor lighting and entertainment appliances such as televisions. ANT+ is designed and maintained by the ANT+ Alliance, which is owned by Garmin.

- **Bluetooth**: As discussed in Chapter 1, "Computer Network Fundamentals," Bluetooth is a wireless technology that allows devices to communicate over a short distance. In addition to the creation of a personal area network (PAN), Bluetooth also comes into play to enable communications for the IoT.
- **NFC**: Near field communication (NFC) is a set of communication protocols that enables two electronic devices to transfer information. Typically, one of these devices is a portable device such as a smartphone. NFC devices must be close to each other (within 4 cm, or 1.6 in). NFC devices are used in contactless payment systems, similar to those used in credit cards and electronic ticket smartcards, and allow mobile payment to replace/supplement these systems.
- **IR**: Infrared is another wireless technology that permits data transmission in short-range communication among computer peripherals and personal digital assistants. These devices usually conform to standards published by IrDA, the Infrared Data Association. Remote controls and IrDA devices use infrared light-emitting diodes (LEDs) to emit infrared radiation that is focused by a plastic lens into a narrow beam.
- **RFID**: Radio-frequency identification (RFID) uses electromagnetic fields to automatically identify and track tags attached to objects. The tags contain electronically stored information. Passive tags collect energy from a nearby RFID reader's interrogating radio waves. Active tags have a local power source such as a battery and may operate at hundreds of meters from the RFID reader. Unlike a barcode, the tag need not be within the line of sight of the reader, so it may be embedded in the tracked object.
- **802.11**: As detailed in Chapter 8, IEEE 802.11 is a set of Media Access Control and physical layer specifications for implementing wireless local area network (WLAN) computer communication in the 900MHz and 2.4GHz, 3.6GHz, 5GHz, and 60GHz frequency bands. Obviously, these technologies play a great role in the IoT because many appliances and common objects communicate over 802.11 wireless signals to reach a main hub. This is how most smart lights function, for example.

Network Infrastructure Devices

The devices used in a network infrastructure can vary based on the Layer 1 technology used. For example, a Token Ring network (which is rare today) might use a multistation access unit (MAU), whereas an Ethernet network might use a switch.

Because Ethernet-based networks are dominant in today's LANs, however, the infrastructure devices presented here lend themselves to networks using Ethernet as the Layer 1 transport. Some devices (such as a router, for example) function basically the same regardless of the Layer 1 transport being used.

Hubs

As mentioned in Chapter 2, "The OSI Reference Model," a hub (specifically, an Ethernet hub in this discussion) lives at Layer 1 of the OSI model. As a result, a hub does not make forwarding decisions. Instead, a hub receives bits in on one port and then retransmits those bits out all other ports (that is, all ports on the hub other than the port on which the bits were received). This basic function of a hub has caused it to gain the nickname of a *bit spitter*.

Hubs most often use UTP cabling to connect to other network devices; however, some early versions of Ethernet hubs (prior to the popularization of Ethernet switches) supported fiber-optic connections.

The three basic types of Ethernet hubs are as follows:

- **Passive hub:** Does not amplify (that is, electrically regenerate) received bits.
- **Active hub:** Regenerates incoming bits as they are sent out all the ports on a hub, other than the port on which the bits were received.
- **Smart hub:** The term *smart hub* usually implies an active hub with enhanced features, such as Simple Network Management Protocol (SNMP) support.

A significant downside to hubs, and the main reason they have largely been replaced with switches, is that all ports on a hub belong to the same *collision domain*. As discussed in Chapter 4, a *collision domain* represents an area on a LAN on which there can be only one transmission at a time. Because multiple devices can reside in the same collision domain, as is the case with multiple PCs connected to a hub, if two devices transmit at the same time, those transmissions *collide* and have to be retransmitted.

Because of the collision-domain issue, and the inefficient use of bandwidth (that is, bits being sent out all ports rather than only the port needing the bits), hubs are rarely seen in modern LANs. However, hubs are an important piece of the tapestry that makes up the history of Ethernet networks and represent characteristics found in different areas of modern Ethernet networks. For example, a wireless AP is much like a hub, in that all the wireless devices associated with the AP belong to the same collision domain.

Consider Figure 3-14. Notice that the PCs depicted are interconnected using an Ethernet hub, but they are all in the same collision domain. As a result, only one of the connected PCs can transmit at any one time. This characteristic of hubs can limit scalability of hub-based LANs.

Also notice that all devices on a hub belong to the same broadcast domain, which means that a broadcast sent into the hub will be propagated out all of the ports on the hub (other than the port on which the broadcast was received).

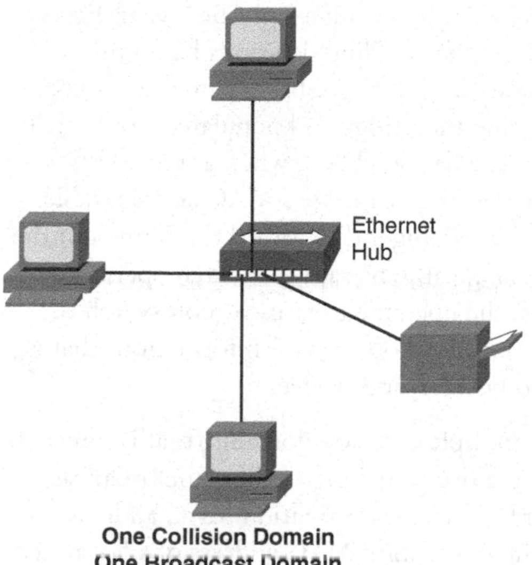

Figure 3-14 Ethernet Hub

Bridges

A bridge joins two or more LAN segments, typically two Ethernet LAN segments. Each LAN segment is in separate collision domains, as shown in Figure 3-15. As a result, an Ethernet bridge can be used to scale Ethernet networks to a larger number of attached devices.

Key Topic

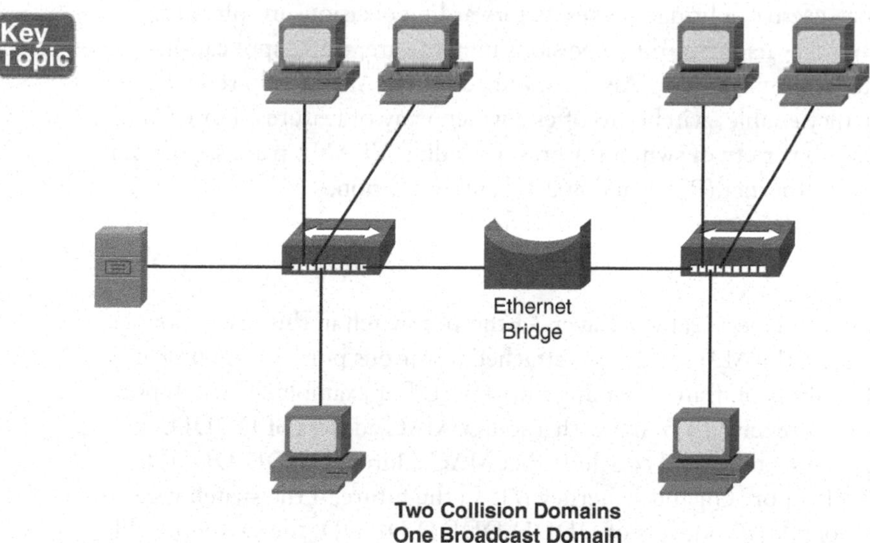

Figure 3-15 Ethernet Bridge

Unlike a hub, which blindly forwards received bits, a bridge (specifically, an Ethernet bridge in this discussion) makes intelligent forwarding decisions based on the destination MAC address present in a frame. Specifically, a bridge analyzes source MAC address information on frames entering the bridge and populates an internal MAC address table based on the learned information. Then, when a frame enters the bridge destined for a MAC address known by the bridge's MAC address table to reside off of a specific port, the bridge can intelligently forward the frame out the appropriate port. Because this operation is logically the same as switch operation, a more detailed description is presented in the upcoming discussion on switches. Because a bridge makes forwarding decisions based on Layer 2 information (that is, MAC addresses), a bridge is considered to be a Layer 2 device.

Although a bridge segments a LAN into multiple collision domains (that is, one collision domain per bridge port), all ports on a bridge belong to the same broadcast domain. To understand this concept, think about the destination MAC address found in a broadcast frame. At Layer 2, the destination MAC address of a broadcast frame is FFFF.FFFF.FFFF in hexadecimal notation. Also, recall that a bridge filters frames (that is, sends frames only out necessary ports) if the bridge has previously learned the destination MAC address in its MAC address table. Because no device on a network will have a MAC address of FFFF.FFFF.FFFF, a bridge will never enter that MAC address in its MAC address table. As a result, broadcast frames are *flooded* out all bridge ports other than the port that received the frame.

Popular in the mid- to late 1980s and early 1990s, bridges have largely been replaced with switches, for reasons including price, performance, and features. From a performance perspective, a bridge makes its forwarding decisions in software, whereas a switch makes its forwarding decisions in hardware, using application-specific integrated circuits (ASICs). Also, not only do these ASICs help reduce the cost of switches, they enable switches to offer a wider array of features. For example, Chapter 4 discusses a variety of switch features, including VLANs, trunks, port mirroring, Power over Ethernet (PoE), and 802.1X authentication.

Switches

Like a bridge, a switch (specifically, a Layer 2 Ethernet switch in this discussion) can dynamically learn the MAC addresses attached to various ports by looking at the source MAC address on frames coming into a port. For example, if switch port Gigabit Ethernet 1/1 received a frame with a source MAC address of DDDD.DDDD.DDDD, the switch could conclude that MAC address DDDD.DDDD.DDDD resided off of port Gigabit Ethernet 1/1. In the future, if the switch receives a frame destined for a MAC address of DDDD.DDDD.DDDD, the switch would only send that frame out of port Gigabit Ethernet 1/1.

Initially, however, a switch is unaware of what MAC addresses reside off of which ports (unless MAC addresses have been statically configured). Therefore, when a switch receives a frame destined for a MAC address not yet present in the switch's MAC address table, the switch floods that frame out of all the switch ports except the port on which the frame was received. Similarly, broadcast frames (that is, frames with a destination MAC address of FFFF.FFFF.FFFF) are always flooded out all switch ports except the port on which the frame was received. As mentioned in the discussion on bridges, the reason broadcast frames are always flooded is that no endpoint will have a MAC address of FFFF.FFFF.FFFF, meaning that the FFFF.FFFF.FFFF MAC address will never be learned in a switch's MAC address table.

To illustrate how a switch's MAC address table becomes populated, consider an endpoint named PC1 that wants to form a Telnet connection with a server. Also, assume that PC1 and its server both reside on the same subnet (that is, no routing is required to get traffic between PC1 and its server). Before PC1 can send a Telnet session to its server, PC1 needs to know the IP address (that is, the Layer 3 address) and the MAC address (Layer 2 address) of the server. The IP address of the server is typically known or is resolved via a Domain Name System (DNS) lookup. In this example, assume the server's IP address is known. To properly form a Telnet segment, however, PC1 needs to know the server's Layer 2 MAC address. If PC1 does not already have the server's MAC address in its ARP cache, PC1 can send an Address Resolution Protocol (ARP) request in an attempt to learn the server's MAC address, as shown in Figure 3-16.

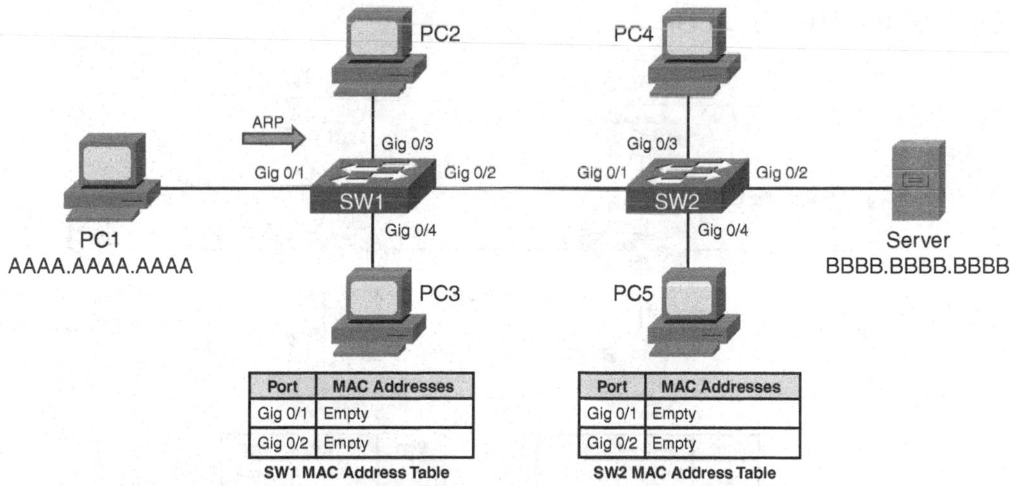

Port	MAC Addresses
Gig 0/1	Empty
Gig 0/2	Empty

Port	MAC Addresses
Gig 0/1	Empty
Gig 0/2	Empty

Figure 3-16 Endpoint Sending an ARP Request

When switch SW1 sees PC1's ARP request enter port Gigabit 0/1, PC1's MAC address of AAAA.AAAA.AAAA is added to switch SW1's MAC address table. Also, because the ARP request is a broadcast, its destination MAC address is FFFF.FFFF.

FFFF. Because the MAC address of FFFF.FFFF.FFFF is not known to switch SW1's MAC address table, switch SW1 floods a copy of the incoming frame out all switch ports, other than the port on which the frame was received, as shown in Figure 3-17.

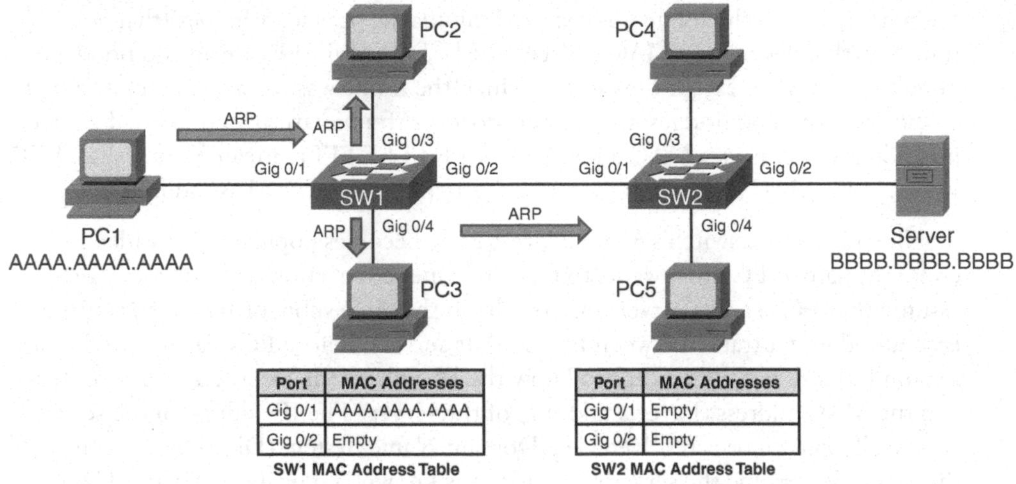

Port	MAC Addresses
Gig 0/1	AAAA.AAAA.AAAA
Gig 0/2	Empty

SW1 MAC Address Table

Port	MAC Addresses
Gig 0/1	Empty
Gig 0/2	Empty

SW2 MAC Address Table

Figure 3-17 Switch SW1 Flooding the ARP Request

When switch SW2 receives the ARP request over its Gig 0/1 trunk port, the source MAC address of AAAA.AAAA.AAAA is added to switch SW2's MAC address table, as illustrated in Figure 3-18. Also, similar to the behavior of switch SW1, switch SW2 floods the broadcast.

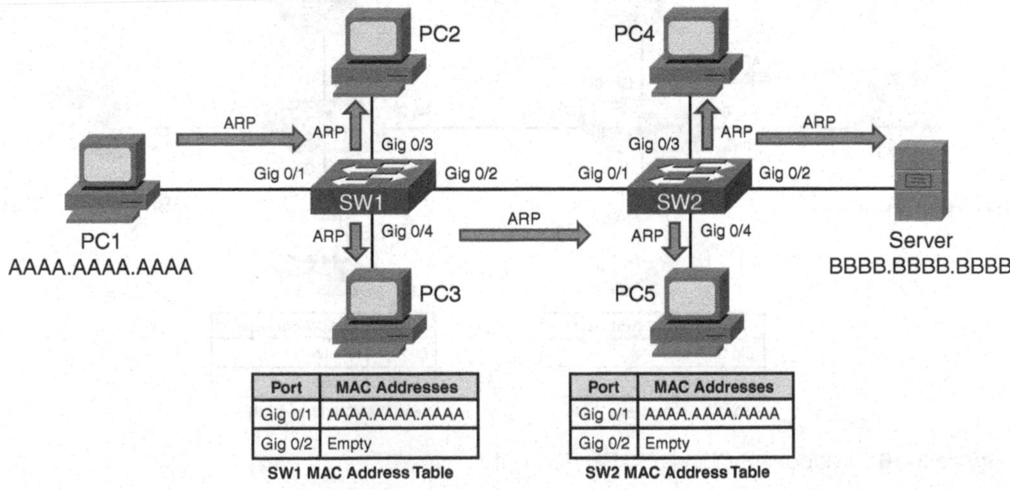

Port	MAC Addresses
Gig 0/1	AAAA.AAAA.AAAA
Gig 0/2	Empty

SW1 MAC Address Table

Port	MAC Addresses
Gig 0/1	AAAA.AAAA.AAAA
Gig 0/2	Empty

SW2 MAC Address Table

Figure 3-18 Switch SW2 Flooding the ARP Request

The server receives the ARP request and responds with an ARP reply, as shown in Figure 3-19. Unlike the ARP request, however, the ARP reply frame is not a broadcast frame. The ARP reply, in this example, has a destination MAC address of AAAA.AAAA.AAAA. This makes the ARP reply a unicast frame.

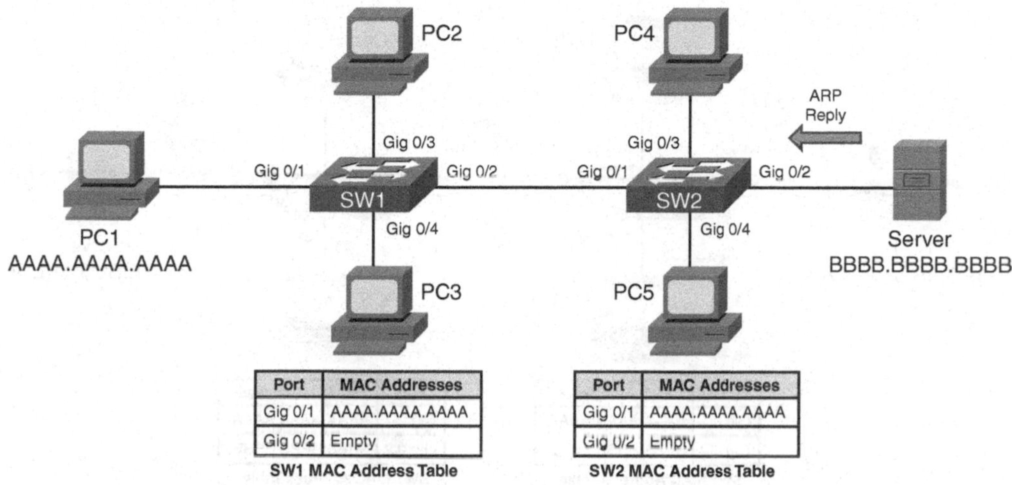

Port	MAC Addresses
Gig 0/1	AAAA.AAAA.AAAA
Gig 0/2	Empty

SW1 MAC Address Table

Port	MAC Addresses
Gig 0/1	AAAA.AAAA.AAAA
Gig 0/2	Empty

SW2 MAC Address Table

Figure 3-19 ARP Reply Sent from the Server

Upon receiving the ARP reply from the server, switch SW2 adds the server's MAC address of BBBB.BBBB.BBBB to its MAC address table, as shown in Figure 3-20. Also, the ARP reply is only sent out port Gig 0/1 because switch SW1 knows that the destination MAC address of AAAA.AAAA.AAAA is available off of port Gig 0/1.

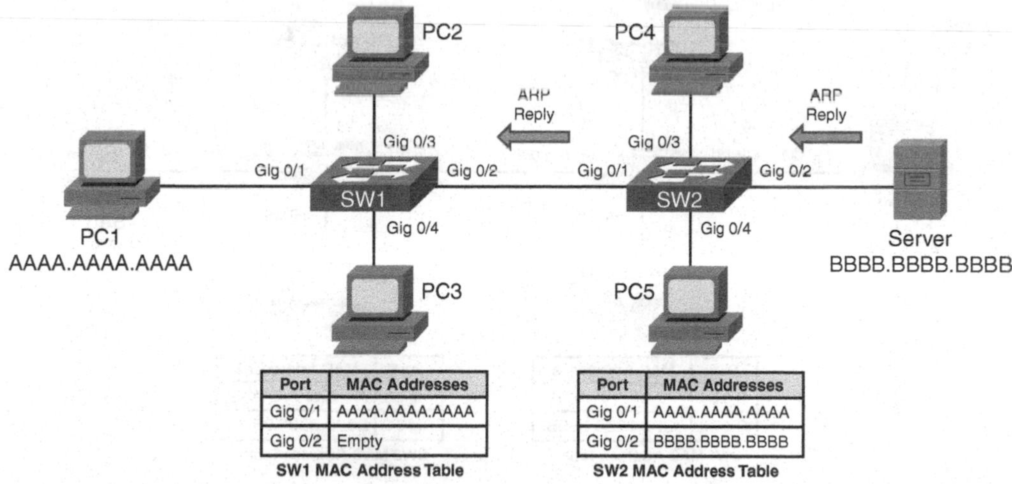

Port	MAC Addresses
Gig 0/1	AAAA.AAAA.AAAA
Gig 0/2	Empty

SW1 MAC Address Table

Port	MAC Addresses
Gig 0/1	AAAA.AAAA.AAAA
Gig 0/2	BBBB.BBBB.BBBB

SW2 MAC Address Table

Figure 3-20 Switch SW2 Forwarding the ARP Reply

When receiving the ARP reply in its Gig 0/2 port, switch SW1 adds the server's MAC address of BBBB.BBBB.BBBB to its MAC address table. Also, like switch SW2, switch SW1 now has an entry in its MAC address table for the frame's destination MAC address of AAAA.AAAA.AAAA. Therefore, switch SW1 forwards the ARP reply out port Gig 0/1 to the endpoint of PC1, as illustrated in Figure 3-21.

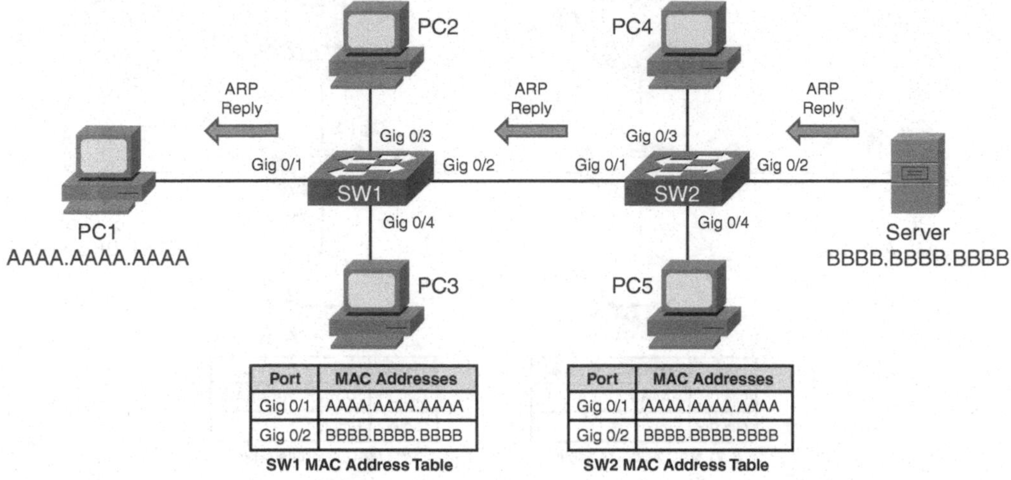

Port	MAC Addresses
Gig 0/1	AAAA.AAAA.AAAA
Gig 0/2	BBBB.BBBB.BBBB

SW1 MAC Address Table

Port	MAC Addresses
Gig 0/1	AAAA.AAAA.AAAA
Gig 0/2	BBBB.BBBB.BBBB

SW2 MAC Address Table

Figure 3-21 Switch SW1 Forwarding the ARP Reply

After receiving the server's ARP reply, PC1 now knows the MAC address of the server. Therefore, PC1 can now properly construct a Telnet segment destined for the server, as depicted in Figure 3-22.

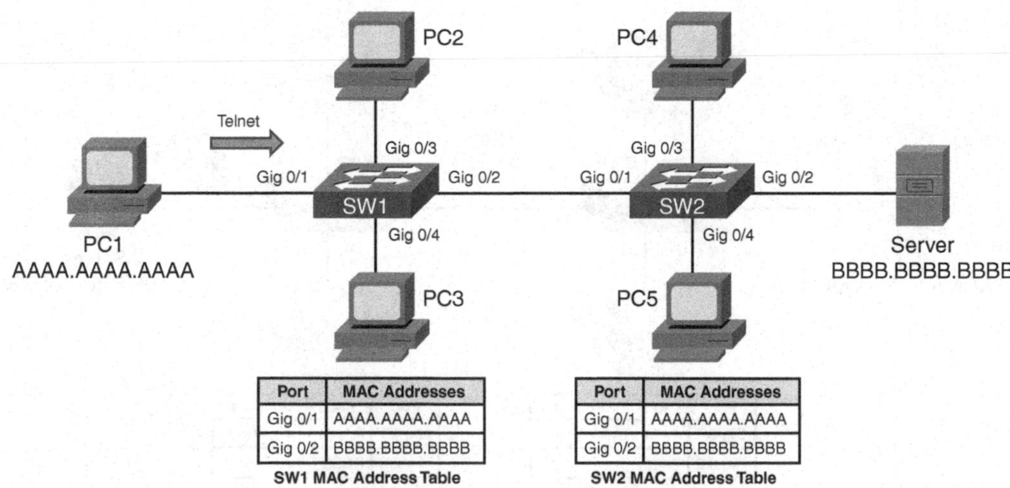

Port	MAC Addresses
Gig 0/1	AAAA.AAAA.AAAA
Gig 0/2	BBBB.BBBB.BBBB

SW1 MAC Address Table

Port	MAC Addresses
Gig 0/1	AAAA.AAAA.AAAA
Gig 0/2	BBBB.BBBB.BBBB

SW2 MAC Address Table

Figure 3-22 PC1 Sending a Telnet Segment

Switch SW1 has the server's MAC address of BBBB.BBBB.BBBB in its MAC address table. Therefore, when switch SW1 receives the Telnet segment from PC1, that segment is forwarded out of switch SW1's Gig 0/2 port, as shown in Figure 3-23.

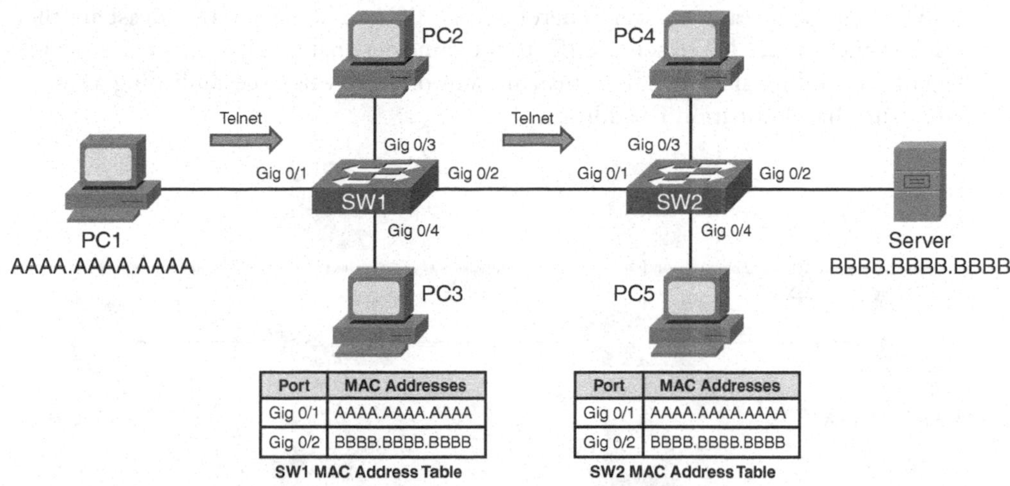

Port	MAC Addresses
Gig 0/1	AAAA.AAAA.AAAA
Gig 0/2	BBBB.BBBB.BBBB

SW1 MAC Address Table

Port	MAC Addresses
Gig 0/1	AAAA.AAAA.AAAA
Gig 0/2	BBBB.BBBB.BBBB

SW2 MAC Address Table

Figure 3-23 Switch SW1 Forwarding the Telnet Segment

Similar to the behavior of switch SW1, switch SW2 forwards the Telnet segment out of its Gig 0/2 port. This forwarding, shown in Figure 3-24, is possible, because switch SW2 has an entry for the segment's destination MAC address of BBBB. BBBB.BBBB in its MAC address table.

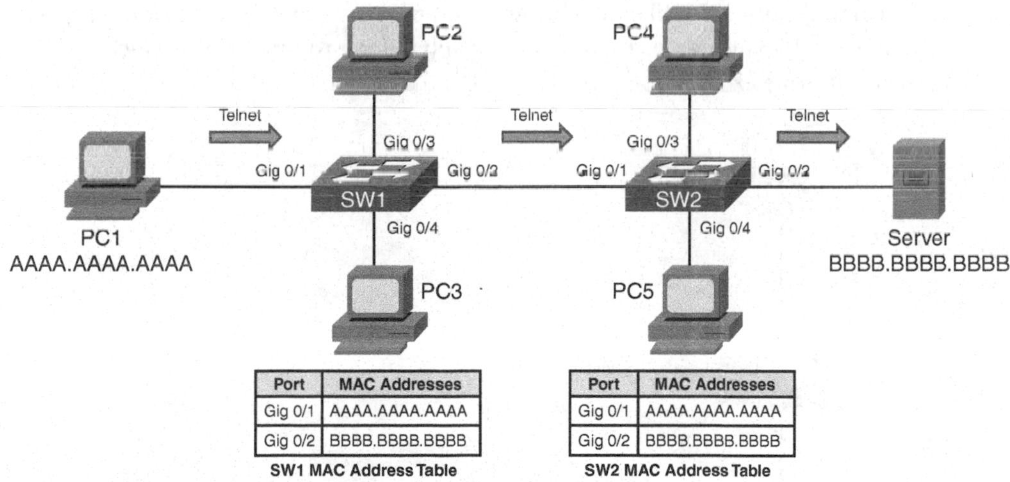

Port	MAC Addresses
Gig 0/1	AAAA.AAAA.AAAA
Gig 0/2	BBBB.BBBB.BBBB

SW1 MAC Address Table

Port	MAC Addresses
Gig 0/1	AAAA.AAAA.AAAA
Gig 0/2	BBBB.BBBB.BBBB

SW2 MAC Address Table

Figure 3-24 Switch SW2 Forwarding the Telnet Segment

Finally, the server responds to PC1, and a bidirectional Telnet session is established between PC1 and the server, as illustrated in Figure 3-25. Because PC1 learned the server's MAC address as a result of its earlier ARP request and stored that result in its local ARP cache, the transmission of subsequent Telnet segments does not require additional ARP requests. However, if unused for a period of time, entries in a PC's ARP cache can time out. Therefore, the PC would have to broadcast another ARP frame if it needed to send traffic to the same destination IP address. The sending of the additional ARP adds a small amount of delay when reestablishing a session with that destination IP address.

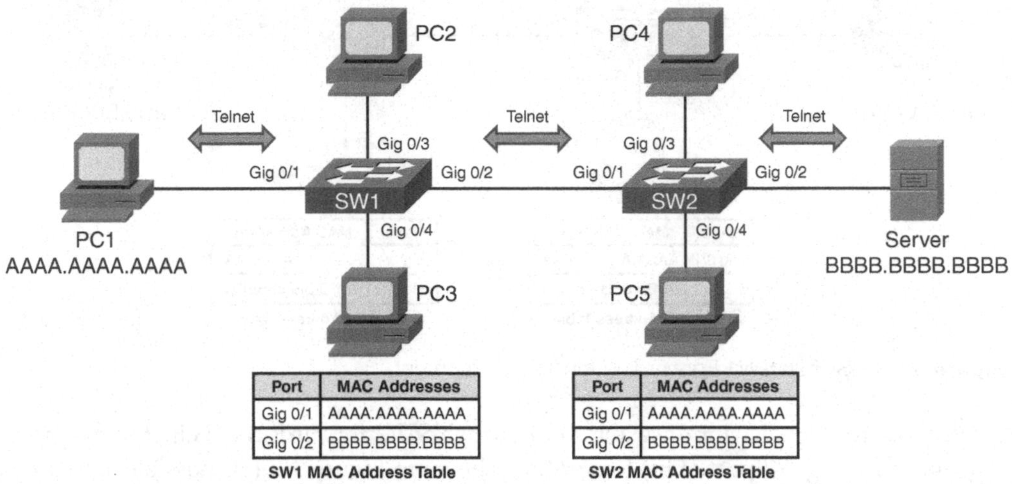

Port	MAC Addresses
Gig 0/1	AAAA.AAAA.AAAA
Gig 0/2	BBBB.BBBB.BBBB

Port	MAC Addresses
Gig 0/1	AAAA.AAAA.AAAA
Gig 0/2	BBBB.BBBB.BBBB

Figure 3-25 Bidirectional Telnet Session Between PC1 and the Server

As shown in Figure 3-26, like on a bridge, each port on a switch represents a separate collision domain. Also, all ports on a switch belong to the same broadcast domain, with one exception.

Key Topic

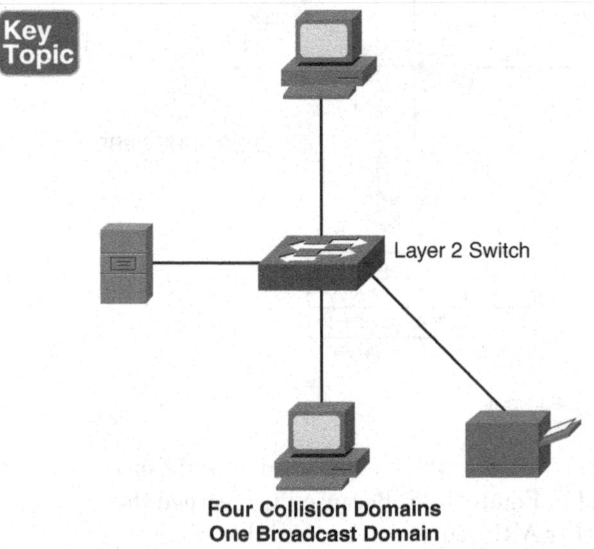

Figure 3-26 Switch Collision and Broadcast Domains

The exception is when the ports on a switch have been divided up into separate virtual LANs (VLANs). As discussed in Chapter 5, "IPv4 and IPv6 Addresses," each VLAN represents a separate broadcast domain, and for traffic to travel from one VLAN to another, that traffic must be routed by a Layer 3 device.

Multilayer Switches

Whereas a Layer 2 switch, as previously described, makes forwarding decisions based on MAC address information, a multilayer switch can make forwarding decisions based on upper-layer information. For example, a multilayer switch could function as a router and make forwarding decisions based on destination IP address information.

Some literature refers to a multilayer switch as a *Layer 3 switch* because of the switch's capability to make forwarding decisions like a router. The term *multilayer switch* is more accurate, however, because many multilayer switches have policy-based routing features that allow upper-layer information (for example, application port numbers) to be used in making forwarding decisions.

Figure 3-27 makes the point that a multilayer switch can be used to interconnect not just network segments, but entire networks. Specifically, Chapter 6, "Routing IP Packets," explains how logical Layer 3 IP addresses are used to assign network devices to different logical networks. For traffic to travel between two networked devices that belong to different networks, that traffic must be *routed*. (That is, a device, such as a multilayer switch, has to make a forwarding decision based on Layer 3 information.)

Key Topic

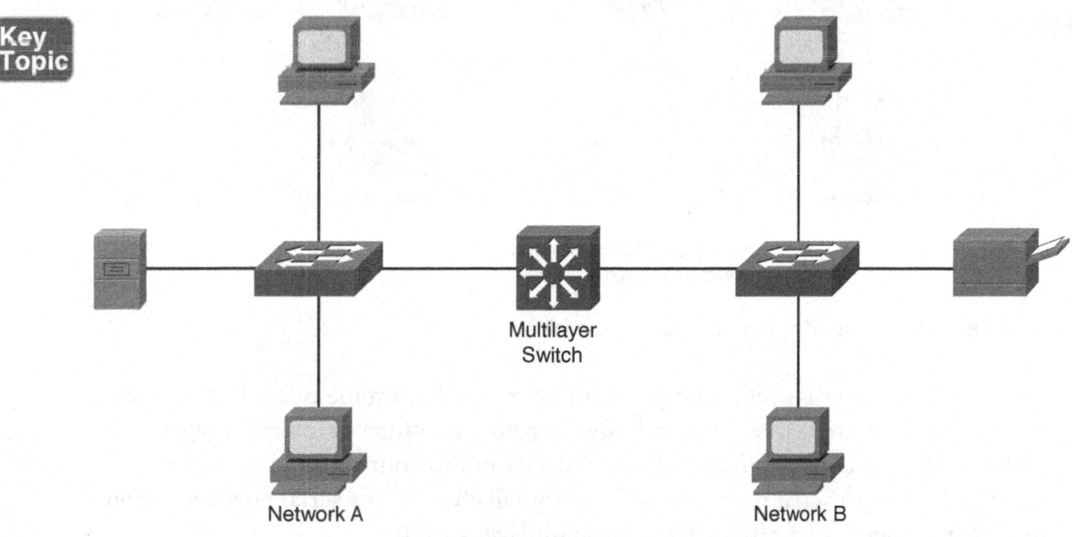

Figure 3-27 Multilayer Ethernet Switch

Like on a Layer 2 switch, each port on a multilayer switch represents a separate collision domain; however, a characteristic of a multilayer switch (and a router) is that it can become a boundary of a broadcast domain. Although all ports on a Layer 2 switch belong to the same broadcast domain, if configured as such, all ports on a multilayer switch can belong to different broadcast domains.

Routers

A router is a Layer 3 device, meaning that it makes forwarding decisions based on logical network address (for example, IP address) information. Although a router is considered to be a Layer 3 device, like a multilayer switch, it has the capability to consider high-layer traffic parameters, such as quality of service (QoS) settings, in making its forwarding decisions.

As shown in Figure 3-28, each port on a router is a separate collision domain and a separate broadcast domain. At this point in the discussion, routers are beginning to sound much like multilayer switches. So, why would network designers select a router rather than a multilayer switch in their design?

Key Topic

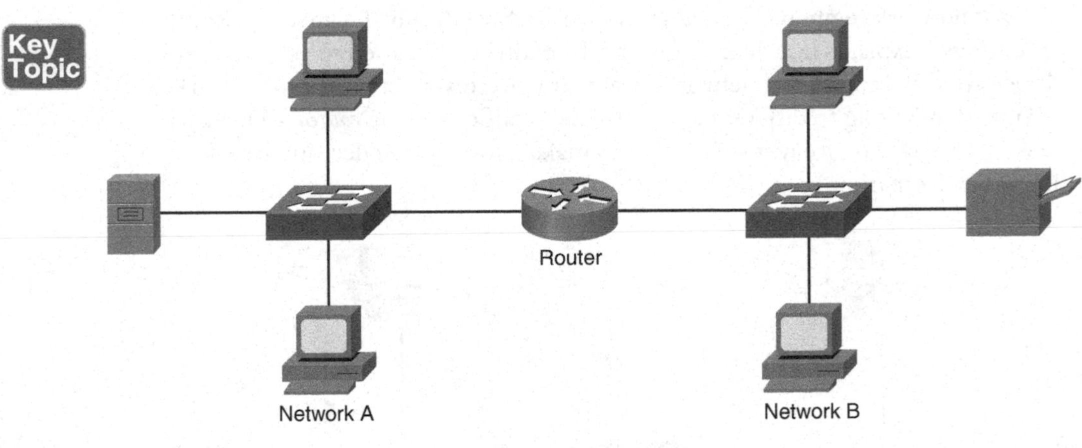

Figure 3-28 Router Broadcast and Collision Domains

One reason a router is preferable to a multilayer switch, in some cases, is that routers are usually more feature rich and support a broader range of interface types. For example, if you need to connect a Layer 3 device out to your Internet service provider (ISP) using a serial port, you will be more likely to find a serial port expansion module for your router rather than your multilayer switch.

Infrastructure Device Summary

Table 3-1 summarizes the characteristics of the network infrastructure devices discussed in this section.

Table 3-1 Network Infrastructure Device Characteristics

Device	Number of Collision Domains Possible	Number of Broadcast Domains Possible	OSI Layer of Operation
Hub	1	1	1
Bridge	1 per port	1	2
Switch	1 per port	1 per port	2
Multilayer switch	1 per port	1 per port	3+
Router	1 per port	1 per port	3+

Specialized Network Devices

Although network infrastructure devices make up the backbone of a network, for added end-user functionality, many networks integrate various specialized network devices such as VPN concentrators, firewalls, DNS servers, DHCP servers, proxy servers, caching engines, and content switches.

VPN Concentrators

Companies with locations spread across multiple sites often require secure communications between those sites. One option is to purchase multiple WAN connections interconnecting those sites. Sometimes, however, a more cost-effective option is to create secure connections through an untrusted network, such as the Internet. Such a secure tunnel is called a *virtual private network* (VPN). Depending on the VPN technology being used, the devices that terminate the ends of a VPN tunnel might be required to perform heavy processing. For example, consider a company headquarters location with VPN connections to each of 100 remote sites. The device at the headquarters terminating these VPN tunnels might have to perform encryption and authentication for each tunnel, resulting in a heavy processor burden on that device.

Although several router models can terminate a VPN circuit, a dedicated device, called a *VPN concentrator*, can be used instead. A VPN concentrator performs the processor-intensive process required to terminate multiple VPN tunnels. Figure 3-29 shows a sample VPN topology, with a VPN concentrator at each corporate location.

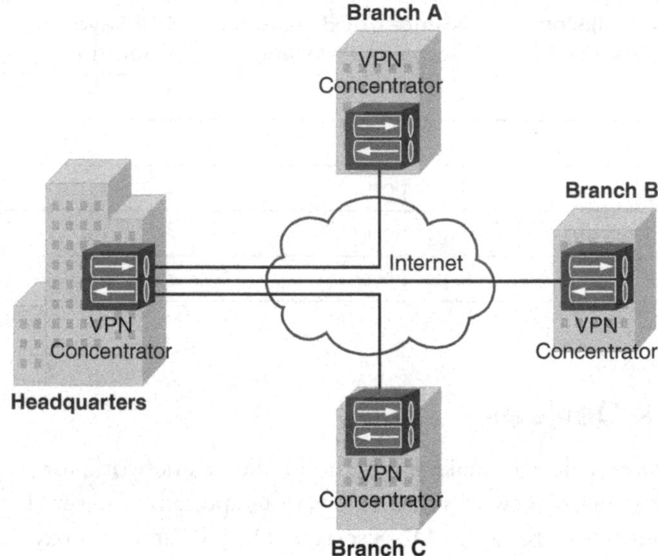

Figure 3-29 VPN Concentrator

The term *encryption* refers to the capability of a device to scramble data from a sender in such a way that the data can be unscrambled by the receiver, but not by any other party who might intercept the data. With a VPN concentrator's capability to encrypt data, it is considered to belong to a class of devices called *encryption devices*, which are devices (for example, routers, firewalls, and VPN concentrators) capable of participating in an encrypted session.

Firewalls

A firewall is primarily a network security appliance, and it is discussed in Chapter 12, "Network Security." As depicted in Figure 3-30, a firewall stands guard at the door of your network, protecting it from malicious Internet traffic.

Key Topic

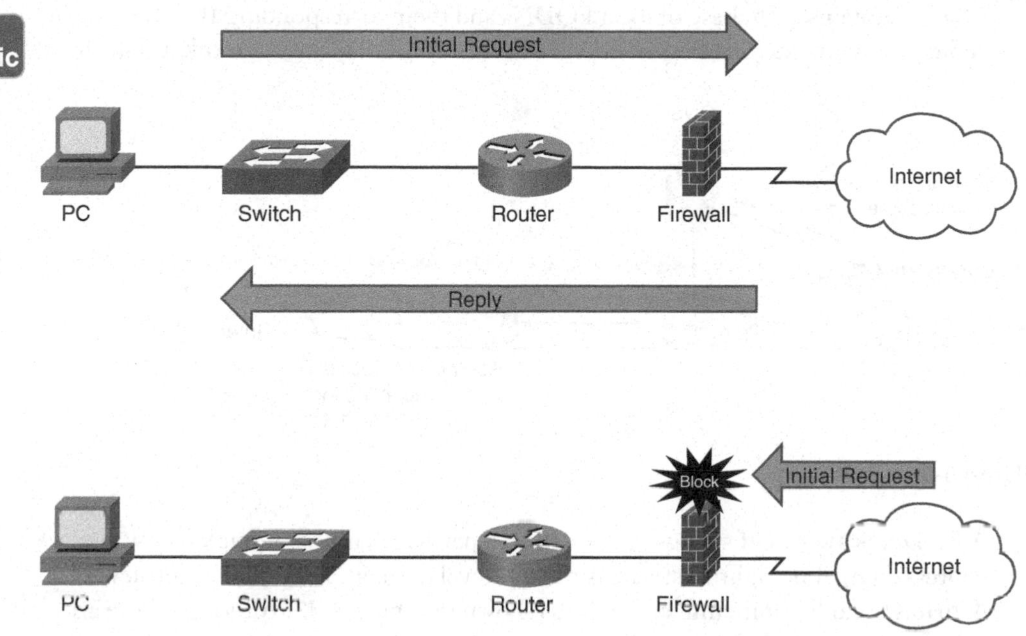

Figure 3-30 Firewall

For example, a *stateful firewall* allows traffic to originate from an inside network (that is, a trusted network) and go out to the Internet (an untrusted network). Likewise, return traffic coming back from the Internet to the inside network is allowed by the firewall. However, if traffic were originated from a device on the Internet (that is, not returning traffic), the firewall blocks that traffic.

DNS Servers

A Domain Name System (DNS) server performs the task of taking a domain name (for example, www.ciscopress.com) and resolving that name into a corresponding IP address (for example, 10.1.2.3). Because routers (or multilayer switches) make their forwarding decisions based on Layer 3 information (for example, IP addresses), an IP packet needs to contain IP address information, not DNS names. However, as humans, we more readily recall meaningful names rather than 32-bit numbers.

As shown in Figure 3-31, an end user who wants to navigate to the www.ciscopress.com website enters that fully qualified domain name (FQDN) into her web browser; however, the browser cannot immediately send a packet destined for www.ciscopress.com. First, the end user's computer needs to take the FQDN of www.ciscopress.com and resolve it into a corresponding IP address, which can be inserted as the destination IP address in an IP packet. This resolution is made possible by a DNS server, which maintains a database of local FQDNs and their corresponding IP addresses, in addition to pointers to other servers that can resolve IP addresses for other domains.

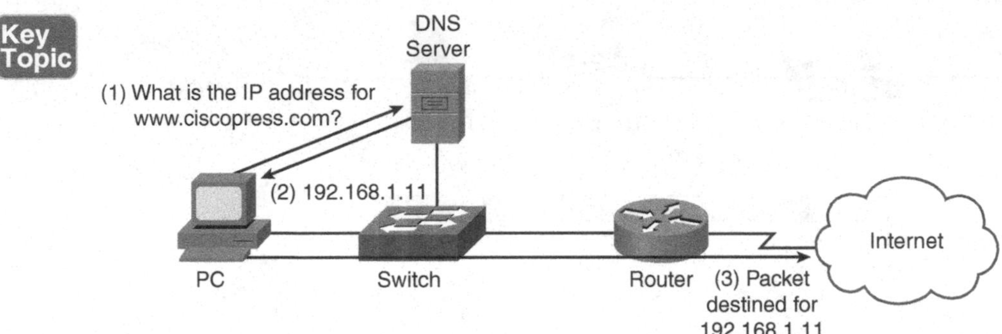

Figure 3-31 DNS Server

A FQDN is a series of strings, delimited by a period (as in the example, www.ciscopress.com). The rightmost part is the top-level domain. Examples of top-level domains include .com, .mil, and .edu, as shown in Figure 3-32. Although there are many other top-level domains, these are among some of the more common top-level domains seen in the United States.

Lower-level domains can point upward to higher-level DNS servers to resolve nonlocal FQDNs, as illustrated in Figure 3-32.

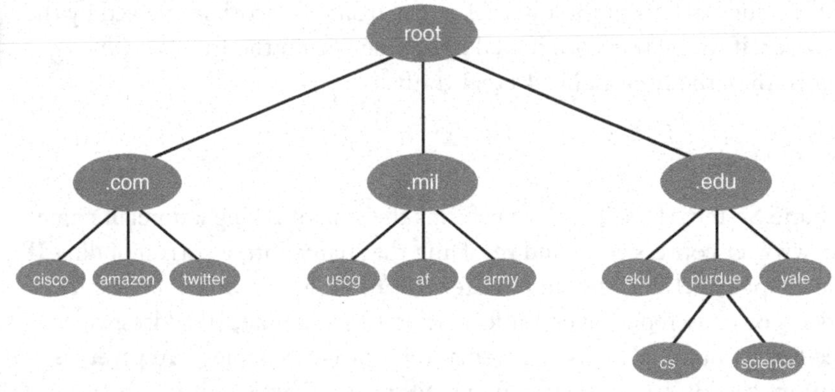

Figure 3-32 Hierarchical Domain Name Structure

A DNS server's database contains not only FQDNs and corresponding IP addresses, but also DNS record types. For example, a Mail Exchange (MX) record would be the record type for an email server. As a few examples, Table 3-2 lists a collection of common DNS record types.

Table 3-2 Common DNS Record Types

Record Type	Description
A	An address record (that is, A record) maps a hostname to an IPv4 address.
AAAA	An IPv6 address record (that is, AAAA record) maps a hostname to an IPv6 address.
CNAME	A canonical name record (that is, CNAME record) is an alias of an existing record, thus allowing multiple DNS records to map to the same IP address.
MX	A mail exchange record (that is, MX record) maps a domain name to an email (or message transfer agent) server for that domain.
NS	Delegates a DNS zone to use the given authoritative name servers.
PTR	A pointer record (that is, PTR record) points to a canonical name. A PTR record is commonly used when performing a reverse DNS lookup, which is a process used to determine what domain name is associated with a known IP address.
SOA	A start of authority record (that is, SOA record) provides authoritative information about a DNS zone, such as email contact information for the zone's administrator, the zone's primary name server, and various refresh timers.
SRV	A generalized service location record. Used for newer protocols instead of creating protocol-specific records such as MX.
TXT	Originally for arbitrary human-readable text in a DNS record. Since the early 1990s, however, this record carries machine-readable data, such as specified by RFC 1464, opportunistic encryption, Sender Policy Framework (SPF), or DomainKeys Identified Email (DKIM).

A potential challenge when setting up DNS records is when you want to point to the IP address of a device that might change its IP address. For example, if you have a cable modem or digital subscriber line (DSL) modem in your home, that device might obtain its IP address from your service provider via DHCP (as discussed in the next section, "DHCP Servers"). As a result, if you add the IP address of your cable modem or DSL modem to a DNS record (to allow users on the Internet to access one or more devices inside your network), that record could be incorrect if your device obtains a new IP address from your service provider.

To overcome such a challenge, you can turn to dynamic DNS (DDNS). A DDNS provider supplies software you run on one of your PCs that monitors the IP address of the device referenced in the DNS record (your cable modem or DSL modem in this example). If the software detects a change in the monitored IP address, that change is reported to your service provider, which is also providing DNS service.

Another option is IP address management (IPAM). This is a means of planning, tracking, and managing the Internet Protocol address space used in a network. IPAM integrates DNS and DHCP so that each is aware of changes in the other (for instance DNS knowing of the IP address taken by a client via DHCP, and updating itself accordingly).

Yet another DNS variant is Extension Mechanisms for DNS (EDNS). The original specification for DNS had size limitations that prevented the addition of certain features, such as security. EDNS supports these additional features, while maintaining backward compatibility with the original DNS implementation. Rather than using new flags in the DNS header, which would negate backwards compatibility, EDNS sends optional pseudo-resource-records between devices supporting EDNS. These records support 16 new DNS flags. If a legacy DNS server were to receive one of these optional records, the record would simply be ignored. Therefore, backward compatibility is maintained, while new features can be added for newer DNS servers.

When you enter a web address into your browser in the form of http://*FQDN* (for example, http://www.ajsnetworking.com), notice that you not only indicate the FQDN of your web address, you also specify that you want to access this location using the HTTP protocol. Such a string, which indicates both an address (for example, www.ajsnetworking.com) and a method for accessing that address (for example, http://), is called a *uniform resource locator* (URL).

Organizations will often implement DNS name resolution using internal and external DNS. This means that clients using DNS to resolve for internal resources will rely on a DNS server installed within the organization, while clients needing to resolve external resources will rely on the Internet (external) DNS servers. You can take steps to ensure the internal use only DNS information is not shared with public, external DNS servers.

Another option often used today for implementing DNS is third-party or cloud-hosted DNS. Amazon Web Services, for example, offers their Route 53 service. This powerful set of DNS services permits everything from domain registrations to name resolution services for your cloud or on-prem servers and clients.

DHCP Servers

Most modern networks have IP addresses assigned to network devices, and those logical Layer 3 addresses are used to route traffic between different networks. However, how does a network device receive its initial IP address assignment?

One option is to manually configure an IP address on a device; however, such a process is time consuming and error prone. A far more efficient method of IP address assignment is to dynamically assign IP addresses to network devices. The most common approach for this auto-assignment of IP addresses is Dynamic Host Configuration Protocol (DHCP). Not only does DHCP assign an IP address to a network device, it can assign a wide variety of other IP parameters, such as a subnet mask, a default gateway, and the IP address of a DNS server.

If you have a cable modem or DSL connection in your home, your cable modem or DSL router might obtain its IP address from your service provider via DHCP. In many corporate networks, when a PC boots, that PC receives its IP address configuration information from a corporate DHCP server.

Figure 3-33 illustrates the exchange of messages that occur as a DHCP client obtains IP address information from a DHCP server. The following list describes each step in further detail:

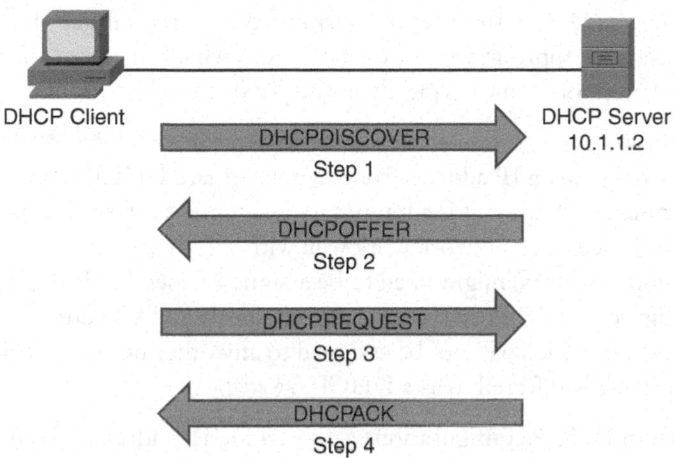

Figure 3-33 Obtaining IP Address Information from a DHCP Server

1. When a DHCP client initially boots, it has no IP address, default gateway, or other such configuration information. Therefore, the way a DHCP client initially communicates is by sending a broadcast message (that is, a DHCPDISCOVER message to a destination address of 255.255.255.255) in an attempt to discover a DHCP server.
2. When a DHCP server receives a DHCPDISCOVER message, it can respond with a unicast DHCPOFFER message. Because the DHCPDISCOVER message is sent as a broadcast, more than one DHCP server might respond to this discover request. However, the client typically selects the server that sent the first DHCPOFFER response received by the client.
3. The DHCP client communicates with this selected server by sending a unicast DHCPREQUEST message asking the DHCP server to provide IP configuration parameters.
4. The DHCP server responds to the client with a unicast DHCPACK message. This DHCPACK message contains a collection of IP configuration parameters.

Notice that in step 1, the DHCPDISCOVER message was sent as a broadcast. By default, a broadcast cannot cross a router boundary. Therefore, if a client resides on a different network than the DHCP server, the client's next-hop router should be configured as a DHCP relay agent, which allows a router to relay DHCP requests to either a unicast IP address or a directed broadcast address for a network. The DHCP relay agent is often referred to as an *IP helper*.

A DHCP server can be configured to assign IP addresses to devices belonging to different subnets. Specifically, the DHCP server can determine the source subnet of the DHCP request and select an appropriate address pool from which to assign an address. One of these address pools (which typically corresponds to a single subnet) is called a *scope*.

When a network device is assigned an IP address from an appropriate DHCP scope, that assignment is not permanent. Rather, it is a temporary assignment referred to as a *lease*. Although most client devices on a network work well with this dynamic addressing, some devices (for example, servers) might need to be assigned a specific IP address. Fortunately, you can configure a DHCP reservation, where a specific MAC address is mapped to a specific IP address, which will not be assigned to any other network device. This static addressing approach is referred to as a DHCP *reservation*.

Another common concern in DHCP configurations is to exclude IP addresses from the scope of addressed you make available. We call these IP exclusions. You might do this for several servers you have in your organization that required configurations with a static IP address in the scope of your overall IP address space. IP exclusions are simple to configure and ensure that an IP address conflict does not result in your subnet.

A method for remembering the four main steps of DHCP is D.O.R.A., with each letter representing the steps discover, offer, request, and acknowledge.

Proxy Servers

Some clients are configured to forward their packets, which are seemingly destined for the Internet, to a proxy server. This proxy server receives the client's request, and on behalf of that client (that is, as that client's proxy), the proxy server sends the request out to the Internet. When a reply is received from the Internet, the proxy server forwards the response on to the client. Figure 3-34 illustrates the operation of a proxy server.

Key Topic

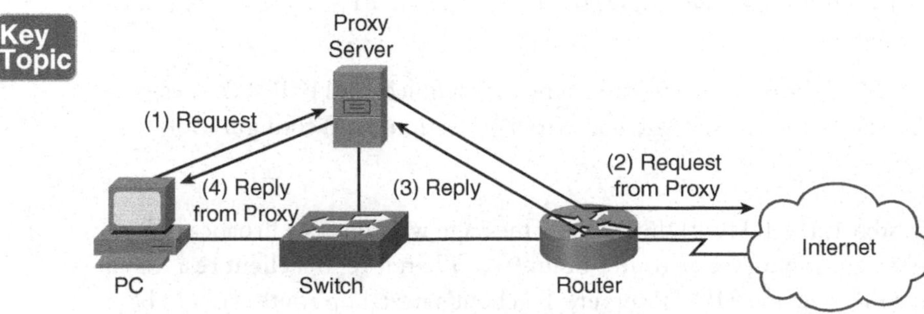

Figure 3-34 Proxy Server Operation

What possible benefit could come from such an arrangement? Security is one benefit. Specifically, because all requests going out to the Internet are sourced from the proxy server, the IP addresses of network devices inside the trusted network are hidden from the Internet.

Yet another benefit could come in the form of bandwidth savings, because many proxy servers perform content caching. For example, without a proxy server, if multiple clients all visited the same website, the same graphics from the home page of the website would be downloaded multiple times (one time for each client visiting the website). However, with a proxy server performing content caching, when the first client navigates to a website on the Internet, and the Internet-based web server returns its content, the proxy server not only forwards this content to the client requesting the web page but stores a copy of the content on its hard drive. Then, when a subsequent client points its web browser to the same website, after the proxy server determines that the page has not changed, the proxy server can locally serve up the content to the client, without having to once again consume Internet bandwidth to download all the graphic elements from the Internet-based website.

As a final example of a proxy server benefit, some proxy servers can perform content filtering. Content filtering restricts clients from accessing certain URLs. For example, many companies use content filtering to prevent their employees from accessing popular social networking sites, in an attempt to prevent a loss of productivity. A reverse proxy receives requests on behalf of a server or servers and replies back to the clients on behalf of those servers. This can also be used with load-balancing and caching to better utilize a group of servers.

Content Engines

As previously described, many proxy servers are capable of performing content caching; however, some networks used dedicated appliances to perform this content caching. These appliances are commonly referred to as *caching engines* or *content engines*.

Figure 3-35 demonstrates how a corporate branch office can locally cache information from a server located at the corporate headquarters location. Multiple requests from branch office clients for the content can then be serviced from the content engine at the branch office, thus eliminating the repetitive transfer of the same data. Depending on traffic patterns, such an arrangement might provide significant WAN bandwidth savings.

Key Topic

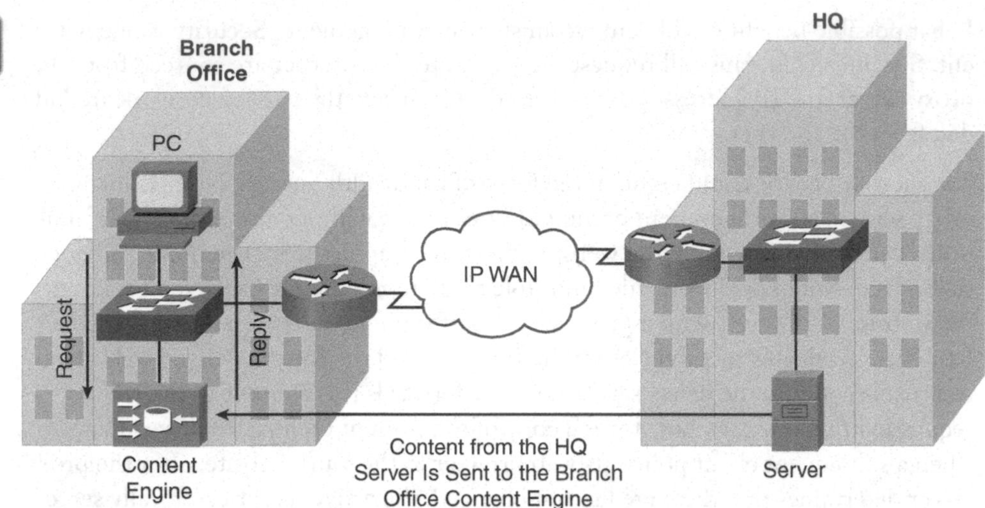

Figure 3-35 Content Engine Operation

Content Switches

Consider the server farm presented in Figure 3-36. The servers making up this server farm house the same data. For companies with a large Internet presence (for example, a search engine company, an online book store, or a social networking site), a single server could be overwhelmed with the glut of requests flooding in from the Internet. To alleviate the burden placed on a single server, a content switch (also known as a *load balancer*) distributes incoming requests across the various servers in the server farm, each of which maintains an identical copy of data and applications.

Key Topic

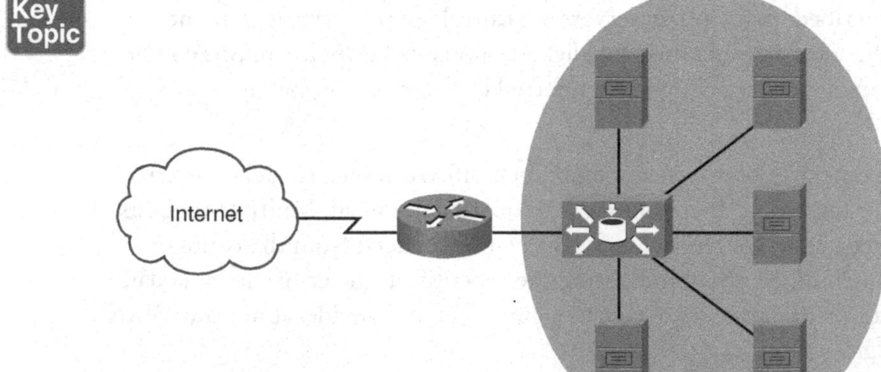

Figure 3-36 Content Switching Operation

A major benefit of content switching is that it allows a server farm to scale. Specifically, as demand increases, new servers can be added to the group of servers across which requests are load balanced. Also, if maintenance (for example, applying an operating system patch) needs to be performed on a server, a server can simply be taken out of the load-balancing rotation, with the remaining servers picking up the slack. Then, after the maintenance is complete, the server can once again be added back to the defined server group.

Other Specialized Devices

Here are some other specialized networking devices not explicitly covered elsewhere in this text:

- **Wireless range extender**: Since all 802.11 wireless technologies have distance limitations, a wireless range extender can amplify the signal and extend the reachability of a wireless cell.
- **Next-generation firewall (NGFW)**: Newer firewalls of today not only can perform stateless and stateful filtering of traffic, but they can also deeply inspect the contents of packets to find and prevent attacks. These devices also can connect to the cloud for the latest updates in global threats.
- **Software-defined networking (SDN) controller**: This appliance-based device is responsible for distributing control plane instructions to network devices downstream for their configuration and management. If you are not familiar with SDN, have no fear: the next section of this chapter explains it to you.

Virtual Network Devices

A major data center paradigm shift is underway. This shift is away from a company having its own data center (with its raised flooring and large air conditioning system) containing multiple physical servers, each of which offering a specific service (for example, email, DNS services, or Microsoft Active Directory).

Virtual Servers

The computing power available in a single high-end server is often sufficient to handle the tasks of multiple independent servers. With the advent of virtualization, multiple servers (which might be running different operating systems) can run in virtual server instances on one physical device. For example, a single high-end server might be running an instance of a Microsoft Windows Server providing Microsoft Active Directory (AD) services to an enterprise, while simultaneously running an instance of a Linux server acting as a corporate web server, and at the same time acting as a Sun Solaris UNIX server providing corporate DNS services. Figure 3-37 illustrates this concept of a virtual server. Although the virtual server in the figure uses a single network interface card (NIC) to connect out to an Ethernet switch, many virtual server platforms support multiple NICs. Having multiple NICs offers increased throughput and load balancing.

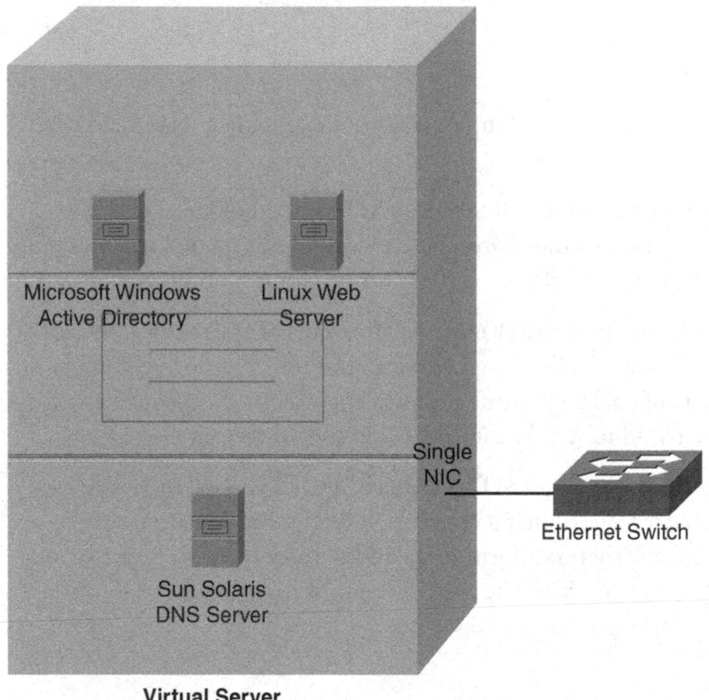

Figure 3-37 Virtual Server

> **NOTE** Although the previous example used a Linux-based web server, be aware that web servers can run on a variety of operating system (OS) platforms. As one example, Microsoft Windows servers support a web server application called *Internet Information Services* (IIS), which was previously known as Internet Information Server.

Virtualization is possible with servers thanks to specialized software called a *hypervisor*. The hypervisor takes physical hardware and abstracts it for the virtual server. The extent of virtualization is amazing, with even the NIC of each virtual server represented virtually (virtual NIC).

The networks and systems supporting virtual servers also commonly have network-attached storage (NAS), where disk storage is delivered as a service over the network.

A technology for network storage is IP-based Small Computer System Interface (iSCSI). With iSCSI, a client using the storage is referred to as an *initiator*, and the system providing the iSCSI storage is called the iSCSI *target*. The networks supporting iSCSI are often configured to support larger-than-normal frame sizes, referred to as *jumbo frames*.

Fibre channel is another technology that can deliver storage services over a network. Thanks to high-speed Ethernet options today, you can even configure Fibre Channel over Ethernet (FCoE) to run a unified network for your SAN and non-storage-data traffic.

NOTE Less commonly encountered is InfiniBand (IB). This communication technology permits high-speed, low-latency communications between supercomputers.

Virtual Routers and Firewalls

Most of the vendors who create physical routers and firewalls also have an offering that includes virtualized routers and firewalls. The benefit of using a virtualized firewall or router is that the same features of routing and security can be available in the virtual environment as they are in the physical environment. As part of interfacing with virtual networks, virtual network adapters can be used. For connectivity between the virtual world and the physical one, there would be physical interfaces involved that connect to the logical virtual interfaces.

Virtual Switches

One potential trade-off you make with the previously described virtual server scenario is that all servers belong to the same IP subnet, which could have QoS and security implications. If these server instances ran on separate physical devices, they could be attached to different ports on an Ethernet switch. These switch ports could belong to different VLANs, which could place each server in a different broadcast domain.

Fortunately, some virtual servers allow you to still have Layer 2 control (for example, VLAN separation and filtering). This Layer 2 control is made possible by the virtual server not only virtualizing instances of servers, but also virtualizing a Layer 2 switch. Figure 3-38 depicts a virtual switch. Notice that the servers logically reside on separate VLANs, and frames from those servers are appropriately tagged when traveling over a trunk to the attached Ethernet switch.

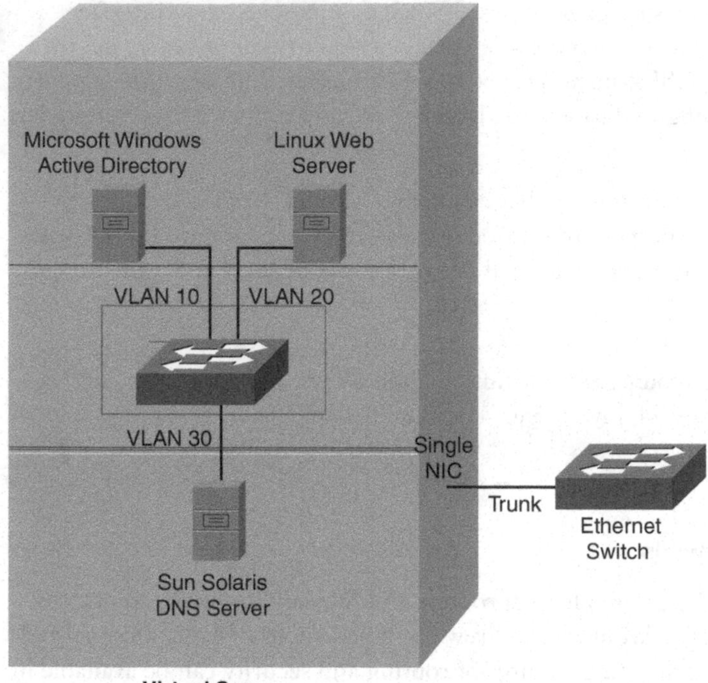

Figure 3-38 Virtual Server with a Virtual Switch

Virtual Desktops

Another emerging virtualization technology is virtual desktops. With today's users being more mobile than ever, they need access to information traditionally stored on their office computers' hard drives from a variety of other locations. For example, a user might be at an airport using their smartphone, and they need access to a document they created on their office computer. With virtual desktops, a user's data is stored in a data center rather than on an office computer's hard drive. By providing authentication credentials, the user can establish a secure connection between the centralized repository of user data and their device, as shown in Figure 3-39, thus allowing the user to remotely access the desired document.

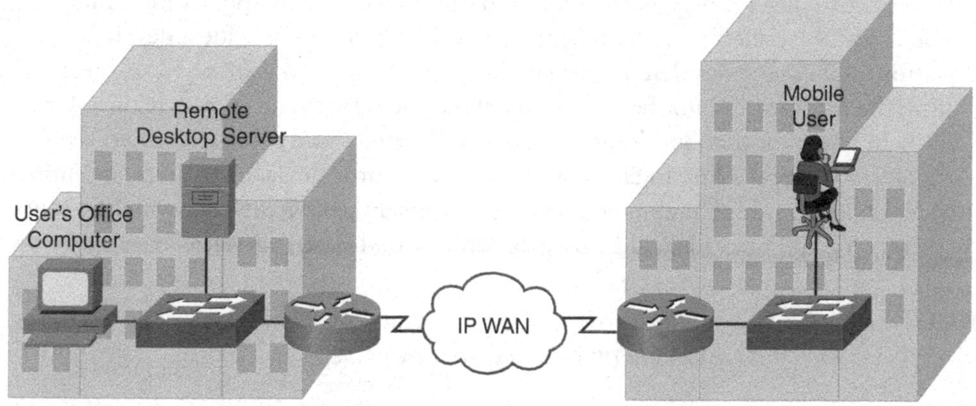

Figure 3-39 Virtual Desktop Topology

Other Virtualization Solutions

Although the previously discussed virtualization technologies (that is, virtual servers, virtual switches, and virtual desktops) were described as residing at a corporate location (that is, *on-site*), some service providers offer *off-site* options. Specifically, if a service provider's customer did not want to house and maintain its own data center, these virtualization technologies could be located at a service provider's data center, and the customer could be billed based on usage patterns. Such a service provider offering is called *network as a service* (NaaS), implying that network features can be provided by a service provider, just as a telephony service provider offers access to the Public Switched Telephone Network (PSTN), and an ISP offers access to the public Internet.

Cloud Computing

Virtualized services and solutions are often offered by service providers as *cloud computing*. A company purchasing cloud computing services has the option of public, private, or hybrid cloud services. Private cloud services include systems that only have interactions and communications with other devices inside that same private cloud or system. Public cloud services interact with devices on public networks such as the Internet and potentially other public clouds. An environment in which there are private cloud services, but some of those services interact with public clouds, is referred to as *hybrid cloud services*. Some of the types of services that can be available as part of cloud computing include *infrastructure as a service* (IaaS), where the company rents virtualized servers (which are hosted by a service provider) and then runs specific applications on those servers. Another type of cloud service is *software as a service* (SaaS), where the details of the servers are hidden from the customer and the customer's experience is similar to using a web-based application. Another cloud service is called *platform as a service* (PaaS), which can provide a development platform for companies that are developing applications and want to focus on creating the software and not have to worry about the servers and infrastructure that are being used for that development. Another type of cloud is the *community cloud*, which is a term referring to cloud services used by individuals, companies, or entities with similar interests. In cloud computing, it is likely that virtualized switches, routers, servers, and firewalls will be used as part of cloud-based services.

NOTE An application service provider (ASP) provides application software access to subscribers. This service is sometimes called *software as a service* (SaaS).

Similar to outsourcing the features of a data network with NaaS, a corporate telephony solution might also be outsourced. Many companies own and maintain their own private branch exchange (PBX), which is a privately owned telephone system. One option for companies that want to outsource their telephony service is to use a service provider's virtual PBX. A virtual PBX is usually a Voice over IP (VoIP) solution, where voice is encapsulated inside data packets for transmission across a data network. Typically, a service provider provides all necessary IP telephony gateways to convert between a customer's existing telephony system and the service provider's virtual PBX.

NOTE A virtual PBX is different from a hosted PBX, which is usually a traditional (that is, not VoIP) PBX hosted by a service provider.

As more and more technology appears in the cloud (either public or private), connectivity (specifically, secured connectivity) becomes paramount. Secure protocols such as HTTPS, TLS, and SSH are a must when accessing most cloud resources. Fortunately, massive cloud providers such as Amazon with Amazon Web Services (AWS) make it simple to securely connect using a wide variety of methods, including hardware VPN appliances located at your corporate or home office. Although your applications and servers might be sharing physical equipment with other customers of Amazon, great pains are taken to ensure this multitenancy does not sacrifice security.

NOTE Amazon makes it very clear. When it comes to your cloud security with Amazon Web Services, it is a shared responsibility model. For example, Amazon will secure your virtual machine from other customer virtual machines, but it is up to you to properly secure the operating system (OS) inside the VM, just as it is your responsibility to control access to and from the VM.

Software-Defined Networking (SDN)

Software-defined networking is changing the landscape of our traditional networks. A well-implemented software-defined network will allow the administrator to implement features, functions, and configurations without the need to do the individual command-line configuration on the network devices. The front end that the administrator interfaces with can alert the administrator to what the network is currently doing, and then through that same graphical user interface the administrator can indicate what he wants done, and then behind the scenes the detailed configurations across multiple network devices can be implemented by the software-defined network.

Voice over IP Protocols and Components

As previously mentioned, a Voice over IP (VoIP) network digitizes the spoken voice into packets and transmits those packets across a data network. This allows voice, data, and even video to share the same medium. In a network with unified communications (UC) such as voice, video, and data, specialized UC servers, controllers, devices, and gateways are also likely to be used. In a cloud computing environment, they may be virtualized as well. Figure 3-40 shows a sample VoIP network topology. Not only can a VoIP network provide significant cost savings over a traditional PBX solution, many VoIP networks offer enhanced services (for example, integration with video conferencing applications and calendaring software to determine availability) not found in traditional corporate telephony environments.

Key Topic

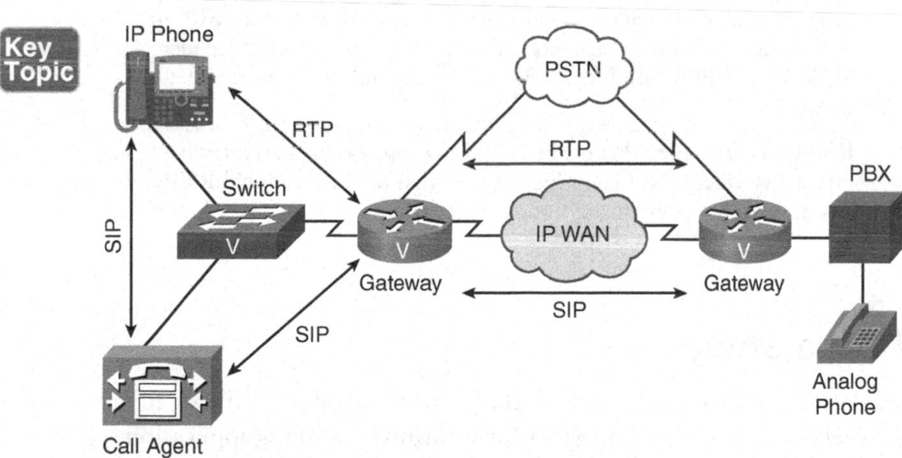

Figure 3-40 Sample VoIP Network Topology

Table 3-3 defines the VoIP devices and protocols shown in Figure 3-40.

Table 3-3 VoIP Network Elements

Protocol/Device	Description
IP phone	An IP phone is a telephone with an integrated Ethernet connection. Although users speak into a traditional analog handset (or headset) on the IP phone, the IP phone digitizes the spoken voice, packetizes it, and sends it out over a data network (via the IP phone's Ethernet port). While an IP phone is a common example of a VoIP endpoint, an alternative is software running on a computer.
Call agent	A call agent is a repository for a VoIP network's dial plan. For example, when a user dials a number from an IP phone, the call agent analyzes the dialed digits and determines how to route the call toward the destination.
Gateway	A gateway in a VoIP network acts as a translator between two different telephony signaling environments. In Figure 3-40, both gateways interconnect a VoIP network with the PSTN. Also, the gateway on the right interconnects a traditional PBX with a VoIP network.
PBX	A Private Branch Exchange (PBX) is a privately owned telephone switch traditionally used in corporate telephony systems. Although a PBX is not typically considered a VoIP device, it connects into a VoIP network through a gateway, as shown in Figure 3-40.
Analog phone	An analog phone is a traditional telephone, like you might have in your home. Even though an analog phone is not typically considered a VoIP device, it can connect into a VoIP network via a VoIP adapter or, as shown in Figure 3-40, via a PBX, which is connected to a VoIP network.
SIP	Session Initiation Protocol (SIP) is a signaling, setup, and management protocol used with voice and video sessions over IP networks. SIP, in conjunction with other protocols, also specifies the encoder/decoder (codec) that will be used for voice and video connections over the network.
RTP	Real-time Transport Protocol (RTP) is a protocol that carries voice (and interactive video). Notice in Figure 3-40 that the bidirectional RTP stream does not flow through the call agent.

Real-World Case Study

Acme, Inc., has decided that to keep pace with the growing customer demand, it will use software as a service from a cloud provider for its primary business application. This will allow the company to focus on its business and use the application instead of managing and maintaining that application.

There will be some desktop computers in the office for the users, and those computers will be networked using UTP cabling that goes to a switch. The switches on each floor of the building will be secured in a locked intermediate distribution frame (IDF) in a wiring closet on each floor. For the interconnections between the switches on each of the floors, multi mode fiber-optic cabling is used. When purchasing hardware and fiber-optic cabling, Acme will want to make sure that the fiber-optic connector type matches the correct fiber interface type on the switches. In the basement of the building is an area for Acme, Inc. to use as its own dedicated main distribution frame (MDF). From the MDF, there will be cabling that goes to the demarcation point for the service provider for the WAN and Internet connectivity provided by the service provider. This connectivity will be used to access the cloud services (SaaS specifically) from the service provider and for WAN and Internet access.

Inside the building, a few of the users have mobile devices. To facilitate network access for these mobile users, wireless APs, which are physically connected through UTP cabling to the switches on each floor, will be used. Hubs will not be used because they are not very secure or effective and because all network traffic is sent to every other port on a hub, whereas a switch only forwards unicast frames to the other ports that need to see that traffic. To consolidate hardware in the MDF, multilayer switches will be used to provide not only Layer 2 forwarding of frames based on MAC addresses, but also Layer 3 forwarding of packets based on IP addresses (routing). On the LAN, Acme intends to use a set of redundant servers near the MDF to provide services such as DHCP, DNS, and time synchronization to each of its offices on each floor. The servers can coordinate DNS and time synchronization with other servers on the public Internet. The local servers can also be used for network authentication to control user access to the network regardless of the source, including wireless, wired, and VPN. Instead of purchasing multiple physical servers, the company is going to virtualize the servers onto specialized hardware that is fault tolerant. With this solution, the company can easily add additional logical servers without purchasing a physical system for every new server. This could include unified communications servers that may be involved with voice, video, and other types of streaming data.

A VPN device will also be installed in the MDF to allow users who are connected to the Internet from their home or other locations to build a secure VPN remote access connection over the Internet to the corporate headquarters. Instead of buying a dedicated VPN device such as a concentrator, Acme is going to use a firewall that has this VPN capability integrated as part of its services.

Summary

Here are the main topics covered in this chapter:

- This chapter contrasted various media types, including coaxial cable, shielded twisted pair, unshielded twisted pair, fiber-optic cable, and wireless technologies.
- The roles of various network infrastructure components were contrasted. These components include hubs, bridges, switches, multilayer switches, and routers.
- This chapter provided examples of specialized network devices and explained how they could add network enhancements. These devices include VPN concentrators, firewalls, DNS servers, DHCP servers, proxy servers, content engines, and content switches.
- Virtual networking components were described. These components include virtual server, virtual switch, virtual desktop, and virtual PBX technologies.
- This chapter introduced VoIP and described some of the protocols and hardware components that make up a VoIP network.

Exam Preparation Tasks

Review All the Key Topics

Review the most important topics from inside the chapter, noted with the Key Topic icon in the outer margin of the page. Table 3-4 lists these key topics and the page numbers where each is found.

Table 3-4 Key Topics for Chapter 3

Key Topic Element	Description	Page Number
List, Figure 3-2	Common coaxial connectors	65
List	Categories of UTP cabling	67
List, Figure 3-5	Common twisted-pair connectors	69
Figure 3-7	Light propagation in multimode fiber	72
Figure 3-8	Light propagation in single-mode fiber	73
List, Figure 3-9	Common fiber-optic connectors	74

Key Topic Element	**Description**	**Page Number**
Figure 3-10	Example: Cable distribution system	75
List	Internet of Things (IoT) Technologies	78
Figure 3-15	Ethernet bridge	81
Figure 3-26	Layer 2 Ethernet switch	88
Figure 3-27	Multilayer Ethernet switch	89
Figure 3-28	Router	90
Table 3-1	Network infrastructure device characteristics	91
Figure 3-29	VPN concentrator	92
Figure 3-30	Firewall	93
Figure 3-31	DNS server	94
Figure 3-32	Hierarchical domain name structure	94
Table 3-2	Common DNS record types	95
Step list	Obtaining IP address information from a DHCP server	97
Figure 3-34	Proxy server operation	98
Figure 3-35	Content engine operation	100
Figure 3-36	Content switching operation	100
Figure 3-37	Virtual server	102
Figure 3-38	Virtual server with a virtual switch	104
Figure 3-39	Virtual desktop topology	105
Figure 3-40	Sample VoIP network topology	107
Table 3-3	VoIP network elements	108

Complete Tables and Lists from Memory

Print a copy of Appendix C, "Memory Tables," or at least the section for this chapter, and complete as many of the tables as possible from memory. Appendix D, "Memory Tables Answer Key," includes the completed tables and lists so you can check your work.

Define Key Terms

Define the following key terms from this chapter, and check your answers in the Glossary:

coaxial cable, twisted-pair cable, shielded twisted-pair cable, unshielded twisted-pair cable, electromagnetic interference (EMI), plenum, multimode fiber (MMF), single-mode fiber (SMF), 66 block, 110 block, hub, switch, router, multilayer switch, firewall, Domain Name System (DNS) server, Dynamic Host Configuration Protocol (DHCP), proxy server, content engine, content switch, virtual server, virtual switch, virtual desktop, on-site, off-site, network as a service (NaaS), virtual PBX, Session Initiation Protocol (SIP), Real-time Transport Protocol (RTP), SaaS, PaaS, IaaS, IPAM, software-defined networking (SDN), SDN controller, Z-Wave, Ant+, Bluetooth, NFC, IR, RFID, 802.11, wireless range extender, NGFW, FCoE, NAS, SAN

Additional Resources

Introducing DHCP: http://www.ajsnetworking.com/dhcp

SDN Controllers: http://www.ajsnetworking.com/sdn

Review Questions

The answers to these review questions appear in Appendix A, "Answers to Review Questions."

1. Which of the following is a VoIP signaling protocol used to set up, maintain, and tear down VoIP phone calls?
   a. MX
   b. RJ-45
   c. SIP
   d. IMAP

2. Which of the following categories of UTP cabling are commonly used for 1000BASE-T networks? (Choose two.)
   a. Cat 5
   b. Cat 5e
   c. Cat 6
   d. Cat 6f

3. Which type of cable might be required for installation in a drop ceiling, which is used as an open-air return duct?
   a. Riser
   b. Plenum
   c. Multimode
   d. Twin-axial

4. Which network infrastructure device primarily makes forwarding decisions based on Layer 2 MAC addresses?
   a. Router
   b. Switch
   c. Hub
   d. Multilayer switch

5. A router operating at Layer 3 primarily makes its forwarding decisions based on what address?
   a. Destination MAC address
   b. Source IP address
   c. Source MAC address
   d. Destination IP address

6. Identify two differences between an Ethernet bridge and an Ethernet switch. (Choose two.)
   a. Switches use ASICs to make forwarding decisions, whereas bridges make their forwarding decisions in software.
   b. Bridges typically operate faster than switches.
   c. Switches usually have higher port densities than bridges.
   d. Bridges can base their forwarding decisions on logical network layer addresses.

7. A router has 12 ports. How many broadcast domains does the router have?
   a. None
   b. 1
   c. 2
   d. 12

8. A switch has 12 ports. How many collision domains does the switch have?
   a. None
   b. 1
   c. 2
   d. 12

9. What is the first DHCP message sent by a client attempting to obtain IP address information from a DHCP server?
   a. DHCPOFFER
   b. DHCPACK
   c. DHCPDISCOVER
   d. DHCPREQUEST

10. What specialized network device is commonly used to load-balance traffic across multiple servers in a group?

a. Content switch

b. Firewall

c. DNS server

d. Content engine

11. What IoT technology is specialized for monitoring sensor data and is ultimately led by Garmin?

a. Z-Wave

b. Ant+

c. Bluetooth

d. RFID

12. Automating the management and configuration of many different network devices thanks to a centralized controller refers to what technology?

a. Content distribution

b. Virtualized networking

c. Software-defined networking

d. Internet of Things

After completion of this chapter, you will be able to answer the following questions:

- What are the characteristics of Ethernet networks, in terms of media access, collisions domains, broadcast domains, and distance/speed limitations of various Ethernet standards?
- Ethernet switches perform what functions? How are these functions related to VLANs, trunks, Spanning Tree Protocol, link aggregation, Power over Ethernet, port monitoring, user authentication, and first-hop redundancy?

CHAPTER 4

Ethernet Technology

Odds are, when you are working with local area networks (LANs), you are working with Ethernet as the Layer 1 technology. Back in the mid-1990s, there was tremendous competition between technologies such as Ethernet, Token Ring, and Fiber Distributed Data Interface (FDDI). Today, however, you can see that Ethernet is the clear winner of those Layer 1 wars.

Of course, over the years, Ethernet has evolved. Several Ethernet standards exist in modern LANs, with a variety of distance and speed limitations. This chapter begins by reviewing the fundamentals of Ethernet networks, including a collection of Ethernet speeds and feeds.

Chapter 3, "Network Components," introduced you to Ethernet switches. Because these switches are such an integral part of LANs, this chapter delves into many of the features offered by some Ethernet switches.

Foundation Topics

Principles of Ethernet

The genesis of Ethernet was 1973, when this technology was developed by Xerox Corporation. The original intent was to create a technology to allow computers to connect with laser printers. A quick survey of most any corporate network reveals that Ethernet rose well beyond its humble beginnings, with Ethernet being used to interconnect such devices as computers, printers, wireless access points, servers, switches, routers, video-game systems, and more. This section discusses early Ethernet implementations and limitations and references up-to-date Ethernet throughput and distance specifications.

Ethernet Origins

In the network-industry literature, you might come upon the term *IEEE 802.3* (where IEEE refers to the Institute of Electrical and Electronics Engineers standards body). In general, you can use the term *IEEE 802.3* interchangeably with the term *Ethernet*. However, be aware that these technologies have some subtle distinctions. For example, an Ethernet frame is a fixed-length frame, whereas an 802.3 frame length can vary.

A popular implementation of Ethernet, in the early days, was called *10BASE5*. The 10 in 10BASE5 referred to network throughput, specifically 10Mbps (that is, 10 million [mega] bits per second). The BASE in 10BASE5 referred to baseband, as opposed to broadband, as discussed in Chapter 2, "The OSI Reference Model." Finally, the 5 in 10BASE5 indicated the distance limitation of 500 meters. The cable used in 10BASE5 networks, as shown in Figure 4-1, was a larger diameter than most types of media. In fact, this network type became known as *thicknet*.

Another early Ethernet implementation was 10BASE2. From the previous analysis of 10BASE5, you might conclude that 10BASE2 was a 10Mbps baseband technology with a distance limitation of 200 meters. That is almost correct. However, 10BASE2's actual distance limitation was 185 meters. The cabling used in 10BASE2 networks was significantly thinner and therefore less expensive than 10BASE5 cabling. As a result, 10BASE2 cabling, as shown in Figure 4-2, was known as *thinnet* or *cheapernet*.

Figure 4-1 10BASE5 Cable

Figure 4-2 Coaxial Cable Used for 10BASE2

10BASE5 and 10BASE2 networks are rarely, if ever, seen today. Other than their 10Mbps bandwidth limitation, the cabling used by these legacy technologies quickly faded in popularity with the advent of unshielded twisted-pair (UTP) cabling, as discussed in Chapter 2. The 10Mbps version of Ethernet that relied on UTP cabling, an example of which is provided in Figure 4-3, is known as *10BASE-T*, where the T in 10BASE-T refers to twisted-pair cabling.

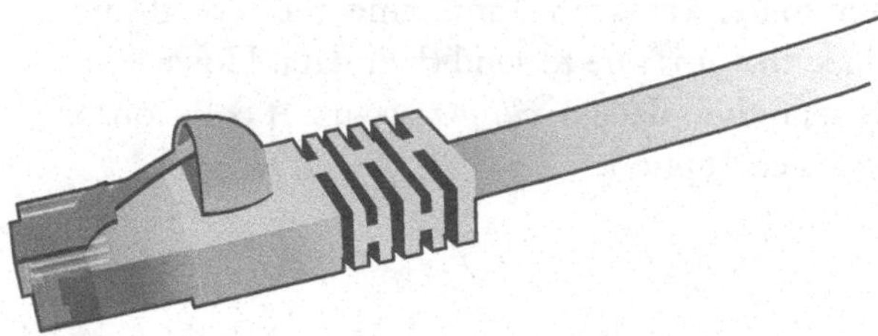

Figure 4-3 UTP Cable Used for 10BASE-T

Carrier-Sense Multiple Access/Collision Detect

Ethernet was based on the philosophy that all networked devices should be eligible, at any time, to transmit on a network. This school of thought is in direct opposition to technologies such as Token Ring, which boasted a *deterministic* media access approach. Specifically, Token Ring networks passed a token around a network in a circular fashion, from one networked device to the next. Only when a networked device was in possession of that token was it eligible to send on the network.

Recall from Chapter 1, "Computer Network Fundamentals," the concept of a bus topology. An example of a bus topology is a long cable (such as thicknet or thinnet) running the length of a building, with various networked devices tapping into that cable to gain access to the network.

Consider Figure 4-4, which depicts an Ethernet network using a shared bus topology.

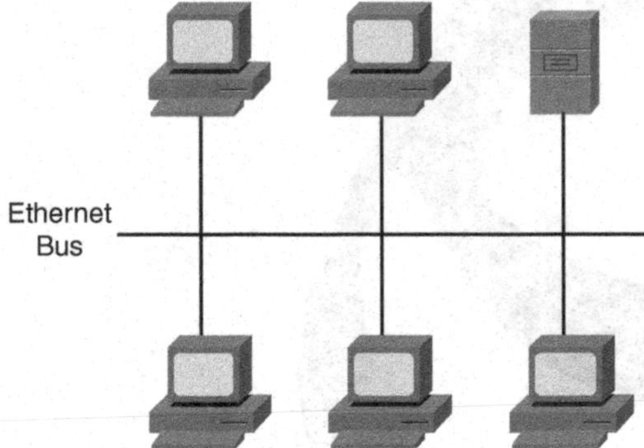

Figure 4-4 Ethernet Network Using a Shared Bus Topology

In this topology, all devices are directly connected to the network and are free to transmit at any time, if they have reason to believe no other transmission currently exists on the wire. Ethernet permits only a single frame to be on a network segment at any one time. So, before a device in this network transmits, it listens to the wire to see if there is currently any traffic being transmitted. If no traffic is detected, the networked device transmits its data. However, what if two devices simultaneously had data to send? If they both listen to the wire at the same time, they could simultaneously, and erroneously, conclude that it is safe to send their data. However, when both devices simultaneously send their data, a *collision* occurs. A collision, as depicted in Figure 4-5, results in data corruption.

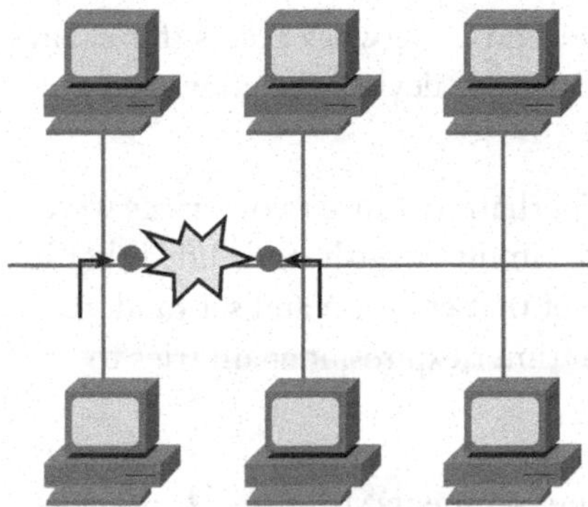

Figure 4-5 Collision on an Ethernet Segment

Fortunately, Ethernet was designed with a mechanism to detect collisions and allow the devices whose transmissions collided to retransmit their data at different times. Specifically, after the devices notice that a collision occurred, they independently set a random *back-off timer*. Each device waits for this random amount of time to elapse before again trying to transmit. Here is the logic: Because each device certainly picked a different amount of time to back off from transmitting, their transmissions should not collide the next time these devices transmit, as illustrated in Figure 4-6.

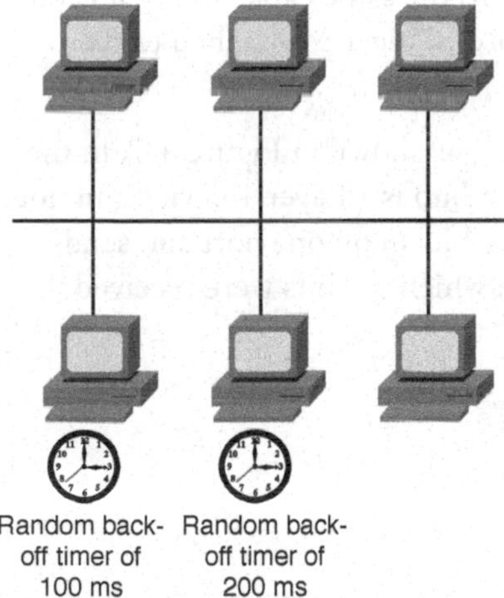

Figure 4-6 Recovering from a Collision with Random Back-off Timers

The procedure used by Ethernet to decide whether it is safe to transmit, detect collisions, and retransmit if necessary is called *carrier-sense multiple access/collision detection* (CSMA/CD).

Key Topic

Let's break down CSMA/CD into its constituent components:

- **Carrier sense:** A device attached to an Ethernet network can listen to the wire, prior to transmitting, to make sure that a frame is not being transmitted on the network segment.

- **Multiple access:** Unlike a deterministic method of network access (for example, the method used by Token Ring), all Ethernet devices simultaneously have access to an Ethernet segment.
- **Collision detection:** If a collision occurs (perhaps because two devices were simultaneously listening to the network and simultaneously concluded that it was safe to send), Ethernet devices can detect that collision and set random back-off timers. After each device's random timer expires, it again tries to transmit its data.

Even with Ethernet's CSMA/CD feature, Ethernet segments still suffer from scalability limitations. Specifically, the likelihood of collisions increases as the number of devices on a shared Ethernet segment increases.

An alternate approach is CSMA/CA. Here, CA refers to using *collision avoidance*. This technology is common in wireless networks and was made famous by Token Ring in early LANs.

Regarding wired Ethernet, devices on a shared Ethernet segment belong to the same *collision domain*. One example of a shared Ethernet segment is a 10BASE5 or 10BASE2 network with multiple devices attaching to the same cable. On that cable, only one device can send at any one time. Therefore, all devices attached to the thicknet or thinnet cable are in the same collision domain.

Similarly, devices connected to an Ethernet hub are, as shown in Figure 4-7, in the same collision domain. As described in Chapter 3, a hub is a Layer 1 device and does not make forwarding decisions. Instead, a hub takes bits in on one port and sends them out all the other hub ports except the one on which the bits were received.

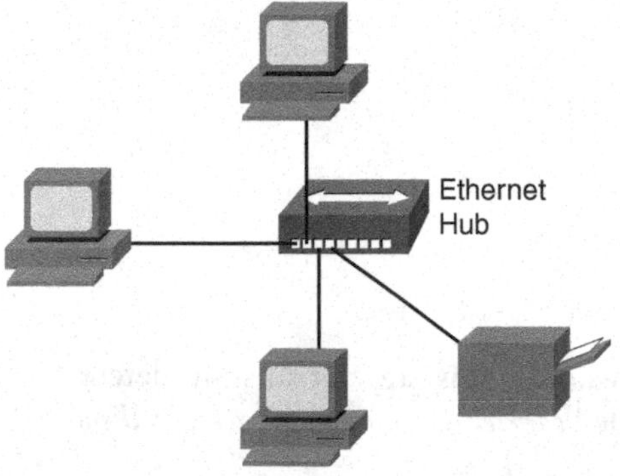

Figure 4-7 Shared Ethernet Hub: One Collision Domain

Ethernet switches, as in Figure 4-8, dramatically increase the scalability of Ethernet networks by creating multiple collision domains. In fact, every port on an Ethernet switch is in its own collision domain.

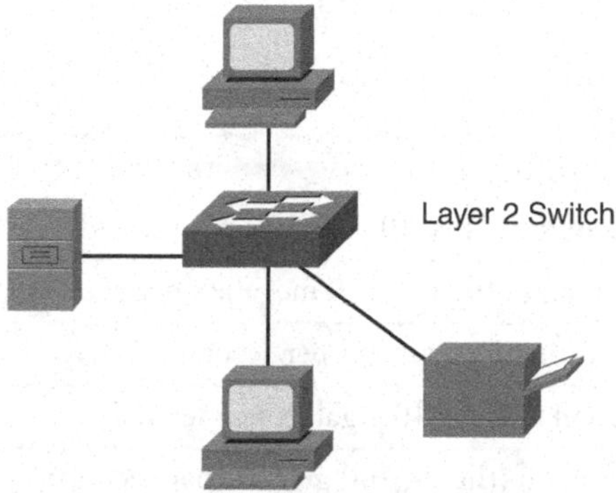

Figure 4-8 Ethernet Switch: One Collision Domain per Port

A less-obvious but powerful benefit also goes with Ethernet switches. Because a switch port is connecting to a single device, there is no chance of having a collision. With no chance of collision, collision detection is no longer needed. With collision detection disabled, network devices can run in *full-duplex* mode rather than *half-duplex* mode. In full-duplex mode, a device can simultaneously send and receive at the same time.

When multiple devices are connected to the same shared Ethernet segment such as a Layer 1 hub, CSMA/CD must be enabled. As a result, the network must work in half-duplex mode, which means that only a single networked device can transmit or receive at any one time. In half-duplex mode, a networked device cannot simultaneously send and receive, which is an inefficient use of a network's bandwidth.

Distance and Speed Limitations

To understand the bandwidth available on networks, you need to define a few terms. You should already know that a *bit* refers to one of two values. These values are represented using binary math, which uses only the numbers 0 and 1. On a cable such as twisted-pair cable, a bit could be represented by the absence or presence of voltage. Fiber-optic cables, however, might represent a bit with the absence or presence of light.

The bandwidth of a network is measured in terms of how many bits the network can transmit during a 1-second period of time. For example, if a network has the capacity to send 10,000,000 (that is, 10 million) bits in a 1-second period of time, the bandwidth capacity is said to be 10 megabits (that is, millions of bits) per second (or *Mbps*). Table 4-1 defines common bandwidths supported on distinct types of Ethernet networks.

Table 4-1 Ethernet Bandwidth Capacities

Ethernet Type	Bandwidth Capacity
Standard Ethernet	10Mbps: 10 million bits per second (that is, 10 megabits per second)
Fast Ethernet	100Mbps: 100 million bits per second (that is, 100 megabits per second)
Gigabit Ethernet	1Gbps: 1 billion bits per second (that is, 1 gigabit per second)
10-Gigabit Ethernet	10Gbps: 10 billion bits per second (that is, 10 gigabits per second)
100-Gigabit Ethernet	100Gbps: 100 billion bits per second (that is, 100 gigabits per second)

The type of cabling used in your Ethernet network influences the bandwidth capacity and the distance limitation of your network. For example, fiber-optic cabling often has a higher bandwidth capacity and a longer distance limitation than twisted-pair cabling.

Recall from Chapter 3 the contrast of single-mode fiber (SMF) to multimode fiber (MMF). Because of the issue of multimode delay distortion, SMF usually has a longer distance limitation than MMF.

When you want to uplink one Ethernet switch to another, you might need different connectors (for example, MMF, SMF, or UTP) for different installations. Fortunately, some Ethernet switches have one or more empty slots in which you can insert a gigabit interface converter (GBIC). GBICs are interfaces that have a bandwidth capacity of 1Gbps and are available with MMF, SMF, and UTP connectors. This allows you to have flexibility in the uplink technology you use in an Ethernet switch.

The various interface converters are commonly called transceivers. Two common characteristics of fiber optic transceivers are that they are bidirectional and (full) duplex. This means they can send data in both directions (bidirectional), and that they can do so simultaneously (full duplex).

NOTE A smaller variant of a regular GBIC is the small form-factor pluggable (SFP), which is sometimes called a *mini-GBIC*. Variations of the SFP include SFP+ and QSFP.

Although not comprehensive, Table 4-2 offers a listing of multiple Ethernet standards, along with their media type, bandwidth capacity, and distance limitation.

Table 4-2 Types of Ethernet

Ethernet Standard	Media Type	Bandwidth Capacity	Distance Limitation
10BASE5	Coax (thicknet)	10Mbps	500 m
10BASE2	Coax (thinnet)	10Mbps	185 m
10BASE-T	Cat 3 (or higher) UTP	10Mbps	100 m
100BASE-TX	Cat 5 (or higher) UTP	100Mbps	100 m
100BASE-FX	MMF	100Mbps	2 km
1000BASE-T	Cat 5e (or higher) UTP	1Gbps	100 m
1000BASE-TX	Cat 6 (or higher) UTP	1Gbps	100 m
1000BASE-SX	MMF	1Gbps	550 km
1000BASE-LX	SMF	1Gbps	5 km
1000BASE-LH	SMF	1Gbps	10 km
1000BASE-ZX	SMF	1Gbps	70 km
10GBASE-SR	MMF	10Gbps	26m–400 m
10GBASE-LR	SMF	10Gbps	10–25 km
10GBASE-ER	SMF	10Gbps	40 km
10GBASE-SW	MMF	10Gbps	300 m
10GBASE-LW	SMF	10Gbps	10 km
10GBASE-EW	SMF	10Gbps	40 km
10GBASE-T	Cat 6a (or higher)	10Gbps	100 m
100GBASE-SR10	MMF	100Gbps	125 m
100GBASE-LR4	SMF	100Gbps	10 km
100GBASE-ER4	SMF	100Gbps	40 km

NOTE Two often-confused terms are *100BASE-T* and *100BASE-TX*. 100BASE-T itself is not a specific standard. Rather, 100BASE-T is a category of standards and includes 100BASE-T2 (which uses two pairs of wires in a Cat 3 cable), 100BASE-T4 (which uses four pairs of wires in a Cat 3 cable), and 100BASE-TX. 100BASE-T2 and 100BASE-T4 were early implementations of 100Mbps Ethernet and are no longer used. Therefore, you can generally use the terms *100BASE-T* and *100BASE-TX* interchangeably.

Similarly, the term *1000BASE-X* is not a specific standard. Rather, 1000BASE-X refers to all Ethernet technologies that transmit data at a rate of 1Gbps over fiber-optic cabling. Additional and creative ways of using Ethernet technology include IEEE 1901-2013, which could be used for Ethernet over HDMI cables and Ethernet over existing power lines to avoid having to run a separate cabling just for networking.

Ethernet Switch Features

Chapter 3 delved into the operation of Layer 2 Ethernet switches (which we generically refer to as *switches*). You read an explanation of how a switch learns which Media Access Control (MAC) addresses live off of which ports and an explanation of how a switch makes forwarding decisions based on destination MAC addresses.

Beyond basic frame forwarding, however, many Layer 2 Ethernet switches offer a variety of other features to enhance such things as network performance, redundancy, security, management, flexibility, and scalability. Although the specific features offered by a switch vary, this section introduces you to some of the more common features found on switches.

Virtual LANs

In a basic switch configuration, all ports on a switch belong to the same *broadcast domain*, as explained in Chapter 3. In such an arrangement, a broadcast received on one port gets forwarded out all other ports.

Also, from a Layer 3 perspective, all devices connected in a broadcast domain have the same *network address*. Chapter 5, "IPv4 and IPv6 Addresses," gets into the binary math behind the scenes of how networked devices can be assigned an IP address (that is, a logical Layer 3 address). A portion of that address is the address of the network to which that device is attached. The remaining portion of that address is the address of the device itself. Devices that have the same network address belong to the same network, or *subnet*.

Imagine that you decide to place PCs from different departments within a company into their own subnet. One reason you might want to do this is for security purposes. For example, by having the Accounting department in a separate subnet (that is, a separate broadcast domain) than the Sales department, devices in one subnet will not see the broadcasts being sent on the other subnet.

A design challenge might be that PCs belonging to these departments are scattered across multiple floors in a building. Consider Figure 4-9 as an example. The Accounting and Sales departments each have a PC on both floors of a building. Because the wiring for each floor runs back to a wiring closet on that floor, to support these two subnets using a switch's default configuration, you would have to install two switches on each floor. For traffic to travel from one subnet to another subnet, that traffic has to be routed, meaning that a device such as a multilayer switch or a router forwards traffic based on a packet's destination network addresses. So, in this example, the Accounting switches are interconnected and then connect to a router, and the Sales switches are connected similarly.

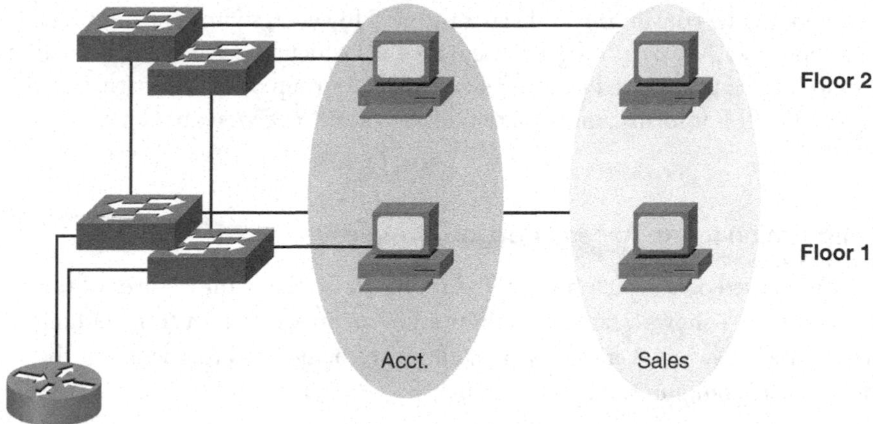

Figure 4-9 Example: All Ports on a Switch Belonging to the Same Subnet

The design presented lacks efficiency, in that you have to install at least one switch per subnet. A more efficient design would be to logically separate a switch's ports into different broadcast domains. Then, in the example, an Accounting department PC and a Sales department PC could connect to the same switch, even though those PCs belong to different subnets. Fortunately, *virtual LANs* (VLANs) make this possible.

With VLANs, as illustrated in Figure 4-10, a switch can have its ports logically divided into more than one broadcast domain (that is, more than one subnet or VLAN). Then, devices that need to connect to those VLANs can connect to the same physical switch, yet logically be separate from one another.

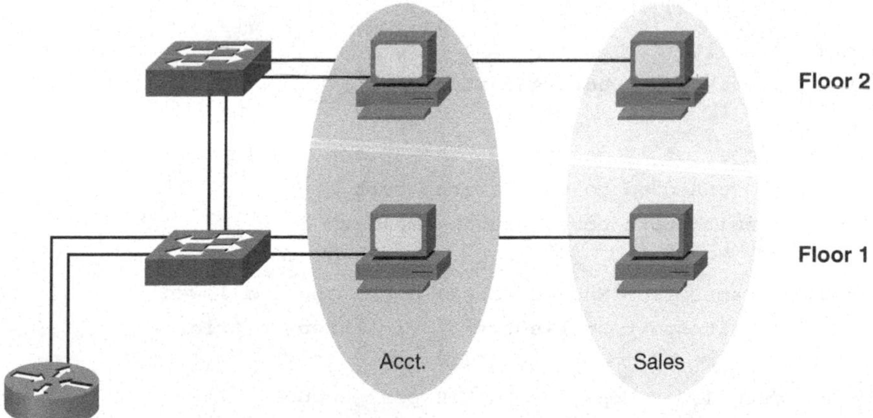

Figure 4-10 Example: Ports on a Switch Belonging to Different VLANs

One challenge with VLAN configuration in large environments is the need to configure identical VLAN information on all switches. Manually performing this configuration is time consuming and error prone. However, switches from Cisco Systems support VLAN Trunking Protocol (VTP), which allows a VLAN created on one switch to be propagated to other switches in a group of switches (that is, a VTP domain). VTP information is carried over a *trunk connection*, which is discussed next.

Switch Configuration for an Access Port

Configurations used on a switch port may vary, based on the manufacturer of the switch. Example 4-1 shows a sample configuration on an access port (no trunking) on a Cisco Catalyst switch. Lines with a leading ! are being used to document the next line(s) of the configuration.

Example 4-1 Switch Access Port Configuration

```
! Move into configuration mode for interface gig 0/21
SW1(config)# interface GigabitEthernet0/21

! Add a text description of what the port is used for
SW1(config-if)# description Access port in Sales VLAN 21

! Define the port as an access port, and not a trunk port
SW1(config-if)# switchport mode access

! Assign the port to VLAN 21
SW1(config-if)# switchport access vlan 21

! Enable port security
SW1(config-if)# switchport port-security

! Control the number of MAC addresses the switch may learn
! from device(s) connected to this switch port
SW1(config-if)# switchport port-security maximum 5

! Restrict any frames from MAC addresses above the 5 allowed
SW1(config-if)# switchport port-security violation restrict

! Set the speed to 1,000 Mbps (1 Gigabit per second)
SW1(config-if)# speed 1000

! Set the duplex to full
SW1(config-if)# duplex full
```

```
! Configure the port to begin forwarding without waiting the
! standard amount of time normally set by Spanning Tree Protocol
SW1(config-if)# spanning-tree portfast
```

Trunks

One challenge with carving a switch up into multiple VLANs is that several switch ports (that is, one port per VLAN) could be consumed connecting a switch to a switch, or a switch to a router. A more efficient approach is to allow traffic for multiple VLANs to travel over a single connection, as shown in Figure 4-11. This type of connection is called a *trunk*.

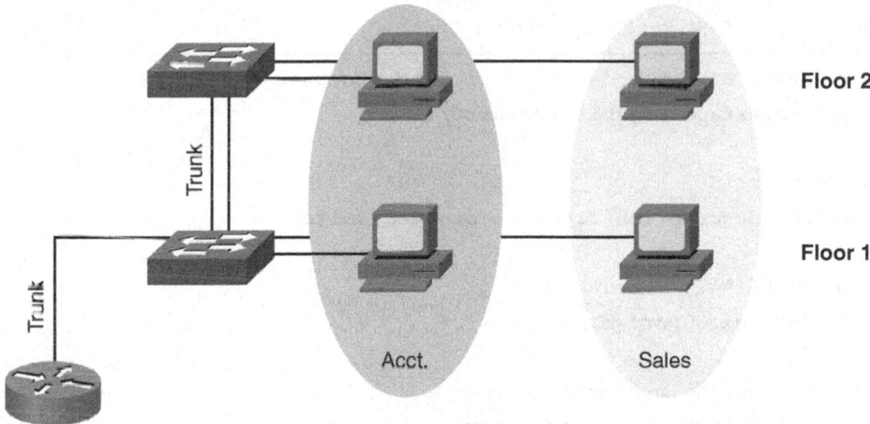

Figure 4-11 Example: Trunking Between Switches

The most popular trunking standard today is IEEE 802.1Q, which is often referred to as *dot1q*. One of the VLANs traveling over an 802.1Q trunk is called a *native VLAN*. Frames belonging to the native VLAN are sent unaltered over the trunk (untagged/no tag). However, to distinguish other VLANs from one another, the remaining VLANs are tagged.

Specifically, a nonnative VLAN has four tag bytes (where a *byte* is a collection of 8 bits) added to the Ethernet frame (tagged frame). Figure 4-12 shows the format of an IEEE 802.1Q header with these 4 bytes.

Preamble 7 Bytes	Start-of-Frame Delimiter 1 Byte	Destination Address 6 Bytes	Source Address 6 Bytes	Tag Protocol Identifier 2 Bytes	Tag Control Identifier 2 Bytes	Type 2 Bytes	Data	CRC/FCS 4 Bytes

4 Bytes Added by IEEE 802.1Q

Figure 4-12 IEEE 8021Q Header

One of these bytes contains a VLAN field. That field indicates to which VLAN a frame belongs. The devices (for example, a switch, a multilayer switch, or a router) at each end of a trunk interrogate that field to determine to which VLAN an incoming frame is associated. As you can see by comparing Figures 4-9, 4-10, and 4-11, VLAN and trunking features allow switch ports to be used far more efficiently than merely relying on a default switch configuration.

Switch Configuration for a Trunk Port

Example 4-2 shows a sample configuration on a trunk port on a Cisco Catalyst switch. Again, lines with a leading ! are being used to document the next line(s) of the configuration.

Example 4-2 Sample Trunk Port Configuration

```
! Go to interface config mode for interface Gig 0/22
SW1(config)# interface GigabitEthernet0/22

! Add a text description
SW1(config-if)# description Trunk to another switch

! Specify that this is a trunk port
SW1(config-if)# switchport mode trunk

! Specify the trunking protocol to use
SW1(config-if)# switchport trunk encapsulation dot1q

! Specify the native VLAN to use for un-tagged frames
SW1(config-if)# switchport trunk native vlan 5

! Specify which VLANs are allowed to go on the trunk
SW1(config-if)# switchport trunk allowed vlan 1-50
```

Spanning Tree Protocol

Administrators of corporate telephone networks often boast about their telephone system—that is, a private branch exchange (PBX) system—having the *five nines* of availability. If a system has five nines of availability, it is up and functioning 99.999 percent of the time, which translates to only about 5 minutes of downtime per year.

Traditionally, corporate data networks struggled to compete with corporate voice networks, in terms of availability. Today, however, many networks that traditionally carried only data now carry voice, video, and data. Therefore, availability becomes an even more important design consideration.

To improve network availability at Layer 2, many networks have redundant links between switches. However, unlike Layer 3 packets, Layer 2 frames lack a Time-to-Live (TTL) field. As a result, a Layer 2 frame can circulate endlessly through a looped Layer 2 topology. Fortunately, IEEE 802.1D Spanning Tree Protocol (STP) allows a network to physically have Layer 2 loops while strategically blocking data from flowing over one or more switch ports to prevent the looping of traffic.

In the absence of STP, if we have parallel paths, two significant symptoms include corruption of a switch's MAC address table and broadcast storms, where frames loop over and over throughout our switched network. An enhancement to the original STP protocol is *802.1w*, which is also called *Rapid Spanning Tree* because it does a quicker job of adjusting to network conditions, such as the addition to or removal of Layer 2 links in the network.

Shortest Path Bridging (IEEE 802.1aq/SPB) is a protocol that is more scalable in larger environments (hundreds of switches interconnected) compared to STP.

Corruption of a Switch's MAC Address Table

As described in Chapter 3, a switch's MAC address table can dynamically learn what MAC addresses are available off its ports. However, in the case of an STP failure, a switch's MAC address table can become corrupted. To illustrate, consider Figure 4-13.

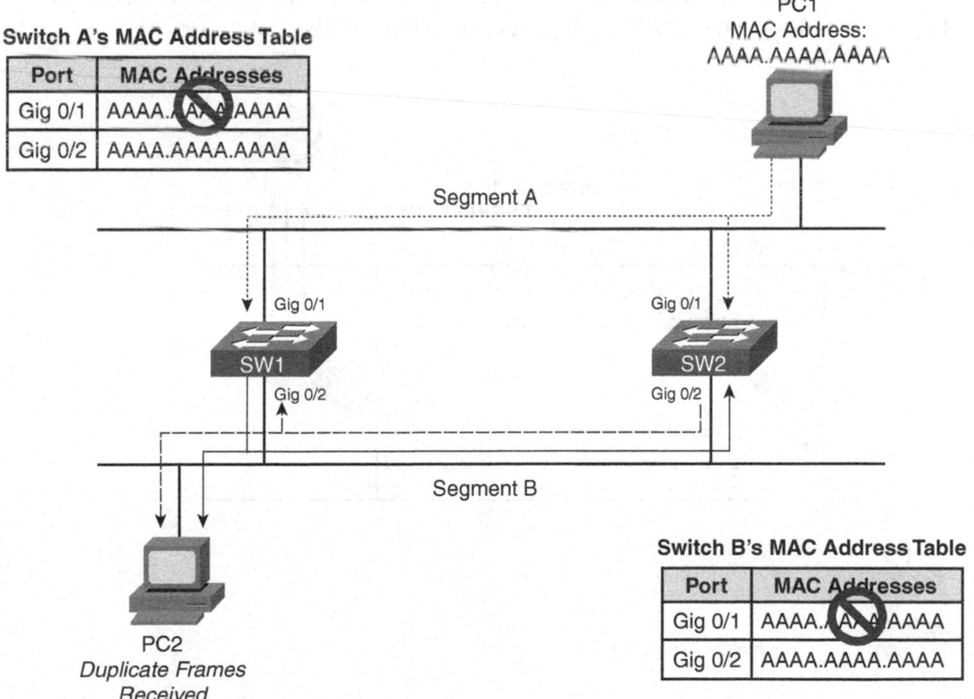

Figure 4-13 MAC Address Table Corruption

PC1 is transmitting traffic to PC2. When the frame sent from PC1 is transmitted on segment A, the frame is seen on the Gig 0/1 ports of switches SW1 and SW2, causing both switches to add an entry to their MAC address tables associating a MAC address of AAAA.AAAA.AAAA with port Gig 0/1. Because STP is not functioning, both switches then forward the frame out on segment B. As a result, PC2 receives two copies of the frame. Also, switch SW1 sees the frame forwarded out of switch SW2's Gig 0/2 port. Because the frame has a source MAC address of AAAA. AAAA.AAAA, switch SW1 incorrectly updates its MAC address table, indicating that a MAC address of AAAA.AAAA.AAAA resides off of port Gig 0/2. Similarly, switch SW2 sees the frame forwarded on to segment B by switch SW1 on its Gig 0/2 port. Therefore, switch SW2 also incorrectly updates its MAC address table.

Broadcast Storms

As previously mentioned, when a switch receives a broadcast frame (that is, a frame destined for a MAC address of FFFF.FFFF.FFFF), the switch floods the frame out of all switch ports, other than the port on which the frame was received. Because a Layer 2 frame does not have a TTL field, a broadcast frame endlessly circulates through the Layer 2 topology, consuming resources on both switches and attached devices (for example, user PCs).

Figure 4-14 and the following list illustrate how a broadcast storm can form in a Layer 2 topology when STP is not functioning correctly:

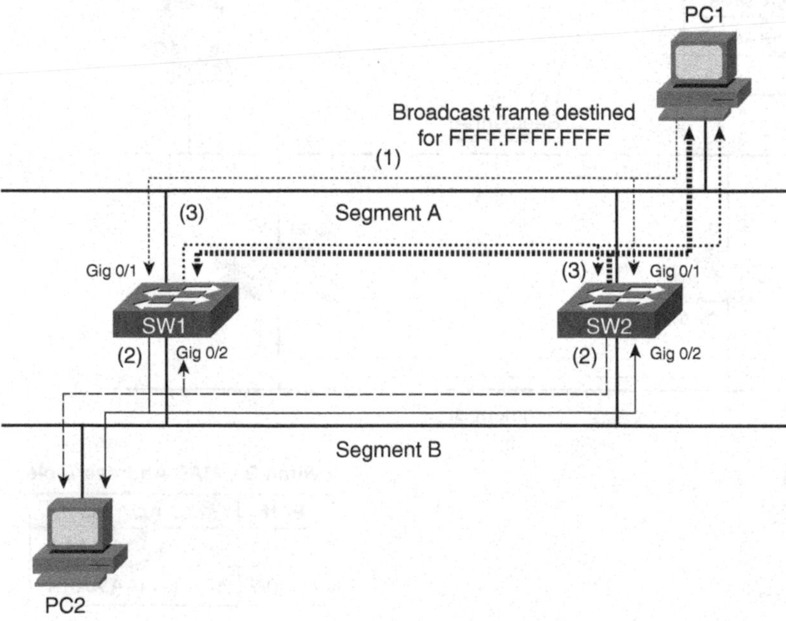

Figure 4-14 Broadcast Storm

1. PC1 sends a broadcast frame on to segment A, and the frame enters each switch on port Gig 0/1.

2. Both switches flood a copy of the broadcast frame out of their Gig 0/2 ports (that is, on to segment B), causing PC2 to receive two copies of the broadcast frame.

3. Both switches receive a copy of the broadcast frame on their Gig 0/2 ports (that is, from segment B) and flood the frame out of their Gig 0/1 ports (that is, on to segment A), causing PC1 to receive two copies of the broadcast frame.

This behavior continues as the broadcast frame copies continue to loop through the network. The performance of PC1 and PC2 is affected because they also continue to receive copies of the broadcast frame.

STP Operation

STP prevents Layer 2 loops from occurring in a network because such an occurrence might result in a broadcast storm or corruption of a switch's MAC address table. Switches in an STP topology are classified as one of the following:

- **Root bridge:** A switch elected to act as a reference point for a spanning tree. The switch with the lowest bridge ID (BID) is elected as the root bridge. The BID is made up of a priority value and a MAC address.
- **Nonroot bridge:** All other switches in the STP topology are nonroot bridges.

Figure 4-15 illustrates the root bridge election in a network. Notice that because the bridge priorities are both 32768, the switch with the lowest MAC address (that is, SW1) is elected as the root bridge.

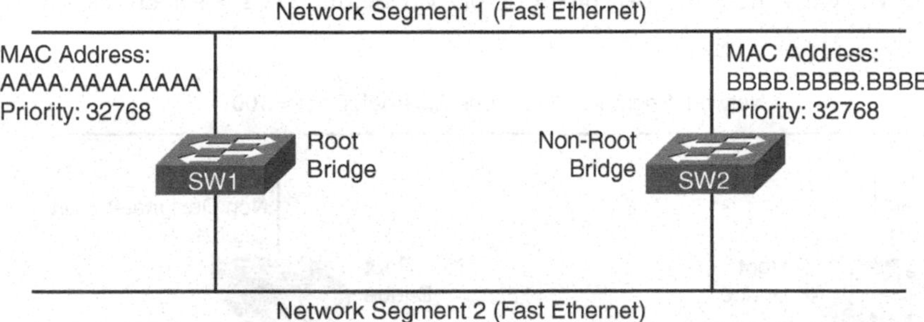

Figure 4-15 Root Bridge Election

Ports that interconnect switches in an STP topology are categorized as one of the port types described in Table 4-3.

Table 4-3 STP Port Types

Port Type	Description
Root port	Every nonroot bridge has a single root port, which is the port on that switch that is closest to the root bridge in terms of cost.
Designated port	Every network segment has a single designated port, which is the port on that segment that is closest to the root bridge in terms of cost. Therefore, all ports on a root bridge are designated ports.
Nondesignated port	Nondesignated ports block traffic to create a loop-free topology.

Figure 4-16 illustrates these port types. Notice the root port for switch SW2 is selected based on the lowest port ID because the costs of both links are equal. Specifically, each link has a cost of 19, because both links are Fast Ethernet links.

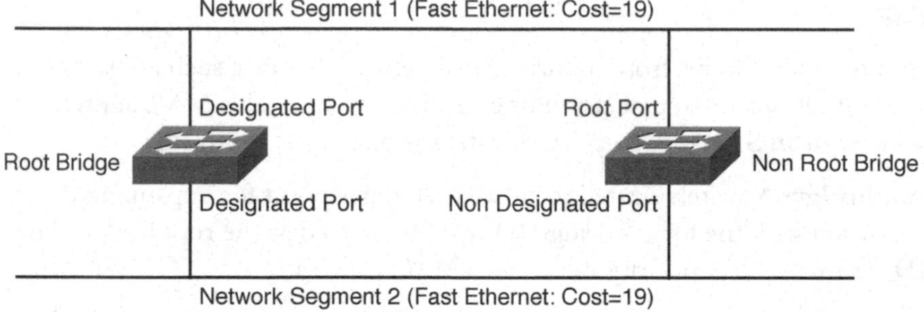

Figure 4-16 Identifying STP Port Roles

Figure 4-17 shows a similar topology to Figure 4-16. In Figure 4-17, however, the top link is running at a speed of 10Mbps, whereas the bottom link is running at a speed of 100Mbps. Because switch SW2 seeks to get back to the root bridge (that is, switch SW1) with the least cost, port Gig 0/2 on switch SW2 is selected as the root port.

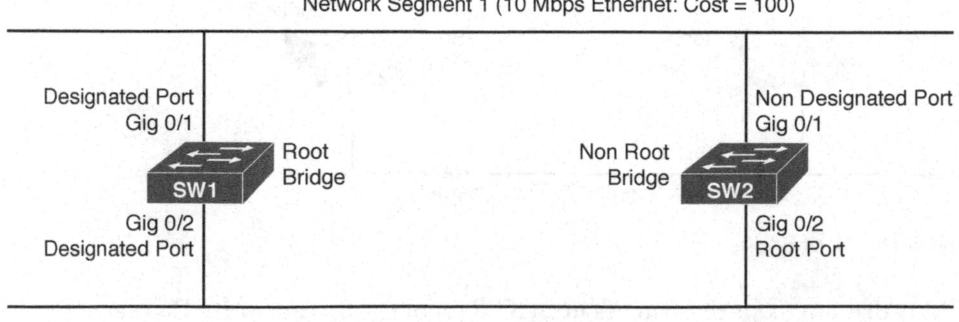

Figure 4-17 STP with Different Port Costs

Specifically, port Gig 0/1 has a cost of 100, and Gig 0/2 has a cost of 19. Table 4-4 shows the port costs for various link speeds.

Table 4-4 STP Port Cost

Link Speed	STP Port Cost
10Mbps (Ethernet)	100
100Mbps (Fast Ethernet)	19
1Gbps (Gigabit Ethernet)	4
10Gbps (10-Gigabit Ethernet)	2

NOTE A new standard for STP port costs, called *long STP*, will be increasingly adopted over the coming years because of link speeds exceeding 10Gbps. Long STP values range from 2,000,000 for 10Mbps Ethernet to as little as 2 for 10Tbps (that is, 10 trillion [tera] bits per second).

Nondesignated ports do not forward traffic during normal operation but do receive bridge protocol data units (BPDUs). Switches exchange STP information in the form of BPDUs. These contain useful information for STP elections, path cost calculation, link suppression, and loop detection. If a link in the topology goes down, the nondesignated port detects the link failure and determines whether it needs to transition to the forwarding state.

If a nondesignated port needs to transition to the forwarding state, it does not do so immediately. Rather, it transitions through the following states:

- **Blocking:** The port remains in the blocking state for 20 seconds by default. During this time, the nondesignated port evaluates BPDUs in an attempt to determine its role in the spanning tree.
- **Listening:** The port moves from the blocking state to the listening state and remains in this state for 15 seconds by default. During this time, the port sources BPDUs, which inform adjacent switches of the port's intent to forward data.
- **Learning:** The port moves from the listening state to the learning state and remains in this state for 15 seconds by default. During this time, the port begins to add entries to its MAC address table.
- **Forwarding:** The port moves from the learning state to the forwarding state and begins to forward frames.

Link Aggregation

If all ports on a switch are operating at the same speed (for example, 1Gbps), the most likely ports to experience congestion are ports connecting to another switch or router. For example, imagine a wiring closet switch connected (via Fast Ethernet ports) to multiple PCs. That wiring closet switch has an uplink to the main switch for a building. Because this uplink port aggregates multiple 100Mbps connections and the uplink port is also operating at 100Mbps, it can quickly become congested if multiple PCs are transmitting traffic that needs to be sent over that uplink, as shown in Figure 4-18.

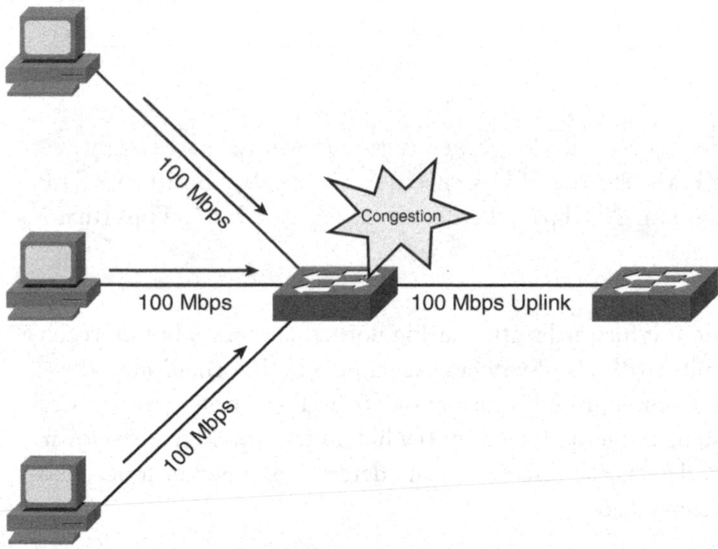

Figure 4-18 Uplink Congestion

To help alleviate congested links between switches, you can (on some switch models) logically combine multiple physical connections into a single logical connection, over which traffic can be sent. This feature, as illustrated in Figure 4-19, is called *link aggregation*.

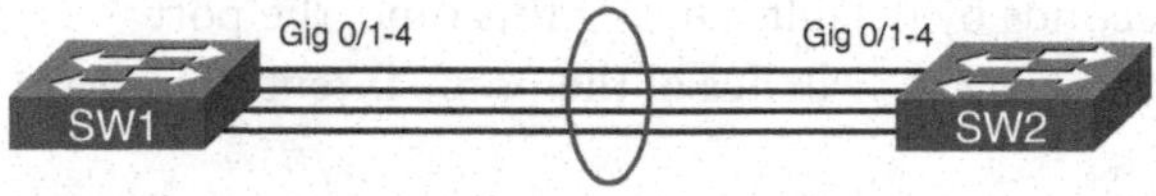

Figure 4-19 Link Aggregation

Although vendor-proprietary solutions for link aggregation have existed for some time, a couple of common issues existed with some solutions:

- Each link in the logical bundle was a potential single point of failure.
- Each end of the logical bundle had to be manually configured.

In 2000, the IEEE ratified the 802.3ad standard for link aggregation. The IEEE 802.3ad standard supports Link Aggregation Control Protocol (LACP). Unlike some of the older vendor proprietary solutions, LACP supports automatic configuration and prevents an individual link from becoming a single point of failure. Specifically, with LACP, if a link fails, that link's traffic is forwarded over a different link. Groups of interfaces that make up an EtherChannel bundle are often referred to as a *link aggregation group* (LAG). Cisco Systems implementation is referred to as *EtherChannel*, and the terms *LACP* and *EtherChannel* are both commonly used. An EtherChannel group could be configured to act as a Layer 2 access port, and only support a single VLAN, or it could be configured to act as a Layer 2 802.1Q trunk to support multiple VLANs of the LAG. LAGs could also be configured as a Layer 3 routed interface if the switch supports that feature. In the case of a Layer 3 EtherChannel, an IP address would be applied to the logical interface that represents the LAG. Another term related to LACP and LAGs is *port bonding*, which also refers to the same concept of grouping multiple ports and using them as a single logical interface.

LACP Configuration

Example 4-3 shows a sample configuration of LACP on a Cisco switch. Comment lines are preceded by an exclamation mark (!).

Example 4-3 LACP Configuration

```
! Move to interface that will be part of the LACP group
SW1(config)# interface GigabitEthernet0/16

! Assign this interface to the LACP group 1
SW1(config-if)# channel-group 1 mode active


! Move to the other interface(s) that will be part of
! the same group
SW1(config-if)# interface GigabitEthernet0/17
SW1(config-if)# channel-group 1 mode active

! Configure the group of interfaces as a logical group
! Configuration here will also apply the individual
! interfaces that are part of the group
SW1(config-if)# interface Port-channel 1

! Apply the configuration desired for the group
! LACP groups can be access or trunk ports depending
```

```
! on how the configuration of the logical port-channel interface
! In this example the LAG will be acting as a trunk
SW1(config-if)# switchport mode trunk
SW1(config-if)# switchport trunk encapsulation dot1q
```

Power over Ethernet

Some switches not only transmit data over a connected UTP cable, but they use that cable to provide power to an attached device. For example, imagine that you want to mount a wireless access point (AP) on the ceiling. Although no electrical outlet is available near the AP's location, you can, as an example, run a Cat 5 UTP plenum cable above the drop ceiling and connect it to the AP. Some APs allow the switch at the other end of the UTP cable to provide power over the same wires that carry data. Examples of other devices that might benefit by receiving power from an Ethernet switch include security cameras and IP phones.

The switch feature that gives power to attached devices is called *Power over Ethernet* (PoE), and it is defined by the IEEE 802.3af standard. As shown in Figure 4-20, the PoE feature of a switch checks for 25k ohms (25,000 ohms) of resistance in the attached device. To check the resistance, the switch applies as much as 10V of direct current (DC) across specific pairs of wires (that is, pins 1 and 2 combine to form one side of the circuit, and pins 3 and 6 combine to form the other side of the circuit) connecting back to the attached device and checks to see how much current flows over those wires. For example, if the switch applied 10V DC across those wires and noticed 0.4 mA (milliamps) of current, the switch concludes the attached device had 25k ohms of resistance across those wires (based on the formula $E = IR$, where E represents voltage, I represents current, and R represents resistance). The switch could then apply power across those wires.

Switch applies 2.8 – 10 V DC to two pairs of leads to detect a 25K Ohm resistor in the attached device

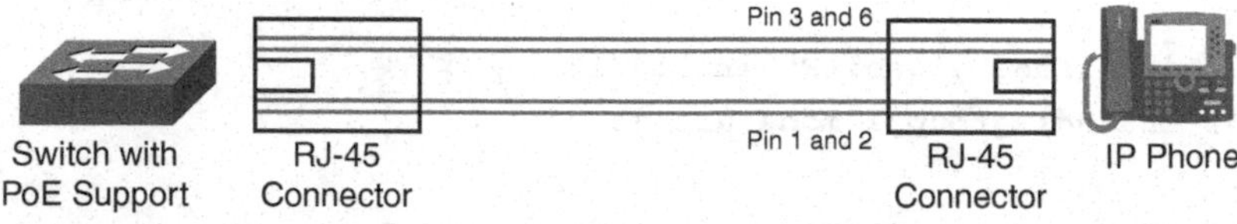

Figure 4-20 PoE

The next thing the switch must determine is how much power the attached device needs. The switch makes this determination by applying 15.5 V–20.5V DC (making sure that the current never exceeds 100 mA) to the attached device, for a brief period of time (less than one-tenth of a second). The amount of current flowing to the attached device tells the switch the *power class* of the attached device. The switch then knows how much power should be made available on the port connecting to the device requiring power, and it begins supplying an appropriate amount of voltage (in the range 44V–57V) to the attached device.

The IEEE 802.3af standard can supply a maximum of 15.4W (watts) of power. However, a more recent standard, IEEE 802.3at, offers as much as 32.4W of power, enabling PoE to support a wider range of devices.

Port Monitoring

For troubleshooting purposes, you might want to analyze packets flowing over the network. To capture packets (that is, store a copy of packets on a local hard drive) for analysis, you could attach a *network sniffer* to a hub. Because a hub sends bits received on one port out all other ports, the attached network sniffer sees all traffic entering the hub.

Although several standalone network sniffers are on the market, a low-cost way to perform packet capture and analysis is to use software such as Wireshark (www.wireshark.org), as shown in Figure 4-21.

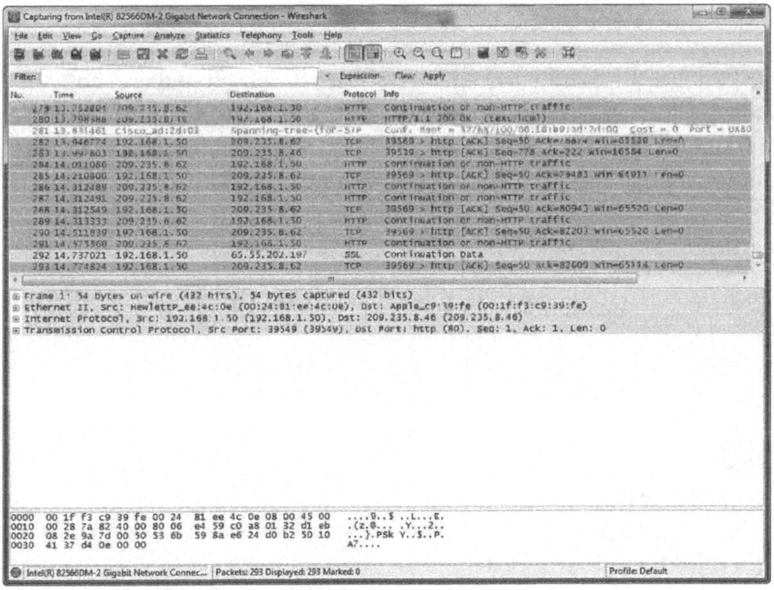

Figure 4-21 Example: Wireshark Packet-Capture Software

A challenge arises, however, if you connect your network sniffer (for example, a laptop running the Wireshark software) to a switch port rather than a hub port. Because a switch, by design, forwards frames out ports containing the frames' destination addresses, a network sniffer attached to one port would not see traffic destined for a device connected to a different port.

Consider Figure 4-22. Traffic enters a switch on port 1 and, based on the destination MAC addresses, exits via port 2. However, a network sniffer is connected to port 3 and is unable to see (and therefore capture) the traffic flowing between ports 1 and 2.

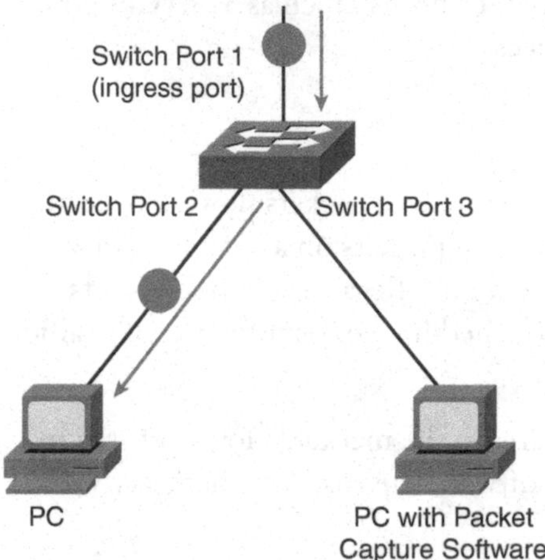

Figure 4-22 Example: Network Sniffer Unable to Capture Traffic

Fortunately, some switches support a *port mirroring* feature, which makes a copy of traffic seen on one port and sends that duplicated traffic out another port (to which a network sniffer could be attached). As shown in Figure 4-23, the switch is configured to mirror traffic on port 2 to port 3. This allows a network sniffer to capture the packets that need to be analyzed. Depending on the switch, locally captured traffic could be forwarded to a remote destination for centralized analysis of that traffic.

Key Topic

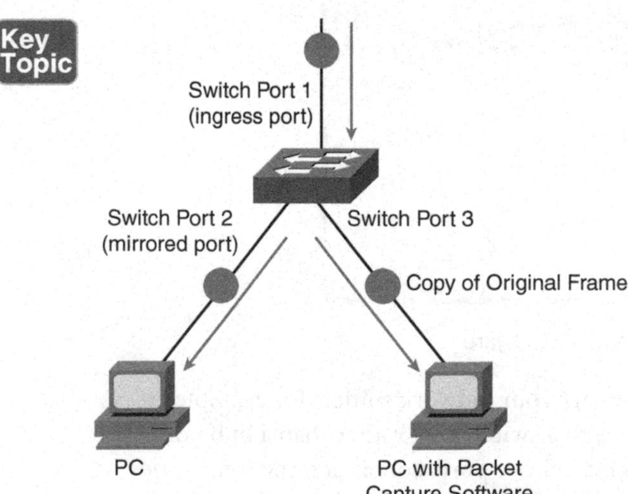

Figure 4-23 Example: Network Sniffer with Port Mirroring Configured on the Switch

Port Mirroring Configuration

Example 4-4 shows a sample configuration from a Cisco Catalyst switch that captures all the frames coming in on port Gig 0/1 and forwards them to port Gig 0/3.

Example 4-4 Port Mirroring Configuration

```
SW1(config)# monitor session 1 source interface Gi0/1
SW1(config)# monitor session 1 destination interface Gi0/3
```

User Authentication

For security purposes, some switches require users to *authenticate* themselves (that is, provide credentials, such as a username and password, to prove who they are) before gaining access to the rest of the network. A standards-based method of enforcing user authentication is IEEE 802.1X.

With 802.1X enabled, a switch requires a client to authenticate before communicating on the network. After the authentication occurs, a key is generated that is shared between the client and the device to which it attaches (for example, a wireless LAN controller or a Layer 2 switch). The key then encrypts traffic coming from and being sent to the client.

In Figure 4-24, you see the three primary components of an 802.1X network, which are described in the following list:

Key Topic

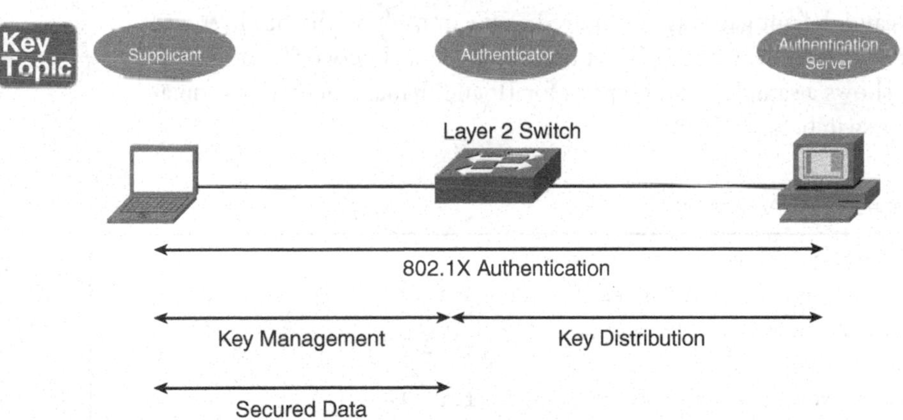

Figure 4-24 8021X User Authentication

- **Supplicant:** The device that wants to gain access to the network.
- **Authenticator:** The authenticator forwards the supplicant's authentication request on to an authentication server. After the authentication server authenticates the supplicant, the authenticator receives a key that is used to communicate securely during a session with the supplicant.

- **Authentication server:** The authentication server (for example, a Remote Authentication Dial In User Service [RADIUS] server) checks a supplicant's credentials. If the credentials are acceptable, the authentication server notifies the authenticator that the supplicant is allowed to communicate on the network. The authentication server also gives the authenticator a key that can be used to securely transmit data during the authenticator's session with the supplicant.

An even more sophisticated approach to admission control is the Network Admission Control (NAC) feature offered by some authentication servers. Beyond just checking credentials, NAC can check characteristics of the device seeking admission to the network. The client's operating system (OS) and version of antivirus software are examples of these characteristics.

Management Access and Authentication

To configure a managed switch, you could use Secure Shell (SSH) or connect directly to the console port of the switch. An unmanaged switch is one that does not support the use of an IP address or a console port to connect to for management purposes. When possible, using a separate network for management of a managed switch is desired. This is referred to as *out-of-band* (OOB) management when the management traffic is kept on a separate network than the user traffic. To use remote SSH access, SSH must be enabled on the switch and the switch must have an IP address and default gateway configured so it can reply to the SSH requests when the administrator using SSH is not on the same local network as the switch. Example 4-5 shows a sample configuration for IP and management access on a Cisco Catalyst switch.

Example 4-5 Management Access

```
! Move to the logical Layer 3 interface that will
! receive the management IP address for the switch
SW1(config)# interface vlan 1

! Configure an IP address that is available for the
! switch to use
SW1(config-if)# ip address 172.16.55.123 255.255.255.0
SW1(config-if)# exit

! Configure a domain name, required for creating the
! keys used for SSH cryptography
SW1(config)# ip domain-name pearson.com
```

```
! Create the public/private key pair SSH can use
SW1(config)# crypto key generate rsa modulus 1024

! Specify the version of SSH to allow
SW1(config)# ip ssh version 2

! Create a user account on the local switch
SW1(config)# username admin privilege 15 secret pears0nR0cks!

! Move to the logical VTY lines used for SSH access
SW1(config)# line vty 0 15

! Allow only SSH on the logical range 16 VTY lines (0 - 15)
SW1(config line)# transport input ssh

! Require using an account from the local switch to log in
SW1(config-line)# login local
SW1(config-line)# exit

! Set the default gateway the switch can use when communicating
! over an SSH session with an administrator who is on a different
! network than the switch's interface VLAN 1
SW1(config)# ip default-gateway 172.16.55.1

! Move to the console port of the switch
SW1(config)# line console 0

! Require authentication using the local switch before allowing
! access to the switch through the console port
SW1(config-line)# login local
```

NOTE The virtual terminal (VTY) lines (lines 0–15 in the example) allow for 16 simultaneous connections to the switch by administrators. If more simultaneous connections are required, additional virtual terminal lines could be configured on the switch.

First-Hop Redundancy

Many devices, such as PCs, are configured with a default gateway. The *default gateway* parameter identifies the IP address of a next-hop router. As a result, if that router were to become unavailable, devices that relied on the default gateway's IP address would be unable to send traffic off their local subnet, even if a backup router exists.

Fortunately, a variety of technologies are available for providing first-hop redundancy. One such technology is Hot Standby Router Protocol (HSRP), which is a Cisco proprietary protocol. HSRP can run on routers or multilayer switches.

HSRP uses virtual IP and virtual MAC addresses. One router, known as the *active router*, services requests destined for the virtual IP and virtual MAC. Another router, known as the *standby router*, can service such requests in the event the active router becomes unavailable. Figure 4-25 illustrates a sample HSRP topology.

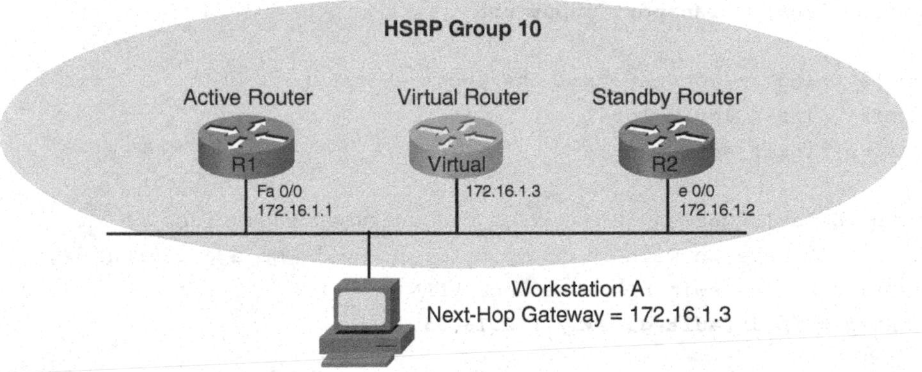

Figure 4-25 Sample HSRP Topology

Notice that router R1 is acting as the active router, and router R2 is acting as the standby router. When workstation A sends traffic destined for a remote network, it sends traffic to its default gateway of 172.16.1.3, which is the virtual IP address shared by the HSRP routers. When router R1 is the active router, it assumes the virtual IP and virtual MAC, and it forwards the traffic off the local network. However, if R2 notices that R1 has become unavailable (because hello messages are no longer received from router R1), R2 transitions to the active router role and assumes the virtual IP and virtual MAC. With default timer settings, the time required to fail over to router R2 is approximately 10 seconds. However, timers can be adjusted such that the failover time is as little as 1 second.

NOTE Cisco has another first-hop proprietary redundancy protocol named *Gateway Load Balancing Protocol* (GLBP). Whereas GLBP and HSRP are Cisco proprietary solutions, Virtual Router Redundancy Protocol (VRRP) and Common Address Redundancy Protocol (CARP) are open standard options for first-hop redundancy.

Other Switch Features

Switch features, such as those previously described, vary widely by manufacturer, and some switches offer a variety of security features. For example, MAC filtering might be supported, which allows traffic to be permitted or denied based on a device's MAC address. Other types of traffic filtering might also be supported, based on criteria such as IP address information (for multilayer switches).

For monitoring and troubleshooting purposes, interface *diagnostics* might be accessible. This diagnostic information might contain information including various error conditions—for example, late collisions or cyclic redundancy check (CRC) errors, which might indicate a duplex mismatch.

Some switches also support *quality of service* (QoS) settings. QoS can forward traffic based on the traffic's priority markings. Also, some switches have the ability to perform marking and remarking of traffic priority values.

NOTE QoS technologies are covered in more detail in Chapter 9, "Network Optimization."

Real-World Case Study

Acme, Inc., has made some decisions regarding the setup of its LAN. For connections from the client machines to the switches in the wiring closets (IDF), it will use unshielded twisted-pair Category 5 cabling with the switch ports configured as access ports and set to 100Mbps to match the Fast Ethernet capabilities of the client computers that will be connecting to the switch.

Multiple VLANs will be used. The computers that are being used by the Sales department will be connected to ports on a switch that are configured as access ports for the specific VLAN for Sales. Computers used by Human Resources will connect to switch ports that are configured as access ports for the Human Resources VLAN. There will be separate IP subnetworks associated with each of the VLANs.

To provide a fault-tolerant default gateway for the clients in each of the VLANs, a first-hop redundancy protocol will be used, such as HSRP, GLBP, or VRRP.

The fiber connections that will go vertically through the building and connect the switches in the IDFs to the MDF in the basement will be running at 1Gbps each, and multiple fiber cables will be used. Link Aggregation Control Protocol will be used for these vertical connections to make the multiple fiber links work together as part of one logical EtherChannel interface. For the LACP connections between the IDFs and MDF to support multiple VLANs, the LAG will be configured as a trunk using 802.1Q tagging. Routing between the VLANs will be done by multilayer switches that are located near the MDF.

Spanning tree will be enabled on the switches so that in the event of parallel paths between switches, a Layer 2 loop can be prevented.

To support IP-based telephones in the offices, the switches will also provide Power over Ethernet, which can supply power to the IP phones over the Ethernet cables that run between the switch in the IDF and the IP telephones.

If protocol analysis needs to be done, the switches that will be purchased need to support port mirroring so that frames from one port can be captured and forwarded to an alternate port for analysis.

To authenticate devices that are connecting to the switch ports, 802.1X can be used. To authenticate administrators who are connecting to switches for management, authentication can be forced at the logical VTY lines. SSH will be enabled and enforced because it is a secure management protocol. The switches will be given their own IP address, in addition to a default gateway to use so that they can be remotely managed. Local user accounts will be created on the switches so that local authentication can be implemented as each administrator connects either to the console or via SSH.

Summary

Here are the main topics covered in this chapter:

- The origins of Ethernet, including a discussion of Ethernet's CSMA/CD features.
- A variety of Ethernet standards were contrasted in terms of media type, network bandwidth, and distance limitation.
- Various features that might be available on modern Ethernet switches. These features include VLANs, trunking, STP, link aggregation, PoE, port monitoring, user authentication, and first-hop redundancy.

Exam Preparation Tasks

Review All the Key Topics

Review the most important topics from inside the chapter, noted with the Key Topic icon in the outer margin of the page. Table 4-5 lists these key topics and the page numbers where each is found.

Table 4-5 Key Topics for Chapter 4

Key Topic Element	Description	Page Number
List	Components of CSMA/CD	121
Table 4-1	Ethernet bandwidth capacities	124
Table 4-2	Types of Ethernet	125
Figure 4-12	IEEE 802.1Q tag bytes	129
Step list	Broadcast storm	132
List	STP switch classification	133
Table 4-3	STP port types	134
Table 4-4	STP port cost	135
List	STP port states	135
Figure 4-20	Power over Ethernet	138
Figure 4-23	Example: Network sniffer with port mirroring configured on the switch	140
List	IEEE 802.1X network components	141

Complete Tables and Lists from Memory

Print a copy of Appendix C, "Memory Tables," or at least the section for this chapter, and complete as many of the tables as possible from memory. Appendix D, "Memory Tables Answer Key," includes the completed tables and lists so you can check your work.

Define Key Terms

Define the following key terms from this chapter, and check your answers in the Glossary:

Ethernet, collision, carrier-sense multiple access/collision detection (CSMA/CD), full-duplex, half-duplex, virtual LAN (VLAN), trunk, Spanning Tree Protocol (STP), root port, designated port, nondesignated port, link aggregation, Power over Ethernet (PoE), supplicant, authenticator, authentication server

Additional Resources

Topology Change with STP: http://www.ajsnetworking.com/stp

Increasing Throughput with EtherChannel: https://youtu.be/CTcToRNonB8

Review Questions

The answers to these review questions appear in Appendix A, "Answers to Review Questions."

1. Identify the distance limitation of a 1000BASE-T Ethernet network.
   - a. 100 m
   - b. 185 m
   - c. 500 m
   - d. 2 km

2. If two devices simultaneously transmit data on an Ethernet network and a collision occurs, what does each station do in an attempt to resend the data and avoid another collision?
   - a. Each device compares the other device's priority value (determined by IP address) with its own, and the device with the highest priority value transmits first.
   - b. Each device waits for a clear-to-send (CTS) signal from the switch.
   - c. Each device randomly picks a priority value, and the device with the highest value transmits first.
   - d. Each device sets a random back-off timer, and the device will attempt retransmission after the timer expires.

3. What kind of media is used by 100GBASE-SR10 Ethernet?
   - a. UTP
   - b. MMF
   - c. STP
   - d. SMF

4. Which of the following statements are true regarding VLANs? (Choose two.)
   a. A VLAN has a single broadcast domain.
   b. For traffic to pass between two VLANs, that traffic must be routed.
   c. Because of a switch's MAC address table, traffic does not need to be routed to pass between two VLANs.
   d. A VLAN has a single collision domain.

5. What name is given to a VLAN on an IEEE 802.1Q trunk whose frames are not tagged?
   a. Native VLAN
   b. Default VLAN
   c. Management VLAN
   d. VLAN 0

6. In a topology running STP, every network segment has a single _____________ port, which is the port on that segment that is closest to the root bridge in terms of cost.
   a. Root
   b. Designated
   c. Nondesignated
   d. Nonroot

7. What is the IEEE standard for link aggregation?
   a. 802.1Q
   b. 802.3ad
   c. 802.1d
   d. 802.3af

8. What is the maximum amount of power a switch is allowed to provide per port according to the IEEE 802.3af standard?
   a. 7.7W
   b. 15.4W
   c. 26.4W
   d. 32.4W

9. What switch feature allows you to connect a network sniffer to a switch port and tells the switch to send a copy of frames seen on one port out the port to which your network sniffer is connected?
   a. Port interception
   b. Port duplexing
   c. Port mirroring
   d. Port redirect

10. Which IEEE 802.1X component checks the credentials of a device wanting to gain access to the network?
    a. Supplicant
    b. Authentication server
    c. Access point
    d. Authenticator

After completion of this chapter, you will be able to answer the following questions:

- How are decimal numbers represented in binary format?
- What is the format of an IP Version 4 (IPv4) address, and what are the distinctions between unicast, broadcast, and multicast addresses?
- Which options are available for assigning IP addresses to networked devices?
- Given a subnet design need (for example, a number of required subnets and a number of required hosts per subnet), how do you decide the right subnet mask for a network?
- What are the primary characteristics of IPv6?

CHAPTER 5

IPv4 and IPv6 Addresses

When two devices on a network want to communicate, they need logical addresses (that is, Layer 3 addresses as described in Chapter 2, "The OSI Reference Model"). Most modern networks use Internet Protocol (IP) addressing, as opposed to other Layer 3 addressing schemes, such as Apple's AppleTalk or Novell's Internetwork Packet Exchange (IPX). Therefore, the focus of this chapter is IP.

This chapter covers two versions of IP: IP Version 4 (IPv4) and IP Version 6 (IPv6). First, it discusses how IP concepts apply to IPv4. This discussion introduces you to how the IP addresses are represented in binary notation. You examine the structure of an IPv4 address and distinguish between different categories of IPv4 addresses.

Next, this chapter details various options for assigning IP addresses to end stations. Also, one of the benefits of IP addressing is that you have flexibility in how you can take a network address and subdivide that address into multiple subnets. This discussion of subnetting tends to get a bit mathematical. As a result, multiple practice exercises are offered to help solidify these concepts in your mind.

Although IPv4 is the most widely deployed Layer 3 addressing scheme in today's networks, its scalability limitation is causing available IPv4 addresses to quickly become depleted. Fortunately, a newer version of IP, IP Version 6 (IPv6), is scalable beyond anything you will need in your lifetime. So, after focusing on the foundation of IP addressing laid by IPv4, this chapter concludes by introducing you to the fundamental characteristics of IPv6 addressing.

Foundation Topics

Binary Numbering

Chapter 2 described how a network transmitted data as a series of binary 1s and 0s. Similarly, the IP addresses are represented as a series of binary digits (that is, *bits*). IPv4 consists of 32 bits, and IPv6 has a whopping 128 bits.

Later in this chapter, you need to be able to convert between the decimal representation of a number and that number's binary equivalent. This skill is needed for things such as subnet mask calculations. This section describes this mathematical procedure and provides you with practice exercises.

Principles of Binary Numbering

You are accustomed to using Base-10 numbering on a day-to-day basis. In a Base-10 numbering system, there are ten digits, in the range of 0 through 9, at your disposal. Binary numbering, however, uses a Base-2 numbering system, where there are only two digits: zero (0) and one (1).

Because computer systems divide 32-bit IPv4 addresses into four 8-bit octets, this discussion focuses on converting between 8-bit binary numbers and decimal numbers. To convert a binary number to decimal, you can create a table like Table 5-1.

Table 5-1 Binary Conversion Table

128	64	32	16	8	4	2	1

Note the structure of the table. There are eight columns, representing the 8 bits in an octet. The column headings are the powers of 2 (the powers of 0–7), beginning with the rightmost column. Specifically, 2 raised to the power of 0 (2^0) is 1. (In fact, any number raised to the 0 power is 1.) If you raise a 2 to the first power (2^1), that equals 2. A 2 raised to the second power (that is, 2 * 2, or 2^2) is 4. This continues through 2 raised to the power of 7 (that is, 2 * 2 * 2 * 2 * 2 * 2 * 2, or 2^7), which equals 128. You can use this table for converting binary numbers to decimal and decimal numbers to binary. The skill of binary-to-decimal and decimal-to-binary conversion is critical for working with subnet masks, as discussed later in this chapter.

Converting a Binary Number to a Decimal Number

To convert a binary number to a decimal number, you populate the previously described binary table with the given binary digits. Then you add up the column heading values for those columns containing a 1.

For example, consider Table 5-2. Only the 128, 16, 4, and 2 columns contain a 1, and all the other columns contain a 0. If you add all the column headings containing a 1 in their column (that is, 128 + 16 + 4 + 2), you get a result of 150. Therefore, you can conclude that the binary number of 10010110 equates to a decimal value of 150.

Table 5-2 Binary Conversion Example 1

128	64	32	16	8	4	2	1
1	0	0	1	0	1	1	0

Converting a Decimal Number to a Binary Number

To convert numbers from decimal to binary, staring with the leftmost column, ask the question, "Is this number equal to or greater than the column heading?" If the answer to that question is no, place a 0 in that column and move to the next column. If the answer is yes, place a 1 in that column and subtract the value of the column heading from the number you are converting. When you then move to the next column (to your right), again ask yourself, "Is this number (which is the result of your earlier subtraction) equal to or greater than the column heading?" This process continues (to the right) for all the remaining column headings.

For example, imagine that you want to convert the number 167 to binary. The following steps walk you through the process:

Step 1. Ask the question, "Is 167 equal to or greater than 128?" Because the answer is yes, you place a 1 in the 128 column, as shown in Table 5-3, and subtract 128 from 167, which yields a result of 39.

Table 5-3 Binary Conversion Example 2: Step 1

128	64	32	16	8	4	2	1
1							

Step 2. Now that you are done with the 128 column, move (to the right) to the 64 column. Ask the question, "Is 39 equal to or greater than 64?" Because the answer is no, you place a 0 in the 64 column, as shown in Table 5-4, and continue to the next column (the 32 column).

Table 5-4 Binary Conversion Example 2: Step 2

128	64	32	16	8	4	2	1
1	0						

Step 3. Under the 32 column, ask the question, "Is 39 equal to or greater than 32?" Because the answer is yes, you place a 1 in the 32 column, as shown in Table 5-5, and subtract 32 from 39, which yields a result of 7.

Table 5-5 Binary Conversion Example 2: Step 3

128	64	32	16	8	4	2	1
1	0	1					

Step 4. Now you are under the 16 column and ask, "Is 7 equal to or greater than 16?" Because the answer is no, you place a 0 in the 16 column, as shown in Table 5-6, and move to the 8 column.

Table 5-6 Binary Conversion Example 2: Step 4

128	64	32	16	8	4	2	1
1	0	1	0				

Step 5. Similar to the 16 column, the number 7 is not equal to or greater than an 8. So, a 0 is placed in the 8 column, as shown in Table 5-7.

Table 5-7 Binary Conversion Example 2: Step 5

128	64	32	16	8	4	2	1
1	0	1	0	0			

Step 6. Because 7 is greater than or equal to 4, a 1 is placed in the 4 column, as shown in Table 5-8, and 4 is subtracted from 7, yielding 3 as the result.

Table 5-8 Binary Conversion Example 2: Step 6

128	64	32	16	8	4	2	1
1	0	1	0	0	1		

Step 7. Now under the 2 column, you ask the question, "Is 3 greater than or equal to 2?" Because the answer is yes, you place a 1 in the 2 column, as shown in Table 5-9, and subtract 2 from 3.

Table 5-9 Binary Conversion Example 2: Step 7

128	64	32	16	8	4	2	1
1	0	1	0	0	1	1	

Step 8. Finally, in the rightmost column (that is, the 1 column), you ask whether the number 1 is greater than or equal to 1. Because it is, you place a 1 in the 1 column, as shown in Table 5-10.

Table 5-10 Binary Conversion Example 2: Step 8

128	64	32	16	8	4	2	1
1	0	1	0	0	1	1	1

You can now conclude that a decimal number of 167 equates to a binary value of 10100111. In fact, you can check your work by adding up the values for the column headings that contain a 1 in their column. In this example, the 128, 32, 4, 2, and 1 columns contain a 1. If you add these values, the result is 167 (that is, 128 + 32 + 4 + 2 + 1 = 167).

Binary Numbering Practice

Because binary number conversion is a skill developed through practice, you will now be challenged with a few conversion exercises. The first two exercises ask you to convert a binary number to a decimal number, and the last two exercises ask you to convert a decimal number to a binary number.

Binary Conversion Exercise 1

Using Table 5-11 as a reference, convert the binary number 01101011 to a decimal number.

Table 5-11 Binary Conversion Exercise 1: Base Table

128	64	32	16	8	4	2	1

Write your answer here: __________

Binary Conversion Exercise 1: Solution

Given a binary number of 01101011 and filling in a binary conversion table, as shown in Table 5-12, we notice that the 64, 32, 8, 2, and 1 columns contain a 1. Each of the other columns contains a 0. By adding up the value of these column headings (that is, 64 + 32 + 8 + 2 + 1), we get a decimal value of 107.

Table 5-12 Binary Conversion Exercise 1: Solution Table

128	64	32	16	8	4	2	1
0	1	1	0	1	0	1	1

Binary Conversion Exercise 2

Using Table 5-13 as a reference, convert the number binary number 10010100 to a decimal number.

Table 5-13 Binary Conversion Exercise 2: Base Table

128	64	32	16	8	4	2	1

Write your answer here: ___________

Binary Conversion Exercise 2: Solution

Given a binary number of 10010100 and filling in a binary conversion table, as shown in Table 5-14, we notice that the 128, 16, and 4 columns contain a 1. Each of the other columns contains a 0. By adding up the value of these column headings (that is, 128 + 16 + 4), we get a decimal value of 148.

Table 5-14 Binary Conversion Exercise 2: Solution Table

128	64	32	16	8	4	2	1
1	0	0	1	0	1	0	0

Binary Conversion Exercise 3

Using Table 5-15 as a reference, convert the number decimal number 49 to a binary number.

Table 5-15 Binary Conversion Exercise 3: Base Table

128	64	32	16	8	4	2	1

Write your answer here: ___________

Binary Conversion Exercise 3: Solution

You can begin your conversion of the decimal number 49 to a binary number by asking the following questions and performing the following calculations:

1. Is 49 greater than or equal to 128? → No → Put a 0 in the 128 column.
2. Is 49 greater than or equal to 64? → No → Put a 0 in the 64 column.
3. Is 49 greater than or equal to 32? → Yes → Put a 1 in the 32 column, and subtract 32 from 49. → 49 – 32 = 17.
4. Is 17 greater than or equal to 16? → Yes → Put a 1 in the 16 column, and subtract 16 from 17. → 17 – 16 = 1.
5. Is 1 greater than or equal to 8? → No → Put a 0 in the 8 column.
6. Is 1 greater than or equal to 4? → No → Put a 0 in the 4 column.
7. Is 1 greater than or equal to 2? → No → Put a 0 in the 2 column.
8. Is 1 greater than or equal to 1? → Yes → Put a 1 in the 1 column.

Combining these eight binary digits forms a binary number of 00110001, as shown in Table 5-16. Verify your work by adding the values of the column headings whose columns contain a 1. In this case, columns 32, 16, and 1 each have a 1 in their column. By adding these values (that is, 32 + 16 + 1), you get a value of 49.

Table 5-16 Binary Conversion Exercise 3: Solution Table

128	64	32	16	8	4	2	1
0	0	1	1	0	0	0	1

Binary Conversion Exercise 4

Using Table 5-17 as a reference, convert the number decimal number 236 to a binary number.

Table 5-17 Binary Conversion Exercise 4: Base Table

128	64	32	16	8	4	2	1

Write your answer here: ___________

Binary Conversion Exercise 4: Solution

You can begin your conversion of the decimal number 236 to a binary number by asking the following questions and performing the following calculations:

1. Is 236 greater than or equal to 128? → Yes → Put a 1 in the 128 column, and subtract 128 from 236. → 236 – 128 = 108.
2. Is 108 greater than or equal to 64? → Yes → Put a 1 in the 64 column, and subtract 64 from 108. → 108 – 64 = 44.
3. Is 44 greater than or equal to 32? → Yes → Put a 1 in the 32 column, and subtract 32 from 44. → 44 – 32 = 12.
4. Is 12 greater than or equal to 16? → No → Put a 0 in the 16 column.
5. Is 12 greater than or equal to 8? → Yes → Put a 1 in the 8 column, and subtract 8 from 12. → 12 – 8 = 4.
6. Is 4 greater than or equal to 4? → Yes → Put a 1 in the 4 column, and subtract 4 from 4. 4 – 4 = 0.
7. Is 0 greater than or equal to 2? → No → Put a 0 in the 2 column.
8. Is 0 greater than or equal to 1? → No → Put a 0 in the 1 column.

Combining these eight binary digits forms a binary number of 11101100, as shown in Table 5-18. You can verify your work by adding the values of the column headings whose columns contain a 1. In this case, columns 128, 64, 32, 8, and 4 each have a 1 in their column. By adding these values (that is, 128 + 64 + 32 + 8 + 4), you get a value of 236.

Table 5-18 Binary Conversion Exercise 4: Solution Table

128	64	32	16	8	4	2	1
1	1	1	0	1	1	0	0

IPv4 Addressing

Although IPv6 is increasingly being adopted in corporate networks, IPv4 is by far the most popular Layer 3 addressing scheme in today's networks. For brevity in this section, the term *IPv4 address* is used interchangeably with the more generic term *IP address*.

Devices on an IPv4 network use unique IP addresses to communicate with one another. Metaphorically, you can relate this to sending a letter through the postal service. You place a destination address on an envelope containing the letter, and in the upper-left corner of the envelope you place your return address. Similarly, when an IPv4 network device sends data on a network, it places both a destination IP address and a source IP address in the packet's IPv4 header.

IPv4 Address Structure

An IPv4 address is a 32-bit address. However, rather than writing out each individual bit value, you write the address in *dotted-decimal* notation. Consider the IP address of 10.1.2.3. Notice that the IP address is divided into four separate numbers, separated by periods. Each number represents one-fourth of the IP address. Specifically, each number represents an 8-bit portion of the 32 bits in the address. Because each of these four divisions of an IP address represent 8 bits, these divisions are called *octets*. For example, Figure 5-1 shows the binary representation of the 10.1.2.3 IP address. In Figure 5-1, notice that the eight leftmost bits of 00001010 equate to a decimal value of 10 (the calculation for this was described in the previous section). Similarly, 00000001 in binary equates to a 1 in decimal, and 00000010 in binary equals 2 in decimal. Finally, 00000011 yields a decimal value of 3.

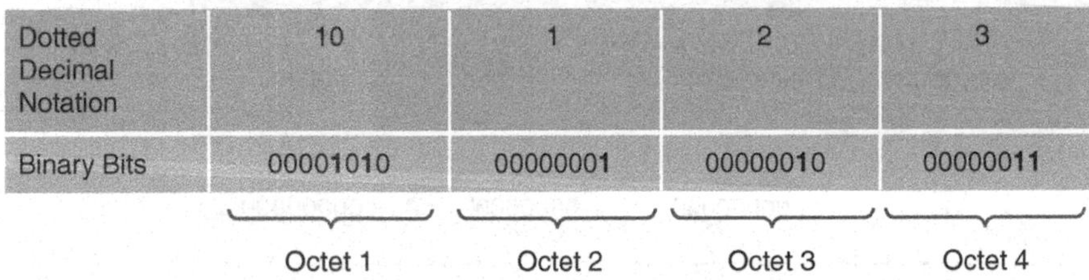

Figure 5-1 Binary Representation of Dotted-Decimal IP Address

Interestingly, an IP address is composed of two types of addresses: a network address and a host address. Specifically, a group of contiguous left-justified bits represent the network address, and the remaining bits (that is, a group of contiguous right-justified bits) represent the address of a host on a network. The IP address component that determines which bits refer to the network and which bits refer to the host is called the *subnet mask*. You can think of the subnet mask as a dividing line separating an IP address's 32 bits into a group of network bits (on the left) and a group of host bits (on the right).

A subnet mask typically consists of a series of contiguous 1s followed by a set of continuous 0s. In total, a subnet mask contains 32 bits, which correspond to the 32 bits found in an IPv4 address. The 1s in a subnet mask correspond to network bits in an IPv4 address, and 0s in a subnet mask correspond to host bits in an IPv4 address.

For example, consider Figure 5-2. The eight leftmost bits of the subnet mask are 1s, and the remaining 24 bits are 0s. As a result, the 8 leftmost bits of the IP address represent the network address, and the remaining 24 bits represent the host address.

Dotted Decimal Notation	10	1	2	3
IP Address (in Binary)	00001010	00000001	00000010	00000011
Subnet Mask	11111111	00000000	00000000	00000000
	Network Bits	Host Bits		

Figure 5-2 Dividing an IP Address into a Network Portion and a Host Portion

When you write a network address, all host bits are set to 0s. Once again, consider the example shown in Figure 5-2. The subnet mask in this example is an *8-bit subnet mask*, meaning that the 8 leftmost bits in the subnet mask are 1s. If the remaining bits were set to 0, as shown in Figure 5-3, the network address of 10.0.0.0 can be seen.

Network Address (in Dotted Decimal)	10	0	0	0
Network Address (in Binary)	00001010	00000000	00000000	00000000
Subnet Mask	11111111	00000000	00000000	00000000
	Network Bits	Host Bits		

Figure 5-3 Network Address Calculation

When writing a network address, or an IP address for that matter, you need to provide more detail than just a dotted-decimal representation of an IP address's 32 bits. For example, just being told that a device has an IP address of 10.1.2.3 does not tell you the network on which the IP address resides. To know the network address, you need to know the subnet mask, which could be written in dotted-decimal notation or in *prefix notation* (also known as *slash notation*). In the example, where there is an IP address of 10.1.2.3 and an 8-bit subnet mask, the IP address could be written as

10.1.2.3 255.0.0.0 or 10.1.2.3 /8. Similarly, the network address could be written as 10.0.0.0 255.0.0.0 or 10.0.0.0 /8.

Classes of Addresses

Although an IP address (or a network address) needs subnet mask information to determine which bits represent the network portion of the address, there are default subnet masks with which you should be familiar. The default subnet mask for a given IP address is solely determined by the value in the IP address's first octet. Table 5-19 shows the default subnet masks for various ranges of IP addresses.

Table 5-19 IP Address Classes

Address Class	Value in First Octet	Classful Mask (Dotted Decimal)	Classful Mask (Prefix Notation)
Class A	1–126	255.0.0.0	/8
Class B	128–191	255.255.0.0	/16
Class C	192–223	255.255.255.0	/24
Class D	224–239	—	—
Class E	240–255	—	—

These ranges of IP address, which you should memorize, are referred to as different *classes* of addresses. Classes A, B, and C are those ranges of addresses assigned to network devices. Class D addresses are used as destination IP addresses (that is, not assigned to devices sourcing traffic) for multicast networks, and Class E addresses are reserved for experimental use. The default subnet masks associated with address classes A, B, and C are called *classful masks*.

For example, consider an IP address of 172.16.40.56. If you are told that this IP address used its classful mask, you should know that it has a subnet mask of 255.255.0.0, which is the classful mask for a Class B IP address. You should know that 172.16.40.56 is a Class B IP address, based on the value of the first octet (172), which falls in the Class B range of 128–191.

NOTE You might have noticed that in the ranges of values in the first octet, the number 127 seems to have been skipped. The reason is that 127 is used as a *loopback* IP address, meaning a locally significant IP address representing the device itself. For example, if you were working on a network device and wanted to verify that device had a TCP/IP stack loaded, you could try to ping an IP address of 127.1.1.1. If you received ping responses, you could conclude that the device is running a TCP/IP stack. This text discusses the ping function in Chapter 10, "Command-Line Tools."

The Internet Corporation for Assigned Names and Numbers (ICANN) nonprofit corporation globally manages publicly routable IP addresses. ICANN does not directly assign a block of IP addresses to your Internet service provider (ISP) but rather assigns a block of IP addresses to a regional Internet registry. One example of a regional Internet registry is the American Registry for Internet Numbers (ARIN), which acts as an Internet registry for North America.

The Internet Assigned Numbers Authority (IANA) is yet another entity responsible for IP address assignment. The ICANN operates IANA and is responsible for IP address assignment outside of North America.

NOTE Some literature references the *Internet Network Information Center* (InterNIC). InterNIC was the predecessor to ICANN (until September 18, 1998).

When an organization is assigned one or more publicly routable IP addresses by its service provider, that organization often needs more IP addresses to accommodate all of its devices. One solution is to use private IP addressing within an organization, in combination with Network Address Translation (NAT). Specific Class A, B, and C networks have been designed for private use. Although these networks are routable (with the exception of the 169.254.0.0–169.254.255.255 address range) within the organization, ISPs do not route these private networks over the public Internet. Table 5-20 shows these IP networks reserved for internal use.

Table 5-20 Private IP Networks

Address Class	Address Range	Default Subnet Mask
Class A	10.0.0.0–10.255.255.255	255.0.0.0
Class B	172.16.0.0–172.31.255.255	255.255.0.0
Class B	169.254.0.0–169.254.255.255	255.255.0.0
Class C	192.168.0.0–192.168.255.255	255.255.255.0

NOTE The 169.254.0.0–169.254.255.255 address range is not routable. Addresses in the range are only usable on their local subnet and are dynamically assigned to network hosts using the Automatic Private IP Addressing (APIPA) feature, which is discussed later in this section.

NAT is a feature available on routers that allows private IP addresses used within an organization to be translated into a pool of one or more publicly routable IP addresses. Chapter 6, "Routing IP Packets," describes the operation of NAT.

Types of Addresses

For the real world and for the Network+ exam, you need to be familiar with the following three categories of IPv4 addresses: unicast, broadcast, and multicast. The following sections describe these in detail.

Unicast

Most network traffic is unicast in nature, meaning that traffic travels from a single source device to a single destination device. Figure 5-4 illustrates an example of a unicast transmission.

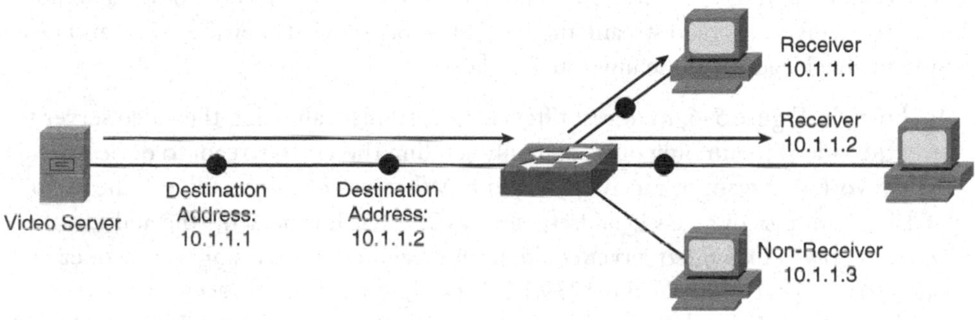

Figure 5-4 Sample Unicast Transmission

Broadcast

Broadcast traffic travels from a single source to all destinations on a network (that is, a *broadcast domain*). A broadcast address of 255.255.255.255 might seem that it would reach all hosts on all interconnected networks. However, 255.255.255.255 targets all devices on a single network—specifically, the network local to the device sending a packet destined for 255.255.255.255. Another type of broadcast address is a *directed broadcast address*, which targets all devices in a remote network. For example, the address 172.16.255.255 /16 is a directed broadcast targeting all devices in the 172.16.0.0 /16 network. Figure 5-5 illustrates an example of a broadcast transmission.

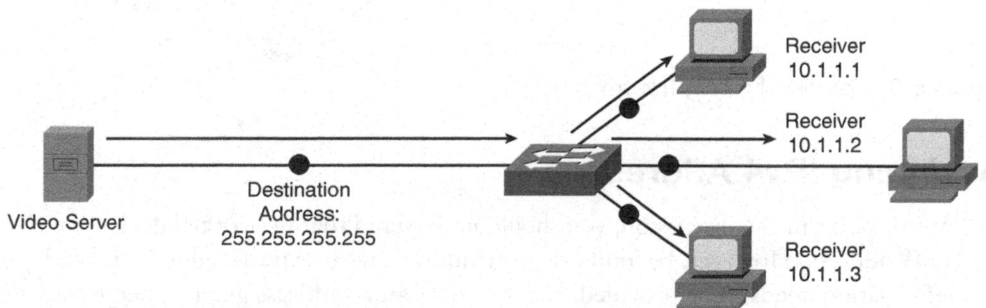

Figure 5-5 Sample Broadcast Transmission

Multicast

Multicast technology offers an efficient mechanism for a single host to send traffic to multiple, yet specific destinations. For example, imagine a network with 100 users. Twenty of those users want to receive a video stream from a video server. With a unicast solution, the video server would have to send 20 individual streams, one stream for each recipient. Such a solution could consume a significant amount of network bandwidth and put a heavy processor burden on the video server.

With a broadcast solution, the video server would only have to send the video stream once; however, it would be received by every device on the local subnet, even devices not wanting to receive the video stream. Even though those devices do not want to receive the video stream, they still must pause what they are doing and take time to check each of these unwanted packets.

As shown in Figure 5-6, multicast offers a compromise, allowing the video server to send the video stream only once, and only sending the video stream to devices on the network that want to receive the stream. What makes this possible is the use of a Class D address. A Class D address, such as 239.1.2.3, represents the address of a *multicast group*. The video server could, in this example, send a single copy of each video stream packet destined for 239.1.2.3. Devices wanting to receive the video stream can join the multicast group. Based on the device request, switches and routers in the topology can then dynamically determine out of which ports the video stream should be forwarded.

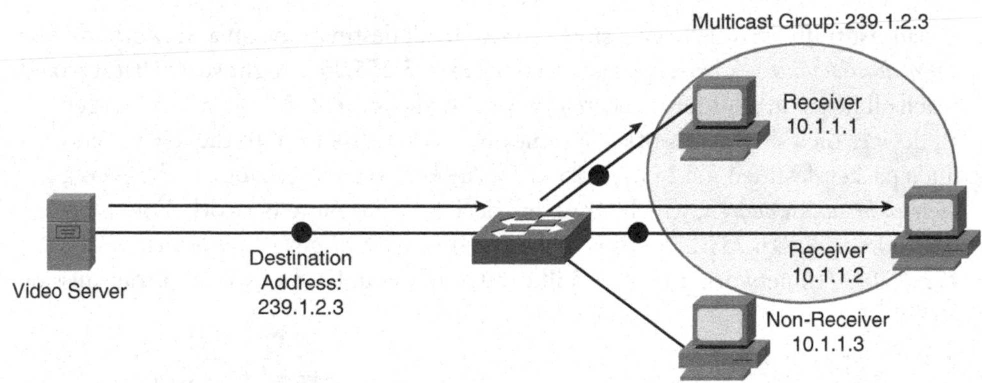

Figure 5-6 Sample Multicast Transmission

Assigning IPv4 Addresses

At this point in the discussion, you should understand that networked devices need an IP address. However, beyond just an IP address, what extra IP address–related information needs to be provided, and how does an IP address get assigned to one of those devices?

This section begins by discussing various parameters that might be assigned to a networked device, followed by discussions covering various approaches to assign IP addresses to devices.

IP Addressing Components

As discussed in the previous section, an IP address has two portions: a network portion and a host portion. A subnet mask is required to delineate between these two portions.

In addition, if traffic is destined for a different subnet than the subnet on which the traffic originates, a *default gateway* needs to be defined. A default gateway routes traffic from the sender's subnet toward the destination subnet. Chapter 6 covers the concept of routing.

Another consideration is that end users typically do not type in the IP address of the destination device with which they want to connect (for example, a web server on the Internet). Instead, end users typically type in fully qualified domain names (FQDNs), such as www.ajsnetworking.com. When connecting to devices on the public Internet, a Domain Name System (DNS) server takes an FQDN and translates it into a corresponding IP address.

In a company's internal network (that is, an *intranet*), a Microsoft Windows Internet Name Service (WINS) server might be used, as an example, to convert the names of network devices into their corresponding IP addresses. For example, you might attempt to navigate to a shared folder of \\server1\hrdocs. A WINS server could then be used to resolve the network device name of *server1* to a corresponding IP address. The path of \\server1\hrdocs is in *universal naming convention* (UNC) form, where you are specifying a network device name (for example, server1) and a resource available on that device (for example, hrdocs). Increasingly, companies today are transitioning to DNS even for internal network name resolution.

To summarize, network devices (for example, an end-user PC) can benefit from a variety of IP address parameters, such as the following:

- IP address
- Subnet mask
- Default gateway
- Server addresses

Remember as well that an IP address no longer needs to be assigned to a single entity or interface. A virtual IP address is commonly used and can fulfill many purposes, such as the following:

- Provide key addresses used in address translation.
- Represent any actual IP address assigned to a network device interface.
- Permit the sending of traffic to multiple different network devices all configured to respond based on the virtual IP address.

Static Configuration

A simple way of configuring a PC, for example, with IP address parameters is to statically configure that information. For example, on a PC running Microsoft Windows as the operating system, you can navigate to the Control Panel, as shown in Figure 5-7, and click **Network and Internet**.

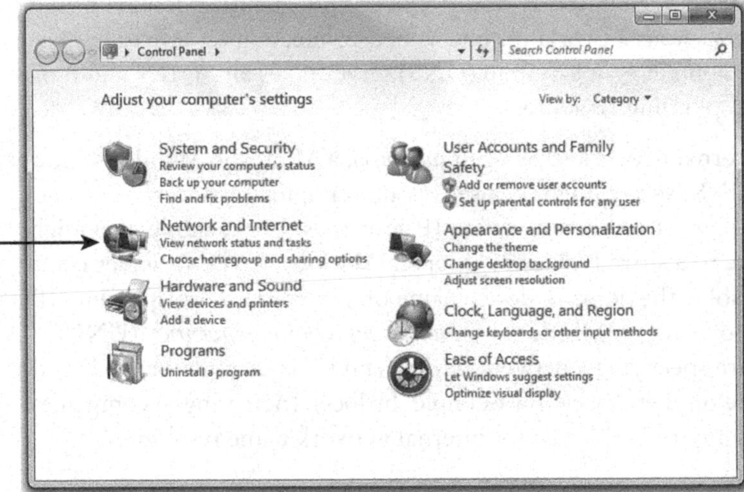

Figure 5-7 Windows Control Panel

From the Network and Internet control panel, click **Network and Sharing Center**, as shown in Figure 5-8.

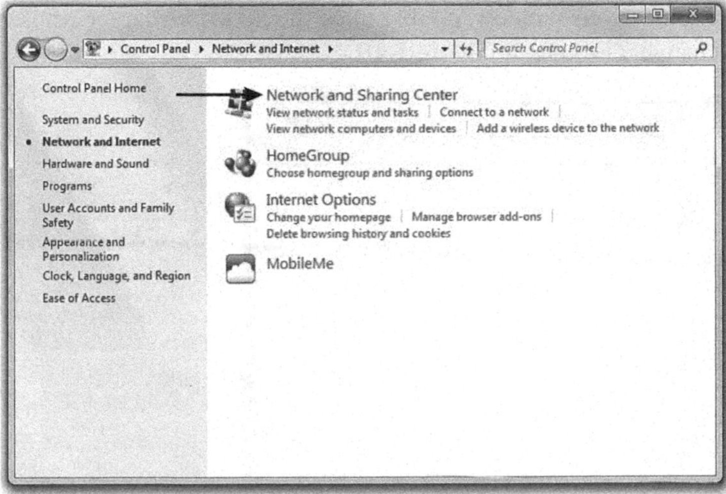

Figure 5-8 Network and Internet Control Panel

You can then click the **Change adapter settings** link, as shown in Figure 5-9.

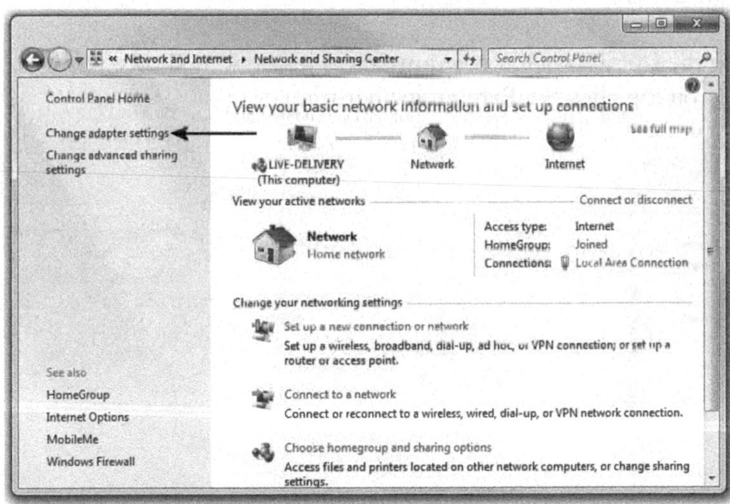

Figure 5-9 Network and Sharing Center

From the **Network Connections** window, double-click the network adapter whose settings you want to change, as shown in Figure 5-10.

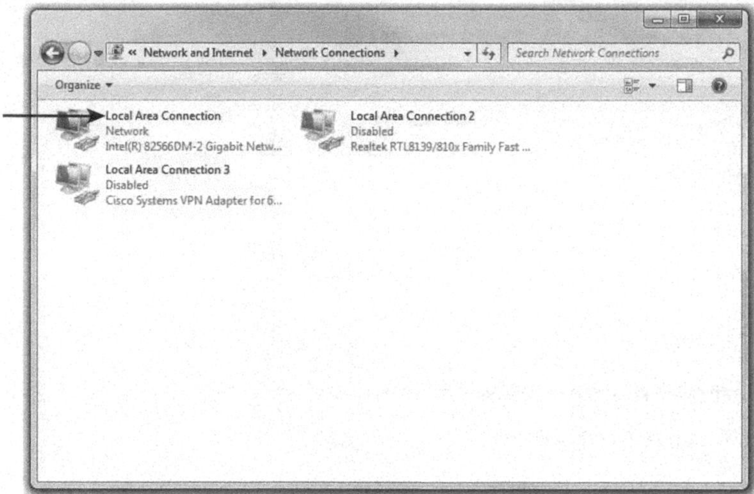

Figure 5-10 Network Connections Window

You are then taken to the Local Area Connection Status window, as shown in Figure 5-11. From here, you can click the **Properties** button.

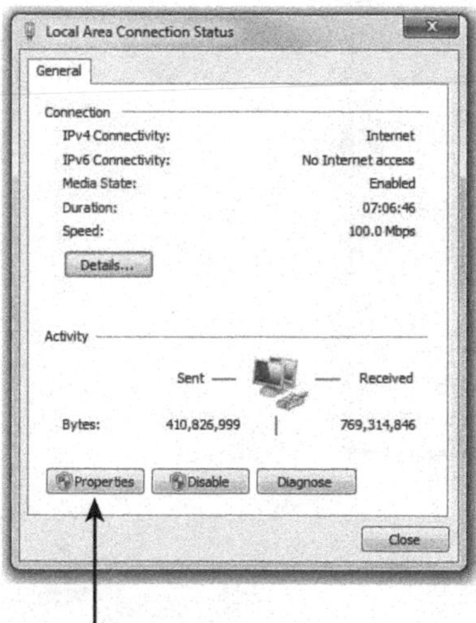

Figure 5-11 Local Area Connection Status Window

As shown in Figure 5-12, you can highlight **Internet Protocol Version 4 (TCP/IPv4)** and click the **Properties** button.

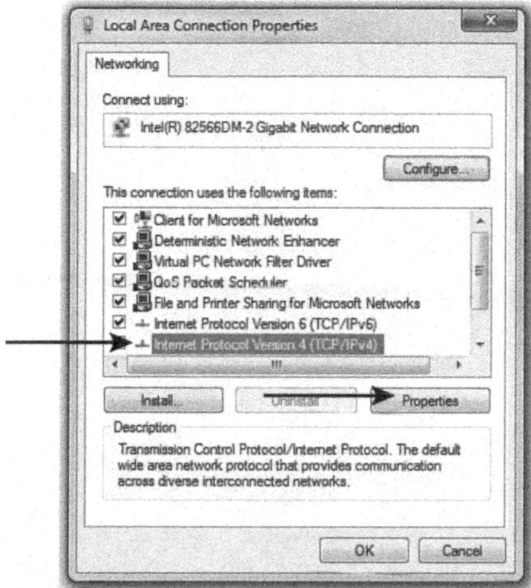

Figure 5-12 Local Area Connection Properties

An IP address, subnet mask, default gateway, and DNS server information can be entered into the Internet Protocol Version 4 (TCP/IPv4) Properties window, as depicted in Figure 5-13. Although DNS server information can be entered in this window, more advanced DNS options and WINS options are available by clicking the **Advanced** button.

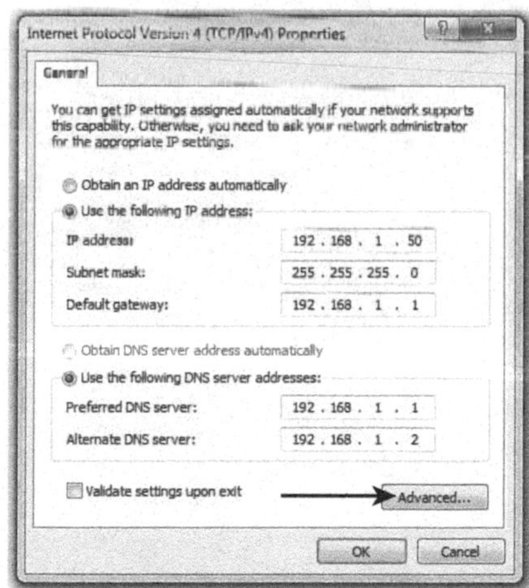

Figure 5-13 Internet Protocol Version 4 (TCP/IPv4) Properties

By clicking the **DNS** tab in the Advanced TCP/IP Settings window, as shown in Figure 5-14, you can add, remove, or reorder DNS servers, in addition to adjusting various other DNS parameters. Recall that a DNS server converts an FQDN to an IP address. Also, although Figure 5-13 shows the same IP address for the default gateway and a DNS server, these are not always located on the same device.

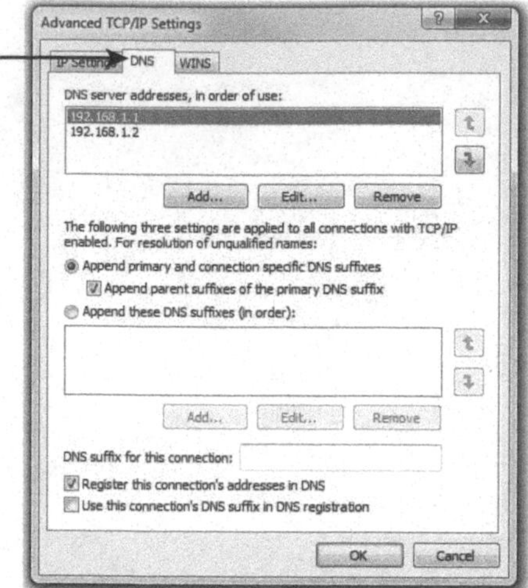

Figure 5-14 Advanced TCP/IP Settings: DNS Tab

Similarly, Windows Internet Name Service (WINS) servers can be configured in the WINS tab of the Advanced TCP/IP Settings window, as shown in Figure 5-15. Similar to a DNS server, a WINS server converts a NetBIOS computer name to a corresponding IP address.

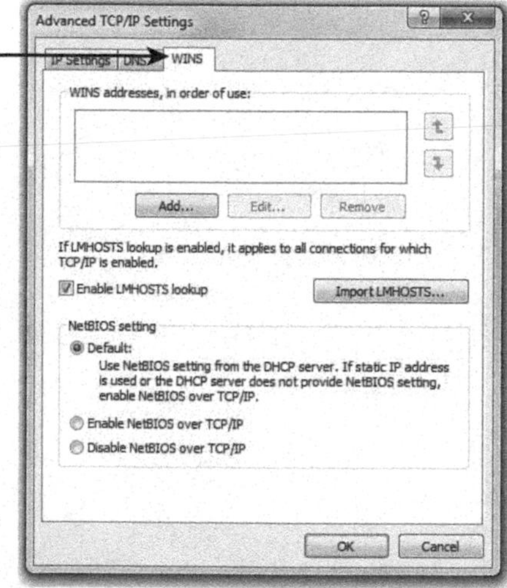

Figure 5-15 Advanced TCP/IP Settings: WINS Tab

Dynamic Configuration

Statically assigning IP address information to individual networked devices can be time consuming, error-prone, and lacking in scalability. Instead of static IP address assignments, many corporate networks dynamically assign IP address parameters to their devices. An early choice for performing this automatic assignment of IP addresses was the *Bootstrap Protocol* (BOOTP for short). Currently, however, the most popular approach for dynamic IP address assignment is Dynamic Host Configuration Protocol (DHCP).

BOOTP

Engineers developed BOOTP as a method of assigning IP address, subnet mask, and default gateway information to diskless workstations. In the early days of Microsoft Windows (for example, Microsoft Windows 3.1), Microsoft Windows did not natively support TCP/IP. To include TCP/IP support, an add-on TCP/IP application (for example, Trumpet Winsock) could be run. Such an application would typically support BOOTP.

When a device needed to obtain IP address information, a BOOTP broadcast would be sent out from the device needing an IP address. If a BOOTP server (BOOTPS) received the broadcast, it could match the source MAC address in the received frame (the MAC address from the device wanting to obtain an IP address) with a corresponding IP address in a database stored on the BOOTP server. The BOOTPS would then respond to the requesting client with IP address information. Because BOOTP requests were based on broadcasts, by default, a BOOTP request could not propagate beyond a device's local subnet. However, most enterprise-class routers can be configured to forward selected broadcast types, including BOOTP broadcasts.

DHCP

DHCP offers a more robust solution to IP address assignment than the solution offered by BOOTP. DHCP does not require a statically configured database of MAC-address-to-IP-address mappings. Also, DHCP has a wide variety of options beyond basic IP address, subnet mask, and default gateway parameters. For example, a DHCP server can educate a DHCP client about the IP address of a WINS server, or even an administrator-defined parameter (for example, the IP address of a TFTP server from which a configuration file could be downloaded).

Refer to Chapter 3, "Network Components," for more information about the operation of DHCP. However, realize that, like BOOTP, DHCP's initial request is a broadcast, requiring a client's local router be configured to appropriately forward DHCP requests to a DHCP server if that DHCP server is not on the local subnet of the requesting client.

In setting up a DHCP server, you would identify a range of IP addresses to hand out, and this would be referred to as the *scope*. In addition, a DHCP server can be configured to have reservations, which reserves a specific IP address for a specific Layer 2 Ethernet MAC address. The lease time can also be configured and is usually set to one day. The DHCP server also provides options such as DNS server addresses, the default gateway to use, domain suffixes to use, and more. If a DHCP client is not on the same subnet as a DHCP server, a router or other device that is connected to the same subnet as the DHCP client can be configured as a DHCP relay agent. The device takes the discover packet from the client (broadcast) and routes it to where the DHCP server is (unicast). This feature is also sometimes referred to as *IP helper*.

As an example of DHCP client configuration, in Microsoft Windows 10, you can select the **Obtain an IP address automatically** and **Obtain DNS server address automatically** options in the Internet Protocol Version 4 (TCP/IPv4) Properties window, as shown in Figure 5-16.

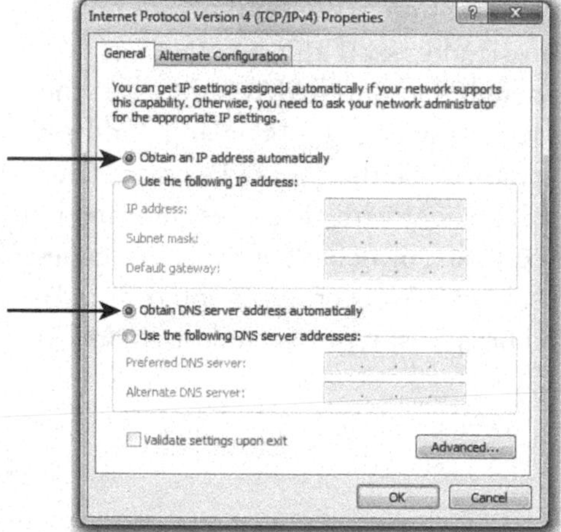

Figure 5-16 Configuring Microsoft Windows 10 to Obtain IP Address Information via DHCP

NOTE A protocol made obsolete by BOOTP and DHCP is Reverse Address Resolution Protocol (RARP). Whereas Address Resolution Protocol (ARP) requests a MAC address that corresponds to a known IP address, RARP requested an IP address (from a preconfigured host) that corresponded to a station's MAC address. Although RARP did allow a station to dynamically obtain an IP address, both BOOTP and DHCP offer additional features.

Automatic Private IP Addressing

If a networked device does not have a statically configured IP address and is unable to contact a DHCP server, it still might be able to communicate on an IP network thanks to Automatic Private IP Addressing (APIPA). The APIPA feature allows a networked device to self-assign an IP address from the 169.254.0.0/16 network. Note that this address is usable only on the device's local subnet. (The IP address is not routable.)

As shown in Figure 5-17, Microsoft Windows 10 defaults to APIPA if a client is configured to automatically obtain IP address information and that client fails to obtain IP address information from a DHCP server.

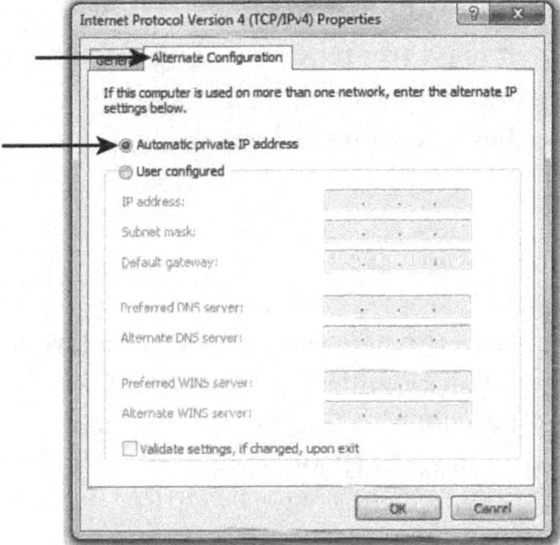

Figure 5-17 APIPA Configuration Enabled by Default

APIPA was designed as a solution for quickly setting up a localized network without the need to configure a DHCP server or the need to statically assign IP address information. However, there remains a need for devices on this localized network to perform name resolution and discover network services. Fortunately, these needs are covered by Zero Configuration (Zeroconf). Zeroconf is a technology supported on most modern operating systems and performs three basic functions:

- **Assigning link-local IP addresses:** A link-local IP address is a nonroutable IP address usable only on a local subnet. APIPA is an example of a technology that assigns link-local IP addresses.
- **Resolving computer names to IP addresses:** Multicast Domain Name Service (mDNS) is an example of a technology that can resolve computer names to their corresponding IP address on a local subnet, without the aid of a DNS server or a WINS server.
- **Locating network services:** Examples of service discovery protocols include the standards-based Service Location Protocol (SLP), Microsoft's Simple Service Discovery Protocol (SSDP), and Apple's DNS-based Service Discovery (DNS-SD).

If devices supporting these three Zeroconf features are interconnected on a local subnet, they can dynamically obtain link-local IP addresses, resolve one another's names to IP addresses, and discover services available on a network.

Subnetting

Earlier in this chapter, you were introduced to the purpose of a subnet mask and the default subnet masks for the various IP addresses classes. Default subnet masks (that is, classful subnet masks) are not always the most efficient choice. Fortunately, you can add additional network bits to a subnet mask (thereby extending the subnet mask) to create subnets within a classful network. This section explains why you might want to perform this process and describes how you mathematically perform subnet calculations.

Purpose of Subnetting

Consider the number of assignable IP addresses in the various classes of IP addresses shown in Table 5-21. Recall that the host bits of an IP address cannot be all 0s (which represents the network address) or all 1s (which represents the directed broadcast address). Therefore, the number of assignable IP addresses in a subnet can be determined by the following formula:

Number of assignable IP addresses in a subnet = $2^h - 2$,

where h is the number of host bits in a subnet mask

Table 5-21 Assignable IP Addresses

Address Class	Assignable IP Addresses
Class A	16,777,214 (2^{24}–2)
Class B	65,534 (2^{16}–2)
Class C	254 (2^{8}–2)

Suppose that you decide to use a private Class B IP address (for example, 172.16.0.0/16) for your internal IP addressing. For performance reasons, you would not want to support as many as 65,534 hosts in a single broadcast domain. Therefore, a best practice is to take such a network address and subnet the network (thereby extending the number of network bits in the network's subnet mask) into additional subnetworks. In fact, you could subnet your major network address space and then further subnet one of your unused subnet addresses! This practice is known as Variable-Length Subnet Masking (VLSM) and allows you to design the network as best as possible regarding the number of IP addresses required in different areas. Of course, this network also uses a variety of subnet masks in order to accomplish this task.

Subnet Mask Notation

As previously mentioned, the number of bits in a subnet mask can be represented in dotted-decimal notation (for example, 255.255.255.0) or in prefix notation (for example, /24). As a reference, Table 5-22 shows valid subnet masks in dotted-decimal notation and the corresponding prefix notation.

Table 5-22 Dotted-Decimal and Prefix-Notation Representations for IPv4 Subnets

Dotted-Decimal Notation	Prefix Notation
255.0.0.0	/8 (classful subnet mask for Class A networks)
255.128.0.0	/9
255.192.0.0	/10
255.224.0.0	/11
255.240.0.0	/12
255.248.0.0	/13
255.252.0.0	/14
255.254.0.0	/15
255.255.0.0	/16 (classful subnet mask for Class B networks)
255.255.128.0	/17
255.255.192.0	/18
255.255.224.0	/19
255.255.240.0	/20
255.255.248.0	/21
255.255.252.0	/22
255.255.254.0	/23
255.255.255.0	/24 (classful subnet mask for Class C networks)
255.255.255.128	/25
255.255.255.192	/26
255.255.255.224	/27
255.255.255.240	/28
255.255.255.248	/29
255.255.255.252	/30

Recall that any octet with a value of 255 contains eight 1s. Also, you should memorize valid octet values for an octet and the corresponding number of 1s (that is, continuous, left-justified 1s) in that octet, as shown in Table 5-23. Based on this information, you should be able to see the dotted-decimal notation of a subnet mask and quickly determine the corresponding prefix notation.

Table 5-23 Subnet Octet Values

Subnet Octet Value	Number of Contiguous Left-Justified Ones
0	0
128	1
192	2
224	3
240	4
248	5
252	6
254	7
255	8

For example, consider the subnet mask of 255.255.192.0. Because each of the first two octets has a value of 255, you know that you have sixteen 1s from the first two octets. You then recall that a value of 192 in the third octet requires two 1s from that octet. By adding the sixteen 1s from the first two octets to the two 1s from the third octet, you can determine that the subnet mask of 255.255.192.0 has a corresponding prefix notation of /18.

To help you develop the skill of making these calculations quickly, work through the following two exercises.

Subnet Notation: Practice Exercise 1

Given a subnet mask of 255.255.255.248, what is the corresponding prefix notation?

____

Subnet Notation: Practice Exercise 1 Solution

Given a subnet mask of 255.255.255.248, you should recognize that the first three octets, each containing a value of 255, represent twenty-four 1s. To those twenty-four 1s, you add five additional 1s, based on your memorization of how many contiguous, left-justified 1s in an octet are required to produce various octet values. The sum of 24 bits (from the first three octets) and the 5 bits (from the fourth octet) give you a total of 29 bits. Therefore, you can conclude that a subnet mask with a dotted-decimal notation of 255.255.255.248 has an equivalent prefix notation of /29.

Subnet Notation: Practice Exercise 2

Given a subnet mask of /17, what is the corresponding dotted-decimal notation?

____

Subnet Notation: Practice Exercise 2 Solution

You know that each octet contains 8 bits. So, given a subnet mask of /17, you can count by 8s to determine that there are eight 1s in the first octet, eight 1s in the second octet, and one 1 in the third octet. You already knew that an octet containing all 1s has a decimal value of 255. From that knowledge, you conclude that each of the first two octets has a value of 255. Also, based on your memorization of Table 5-23, you know that one 1 (that is, a left-justified 1) in an octet has a decimal equivalent value of 128. Therefore, you can conclude that a subnet mask with a prefix notation of /17 can be represented in dotted-decimal notation as 255.255.128.0.

Extending a Classful Mask

The way to take a classful network (that is, a network using a classful subnet mask) and divide that network into multiple subnets is by adding 1s to the network's classful subnet mask. However, the class of the IP address does not change, regardless of the new subnet mask. For example, if you took the 172.16.0.0/16 network and subnetted it into multiple networks using a 24-bit subnet mask (172.16.0.0/24, 172.16.1.0/24, 172.16.2.0/24, …), those networks would still be Class B networks.

Specifically, the class of a network is entirely determined by the value of the first octet. The class of a network has nothing to do with the number of bits in a subnet, making this an often-misunderstood concept.

As another example, the network 10.2.3.0/24 has the subnet mask of a Class C network (that is, a 24-bit subnet mask). However, the 10.2.3.0/24 network is a Class A network because the value of the first octet is 10. It is simply a Class A network that happens to have a 24-bit subnet mask.

Borrowed Bits

When you add bits to a classful mask, the bits you add are referred to as *borrowed bits*. The number of borrowed bits you use determines how many subnets are created and the number of usable hosts per subnet.

Calculating the Number of Created Subnets

To determine the number of subnets created when adding bits to a classful mask, you can use the following formula:

Number of created subnets = 2^s

where s is the number of borrowed bits

For example, let's say you subnetted the 192.168.1.0 network with a 28-bit subnet mask, and you want to determine how many subnets were created. First, you determine how many borrowed bits you have. Recall that the number of borrowed bits is the number of bits in a subnet mask beyond the classful mask. In this case, because the first octet in the network address has a value of 192, you can conclude that this is a Class C network. You also recall that a Class C network has 24 bits in its classful (that is, its default) subnet mask. Because you now have a 28-bit subnet mask, the number of borrowed bits can be calculated as follows:

Number of borrowed bits = Bits in custom subnet mask – Bits in classful subnet mask

Number of borrowed bits = 28 – 24 = 4

Now that you know you have 4 borrowed bits, you can raise 2 to the power of 4 (2^4, or 2 * 2 * 2 * 2), which equals 16. From this calculation, you conclude that subnetting 192.168.1.0/24 with a 28-bit subnet mask yields 16 subnets.

Calculating the Number of Available Hosts

Earlier in this section you were given the formula for calculating the number of available (that is, assignable) host IP addresses, based on the number of host bits in a subnet mask. The formula is

Number of assignable IP address in a subnet = $2^h - 2$

where h is the number of host bits in the subnet mask

Using the previous example, let's say you want to determine the number of available host IP addresses in one of the 192.168.1.0/28 subnets. First, you need to determine the number of host bits in the subnet mask. Because you know that an IPv4 address consists of 32 bits, you can subtract the number of bits in the subnet mask (28, in this example) from 32 to determine the number of host bits:

Number of host bits = 32 – Number of bits in subnet mask

Number of host bits = 32 – 28 = 4

Now that you know the number of host bits, you can apply it to the previously presented formula:

Number of assignable IP addresses in a subnet = $2^h - 2$

where h is the number of host bits in the subnet mask

Number of assignable IP addresses in a subnet = $2^4 - 2 = 14$

From this calculation, you can conclude that each of the 192.168.1.0/28 subnets has 14 usable IP addresses.

To reinforce your skill with these calculations, you are now challenged with a few practice exercises.

Basic Subnetting Practice: Exercise 1

Using a separate sheet of paper, solve the following scenario:

Your company has been assigned the 172.20.0.0/16 network for use at one of its sites. You need to use a subnet mask that will accommodate 47 subnets while simultaneously accommodating the maximum number of hosts per subnet. What subnet mask will you use?

Basic Subnetting Practice: Exercise 1 Solution

To determine how many borrowed bits are required to accommodate 47 subnets, you can write out a table that lists the powers of 2, as shown in Table 5-24. In fact, you might want to sketch out a similar table on the dry-erase card you are given when you take the Network+ exam.

Table 5-24 Number of Subnets Created by a Specified Number of Borrowed Bits

Borrowed Bits	Number of Subnets Created (2s, Where s Is the Number of Borrowed Bits)
0	1
1	2
2	4
3	8
4	16
5	32
6	64
7	128

Borrowed Bits	**Number of Subnets Created (2s, Where s Is the Number of Borrowed Bits)**
8	256
9	512
10	1024
11	2048
12	4096

In this example, where you want to support 47 subnets, 5 borrowed bits are not enough, and 6 borrowed bits are more than enough. Because 5 borrowed bits are not enough, you round up and use 6 borrowed bits.

The first octet in the network address 172.20.0.0 has a value of 172, meaning that you are dealing with a Class B address. Because a Class B address has 16 bits in its classful mask, you can add the 6 borrowed bits to the 16-bit classful mask, which results in a 22-bit subnet mask.

One might argue that although a 22-bit subnet mask would accommodate 47 subnets, so would a 23-bit subnet mask or a 24-bit subnet mask. Although that is true, recall that the scenario said you should have the maximum number of hosts per subnet. This suggests that you should not use more borrowed bits than necessary. Therefore, you can conclude that to meet the scenario's requirements, you should use a subnet mask of /22, which could also be written as 255.255.252.0.

Basic Subnetting Practice: Exercise 2

Using a separate sheet of paper, solve the following scenario:

Your company has been assigned the 172.20.0.0/16 network for use at one of its sites. You need to calculate a subnet mask that will accommodate 100 hosts per subnet while maximizing the number of available subnets. What subnet mask will you use?

Basic Subnetting Practice: Exercise 2 Solution

To determine how many host bits are required to accommodate 100 hosts, you can write out a table that shows the number of hosts supported by a specific number of hosts bits, as shown in Table 5-25. Like the previous table, you might want to sketch out a similar table on the dry-erase card you are given when taking the Network+ exam.

Table 5-25 Number of Supported Hosts Given a Specified Number of Host Bits

Host Bits	Number of Supported Hosts (2^h–2, Where h Is the Number of Host Bits)
2	2
3	6
4	14
5	30
6	62
7	126
8	254
9	510
10	1022
11	2046
12	4094

In this example, where you want to support 100 hosts, 6 host bits are not enough, and 7 host bits are more than enough. Because 6 host bits are not enough, you round up and use 7 host bits.

Because an IPv4 address has 32 bits and you need 7 host bits, you can calculate the number of subnet bits by subtracting the 7 host bits from 32 (that is, the total number of bits in an IPv4 address). This results in a 25-bit subnet mask (that is, 32 total bits – 7 host bits = 25 subnet mask bits). Therefore, you can conclude that to meet the scenario's requirements, you should use a subnet mask of /25, which could also be written as 255.255.255.128.

Calculating New IP Address Ranges

Now that you can calculate the number of subnets created based on a given number of borrowed bits, the next logical step is to calculate the IP address ranges making up those subnets. For example, if you took 172.25.0.0/16 and subnetted it with a 24-bit subnet mask, the resulting subnets would be as follows:

172.25.0.0/24

172.25.1.0/24

172.25.2.0/24

...

172.25.255.0/24

Let's consider how such a calculation is performed. Notice in the previous example that you count by 1 in the third octet to calculate the new networks. To decide in what octet you start counting and by what increment you count, a new term needs to be defined. The *interesting octet* is the octet containing the last 1 in the subnet mask.

In this example, the subnet mask was a 24-bit subnet mask, which has a dotted-decimal equivalent of 255.255.255.0 and a binary equivalent of 11111111.11111111.11111111.00000000. From any of these subnet mask representations, you can determine that the third octet is the octet to contain the last 1 in the subnet mask. Therefore, you will be changing the value of the third octet to calculate the new networks.

Now that you know the third octet is the interesting octet, you need to know by what increment you will be counting in that octet. This increment is known as the *block size*. The block size can be calculated by subtracting the subnet mask value in the interesting octet from 256. In this example, the subnet mask had a value of 255 in the interesting octet (that is, the third octet). If you subtract 255 from 256, you get a result of 1 (that is, 256 – 255 = 1). The first subnet will be the original network address, with all of the borrowed bits set to 0. After this first subnet, you start counting by the block size (1 in this example) in the interesting octet to calculate the remainder of the subnets.

The preceding process for calculating subnets can be summarized as follows:

Step 1. Determine the interesting octet by determining the last octet in the subnet mask to contain a 1.

Step 2. Determine the block size by subtracting the decimal value in the subnet's interesting octet from 256.

Step 3. Determine the first subnet by setting all the borrowed bits (which are bits in the subnet mask beyond the bits in the classful subnet mask) to 0.

Step 4. Determine additional subnets by taking the first subnet and counting by the block size increment in the interesting octet.

To reinforce this procedure, consider another example. A 27-bit subnet mask is applied to a network address of 192.168.10.0/24. To calculate the created subnets, you can perform the following steps:

Step 1. The subnet mask /27 (in binary) is 11111111.11111111.11111111.11100000. The interesting octet is the fourth octet because the fourth octet contains the last 1 in the subnet mask.

Step 2. The decimal value of the fourth octet in the subnet mask is 224 (11100000 in decimal). Therefore, the block size is 32 (256 – 224 = 32).

Step 3. The first subnet is 192.168.10.0/27—the value of the original 192.168.10.0 network with the borrowed bits (the first three bits in the fourth octet) set to 0.

Step 4. Counting by 32 (the block size) in the interesting octet (the fourth octet) allows you to calculate the remaining subnets:

192.168.10.0

192.168.10.32

192.168.10.64

192.168.10.96

192.168.10.128

192.168.10.160

192.168.10.192

192.168.10.224

Now that you know the subnets created from a classful network given a subnet mask, the next logical step is to determine the usable addresses within those subnets. Recall that you cannot assign an IP address to a device if all the host bits in the IP address are set to 0, because an IP address with all host bits set to 0 is the address of the subnet itself.

Similarly, you cannot assign an IP address to a device if all the host bits in the IP address are set to 1 because an IP address with all host bits set to 1 is the directed broadcast address of a subnet.

By excluding the network and directed broadcast addresses from the 192.168.10.0/27 subnets (as previously calculated), the usable addresses shown in Table 5-26 can be determined.

Table 5-26 Usable IP Address Ranges for the 192.168.10.0/27 Subnets

Subnet Address	Directed Broadcast Address	Usable IP Addresses
192.168.10.0	192.168.10.31	192.168.10.1–192.168.10.30
192.168.10.32	192.168.10.63	192.168.10.33–192.168.10.62
192.168.10.64	192.168.10.95	192.168.10.65–192.168.10.94
192.168.10.96	192.168.10.127	192.168.10.97–192.168.10.126
192.168.10.128	192.168.10.159	192.168.10.129–192.168.10.158
192.168.10.160	192.168.10.191	192.168.10.161–192.168.10.190

Subnet Address	Directed Broadcast Address	Usable IP Addresses
192.168.10.192	192.168.10.223	192.168.10.193–192.168.10.222
192.168.10.224	192.168.10.255	192.168.10.225–192.168.10.254

To help develop your subnet-calculation skills, you are now challenged with a few practice subnetting exercises.

Advanced Subnetting Practice: Exercise 1

Using a separate sheet of paper, solve the following scenario:

Based on your network design requirements, you determine that you should use a 26-bit subnet mask applied to your 192.168.0.0/24 network. You now need to calculate each of the created subnets. Additionally, you want to know the broadcast address and the range of usable addresses for each of the created subnets.

Advanced Subnetting Practice: Exercise 1 Solution

As described earlier, you can go through the following four-step process to determine the subnet address:

Step 1. The subnet mask /26 (in binary) is 11111111.11111111.11111111.11000000. The interesting octet is the fourth octet because the fourth octet contains the last 1 in the subnet mask.

Step 2. The decimal value of the fourth octet in the subnet mask is 192 (11000000 in decimal). Therefore, the block size is 64 (256 – 192 = 64).

Step 3. The first subnet is 192.168.0.0/26—the value of the original 192.168.0.0 network with the borrowed bits (the first 2 bits in the last octet) set to 0.

Step 4. Counting by 64 (the block size) in the interesting octet (the fourth octet) allows you to calculate the remaining subnets, resulting in the following subnets:

192.168.0.0

192.168.0.64

192.168.0.128

192.168.0.192

The directed broadcast addresses for each of the preceding subnets can be calculated by adding 63 (that is, one less than the block size) to the interesting octet for each subnet address. Excluding the subnet addresses and directed broadcast addresses, you can calculate a range of usable addresses, the results of which are seen in Table 5-27.

Table 5-27 Usable IP Address Ranges for the 192.168.0.0/26 Subnets

Subnet Address	Directed Broadcast Address	Usable IP Addresses
192.168.0.0	192.168.0.63	192.168.0.1–192.168.0.62
192.168.0.64	192.168.0.127	192.168.0.65–192.168.0.126
192.168.0.128	192.168.0.191	192.168.0.129–192.168.0.190
192.168.0.192	192.168.0.255	192.168.0.193–192.168.0.254

Advanced Subnetting Practice: Exercise 2

Using a separate sheet of paper, solve the following scenario:

The network shown in Figure 5-18 has subnetted the 172.16.0.0/16 network by using a 20-bit subnet mask. Notice that two VLANs (two subnets) are configured; however, one of the client PCs is assigned an IP address that is not in that PC's VLAN. Which client PC is assigned an incorrect IP address?

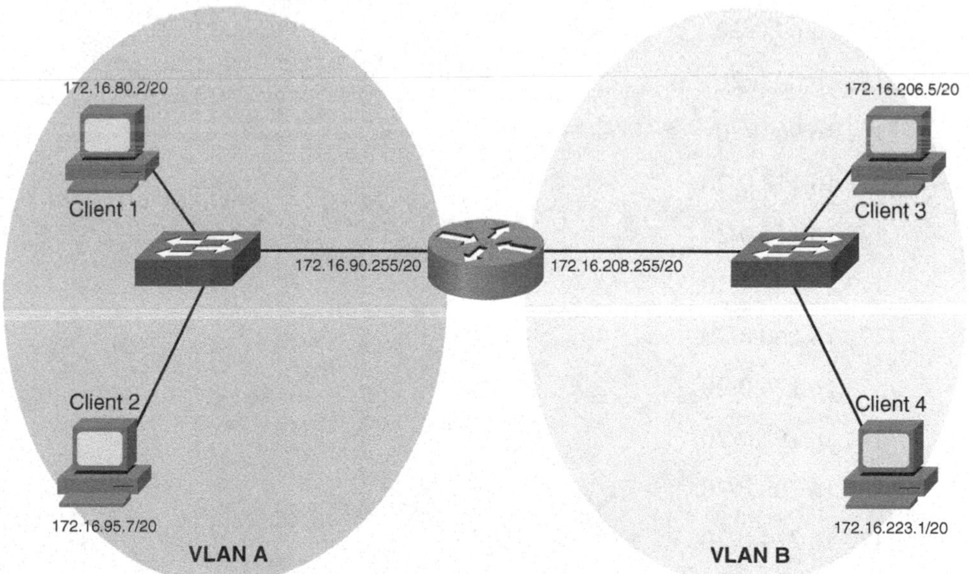

Figure 5-18 Topology for Advanced Subnetting Practice: Exercise 2

Advanced Subnetting Practice: Exercise 2 Solution

To determine which client PC is assigned an IP address outside of its local VLAN, you need to determine the subnets created by the 20-bit subnet mask applied to the 172.16.0.0/16 network:

1. The interesting octet for a 20-bit subnet mask is the third octet because the third octet is the last octet to contain a 1 in the 20-bit subnet mask (11111111.11111111.11110000.00000000, which could also be written as 255.255.240.0).
2. The decimal value of the third octet in the subnet mask is 240. Therefore, the block size is 16 (256 – 240 = 16).
3. The first 172.16.0.0/20 subnet is 172.16.0.0 (172.16.0.0/20 with the 4 borrowed bits in the third octet set to 0).
4. Beginning with the first subnet of 172.16.0.0/20 and counting by the block size of 16 in the interesting octet yields the following subnets:

   172.16.0.0/20

   172.16.16.0/20

   172.16.32.0/20

   172.16.48.0/20

   172.16.64.0/20

   172.16.80.0/20

   172.16.96.0/20

   172.16.112.0/20

   172.16.128.0/20

   172.16.144.0/20

   172.16.160.0/20

   172.16.176.0/20

   172.16.192.0/20

   172.16.208.0/20

   172.16.224.0/20

   172.16.240.0/20

Based on the IP addresses of the router interfaces, you can figure out the subnets for VLAN A and VLAN B. Specifically, the router interface in VLAN A has an IP address of 172.16.90.255/20. Based on the previous listing of subnets, you can determine that this interface resides in the 172.16.80.0/20 network, whose range of usable addresses is 172.16.80.1–172.16.95.254. Then you can examine the IP addresses of Client 1 and Client 2 to determine whether their IP addresses reside in that range of usable addresses.

Similarly, for VLAN B, the router's interface has an IP address of 172.16.208.255/20. Based on the previous subnet listing, you notice that this interface has an IP address that is part of the 172.16.208.0/20 subnet. As you did for VLAN A, you can check the IP address of Client 3 and Client 4 to decide whether their IP addresses live in VLAN B's range of usable IP addresses (that is, 172.16.208.1–172.16.223.254).

Table 5-28 shows these comparisons.

Table 5-28 IP Address Comparison for Advanced Subnetting Practice: Exercise 2

Client	VLAN	Range of Usable Addresses	Client IP Address	Is Client in Range of Usable Addresses?
Client 1	A	172.16.80.1–172.16.95.254	172.16.80.2	Yes
Client 2	A	172.16.80.1–172.16.95.254	172.16.95.7	Yes
Client 3	B	172.16.208.1–172.16.223.254	172.16.206.5	No
Client 4	B	172.16.208.1–172.16.223.254	172.16.223.1	Yes

The comparison in Table 5-28 reveals that Client 3 (with an IP address of 172.16.206.5) does not have an IP address in VLAN B's subnet (with a usable address range of 172.16.208.1–172.16.223.254).

Additional Practice

If you want to continue practicing these concepts, make up your own subnet mask and apply it to a classful network of your choosing. Then you can calculate the created subnets, the directed broadcast IP address for each subnet, and the range of usable IP addresses for each subnet.

To check your work, you can use a subnet calculator. An example of such a calculator is the free IP Address Manager available for download from http://www.solarwinds.com/downloads, as shown in Figure 5-19.

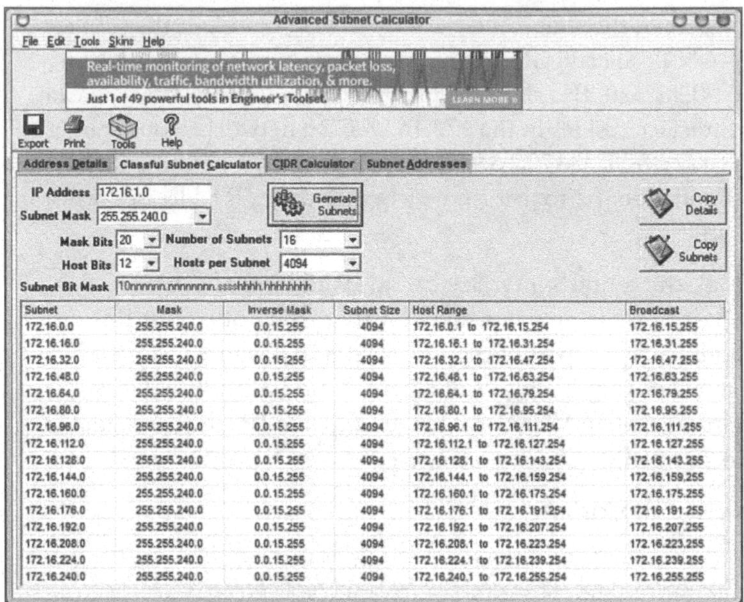

Figure 5-19 Free IP Address Manager

> **NOTE** As you read through different networking literature, you might come across other approaches to performing subnetting. Various shortcuts exist (including the one presented in this chapter), and some approaches involve much more binary math. The purpose of this section was not to be an exhaustive treatment of all available subnetting methods, but to provide a quick and easy approach to performing subnet calculations in the real world and on the Network+ certification exam.

Classless Interdomain Routing

Whereas subnetting is the process of extending a classful subnet mask (that is, adding 1s to a classful mask), classless interdomain routing (CIDR) does just the opposite. Specifically, CIDR shortens a classful subnet mask by removing 1s from the classful mask. As a result, CIDR allows contiguous classful networks to be aggregated. This process is sometimes called *route aggregation*.

A typical use of CIDR is a service provider summarizing multiple Class C networks, assigned to their various customers. For example, imagine that a service provider is responsible for advertising the following Class C networks:

192.168.32.0/24

192.168.33.0/24

192.168.34.0/24

192.168.35.0/24

The service provider could advertise all four networks with a single route advertisement of 192.168.32.0/22. To calculate this advertisement, convert the values in the third octet (that is, the octet where the values start to differ) to binary, as shown in Figure 5-20. Then determine how many bits the networks have in common. The number of common bits then becomes the number of bits in the CIDR mask.

Network Address	1st Octet	2nd Octet	3rd Octet	4th Octet
192.168.32.0	11000000	10101000	001000 00	00000000
192.168.33.0	11000000	10101000	001000 01	00000000
192.168.34.0	11000000	10101000	001000 10	00000000
192.168.35.0	11000000	10101000	001000 11	00000000

All Networks Have 22 Bits in Common

Figure 5-20 CIDR Calculation Example

Because all four of the network addresses have the first 22 bits in common, and because setting the remaining bits to 0 (11000000.10101000.00100000.0000000 0) creates a network address of 192.168.32.0, these networks can be summarized as 192.168.32.0/22.

IP Version 6

With the global proliferation of IP-based networks, available IPv4 addresses are rapidly becoming extinct. Fortunately, IPv6 provides enough IP addresses for many generations to come. This section introduces IPv6's address structure and discusses some of its unique characteristics.

Need for IPv6

With the worldwide depletion of IP Version 4 (IPv4) addresses, many organizations have migrated, are in the process of migrating, or are considering migrating their IPv4 addresses to IPv6 addresses. IPv6 dramatically increases the number of available IP addresses. In fact, IPv6 offers approximately $5 * 10^{28}$ IP addresses for each person on the planet.

Beyond the increased address space, IPv6 offers many other features:

- Simplified header:
  - IPv4 header uses 12 fields.
  - IPv6 header uses five fields.
- No broadcasts.
- No fragmentation (performs MTU discovery for each session).
- Can coexist with IPv4 during a transition.
  - Dual stack (running IPv4 and IPv6 simultaneously on a network interface or device).
  - IPv6 over IPv4 (tunneling IPv6 over an IPv4 tunnel).

Even if you are designing a network based on IPv4 addressing, a good practice is to consider how readily an IPv6 addressing scheme could be overlaid on that network at some point in the future. Using Teredo tunneling, an IPv6 host could provide IPv6 connectivity even when the host is directly connected to an IPv4-only network. Miredo is a client that can be used to implement the Teredo protocol and is included in many versions of Linux. IPv6/IPv4 tunneling is often referred to as 6to4 or 4to6 tunneling, depending on which protocol is being tunneled (IPv4 or IPv6). These are just some of the many tunneling mechanisms devised to ensure a smooth transition from IPv4 to IPv6. In fact, thanks to dual stack and tunneling features, it is very unlikely that you will see IPv4 ever completely go away in your lifetime.

IPv6 Address Structure

An IPv6 address has the following address format, where X = a hexadecimal digit in the range of 0 to F:

XXXX:XXXX:XXXX:XXXX:XXXX:XXXX:XXXX:XXXX

A hexadecimal digit is 4 bits in size (4 binary bits can represent 16 values). Notice that an IPv6 address has eight fields, and each field contains four hexadecimal digits. The following formula reveals why an IPv6 address is a 128-bit address:

4 bits per digit * 4 digits per field * 8 fields = 128 bits in an IPv6 address

IPv6 addresses can be difficult to work with because of their size. Fortunately, the following rules exist for abbreviating these addresses:

- Leading 0s in a field can be omitted.

- Contiguous fields containing all 0s can be represented with a double colon. (Note that this can be done only once for a single IPv6 address.)

For example, consider the following IPv6 address:

ABCD:0123:4040:0000:0000:0000:000A:000B

Using the rules for abbreviation, the IPv6 address can be rewritten as follows:

ABCD:123:4040::A:B

Also, the Extended Unique Identifier (EUI-64) format can be used to cause a router to automatically populate the low-order 64 bits of an IPv6 address based on an interface's MAC address.

IPv6 Address Types

The following are some of the many unique aspects to IPv6 addressing and many interesting address types:

- IPv6 globally routable unicast addresses start with the first four hex characters in the range of 2000 to 3999.
- An IPv6 link-local address is also used on each IPv6 interface. The link-local address begins with FE80.
- Multicast addresses begin with FF as the first two hex characters.
- IPv6 can use autoconfiguration to discover the current network and select a host ID that is unique on that network. Automatic generation of a unique host ID is made possible through a process known as EUI64, which uses the 48-bit MAC address on the device to aid in the generation of the unique 64-bit host ID. Notice that the autoconfiguration capabilities described here permit you to create an IPv6 network free of DHCP-type services.
- IPv6 can also use a special version of DHCP for IPv6. Not surprisingly, this version is called DHCPv6.
- The protocol that is used to discover the network address and learn the Layer 2 address of neighbors on the same network is Neighbor Discovery Protocol (NDP).

Neighbor Discovery Protocol is hugely important in IPv6. It defines five ICMPv6 packet types for important jobs:

- **Router Solicitation**: Hosts inquire with Router Solicitation messages to locate routers on an attached link.

- **Router Advertisement**: Routers advertise their presence together with various link and Internet parameters, either periodically or in response to a Router Solicitation message.
- **Neighbor Solicitation**: Neighbor solicitations are used by nodes to determine the link layer address of a neighbor, or to verify that a neighbor is still reachable via a cached link layer address.
- **Neighbor Advertisement**: Neighbor advertisements are used by nodes to respond to a Neighbor Solicitation message.
- **Redirect**: Routers may inform hosts of a better first-hop router for a destination.

IPv6 Data Flows

IPv6 has three types of data flows:

- Unicast
- Multicast
- Anycast

The following sections summarize the characteristics of each address type.

Unicast

With unicast, a single IPv6 address is applied to a single interface, as illustrated in Figure 5-21. The communication flow can be thought of as a one-to-one communication flow.

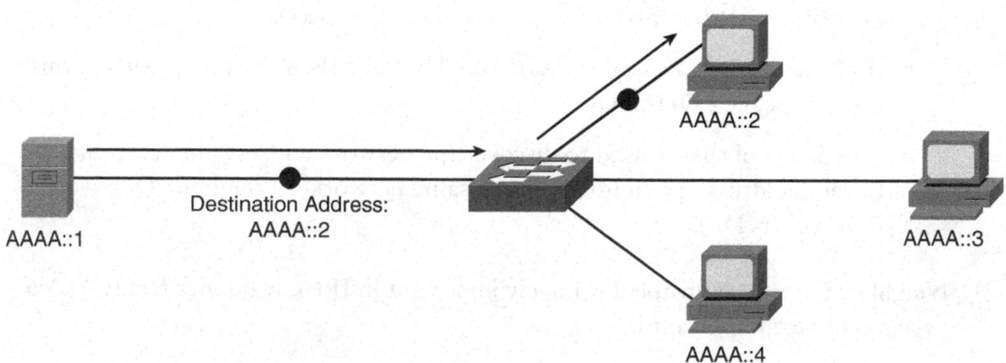

Figure 5-21 IPv6 Unicast Example

In Figure 5-21, a server (AAAA::1) is sending traffic to a single client (AAAA::2).

Multicast

With multicast, a single IPv6 address (a multicast group) can represent multiple devices on a network, as shown in Figure 5-22. The communication flow is a one-to-many communication flow.

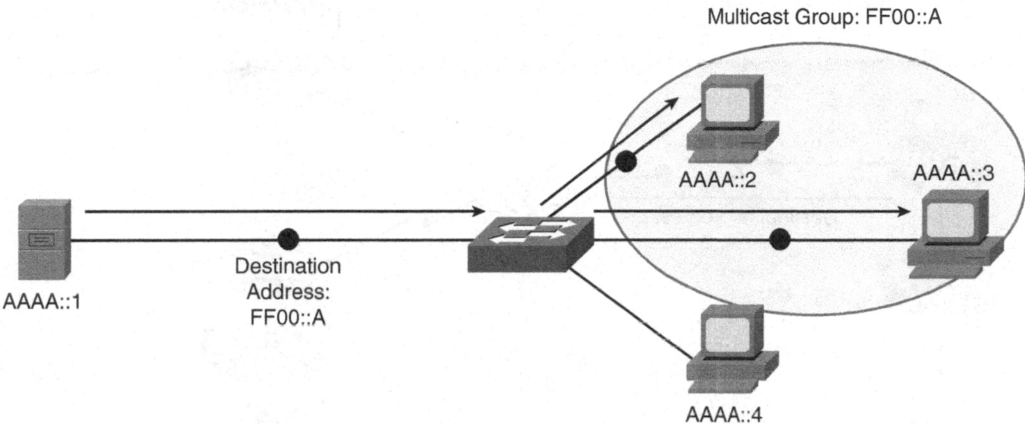

Figure 5-22 IPv6 Multicast Example

In Figure 5-22, a server (AAAA::1) is sending traffic to a multicast group (FF00::A). Two clients (AAAA::2 and AAAA::3) have joined this group. Those clients receive the traffic from the server, while any client that did not join the group (for example, AAAA::4) does not receive the traffic.

Remember, IPv6 replaces broadcast behavior thanks to the "all nodes" multicast group. This reserved address is FF01:0:0:0:0:0:0:1 (FF01::1). All IPv6 nodes join this group, which represents a simple and efficient method for sending traffic to all nodes.

Anycast

With anycast, a single IPv6 address is assigned to multiple devices, as depicted in Figure 5-23. It is a one-to-nearest (from the perspective of a router's routing table) communication flow.

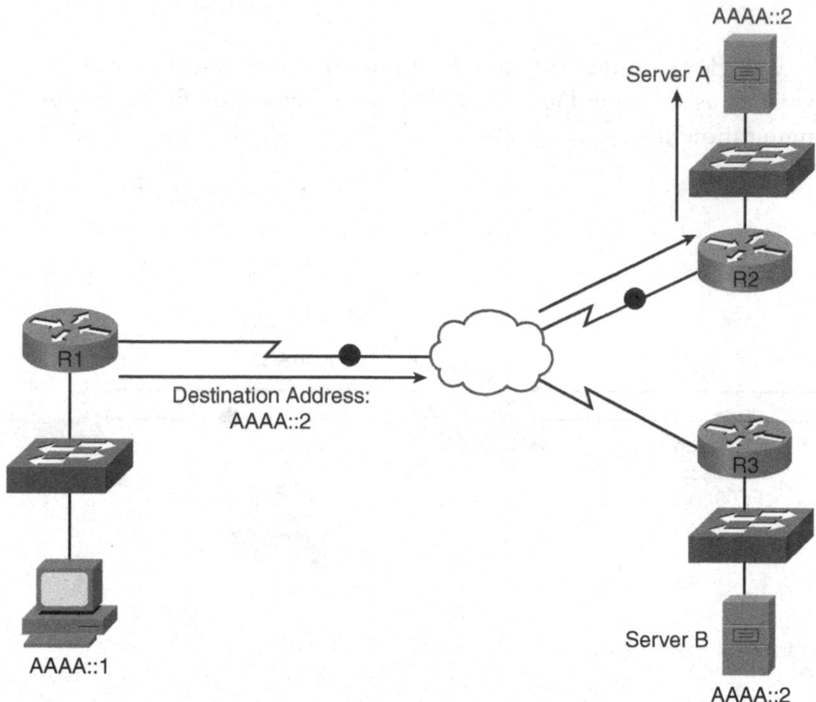

Figure 5-23 IPv6 Anycast Example

In Figure 5-23, a client with an IPv6 address of AAAA::1 wants to send traffic to a destination IPv6 address of AAAA::2. Notice that two servers (server A and server B) have an IPv6 address of AAAA::2. In the figure, the traffic destined for AAAA::2 is sent to server A, via router R2, because the network on which server A resides appears to be closer than the network on which server B resides, from the perspective of router R1's IPv6 routing table.

Real-World Case Study

Acme, Inc. has decided to use private IP addresses for its internal LAN and for the WAN. The company will use the private block of 10.0.0.0/8 and create subnets to provide enough subnets to cover the number of VLANs it will be using on the LANs at the headquarters site and at each of the remote offices. The association between the Layer 2 VLANs and the Layer 3 IP subnets will be one-to-one, with each VLAN having its own subnet associated with it.

The company will have nine VLANs and will use a couple subnets for the WAN connections. For the VLANs, the company plans to use a network mask of /12, which will offer enough subnets to meet its needs based on the starting mask of /8 for the Class A private address of 10.0.0.0/8.

For the WAN connectivity Acme is purchasing from a service provider for connectivity between the remote branch offices and the headquarters site, the company will use masks of /30, which will allow for two hosts on each of the WAN connections. This is enough for each device at the end of the point-to-point WAN connections.

To connect its LANs to the Internet, Acme plans to use Network Address Translation (NAT), which is going to be performed by its service provider so that traffic going to the Internet will appear to be coming from a globally routable IP address and not from a private address (more about NAT in Chapter 6).

Summary

Here are the main topics covered in this chapter:

- The binary math tutorial gave you a basic understanding of why binary math is necessary for working with subnet masks.
- The characteristics of IPv4 were presented, including IPv4's address format and a contrast of unicast, broadcast, and multicast data flows.
- You examined various approaches for assigning IP address information to network devices. These approaches included static assignment, dynamic assignment (BOOTP and DHCP), and APIPA (a Zeroconf component).
- Multiple examples and practice exercises were provided for various subnet calculations.
- The characteristics of IPv6 were highlighted, including the IPv6 address format and IPv6 data flows (unicast, multicast, and anycast).

Exam Preparation Tasks

Review All the Key Topics

Review the most important topics from inside the chapter, noted with the Key Topic icon in the outer margin of the page. Table 5-29 lists these key topics and the page numbers where each is found.

Table 5-29 Key Topics for Chapter 5

Key Topic Element	Description	Page Number
Table 5-1	Binary conversion table	154
Section	Converting a decimal number to a binary number	155
Figure 5-2	Dividing an IP address into a network portion and a host portion	162
Table 5-19	IP address classes	163
Table 5-20	Private IP networks	164
List	Basic functions of Zeroconf	175
Formula	Number of assignable IP addresses in a subnet	176
Table 5-22	Dotted-decimal and prefix-notation representations for IPv4 subnets	177
Table 5-23	Subnet octet values	178
Formula	Number of created subnets	180
Formula	Number of borrowed bits	180
Formula	Number of host bits	180
Table 5-25	Number of subnets created by a specified number of borrowed bits	183
Step list	Steps for calculating subnets	184
Table 5-26	Number of supported hosts given a specified number of host bits	185
Figure 5-20	CIDR calculation example	191
List	Rules for abbreviating IPv6 addresses	192
List	List of NDP packets	193
List	Types of IPv6 data flows	194

Complete Tables and Lists from Memory

Print a copy of Appendix C, "Memory Tables," or at least the section for this chapter, and complete as many of the tables as possible from memory. Appendix D, "Memory Tables Answer Key," includes the completed tables and lists so you can check your work.

Define Key Terms

Define the following key terms from this chapter, and check your answers in the Glossary:

classful masks, private IP addresses, loopback, octet, prefix notation, slash notation, dotted-decimal notation, subnet mask, classful mask, default gateway, VLSM, Bootstrap Protocol, Dynamic Host Configuration Protocol (DHCP), Zeroconf, link-local IP address, Automatic Private IP Addressing, borrowed bits, block size, classless interdomain routing (CIDR), unicast, multicast, anycast, tunneling, dual stack, router advertisement, neighbor discovery, DHCPv6, EUI64

Complete Chapter 5 Hands-On Labs in Network+ Simulator Lite

- IPv4 Address Types
- Configuring a Client Network Adapter with an IPv4 Address

Additional Resources

Subnetting – Hosts Per Subnet: http://www.ajsnetworking.com/subnetting

Subnetting – What Mask to Use: http://www.ajsnetworking.com/subnetting2

Subnetting – "I Feel the Need, the Need for Speed": http://www.ajsnetworking.com/subnetting3

IPv6 Shortcuts: https://youtu.be/66XwxVELFIk

Review Questions

The answers to these review questions appear in Appendix A, "Answers to Review Questions."

1. What is the binary representation of the decimal number 117?
   - a. 10110101
   - b. 01110101
   - c. 10110110
   - d. 01101001

2. The binary number 10110100 has what decimal equivalent?
   - a. 114
   - b. 190
   - c. 172
   - d. 180

3. What is the class of IP address 10.1.2.3/24?
   - a. Class A
   - b. Class B
   - c. Class C
   - d. Class D

4. What type of IPv4 address is 239.1.2.3?
   - a. Unicast
   - b. Experimental
   - c. Private use only
   - d. Multicast

5. Which of the following are dynamic approaches to assigning routable IP addresses to networked devices? (Choose two.)
   - a. BOOTP
   - b. APIPA
   - c. Zeroconf
   - d. DHCP

6. How many assignable IP addresses exist in the 172.16.1.10/27 network?

a. 30

b. 32

c. 14

d. 64

7. What is the prefix notation for a subnet mask of 255.255.255.240?

a. /20

b. /24

c. /28

d. /29

8. Your company has been assigned the 192.168.30.0/24 network for use at one of its sites. You need to use a subnet mask that will accommodate seven subnets while simultaneously accommodating the maximum number of hosts per subnet. What subnet mask should you use?

a. /24

b. /26

c. /27

d. /28

9. A client with an IP address of 172.16.18.5/18 belongs to what network?

a. 172.16.0.0/18

b. 172.16.64.0/18

c. 172.16.96.0/18

d. 172.16.128.0/18

10. How can the following IPv6 address be condensed?

2009:0123:4040:0000:0000:000:000A:100B

a. 2009::123:404:A:100B

b. 2009::123:404:A:1B

c. 2009:123:4040::A:100B

d. 2009:0123:4040::0::000A:100B

11. What technology allows for the automatic assignment of the host portion of an IPv6 address?

    a. Dual Stack

    b. EUI64

    c. Neighbor discovery

    d. Anycast

After completion of this chapter, you will be able to answer the following questions:

- How are source and destination IP addresses used to route traffic through a network?
- What are sources for routing information used to populate a router's routing table?
- How do routed protocols differ from routing protocols?
- When multiple routing protocols know how to reach a destination network, which route is chosen?
- When a single routing protocol knows of multiple routes to reach a destination network, how is the preferred path (or paths) chosen?
- What is the distinction between an Interior Gateway Protocol (IGP) and an Exterior Gateway Protocol (EGP)?
- What are the primary differences between distance-vector and link-state routing protocols?
- What are the characteristics of the following routing protocols? Routing Information Protocol (RIP), Open Shortest Path First (OSPF) protocol, Intermediate System-to-Intermediate System (IS-IS) protocol, Enhanced Interior Gateway Routing Protocol (EIGRP), and Border Gateway Protocol (BGP)
- How does Network Address Translation (NAT) perform IP address translation, and how do the Port Address Translation (PAT), Static NAT (SNAT), and Dynamic NAT (DNAT) approaches to NAT differ?
- What protocols are used to route multicast traffic?

CHAPTER 6

Routing IP Packets

In Chapter 5, "IPv4 and IPv6 Addresses," you learned how Internet Protocol (IP) networks can be divided into subnets. Each subnet is its own broadcast domain, and the device that separates broadcast domains is a router (which this text considers synonymous with a multilayer switch). A multilayer switch is a network device that can perform the Layer 2 switching of frames as well as the Layer 3 routing of IP packets. Multilayer switches generally use dedicated chips to perform these functions and, as a result, may be faster than a traditional router in forwarding packets.

For traffic to flow between subnets, that traffic has to be routed, which is a router's primary job. This chapter discusses how routing occurs and introduces you to a variety of approaches for performing address translation. This chapter concludes with a discussion of how devices route multicast traffic.

Foundation Topics

Basic Routing Processes

To understand basic routing processes, consider Figure 6-1. In this topology, PC1 needs to send traffic to Server1. Notice that these devices are on different networks. Therefore, the question becomes, "How does a packet from a source IP address of 192.168.1.2 get routed to a destination IP address of 192.168.3.2?"

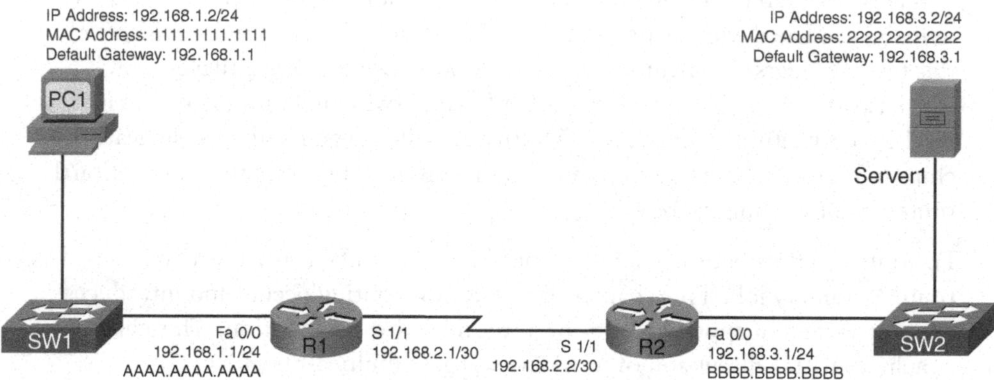

Figure 6-1 Basic Routing Topology

It might help to walk through this process systematically:

Step 1. PC1 compares its IP address and subnet mask of 192.168.1.2/24 with the destination IP address and subnet mask of 192.168.3.2/24. PC1 concludes that the destination IP address resides on a remote subnet. Therefore, PC1 needs to send the packet to its default gateway, which could have been manually configured on PC1 or dynamically learned via Dynamic Host Configuration Protocol (DHCP). In this example, PC1 has a default gateway of 192.168.1.1 (router R1). However, to construct a Layer 2 frame, PC1 also needs the MAC address of its default gateway. PC1 sends an Address Resolution Protocol (ARP) request for router R1's MAC address. After PC1 receives an ARP reply from router R1, PC1 adds router R1's MAC address to its ARP cache. PC1 now sends its data in a frame destined for Server1, as shown in Figure 6-2.

> **NOTE** ARP is a broadcast-based protocol and, therefore, does not travel beyond the local subnet of the sender.

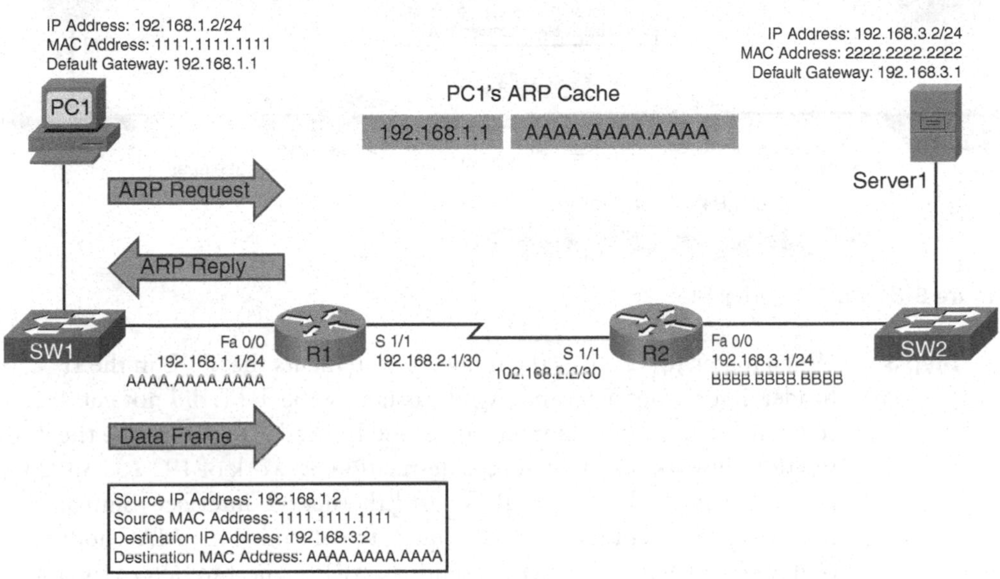

Figure 6-2 Basic Routing: Step 1

Step 2. Router R1 receives the frame sent from PC1 and interrogates the IP header. An IP header contains a Time To Live (TTL) field, which is decremented once for each router hop. Therefore, router R1 decrements the packet's TTL field. If the value in the TTL field is reduced to 0, the router discards the frame and sends a "time exceeded" Internet Control Message Protocol (ICMP) message back to the source. Assuming the TTL is not decremented to 0, router R1 checks its routing table to determine the best path to reach network 192.168.3.0/24. In this example, router R1's routing table has an entry stating that network 192.168.3.0/24 is accessible via interface Serial 1/1. Note that ARPs is not required for serial interfaces because these interface types do not have MAC addresses. Router R1, therefore, forwards the frame out of its Serial 1/1 interface, as shown in Figure 6-3.

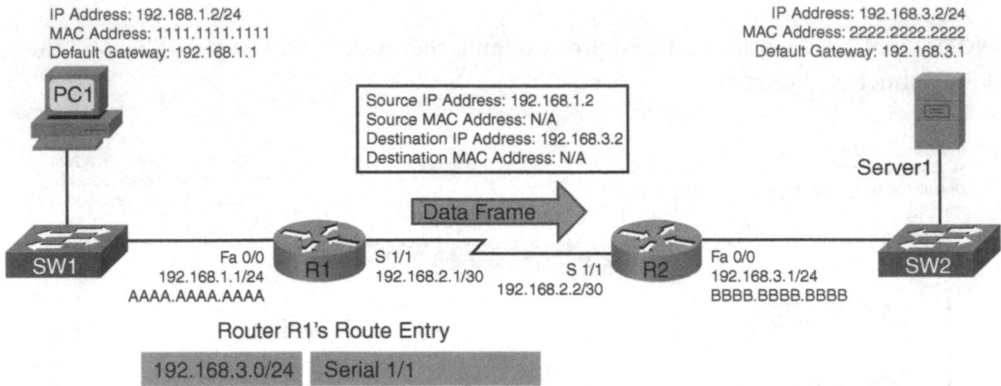

Figure 6-3 Basic Routing: Step 2

Step 3. When router R2 receives the frame, it decrements the TTL in the IP header, just as router R1 did. Again, assuming the TTL did not get decremented to 0, router R2 interrogates the IP header to determine the destination network. In this case, the destination network of 192.168.3.0/24 is directly attached to router R2's Fast Ethernet 0/0 interface. Similar to the way PC1 sent out an ARP request to determine the MAC address of its default gateway, router R2 sends an ARP request to determine the MAC address of Server1. After an ARP reply is received from Server1, router R2 forwards the frame out of its Fast Ethernet 0/0 interface to Server1, as illustrated in Figure 6-4.

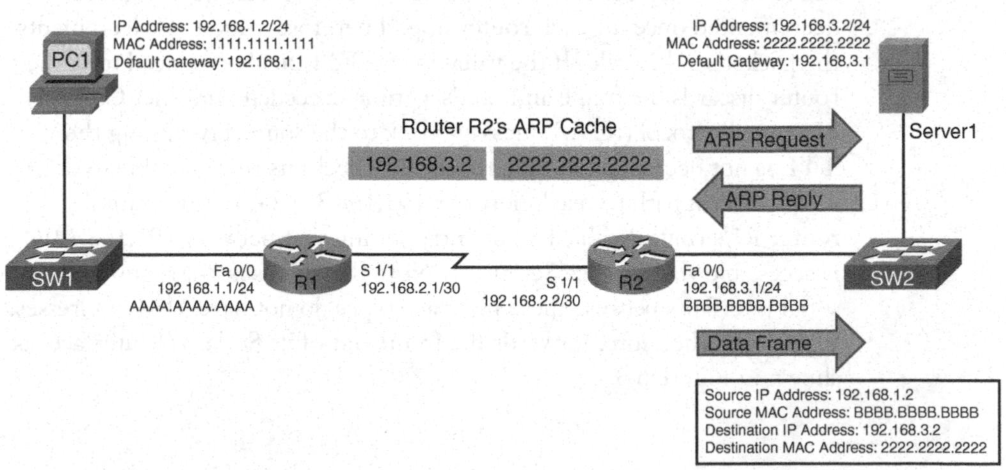

Figure 6-4 Basic Routing: Step 3

The previous steps identified two router data structures:

- **IP routing table:** When a router needed to route an IP packet, it consulted its IP routing table to find the best match. The best match is the route that has the longest prefix. Specifically, a route entry with the longest prefix is the most specific network. For example, imagine that a router has an entry for network 10.0.0.0/8 and for network 10.1.1.0/24. Also, imagine the router is seeking the best match for a destination address of 10.1.1.1/24. The router would select the 10.1.1.0/24 route entry as the best entry because that route entry has the longest prefix (/24 is longer than /8, which is a more specific entry).

- **Layer 3 to Layer 2 mapping:** In the previous example, router R2's ARP cache contained Layer 3 to Layer 2 mapping information. Specifically, the ARP cache had a mapping that said a MAC address of 2222.2222.2222 corresponded to an IP address of 192.168.3.2.

As shown in the preceding example, routers rely on their internal routing table to make packet-forwarding decisions. Therefore, at this point, a logical question is, "How does a router's routing table become populated with entries?" This is the focus of the next section.

Sources of Routing Information

A router's routing table can be populated from various sources. As an administrator, you could statically configure a route entry. A route could be learned via a dynamic routing protocol (for example, OSPF or EIGRP), or a router could know how to get to a specific network, because the router is physically attached to that network.

Directly Connected Routes

One way for a router to know how to reach a specific destination network is by virtue of the fact that the router has an interface directly participating in that network. For example, consider Figure 6-5.

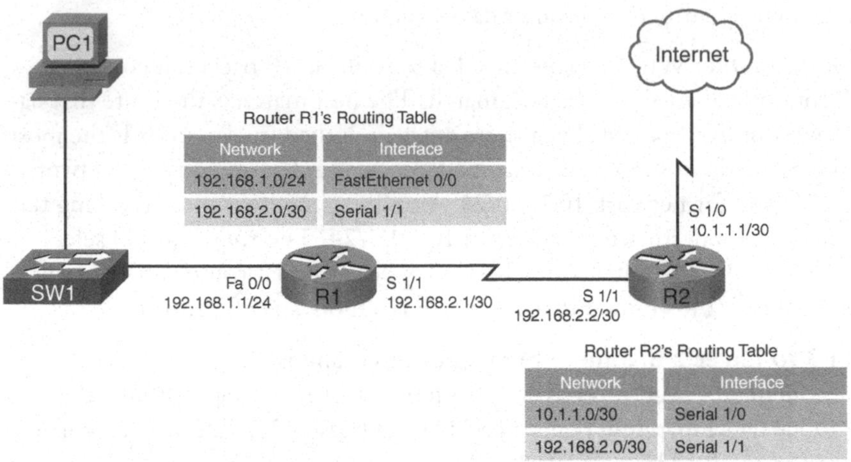

Figure 6-5 Directly Connected Routes

In Figure 6-5, router R1's routing table knows how to reach the 192.168.1.0/24 and 192.168.2.0/30 networks because router R1 has an interface physically attached to each network. Similarly, router R2 has interfaces participating in the 10.1.1.0/30 and 192.168.2.0/30 networks and therefore knows how to reach those networks. The entries currently shown to be in the routing tables of routers R1 and R2 are called *directly connected routes*.

Static Routes

Routes can also be statically configured in a router's routing table. Continuing to expand on the previous example, consider router R1. As shown in Figure 6-6, router R1 does not need knowledge of each route on the Internet. Specifically, router R1 already knows how to reach devices on its locally attached networks. All router R1 really needs to know at this point is how to get out to the rest of the world. As you can see from Figure 6-6, any traffic destined for a nonlocal network (for example, any of the networks available on the public Internet) can simply be sent to router R2. Because R2 is the next router hop along the path to reach all those other networks, router R1 could be configured with a *default static route*, which says, "If traffic is destined for a network not currently in the routing table, send that traffic out of interface Serial 1/1."

> **NOTE** A static route does not always reference a local interface. Instead, a static route might point to a *next-hop* IP address (an interface's IP address on the next router to which traffic should be forwarded). The network address of a default route is 0.0.0.0/0.

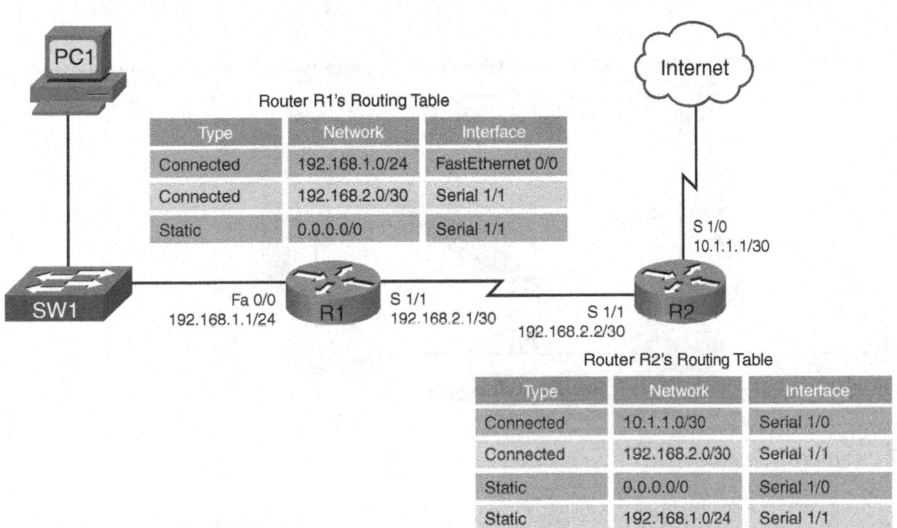

Router R1's Routing Table

Type	Network	Interface
Connected	192.168.1.0/24	FastEthernet 0/0
Connected	192.168.2.0/30	Serial 1/1
Static	0.0.0.0/0	Serial 1/1

Router R2's Routing Table

Type	Network	Interface
Connected	10.1.1.0/30	Serial 1/0
Connected	192.168.2.0/30	Serial 1/1
Static	0.0.0.0/0	Serial 1/0
Static	192.168.1.0/24	Serial 1/1

Figure 6-6 Static Routes

Similarly, router R2 can reach the Internet by sending traffic out of its Serial 1/0 interface. However, router R2 does need information about how to reach the 192.168.1.0/24 network available off of router R1. To educate router R2 as to how this network can be reached, a static route, pointing to 192.168.1.0/24, can be statically added to router R2's routing table.

Dynamic Routing Protocols

If you want to add routing information to routers in more complex networks, such as the topology shown in Figure 6-7, static routing does not scale well. Fortunately, a variety of dynamic routing protocols are available that allow a router's routing table to be updated as network conditions change.

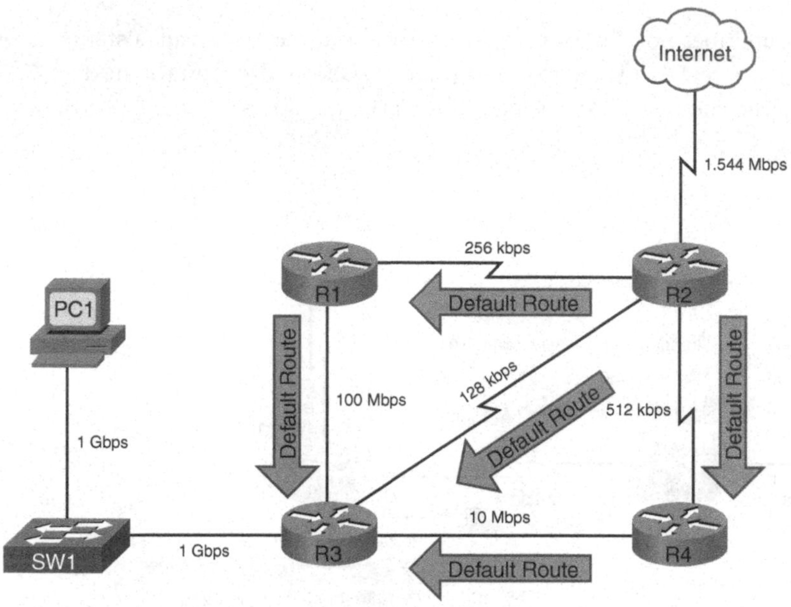

Figure 6-7 Dynamic Routes

In Figure 6-7, router R2 is advertising a default route to its neighbors (routers R1, R3, and R4). What happens if PC1 wants to send traffic to the Internet? PC1's default gateway is router R3, and router R3 has received three default routes. Which one does it use?

Router R3's path selection depends on the dynamic routing protocol being used. As you see later in this chapter, a routing protocol such as Routing Information Protocol (RIP) would make the path selection based on the number of routers that must be used to reach the Internet (that is, *hop count*). Based on the topology presented, router R3 would select the 128Kbps link (where Kbps stands for kilobits per second, meaning thousands of bits per second) connecting to router R2 because the Internet would be only one hop away. If router R3 had instead selected a path pointing to either router R1 or R4, the Internet would be two hops away.

However, based on the link bandwidths, you can see that the path from router R3 to router R2 is suboptimal. Unfortunately, RIP does not consider available bandwidth when making its route selection. Some other protocols, such as Open Shortest Path First (OSPF), can consider available bandwidth when making their routing decisions.

Dynamic routes also allow a router to reroute around a failed link. For example, in Figure 6-8, router R3 had preferred to reach the Internet via router R4. However, the link between routers R3 and R4 went down. Thanks to a dynamic routing protocol, router R3 knows of two other paths to reach the Internet, and it selects the next-best path, which is via router R1 in this example. You call this process of failing over from one route to a backup route *convergence*.

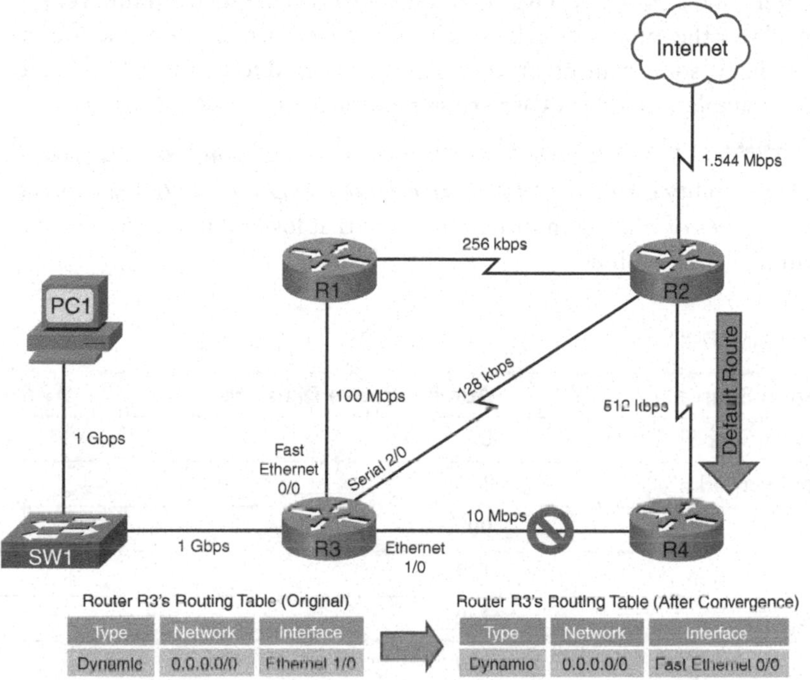

Figure 6-8 Route Redundancy

Routing Protocol Characteristics

Before examining the characteristics of routing protocols, an important distinction to make is the difference between a *routing* protocol and a *routed* protocol. A *routing* protocol (for example, RIP, OSPF, or EIGRP) is a protocol that advertises route information between routers.

Conversely, a *routed* protocol is a protocol with an addressing scheme (for example, IP) that defines different network addresses. Traffic can then be routed between defined networks, perhaps with the assistance of a routing protocol.

This section looks at routing protocol characteristics, such as how believable a routing protocol is versus other routing protocols. In addition, in the presence of multiple routes, different routing protocols use different metrics to determine the best path. A distinction is made between Interior Gateway Protocols (IGPs) and Exterior Gateway Protocols (EGPs). Finally, this section discusses different approaches to making route advertisements.

Believability of a Route

If a network is running more than one routing protocol (maybe as a result of a corporate merger), and a router receives two route advertisements from different routing protocols for the same network, which route advertisement does the router believe? Interestingly, some routing protocols are considered to be more believable that others. An example would be a Cisco router considering EIGRP to be more believable than RIP.

The index of believability is called *administrative distance* (AD). Table 6-1 shows the AD for various sources of routing information. Note that lower AD values are more believable than higher AD values.

Table 6-1 Administrative Distance

Routing Information Source	Administrative Distance
Directly connected network	0
Statically configured network	1
EIGRP	90
OSPF	110
RIP	120
External EIGRP	170
Unknown of unbelievable	255 (considered to be unreachable)

Metrics

Some networks might be reachable via more than one path. If a routing protocol knows of multiple paths to reach such a network, which route (or routes) does the routing protocol select? Actually, it varies depending on the routing protocol and what that routing protocol uses as a *metric* (a value assigned to a route). Lower metrics are preferred over higher metrics.

If a routing protocol knows of more than one route to reach a destination network and those routes have equal metrics, some routing protocols support load balancing across equal-cost paths. EIGRP can even be configured to load-balance across unequal-cost paths.

Different routing protocols can use different parameters in their calculation of a metric. The specific parameters used for a variety of routing protocols are presented later in this chapter.

Interior Versus Exterior Gateway Protocols

Routing protocols can also be categorized based on the scope of their operation. Interior Gateway Protocols (IGPs) operate within an autonomous system, where an autonomous system is a network under a single administrative control. Conversely, Exterior Gateway Protocols (EGPs) operate between autonomous systems.

Consider Figure 6-9. Routers R1 and R2 are in one autonomous system (AS 65002), and routers R3 and R4 are in another autonomous system (AS 65003). Within those autonomous systems, an IGP is used to exchange routing information. However, router ISP1 is a router in a separate autonomous system (AS 65001) run by a service provider. An EGP (typically, Border Gateway Protocol) is used to exchange routing information between the service provider's autonomous system and each of the other autonomous systems.

Key Topic

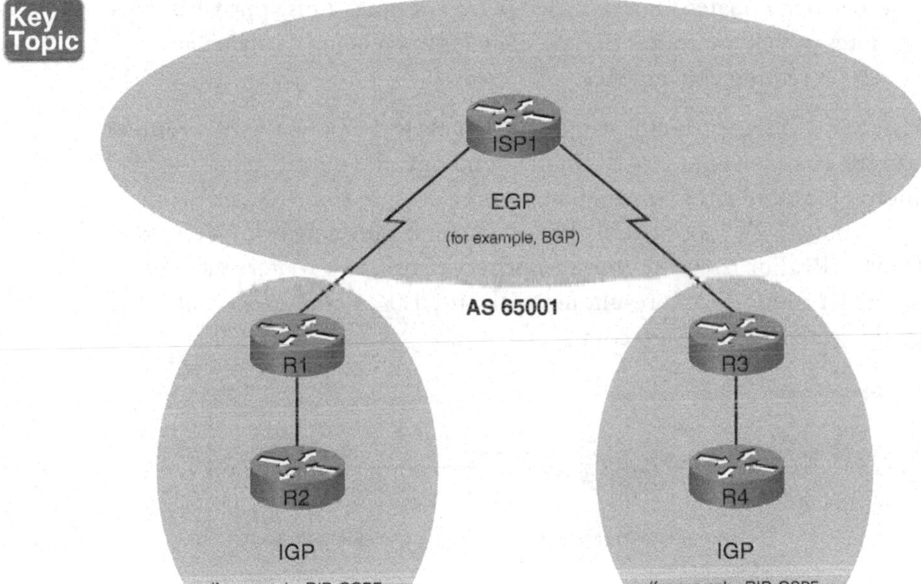

Figure 6-9 IGPs Versus EGPs

Route Advertisement Method

Another characteristic of a routing protocol is how it receives, advertises, and stores routing information. The two fundamental approaches are *distance vector* and *link state*.

Distance Vector

A *distance-vector* routing protocol sends a full copy of its routing table to its directly attached neighbors. This is a periodic advertisement, meaning that even if there have been no topological changes, a distance-vector routing protocol will, at regular intervals, advertise again its full routing table to its neighbors.

Obviously, this periodic advertisement of redundant information is inefficient. Ideally, you want a full exchange of route information to occur only once and subsequent updates to be triggered by topological changes.

Another drawback to distance-vector routing protocols is the time they take to converge, which is the time required for all routers to update their routing table in response to a topological change in a network. *Hold-down* timers can speed the convergence process. After a router makes a change to a route entry, a hold-down timer prevents any subsequent updates for a specified period of time. This approach helps stop flapping routes (which are routes that oscillate between being available and unavailable) from preventing convergence.

Yet another issue with distance-vector routing protocols is the potential of a routing loop. To illustrate, consider Figure 6-10. In this topology, the metric being used is *hop count*, which is the number of routers that must be crossed to reach a network. As one example, router R3's routing table has a route entry for network 10.1.1.0/24 available off router R1. For router R3 to reach that network, two routers must be transited (routers R2 and R1). As a result, network 10.1.1.0/24 appears in router R3's routing table with a metric (hop count) of 2.

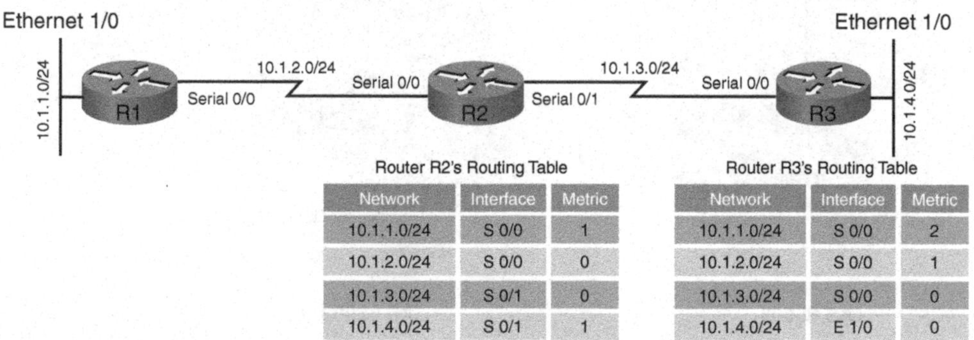

Router R2's Routing Table

Network	Interface	Metric
10.1.1.0/24	S 0/0	1
10.1.2.0/24	S 0/0	0
10.1.3.0/24	S 0/1	0
10.1.4.0/24	S 0/1	1

Router R3's Routing Table

Network	Interface	Metric
10.1.1.0/24	S 0/0	2
10.1.2.0/24	S 0/0	1
10.1.3.0/24	S 0/0	0
10.1.4.0/24	E 1/0	0

Figure 6-10 Routing Loop: Before Link Failure

Continuing with the example, imagine that interface Ethernet 1/0 on router R3 goes down. As shown in Figure 6-11, router R3 loses its directly connected route (with a metric of 0) to network 10.1.4.0/24. However, router R2 had a route to 10.1.4.0/24 in its routing table (with a metric of 1), and this route was advertised to router R3. Router R3 adds this entry for 10.1.4.0 to its routing table and increments the metric by 1.

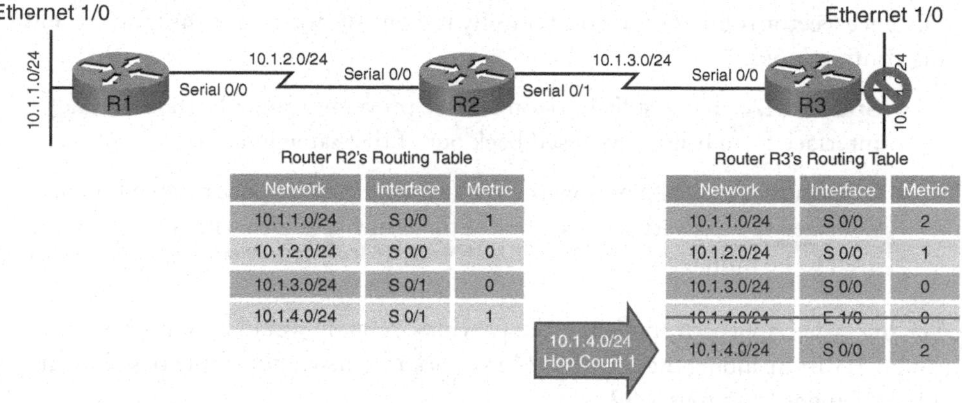

Figure 6-11 Routing Loop: After Link Failure

The problem with this scenario is that the 10.1.4.0/24 entry in router R2's routing table was due to an advertisement router R2 received from router R3. Now, router R3 is relying on that route, which is no longer valid. The routing loop continues as router R3 advertises its newly learned route of 10.1.4.0/24 with a metric of 2 to its neighbor, router R2. Because router R2 originally learned the 10.1.4.0/24 network from router R3, when it sees router R2 advertising that same route with a metric of 2, the network gets updated in router R2's routing table to have a metric of 3, as shown in Figure 6-12.

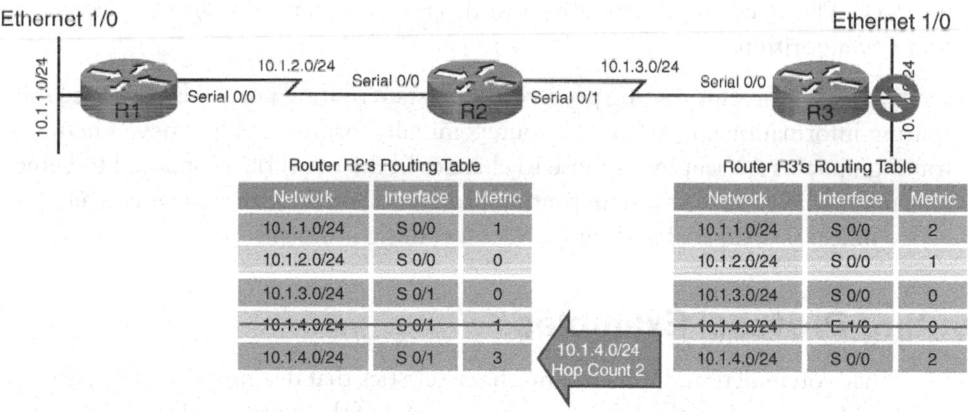

Figure 6-12 Routing Loop: Routers R2 and R3 Incrementing the Metric for 10.1.4.0/24

The metric for the 10.1.4.0/24 network continues to increment in the routing tables for both routers R2 and R3, until the metric reaches a value considered to be an unreachable value (for example, 16 in the case of RIP). This process is referred to as a *routing loop*.

Distance-vector routing protocols typically use one of two approaches for preventing routing loops:

- **Split horizon:** The split-horizon feature prevents a route learned on one interface from being advertised back out of that same interface.
- **Poison reverse:** The poison-reverse feature causes a route received on one interface to be advertised back out of that same interface with a metric considered to be infinite.

Having either approach applied to the previous example would have prevented router R3 from adding the 10.1.4.0/24 network into its routing table based on an advertisement from router R2.

Link State

Rather than having neighboring routers exchange their full routing tables with one another, a *link-state* routing protocol allows routers to build a topological map of the network. Then, similar to a global positioning system (GPS) in a car, a router can execute an algorithm to calculate an optimal path (or paths) to a destination network.

Routers send link-state advertisements (LSAs) to advertise the networks they know how to reach. Routers then use those LSAs to construct the topological map of a network. The algorithm that runs against this topological map is *Dijkstra's shortest path first* algorithm.

Unlike distance-vector routing protocols, link-state routing protocols exchange full routing information only when two routers initially form their adjacency. Then routing updates are sent in response to changes in the network, as opposed to being sent periodically. Also, link-state routing protocols benefit from shorter convergence times, as compared to distance-vector routing protocols.

Routing Protocol Examples

Now that you understand some of the characteristics that distinguish one routing protocol from another, this section contrasts some of the most popular routing protocols found in modern networks:

- **Routing Information Protocol (RIP):** A distance-vector routing protocol that uses a metric of *hop count*. The maximum number of hops between two routers in an RIP-based network is 15. Therefore, a hop count of 16 is considered to be infinite. Also, RIP is an IGP.

- **Open Shortest Path First (OSPF):** A link-state routing protocol that uses a metric of *cost*, which is based on the link speed between two routers. OSPF is a popular IGP because of its scalability, fast convergence, and vendor-interoperability.
- **Intermediate System-to-Intermediate System (IS-IS):** This link-state routing protocol is similar in its operation to OSPF. It uses a configurable, yet dimensionless, metric associated with an interface and runs Dijkstra's shortest path first algorithm. Although IS-IS as an IGP offers the scalability, fast convergence, and vendor-interoperability benefits of OSPF, it has not been as widely deployed as OSPF.
- **Enhanced Interior Gateway Routing Protocol (EIGRP):** EIGRP is a Cisco proprietary protocol. It is popular in Cisco-only networks, but less popular in mixed-vendor environments. Like OSPF, EIGRP is an IGP with fast convergence and is very scalable. EIGRP is more challenging to classify as a distance-vector or a link-state routing protocol.

  By default, EIGRP uses bandwidth and delay in its metric calculation; however, other parameters can be considered. These optional parameters include reliability, load, and maximum transmission unit (MTU) size. Using delay as part of the metric, EIGRP can take into consideration the latency caused from the slowest links in the path.

  Some literature calls EIGRP an *advanced distance-vector* routing protocol, and some literature calls it a *hybrid* routing protocol (mixing characteristics of both distance-vector and link-state routing protocols). EIGRP uses information from its neighbors to help it select an optimal route (like distance-vector routing protocols). However, EIGRP also maintains a database of topological information (like a link-state routing protocol). The algorithm EIGRP uses for its route selection is not Dijkstra's shortest path first algorithm. Instead, EIGRP uses diffusing update algorithm (DUAL).
- **Border Gateway Protocol (BGP):** The only EGP in widespread use today. In fact, BGP is considered to be the routing protocol that runs the Internet, which is an interconnection of multiple autonomous systems. Although some literature classifies BGP as a distance-vector routing protocol, it can more accurately be described as a *path-vector* routing protocol, meaning that it can use as its metric the number of autonomous system hops that must be transited to reach a destination network, as opposed to a number of required router hops. BGP's path selection is not solely based on autonomous system hops, however. BGP has a variety of other parameters that it can consider. Interestingly, none of those parameters are based on link speed. In addition, although BGP is incredibly scalable, it does not quickly converge in the event of a topological change.

A network can simultaneously support more than one routing protocol through the process of *route redistribution*. For example, a router could have one of its interfaces participating in an OSPF area of the network and have another interface participating in an EIGRP area of the network. This router could then take routes learned via OSPF and inject those routes into the EIGRP routing process. Similarly, EIGRP-learned routes could be redistributed into the OSPF routing process.

Address Translation

As described in Chapter 5, some IP addresses are routable through the public Internet, and other IP addresses are considered private and are intended for use within an organization. Network Address Translation (NAT) allows private IP addresses (as defined in RFC 1918) to be translated into Internet-routable IP addresses (public IP addresses). This section examines the operation of basic NAT and a variant called *Port Address Translation* (PAT). Address translation can also be done for specific ports associated with an IP address. When this is done, it's often referred to as *port forwarding*.

NAT

Consider Figure 6-13, which shows a basic NAT topology. Note that, even though the IP networks of 172.16.1.0/24 and 192.168.1.0/24 are actually private IP networks, for this discussion, assume that they are publicly routable IP addresses. The reason for the use of these private IP addresses to represent public IP addresses is to avoid using an entity's registered IP addresses in the example.

Key Topic

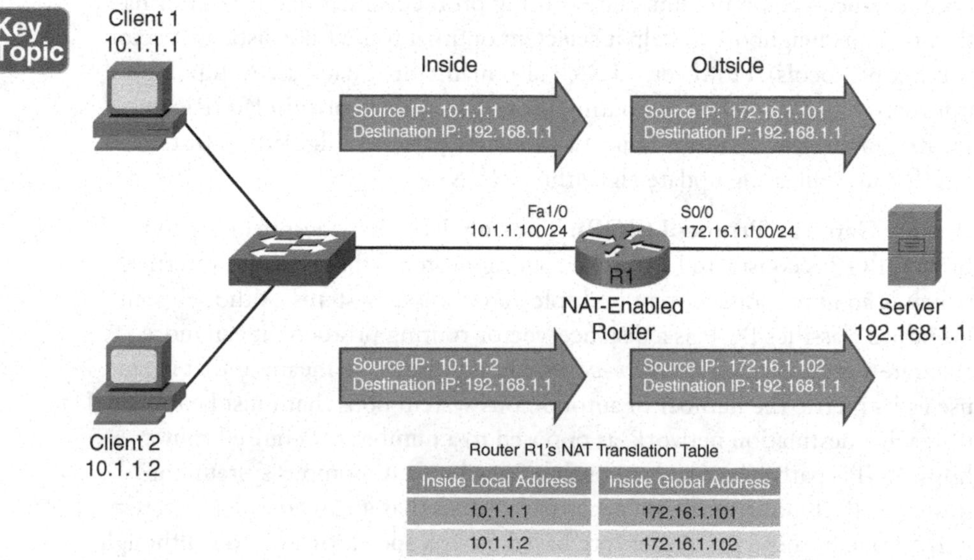

Figure 6-13 Basic NAT Topology

In Figure 6-13's topology, two clients with private IP addresses of 10.1.1.1 and 10.1.1.2 want to communicate with a web server on the public Internet. The server's IP address is 192.168.1.1. Router R1 is configured for NAT. As an example, router R1 takes packets coming from 10.1.1.1 destined for 192.168.1.1 and changes the source IP address in the packets' headers to 172.16.1.101 (which we assume is a publicly routable IP address for the purposes of this discussion). When the server at IP address 192.168.1.1 receives traffic from the client, the server's return traffic is sent to a destination address of 172.16.1.101. When router R1 receives traffic from the outside network destined for 172.16.1.101, the router translates the destination IP address to 10.1.1.1 and forwards the traffic to the inside network, where client 1 receives the traffic. Similarly, client 2's IP address of 10.1.1.2 is translated into an IP address of 172.16.1.102.

Table 6-2 introduces the terminology used when describing the various IP addresses involved in a translation.

Table 6-2 Names of NAT IP Addresses

NAT IP Address	Definition
Inside local	A private IP address referencing an inside device
Inside global	A public IP address referencing an inside device
Outside local	A private IP address referencing an outside device
Outside global	A public IP address referencing an outside device

As a memory aid, remember that *inside* always refers to an inside device (source), and *outside* always refers to an outside device (destination). Also, think of the word *local* being similar to the Spanish word *loco*, meaning crazy. That is what a local address could be thought of. It is a crazy, made-up address (a private IP address that is not routable on the Internet). Finally, let the *g* in *global* remind you of the *g* in *good*, because a global address is a good (routable on the Internet) IP address.

Based on these definitions, Table 6-3 categorizes the IP addresses previously shown in Figure 6-13.

Table 6-3 Classifying the NAT IP Addresses in Figure 6-13

NAT IP Address	NAT IP Address Type
Inside local	10.1.1.1
Inside local	10.1.1.2
Inside global	172.16.1.101

NAT IP Address	NAT IP Address Type
Inside global	172.16.1.102
Outside local	None
Outside global	192.168.1.1

NAT does not always have to be between private and public addresses. For example, NAT could be implemented between two private address ranges or two public address ranges as well.

Whether an inside local address is randomly assigned an inside global address from a pool of available addresses or is assigned an address from a static configuration determines the type of NAT you are using. These two approaches to NAT are called *DNAT* and *SNAT*:

- **DNAT:** In the preceding example, the inside local addresses were automatically assigned an inside global address from a pool of available public addresses. This approach to NAT is referred to as Dynamic NAT (DNAT). This is often referred to as "many-to-many," as many inside local users (a network) are mapped to a pool of inside global addresses.
- **SNAT:** Sometimes, you want to statically configure the inside global address assigned to a specific device inside your network. For example, you might have an email server inside your company, and you want other email servers on the Internet to send email messages to your server. Those email servers on the Internet need to point to a specific IP address, not one that was randomly picked from a pool of available IP addresses. In such a case, you can statically configure the mapping of an inside local address (the IP address of your internal email server) to an inside global address (the IP address to which email servers on the Internet will send email for your company). This approach to NAT is referred to as Static NAT (SNAT). This is often called a "one-to-one" mapping.

PAT

A challenge with basic NAT, however, is that there is a one-to-one mapping of inside local addresses to inside global addresses, meaning that a company would need as many publicly routable IP addresses as it had internal devices needing IP addresses. This does not scale well because, often, a service provider will provide a customer with only a single IP address or a small block of IP addresses.

Fortunately, many routers support Port Address Translation (PAT), which allows multiple inside local addresses to share a single inside global address (a single publicly routable IP address). For this reason PAT is referred to as "many-to-one." In Chapter 2, "The OSI Reference Model," you learned about how IP communications rely on port numbers. As a review, when a client sends an IP packet, not only does that packet have a source and destination IP address, it has a source and destination port number. PAT leverages these port numbers to track separate communication flows.

For instance, consider Figure 6-14. Unlike the example shown in Figure 6-13, in which each inside local address was translated to its own inside global address, the example shown in Figure 6-14 has only one inside global address. This single inside global address is shared among all the devices inside a network. The different communication flows are kept separate in router R1's NAT translation table by considering port numbers.

Key Topic

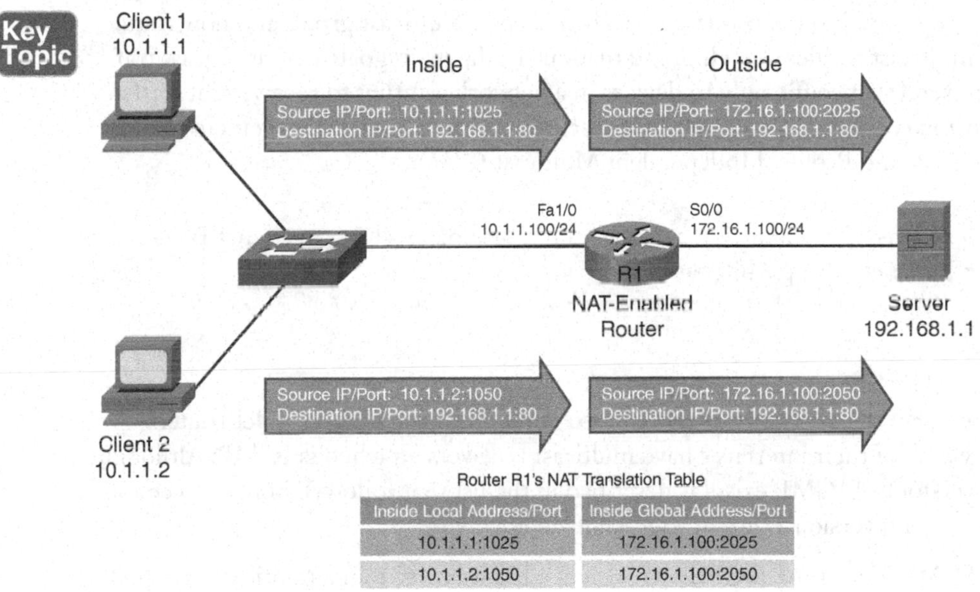

Inside Local Address/Port	Inside Global Address/Port
10.1.1.1:1025	172.16.1.100:2025
10.1.1.2:1050	172.16.1.100:2050

Figure 6-14 PAT Topology

When client 1 sends a packet to the web server (with an IP address of 192.168.1.1), the client's ephemeral port number (its source port selected, which is greater than 1023) is 1025. Router R1 notes that port number and translates the inside local address of 10.1.1.1 with a port number of 1025 to an inside global address of 172.16.1.100 with a port number of 2025. When client 2 sends a packet to the same web server, its inside local address of 10.1.1.2 with a port number of 1050 is translated into an inside global address of 172.16.1.100 with a port number of 2050.

Notice that both client 1 and client 2 had their inside local addresses translated into the same inside global address of 172.16.1.100. Therefore, when the web server sends packets back to client 1 and client 2, those packets are destined for the same IP address (172.16.1.100). However, when router R1 receives those packets, it knows to which client each packet should be forwarded based on the destination port number. For example, if a packet from the web server (192.168.1.1) arrived at router R1 with a destination IP address of 172.16.1.100 and a destination port number of 2050, router R1 would translate the destination IP address to 10.1.1.2 with a port number of 1050, which would be forwarded to client 2.

Multicast Routing

Chapter 5 introduced the concept of multicast transmission, where a multicast sender could send traffic destined for a Class D IP address, known as a *multicast group*, and devices on a network wanting to receive that transmission could join that multicast group. Now consider how a client joins a multicast group and how routers route multicast traffic. Keep in mind that one of the main goals with multicast traffic is to send that traffic only to devices in a network wanting to receive that traffic. Two primary protocols used for multicast are Internet Group Management Protocol (IGMP) and Protocol Independent Multicast (PIM).

NOTE A surprising amount of networking literature incorrectly states that IGMP stands for Internet Group Multicast Protocol.

IGMP

The protocol used between clients (for example, PCs) and routers to let routers know which of their interfaces have multicast receivers attached is IGMP. Although three versions of IGMP exist (as described in the list that follows), only two versions (version 1 and version 2) are in wide-scale deployment:

- **IGMP Version 1 (IGMPv1):** When a PC wants to join a multicast group, it sends an IGMP report message to its router, letting the router know it wants to receive traffic for a specific group. Every 60 seconds, by default, the router sends an IGMP query message to determine if the PC still wants to belong to the group. There can be up to a 3-minute delay before a router realizes the receiver left the group. The destination address of this router query is 224.0.0.1, which addresses all IP multicast hosts.
- **IGMP Version 2 (IGMPv2):** Similar to IGMPv1, except IGMP version 2 can send queries to a specific group and support a *leave* message. Specifically, a receiver can proactively send a leave message when it no longer wants to participate in a multicast group, allowing the router to prune its interface earlier than it would have with IGMPv1.

- **IGMP Version 3 (IGMPv3):** Adds a feature called *source-specific multicast* (SSM), which allows a client to request traffic not only destined for a particular multicast group but also sourced from a specific server. For example, you could have multiple video servers streaming different video streams, all destined for the same multicast group. However, when a client joins that group, with SSM (as supported by IGMPv3), that client could request that it only receive traffic sourced from a specific server. This would provide support for multiple multicast sessions while consuming only one Class D IP address.

Consider Figure 6-15, which shows a basic multicast topology. Of the three PCs on the network, only PC2 wants to receive the multicast traffic. How do the switch and router know to only forward traffic out ports leading to PC2 (the multicast receiver)?

Key Topic

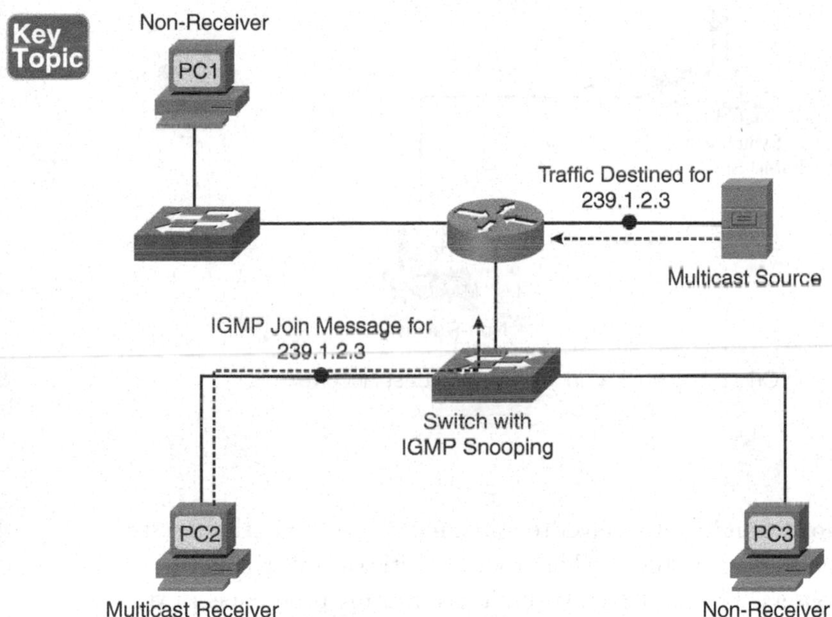

Figure 6-15 Multicast Receiver Joining a Multicast Group

PC2 indicates it wants to belong to the multicast group of 239.1.2.3 by sending an IGMP join message to its default gateway. The switch through which the IGMP join message passes is enabled with the *IGMP snooping* feature, which allows the switch to eavesdrop on the IGMP join message and determine the multicast group that PC2 wants to join. Then, in the future, when the switch receives traffic from the router destined for 239.1.2.3, the switch will only forward those packets out the port connected to PC2.

When the router receives the IGMP join message from PC2, it knows that it should only forward traffic destined for 239.1.2.3 out the interface on which a IGMP join message was received. As a result, when the multicast source sends a stream of traffic, that traffic is only forwarded out the router port and the switch port leading to PC2, as shown in Figure 6-16.

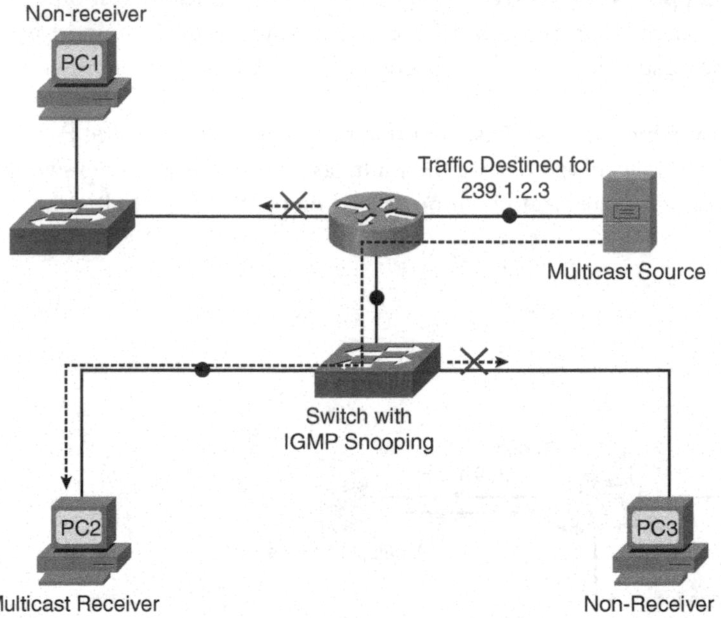

Figure 6-16 Multicast Traffic Only Being Forwarded to the Multicast Receiver

PIM

Although IGMP allows a multicast receiver to join a multicast group, there is still a need for a multicast routing protocol, which routes multicast traffic between multicast-enabled routers. The most popular multicast routing protocol is PIM. PIM's main purpose is to form a *multicast distribution tree*, which is the path (or paths) over which multicast traffic flows. PIM has two modes of operation: PIM dense mode (PIM-DM) and PIM sparse mode (PIM-SM).

PIM-DM

PIM-DM uses a *source distribution tree*, meaning that an optimal path is formed between the source router in a multicast network (that is, the router closest to the multicast sender) and each last-hop router (the router closest to each multicast receiver). However, before this optimal source distribution tree is formed, traffic from the multicast source is initially flooded throughout the entire network, as shown in Figure 6-17.

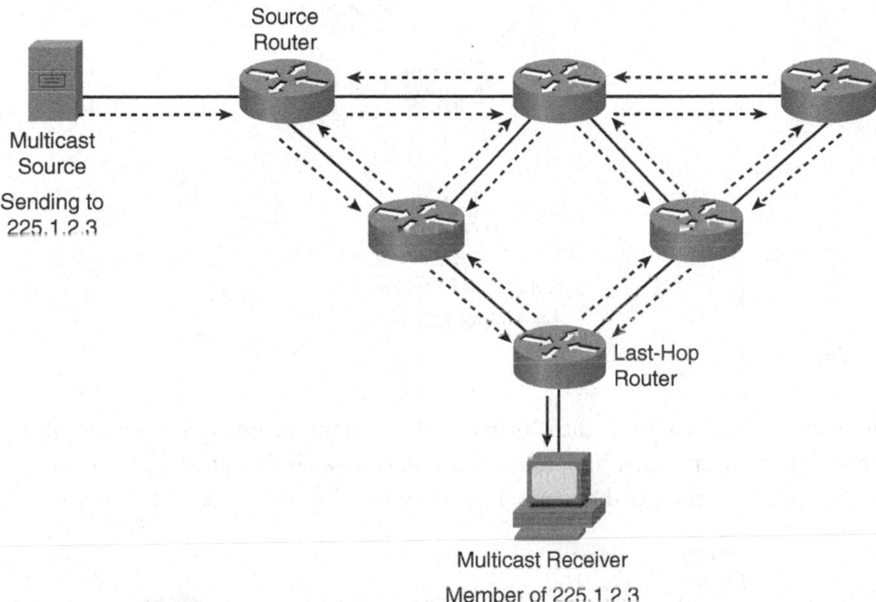

Figure 6-17 PIM-DM Flooding

Obviously, this initial flooding of multicast traffic causes traffic to be sent to routers not needing the multicast traffic, and it can unnecessarily consume bandwidth on the links between routers. After this initial flooding occurs, if a router interface receives the multicast traffic, and that traffic is not needed by the router (or if the traffic is needed by the router, but on a different interface), the router interface sends a *prune* message to its neighboring router, asking that it be pruned off of the source distribution tree, as shown in Figure 6-18.

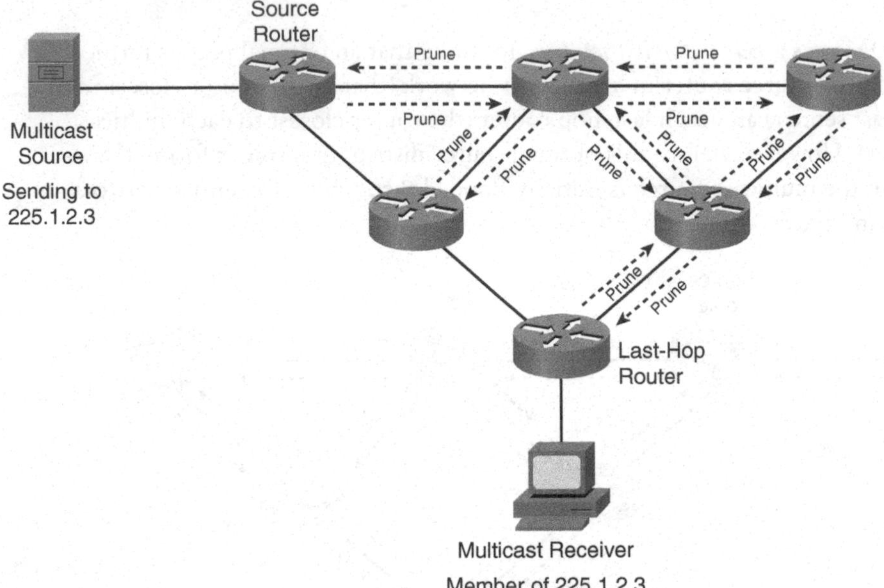

Figure 6-18 PIM-DM Pruning

After the router interface sends these prune messages, the resulting source distribution tree (the path over which the multicast packets flow) is an optimal path between the source router and the last-hop router, as shown in Figure 6-19.

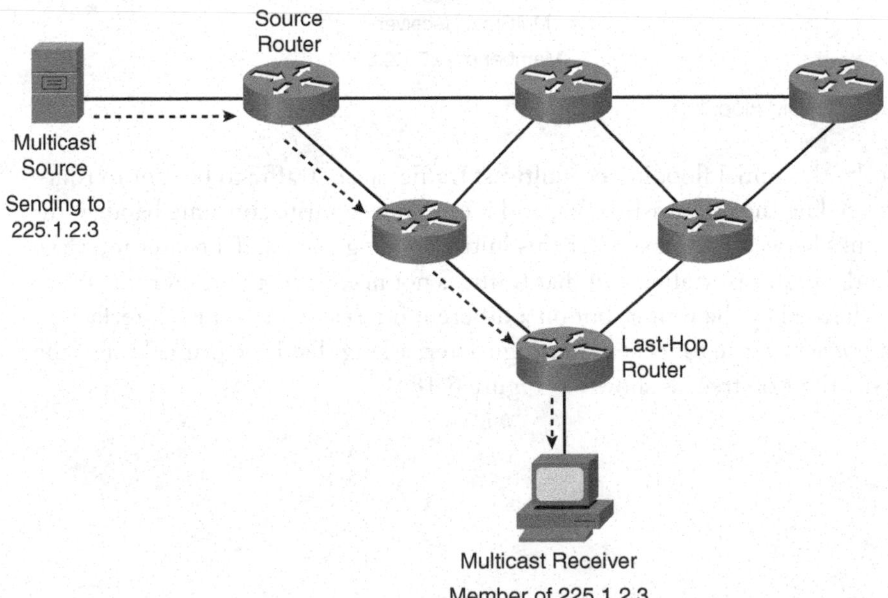

Figure 6-19 PIM-DM Source Distribution Tree After Pruning

A benefit of PIM-DM is that an optimal path is formed between the source router and each last-hop router. However, the drawback of PIM-DM is that a network must undergo the *flood-and-prune behavior*, as previously described, to form the optimal distribution tree. In addition, even after the optimal distribution tree is formed, the flooding and pruning repeat every 3 minutes. Such a periodic flooding of traffic might cause a significant performance impact on a network.

PIM-SM

PIM-SM uses a shared distribution tree. A shared distribution tree does not initially form an optimal path between a source router and each last-hop router. Instead, a multicast source sends traffic directly to another router, called a *rendezvous point* (RP). When another router in the multicast network wants to join the multicast distribution tree (because it received an IGMP join message from a client), that last-hop router sends a join message to the RP to join the shared distribution tree, as shown in Figure 6-20. The tree is called a *shared distribution tree* because all last-hop routers (routers with downstream multicast receivers) send join messages to the same RP.

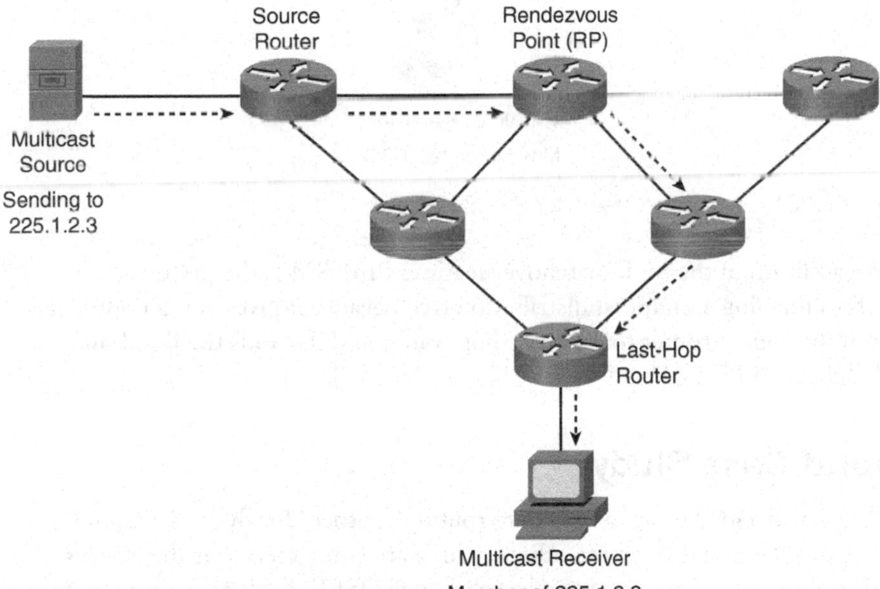

Figure 6-20 PIM-SM Shared Distribution Tree

The benefit of PIM-SM is that the flood-and-prune behavior of PIM-DM is avoided. However, by inspecting Figure 6-20, you might conclude that a drawback of PIM-SM is that a suboptimal distribution tree might be formed. Although that is initially true, after a last-hop router receives the first multicast packet from the multicast source, it can see the IP address of the multicast source. Then, based on its unicast routing table, a last-hop router can form an optimal distribution tree and then prune off the branch of the tree connecting it to the RP. This behavior is called *shortest path tree* (SPT) *switchover*. Figure 6-21 shows the resulting distribution tree.

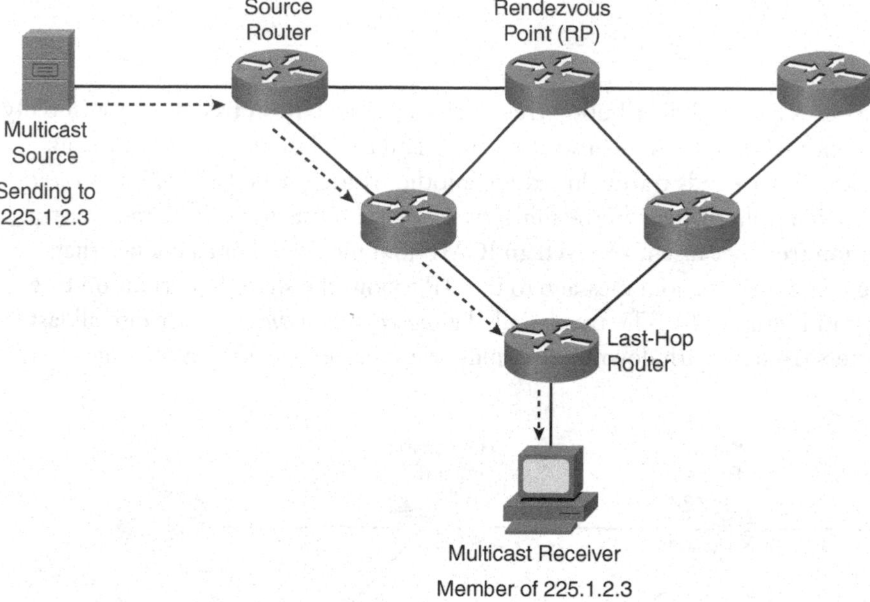

Figure 6-21 PIM-SM Distribution Tree After SPT Switchover

With the addition of the SPT switchover feature, PIM-SM is the preferred approach to forming a multicast distribution tree because it gives you an optimal path from the source router to each last-hop router and it avoids the flood-and-prune behavior of PIM-DM.

Real-World Case Study

Acme, Inc. has decided to use a link-state routing protocol for dynamic routing between its LANs and the remote offices, which are connected over the WANs. The link-state protocol the company has chosen is OSPF. Each of the routers that has connections to the LAN and WAN subnets will learn about and advertise OSPF routes with its OSPF neighbors.

The branch offices will have a default route that points toward the headquarters' routers, and at the headquarters' site, they will use a default route that points toward the service provider. Acme, Inc. itself will not be using BGP, but its WAN and Internet service provider, which is interacting with other service providers, will use BGP.

IP packets from Acme's LAN, which are using private IP addresses, will have a DNAT translation performed as those packets are routed out to the Internet through the service provider's network. The globally routed addresses used for DNAT are provided to Acme from the ISP. Traffic between the headquarters' office and the remote branch offices will be routed normally, without NAT being added for the intracompany connections.

Acme may use multicast routing internally for video streams that deliver a morning status report from Acme's president on a daily basis. By using multicast, the server can send out one stream of data, and the multicast-enabled network can deliver the multicast content to employees who have requested and joined that multicast group and have the software running on their computers or mobile devices to enable them to see it.

Summary

Here are the main topics covered in this chapter:

- This chapter discussed how routers forward traffic through a network based on source and destination IP addresses.
- The sources of route information used to populate a router's routing table were also covered. These sources include directly connected routes, statically configured routes, and dynamically learned routes.
- This chapter distinguished between routed protocols (for example, IP) and routing protocols (such as OSPF or EIGRP).
- Some routing sources are more trustworthy than other routing sources, based on their administrative distances.
- Different routing protocols use different metrics to select the best route in the presence of multiple routes.
- This chapter distinguished between IGPs (which run within an autonomous system) and EGPs (which run between autonomous systems).
- The behavior of distance-vector and link-state routing protocols was contrasted, and you saw how spilt horizon and poison reverse could prevent a routing loop in a distance-vector routing protocol environment.
- Today's most popular routing protocols (including RIP, OSPF, IS-IS, EIGRP, and BGP) were presented, along with their characteristics.

- NAT can be used to translate private IP addresses inside a network to publicly routable IP addresses. Additionally, this chapter contrasted variations of NAT: PAT, SNAT, and DNAT.
- This chapter discussed the IGMP and PIM protocols used in multicast networks. These protocols work together to allow a network to forward only multicast traffic over links needing that traffic.

Exam Preparation Tasks

Review All the Key Topics

Review the most important topics from inside the chapter, noted with the Key Topic icon in the outer margin of the page. Table 6-4 lists these key topics and the page numbers where each is found.

Table 6-4 Key Topics for Chapter 6

Key Topic Element	Description	Page Number
Step list	Basic routing processes	206
Table 6-1	Administrative distance	214
Figure 6-9	IGPs versus EGPs	215
List	Approaches for preventing routing loops	218
List	Routing protocol examples	218
Figure 6-13	Basic NAT topology	220
Table 6-2	Names of NAT IP addresses	221
List	NAT variations	222
Figure 6-14	PAT topology	223
Figure 6-15	Multicast receiver joining a multicast group	225

Complete Tables and Lists from Memory

Print a copy of Appendix C, "Memory Tables," or at least the section for this chapter, and complete as many of the tables as possible from memory. Appendix D, "Memory Tables Answer Key," includes the completed tables and lists so you can check your work.

Define Key Terms

Define the following key terms from this chapter, and check your answers in the Glossary:

ARP, TTL, default static route, next-hop, routed protocol, routing protocol, administrative distance, metric, IGP, EGP, distance-vector, link-state, hold-down timer, split horizon, poison reverse, LSA, RIP, OSPF, IS-IS, EIGRP, BGP, route redistribution, NAT, DNAT, SNAT, PAT, IGMP, PIM

Additional Resources

Inter-VLAN Routing on a Cisco Router: http://www.ajsnetworking.com/inter-vlan

EIGRP's Composite Metric: http://www.ajsnetworking.com/eigrp-metric

Review Questions

The answers to these review questions appear in Appendix A, "Answers to Review Questions."

1. If a PC on an Ethernet network attempts to communicate with a host on a different subnet, what destination IP address and destination MAC address will be placed in the packet/frame header sent by the PC?

- **a. Dest. IP:** IP address of default gateway. **Dest. MAC:** MAC address of default gateway.
- **b. Dest. IP:** IP address of remote host. **Dest. MAC:** MAC address of default gateway.
- **c. Dest. IP:** IP address of remote host. **Dest. MAC:** MAC address of remote host.
- **d. Dest. IP:** IP address of remote host. **Dest. MAC:** MAC address of local PC.

2. What protocol is used to request a MAC address that corresponds to a known IPv4 address on the local network?

- **a.** IGMP
- **b.** TTL
- **c.** ICMP
- **d.** ARP

3. What is the network address and subnet mask of a default route?

- **a.** 255.255.255.255/32
- **b.** 0.0.0.0/32
- **c.** 255.255.255.255/0
- **d.** 0.0.0.0/0

4. What routing protocol characteristic indicates the believability of the routing protocol (as opposed to other routing protocols)?

- **a.** Weight
- **b.** Metric
- **c.** Administrative distance
- **d.** SPF algorithm

5. Which of the following are distance-vector routing protocol features that can prevent routing loops? (Choose two.)
   a. Reverse path forwarding (RPF) check
   b. Split horizon
   c. Poison reverse
   d. Rendezvous point

6. Which of the following is a distance-vector routing protocol with a maximum usable hop count of 15?
   a. BGP
   b. IS-IS
   c. RIP
   d. OSPF

7. Which of the following routing protocols is an EGP?
   a. BGP
   b. IS-IS
   c. RIP
   d. OSPF

8. What NAT IP address is a public IP address that maps to an inside device?
   a. Inside local
   b. Inside global
   c. Outside local
   d. Outside global

9. What NAT variation automatically assigns an inside global address from a pool of available addresses?
   a. SNAT
   b. DNAT
   c. PAT
   d. GNAT

10. What multicast protocol is used between clients and routers to let routers know which of their interfaces are connected to a multicast receiver?
    a. IGMP
    b. PIM-DM
    c. PIM-SM
    d. SPT switchover

After completion of this chapter, you will be able to answer the following questions:

- What are three categories of wide area network (WAN) connections?
- How are data rates measured on various WAN technologies?
- Which types of media (or wireless technologies) might you use in WAN connections?
- What are the characteristics of the following WAN technologies? Dedicated leased line, digital subscriber line (DSL), cable modem, Synchronous Optical Network (SONET), satellite, plain old telephone service (POTS), Integrated Services Digital Network (ISDN), Frame Relay, Asynchronous Transfer Mode (ATM), and Multiprotocol Label Switching (MPLS)

Wide Area Networks (WANs)

The *Pareto principle* states that 80% of the effects come from 20% of the causes. In the early 1990s, computer-networking design guides invoked the Pareto principle and said that 80% of your network traffic stays local, while only 20% of your network traffic leaves the local network. This was an information technology (IT) extrapolation of Vilfredo Pareto's *80-20 rule*. With the advent of Internet browsers, cloud storage, and streaming audio and video, today's network traffic patterns are more closely approximated with a 20-80 rule, meaning that the clear majority of network traffic leaves the local network over a wide area network (WAN) connection.

As defined in Chapter 1, "Computer Network Fundamentals," a WAN is a network that spans large geographical distances. This chapter discusses the properties of WAN connections, followed by a survey of common WAN technologies.

Foundation Topics

WAN Properties

To select the right WAN technology for a network you are designing or to better understand a WAN technology in a currently installed network, you need the ability to compare one WAN technology to another. This section shows a collection of WAN connection properties that can be used to contrast various WAN technologies.

WAN Connection Types

Some WAN connections are considered to be *always on*, in that the connection is always available without having to first set up the connection. Conversely, some WAN technologies are *on demand*, meaning that the connection is not established until needed. Then, when the connection is needed, it is brought up.

Another distinguishing characteristic of WAN connections is whether multiple users share bandwidth. For example, some WAN connections offer dedicated bandwidth to a service provider's customer, while other WAN connections allow multiple customers of a service provider to share a common pool of available bandwidth.

A WAN connection can be classified into one of three categories:

- **Dedicated leased line:** A connection interconnecting two sites. This logical connection might physically connect through a service provider's facility or a telephone company's central office (CO). The expense of a dedicated leased line is typically higher than other WAN technologies offering similar data rates because with a dedicated leased line, a customer does not have to share bandwidth with other customers.

  As discussed in the section "WAN Technologies," a T1 circuit, as shown in Figure 7-1, is an example of a dedicated leased line technology found in North America. A common Layer 2 protocol that could run over a dedicated leased line is Point-to-Point Protocol (PPP), which is discussed later in this chapter.

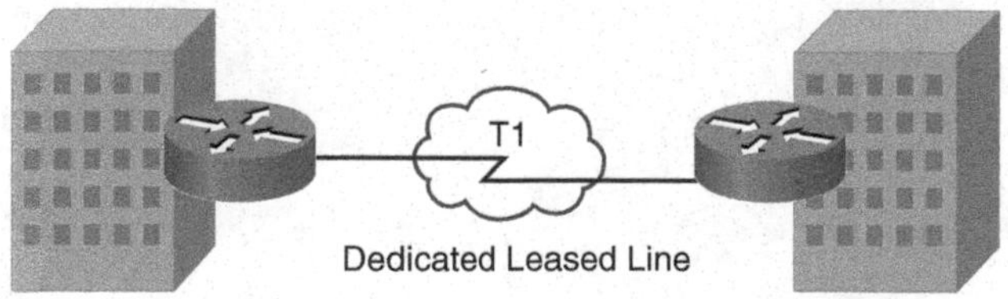

Figure 7-1 Dedicated Leased Line Sample Topology

- **Circuit-switched connection:** A connection that is brought up on an as-needed basis. In fact, a circuit-switched connection is analogous to a phone call, where you pick up your phone, dial a number, and a connection is established based on the number you dial. As discussed later in this chapter, Integrated Services Digital Network (ISDN) can operate as a circuit-switched connection, bringing up a virtual circuit (VC) on demand. This approach to on-demand bandwidth can be a cost savings for some customers who only need periodic connectivity to a remote site. Figure 7-2 illustrates a circuit-switched connection.

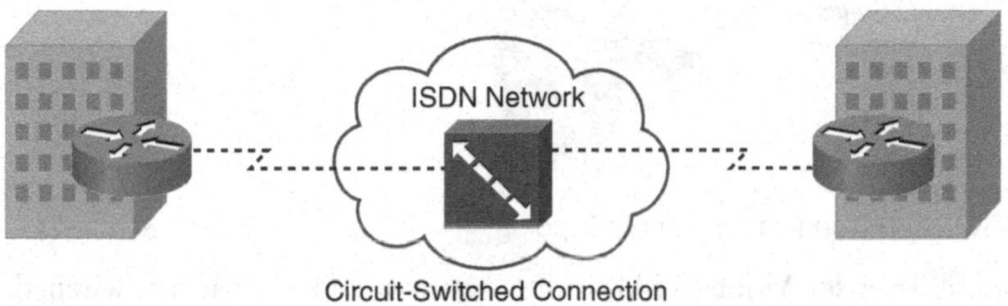

Figure 7-2 Circuit-Switched Connection Sample Topology

- **Packet-switched connection:** Like a dedicated leased line, because most packet-switched networks are always on. However, unlike a dedicated leased line, packet-switched connections allow multiple customers to share a service provider's bandwidth.

  Even though bandwidth is being shared among customers, customers can buy a service-level agreement (SLA), which specifies performance metrics (for example, available bandwidth and maximum delay) guaranteed for a certain percentage of time. For example, an SLA might guarantee customers that they have a minimum of 5Mbps of bandwidth available 80% of the time.

  Frame Relay, which is discussed in the section "WAN Technologies," is an example of a packet-switched connection. As shown in Figure 7-3, a Frame Relay network allows multiple customers to connect to a service provider's network, and virtual circuits (VCs, shown as dashed lines) logically interconnect customer sites.

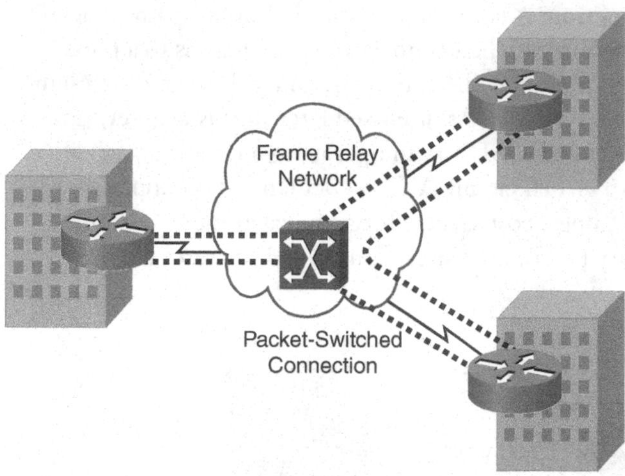

Figure 7-3 Packet-Switched Connection Sample Topology

Asynchronous Transfer Mode (ATM) is often categorized as a packet-switched connection. However, to be technically correct, ATM is a cell-switched connection because ATM uses fixed-length (53-byte) cells, as opposed to variable-length frames.

> **NOTE** These connection types are meant to be general categories, and not all WAN technologies will meet the previous definitions. For example, digital subscriber line (DSL) is a technology that could be configured for on-demand access (like a circuit-switched connection), or it could be configured for always-on access. Also, DSL typically provides a customer with an amount of bandwidth that the customer does not have to share with other customers (like a dedicated leased line). However, DSL uses ATM technologies to connect back to the service provider's equipment (like a cell-switched connection). So, use these three categories of WAN connection types as general guidelines, not strict definitions.

WAN Data Rates

LAN links are typically faster than WAN links; however, some WAN technologies, such as Synchronous Optical Network (SONET), boast a bandwidth capacity in the tens of gigabits per second (Gbps). One could argue that some of these higher-speed WAN technologies are metropolitan area network (MAN) technologies. However, this chapter considers a WAN to be an interconnection of geographically dispersed networks that also encompass MAN technologies.

Aside from measuring bandwidth in kilobits per second (Kbps), megabits per second (Mbps), or gigabits per second (Gbps), high-speed optical networks often use optical carrier (OC) levels to indicate bandwidth. As a base reference point, the speed of an OC-1 link is 51.84Mbps. Other OC levels are simply multiples of an OC-1. For example, an OC-3 link has three times the bandwidth of an OC-1 link (that is, 3 * 51.84Mbps = 155.52Mbps).

Here are some OC level examples:

- OC-1 51.48Mbps
- OC-3 155.52Mbps
- OC-12 622.08Mbps
- OC-48 2.4Gbps
- OC-192 9.6Gbps

Although a variety of speeds are available from different service providers, Table 7-1 offers typical bandwidths of several common WAN technologies.

Table 7-1 Typical WAN Data Rates

WAN Technology	Typical Available Bandwidth
Frame Relay	56Kbps to 1.544Mbps
T1	1.544Mbps
T3	44.736Mbps
E1	2.048Mbps
E3	34.4Mbps
ATM	155Mbps to 622Mbps
SONET	51.84Mbps (OC-1) to 159.25Gbps (OC-3072)

WAN Media Types

WAN links might be physical hard-wired links (for example, copper or fiber-optic cable running from your site back to your service provider's site and then to the remote site with which your site communicates). Alternatively, some WAN links are wireless. These wireless solutions might be right for locations where more conventional WAN technologies are unavailable or for accommodating the needs of mobile users.

Physical Media

The physical media used for WAN connections is like the physical media found in LAN connections:

- **Unshielded twisted pair (UTP):** Both analog and digital circuits coming into your location from a local telephone central office use UTP cabling. This cabling might be Category 3 (Cat 3) cabling, as opposed to higher categories used in LANs. Examples of WAN technologies using UTP cabling include T1 circuits, DSL connections, dial-up analog modems, and ISDN circuits.

- **Coaxial cable:** A common residential WAN solution (primarily for connecting out to the Internet) is a cable modem. As the name suggests, a cable modem uses a coaxial cable (for example, an RG-6 coaxial cable) for transmission. In fact, the same coaxial cable providing a variety of television programming for your home might also be used to carry data (upstream and downstream) using specific frequency ranges.
- **Fiber-optic cable:** WAN connections needing a high-bandwidth capacity or needing to span a large distance might use fiber-optic cabling. Another benefit of fiber-optic cabling is its immunity from electromagnetic interference (EMI).
- **Electric power lines:** With such an expansive existing infrastructure, electric power lines can be attractive candidates to offer broadband Internet access to residential locations. This is made possible with broadband over power lines (BPL) technology. Although implementations vary widely, bandwidth offered to an end user typically maxes out at approximately 2.7Mbps.

Although the physical media on a WAN closely resembles LAN media, keep in mind that the Layer 2 protocols running over the media are usually different for WAN links than they are for LAN links.

Wireless Media

Wireless media adds flexibility to WAN connections and often reduces cost. Here are some examples of wireless media:

- **Cellular phone:** Some cellular phone technologies, such as Long-Term Evolution (LTE), which supports a 100Mbps data rate to mobile devices and a 1Gbps data rate for stationary devices, can be used to connect a mobile device such as a smartphone to the Internet. Other technologies for cellular phones include the older 2G edge, which offers slow data rates. 2G edge was improved upon with 3G, in addition to the newer 4G, LTE, and Evolved High-Speed Packet Access (HSPA+). The term *tethering* is used with today's smartphones. Tethering allows a smartphone's data connection to be used by another device, such as a laptop. Also, mobile hotspots are growing in popularity because these devices connect to a cell phone company's data network and make that data network available to nearby devices (typically, a maximum of five devices) via wireless networking technologies. This, for example, allows multiple passengers in a car to share a mobile hotspot and have Internet connectivity from their laptops when riding down the road. Code Division Multiple Access (CDMA) and Global System for Mobiles (GSM) are the two major radio systems used in cell phones. GSM uses Time Division Multiple Access (TDMA) in its operation.

NOTE The term *Internet connection sharing* (ICS) is sometimes used interchangeably with the term *tethering*. However, be aware that ICS is a Microsoft Windows solution, allowing a Microsoft Windows–based computer with an Internet connection (possibly via an internal cellular data card) to share its connection with other devices.

- **Satellite:** Some locations do not have WAN connectivity options, such as DSL connections or cable modems, available in urban areas. However, these locations might be able to connect to the Internet or to a remote office using satellite communications, where a transmission is bounced off a satellite, received by a satellite ground station, and then sent to its destination using either another satellite hop or a wired WAN connection.
- **WiMAX:** Worldwide Interoperability for Microwave Access (WiMAX) offers wireless broadband access to fixed locations (as an alternative to technologies such as DSL) and mobile devices. Depending on the WiMAX service provider, WiMAX coverage areas could encompass entire cities or small countries.
- **HSPA+:** Like WiMAX, Evolved High-Speed Packet Access (HSPA+) is a technology offering wireless broadband service. The maximum data rate for HSPA+ is 84Mbps.
- **Radio:** The range of frequencies (measured in Hertz [Hz], which represents the number of cycles of a waveform per second) typically considered to be in the radio frequency spectrum includes frequencies of 3KHz through 300GHz. Different countries have their own standards bodies that dictate which frequency ranges can be used for what purposes. For example, in the United States, the Federal Communications Commission (FCC) regulates the use of frequencies in the radio frequency spectrum. Therefore, while multiple radio-based WAN solutions exist, their implementation might vary by country.

A couple of potential downsides of wireless WAN media include experiencing increased delay and higher packet error rates, as compared with physical links.

WAN Technologies

The previous section presented a collection of WAN connection properties. Understanding these properties can now help you better understand the collection of WAN technologies presented in this section.

Dedicated Leased Line

A dedicated leased line is typically a *point-to-point* connection interconnecting two sites. All the bandwidth on that dedicated leased line is available to those sites. This means that, unlike a packet-switched connection, the bandwidth of a dedicated leased line connection does not need to be shared among multiple service provider customers.

WAN technologies used with dedicated leased lines include digital circuits, such as T1, E1, T3, and E3. These circuits can use multiplexing technology to simultaneously carry multiple conversations in different 64Kbps channels. A single 64Kbps channel is called a *Digital Signal 0* (DS0).

When one of these circuits comes into your location, it terminates on a device called a channel service unit/data service unit (CSU/DSU). Also, be aware that a common Layer 2 protocol used on dedicated leased lines is Point-to-Point Protocol (PPP). A common connection type used to connect to a CSU/DSU is an RJ-48C, which looks like an RJ-45(Ethernet) connector.

NOTE A less common protocol used on dedicated leased lines (as compared to PPP) is High-Level Data Link Control (HDLC). HDLC lacks many of the features of PPP, and in its standards-based implementation, it can only support a single Layer 3 protocol on a circuit. However, Cisco has its own HDLC implementation in which the HDLC header has a protocol field, thus allowing the simultaneous transmission of multiple Layer 3 protocols.

T1

T1 circuits were originally used in telephony networks, with the intent of one voice conversation being carried in a single channel (that is, a single DS0). A T1 circuit is composed of 24 DS0s, which is called a *Digital Signal 1* (DS1). The bandwidth of a T1 circuit is 1.544Mbps:

- The size of a T1 frame = 193 bits (that is, 24 channels * 8 bits per channel + 1 framing bit = 193 bits).
- The *Nyquist theorem* needs 8,000 samples to be sent per second for a voice conversation (that is, a rate at least twice the highest frequency of 4,000Hz).
- Total bandwidth = 193-bit frames * 8,000 samples per second = 1.544Mbps.

In a T1 environment, more than one frame is sent at once. Here are two popular approaches to grouping these frames:

- **Super Frame (SF):** Combines 12 standard 193-bit frames into a *super frame*
- **Extended Super Frame (ESF):** Combines 24 standard 193-bit frames into an *extended super frame*

T1 circuits are popular in North America and Japan.

E1

An E1 circuit contains 32 channels, in contrast to the 24 channels on a T1 circuit. Only 30 of those 32 channels, however, can transmit data (or voice or video). Specifically, the first of those 32 channels is reserved for framing and synchronization, and the seventeenth channel is reserved for signaling (that is, setting up, maintaining, and tearing down a call).

Because an E1 circuit has more DS0s than a T1, it has a higher bandwidth capacity. Specifically, an E1 has a bandwidth capacity of 2.048Mbps (8,000 samples per second, as required by the Nyquist theorem 8 bits per sample * 32 channels = 2,048,000 bits per second).

Unlike a T1 circuit, an E1 circuit does not group frames in an SF or an ESF. Rather, an E1 circuit groups 16 frames in a *multiframe*.

E1 circuits are popular outside of North America and Japan.

T3

In the same T-carrier family of standards as T1, a T3 circuit offers an increased bandwidth capacity. Whereas a T1 circuit combines 24 DS0s into a single physical connection to offer 1.544Mbps of bandwidth, a T3 circuit combines 672 DS0s into a single physical connection, delivered to the customer over coaxial cable, which is called a Digital Signal 3 (DS3). A T3 circuit has a bandwidth capacity of 44.7Mbps.

E3

Just as a T3 circuit provides more bandwidth than a T1 circuit, an E3 circuit's available bandwidth of 34.4Mbps is significantly more than the 2.048Mbps of bandwidth offered by an E1 circuit. A common misconception is that the bandwidth of E3 is greater than the bandwidth of T3 because E1's bandwidth is greater than T1's bandwidth. However, that is not the case, with T3 having a greater bandwidth (that is, 44.7Mbps) than an E3 (that is, 34.4Mbps).

CSU/DSU

Although far less popular than they once were, analog modems allowed a phone line to come into a home or business and terminate on analog modems, which provided data connections for devices such as PCs. These analog modems supported a single data conversation per modem.

However, digital circuits (for example, T1, E1, T3, and E3 circuits) usually have multiple data conversations multiplexed together on a single physical connection. Therefore, a digital modem is needed, as opposed to an analog modem. This digital modem needs to be able to distinguish between data arriving on various DS0s. Such a digital modem is called a *channel service unit/data service unit* (CSU/DSU).

As shown in Figure 7-4, a CSU/DSU circuit can terminate an incoming digital circuit from a service provider and send properly formatted bits to a router. A CSU/DSU uses clocking (often provided by the service provider) to determine when one bit stops and another bit starts. Therefore, the circuit coming from a service provider and terminating on a CSU/DSU is a synchronous circuit (where the synchronization is made possible by clocking).

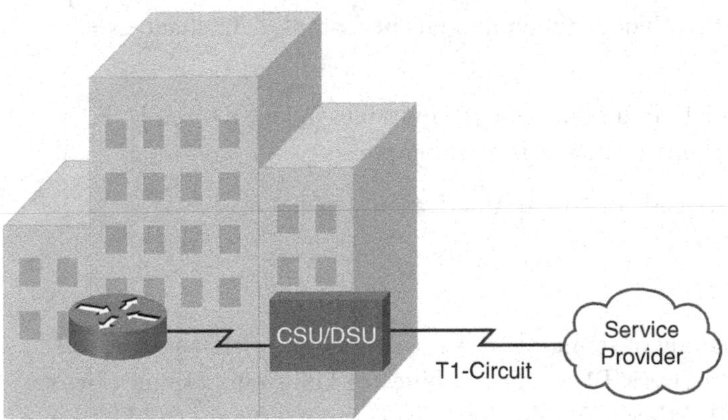

Figure 7-4 CSU/DSU Terminating a Synchronous Circuit

> **NOTE** Because a CSU/DSU works with bits, it is classified as a Layer 1 device.

Metro Ethernet

Ethernet ports (using an RJ-45 connecter) are very common and less expensive than specialized serial ports and associated cables. A service provider can provide an Ethernet interface to its customers for their WAN connectivity. The service provider would configure the logical connections (in the provider network) required to connect the customer sites. The technology used in the provider's network is hidden from the customer, providing what appears to be Ethernet connectivity to each of the customer sites. Actual throughput between sites is controlled by the provider based on the level of service purchased by the customer.

Point-to-Point Protocol

A common Layer 2 protocol used on dedicated leased lines is Point-to-Point Protocol (PPP). PPP has the capability to simultaneously transmit multiple Layer 3 protocols (for example, IP and IPX) through the use of control protocols (CPs). IP, as an example, uses the IP control protocol (IPCP).

Each Layer 3 CP runs an instance of PPP's Link Control Protocol (LCP).

Four primary features are offered by LCP:

- **Multilink interface:** PPP's multilink interface feature allows multiple physical connections to be bonded together into a logical interface. This logical interface allows load balancing across multiple physical interfaces. This is referred to as Multilink PPP.
- **Looped link detection:** A Layer 2 loop (of PPP links) can be detected and prevented.
- **Error detection:** Frames containing errors can be detected and discarded by PPP.
- **Authentication:** A device at one end of a PPP link can authenticate the device at the other end of the link. Three approaches are used to perform PPP authentication:
  - **Password Authentication Protocol (PAP):** PAP performs one-way authentication (a client authenticates with a server), as shown in Figure 7-5. A significant drawback to PPP, other than its unidirectional authentication, is the security vulnerability of its clear-text transmission of credentials, which could permit an eavesdropper to learn the authentication credentials being used.

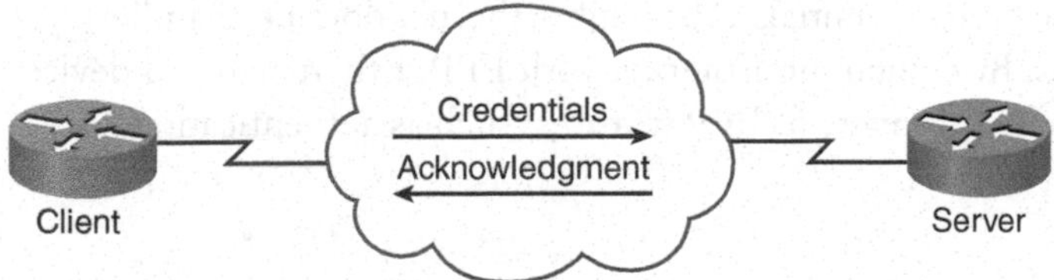

Figure 7-5 PAP Authentication

- **Challenge-Handshake Authentication Protocol (CHAP):** Like PAP, CHAP performs a one-way authentication. However, authentication is performed through a three-way handshake (challenge, response, and acceptance messages) between a server and a client, as shown in Figure 7-6. The three-way handshake allows a client to be authenticated without sending credential information across a network

Figure 7-6 CHAP Authentication

- **Microsoft Challenge-Handshake Authentication Protocol (MS-CHAP):** MS-CHAP is a Microsoft-enhanced version of CHAP, offering a collection of additional features, including two-way authentication.

> **NOTE** These PPP features are optional and are not necessarily going to be found in a given PPP connection.

Point-to-Point Protocol over Ethernet

A popular WAN technology (specifically, an Internet access technology) in residences and in businesses is digital subscriber line (DSL). DSL is described later in this section. However, as part of the PPP discussion, note that DSL connections use a variant of PPP called *PPP over Ethernet* (PPPoE).

As Figure 7-7 illustrates, PPPoE is commonly used between a DSL modem in a home (or business) and a service provider. Specifically, PPPoE encapsulates PPP frames within Ethernet frames. PPP is used to leverage its features, such as authentication. For example, when you set up a DSL modem in your home, you typically have to provide authentication credentials. Although Ethernet does not handle authentication, PPP does. By combining Ethernet with PPP, Ethernet-based devices (for example, PCs) can take advantage of PPP features, such as authentication.

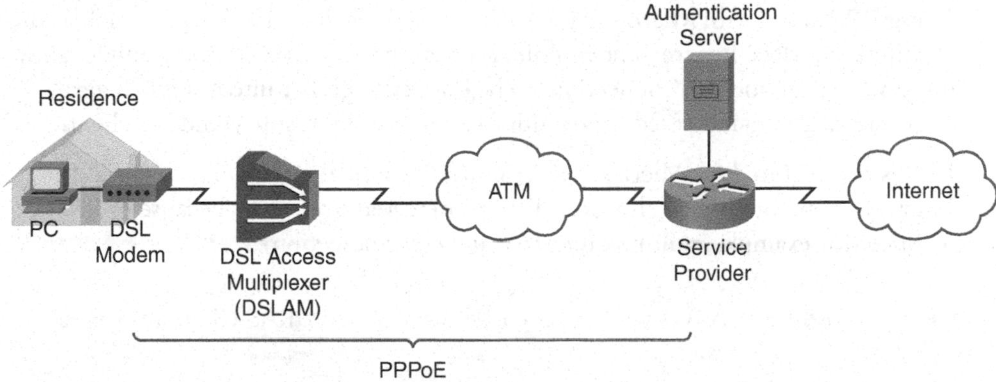

Figure 7-7 PPPoE Sample Topology

Microsoft RRAS

PPP is often the protocol used by Microsoft Routing and Remote Access Server (RRAS), which is a Microsoft Windows Server feature that allows Microsoft Windows clients to remotely access a Microsoft Windows network. Figure 7-8 shows the RRAS configuration window being used to configure a static route.

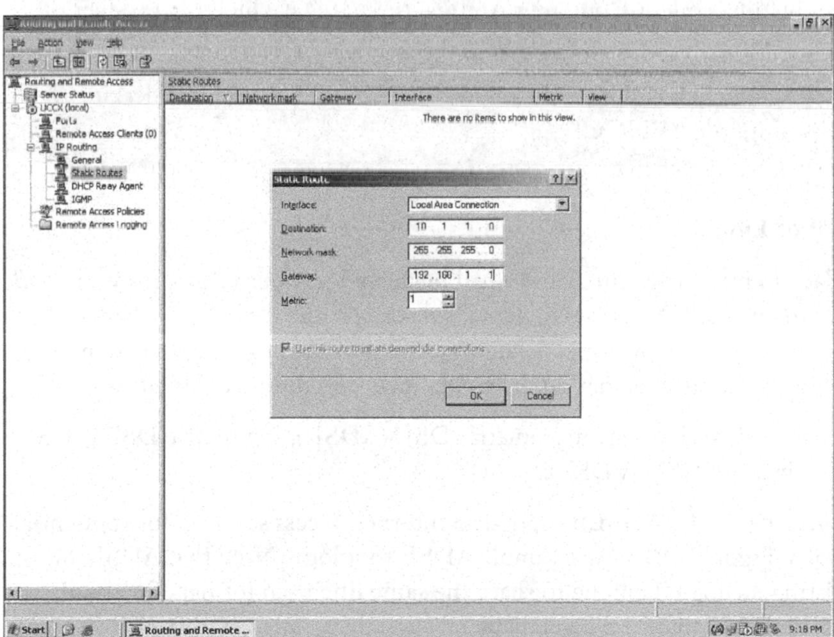

Figure 7-8 Microsoft RRAS

Using PPP along with Microsoft RRAS allows support for PPP features, such as the multilink interface feature. The multilink interface feature could, for example, allow multiple dial-up modem connections to be bonded together into a single logical connection, giving increased bandwidth to a remote Microsoft Windows client.

PPP is not required for Microsoft RRAS, which could alternatively use Serial Line Internet Protocol (SLIP). However, PPP is preferred over SLIP because of PPP's features (for example, multilink interface and error detection).

NOTE Microsoft RRAS was previously known as Microsoft RAS (Remote Access Server).

NOTE An alternative to RRAS, where remote clients can become members of a Microsoft Windows network, is *remote desktop control*. With remote desktop control, a remote computer does not directly become a member of an internal network (for example, a network inside a corporation). Rather, it controls a computer that is already part of an internal network (which could be Microsoft Windows based or based on some other operating system, such as Linux or macOS). With remote desktop control, a remote user can see the screen of the internal computer and control the computer with a keyboard and mouse. One example of a protocol that supports remote desktop control is Independent Computer Architecture (ICA), which is a product of Citrix.

Yet another technology that supports the remote control of a computer's desktop is virtual network computing (VNC).

Digital Subscriber Line

Commonplace in many residential and small business locations (also known as *small office/home office* or SOHO locations), digital subscriber line (DSL) is a group of technologies that provide high-speed data transmission over existing telephone wiring. DSL has several variants that differ in data rates and distance limitations.

Three popular DSL variants are asymmetric DSL (ADSL), symmetric DSL (SDSL), and very high bit-rate DSL (VDSL):

- **Asymmetric DSL (ADSL):** A popular Internet-access solution for residential locations. Figure 7-9 shows a sample ADSL topology. Note that ADSL allows an existing analog telephone to share the same line used for data for simultaneous transmission of voice and data.

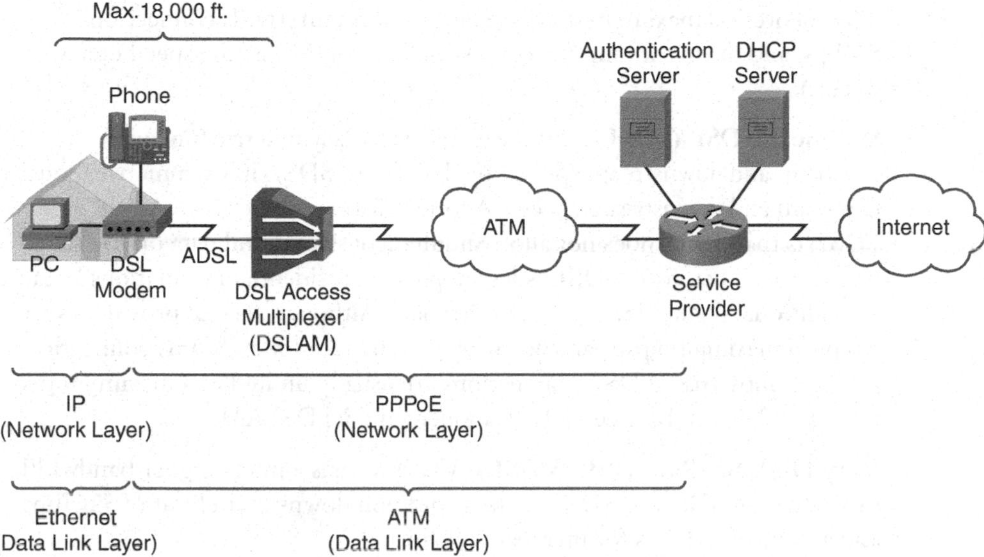

Figure 7-9 ADSL Sample Topology

Also notice in Figure 7-9 that the maximum distance from a DSL modem to a DSL access multiplexer (DSLAM) is 18,000 ft. This limitation stems from a procedure telephone companies have used for decades to change the impedance of telephone lines.

Here is a brief history: If wires in a telephone cable run side-by-side for several thousand feet, capacitance builds up in the line (which can cause echo). To counteract this capacitance, after 18,000 ft. of cable, telephone companies insert a *load coil*, which adds inductance to the line. Electrically speaking, inductance is the opposite of capacitance. So, by adding a load coil, much of the built-up capacitance in a telephone cable is reduced. However, ADSL signals cannot cross a load coil, thus the 18,000 ft. distance limitation for ADSL.

Figure 7-9 also shows how a telephone line leaving a residence terminates on a DSLAM. A DSLAM acts as an aggregation point for multiple connections, and it connects via an ATM network back to a service provider's router. The service provider authenticates user credentials, given via PPPoE, using an authentication server. Also, the service provider has a DHCP server to hand out IP address information to end-user devices (for example, a PC or a wireless router connected to a DSL modem).

The term *asymmetric* in asymmetric DSL implies the upstream and downstream speeds can be different. Typically, downstream speeds are greater than upstream speeds in an ADSL connection.

The theoretical maximum downstream speed for an ADSL connection is 8Mbps, and the maximum upstream speed is 1.544Mbps (the speed of a T1 circuit).

- **Symmetric DSL (SDSL):** Whereas ADSL has asymmetric (unequal) upstream and downstream speeds, by definition, SDSL has symmetric (equal) upstream and downstream speeds. Another distinction between ADSL and SDSL is that SDSL does not allow simultaneous voice and data on the same phone line. Therefore, SDSL is less popular in residential installations because an additional phone line is required for data. Although service providers vary, a typical maximum upstream/downstream data rate for an SDSL connection is 1.168Mbps. Also, SDSL connections are usually limited to a maximum distance of 12,000 ft. between a DSL modem and its DSLAM.
- **Very High Bit-Rate DSL (VDSL):** VDSL boasts a much higher bandwidth capacity than ADSL or SDSL, with a common downstream limit of 52Mbps and a limit of 12Mbps for upstream traffic.

  VDSL's distance limitation is 4000 ft. of telephone cable between a cable modem and a DSLAM. This constraint might seem too stringent for many potential VDSL subscribers, based on their proximity to their closest telephone central office (CO). However, service providers and telephone companies offering VDSL service often extend their fiber-optic network into their surrounding communities. This allows VDSL gateways to be located in multiple communities. The 4000 ft. limitation then becomes a distance limitation between a DSL modem and the nearest VDSL gateway, thus increasing the number of potential VDSL subscribers.

Cable Modem

Cable television companies have a well-established and wide-reaching infrastructure for television programming. This infrastructure might contain both coaxial and fiber-optic cabling. Such an infrastructure is called a *hybrid fiber-coax* (HFC) distribution network. These networks can designate specific frequency ranges for upstream and downstream data transmission. The device located in a residence (or a business) that can receive and transmit in those data frequency ranges is known as a *cable modem*, as illustrated in Figure 7-10.

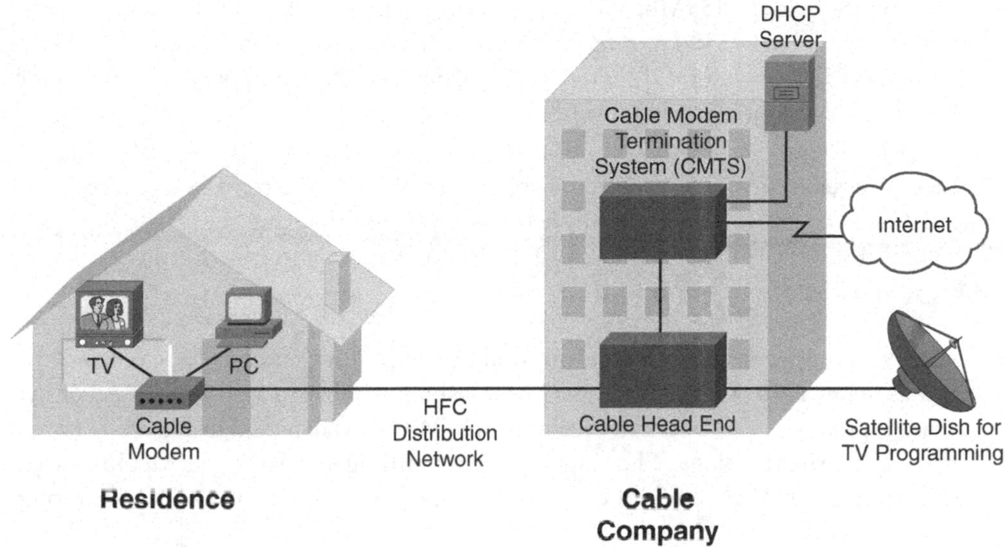

Figure 7-10 Cable Modem Sample Topology

The frequency ranges typically given for upstream and downstream data are as follows:

- **Upstream data frequencies:** 5MHz to 42MHz
- **Downstream data frequencies:** 50MHz to 860MHz

Although the theoretical maximum upstream/downstream bandwidth limits are greater (and are dependent on the HFC distribution network in use), most upstream speeds are limited to 2Mbps, with downstream speeds limited to 10Mbps. As HFC distribution networks continue to evolve, greater bandwidth capacities will be available. The current theoretical maximums are 1Gbps upstream and 10Gbps downstream.

The frequencies dedicated to data transmission are specified by a Data-Over-Cable Service Interface Specification (DOCSIS) version. Although DOCSIS is an international standard, European countries use their own set of frequency ranges; their own standard is known as *Euro-DOCSIS*.

Synchronous Optical Network

Synchronous Optical Network (SONET) is a Layer 1 technology that uses fiber-optic cabling as its media. Because SONET is a Layer 1 technology, it can be used to transport various Layer 2 encapsulation types, such as Asynchronous Transfer Mode (ATM). Also, because SONET uses fiber-optic cabling, it offers high data rates, typically in the 155Mbps to 10Gbps range, and long-distance limitations, typically in the 20 km to 250 km range. Optical Carrier transmission rates, such as OC3 (close to 155Mbps) and OC12 (close to 622Mbps), are examples of specifications for digital signal transmission bandwidth.

NOTE The term *SONET* is often used synonymously with the term *Synchronous Digital Hierarchy* (SDH), which is another fiber-optic multiplexing standard. Although these standards are similar, SONET is usually seen in North America, whereas SDH has greater worldwide popularity.

A SONET network can vary in its physical topology. For example, devices can connect as many as 16 other devices in a linear fashion (similar to a bus topology) or in a ring topology. A metropolitan area network (MAN), as depicted in Figure 7-11, often uses a ring topology. The ring might circumnavigate a large metropolitan area. Sites within that MAN could then connect to the nearest point on the SONET ring.

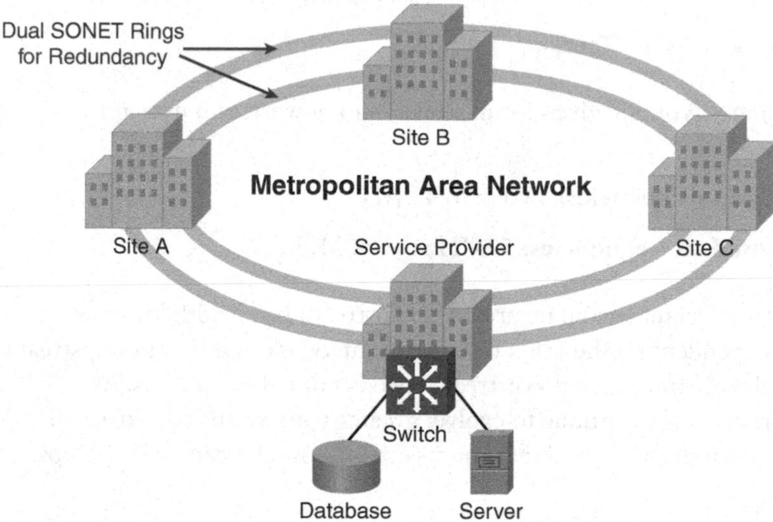

Figure 7-11 SONET Sample Topology

NOTE A SONET network uses a single wavelength of light, along with time-division multiplexing (TDM), to support multiple data flows on a single fiber. This approach differs from dense wavelength-division multiplexing (DWDM), which is another high-speed optical network commonly used in MANs. DWDM uses as many as 32 light wavelengths on a single fiber, where each wavelength can support as many as 160 simultaneous transmissions using more than eight active wavelengths per fiber. Coarse wavelength-division multiplexing (CWDM) uses fewer than eight active wavelengths per fiber.

NOTE Another optical WAN technology to be aware of is passive optical network (PON), which allows a single fiber cable to service as many as 128 subscribers. This is made possible via unpowered (that is, passive) optical splitters.

Satellite

Many rural locations lack the option of connecting to an IP WAN or to the Internet via physical media (for example, a DSL modem or a broadband cable modem connection). For such locations, a satellite WAN connection, as shown in Figure 7-12, might be an option.

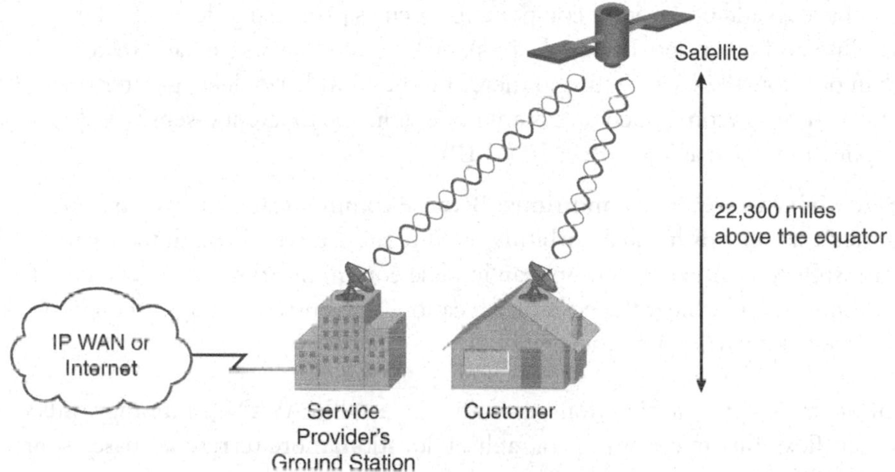

Figure 7-12 Satellite WAN Sample Topology

Most satellites used for WAN connectivity are in orbit above the earth's equator, about 22,300 miles high. Therefore, if a customer in North America, for example, had a clear view of the southern sky, they would be able to install a satellite dish and establish a line-of-sight communication path with the orbiting satellite.

The satellite would then relay transmissions back and forth between the customer's site and the service provider's ground station. The ground station could then provide connectivity, via physical media, to an IP WAN or to the Internet.

Two significant design considerations need to be taken into account:

- **Delay:** Radio waves travel at the speed of light, which is 186,000 miles per second, or $3 * 10^8$ meters per second. This speed is specifically the speed of light (and radio waves) in a vacuum; however, for the purposes of this discussion, assume these known values, even though, technically, the speed of light (and radio waves) is a bit slower when traveling through air, as opposed to traveling through a vacuum. Although these are fast speeds, consider the distance between a customer and the satellite. If a customer were located 2,000 miles north of the equator, the approximate distance between the customer site and the satellite could be calculated using the Pythagorean Theorem: $d^2 = 2000^2 + 22{,}300^2$. Solving the equation for d, which is the distance between the customer and the satellite, yields a result of approximately 22,390 miles.

A transmission from a customer to a destination on the Internet (or IP WAN) would have to travel from the customer to the satellite, from the satellite to the ground station, and then out to the Internet (or IP WAN). The propagation delay alone introduced by bouncing a signal off the satellite is approximately 241 ms—that is, (22,390 * 2) / 186,000 = .241 seconds = 241 ms). And to that, you have to add other delay components, such as processing delay (by the satellite and other networking devices), making the one-way delay greater than one-fourth of a second, and therefore the round-trip delay greater than one-half of a second. Such delays are not conducive to latency-sensitive applications such as Voice over IP (VoIP).

- **Sensitivity to weather conditions:** Because communication between a customer's satellite dish and an orbiting satellite must travel through the earth's atmosphere, weather conditions can impede communications. For example, if a thunderstorm is near the customer location, that customer might temporarily lose connectivity with their satellite.

Based on these design considerations, even though satellite WAN technology offers tremendous flexibility in terms of geographical location, more terrestrial-based solutions are preferred.

Plain Old Telephone Service

The *Public Switched Telephone Network* (PSTN) is composed of multiple telephone carriers from around the world. An end-user location (for example, a home or business) gets to the PSTN by connecting to its local telephone company, known as a *local exchange carrier* (LEC). Analog connections (both voice and data connections) using the PSTN are referred to as *plain old telephone service* (POTS) connections.

With the PSTN as we know it today, you can place a telephone call to anywhere in the world from just about anywhere in the world. Although the bandwidth available on the PSTN is limited, the PSTN is such an expansive network, it is more likely to be available in each location than other wired WAN solutions. Therefore, the benefit of availability has the trade-off of performance.

A POTS connection can be used to access the Internet (or an IP WAN) by connecting a computer to a modem with a serial cable using either a DB-9 (nine-pin) or DB-25 (25-pin) RS232/EIA232 serial port, a USB with an adapter, or a computer with an internal modem, and then connecting the modem to a POTS phone line and dialing in to a service provider. The service provider can then connect to the Internet (or an IP WAN), as shown in Figure 7-13.

Key Topic

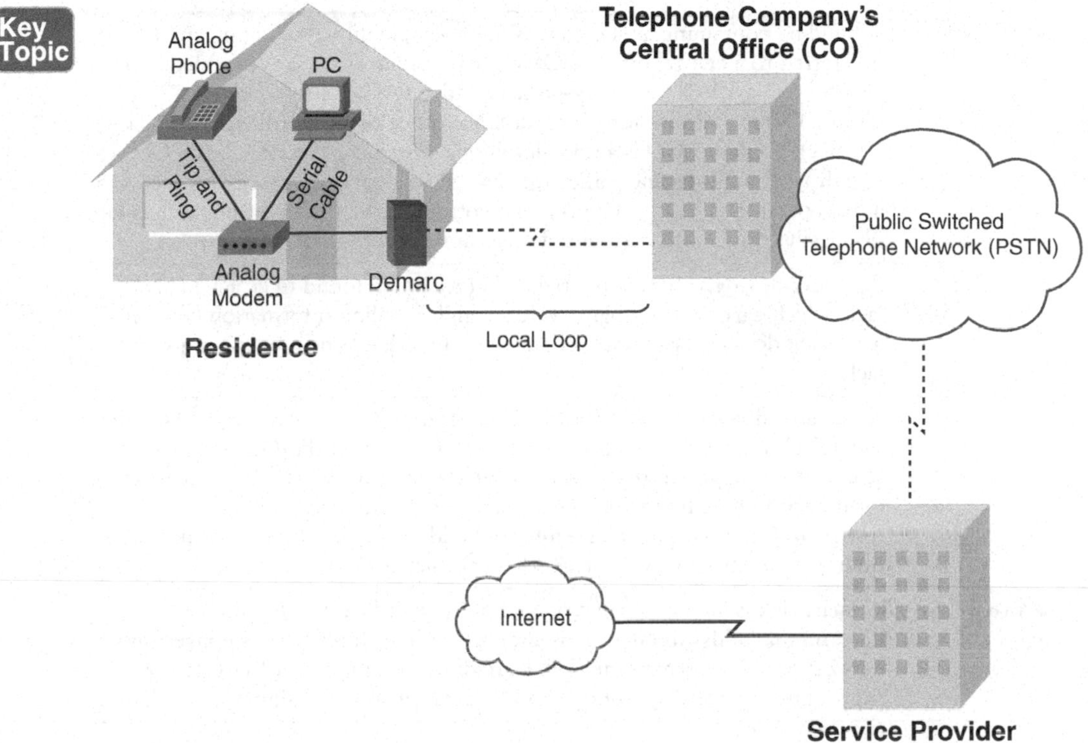

Figure 7-13 Dial-Up Modem Sample Topology

As previously stated, the performance of a POTS connection (using a dial-up modem) is limited. Although modems are rated as 56Kbps modems, in the United States and Canada, a modem's upstream data rate is limited to 48.0Kbps, and its downstream data rate is limited to 53.3Kbps. These limits are imposed not based on a technical limitation but rather on regulations from these countries' communications commissions.

Table 7-2 offers a collection of common terms used when working with POTS connections, for both voice and data.

Table 7-2 Common POTS Terms

Term	Definition
Telco	A telco is a telephone company. Some countries have government-maintained telcos, whereas other countries have multiple competitive telcos.
Local loop	A local loop is a connection between a customer's premises and their local telephone central office (CO).
Central office (CO)	A building containing a telephone company's telephone switching equipment is referred to a central office (CO). COs are categorized into five hierarchical classes. A Class 1 CO is a long-distance office serving a regional area. A Class 2 CO is a second-level long-distance office (it's subordinate to a Class 1 office). A Class 3 CO is a third-level long-distance office. A Class 4 CO is a fourth-level long-distance office that provides telephone subscribers access to a live operator. A Class 5 CO is at the bottom of the five-layer hierarchy and physically connects to customer devices in the local area.
Tip and ring	The tip and ring wires are the red and green wires found in an RJ-11 wall jack, which carry voice, ringing voltage, and signaling information between an analog device (for example, a phone or a modem) and a telephone's wall jack.
Demarc	A demarc (also known as a *demarcation point* or a *demarc extension*) is the point in a telephone network where the maintenance responsibility passes from a telephone company to the subscriber (unless the subscriber has purchased inside wiring maintenance). This demarc is typically located in a box mounted to the outside of a customer's building (for example, a residential home). This box is called a *network interface device* (NID).
Smart jack	A smart jack is a type of network interface device (see the definition for demarc) that adds circuitry. This circuitry adds such features as converting between framing formats on digital circuit (for example, a T1 circuit), supporting remote diagnostics, and regenerating a digital signal.

Integrated Services Digital Network

Integrated Services Digital Network (ISDN) is a digital telephony technology that supports multiple 64Kbps channels (known as *bearer channels*, or *B channels*) on a single connection. ISDN was popular back in the 1980s and was used to connect private branch exchanges (PBXs), which are telephone switches owned by and operated by a company, to a CO. ISDN has the capability to carry voice, video, or data over its B channels. ISDN also offers a robust set of signaling protocols: Q.921 for Layer 2 signaling and Q.931 for Layer 3 signaling. These signaling protocols run on a separate channel in an ISDN circuit (known as the *delta channel*, *data channel*, or *D channel*).

ISDN circuits are classified as either a basic rate interface (BRI) circuit or a primary rate interface (PRI) circuit:

- **BRI:** A BRI circuit contains two 64Kbps B channels and one 16Kbps D channel. Although such a circuit can carry two simultaneous voice conversations, the B channels can be logically bonded into a single VC (using the multilink interface feature of PPP, as discussed earlier in this chapter) to offer a 128Kbps data path.
- **PRI:** A PRI circuit is an ISDN circuit built on a T1 or E1 circuit. Recall that a T1 circuit has 24 channels. Therefore, if a PRI circuit is built on a T1 circuit, the ISDN PRI circuit has 23 B channels and one 64Kbps D channel. The twenty-fourth channel in the T1 circuit is used as the ISDN D channel (the channel used to carry the Q.921 and Q.931 signaling protocols, which are used to set up, maintain, and tear down connections).

  Also, recall that an E1 circuit has 32 channels, with the first channel being reserved for framing and synchronization and the seventeenth channel being served for signaling. Therefore, an ISDN PRI circuit built on an E1 circuit has 30 B channels and one D channel, which is the seventeenth channel.

Figure 7-14 depicts the constituent elements of an ISDN network.

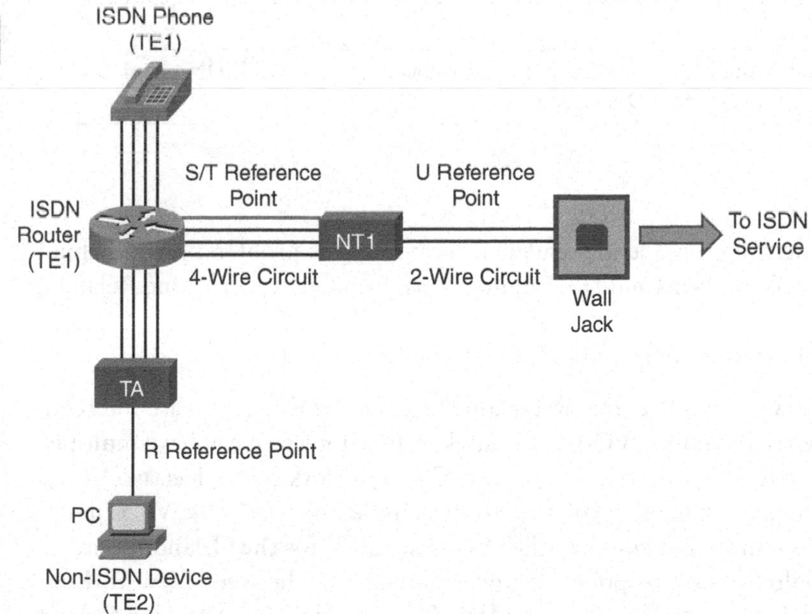

Figure 7-14 ISDN Sample Topology

Some ISDN circuits are four-wire circuits, and some are two-wire. Also, some devices in an ISDN network might not natively be ISDN devices, or they might need to connect to a four-wire ISDN circuit or a two-wire ISDN circuit. Because of all these variables, an ISDN network, as pictured in Figure 7-14, categorizes various reference points in the network and various elements in the network. Table 7-3 presents some definitions of these reference points and elements.

Table 7-3 ISDN Network Reference Points and Elements

Term	Definition
R reference point	The R reference point resides between a non-ISDN device and a terminal adapter (TA).
S/T reference point	The S/T reference point resides between a network termination 1 (NT1) and a terminal endpoint 1 (TE1).
U reference point	The U reference point resides between a network termination 1 (NT1) and the wall jack connecting back to an ISDN service provider.
Terminal adapter (TA)	A TA performs protocol conversion between a non-ISDN device and a terminal endpoint 1 (TE1) device.
Terminal endpoint 1 (TE1)	A TE1 is a device (such as an ISDN phone) that natively supports ISDN.
Terminal endpoint 2 (TE2)	A TE2 is a device (such as a PC) that does not natively support ISDN.
Network termination 1 (NT1)	An NT1 is a device that interconnects a four-wire ISDN circuit and a two-wire ISDN circuit.

Frame Relay

Although it is starting to wane in popularity because of the proliferation of technologies such as cable modems and DSL connections, for many years Frame Relay was *the* WAN technology of choice for many companies. Frame Relay offers widespread availability and low cost compared to leased lines.

Figure 7-15 shows a sample Frame Relay topology. Frame Relay sites are interconnected using virtual circuits (VCs). So, a single router interface can have multiple VCs. For example, in Figure 7-15, notice that the New York router has two VCs (as indicated by the dashed lines) emanating from a single interface. One VC is destined for the Austin router, and the other VC is destined for the Orlando router. These VCs could be point-to-point circuits, where the VC between New York and Austin belongs to the same IP subnet, and the VC between New York and Orlando belongs to a separate subnet. Alternatively, the connection from New York to Austin and Orlando could be a point-to-multipoint connection, where all routers belong to the same subnet.

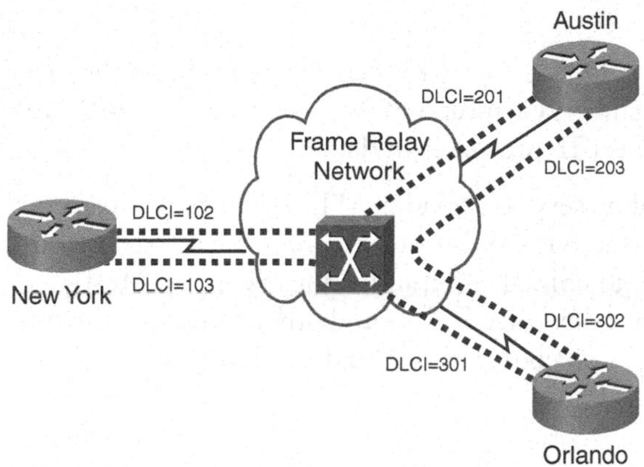

Figure 7-15 Frame Relay Sample Topology

Frame Relay is a Layer 2 technology, and a router uses locally significant identifiers for each VC. These identifiers are called *data-link connection identifiers* (DLCIs). Because DLCIs are locally significant, DLCIs at the different ends of a VC do not need to match (although they could). For example, note the VC that interconnects New York with Orlando. From the perspective of the New York router, the VC is denoted with a DLCI of 103. However, from the perspective of the Orlando router, the same VC is referenced with a DLCI of 301.

If a VC is always connected, it is considered to be a permanent virtual circuit (PVC). However, some VCs can be brought up on an as-needed basis, and they are referred to as switched virtual circuits (SVCs).

Unlike a dedicated leased line, Frame Relay shares a service provider's bandwidth with other customers of its service provider. Therefore, subscribers might purchase an SLA (previously described) to guarantee a minimum level of service. In SLA terms, a minimum bandwidth guarantee is called a *committed information rate* (CIR).

During times of congestion, a service provider might need a sender to reduce their transmission rate below the CIR. A service provider can ask a sender to reduce their rate by setting the *backward explicit congestion notification* (BECN) bit in the Frame Relay header of a frame destined for the sender that needs to slow down. If the sender is configured to respond to BECN bits, they can reduce their transmission rate by as much as 25% per timing interval (which is 125 ms by default). Both CIR and BECN configurations are considered elements of Frame Relay Traffic Shaping (FRTS). A device that does packet shaping is referred to as a *packet shaper*.

Another bit to be aware of in a Frame Relay header is the discard eligible (DE) bit. Recall that a CIR is a minimum bandwidth guarantee for a service provider's customer. However, if the service is not congested, a customer might be able to temporarily transmit at a higher rate. However, frames sent in excess of the CIR have the DE bit in their header set. Then, if the Frame Relay service provider experiences congestion, it might first drop those frames marked with a DE bit.

SIP Trunk

A SIP Trunk is a Voice over Internet Protocol (VoIP) technology based on the Session Initiation Protocol (SIP). Remember, Chapter 3, "Network Components," covers many of these important Voice over IP protocols in detail.

A SIP Trunk allows Internet telephony service providers (ITSPs) to deliver telephone services and unified communications to customers equipped with SIP-based private branch exchange (IP-PBX) and unified communications facilities. Most unified communications applications offer voice, video, and other streaming media applications such as desktop sharing, web conferencing, and shared whiteboard technologies.

Asynchronous Transfer Mode

Like Frame Relay, Asynchronous Transfer Mode (ATM) is a Layer 2 WAN technology that operates using the concept of PVCs and SVCs. However, ATM uses fixed-length *cells* as its protocol data unit (PDU), as opposed to the variable frames used by Frame Relay.

As shown in Figure 7-16, an ATM cell contains a 48-byte payload and a 5-byte header. Table 7-4 describes the fields of an ATM header.

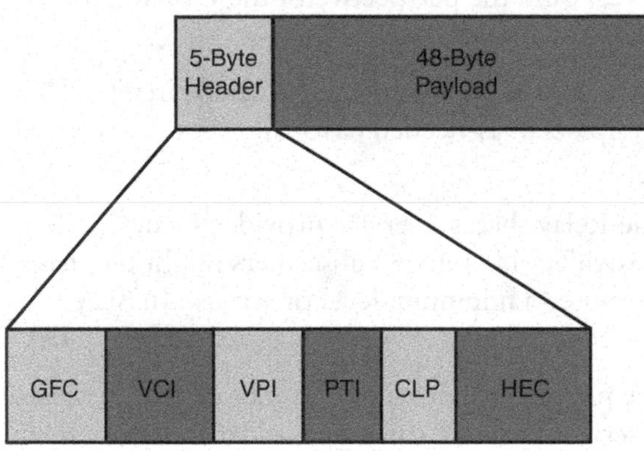

Figure 7-16 ATM Cell Structure

Table 7-4 ATM Header Fields

Field	Description
GFC (4 bits)	The Generic Flow Control (GFC) field uses 4 bits to locally indicate a congestion condition.
VCI (16 bits)	The Virtual Circuit Identifier (VCI) field usually uses 16 bits to indicate a VC. However, to fully identify a VC, the virtual path within which that VC resides must also be defined.
VPI (8 bits)	The Virtual Path Identifier (VPI) field uses 8 bits to identify an ATM virtual path, which could contain multiple virtual circuits.

Field	Description
PTI (3 bits)	The Payload Type Indicator (PTI) field uses 3 bits to indicate the type of payload being carried in a cell (for example, user data versus ATM management data).
HEC (8 bits)	The Header Error Control (HEC) field uses 8 bits to detect and correct errors in an ATM cell header.

An ATM cell's 48-byte payload size resulted from a compromise between the wishes of different countries as an international standard for ATM was being developed. Some countries, such as France and Japan, wanted a 32-byte payload size because smaller payload sizes worked well for voice transmission. However, other countries, including the United States, wanted a 64-byte payload size because they felt such a size would better support the transmission of both voice and data. In the end, the compromise was to use the average of 32 bytes and 64 bytes (that is, 48 bytes).

Although ATM uses VCs to send voice, data, and video, those VCs are not identified with DLCIs. Rather, ATM uses a pair of numbers to identify a VC. One of the numbers represents the identifier of an ATM virtual path. A single virtual path can contain multiple virtual circuits, as shown in Figure 7-17.

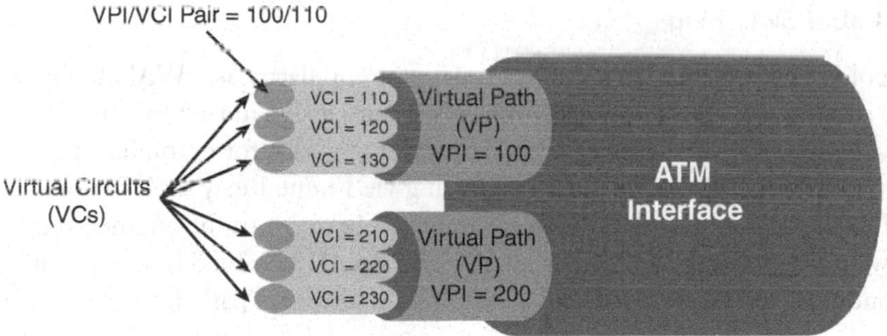

Figure 7-17 ATM Virtual Circuits

Also note in Figure 7-17 that a virtual path is labeled with a virtual path identifier (VPI), and a virtual circuit is labeled with a virtual circuit identifier (VCI). Therefore, an ATM VC can be identified with a *VPI/VCI pair* of numbers. For example, 100/110 can be used to represent a VC with a VPI of 100 and a VCI of 110.

Figure 7-18 provides an example of an ATM network topology. Notice that interconnections between ATM switches and ATM endpoints are called *user-network interfaces* (UNIs), whereas interconnections between ATM switches are called *network-node interfaces* (NNIs).

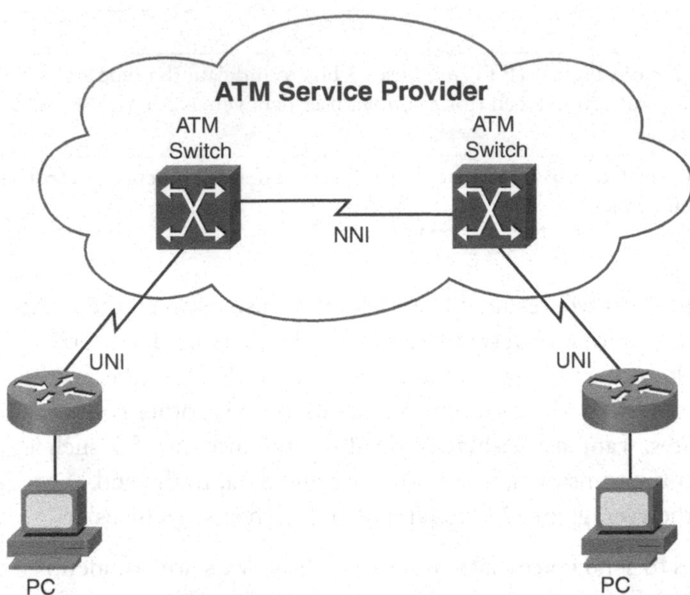

Figure 7-18 ATM Sample Topology

Multiprotocol Label Switching

Multiprotocol Label Switching (MPLS) is growing in popularity as a WAN technology used by service providers. This growth in popularity is due in part to MPLS's capability to support multiple protocols on the same network—for example, an MPLS network can accommodate users connecting via Frame Relay or ATM on the same MPLS backbone—and MPLS's capability to perform traffic engineering (which allows traffic to be dynamically routed within an MPLS cloud based on current load conditions of specific links and availability of alternate paths).

MPLS inserts a 32-bit header between Layer 2 and Layer 3 headers. Because this header is shimmed between the Layer 2 and Layer 3 headers, it is sometimes referred to as a *shim header*. Also, because the MPLS header resides between the Layer 2 and Layer 3 headers, MPLS is considered to be a Layer 2 1/2 technology.

The 32-bit header contains a 20-bit label. This label is used to make forwarding decisions within an MPLS cloud. Therefore, the process of routing MPLS frames through an MPLS cloud is referred to as *label switching*.

Figure 7-19 shows a sample MPLS network. Table 7-5 defines the various MPLS network elements shown in the figure.

Key Topic

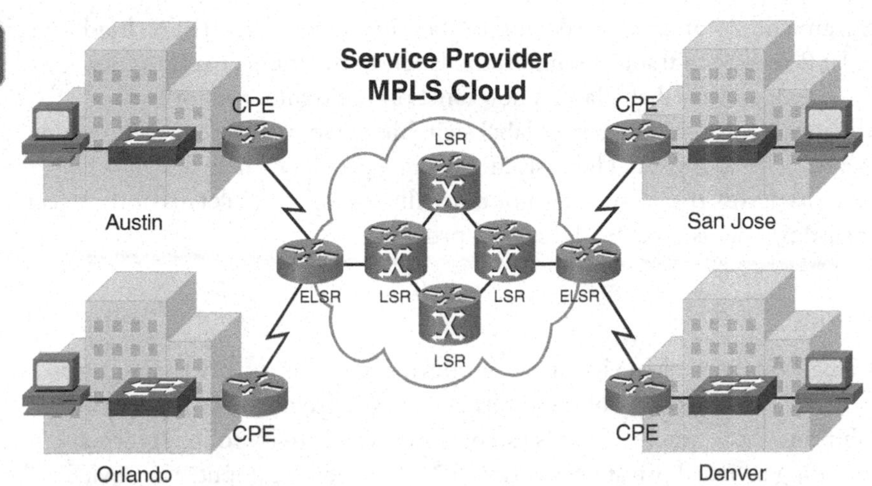

Figure 7-19 MPLS Sample Topology

Table 7-5 MPLS Network Elements

Element	Description
CPE	A customer premises equipment (CPE) device resides at a customer site. A router, as an example, could be a CPE that connects a customer with an MPLS service provider.
CE	A customer edge (CE) router is a customer router that provides the connectivity between the customer network and the service provider network. CE routers use static or dynamic routing protocols but do not run MPLS. The MPLS function is done in the service provider network.
ELSR	An edge label switch router (ELSR) resides at the edge of an MPLS service provider's cloud and interconnects a service provider to one or more customers.
PE	A provider edge (PE) router is the MPLS service provider's router that connects to the customer router. A PE is another name for an ELSR.
LSR	A label switch router (LSR) resides as part of a service provider's MPLS cloud and makes frame-forwarding decisions based on labels applied to frames.
P	A provider (P) router is a service provider internal router that doesn't directly interface with the customer routers. A P router is internal to the service provider's network.

An MPLS frame does not maintain the same label throughout the MPLS cloud. Rather, an LSR receives a frame, examines the label on the frame, makes a forwarding decision based on the label, places a new label on the frame, and forwards the frame to the next LSR. This process of label switching is more efficient than routing based on Layer 3 IP addresses. The customer using a provider's network and the MPLS transport across that network is not normally aware of the details of the exact MPLS forwarding that is done by the service provider.

Overlay Networks

In today's environments, when virtually every device has connectivity to the Internet, using the basic connectivity of the Internet can also provide wide area network (WAN) solutions. An example of this is establishing connectivity to the Internet and then building a virtual private network (VPN) between a computer or device on one part of the Internet and a computer or device on another part of the Internet. This is an example of an "overlay" network, because the VPN is overlaid on top of another network (in this case the Internet). The benefit of a virtual private network is that authentication and encryption can be done so that anyone on the Internet who may happen to see packets associated with the VPN will not be able to decrypt or understand them without the correct keys, which keeps the VPN content confidential.

A small company that does not want to purchase explicit WAN connectivity between two or more sites could instead simply purchase Internet connectivity and build site-to-site VPNs or remote-access VPNs for its WAN connectivity. VPNs are discussed again in Chapter 12, "Network Security."

A popular method of implementation for overlay networks today is the Dynamic Multipoint VPN (DMVPN). This Cisco invention has the ability to automate the creation of VPN connections in a WAN topology. Although a DMVPN can technically be used in any layout, it is most often seen implemented with the popular hub-and-spoke (partial mesh) WAN topology.

The DMVPN uses multiple GRE (mGRE) tunnels and the Next-Hop Resolution Protocol (NHRP) to dynamically discover and form the VPN. IPSec (IP Security) provides the necessary authentication, integrity, and encryption for the connections.

Real-World Case Study

Acme, Inc. has its headquarters in a building where multiple service providers are offering high-speed serial and Ethernet-based connectivity options. The company has decided that for the connectivity between the headquarters and the two branch offices, it will use a service provider with MPLS-based services. The MPLS connectivity will be delivered to the customer's CE routers as Ethernet connections. This same service provider will be providing the Internet access, as well, for all three locations. For fault tolerance, the company decided to also purchase Internet access using a serial HDLC connection with a second service provider. In the event the primary service provider fails, the headquarters and two branch office sites will connect to each other using site-to-site VPNs and the Internet as the backbone network for the VPN.

If either of the branch offices loses all connectivity to the Internet (and to the service providers and PLS network), the router at each branch office will be connected to the PSTN so that in a worst-case scenario, dial-up connectivity will be established to those routers for management purposes. The dial-up connectivity over the public telephone network would use PPP encapsulation and CHAP authentication.

Remote workers who need to access either the branch or the headquarter locations can do so by using their computer and a VPN connection going to the router or firewall at the site they want to connect to. To enable this, the remote workers would need connectivity to the Internet, which could be through DSL, cable modem, dial-up, or a wireless service provider network that is available to the remote worker, such as a cell phone company that provides data services.

Summary

Here are the main topics covered in this chapter:

- This chapter identified the three categories of WAN connections: dedicated leased lines, circuit-switched connections, and packet-switched connections.
- Data rates of various WAN technologies were contrasted.
- Various types of WAN media were identified. These types could be categorized either as physical media, including unshielded twisted pair (UTP), coaxial cable, fiber-optic cable, and electric power lines, or as wireless technologies, including cellular phone, satellite, WiMAX, HSPA+, and radio technologies.
- The basic theory and operation of various WAN technologies were discussed, including dedicated leased line, digital subscriber line (DSL), cable modem, Synchronous Optical Network (SONET), satellite, plain old telephone service (POTS), Integrated Services Digital Network (ISDN), Frame Relay, Asynchronous Transfer Mode (ATM), and Multiprotocol Label Switching (MPLS).

Exam Preparation Tasks

Review All the Key Topics

Review the most important topics from inside the chapter, noted with the Key Topic icon in the outer margin of the page. Table 7-6 lists these key topics and the page numbers where each is found.

Table 7-6 Key Topics for Chapter 7

Key Topic Element	Description	Page Number
List	WAN connection types	240
Table 7-1	Typical WAN data rates	243
List	Types of physical WAN media	243
List	Types of wireless WAN technologies	244
List	PPP features	249
List	Types of DSL connections	252
Figure 7-10	Cable modem sample topology	255
Figure 7-12	Satellite sample topology	257
Figure 7-13	Dial-up modem sample topology	259
Table 7-2	Common POTS terms	260
List	Types of ISDN circuits	261
Figure 7-14	ISDN sample topology	261
Figure 7-15	Frame Relay sample topology	263
Figure 7-16	ATM cell structure	264
Figure 7-19	MPLS sample topology	267

Complete Tables and Lists from Memory

Print a copy of Appendix C, "Memory Tables," or at least the section for this chapter, and complete as many of the tables as possible from memory. Appendix D, "Memory Tables Answer Key," includes the completed tables and lists so you can check your work.

Define Key Terms

Define the following key terms from this chapter, and check your answers in the Glossary:

dedicated leased line, circuit-switched connection, packet-switched connection, optical carrier, T1, E1, T3, E3, channel service unit/data service unit (CSU/DSU), Point-to-Point Protocol (PPP), Password Authentication Protocol (PAP), Challenge-Handshake Authentication Protocol (CHAP), Microsoft Challenge-Handshake Authentication Protocol (MS-CHAP), Point-to-Point Protocol over Ethernet (PPPoE), Microsoft Routing and Remote Access Server (RRAS), digital subscriber line (DSL), cable modem, Synchronous Optical Network (SONET), satellite (WAN technology), Public Switched Telephone Network (PSTN), plain old telephone service (POTS), telco, local loop, central office (CO), tip and ring, demarc, Integrated Services Digital Network (ISDN), basic rate interface (BRI), primary rate interface (PRI), Frame Relay, Asynchronous Transfer Mode (ATM), Multiprotocol Label Switching (MPLS), Dynamic Multipoint VPN (DMVPN), customer premises equipment (CPE), edge label switch router (ELSR), label switch router (LSR), GSM, TDMA, CDMA

Additional Resources

Introducing WANs: http://www.ajsnetworking.com/wan

What Is a Dynamic Multi-Point Virtual Private Network? https://youtu.be/sbtr632ShiM

Review Questions

The answers to these review questions appear in Appendix A, "Answers to Review Questions."

1. ISDN is considered to be what type of WAN connection?
   - **a.** Dedicated leased line
   - **b.** Circuit-switched connection
   - **c.** Packet-switched connection
   - **d.** Cell-switched connection

2. What is the data rate of an OC-3 connection?
   a. 51.84Mbps
   b. 622Mbps
   c. 155.52Mbps
   d. 159.25Gbps

3. Which of the following WAN technologies use unshielded twisted pair (UTP)? (Choose three.)
   a. Cable modem
   b. ISDN
   c. DSL modem
   d. POTS dial-up modem

4. How many channels on an E1 circuit are available for voice, video, or data?
   a. 23
   b. 24
   c. 30
   d. 32

5. Which PPP authentication method offers one-way authentication and sends credentials in clear text?
   a. WEP
   b. MS-CHAP
   c. PAP
   d. CHAP

6. What DSL variant has a distance limitation of 18,000 ft. between a DSL modem and its DSLAM?
   a. HDSL
   b. ADSL
   c. SDSL
   d. VDSL

7. What kind of network is used by many cable companies to service their cable modems and has both fiber-optic and coaxial cabling?
   a. Head-end
   b. DOCSIS
   c. Composite
   d. HFC

8. What locally significant identifier is used by a Frame Relay network to reference a virtual circuit?
   a. VPI/VCI
   b. DLCI
   c. TEI
   d. MAC

9. How big is the payload part of an ATM cell?
   a. 5 bytes
   b. 48 bytes
   c. 53 bytes
   d. 64 bytes

10. What is the size of an MPLS header?
   a. 4 bits
   b. 8 bits
   c. 16 bits
   d. 32 bits

11. What is the most common topology seen with a DMVPN?
   a. Full mesh
   b. Ring
   c. Bus
   d. Hub and spoke (partial mesh)

After completion of this chapter, you will be able to answer the following questions:

- How do various wireless LAN technologies function, and what wireless standards are in common use?
- What are some of the most important WLAN design considerations?
- What WLAN security risks exist, and how can you mitigate those risks?

CHAPTER 8

Wireless Technologies

The popularity of wireless LANs (WLANs) has exploded over the past decade, allowing users to roam within a WLAN coverage area, take their laptops with them, and maintain network connectivity as they move throughout a building or campus environment. Many other devices, however, can take advantage of wireless networks, such as gaming consoles, smartphones, and printers.

This chapter introduces WLAN technology, along with various wireless concepts, components, and standards. WLAN design considerations are then presented, followed by a discussion of WLAN security.

Foundation Topics

Introducing Wireless LANs

This section introduces the basic building blocks of WLANs and discusses how WLANs connect into a wired local area network (LAN). Various design options, including antenna design, frequencies, and communications channels, are discussed, along with a comparison of today's major wireless standards, which are all some variant of IEEE 802.11.

WLAN Concepts and Components

Wireless devices, such as laptops and smartphones, often have a built-in wireless card that allows those devices to communicate on a WLAN. But what is the device to which they communicate? It could be another laptop with a wireless card. This would be an example of an *ad hoc* WLAN. However, enterprise-class WLANs, and even most WLANs in homes, are configured in such a way that a wireless client connects to some sort of a wireless base station, such as a wireless access point (AP) or a wireless router. Many companies offer Wi-Fi as a service, and when in range of an AP, it is also referred to as a *hotspot*, indicating that Wi-Fi is available through the AP.

This communication might be done using a variety of antenna types, frequencies, and communication channels. The following sections consider some of these elements in more detail.

Wireless Routers

Consider the basic WLAN topology shown in Figure 8-1. Such a WLAN might be found in a residence whose Internet access is provided by digital subscriber line (DSL) modem. In this topology, a wireless router and switch are shown as separate components. However, in many residential networks, a wireless router integrates switch ports and wireless routing functionality into a single device.

Key Topic

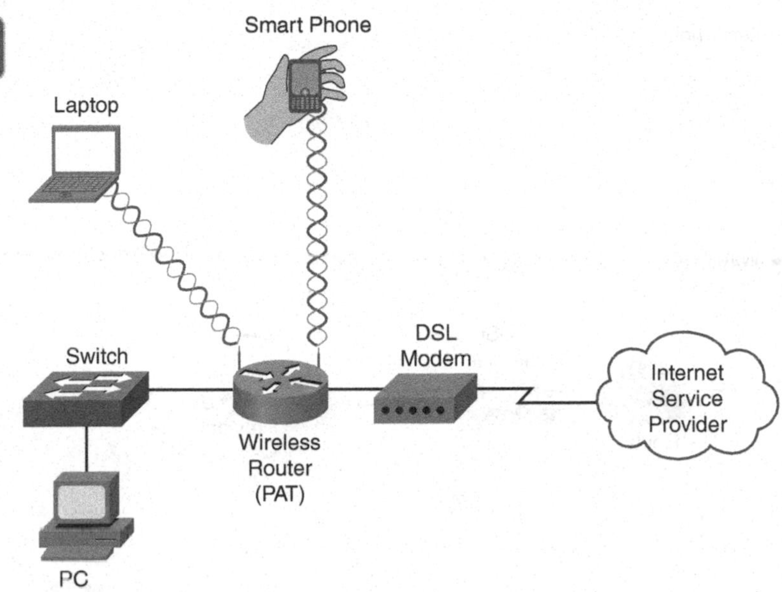

Figure 8-1 Basic WLAN Topology with a Wireless Router

In Figure 8-1, the DSL modem obtains an IP address via DHCP from the Internet service provider (ISP). The wireless router behind the modem also uses DHCP to provide IP addresses to LAN devices attaching to it wirelessly or through a wired connection. The process through which a wireless client (for example, a laptop or a smartphone) attaches with a wireless router (or wireless AP) is called *association*. All wireless devices associating with a single AP share a collision domain. Therefore, for scalability and performance reasons, WLANs might include multiple APs. The router then uses Port Address Translation (PAT), as described in Chapter 6, "Routing IP Packets," to allow packets to leave the LAN heading to the Internet.

Wireless Access Point

Although a wireless access point (AP) interconnects a wired LAN with a WLAN, it does not interconnect two networks (for example, the service provider's network with an internal network). Figure 8-2 shows a typical deployment of an AP.

Key Topic

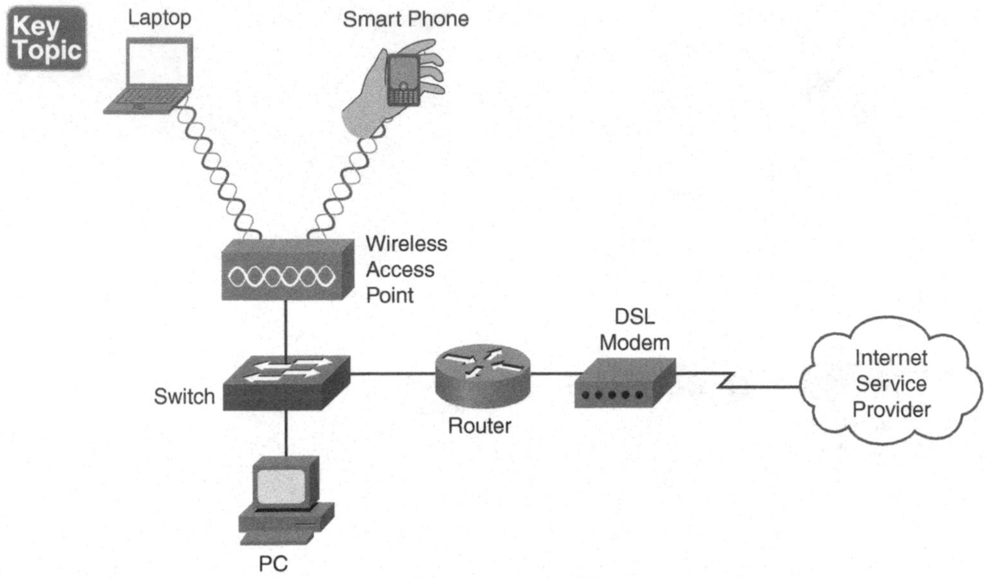

Figure 8-2 Basic WLAN Topology with a Wireless AP

The AP connects to the wired LAN, and the wireless devices that connect to the wired LAN via the AP are on the same subnet as the AP. (No Network Address Translation [NAT] or PAT is being performed.) This is acting as a wireless bridge between the wireless clients connected to the AP and the wired devices connected to the switch in the same Layer 2 domain.

To manage multiple APs, a company will use a wireless LAN controller (WLC) for centralized management and control of the APs. A Cisco model 5760 WLC would be an example of a network controller for multiple APs. The protocols used to communicate between an AP and a WLC could be the older Lightweight Access Point Protocol (LWAPP) or the more current Control And Provisioning of Wireless Access Points (CAPWAP). Using a WLC, VLAN pooling can be used to assign IP addresses to wireless clients from a pool of IP subnets and their associated VLANs.

Antennas

The coverage area of a WLAN is largely determined by the type of antenna used on a wireless AP or a wireless router. Although some lower-end, consumer-grade wireless APs have fixed antennas, higher-end, enterprise-class wireless APs often support various antenna types.

Design goals to keep in mind when selecting an antenna include the following:

- Required distance between an AP and a wireless client.
- Pattern of coverage area. (For example, the coverage area might radiate out in all directions, forming a spherical coverage area around an antenna, or an antenna might provide increased coverage in only one or two directions.)
- Indoor or outdoor environment.
- Avoiding interference with other APs.

The strength of the electromagnetic waves being radiated from an antenna is referred to as *gain*, which involves a measurement of both direction and efficiency of a transmission. For example, the gain measurement for a wireless AP's antenna transmitting a signal is a measurement of how efficiently the power being applied to the antenna is converted into electromagnetic waves being broadcast in a specific direction. Conversely, the gain measurement for a wireless AP's antenna receiving a signal is a measurement of how efficiently the received electromagnetic waves arriving from a specific direction are converted back into electricity leaving the antenna.

Gain is commonly measured using the dBi unit of measure. In this unit of measure, the *dB* stands for *decibels* and the *i* stands for *isotropic*. A decibel, in this context, is a ratio of radiated power to a reference value. In the case of dBi, the reference value is the signal strength (power) radiated from an isotropic antenna, which represents a theoretical antenna that radiates an equal amount of power in all directions (in a spherical pattern). An isotropic antenna is considered to have gain of 0 dBi.

Here is the most common formula used for antenna gain:

$$GdBi = 10 * \log^{10} (G)$$

Based on this formula, an antenna with a peak power gain of 4 (*G*) would have a gain of 6.02 dBi. Antenna theory can become mathematical (heavily relying on the use of Maxwell's equations). However, to put this discussion in perspective, generally speaking, if one antenna has 3 dB more gain than another antenna, it has approximately twice the effective power.

Antennas are classified not just by their gain but also by their coverage area. The two broad categories of antennas, which are based on coverage area, are omnidirectional and unidirectional:

- **Omnidirectional:** An omnidirectional antenna radiates power at relatively equal power levels in all directions (somewhat similar to the theoretical isotropic antenna). Omnidirectional antennas, an example of which is depicted in Figure 8-3, are popular in residential WLANs and small office/home office (SOHO) locations.

Key Topic

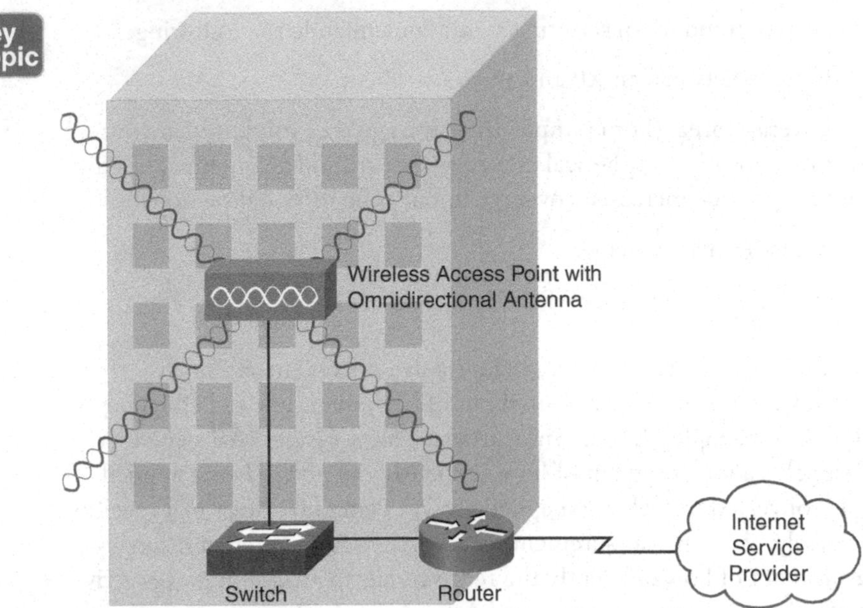

Figure 8-3 Omnidirectional Antenna Coverage

- **Unidirectional:** Unidirectional antennas can focus their power in a specific direction, thus avoiding potential interference with other wireless devices and perhaps reaching greater distances than those possible with omnidirectional antennas. One application for unidirectional antennas is interconnecting two nearby buildings, as shown in Figure 8-4.

Key Topic

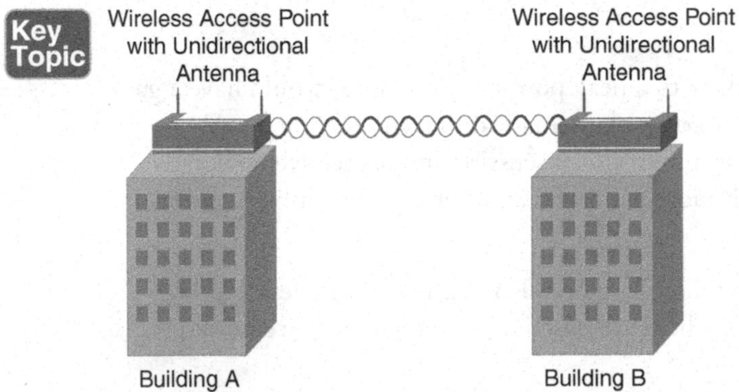

Figure 8-4 Unidirectional Antenna Coverage

Another consideration for antenna installation is the horizontal or vertical orientation of the antenna. For best performance, if two wireless APs communicate with one another, they have matching antenna orientations, which is referred to as the *polarity* of the antenna.

Frequencies and Channels

Later in this chapter, you are introduced to a variety of wireless standards, which are all variants of the IEEE 802.11 standard. As you contrast one standard with another, a characteristic to watch out for is the frequencies at which these standards operate. Although there are some country-specific variations, certain frequency ranges (or *frequency bands*) have been reserved internationally for industrial, scientific, and medical purposes. These frequency bands are called the *ISM bands*, where ISM derives from *i*ndustrial, *s*cientific, and *m*edical.

Two of these bands are commonly used for WLANs. Specifically, WLANs use the range of frequencies in the 2.4GHz-to-2.5GHz range (commonly referred to as the *2.4GHz band*) or in the 5.725GHz-to-5.875GHz range (commonly referred to as the *5GHz band*). In fact, some WLANs support a mixed environment, where 2.4GHz devices run alongside 5GHz devices.

Within each band are specific frequencies (or *channels*) at which wireless devices operate. To avoid interference, nearby wireless APs should use frequencies that do not overlap with one another. Using wireless survey tools such as AirMagnet from Fluke Networks can provide analysis of what is currently in use, allowing you to set up a new wireless system that does not compete for the same frequencies that are already in use. Those same tools can assist in identifying wireless channel utilization as well in existing and new wireless networks. Regarding channel selection, merely selecting different channels is not sufficient because transmissions on one channel spill over into nearby channels. Site survey tools can collect data to show the relative strength of signals in the areas being serviced by the APs. This output can be color-coded and overlaid on top of the floor plan and is often referred to as a *heat map* of the wireless signals.

Consider, for example, the 2.4GHz band. Here, channel frequencies are separated by 5MHz (with the exception of channel 14, which has 12MHz of separation from channel 13). However, a single channel's transmission can spread over a frequency range of 22MHz. As a result, channels must have five channels of separation (5 * 5MHz = 25MHz, which is greater than 22MHz). You can see from Figure 8-5 that, in the United States, you could select nonoverlapping channels of 1, 6, and 11.

Key Topic

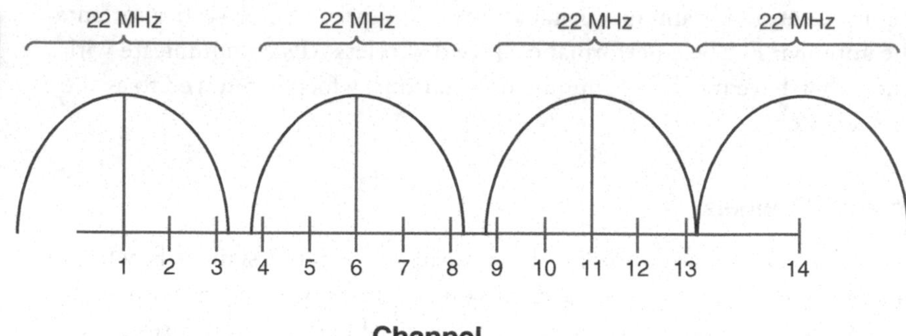

Figure 8-5 Nonoverlapping Channels in the 2.4GHz Band

> **NOTE** Even though some countries use channel 14 as a nonoverlapping channel, it is not supported in the United States.

As a reference, Table 8-1 shows the specific frequencies for each of the channels in the 2.4GHz band.

Table 8-1 Channel Frequencies in the 2.4GHz Band

Channel	Frequency (GHz)	Recommended as a Nonoverlapping Channel
1	2.412	Yes
2	2.417	No
3	2.422	No
4	2.427	No
5	2.432	No
6	2.437	Yes
7	2.442	No
8	2.447	No
9	2.452	No
10	2.457	No
11	2.462	Yes
12	2.467	No
13	2.472	No
14	2.484	Yes (not supported in the United States)

The 5GHz band has a higher number of channels, as compared to the 2.4GHz band. Table 8-2 lists the recommended nonoverlapping channels for the 5GHz band in the United States. Note that additional channels are supported in some countries.

Table 8-2 Nonoverlapping Channels in the 5GHz Band Recommended for Use in the United States

Channel	Frequency (GHz)
36	5.180
40	5.200
44	5.220
48	5.240
52	5.260*
56	5.280*
60	5.300*
64	5.320*
100	5.500**
104	5.520**
108	5.540**
112	5.560**
116	5.580**
136	5.680**
140	5.700**
149	5.745
153	5.765
157	5.785
161	5.805
165	5.825

*Must support dynamic frequency selection to prevent interference with RADAR

**Must be professionally installed

CSMA/CA

In Chapter 4, "Ethernet Technology," you learned about Ethernet's *carrier-sense multiple access/collision detection* (CSMA/CD) technology. WLANs use a similar technology called carrier-sense multiple access/collision avoidance (CSMA/CA). Just as

CSMA/CD is needed for half-duplex Ethernet connections, CSMA/CA is needed for WLAN connections because of their half-duplex operation. Similar to the way an Ethernet device listens to an Ethernet segment to determine whether a frame exists on the segment, a WLAN device listens for a transmission on a wireless channel to determine whether it is safe to transmit. In addition, the collision-avoidance part of the CSMA/CA algorithm causes wireless devices to wait for a random back-off time before transmitting.

Transmission Methods

In the previous discussion, you saw the frequencies used for various wireless channels. However, be aware that those frequencies are considered to be the *center frequencies* of a channel. In actual operation, a channel uses more than one frequency, which is a transmission method called *spread spectrum*. These frequencies are, however, very close to one another, which results in a *narrowband transmission*.

Here are the three variations of spread-spectrum technology to be aware of for your study of WLANs:

- **Direct-sequence spread spectrum (DSSS):** Modulates data over an entire range of frequencies using a series of symbols called *chips*. A chip is shorter in duration than a bit, meaning that chips are transmitted at a higher rate than the actual data. These chips encode not only the data to be transmitted, but also what appears to be random data. Although both parties involved in a DSSS communication know which chips represent actual data and which chips do not, if a third party intercepted a DSSS transmission, it would be difficult for them to eavesdrop on the data because they would not easily know which chips represented valid bits. DSSS is more subject to environmental factors, as opposed to FHSS and OFDM, because of its use of an entire frequency spectrum.
- **Frequency-hopping spread spectrum (FHSS):** Allows the participants in a communication to hop between predetermined frequencies. Security is enhanced because the participants can predict the next frequency to be used, but a third party cannot easily predict the next frequency. FHSS can also provision extra bandwidth by simultaneously using more than one frequency.
- **Orthogonal frequency-division multiplexing (OFDM):** Whereas DSSS uses a high modulation rate for the symbols it sends, OFDM uses a relatively slow modulation rate for symbols. This slower modulation rate, combined with the simultaneous transmission of data over 52 data streams, helps OFDM support high data rates while resisting interference between the various data streams.

Of these three wireless modulation techniques, only DSSS and OFDM are commonly used in today's WLANs.

WLAN Standards

Most modern WLAN standards are variations of the original IEEE 802.11 standard, which was developed in 1997. This original standard supported a DSSS and an FHSS implementation, both of which operated in the 2.4GHz band. However, with supported speeds of 1Mbps or 2Mbps, the original 802.11 standard lacks sufficient bandwidth to meet the needs of today's WLANs. The most popular variants of the 802.11 standard in use today are 802.11a, 802.11b, 802.11g, 802.11n, and 802.11ac, as described in detail in the following sections.

802.11a

The 802.11a WLAN standard, which was ratified in 1999, supports speeds as high as 54Mbps. Other supported data rates (which can be used if conditions are not suitable for the 54Mbps rate) include 6, 9, 12, 18, 24, 36, and 48Mbps. The 802.11a standard uses the 5GHz band and uses the OFDM transmission method. Interestingly, 802.11a never gained widespread adoption because it was not backward compatible with 802.11b, whereas 802.11g was backward compatible. Although this is true, it is worth noting that 802.11a is a possible alternative to 802.11b/g, as the 2.4GHz is often far more crowded than the 5GHz band.

802.11b

The 802.11b WLAN standard, which was ratified in 1999, supports speeds as high as 11Mbps. However, 5.5Mbps is another supported data rate. The 802.11b standard uses the 2.4GHz band and uses the DSSS transmission method.

802.11g

The 802.11g WLAN standard, which was ratified in 2003, supports speeds as high as 54Mbps. Like 802.11a, other supported data rates include 6, 9, 12, 18, 24, 36, and 48Mbps. However, like 802.11b, 802.11g operates in the 2.4GHz band, which allows it to offer backward compatibility to 802.11b devices. 802.11g can use either the OFDM or the DSSS transmission method.

802.11n

The 802.11n WLAN standard, which was ratified in 2009, supports a wide variety of speeds, depending on its implementation. Although the speed of an 802.11n network could exceed 300Mbps (through the use of *channel bonding*, as discussed later), many 802.11n devices on the market have speed ratings in the 130 Mbps–150Mbps range. Interestingly, an 802.11n WLAN could operate in the 2.4GHz band, the 5GHz band, or both simultaneously. 802.11n uses the OFDM transmission method.

One way 802.11n achieves superior throughput is through the use of a technology called *multiple input, multiple output* (MIMO). MIMO uses multiple antennas for transmission and reception. These antennas do not interfere with one another, thanks to MIMO's use of *spatial multiplexing*, which encodes data based on the antenna from which the data will be transmitted. Both reliability and throughput is increased with MIMO's simultaneous use of multiple antennas.

Yet another technology implemented by 802.11n is *channel bonding*. With channel bonding, two wireless bands are logically bonded together, forming a band with twice the bandwidth of an individual band. Some literature refers to channel bonding as *40MHz mode*, which is the bonding of two adjacent 20MHz bands into a 40MHz band.

The 802.11n high throughput (HT) standard defines modes for ensuring that older a/b/g devices and newer 802.11n devices avoid collisions with each other.

802.11ac

The 802.11ac is a 5GHz standard that uses more simultaneous streams than 802.11n and features multi-user MIMO (MU-MIMO). A single 80MHz wide stream supports 433Mbps.

802.11x Standard Summary

Table 8-3 acts as a reference to help you contrast the characteristics of the 802.11 standards.

Table 8-3 Characteristics of 802.11 Standards

Standard	Band	Max. Bandwidth	Transmission Method	Max. Range
802.11	2.4GHz	1Mbps or 2Mbps	DSSS or FHSS	20 m indoors / 100 m outdoors
802.11a	5GHz	54Mbps	OFDM	35 m indoors/ 120 m outdoors
802.11b	2.4GHz	11Mbps	DSSS	32 m indoors/ 140 m outdoors
802.11g	2.4GHz	54Mbps	OFDM or DSSS	32 m indoors/ 140 m outdoors
802.11n	2.4GHz or 5GHz (or both)	> 300Mbps (with channel bonding)	OFDM	70 m indoors/ 250 m outdoors
802.11ac	5GHz	> 3Gbps (with MU-MIMO and several antennas)	OFDM	Similar to 802.11n operating at 5 GHz

NOTE Others forms of wireless technologies are in a group termed *cellular* because the tech is found on cell phones (among other mobile devices). Cellular technology is covered in Chapter 7, "Wide Area Networks (WANs)."

Deploying Wireless LANs

When designing and deploying WLANs, you have a variety of installation options and design considerations. This section delves into your available options and provides you with some best practice recommendations.

Types of WLANs

WLANs can be categorized based on their use of wireless APs. The three main categories are independent basic service set (IBSS), basic service set (BSS), and extended service set (ESS). An IBSS WLAN operates in an ad hoc fashion, whereas BSS and ESS WLANs operate in infrastructure mode. The following sections describe the three types of WLANs in detail.

IBSS

As shown in Figure 8-6, a WLAN can be created without the use of an AP. Such a configuration, called an IBSS, is said to work in an ad hoc fashion. An ad hoc WLAN is useful for temporary connections between wireless devices. For example, you might temporarily interconnect two laptop computers to transfer a few files.

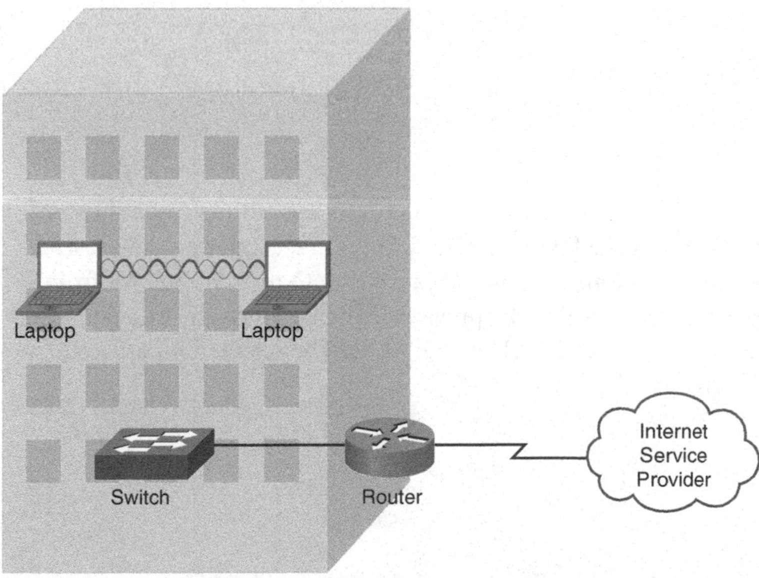

Figure 8-6 Independent Basic Service Set (IBSS) WLAN

BSS

Figure 8-7 depicts a WLAN using a single AP. WLANs that have just one AP are called BSS WLANs. BSS WLANs are said to run in infrastructure mode because wireless clients connect to an AP, which is typically connected to a wired network infrastructure. A BSS network is often used in residential and SOHO locations, where the signal strength provided by a single AP is sufficient to service all the WLAN's wireless clients.

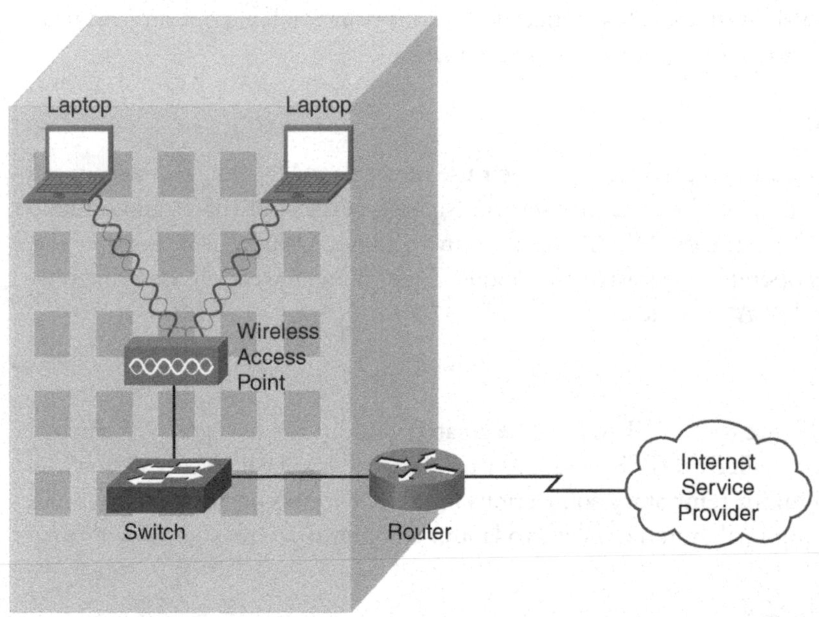

Figure 8-7 Basic Service Set (BSS) WLAN

ESS

Figure 8-8 illustrates a WLAN using two APs. WLANs containing more than one AP are called *ESS WLANs*. Like BSS WLANs, ESS WLANs operate in infrastructure mode. When you have more than one AP, take care to prevent one AP from interfering with another. Specifically, the previously discussed nonoverlapping channels (channels 1, 6, and 11 for the 2.4GHz band) should be selected for adjacent wireless coverage areas.

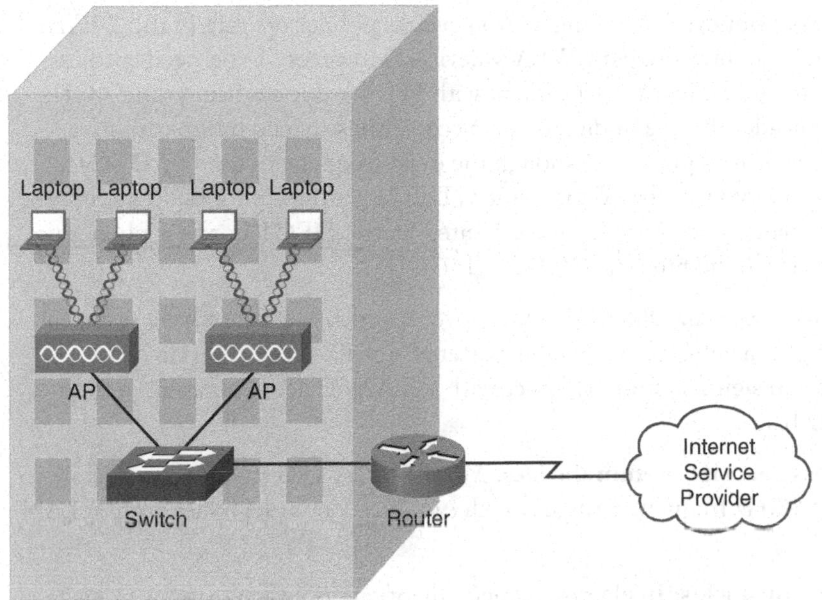

Figure 8-8 Extended Service Set (ESS) WLAN

Mesh Topology

A mesh wireless network is a collection of wireless devices that may not use centralized control (decentralized management). The combined wireless coverage range defines the range of the network. This could also be referred to as a *mesh cloud*. Additional wireless technologies (besides Wi-Fi) could be used to build a mesh wireless topology. This type of network could be used for hosts to communicate with other devices in the mesh, or the network could provide a gateway to the Internet or other networks.

Sources of Interference

A major issue for WLANs is radio frequency interference (RFI) caused by other devices using similar frequencies to the WLAN devices. Also, physical obstacles can impede or reflect WLAN transmissions. The following are some of the most common sources of interference:

- **Other WLAN devices:** Earlier in this chapter, you read about nonoverlapping channels for both the 2.4GHz and 5GHz bands. However, if two or more WLAN devices are in close proximity and use overlapping channels, those devices could interfere with one another.

- **Cordless phones:** Several models of cordless phones operate in the 2.4GHz band and can interfere with WLAN devices. However, if you need cordless phones to coexist in an environment with WLAN devices using the 2.4GHz band, consider the use of digital enhanced cordless telecommunications (DECT) cordless phones. Although the exact frequencies used by DECT cordless phones vary based on country, DECT cordless phones do not use the 2.4GHz band. For example, in the United States, DECT cordless phones use frequencies in the range 1.92GHz to 1.93GHz.
- **Microwave ovens:** Older microwave ovens, which might not have sufficient shielding, can emit relatively high-powered signals in the 2.4GHz band, resulting in significant interference with WLAN devices operating in the 2.4GHz band.
- **Wireless security system devices:** Most wireless security cameras operate in the 2.4GHz frequency range, which can cause potential issues with WLAN devices.
- **Physical obstacles:** In electromagnetic theory, radio waves cannot propagate through a perfect conductor. So, although metal filing cabinets and large appliances are not perfect conductors, they are sufficient to cause degradation of a WLAN signal. For example, a WLAN signal might hit a large air conditioning unit, causing the radio waves to be reflected and scattered in multiple directions. Not only does this limit the range of the WLAN signal, but radio waves carrying data might travel over different paths. This *multipath issue* can cause data corruption. Concrete walls, metal studs, or even window film could reduce the quality of the wireless network signals.
- **Signal strength:** The range of a WLAN device is a function of the device's signal strength. Lower-cost consumer-grade APs do not typically allow an administrative adjustment of signal strength. However, enterprise-class APs often allow signal strength to be adjusted to ensure sufficient coverage of a specific area, while avoiding interference with other APs using the same channel.

As you can see from this list, most RFI occurs in the 2.4GHz band as opposed to the 5GHz band. Therefore, depending on the wireless clients you need to support, you might consider using the 5GHz band, which is an option for 802.11a and 802.11n WLANs. With the increased use of wireless, both coverage and capacity-based planning should be done to provide acceptable goodput. *Goodput* refers to the number of useful information bits that the network can deliver (not including overhead for the protocols being used). Another factor is the density (ratio of users to APs), which if too high could harm performance of the network. Areas expecting high density would include classrooms, hotels, and hospitals. Device or bandwidth saturation could impact performance.

Wireless AP Placement

WLANs using more than one AP (an ESS WLAN) require careful planning to prevent the APs from interfering with one another, while still servicing a desired coverage area. Specifically, an overlap of coverage between APs should exist to allow uninterrupted roaming from one WLAN *cell* (which is the coverage area provided by an AP) to another. However, those overlapping coverage areas should not use overlapping frequencies.

Figure 8-9 shows how nonoverlapping channels in the 2.4GHz band can overlap their coverage areas to provide seamless roaming between AP coverage areas. A common WLAN design recommendation is to have a 10% to 15% overlap of coverage between adjoining cells.

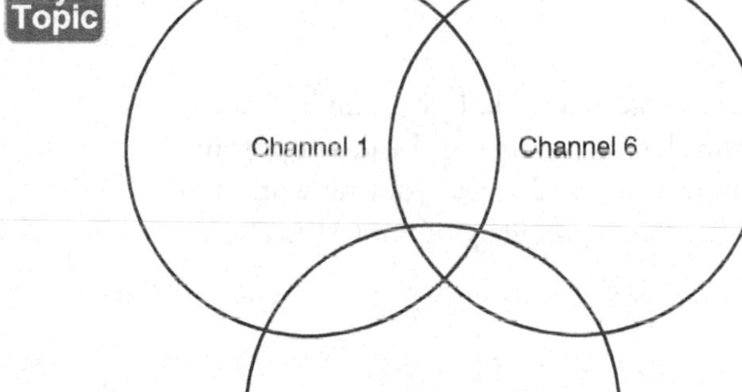

Figure 8-9 Coverage Overlap in Coverage Areas for Nonoverlapping Channels

If a WLAN has more than three APs, the APs are deployed in a honeycomb fashion to allow an overlap of AP coverage areas while avoiding an overlap of identical channels. The example in Figure 8-10 shows an approach to channel selection for adjoining cells in the 2.4GHz band. Notice that cells using the same nonoverlapping channels (channels 1, 6, and 11) are separated by another cell. For example, notice that none of the cells using channel 11 overlap another cell using channel 11.

Key Topic

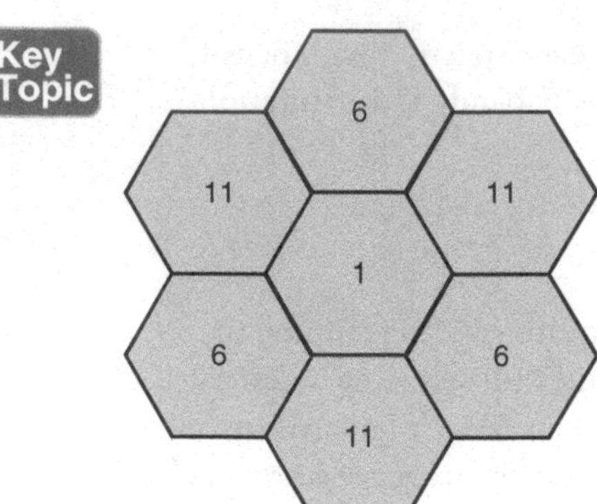

Figure 8-10 Nonoverlapping Coverage Cells for the 2.4GHz Band

NOTE Although a honeycomb channel assignment scheme can be used for the 5GHz band, identical channels should be separated by at least two cells, rather than the single cell shown for the 2.4GHz band.

Securing Wireless LANs

WLANs introduce some unique concerns to your network. For example, improperly installed wireless APs are roughly equivalent to putting an Ethernet port in a building's parking lot, where someone can drive up and access your network. Fortunately, various features are available to harden the security of your WLAN, as discussed in this section.

Security Issues

In the days when dial-up modems were popular, malicious users could run a program on their computer to call all phone numbers in a certain number range. Phone numbers that answered with modem tone became targets for later attacks. This type of reconnaissance was known as *war dialing*. A modern-day variant of war dialing is *war driving*, where potentially malicious users drive around looking for unsecured WLANs. These users might be identifying unsecured WLANs for nefarious purposes or simply looking for free Internet access. Devices such as cell phones, laptops, tablets, and gaming and media devices could act as wireless clients as well as be used in a wireless attack because they have potential Wi-Fi access to the network.

Other WLAN security threats include the following:

- **War chalking:** Once an open WLAN (or a WLAN whose SSID and authentication credentials are known) is found in a public place, a user might write a symbol on a wall (or some other nearby structure) to let others know the characteristics of the discovered network. This practice, which is a variant of the decades-old practice of hobos leaving symbols as messages to fellow hobos, is called *war chalking*. Figure 8-11 shows common war-chalking symbols.

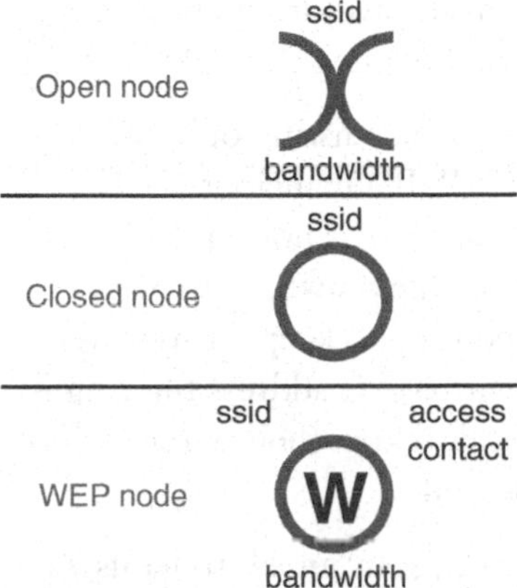

Figure 8-11 War-Chalking Symbols

- **WEP and WPA security cracking:** As discussed later in this chapter, various security standards are available for encrypting and authenticating a WLAN client with an AP. Two of the less secure standards are Wired Equivalent Privacy (WEP) and Wi-Fi Protected Access (WPA). Although WPA is considered more secure than WEP, utilities are available on the Internet for cracking each of these approaches to wireless security. By collecting enough packets transmitted by a secure AP, these cracking utilities can use mathematical algorithms to determine the preshared key (PSK) configured on a wireless AP with which an associating wireless client must also be configured.
- **Rogue access point:** A malicious user could set up their own AP to which legitimate users would connect. Such an AP is called a *rogue access point*. That malicious user could then use a packet sniffer (which displays information about unencrypted traffic, including the traffic's data and header information) to eavesdrop on communications flowing through the rogue AP. To cause unsuspecting users to connect to the rogue AP, the malicious user could configure the rogue AP with the same service set identifier (SSID) as used by a legitimate AP. When a rogue AP is configured with the SSID of a legitimate AP, the rogue AP is commonly referred to as an *evil twin*.

NOTE An SSID is a string of characters identifying a WLAN. APs participating in the same WLAN (in an ESS) can be configured with identical SSIDs. An SSID shared among multiple APs is called an *extended service set identifier* (ESSID).

Approaches to WLAN Security

A WLAN that does not require authentication or provide encryption for wireless devices (for example, a publicly available WLAN found in many airports) is said to be using *open authentication*. To protect WLAN traffic from eavesdroppers, a variety of security standards and practices have been developed, including the following:

- **MAC address filtering:** An AP can be configured with a listing of MAC addresses that are permitted to associate with the AP. If a malicious user attempts to connect via their laptop (whose MAC address is not on the list of trusted MAC addresses), that user is denied access. One drawback to MAC address filtering is the administrative overhead required to keep an approved list of MAC addresses up to date. Another issue with MAC address filtering is that a knowledgeable user could falsify the MAC address of their wireless network card, making their device appear to be approved.

- **Disabling SSID broadcast:** An SSID can be broadcast by an AP to let users know the name of the WLAN. For security purposes, an AP might be configured not to broadcast its SSID. However, knowledgeable users could still determine the SSID of an AP by examining captured packets.

- **Preshared key:** To encrypt transmission between a wireless client and an AP (in addition to authenticating a wireless client with an AP), both the wireless client and the AP could be preconfigured with a matching string of characters (a PSK, as previously described). The PSK could be used as part of a mathematical algorithm to encrypt traffic, such that if an eavesdropper intercepted the encrypted traffic, they would not be able to decrypt the traffic without knowing the PSK. Although using a PSK can be effective in providing security for a small network (for example, a SOHO network), it lacks scalability. For example, in a large corporate environment, a PSK being compromised would necessitate the reconfiguration of all devices configured with that PSK.

NOTE WLAN security based on a PSK technology is called *personal mode*.

- **IEEE 802.1X:** Rather than having all devices in a WLAN be configured with the same PSK, a more scalable approach is to require all wireless users to authenticate using their own credentials (for example, a username and password). Allowing users to have their own set of credentials prevents the compromising of one password from impacting the configuration of all wireless devices. IEEE 802.1x is a technology that allows wireless clients to authenticate with an authentication server—typically, a Remote Authentication Dial-In User Service (RADIUS) server.

NOTE WLAN security based on IEEE 802.1x, and a centralized authentication server such as RADIUS is called *enterprise mode*.

Chapter 4 discussed IEEE 802.1X in detail and described the role of a supplicant, an authenticator, and an authentication server, but Chapter 4 showed how IEEE 802.1X was used in a wired network. Figure 8-12 shows a wireless implementation of IEEE 802.1X.

Key Topic

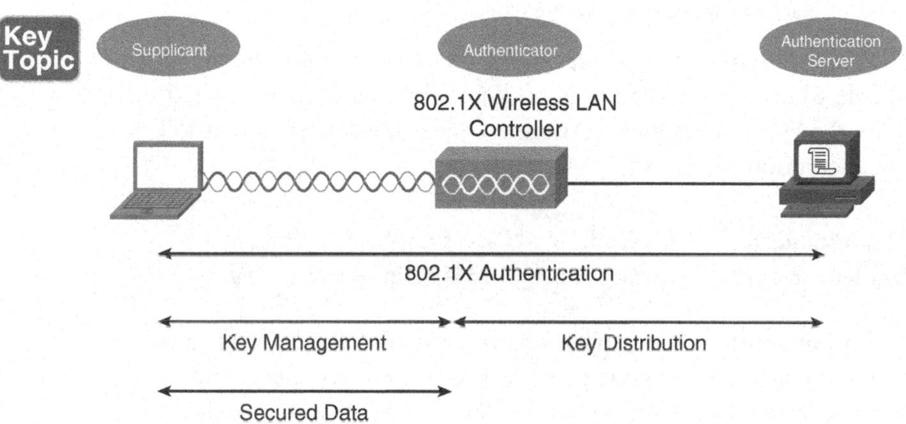

Figure 8-12 IEEE 802.1X Security for a WLAN

NOTE IEEE 802.1X works in conjunction with an Extensible Authentication Protocol (EAP) to perform its job of authentication. A variety of EAP types exist, including Lightweight Extensible Authentication Protocol (LEAP), EAP-Flexible Authentication via Secure Tunneling (EAP-FAST), EAP-Transport Layer Security (EAP-TLS), EAP-Tunneled Transport Layer Security (EAP-TTLS), Protected EAP–Generic Token Card (PEAP-GTC), and Protected EAP–Microsoft Challenge Handshake Authentication Protocol version 2 (PEAP-MSCHAPv2). Although these EAP types differ in their procedures, the overriding goal for each EAP type is to securely authenticate a supplicant and provide the supplicant and the authenticator a session key that can be used during a single session in the calculation of security algorithms (for example, encryption algorithms).

Security Standards

When you're configuring a wireless client for security, the most common security standards from which you can select are as follows:

- Wired Equivalent Privacy (WEP)
- Wi-Fi Protected Access (WPA)
- Wi-Fi Protected Access Version 2 (WPA2)

The following sections describe these standards in detail.

WEP

The original 802.11 standard did address security; however, the security was a WEP key. With WEP, an AP is configured with a static WEP key. Wireless clients needing to associate with an AP are configured with an identical key (making this a PSK approach to security). The 802.11 standard specifies a 40-bit WEP key, which is considered to be a relatively weak security measure.

Because a WEP key is a static string of characters, it could be compromised with a brute-force attack, where an attacker attempts all possible character combinations until a match for the WEP key is found. Another concern, however, is that WEP uses RC4 as its encryption algorithm.

NOTE RC4 (which stands for "Ron's Code" or "Rivest Cipher" because it was developed by Ron Rivest of RSA Security) is sometimes pronounced *arc four*.

RC4 uses a 24-bit initialization vector (IV), which is a string of characters added to the transmitted data, such that the same plain-text data frame will never appear as the same WEP-encrypted data frame. However, the IV is transmitted in clear text. So, because a malicious user can see the IV in clear text, if they use packet-capture software and capture enough packets having the same WEP key, they can use a mathematical algorithm to determine the static WEP key (which can be performed with WEP-cracking software found on the Internet).

Some WEP implementations support the use of a longer WEP key (for example, 128 bits instead of 40 bits), making a WEP key more difficult to crack; however, both the wireless clients and their AP must support the longer WEP key.

WPA

The Wi-Fi Alliance (a nonprofit organization formed to certify interoperability of wireless devices) developed its own security standard, WPA, to address the weaknesses of WEP. Here are some of the security enhancements offered by WPA:

- WPA operating in enterprise mode can require a user to be authenticated before keys are exchanged.
- In enterprise mode, the keys used between a wireless client and an access point are temporary session keys.
- WPA uses Temporal Key Integrity Protocol (TKIP) for enhanced encryption. Although TKIP does rely on an initialization vector, the IV is expanded from WEP's 24-bit IV to a 48-bit IV. Also, broadcast key rotation can be used, which causes a key to change so quickly that an eavesdropper would not

have time to exploit a derived key. TKIP uses Rivest Cipher 4 (RC4) for the encryption algorithm, and this is why the CompTIA Network+ exam may reference TKIP-RC4 in a discussion of wireless.

- TKIP leverages Message Integrity Check (MIC), which is sometimes referred to as *Message Integrity Code*. MIC can confirm that data was not modified in transit.

Although the term *WPA* is not typically written as WPA1, when you see it, consider it to be WPA Version 1 (WPA1). WPA Version 2, however, is written as *WPA2*.

WPA2

In 2004, the IEEE 802.11i standard was approved and required stronger algorithms for encryption and integrity checking than those seen in previous WLAN security protocols such as WEP and WPA. The requirements set forth in the IEEE 802.11i standard are implemented in the Wi-Fi Alliance's WPA Version 2 (WPA2) security standard. WPA2 uses Counter Mode with Cipher Block Chaining Message Authentication Code Protocol (CCMP) for integrity checking and Advanced Encryption Standard (AES) for encryption. In the Network+ exam, you might find this referenced as simply CCMP-AES. WPA2 that uses a centralized server for authenticating users is referred to as *Enterprise* mode. An implementation of WPA2 that uses a configured password or PSK instead of a centralized server is referred to as *Personal* mode.

Additional Wireless Options

Other wireless technologies, such as Bluetooth, infrared (IR), and near-field communications (NFC), which are often integrated into smartphones, can also provide connectivity for a personal area network (PAN) or other short-range networking applications. Many of these technologies help facilitate the Internet of Things (IoT) and are covered in Chapter 3, "Network Components."

Another interesting wireless technology is *geofencing*, which often uses the global positioning system (GPS) or radio frequency identification (RFID) to define geographical boundaries. Geofencing allows you to define triggers so that when a device enters (or exits) the boundaries defined by the administrator, an alert is issued.

Geofence virtual barriers can be active or passive. Active geofences require an end user to opt in to location services and require a mobile app to be open. Passive geofences are always on; they rely on Wi-Fi and/or cellular data instead of GPS or RFID and can work in the background.

How might this be used in a practical application? Consider a hospital with patient information on iPads that the hospital distributes to staff. If these iPads travel beyond the geofence, an administrative alert can trigger.

Real-World Case Study

Acme, Inc. hired an outside contractor who specializes in Wi-Fi. The consultants came in and did a needs assessment and performed a wireless site survey. Recommendations were then made about the need for 15 access points in the headquarters office spaces and three access points at each of the remote branch offices. Three wireless LAN controllers, one for each office, will be used to manage the respective access points. The management of the access points through the wireless LAN controllers will be done primarily through the headquarters office using the WAN that is connecting the branch offices to the headquarters office.

Because of the high number of other Wi-Fi access points being used in the same building as the headquarters office, Acme decided to use the 5GHz range (due to less competition in that space) and to use 802.11n.

For security, Acme will use WPA2 in conjunction with a RADIUS server. Acme will use Enterprise mode for authentication of each user before allowing them access on the wireless network(s). The RADIUS server is integrated with Microsoft Active Directory so that Acme will not have to re-create every user account; the RADIUS server can check with the Active Directory server to verify user credentials and passwords.

Separate SSIDs were set up that map to the various VLANs and departments currently on the wired network. Also, a separate SSID was set up as a wireless guest network that has limited access but does provide Internet access for guest users.

Once all this was in place, a site survey was done again to verify the signal strengths and to identify any interference related to the wireless implementation. A heat map was provided to visually represent the signal strengths in the coverage areas in the respective office spaces.

Summary

Here are the main topics covered in this chapter:

- Various components, technologies, and terms used in WLANs were identified.
- WLAN design considerations were presented, such as the selection of WLAN standards, bands, and nonoverlapping channels. Potential sources of interference were also identified.
- Some of the security risks posed by a WLAN were described and the technologies available for mitigating those risks were presented.

Exam Preparation Tasks

Review All the Key Topics

Review the most important topics from inside the chapter, noted with the Key Topic icon in the outer margin of the page. Table 8-4 lists these key topics and the page numbers where each is found.

Table 8-4 Key Topics for Chapter 8

Key Topic Element	Description	Page Number
Figure 8-1	Basic WLAN topology with a wireless router	277
Figure 8-2	Basic WLAN topology with a wireless access point	278
List	Antenna selection criteria	279
Figure 8-3	Omnidirectional antenna coverage	280
Figure 8-4	Unidirectional antenna coverage	280
Figure 8-5	Nonoverlapping channels in the 2.4GHz band	282
List	Spread spectrum transmission methods	284
Table 8-3	Characteristics of 802.11 standards	286
Figure 8-6	Independent basic service set (IBSS) WLAN	287
Figure 8-7	Basic service set (BSS) WLAN	288
Figure 8-8	Extended service set (ESS) WLAN	289
List	Sources of interference	289
Figure 8-9	Coverage overlap in coverage areas for nonoverlapping channels	291
Figure 8-10	Nonoverlapping coverage cells for the 2.4GHz band	292
List	Wireless security threats	292
Figure 8-12	IEEE 802.1X security for a WLAN	295
List	Security standards and best practices	295

Complete Tables and Lists from Memory

Print a copy of Appendix C, "Memory Tables," or at least the section for this chapter, and complete as many of the tables as possible from memory. Appendix D, "Memory Tables Answer Key," includes the completed tables and lists so you can check your work.

Define Key Terms

Define the following key terms from this chapter, and check your answers in the Glossary:

wireless access point (AP), wireless router, decibel (dB), omnidirectional antenna, unidirectional antenna, carrier-sense multiple access/collision avoidance (CSMA/CA), direct-sequence spread spectrum (DSSS), frequency-hopping spread spectrum (FHSS), orthogonal frequency-division multiplexing (OFDM), 802.11a, 802.11b, 802.11g, 802.11n, 802.11ac, multiple input, multiple output (MIMO), channel bonding, independent basic service set (IBSS), basic service set (BSS), extended service set (ESS), war chalking, service set identifier (SSID), Wired Equivalent Privacy (WEP), Wi-Fi Protected Access (WPA), Wi-Fi Protected Access Version 2 (WPA2), Enterprise mode, Personal mode, geofencing

Complete Chapter 8 Hands-On Lab in Network+ Simulator Lite

- Matching Wireless Standards and Terminology

Additional Resources

IT Expertise: Setting Up a Sweet Home WiFi: https://youtu.be/2YQlTDZ3p40

What Is WPA2 Enterprise? https://youtu.be/YCzB7v8n3Xk

Review Questions

The answers to these review questions are in Appendix A, "Answers to Review Questions."

1. What type of antenna, used in wireless APs and wireless routers in SOHO locations, radiates equal power in all directions?
   a. Unidirectional
   b. Yagi
   c. Parabolic
   d. Omnidirectional

2. When you're using the 2.4GHz band for multiple access points in a WLAN found in the United States, which nonoverlapping channels should you select? (Choose three.)
   a. 0
   b. 1
   c. 5
   d. 6
   e. 10
   f. 11
   g. 14

3. What technology do WLANs use to decide when they gain access to the wireless media?
   a. SPF
   b. CSMA/CA
   c. RSTP
   d. DUAL

4. Which IEEE 802.11 variant supports a maximum speed of 54Mbps and uses the 2.4GHz band?
   a. 802.11a
   b. 802.11b
   c. 802.11g
   d. 802.11n

5. Which of the following is used by IEEE 802.11n to achieve high throughput using multiple antennas for transmission and reception?
   a. MIMO
   b. DSSS
   c. FHSS
   d. LACP

6. WLAN formed directly between wireless clients (without the use of a wireless AP) is referred to as what type of WLAN?
   a. Enterprise mode
   b. IBSS
   c. Personal mode
   d. BSS

7. When extending the range for a 2.4GHz WLAN, you can use nonoverlapping channels for adjacent coverage cells. However, there should be some overlap in coverage between those cells (using nonoverlapping channels) to prevent a connection from dropping as a user roams from one coverage cell to another. What percentage of coverage overlap should you recommend for these adjacent cells?
   a. 5% to 10%
   b. 10% to 15%
   c. 15% to 20%
   d. 20% to 25%

8. If a WLAN does not need a user to give credentials to associate with a wireless AP and access the WLAN, what type of authentication is in use?
   a. WEP
   b. SSID
   c. Open
   d. IV

9. WEP's RC4 approach to encryption uses a 24-bit string of characters added to transmitted data, such that the same plain-text data frame will never appear as the same WEP-encrypted data frame. What is this string of characters called?
   a. Initialization vector
   b. Chips
   c. Orthogonal descriptor
   d. Session key

10. Which standard developed by the Wi-Fi Alliance implements the requirements of IEEE 802.11i?

    a. TKIP

    b. MIC

    c. WEP

    d. WPA2

11. Which security technique uses wireless technologies to create an invisible boundary around some point?

    a. WPA2

    b. TKIP

    c. War driving

    d. Geofencing

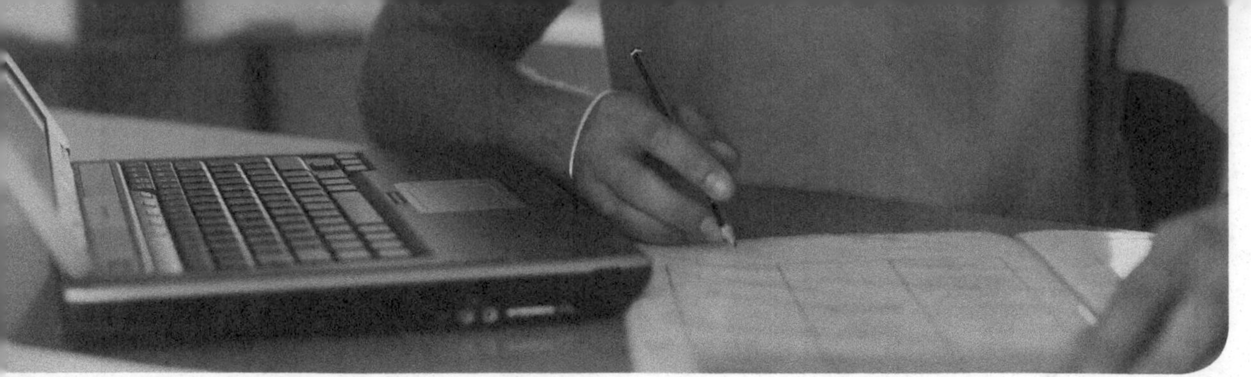

After completion of this chapter, you will be able to answer the following questions:

- Why is high availability a requirement in today's network designs, and what mechanisms can help provide that high availability?
- What various technologies optimize network performance?
- What QoS mechanisms can help optimize network performance?
- Using what you have learned in this and previous chapters, how do you design a SOHO network based on a set of requirements?

CHAPTER 9

Network Optimization

If you saw the movie *Field of Dreams*, you have heard this statement: "If you build it, they will come." That statement has proven itself to be true in today's networks. These networks, which were once relegated to the domain of data, can now carry voice and video. These additional media types, like mission-critical data applications, need a network to be up and available for their users.

For example, think about how often your telephone service has been unavailable versus how often your data network has been unavailable. Unfortunately, data networks have traditionally been less reliable than voice networks; however, today's data networks often *are* voice networks, contributing to this increased demand for uptime. Unified voice services such as call control and communication gateways can be integrated into one or more network devices, leveraging the bandwidth available on the LAN and WAN.

Beyond basic availability, today's networks need optimization tools to make the most of their available bandwidth. This book already addressed several network optimization tools, which are reviewed in this chapter.

Quality of service (QoS) is an entire category of network-optimization tools. QoS, as one example, can give priority treatment to *latency-sensitive* (delay-sensitive) traffic, such as Voice over IP (VoIP). This chapter devotes a section to exploring these tools.

Finally, based on what you learn in this chapter and what you have learned in previous chapters, you are presented with a design challenge. Specifically, a case study presents various design requirements for a small office/home office (SOHO) network. After you create your own network design, you can compare your solution with a suggested solution, keeping in mind that multiple solutions are valid.

Foundation Topics

High Availability

If a network switch or router stops operating correctly (meaning that a *network fault* occurs), communication through the network could be disrupted, resulting in a network becoming unavailable to its users. Therefore, network availability, called *uptime*, is a major design consideration. This consideration might, for example, lead you to add fault-tolerant devices and fault-tolerant links between those devices. This section discusses the measurement of high availability along with a collection of high-availability design considerations.

High-Availability Measurement

The availability of a network is measured by its uptime during a year. For example, if a network has *five nines* of availability, it is up 99.999% of the time, which translates to a maximum of 5 minutes of downtime per year. If a network has *six nines* of availability (meaning it is up 99.9999% of the time), it is down less than 30 seconds per year.

As a designer, one of your goals is to select components, topologies, and features that maximize network *availability* within certain parameters (for example, a budget). Be careful not to confuse *availability* with *reliability*. A *reliable* network, as an example, does not drop many packets, whereas an *available* network is up and operational.

NOTE The availability of a network increases as the mean time to repair (MTTR) of the network devices decreases and as the mean time between failures (MTBF) increases. Therefore, selecting reliable networking devices that are quick to repair is crucial to a high-availability design.

Another goal in your design might be to meet the requirements set forth in a service-level agreement (SLA). An SLA is an official commitment that exists between a service provider and a client. Aspects of the IT services provided—quality, availability, specific responsibilities—are agreed upon between the service provider and the service user. Strict SLAs are more and more common in networking today as more and more cloud services find their way into the IT landscape. The cloud provider is a specialized service provider, and the cloud consumer is the client.

Fault-Tolerant Network Design

Two approaches to designing a fault-tolerant network are as follows:

- **Single points of failure:** If the failure of a single network device or link (for example, a switch, router, or WAN connection) would result in a network becoming unavailable, that single device or link is a potential single point of failure. To eliminate single points of failure from your design, you might include redundant links and redundant hardware. For example, some high-end Ethernet switches support two power supplies, and if one power supply fails, the switch continues to operate by using the backup power supply. Link redundancy, as shown in Figure 9-1, can be achieved by using more than one physical link. If a single link between a switch and a router fails, the network would not go down because of the link redundancy that is in place.

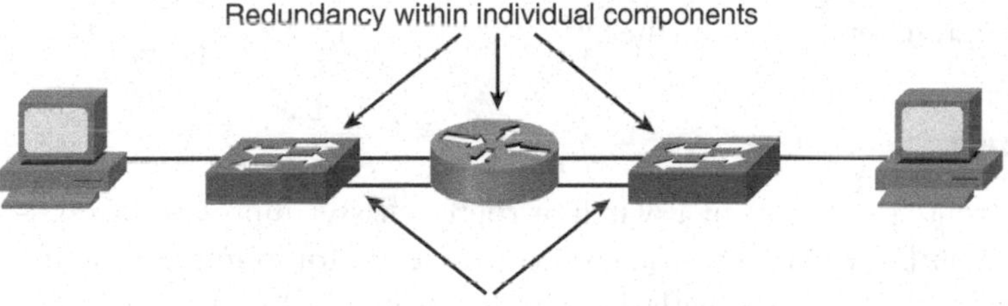

Figure 9-1 Redundant Network with Single Points of Failure

- **No single points of failure:** A network without a single point of failure contains redundant network-infrastructure components (for example, switches and routers). In addition, these redundant devices are interconnected with redundant links. Although a network host could have two network interface cards (NICs), each of which connects to a different switch, such a design is rarely implemented because of the increased costs. Instead, as shown in Figure 9-2, a network with no single points of failure in the backbone allows any single switch or router in the backbone to fail, or any single link in the backbone to fail, while maintaining end-to-end network connectivity.

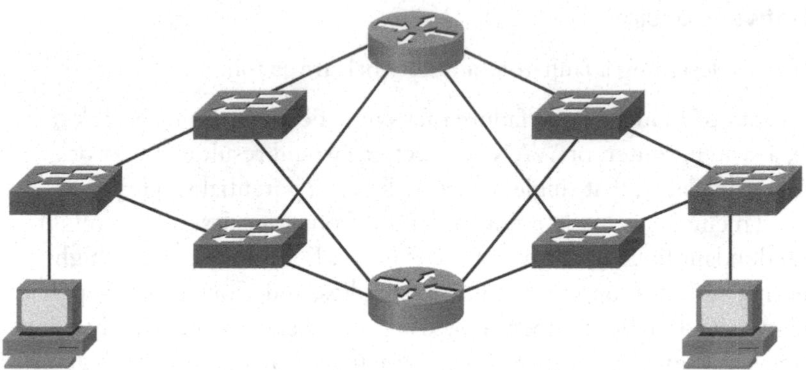

Figure 9-2 Redundant Network with No Single Point of Failure

These two approaches to fault-tolerant network design can be used together to increase a network's availability even further.

Hardware Redundancy

Having redundant route processors in a switch or router chassis improves the chassis' reliability. If a multilayer switch has two route processors, for example, one of the route processors could be active, with the other route processor standing by to take over in the event the active processor became unavailable.

An end system can have redundant NICs. The two modes of NIC redundancy are as follows:

- **Active-active:** Both NICs are active at the same time, and each has its own MAC address. This makes troubleshooting more complex, while giving you slightly better performance than the active-standby approach.
- **Active-standby:** Only one NIC is active at a time. This approach allows the client to appear to have a single MAC address and IP address, even in the event of a NIC failure.

NIC redundancy is most often found in strategic network hosts, rather than in end-user client computers, because of the expense and administrative overhead incurred with a redundant NIC configuration.

> **NOTE** Different vendors use different terms to refer to combining NICs for hardware redundancy. The two most common are *NIC teaming* and *NIC bonding*. CompTIA prefers NIC teaming.

Another powerful method of hardware redundancy comes in the form of computer clustering. A computer cluster consists of a set of tightly connected computers that work together. In many respects, clients view them as a single system.

The servers in a cluster are usually connected to each other through fast local area networks, with each node running its own instance of an operating system. In most circumstances, all of the nodes use the same hardware and the same operating system, although in some setups, different operating systems can be used on each computer, or even different hardware.

Computer clusters emerged as a result of the convergence of a number of computing trends, including the availability of low-cost microprocessors, high-speed networks, and software for high-performance distributed computing. They have a wide range of applicability and deployment, ranging from small business clusters with a handful of nodes to some of the fastest supercomputers in the world.

Layer 3 Redundancy

End systems not running a routing protocol point to a default gateway. The default gateway is traditionally the IP address of a router on the local subnet. However, if the default gateway router fails, the end systems are unable to leave their subnet. Chapter 4, "Ethernet Technology," introduced four first-hop redundancy technologies (which offer Layer 3 redundancy):

- **Hot Standby Router Protocol (HSRP):** A Cisco proprietary approach to first-hop redundancy. Figure 9-3 shows a sample HSRP topology.

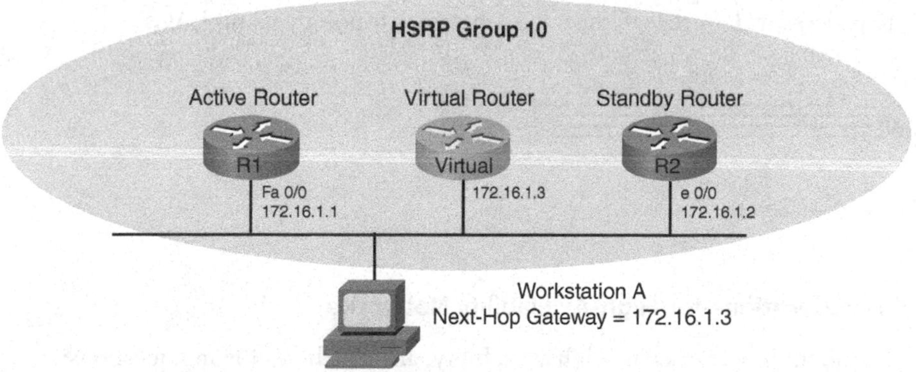

Figure 9-3 HSRP Sample Topology

In Figure 9-3, workstation A is configured with a default gateway (that is, a next-hop gateway) of 172.16.1.3. To prevent the default gateway from becoming a single point of failure, HSRP enables routers R1 and R2 to each act as the default gateway, supporting the virtual IP address of the HSRP group (172.16.1.3), although only one of the routers will act as the default gateway at any one time. Under normal conditions, router R1 (that is, the *active router*) forwards packets sent to virtual IP 172.16.1.3. However, if router R1 is unavailable, router R2 (that is, the *standby router*) can take over and start forwarding traffic sent to 172.16.1.3. Notice that neither router R1 nor R2 has a physical interface with an IP address of 172.16.1.3. Instead, a logical router (called a *virtual router*), which is serviced by either router R1 or R2, maintains the 172.16.1.3 IP address.

- **Common Address Redundancy Protocol (CARP):** CARP is an open-standard variant of HSRP.
- **Virtual Router Redundancy Protocol (VRRP):** VRRP is an IETF open standard that operates in a similar method to Cisco's proprietary HSRP.
- **Gateway Load Balancing Protocol (GLBP):** GLBP is another first-hop redundancy protocol that is proprietary to Cisco Systems.

With each of these technologies, the MAC address and the IP address of a default gateway can be serviced by more than one router (or multilayer switch). Therefore, if a default gateway becomes unavailable, the other router (or multilayer switch) can take over, still servicing the same MAC and IP addresses.

Another type of Layer 3 redundancy is achieved by having multiple links between devices and selecting a routing protocol that load-balances over the links. Link Aggregation Control Protocol (LACP), discussed in Chapter 4, enables you to assign multiple physical links to a logical interface, which appears as a single link to a route processor. Figure 9-4 illustrates a network topology using LACP.

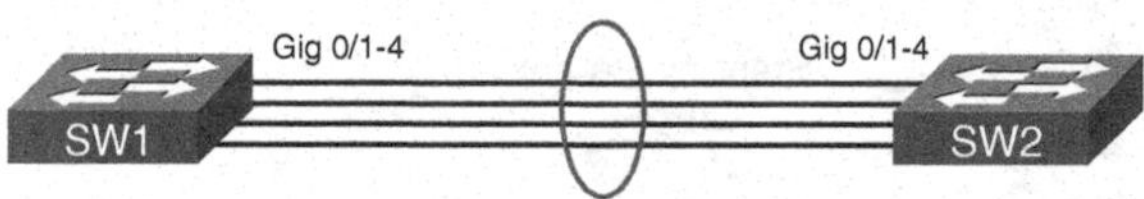

Figure 9-4 LACP Sample Topology

Design Considerations for High-Availability Networks

When designing networks for high availability, answer the following questions:

- Where will module and chassis redundancy be used? Module redundancy provides redundancy within a chassis by allowing one module to take over in the event that a primary module fails. Chassis redundancy provides redundancy by having more than one chassis, thus providing a path from the source to the destination, even in the event of a chassis or link failure.

- What software redundancy features are appropriate?
- What protocol characteristics affect design requirements?
- What redundancy features should be used to provide power to an infrastructure device—for example, using an uninterruptible power supply (UPS), a generator, or dual power supplies?
- What redundancy features should be used to maintain environmental conditions (for example, dual air-conditioning units)?
- Will dual circuits be provided in the event of a loss of connection with one of the circuits?
- What backup strategy exists for infrastructure and user data? Remember, different backup strategies include the following:
    - **Full**: A backup of all of the data set. Although this is the safest and most comprehensive way to ensure data availability, it can be time consuming and costly.
    - **Incremental**: This backs up only data that has changed since the previous backup.
    - **Differential**: This is similar to an incremental backup in that it starts with a full backup, and then subsequent backups only contain data that has changed. The difference is that whereas an incremental backup only includes the data that has changed since the previous backup, a differential backup contains all of the data that has changed since the last full backup
    - **Snapshots**: This is a read-only copy of the data set that is frozen in a point in time. This type of technology for backup is often used with virtual machines and file system objects.

High-Availability Best Practices

The following are the five best practices for designing high-availability networks:

- Examine technical goals.
- Identify the budget to fund high-availability features.
- Categorize business applications into profiles, each of which requires a certain level of availability.
- Establish performance standards for high-availability solutions.
- Define how to manage and measure the high-availability solution.

Although existing networks can be retrofitted to make them highly available networks, network designers can often reduce such expenses by integrating high-availability best practices and technologies into the initial design of a network.

Content Caching

Chapter 3, "Network Components," introduced the concept of a *content engine* (also known as a *caching engine*). A content engine is a network appliance that can receive a copy of content stored elsewhere (for example, a video presentation located on a server at a corporate headquarters) and serve that content to local clients, thus reducing the bandwidth burden on an IP WAN. Figure 9-5 shows a sample topology using a content engine as a network optimization technology.

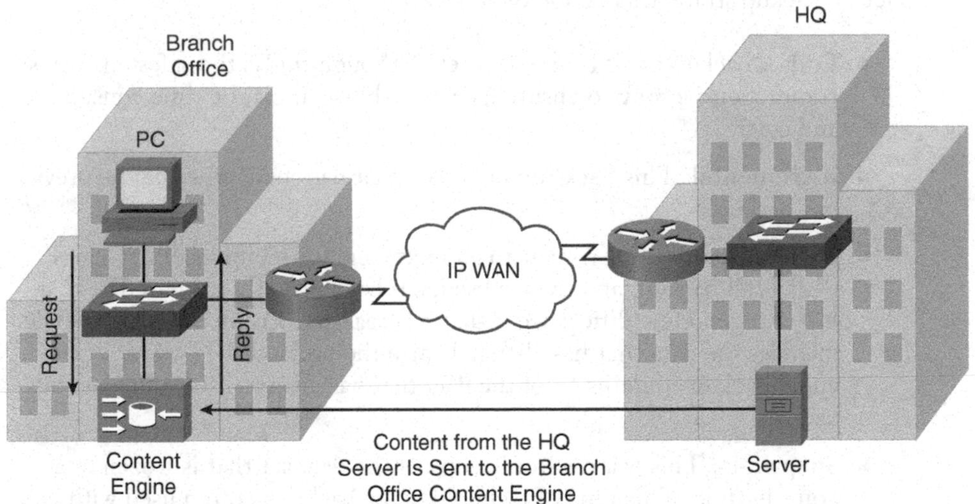

Figure 9-5 Content Engine Sample Topology

Load Balancing

Another network optimization technology introduced in Chapter 3 was *content switching*, which allows a request coming into a server farm to be distributed across multiple servers containing identical content. This approach to load balancing lightens the load on individual servers in a server farm and allows servers to be taken out of the farm for maintenance without disrupting access to the server farm's data. Figure 9-6 illustrates a sample content-switching topology that performs load balancing across five servers (containing identical content) in a server farm.

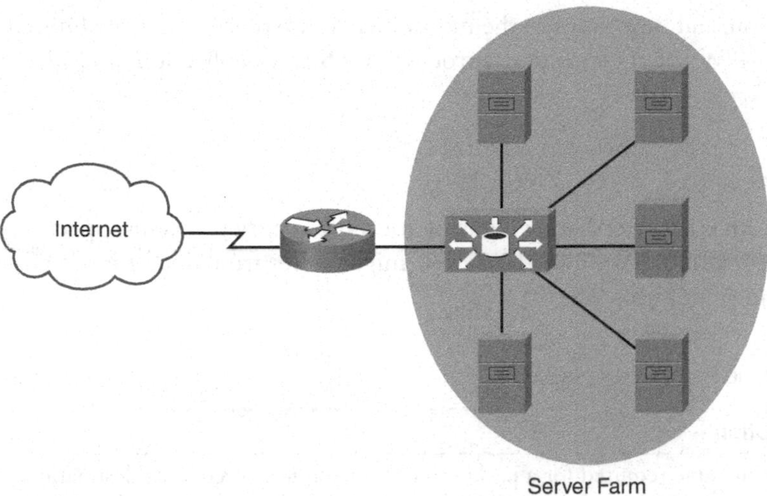

Figure 9-6 Content-Switching Sample Topology

Hardware Redundancy

It is also possible to design entire site redundancy into your network infrastructure. This requires redundant data and equipment located in geographically distant areas. How fast can your IT infrastructure be back up and running should issues arise in your primary site? This is commonly measured as follows:

- **Cold site**: Recovery is possible but is difficult and time consuming.
- **Warm site**: Recovery is possible fairly quickly, but it might not be equal to all the resources and responsiveness of the original site.
- **Hot site**: Downtime is minimal, with a nearly identical service level.

QoS Technologies

Quality of service (QoS) is a suite of technologies that allows you to strategically optimize network performance for select traffic types. For example, in today's converged networks (that is, networks simultaneously transporting voice, video, and data), some applications (for example, voice) might be more intolerant of delay (or *latency*) than other applications (for example, an FTP file transfer is less latency sensitive than a VoIP call). Fortunately, through the use of QoS technologies, you can identify which traffic types need to be sent first, how much bandwidth to allocate to various traffic types, which traffic types should be dropped first in the event of congestion, and how to make the most efficient use of the relatively limited bandwidth of an IP WAN. This section introduces QoS and a collection of QoS mechanisms.

Introduction to QoS

A lack of bandwidth is the overshadowing issue for most quality problems. Specifically, when there is a lack of bandwidth, packets might suffer from one or more of the symptoms shown in Table 9-1.

Table 9-1 Three Categories of Quality Issues

Issue	Description
Delay	Delay is the time required for a packet to travel from its source to its destination. You might have witnessed delay on the evening news when the news anchor is talking via satellite to a foreign news correspondent. Because of the satellite delay, the conversation begins to feel unnatural.
Jitter	Jitter is the uneven arrival of packets. For example, imagine a VoIP conversation where packet 1 arrives at a destination router. Then, 20 ms later, packet 2 arrives. After another 70 ms, packet 3 arrives, and then packet 4 arrives 20 ms behind packet 3. This variation in arrival times (that is, variable delay) is not dropping packets, but the jitter might be interpreted by the listener as dropped packets.
Drops	Packet drops occur when a link is congested and a router's interface queue overflows. Some types of traffic, such as UDP traffic carrying voice packets, are not retransmitted if packets are dropped.

Fortunately, QoS features available on many routers and switches can recognize important traffic and then treat that traffic in a special way. For example, you might want to allocate 128Kbps of bandwidth for your VoIP traffic and give that traffic priority treatment.

Consider water flowing through a series of pipes with varying diameters. The water's flow rate through those pipes is limited to the water's flow rate through the pipe with the smallest diameter. Similarly, as a packet travels from its source to its destination, its effective bandwidth is the bandwidth of the slowest link along that path. For example, consider Figure 9-7. Notice that the slowest link speed is 256Kbps. This weakest link becomes the effective bandwidth between client and server.

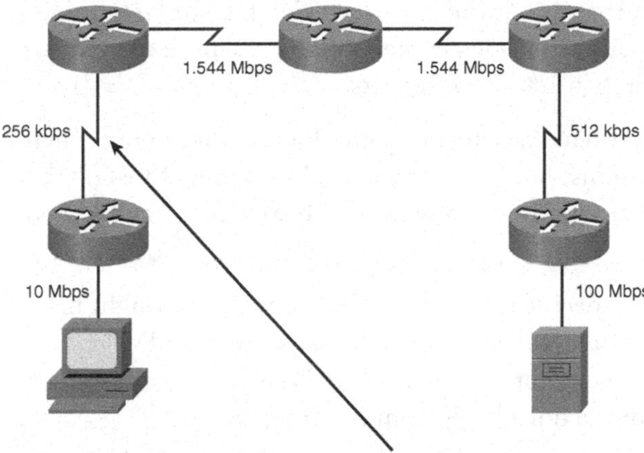

Figure 9-7 Effective Bandwidth of 256Kbps

Because the primary challenge of QoS is a lack of bandwidth, the logical question is, "How do we increase available bandwidth?" A knee-jerk response to that question is often, "Add more bandwidth." Although there is no substitute for more bandwidth, it often comes at a relatively high cost.

Compare your network to a highway system in a large city. During rush hour, the lanes of the highway are congested, but the lanes might be underutilized during other periods of the day. Instead of just building more lanes to accommodate peak traffic rates, the highway engineers might add a carpool lane. Cars with two or more riders can use the reserved carpool lane because they have a higher priority on the highway. Similarly, you can use QoS features to give your mission-critical applications higher-priority treatment in times of network congestion.

QoS Configuration Steps

The mission statement of QoS could read something like this: "To categorize traffic and apply a policy to those traffic categories, in accordance with a QoS policy." Understanding this underlying purpose of QoS can help you better understand the three basic steps to QoS configuration:

Step 1. Determine network performance requirements for various traffic types. For example, consider these design recommendations for voice, video, and data traffic:

- **Voice:** No more than 150 ms of one-way delay; no more than 30 ms of jitter; and no more than 1% packet loss.

- **Video:** No more than 150 ms of one-way delay for interactive voice applications (for example, video conferencing); no more than 30 ms of jitter; no more than 1% of packet loss.
- **Data:** Applications have varying delay and loss requirements. Therefore, data applications should be categorized into predefined *classes* of traffic, where each class is configured with specific delay and loss characteristics.

Step 2. Categorize traffic into specific categories. For example, you might have a category named *Low Delay*, and you decide to place voice and video packets in that category. You might also have a *Low Priority* class, where you place traffic such as music downloads from the Internet.

Step 3. Document your QoS policy and make it available to your users. Then, for example, if a user complains that his network-gaming applications are running slowly, you can point them to your corporate QoS policy, which describes how applications such as network gaming have *best-effort* treatment while VoIP traffic receives *priority* treatment.

The actual implementation of these steps varies based on the specific device you are configuring. In some cases, you might be using the command-line interface (CLI) of a router or switch. In other cases, you might have some sort of graphical user interface (GUI) through which you configure QoS on your routers and switches.

QoS Components

QoS features are categorized into one of the three categories shown in Table 9-2.

Table 9-2 Three Categories of QoS Mechanisms

Issue	Description
Best effort	Best-effort treatment of traffic does not truly provide QoS to that traffic because there is no reordering of packets. Best effort uses a first-in, first-out (FIFO) queuing strategy, where packets are emptied from a queue in the same order that they entered the queue.
Integrated Services (IntServ)	IntServ is often referred to as hard QoS because it can make strict bandwidth reservations. IntServ uses signaling among network devices to provide bandwidth reservations. Resource Reservation Protocol (RSVP) is an example of an IntServ approach to QoS. Because IntServ must be configured on every router along a packet's path, the main drawback of IntServ is its lack of scalability.

Issue	Description
Differentiated services (DiffServ)	DiffServ, as its name suggests, differentiates between multiple traffic flows. Specifically, packets are marked, and routers and switches can then make decisions (for example, dropping or forwarding decisions) based on those markings. Because DiffServ does not make an explicit reservation, it is often called soft QoS. Most modern QoS configurations are based on the DiffServ approach.

Figure 9-8 summarizes these three QoS categories.

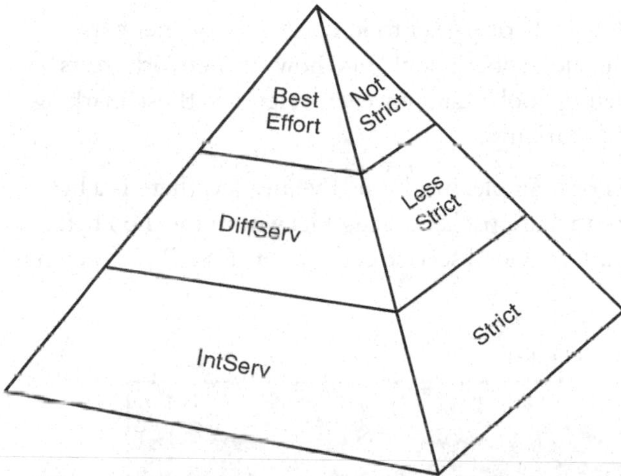

Figure 9-8 QoS Categories

QoS Mechanisms

As previously mentioned, a DiffServ approach to QoS marks traffic. However, for markings to impact the behavior of traffic, a QoS tool must reference those markings and alter the packets' treatment based on them. The following is a collection of commonly used QoS mechanisms:

- Classification
- Marking
- Congestion management
- Congestion avoidance
- Policing and shaping
- Link efficiency

The following sections describe each QoS mechanism in detail.

Classification

Classification is the process of placing traffic into different categories. Multiple characteristics can be used for classification. For example, POP3, IMAP, SMTP, and Exchange traffic could all be placed in an *E-MAIL* class. Classification does not, however, alter any bits in the frame or packet.

Marking

Marking alters bits within a frame, cell, or packet to indicate how the network should treat that traffic. Marking alone does not change how the network treats a packet. Other tools (such as queuing tools) can, however, reference those markings and make decisions based on the markings.

Various packet markings exist. For example, inside an IPv4 header, there is a byte called *type of service* (ToS). You can mark packets, using bits within the ToS byte, using either IP Precedence or differentiated service code point (DSCP), as shown in Figure 9-9.

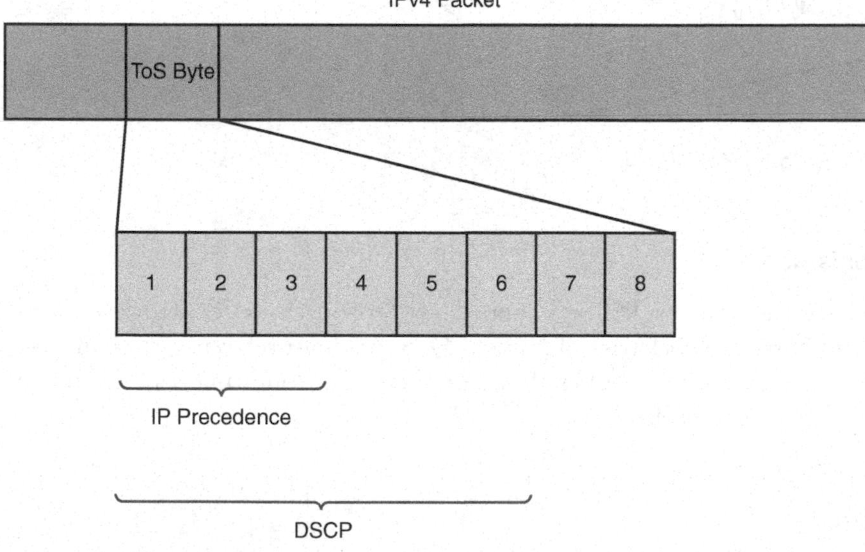

Figure 9-9 ToS Byte

IP Precedence uses the three leftmost bits in the ToS byte. With three bits at its disposal, IP Precedence markings can range from 0 to 7. However, 6 and 7 should not be used because those values are reserved for network use.

For more granularity, you might choose DSCP, which uses the six leftmost bits in the ToS byte. Six bits yield 64 possible values (0–63).

Congestion Management

When a device such as a switch or a router receives traffic faster than it can be transmitted, the device attempts to buffer (or store) the extra traffic until bandwidth becomes available. This buffering process is called *queuing* or *congestion management*. However, a queuing algorithm, such as weighted fair queuing (WFQ), low-latency queuing (LLQ), or weighted round-robin (WRR), can be configured on routers and switches. These algorithms divide an interface's buffer into multiple logical queues, as shown in Figure 9-10. The queuing algorithm then empties packets from those logical queues in a sequence and amount determined by the algorithm's configuration. For example, traffic could first be sent from a priority queue (which might contain VoIP packets) up to a certain bandwidth limit, after which packets could be sent from a different queue.

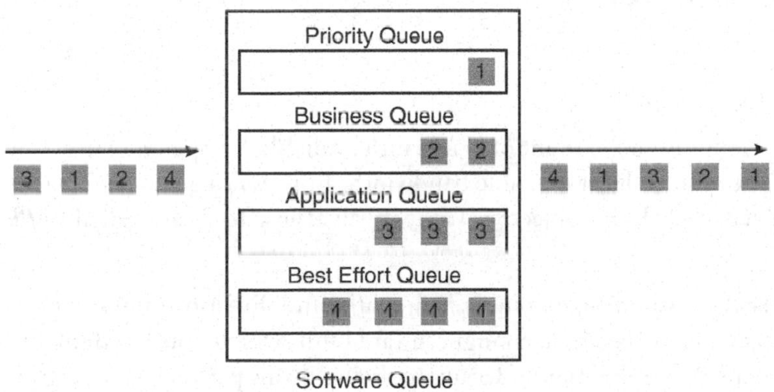

Figure 9-10 Queuing Example

Congestion Avoidance

If an interface's output queue fills to capacity, newly arriving packets are discarded (or *tail dropped*). To prevent this behavior, a congestion-avoidance technique called *random early detection* (RED) can be used, as illustrated in Figure 9-11. After a queue depth reaches a configurable level (*minimum threshold*), RED introduces the possibility of a packet discard. As the queue depth continues to increase, the possibility of a discard increases until a configurable *maximum threshold* is reached. After the queue depth exceeds the maximum threshold for traffic with a specific priority, there is a 100% chance of discard for those traffic types. If those discarded packets are TCP based (connection oriented), the sender knows which packets are discarded and can retransmit those dropped packets. However, if those dropped packets are UDP based (that is, connectionless), the sender does not receive an indication that the packets were dropped.

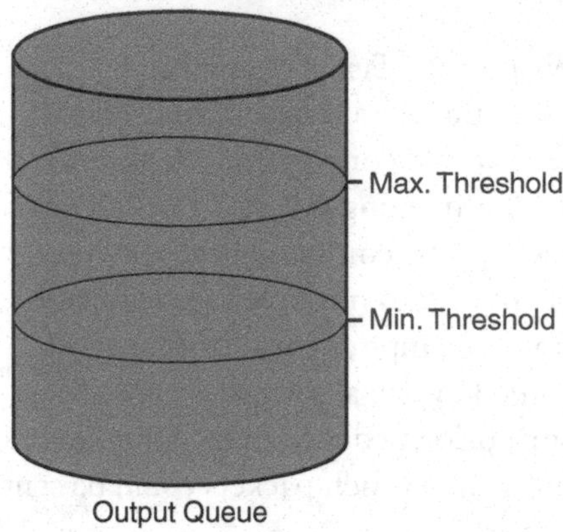

Figure 9-11 Random Early Detection (RED)

Policing and Shaping

Instead of making a minimum amount of bandwidth available for specific traffic types, you might want to limit available bandwidth. Both *policing* and *traffic-shaping* tools can accomplish this objective. Collectively, these tools are called *traffic conditioners*.

Policing can be used in either the inbound or the outbound direction, and it typically discards packets that exceed the configured rate limit, which you can think of as a *speed limit* for specific traffic types. Because policing drops packets, resulting in retransmissions, it is recommended for higher-speed interfaces.

Shaping buffers (and therefore delays) traffic exceeding a configured rate. Therefore, shaping is recommended for slower-speed interfaces.

Because traffic shaping (and policing) can limit the speed of packets exiting a router, a question arises: "How do we send traffic out of an interface at a rate that is less than the physical clock rate of the interface?" For this to be possible, shaping and policing tools do not transmit all the time. Specifically, they send a certain number of bits or bytes at line rate, and then they stop sending, until a specific timing interval (for example, one-eighth of a second) is reached. After the timing interval is reached, the interface again sends a specific amount of traffic at line rate. It stops and waits for the next timing interval to occur. This process continually repeats, allowing an interface to send an average bandwidth that might be below the physical speed of the interface. This average bandwidth is called the *committed information rate* (CIR). The number of bits (the unit of measure used with shaping tools) or bytes (the unit of measure used with policing tools) that is sent during a timing interval is called the *committed burst* (Bc). The timing interval is written as *Tc*.

For example, imagine that you have a physical line rate of 128Kbps, but the CIR is only 64Kbps. Also, assume there are eight timing intervals in a second (that is, Tc = 1/8th of a second = 125 ms), and during each of those timing intervals, 8000 bits (the committed burst parameter) are sent at line rate. Therefore, over the period of a second, 8000 bits were sent (at line rate) eight times, for a grand total of 64,000 bits per second, which is the CIR. Figure 9-12 illustrates this shaping of traffic to 64Kbps on a line with a rate of 128Kbps.

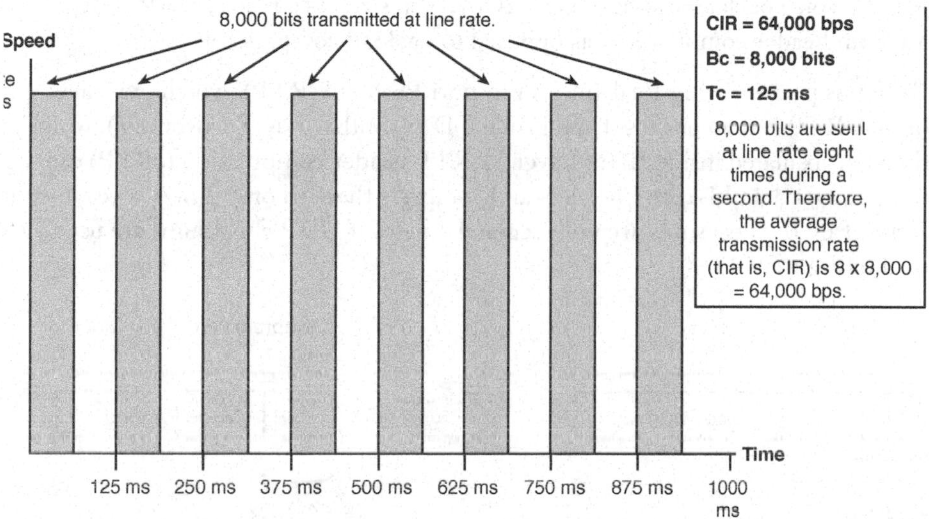

Figure 9-12 Traffic Shaping

If all the Bc bits (or bytes) were not sent during a timing interval, there is an option to *bank* those bits and use them during a future timing interval. The parameter that allows this storing of unused potential bandwidth is called the *excess burst* (Be) parameter. The Be parameter in a shaping configuration specifies the maximum number of bits or bytes that can be sent in excess of the Bc during a timing interval, if those bits are indeed available. For those bits or bytes to be available, they must have gone unused during previous timing intervals. Policing tools, however, use the Be parameter to specify the maximum number of bytes that can be sent during a timing interval. Therefore, in a policing configuration, if the Bc equals the Be, no excess bursting occurs. If excess bursting occurs, policing tools consider this excess traffic as *exceeding traffic*. Traffic that conforms to (does not exceed) a specified CIR is considered by a policing tool to be *conforming traffic*.

The relationship between the Tc, Bc, and CIR is given with this formula: *CIR = Bc / Tc*. Alternately, the formula can be written as *Tc = Bc / CIR*. Therefore, if you want a smaller timing interval, configure a smaller Bc.

Link Efficiency

To make the most of the limited bandwidth available on slower-speed links, you might choose to implement *compression* or *link fragmentation and interleaving* (LFI). Although you could compress a packet's payload or header to conserve bandwidth, as one example, consider header compression. With VoIP packets, the Layer 3 and Layer 4 headers total 40 bytes in size. However, depending on how you encode voice, the voice payload might be only 20 bytes in size. As a result, VoIP benefits most from header compression, as opposed to payload compression.

VoIP sends packets using Real-time Transport Protocol (RTP), which is a Layer 4 protocol. RTP is then encapsulated inside UDP (another Layer 4 protocol), which is then encapsulated inside IP (at Layer 3). RTP header compression (cRTP) can take the Layer 3 and Layer 4 headers and compress them to only 2 or 4 bytes in size (2 bytes if UDP checksums are not used and 4 bytes if UDP checksums are used), as shown in Figure 9-13.

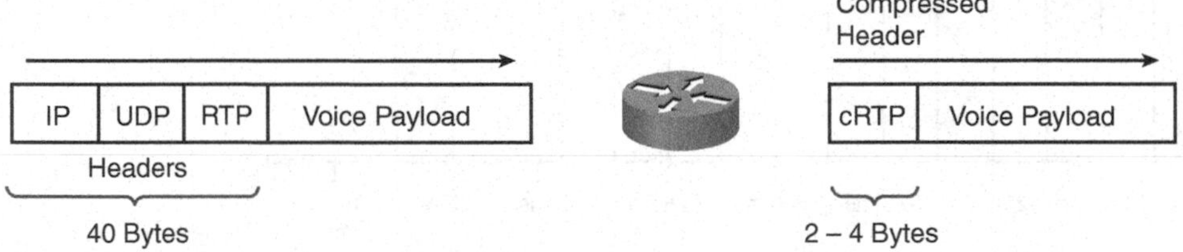

Figure 9-13 RTP Header Compression (cRTP)

LFI addresses the issue of serialization delay, which is the amount of time required for a packet to exit an interface. A large data packet, for example, on a slower-speed link might create excessive delay for a voice packet because of the time required for the data packet to exit the interface. LFI fragments the large packets and interleaves the smaller packets among the fragments, reducing the serialization delay experienced by the smaller packets. Figure 9-14 shows the operation of LFI, where the packets labeled *D* are data packets, and the packets labeled *V* are voice packets.

Figure 9-14 Link Fragmentation and Interleaving (LFI)

Case Study: SOHO Network Design

Based on what you learned from previous chapters and this chapter, this section challenges you to create a network design to meet a collection of criteria. Because network design is part science and part art, multiple designs can meet the specified requirements. However, as a reference, this section presents one solution, against which you can contrast your solution.

Case Study Scenario

While working through your design, consider the following:

- Meeting all requirements
- Media distance limitations
- Network device selection
- Environmental factors
- Compatibility with existing and future equipment

The following are your design scenario and design criteria for this case study:

- Company ABC leases two buildings (building A and building B) in a large office park, as shown in Figure 9-15. The office park has a conduit system that allows physical media to run between buildings. The distance (via the conduit system) between building A and building B is 1 km.

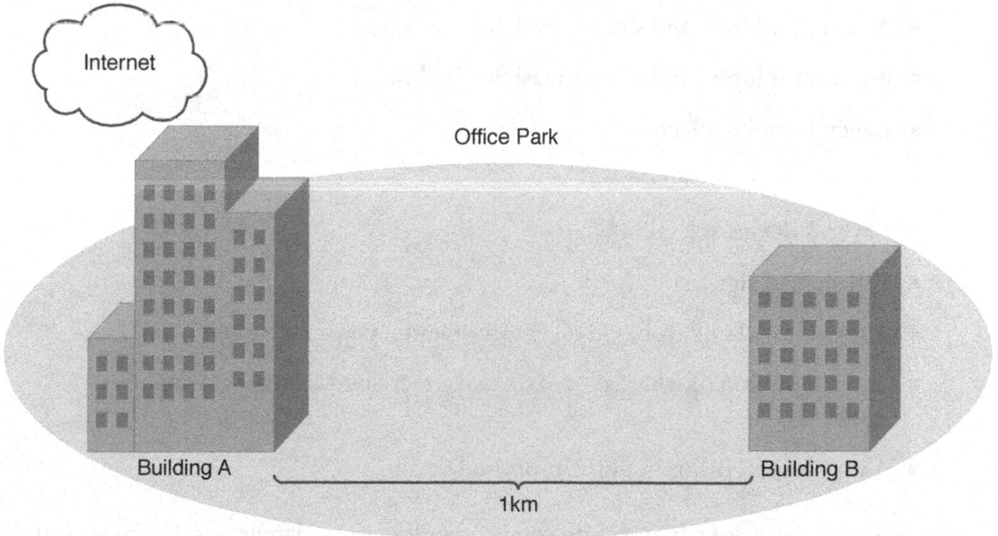

Figure 9-15 Case Study Topology

- Company ABC will use the Class B address of 172.16.0.0/16 for its sites. You should subnet this classful network not only to support the two buildings (one subnet per building), but to allow as many as five total sites in the future, as Company ABC continues to grow.
- Company ABC needs to connect to the Internet, supporting a speed of at least 30Mbps, and this connection should come into building A.
- Cost is a primary design consideration, while performance is a secondary design consideration.
- Each building contains various Wi-Fi client devices (for example, smartphones, tablets, and laptops).
- Table 9-3 identifies the number of hosts contained in each building and the number of floors contained in each building.

Table 9-3 Case Study Information for Buildings A and B

Building	Number of Hosts	Floors (and Wireless Coverage)
A	200	Three floors, each of which can be serviced with a single wireless access point
B	100	One floor, which can be serviced by a single wireless access point

Your design should include the following information:

- Network address and subnet mask for building A
- Network address and subnet mask for building B
- Layer 1 media selection
- Layer 2 device selection
- Layer 3 device selection
- Wireless design
- Any design elements based on environmental considerations
- An explanation of where cost savings were created from performance trade-offs
- A topological diagram of the proposed design

On separate sheets of paper, create your network design. After your design is complete, perform a sanity check by contrasting the listed criteria against your design.

Finally, while keeping in mind that multiple designs could meet the design criteria, you can review the following suggested solution. In the real world, reviewing the logic behind other designs can often give you a fresh perspective for future designs.

Suggested Solution

This suggested solution begins by IP address allocation. Then, consideration is given to the Layer 1 media, followed by Layer 2 and Layer 3 devices. Wireless design decisions are presented. Design elements based on environmental factors are discussed. The suggested solution also addresses how cost savings were achieved through performance trade-offs. Finally, a topological diagram of the suggested solution is presented.

IP Addressing

Questions you might need to ask when designing the IP addressing of a network include the following:

- How many hosts do you need to support (now and in the future)?
- How many subnets do you need to support (now and in the future)?

From the scenario, you know that each subnet must accommodate at least 200 hosts. Also, you know that you must accommodate at least five subnets. In this solution, the subnet mask is based on the number of required subnets. Eight subnets are supported with 3 borrowed bits, while two borrowed only support four subnets, based on this formula:

Number of subnets = 2^s

where s is the number of borrowed bits

With 3 borrowed bits, we have 13 bits left for host IP addressing, which is much more than needed to accommodate 200 host IP addresses. These 3 borrowed bits yield a subnet mask of 255.255.224.0. Because the third octet is the last octet to contain a binary 1 in the subnet mask, the third octet is the *interesting octet*.

The block size can be calculated by subtracting the subnet decimal value in the interesting octet from 256 (that is, 256 – 224 = 32). Because the block size is 32 and the interesting octet is the third octet, the following subnets are created with the 255.255.224.0 (that is, /19) subnet mask:

- 172.16.0.0 /19
- 172.16.32.0 /19
- 172.16.64.0 /19

- 172.16.96.0 /19
- 172.16.128.0 /19
- 172.16.160.0 /19
- 172.16.192.0 /19
- 172.16.224.0 /19

The first two subnets are selected for the building A and building B subnet, as shown in Table 9-4.

Table 9-4 Case Study Suggested Solution: Network Addresses

Building	Subnet
A	172.16.0.0 /19
B	172.16.32.0 /19

Layer 1 Media

Questions you might need to ask when selecting the Layer 1 media types of a network include the following:

- What speeds need to be supported (now and in the future)?
- What distances between devices need to be supported (now and in the future)?

Within each building, Category 6a (Cat 6a) unshielded twisted-pair (UTP) cabling is selected to interconnect network components. The installation is based on Gigabit Ethernet. However, if 10-Gigabit Ethernet devices are installed in the future, Cat 6a is rated for 10GBASE-T for distances as long as 100 m.

The 1-km distance between building A and building B is too far for UTP cabling. Therefore, multimode fiber (MMF) is selected. The speed of the fiber link will be 1Gbps. Table 9-5 summarizes these media selections.

Table 9-5 Case Study Suggested Solution: Layer 1 Media

Connection Type	Media Type
LAN links within buildings	Cat 6a UTP
Link between building A and building B	MMF

Layer 2 Devices

Questions you might need to ask when selecting Layer 2 devices in a network include the following:

- Where will the switches be located?
- What port densities are required on the switches (now and in the future)?
- What switch features need to be supported (for example, STP or LACP)?
- What media types are used to connect to the switches?

A collection of Ethernet switches interconnect network devices within each building. Assume the 200 hosts in building A are distributed relatively evenly across the three floors (each floor contains approximately 67 hosts). Therefore, each floor will have a wiring closet containing two Ethernet switches: one 48-port density switch and one 24-port density switch. Each switch is connected to a multilayer switch located in building A using four connections logically bundled together using Link Aggregation Control Protocol (LACP).

NOTE Link aggregation is also known as *port aggregation*. CompTIA prefers the term port aggregation to link aggregation.

Within building B, two Ethernet switches, each with 48 ports, and one Ethernet switch, with 24 ports, are installed in a wiring closet. These switches are interconnected in a stacked configuration, using four connections logically bundled together with LACP. One of the switches has an MMF port, which allows it to connect via fiber to building A's multilayer switch.

Table 9-6 summarizes the switch selections.

Table 9-6 Case Study Suggested Solution: Layer 2 Devices

Building	Quantity of 48-Port Switches	Quantity of 24-Port Switches
A	3	3
B	2	1

Layer 3 Devices

Questions you might need to ask when selecting Layer 3 devices for a network include the following:

- How many interfaces are needed (now and in the future)?
- What types of interfaces need to be supported (now and in the future)?

- What routing protocol (or protocols) needs to be supported?
- What router features (for example, HSRP or security features) need to be supported?

Layer 3 devices consist of a multilayer switch located in building A. All switches within building A home back to the multilayer switch using four LACP-bundled links. The multilayer switch is equipped with at least one MMF port, which allows a connection with one of the Ethernet switches in building B.

The multilayer switch connects to a router via a Fast Ethernet connection. This router contains a serial interface, which connects to the Internet via a T3 connection.

Wireless Design

Questions you might need to ask when designing the wireless portion of a network include the following:

- What wireless speeds need to be supported (now and in the future)?
- What distances need to be supported between wireless devices and wireless access points (now and in the future)?
- What IEEE wireless standards need to be supported?
- What channels should be used?
- Where should wireless access points be located?

Because the network needs to support various Wi-Fi clients, the 2.4GHz band is chosen. Within building A, a wireless access point (AP) is placed on each floor of the building. To avoid interference, the nonoverlapping channels of 1, 6, and 11 are chosen. The 2.4GHz band also allows compatibility with IEEE 802.11b/g/n.

Within building B, a single wireless AP accommodates Wi-Fi clients. Table 9-7 summarizes the wireless AP selection.

Table 9-7 Case Study Suggested Solution: Wireless AP Selection

AP Identifier	Building	Band	Channel
1	A (1st floor)	2.4GHz	1
2	A (2nd floor)	2.4GHz	6
3	A (3rd floor)	2.4GHz	11
4	B	2.4GHz	1

Environmental Factors

Questions you might need to ask when considering environmental factors of a network design include the following:

- What temperature or humidity controls exist in the rooms containing network equipment?
- What power redundancy systems are needed to provide power to network equipment in the event of a power outage?

Because the multilayer switch in building A could be a single point of failure for the entire network, the multilayer switch is placed in a well-ventilated room, which can help dissipate heat in the event of an air-conditioning failure. To further enhance the availability of the multilayer switch, the switch is connected to a UPS, which can help the multilayer switch continue to run for a brief time in the event of a power outage. Protection against an extended power outage could be achieved with the addition of a generator. However, no generator is included in this design because of budgetary reasons.

Cost Savings Versus Performance

When assimilating all the previously gathered design elements, you need to weigh budgetary constraints against network performance metrics. In this example, Gigabit Ethernet was chosen over 10-Gigabit Ethernet. In addition, the link between building A and building B could become a bottleneck because it runs at a speed of 1Gbps, although it transports an aggregation of multiple 1Gbps links. However, cost savings are achieved by using 1Gbps switch interfaces as opposed to 10Gbps interfaces or a bundle of multiple 1Gbps fiber links.

Topology

Figure 9-16 shows the topology of the proposed design based on the collection of previously listed design decisions.

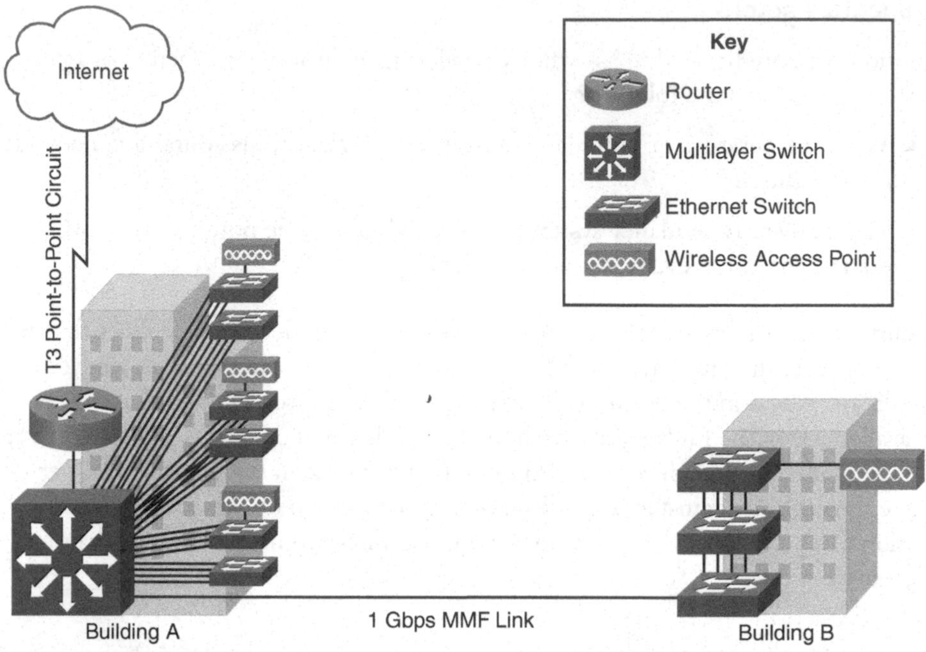

Figure 9-16 Case Study Proposed Topology

Real-World Case Study

The network design for Acme, Inc. includes fault tolerance at several points in the network. The uplinks that go to the wiring closets from the MDF downstairs are implemented as redundant pairs, so that if a single pair fails or a single interface fails, the other fiber pair and associated interfaces can continue to forward traffic. The routing function is located downstairs, and each VLAN (and associated subnet) has a pair of routers acting as an HSRP group.

The firewalls that control traffic at the edge of the company's networks are also set up in an active-active failover pair.

A dedicated VLAN just for voice traffic on the wired network has been set up with the appropriate marking of traffic. Routers and switches have been configured to identify voice traffic based on its markings, and if congestion is present the voice traffic will receive priority treatment for forwarding over the network.

The Active Directory servers that the company is using internally are running on a virtualized hardware platform using VMware's vSphere. The feature of fault tolerance (FT), which is offered by VMware, will have a backup copy of the Active Directory server(s) available in the event the primary servers fail.

A VPN over the Internet will be used (via a second service provider) to connect the branch and headquarters offices if the Multiprotocol Label Switching (MPLS) path over the primary WAN through the primary service provider fails.

Abnormally high levels of Internet Control Message Protocol (ICMP) packets that are heading to the headquarters site from the Internet will be rate-limited at the service provider. This will reduce the potential for an ICMP-based attack that is attempting to consume all the bandwidth available to the HQ site.

Summary

Here are the main topics covered in this chapter:

- Network availability was discussed, including how availability is measured and can be achieved through redundant designs.
- Performance optimization strategies were discussed, including the use of content caching, link aggregation, and load balancing.
- Various QoS technologies were reviewed, with an emphasis on traffic shaping, which can limit the rate of data transmission on a WAN link to the CIR.
- You were given a case study, where you were challenged to design a network to meet a collection of criteria.

Exam Preparation Tasks

Review All the Key Topics

Review the most important topics from inside the chapter, noted with the Key Topic icon in the outer margin of the page. Table 9-8 lists these key topics and the page numbers where each is found.

Table 9-8 Key Topics for Chapter 9

Key Topic Element	Description	Page Number
List	Fault-tolerant network design approaches	307
List	First-hop redundant technologies	309
List	Design considerations for high-availability networks	310
List	High-availability best practices	311

Key Topic Element	Description	Page Number
Table 9-1	Three categories of quality issues	314
Table 9-2	Three categories of quality of service mechanisms	316
Section	QoS Mechanism: Classification	318
Section	QoS Mechanism: Marking	318
Section	QoS Mechanism: Congestion Management	319
Section	QoS Mechanism: Congestion Avoidance	319
Section	QoS Mechanism: Policing and Shaping	320
Section	QoS Mechanism: Link Efficiency	322

Complete Tables and Lists from Memory

Print a copy of Appendix C, "Memory Tables," or at least the section for this chapter, and complete as many of the tables as possible from memory. Appendix D, "Memory Tables Answer Key," includes the completed tables and lists so you can check your work.

Define Key Terms

Define the following key terms from this chapter, and check your answers in the Glossary:

availability, reliability, Common Address Redundancy Protocol (CARP), uninterruptible power supply (UPS), latency, jitter, integrated services (IntServ), differentiated services, classification, marking, congestion management, congestion avoidance, policing, traffic shaping, committed information rate (CIR), link efficiency, NIC teaming, port aggregation, clustering, load balancing, cold sites, warm sites, hot sites, full backup, differential backup, incremental backup, snapshots, MTTR, MTFB, SLA

Complete Chapter 9 Hands-On Lab in Network+ Simulator Lite

- Contrast Virtualization Technologies and Services

Additional Resources

Configuring HSRP: http://www.ajsnetworking.com/hsrp

Using Quality of Service Tools: https://youtu.be/TMEIzlBaQcM

Review Questions

The answers to these review questions are in Appendix A, "Answers to Review Questions."

1. If a network has the five nines of availability, how much downtime does it experience per year?
   a. 30 seconds
   b. 5 minutes
   c. 12 minutes
   d. 26 minutes

2. What mode of NIC redundancy has only one NIC active at a time?
   a. Publisher-subscriber
   b. Client-server
   c. Active-standby
   d. Active-subscriber

3. What performance optimization technology uses a network appliance, which can receive a copy of content stored elsewhere (for example, a video presentation located on a server at a corporate headquarters), and serves that content to local clients, thus reducing the bandwidth burden on an IP WAN?
   a. Content engine
   b. Load balancer
   c. LACP
   d. CARP

4. What type of backup solution is a point-in-time, read-only copy of data?
   a. Differential
   b. Incremental
   c. Snapshot
   d. Virtual

5. What site provides a nearly identical level of service with virtually no downtime?
   a. Warm
   b. Cold
   c. Hot
   d. Remote

6. A lack of bandwidth can lead to which QoS issues? (Choose three.)
   a. Delay
   b. Jitter
   c. Prioritization
   d. Packet drops

7. What is the maximum recommended one-way delay for voice traffic?
   a. 25 ms
   b. 75 ms
   c. 100 ms
   d. 150 ms

8. Which of the following QoS mechanisms is considered an IntServ mechanism?
   a. LLQ
   b. RSVP
   c. RED
   d. cRTP

9. Identify the congestion-avoidance mechanism from the following list of QoS tools.
   a. LLQ
   b. RSVP
   c. RED
   d. cRTP

After completion of this chapter, you will be able to answer the following questions:

- What are some of the more useful Microsoft Windows commands for configuring and troubleshooting network clients and servers?
- What are some of the more useful UNIX commands for configuring and troubleshooting network clients and servers?

CHAPTER 10

Command-Line Tools

Your configuration and troubleshooting of networks will undoubtedly involve issuing commands at an operating system (OS) prompt of an end-user computer (a client) or a server. This chapter provides you with a collection of commands you can use at those OS prompts. The two operating systems for which commands are provided are Microsoft Windows and UNIX.

Some commands, you will notice, exist on both Microsoft Windows and UNIX platforms. For example, both platforms can use the **ping** command to check network reachability; however, other commands are OS specific. For example, the IP address settings on a Microsoft Windows PC can be viewed by entering the **ipconfig** command. However, a slightly different command, the **ifconfig** command, is used to gather similar information on UNIX hosts.

Many of the commands presented in this chapter have multiple command-line arguments; however, this chapter focuses on the more popular options for these commands. As a result, this chapter is not an exhaustive reference listing all available options for the commands presented.

Foundation Topics

Windows Commands

The Microsoft Windows OS (generically referred to as *Windows* in this chapter) allows you to access a command prompt by opening the Command Prompt application or by typing **cmd** in the **Start > Run** dialog box (on some Windows platforms, such as Windows XP) or in the **Start > Search Programs and Files** dialog box (on other Windows platforms, such as Windows 7). Although slight variations exist in these Windows commands based on your version of Windows, this chapter describes these Windows commands as they exist in Windows 7. Also, note that all the commands listed in this section are commands on the Network+ exam (N10-006) blueprint.

arp

You can use the **arp** command to see what a Layer 2 MAC address corresponds to as a known Layer 3 IP address. In addition, you can use the **arp** command to statically add a MAC-address-to-IP-address mapping to a PC's Address Resolution Protocol (ARP) MAC address lookup table (sometimes called the *ARP cache*).

The syntax of the **arp** command is as follows:

```
arp -s inet_addr eth_addr [if_addr]
arp -d inet_addr [if_addr]
arp -a [inet_addr] [-N if_addr] [-v]
```

Table 10-1 describes the previously listed *switches* (for example, **-s**, **-d**, and **-a**) and *arguments* (for example, *inet_addr* and *if_addr*).

Table 10-1 Parameters for the Windows **arp** Command

Parameter	Purpose
-a or -g	These options display current entries in a PC's ARP table.
-v	This option, where the **v** stands for verbose, includes any invalid and loopback interface entries in an ARP table.
inet_addr	This option is a specific IP address.
-N *if_addr*	This option shows ARP entries learned for a specified network.
-d	An ARP entry for a host can be deleted with this option, in combination with the *inet_addr* parameter. A wildcard character of * can delete all host entries.

Parameter	Purpose
-s	This option, used in conjunction with the *inet_addr* and *eth_addr* parameters, statically adds a host entry in the ARP table.
eth_addr	This parameter is a 48-bit MAC address.
if_addr	If a host has multiple interfaces, an ARP entry might be associated with a specific interface. This option can be used for statically adding or deleting an ARP entry to or from a specified interface.

Example 10-1 shows the **arp -a** command being issued on a PC. The output shows what MAC addresses have been learned for the listed IP addresses. The dynamically learned addresses have *dynamic* listed in the Type column, and statically configured addresses (which are addresses configured by a user or the OS) are listed with *static* in the Type column. From the output, as one example, you can determine that the network device with an IP address of 172.16.202.1 has a MAC address of 00-50-56-c0-00-08, which could alternatively be written as 0050.56c0.0008. Also, you can determine from the output that this information was dynamically learned, as opposed to being statically configured.

Example 10-1 Sample Output from the Windows **arp -a** Command

```
C:\> arp -a
Interface: 172.16.202.128 --- 0xb
   Internet Address      Physical Address       Type
   172.16.202.1          00-50-56-c0-00-08      dynamic
   172.16.202.2          00-50-56-fd-65-2c      dynamic
   172.16.202.254        00-50-56-e8-84-fc      dynamic
   172.16.202.255        ff-ff-ff-ff-ff-ff      static
   224.0.0.22            01-00-5e-00-00-16      static
   224.0.0.252           01-00-5e-00-00-fc      static
   255.255.255.255       ff-ff-ff-ff-ff-ff      static

Interface: 172.16.202.129 --- 0x14
   Internet Address      Physical Address       Type
   172.16.202.1          00-50-56-c0-00-08      dynamic
   172.16.202.2          00-50-56-fd-65-2c      dynamic
   172.16.202.254        00-50-56-e8-84-fc      dynamic
   172.16.202.255        ff-ff-ff-ff-ff-ff      static
   224.0.0.22            01-00-5e-00-00-16      static
   224.0.0.252           01-00-5e-00-00-fc      static
   224.0.1.60            01-00-5e-00-01-3c      static
   255.255.255.255       ff-ff-ff-ff-ff-ff      static
```

From a troubleshooting perspective, keep in mind that static ARP entries tend to be more problematic than dynamic entries. For example, a static entry might be added to a laptop computer, and the computer might later connect to a different network. If a PC then attempts to reach the IP address specified in the static ARP entry, the Layer 2 frame would have the incorrect destination MAC address (which should then be the MAC address of the PC's default gateway) in its header.

ipconfig

You can use the **ipconfig** command to display IP address configuration parameters on a Windows PC. In addition, if the PC uses Dynamic Host Configuration Protocol (DHCP), you can use the **ipconfig** command to release and renew a DHCP lease, which is often useful when troubleshooting.

The syntax of the **ipconfig** command, along with some of its more commonly used parameters, is as follows:

```
ipconfig [/all | /renew | /release | /renew6 | /release6]
```

Table 10-2 describes the previously listed parameters for the **ipconfig** command.

Table 10-2 Parameters for the Windows **ipconfig** Command

Parameter	Purpose
/all	The **ipconfig** command entered by itself displays summary information about a PC's IP address configuration. This parameter gives more verbose information, including such information as DNS, MAC address, and IPv6 address information.
/release and /release6	These options release a DHCP lease for an IPv4 and IPv6 address, respectively.
/renew and /renew6	These options renew a DHCP lease for an IPv4 and IPv6 address, respectively.

Example 10-2 shows the **ipconfig** command, without extra parameters, being issued on a PC. The PC contains an Ethernet and a wireless network interface card (NIC). From the output, you can conclude that one of the NICs has an IP address of 172.16.202.129, while the other NIC has an IP address of 172.16.202.128. Also, you can see that these two NICs share a common default gateway of 172.16.202.2.

Example 10-2 Sample Output from the Windows **ipconfig** Command

```
C:\> ipconfig
Windows IP Configuration
Ethernet adapter Local Area Connection 3:
   Connection-specific DNS Suffix . : localdomain
   Link-local IPv6 Address . . . . . : fe80::5101:b420:4354:d496%20
   IPv4 Address. . . . . . . . . . . : 172.16.202.129
   Subnet Mask . . . . . . . . . . . : 255.255.255.0
   Default Gateway . . . . . . . . . : 172.16.202.2
Ethernet adapter Local Area Connection:
   Connection-specific DNS Suffix . : localdomain
   Link-local IPv6 Address . . . . . : fe80::a10f:cff4:15e4:aa6%11
   IPv4 Address. . . . . . . . . . . : 172.16.202.128
   Subnet Mask . . . . . . . . . . . : 255.255.255.0
   Default Gateway . . . . . . . . . : 172.16.202.2
OUTPUT OMITTED...
```

Example 10-3 shows the **ipconfig /all** command being issued on a PC. Notice the additional output from this command, not shown in the output of the **ipconfig** command. As a couple of examples, you can see the MAC address (labeled as the *physical address*) for each NIC and the DNS server's IP address of 172.16.202.2.

Example 10-3 Sample Output from the Windows **ipconfig /all** Command

```
C:\> ipconfig /all
Windows IP Configuration
   Host Name . . . . . . . . . . . . : WIN-OD1IG7JF47P
   Primary Dns Suffix . . . . . . . :
   Node Type . . . . . . . . . . . . : Hybrid
   IP Routing Enabled. . . . . . . . : No
   WINS Proxy Enabled. . . . . . . . : No
   DNS Suffix Search List. . . . . . : localdomain
Ethernet adapter Local Area Connection 3:
   Connection-specific DNS Suffix . : localdomain
   Description . . . . . . . . . . . : Intel(R) PRO/1000 MT Network
Connection #2
   Physical Address. . . . . . . . . : 00-0C-29-3A-21-67
   DHCP Enabled. . . . . . . . . . . : Yes
   Autoconfiguration Enabled . . . . : Yes
   Link-local IPv6 Address . . . . . : fe80::5101:b420:4354:d496%20
(Preferred)
```

```
   IPv4 Address. . . . . . . . . . . : 172.16.202.129(Preferred)
   Subnet Mask . . . . . . . . . . . : 255.255.255.0
   Lease Obtained. . . . . . . . . . : Saturday, May 28, 2011 6:28:08 PM
   Lease Expires . . . . . . . . . . : Saturday, May 28, 2011 9:28:08 PM
   Default Gateway . . . . . . . . . : 172.16.202.2
   DHCP Server . . . . . . . . . . . : 172.16.202.254
   DHCPv6 IAID . . . . . . . . . . . : 419433513
   DHCPv6 Client DUID. . . . . . . . : 00-01-00-01-14-A6-11-77-00-0C-
29-3A-21-5D
   DNS Servers . . . . . . . . . . . : 172.16.202.2
   Primary WINS Server . . . . . . . : 172.16.202.2
   NetBIOS over Tcpip. . . . . . . . : Enabled
Ethernet adapter Local Area Connection:
   Connection-specific DNS Suffix . : localdomain
   Description . . . . . . . . . . . : Intel(R) PRO/1000 MT Network
Connection
   Physical Address. . . . . . . . . : 00-0C-29-3A-21-5D
   DHCP Enabled. . . . . . . . . . . : Yes
   Autoconfiguration Enabled . . . . : Yes
   Link-local IPv6 Address . . . . . : fe80::a10f:cff4:15e4:aa6%11
(Preferred)
   IPv4 Address. . . . . . . . . . . : 172.16.202.128(Preferred)
   Subnet Mask . . . . . . . . . . . : 255.255.255.0
   Lease Obtained. . . . . . . . . . : Saturday, May 28, 2011 6:27:56 PM
   Lease Expires . . . . . . . . . . : Saturday, May 28, 2011 9:28:08 PM
   Default Gateway . . . . . . . . . : 172.16.202.2
   DHCP Server . . . . . . . . . . . : 172.16.202.254
   DHCPv6 IAID . . . . . . . . . . . : 234884137
   DHCPv6 Client DUID. . . . . . . . : 00-01-00-01-14-A6-11-77-00-0C-
29-3A-21-5D
   DNS Servers . . . . . . . . . . . : 172.16.202.2
   Primary WINS Server . . . . . . . : 172.16.202.2
   NetBIOS over Tcpip. . . . . . . . : Enabled
OUTPUT OMITTED...
```

If you are troubleshooting a PC and suspect that IP addressing might be an issue, you can release the PC's current DHCP lease with the **ipconfig /release** command, as shown in Example 10-4. Then you can renew the DHCP lease with the **ipconfig /renew** command, as shown in Example 10-5.

Example 10-4 Sample Output from the Windows **ipconfig /release** Command

```
C:\> ipconfig /release
Windows IP Configuration
Ethernet adapter Local Area Connection 3:
   Connection-specific DNS Suffix . :
   Link-local IPv6 Address . . . . . : fe80::5101:b420:4354:d496%20
   Default Gateway . . . . . . . . . :
Ethernet adapter Local Area Connection:
   Connection-specific DNS Suffix . :
   Link-local IPv6 Address . . . . . : fe80::a10f:cff4:15e4:aa6%11
   Default Gateway . . . . . . . . . :
OUTPUT OMITTED...
```

Example 10-5 Sample Output from the Windows **ipconfig /renew** Command

```
C:\> ipconfig /renew
Windows IP Configuration
Ethernet adapter Local Area Connection 3:
   Connection-specific DNS Suffix .  : localdomain
   Link-local IPv6 Address . . . . . : fe80::5101:b420:4354:d496%20
   IPv4 Address. . . . . . . . . . . : 172.16.202.129
   Subnet Mask . . . . . . . . . . . : 255.255.255.0
   Default Gateway . . . . . . . . . : 172.16.202.2
Ethernet adapter Local Area Connection:
   Connection-specific DNS Suffix .  : localdomain
   Link-local IPv6 Address . . . . . : fe80::a10f:cff4:15e4:aa6%11
   IPv4 Address. . . . . . . . . . . : 172.16.202.128
   Subnet Mask . . . . . . . . . . . : 255.255.255.0
   Default Gateway . . . . . . . . . : 172.16.202.2
OUTPUT OMITTED...
```

nbtstat

The **nbtstat** command displays NetBIOS information for IP-based networks. The *nbt* prefix of the **nbtstat** command refers to NetBIOS over TCP/IP, which is called *NBT* or *NetBT*. This command can, for example, display a listing of NetBIOS device names learned by a Windows PC.

The syntax of the **nbtstat** command is as follows:

```
nbtstat [ [-a remote_name] [-A ip_address] [-c] [-n] [-r] [-R] [-S] ]
```

Table 10-3 describes the previously listed parameters for the **nbtstat** command.

Table 10-3 Parameters for the Windows **nbtstat** Command

Parameter	Purpose
-a ***remote_name***	This option allows you to see the NetBIOS table of a remote PC with a NetBIOS name as specified by the *remote_name* argument.
-A ***ip_address***	This option allows you to see the NetBIOS table of a remote PC with an IP address as specified by the *ip_address* argument.
-c	This option displays the contents of a PC's NetBIOS name cache along with the IP addresses corresponding to those NetBIOS names.
-n	This option displays NetBIOS names that have been registered by an application, such as a server application.
-r	This option shows statistical NetBIOS information, such as the number of NetBIOS names resolved by broadcasting and the number of NetBIOS names resolved by a WINS server.
-R	This option purges a PC's NetBIOS cache and reloads entries from a PC's LMHOSTS file (which is a text file containing NetBIOS to IP address mappings) that have #PRE following the entry. The **#PRE** option in an LMHOSTS file causes those entries to be preloaded into a PC's NetBIOS cache.
-S	This option provides a listing of the NetBIOS session table, along with the IP addresses of the listed NetBIOS names.

When you are troubleshooting, it often helps to know the IP address of a known NetBIOS name. You can view a PC's NetBIOS name cache, which lists this information, with the **nbtstat -c** command, as shown in Example 10-6.

Example 10-6 Sample Output from the Windows **nbtstat -c** Command

```
C:\> nbtstat -c
Local Area Connection:
Node IpAddress: [192.168.1.50] Scope Id: []

                    NetBIOS Remote Cache Name Table
Name                      Type          Host Address          Life [sec]
192.168.1.150      <20>  UNIQUE         192.168.1.150         440
192.168.1.241      <20>  UNIQUE         192.168.1.241         395
192.168.1.50       <20>  UNIQUE         192.168.1.50          392
AZSCO-CISCO-S2     <00>  UNIQUE         192.168.1.150         555
AZSCO-CISCO-S2     <20>  UNIQUE         192.168.1.150         555
```

```
THE-WALLACES-TI    <20>  UNIQUE          192.168.1.1          202
THE-WALLACES-TI    <00>  UNIQUE          192.168.1.1          202
IMAC-3026FE        <00>  UNIQUE          192.168.1.240        552
IMAC-3026FE        <20>  UNIQUE          192.168.1.240        550
LIVE-DELIVERY      <20>  UNIQUE          192.168.1.50         222
```

If you want to verify that a PC is successfully resolving NetBIOS names, either by using a broadcast or from a WINS server, the **nbtstat -r** command, as demonstrated in Example 10-7, can help.

Example 10-7 Sample Output from the Windows **nbtstat -r** Command

```
C:\> nbtstat -r
    NetBIOS Names Resolution and Registration Statistics
    ----------------------------------------------------
    Resolved By Broadcast     = 6
    Resolved By Name Server   = 0

    Registered By Broadcast   = 4
    Registered By Name Server = 0

    NetBIOS Names Resolved By Broadcast
---------------------------------------------
          AZSCO-CISCO-S2 <00>
          AZSCO-CISCO-S2
          IMAC-3026FE <00>
          IMAC-3026FE
          THE-WALLACES-TI<00>
          THE-WALLACES-TI
```

You can even view the NetBIOS table of a remote PC with the **nbtstat -a** command, as shown in Example 10-8. Note, however, that the *Node IpAddress* parameter shows the IP address of the PC issuing the **nbtstat** command, whereas the *MAC Address* parameter shows the MAC address of the remote PC.

Example 10-8 Sample Output from the Windows **nbtstat -a** Command

```
C:\> nbtstat -a AZSCO-CISCO-S2
Local Area Connection:
Node IpAddress: [192.168.1.50] Scope Id: []
          NetBIOS Remote Machine Name Table
```

```
    Name                     Type          Status
AZSCO-CISCO-S2      <00>     UNIQUE        Registered
KITCHEN             <00>     GROUP         Registered
AZSCO-CISCO-S2      <20>     UNIQUE        Registered
KITCHEN             <1E>     GROUP         Registered
KITCHEN             <1D>     UNIQUE        Registered
..__MSBROWSE__.     <01>     GROUP         Registered
MAC Address = 00-13-72-79-4C-9D
```

netstat

You can use the **netstat** command to display various information about IP-based connections on a PC. For example, you can view information about current sessions, including source and destination IP addresses and port numbers. You can also display protocol statistics. This might be useful for troubleshooting purposes. For example, you might issue the **netstat** command and see that your PC has sessions open to an unknown host on the Internet. These sessions might warrant further investigation to determine why the sessions are open and if they might be resulting in performance issues on your PC or possibly posing a security risk.

The following is the syntax for the **netstat** command and some of its commonly used options:

```
netstat [-a] [-b] [-e] [-f] [-p proto] [-r] [-s]
```

Table 10-4 explains the usage of the previously listed command options.

Table 10-4 Parameters for the Windows **netstat** Command

Parameter	Purpose
-a	This option displays all of a PC's active IP-based sessions, along with the TCP and UDP ports of each session.
-b	This option shows you the names of the program that opened up a session.
-e	This option shows statistical information for an interface's IP-based traffic, such as the number of bytes sent and received.
-f	This option displays fully qualified domain names (FQDN) of destination addresses appearing in a listing of active sessions.
-p *proto*	This option displays connections for a specific protocol, which might be **icmp**, **icmpv6**, **ip**, **ipv6**, **tcp**, **tcpv6**, **udp**, or **udpv6**.

Parameter	Purpose
-r	This option displays a PC's IP routing table. (Note that this command generates the same output as the **route print** command.)
-s	This option displays statistical information for the following protocols: **icmpv4**, **icmpv6**, **ipv4**, **ipv6**, **tcpv4**, **tcpv6**, **udpv4**, and **udpv6**.

The **netstat** command issued without any options lists source and destination IP addresses and port numbers for all IP-based sessions. Example 10-9 shows sample output from this command.

Example 10-9 Sample Output from the Windows **netstat** Command

```
C:\> netstat
OUTPUT OMITTED...
  TCP   127.0.0.1:27015       LIVE-DELIVERY:1309             ESTABLISHED
  TCP   192.168.1.50:1045     172.16.224.200:https           CLOSE_WAIT
  TCP   192.168.1.50:1058     THE-WALLACES-TI:microsoft-ds   ESTABLISHED
  TCP   192.168.1.50:1079     tcpep:https                    ESTABLISHED
  TCP   192.168.1.50:1081     174:http                       ESTABLISHED
  TCP   192.168.1.50:1089     by2msg4020609:msnp             ESTABLISHED
  TCP   192.168.1.50:1111     HPB81308:netbios-ssn           ESTABLISHED
  TCP   192.168.1.50:1115     10.65.228.81:https             ESTABLISHED
  TCP   192.168.1.50:1116     10.65.228.81:https             ESTABLISHED
  TCP   192.168.1.50:1117     10.65.228.81:https             ESTABLISHED
  TCP   192.168.1.50:1118     10.65.228.81:https             ESTABLISHED
  TCP   192.168.1.50:1126     10.65.228.81:https             ESTABLISHED
  TCP   192.168.1.50:1417     vip1:http                      CLOSE_WAIT
  TCP   192.168.1.50:1508     208:https                      CLOSE_WAIT
  TCP   192.168.1.50:1510     208:https                      CLOSE_WAIT
  TCP   [::1]:2869            LIVE-DELIVERY:1514             TIME_WAIT
  TCP   [::1]:286             LIVE-DELIVERY:1515             ESTABLISHED
OUTPUT OMITTED...
```

You might notice an open connection using a specific port and be unsure what application opened that connection. As seen in Example 10-10, the **netstat -b** command shows which application opened a specific connection. In this example, Dropbox.exe, iTunex.exe, firefox.exe, and OUTLOOK.exe are applications that have currently open connections.

Example 10-10 Sample Output from the Windows **netstat -b** Command

```
C:\> netstat -b
Active Connections
OUTPUT OMITTED...
 Proto          Local Address          Foreign Address        State
 TCP            127.0.0.1:1068         LIVE-DELIVERY:19872    ESTABLISHED
[Dropbox.exe]
 TCP            127.0.0.1:1309         LIVE-DELIVERY:27015    ESTABLISHED
[iTunes.exe]
 TCP            127.0.0.1:1960         LIVE-DELIVERY:1961     ESTABLISHED
[firefox.exe]
 TCP            192.168.1.50:1115      10.1.228.81:https      ESTABLISHED
[OUTLOOK.EXE]
 TCP            192.168.1.50:1116      10.1.228.81:https      ESTABLISHED
[OUTLOOK.EXE]
OUTPUT OMITTED...
```

nslookup

Although the **nslookup** command offers various command options, this section focuses on the most common use for the command. Specifically, you can use the **nslookup** command to resolve an FQDN to an IP address. This can, for example, help you to determine whether a DNS record is correct and to verify that your DNS server is operating.

The **nslookup** command can be issued along with an FQDN, or it can be used in an interactive mode, where you are prompted to enter command parameters. Therefore, the syntax can be summarized as follows:

```
nslookup [fqdn]
```

In noninteractive mode, you issue the **nslookup** command followed by an FQDN to display the IP address corresponding to the FQDN. To illustrate, consider Example 10-11, where the **nslookup** command is issued to resolve the IP address of the website cbtnuggets.com, which appears to be 172.31.194.74. (Note that a private IP address is used for illustrative purposes; in a real-world example, a public IP address would display.)

Example 10-11 Sample Output from the Windows **nslookup** Noninteractive Command

```
C:\> nslookup cbtnuggets.com
Server: UnKnown
Address: 192.168.1.1

Non-authoritative answer:
Name: cbtnuggets.com
Address: 172.31.194.74
```

In interactive mode, the **nslookup** command is entered, after which you enter command parameters from the > prompt. In Example 10-12, cbtnuggets.com is entered at the prompt to see the IP address corresponding to that FQDN. Also, notice that entering a question mark (?) displays a help screen that shows command options. Entering **quit** exits you from interactive mode.

Example 10-12 Sample Output from the Windows **nslookup** Interactive Command

```
C:\> nslookup
Default Server: UnKnown
Address: 192.168.1.1

> cbtnuggets.com
Server: UnKnown
Address: 192.168.1.1

Non-authoritative answer:
Name: cbtnuggets.com
Address: 172.31.194.74

> ?
Commands:    (identifiers are shown in uppercase, [] means optional)
NAME         - print info about the host/domain NAME using default server
NAME1 NAME2       - as above, but use NAME2 as server
help or ?         - print info on common commands
set OPTION        - set an option
   all                        - print options, current server and host
   [no]debug                  - print debugging information
   [no]d2                     - print exhaustive debugging information
   [no]defname                - append domain name to each query
   [no]recurse                - ask for recursive answer to query
   [no]search                 - use domain search list
```

```
    [no]vc                      - always use a virtual circuit
    domain=NAME                 - set default domain name to NAME
    srchlist=N1[/N2/.../N6]     - set domain to N1 and search list to N1,N2, etc.
    root=NAME                   - set root server to NAME
OUTPUT OMITTED...
> quit
C:\>
```

ping

The **ping** command is one of the most commonly used command-line commands. You can use it to check IP connectivity between two network devices. Multiple platforms (for example, routers, switches, and hosts) support the **ping** command.

The **ping** command uses Internet Control Message Protocol (ICMP), which is a Layer 4 protocol. If you issue a **ping** command from your PC, your PC sends an ICMP echo message to the specified destination host. Assuming the destination host is reachable, the host responds with an ICMP echo reply message. Other ICMP messages can be returned to your PC, from your PC's default gateway, to indicate that a destination host is unreachable, that an ICMP echo timed out, or that a Time To Live (TTL) value (which is decremented by 1 at each router hop) has expired (decremented to a value of 0).

The syntax of the **ping** command, along with some of its commonly used options, is as follows:

```
ping [-t] [-n count] [-l size] [-f] [-i TTL] [-S srcaddr] target_name
```

Table 10-5 explains the usage of the previously listed command options.

Table 10-5 Parameters for the Windows **ping** Command

Parameter	Purpose
-t	This option repeatedly sends pings (ICMP echo messages) until you stop it by pressing Ctrl+C.
-n ***count***	This option specifies the number of pings to send.
-f	This option sets the "don't fragment" bit in a packet's header. If the packet tries to cross a router that attempts to fragment the packet, the packet is dropped, and an ICMP error message is returned.
-i ***TTL***	This option sets the TTL value in a packet's header. The TTL is decremented for each router hop. A packet is discarded when its TTL value reaches 0.

Parameter	Purpose
-S *srcaddr*	If the PC from which you are issuing the **ping** command has more than one IP address, this option allows you to specify the source IP address from which the ICMP echo messages should be sent.
target_name	This option specifies the name or the IP address of the device to which you are sending ICMP echo messages.

A Windows **ping** command specifying only the *target_name* parameter sends four ICMP echo messages to the specified target, as shown in Example 10-13. In the output, notice that none of the packets were dropped.

Example 10-13 Sample Output from the Windows **ping** Command

```
C:\> ping 192.168.1.2
Pinging 192.168.1.2 with 32 bytes of data:
Reply from 192.168.1.2: bytes=32 time=2ms TTL=64
Reply from 192.168.1.2: bytes=32 time=1ms TTL=64
Reply from 192.168.1.2: bytes=32 time=1ms TTL=64
Reply from 192.168.1.2: bytes=32 time=1ms TTL=64

Ping statistics for 192.168.1.2:
    Packets: Sent = 4, Received = 4, Lost = 0 (0% loss),
Approximate round trip times in milli-seconds:
    Minimum = 1ms, Maximum = 2ms, Average = 1ms
```

If the specified target address is unreachable, output from the **ping** command indicates that the target cannot be reached, as shown in Example 10-14.

Example 10-14 Windows **ping** Command Indicating an Unreachable Destination

```
C:\> ping 192.168.1.200

Pinging 192.168.1.200 with 32 bytes of data:
Reply from 192.168.1.50: Destination host unreachable.
Reply from 192.168.1.50: Destination host unreachable.
Reply from 192.168.1.50: Destination host unreachable.
Reply from 192.168.1.50: Destination host unreachable.

Ping statistics for 192.168.1.200:
    Packets: Sent = 4, Received = 4, Lost = 0 (0% loss),
```

ping with IPv6

Depending on the operating system, ping can natively work to test connectivity using IPv6 when an IPv6 destination address is part of the **ping** command. On some systems the command **ping -6** *IPv6-destination-address*, **ping6** *IPv6-destination-address*, or some variant specific to that operating system may be available for testing IPv6 connectivity.

route

The **route** command can display a PC's current IP routing table. In addition, you can use the **route** command to add or delete entries to or from that routing table. Syntax of the **route** command, with a collection of commonly used options, is as follows:

```
C:\>route [-f] [-p] command [destination] [mask netmask] [gateway]
[metric metric] [if interface]
```

Table 10-6 explains the usage of the previously listed command options.

Table 10-6 Parameters for the Windows **route** Command

Parameter	Purpose
-f	This option clears gateway entries from the routing table. If this option is used with another option, the clearing of gateways from the routing table occurs before any other specified action.
-p	This option can be used with the **add** command to make a statically configured route persistent, meaning that the route will remain in a PC's routing table even after a reboot.
command	Supported commands include **print**, **add**, **delete**, and **change**. The **print** command lists entries in a PC's routing table. The **add** command adds a route entry. The **delete** command removes a route from the routing table, while the **change** command can modify an existing route.
destination	This option specifies the destination host or subnet to add to a PC's routing table.
mask *netmask*	This option, used in conjunction with the *destination* option, specifies the subnet mask of the destination. If the destination is the IP address of a host, the *netmask* parameter is 255.255.255.255.
gateway	This option specifies the IP address of the next-hop router used to reach the specified destination.
metric *metric*	This option specifies the cost to reach a specified destination. If a routing table contains more than one route to reach the destination, the route with the lowest cost is selected.
if *interface*	If you want to forward traffic to a specified destination out of a specific interface, use this option.

Example 10-15 illustrates the use of the **route print** command, which displays the contents of a PC's routing table. Notice that the output identifies a listing of the PC's interfaces, along with IPv4 routes and IPv6 routes. From the output, you see that the 10.0.0.0 255.0.0.0 network is reachable via two gateways (192.168.1.77 and 192.168.1.11). Also, notice that there is a persistent route (a route entry that survives a reboot) to act as a default gateway for the PC, which is 192.168.1.1.

Example 10-15 Sample Output from the Windows **route print** Command

```
C:\> route print
===================================================================
Interface List
 11...00 24 81 ee 4c 0e ......Intel(R) 82566DM-2 Gigabit Network Connection
  1...........................Software Loopback Interface 1
 12...00 00 00 00 00 00 00 e0 Microsoft ISATAP Adapter
 13...00 00 00 00 00 00 00 e0 Teredo Tunneling Pseudo-Interface
===================================================================


IPv4 Route Table
==============================+====================================
Active Routes:
Network Destination    Netmask           Gateway         Interface     Metric
            0.0.0.0    0.0.0.0           192.168.1.1     192.168.1.50  276
           10.0.0.0    255.0.0.0       192.168.1.77      192.168.1.50   21
           10.0.0.0    255.0.0.0       192.168.1.11      192.168.1.50   21
          127.0.0.0    255.0.0.0         On-link         127.0.0.1     306
          127.0.0.1    255.255.255.255   On-link         127.0.0.1     306
    127.255.255.255    255.255.255.255   On-link         127.0.0.1     306
         172.16.0.0    255.255.0.0       192.168.1.1     192.168.1.50   21
        192.168.0.0    255.255.255.0     192.168.1.11    192.168.1.50   21
        192.168.1.0    255.255.255.0     On-link         192.168.1.50  276
       192.168.1.50    255.255.255.255   On-link         192.168.1.50  276
      192.168.1.255    255.255.255.255   On-link         192.168.1.50  276
          224.0.0.0    240.0.0.0         On-link         127.0.0.1     306
          224.0.0.0    240.0.0.0         On-link         192.168.1.50  276
    255.255.255.255    255.255.255.255   On-link         127.0.0.1     306
    255.255.255.255    255.255.255.255   On-link         192.168.1.50  276
===========================================================================
Persistent Routes:
    Network Address    Netmask        Gateway Address    Metric
    0.0.0.0            0.0.0.0        192.168.1.1        Default
```

```
===========================================================================
IPv6 Route Table
===========================================================================
Active Routes:
 If   Metric   Network Destination      Gateway
 13   58 :     :/0                      On-link
 1    306 :    :1/128                   On-link
 13   58       2001::/32 On-link
 13   306      2001:0:4137:9e76:10e2:614f:b34e:ea84/128
                                        On-link
 11   276      fe80::/64                On-link
 13   306      fe80::/64                On-link
 13   306      fe80::10e2:614f:b34e:ea84/128
                                        On-link
 11    276     fe80::f46d:4a34:a9c4:51a0/128
                                        On-link
 1     306     ff00::/8                 On-link
 13    306     ff00::/8                 On-link
 11    276     ff00::/8                 On-link
=====================================================================
Persistent Routes:
  None
```

Imagine that you want to remove one of the route entries for the 10.0.0.0 255.0.0.0 network. Example 10-16 shows how one of the two entries (specifically, the entry pointing to 192.168.1.11) can be removed from the routing table. Notice from the output that after the **route delete 10.0.0.0 mask 255.0.0.0 192.168.1.11** command is issued, the route no longer appears in the routing table.

Example 10-16 Sample Output from the Windows **route delete** Command

```
C:\> route delete 10.0.0.0 mask 255.0.0.0 192.168.1.11
 OK!
C:\> route print
OUTPUT OMITTED...
IPv4 Route Table
=======================================================++++==============
Active Routes:
Network Destination   Netmask            Gateway        Interface      Metric
0.0.0.0               0.0.0.0            192.168.1.1    192.168.1.50   276
```

```
10.0.0.0          255.0.0.0        192.168.1.77  192.168.1.50  21
127.0.0.0         255.0.0.0        On-link       127.0.0.1     306
127.0.0.1         255.255.255.255  On-link       127.0.0.1     306
127.255.255.255   255.255.255.255  On-link       127.0.0.1     306
172.16.0.0        255.255.0.0      192.168.1.11  192.168.1.50  21
192.168.0.0       255.255.255.0    192.168.1.11  192.168.1.50  21
192.168.1.0       255.255.255.0    On-link       192.168.1.50  276
192.168.1.50      255.255.255.255  On-link       192.168.1.50  276
192.168.1.255     255.255.255.255  On-link       192.168.1.50  276
224.0.0.0         240.0.0.0        On-link       127.0.0.1     306
224.0.0.0         240.0.0.0        On-link       192.168.1.50  276
255.255.255.255   255.255.255.255  On-link       127.0.0.1     306
255.255.255.255   255.255.255.255  On-link       192.168.1.50  276
==================================================================
OUTPUT OMITTED...
```

A route can be added by using the **route add** command. Example 10-17 shows and confirms the addition of a route pointing to the 10.2.1.0 255.255.255.0 network, with a next-hop route (gateway) of 192.168.1.1.

Example 10-17 Sample Output from the Windows **route add** Command

```
C:\> route add 10.2.1.0 mask 255.255.255.0 192.168.1.1
 OK!

C:\> route print
OUTPUT OMITTED...
IPv4 Route Table
======================================================================
Active Routes:
Network Destination  Netmask          Gateway       Interface     Metric
0.0.0.0           0.0.0.0          192.168.1.1   192.168.1.50  276
10.0.0.0          255.0.0.0        192.168.1.77  192.168.1.50  21
10.2.1.0          255.255.255.0    192.168.1.1   192.168.1.50  21
127.0.0.0         255.0.0.0        On-link       127.0.0.1     306
127.0.0.1         255.255.255.255  On-link       127.0.0.1     306
127.255.255.255   255.255.255.255  On-link       127.0.0.1     306
172.16.0.0        255.255.0.0      192.168.1.11  192.168.1.50  21
192.168.0.0       255.255.255.0    192.168.1.11  192.168.1.50  21
192.168.1.0       255.255.255.0    On-link       192.168.1.50  276
```

```
192.168.1.50        255.255.255.255  On-link       192.168.1.50  276
192.168.1.255       255.255.255.255  On-link       192.168.1.50  276
224.0.0.0           240.0.0.0        On-link       127.0.0.1     306
224.0.0.0           240.0.0.0        On-link       192.168.1.50  276
255.255.255.255     255.255.255.255  On-link       127.0.0.1     306
255.255.255.255     255.255.255.255  On-link     192.168.1.50    276
===========================================================================
OUTPUT OMITTED...
```

tracert

In an earlier section, you were introduced to the **ping** command, which can verify Layer 3 connectivity to a remote host. If the pings were unsuccessful, or if the round-trip response times seem too long, the **tracert** command might help isolate the issue. Specifically, the **tracert** command pings every router hop from the source to the destination and reports the round-trip time for each router hop.

If a router is not reachable, you might want to investigate the router hop just before or just after the hop that timed out. However, in many cases, a router does not respond to a **tracert** because it has been configured not to respond to ICMP messages (which is what the **tracert** command uses) for security reasons. So, a failed response does not always indicate a router-configuration issue or a bad link between two routers. However, even if the **tracert** output shows every route hop from the source to the destination, the round-trip delay time can help identify congested links.

Although the **tracert** command has a few optional parameters, usually it simply specifies a target IP address or FQDN, as follows:

```
C:\>tracert destination
```

Example 10-18 shows a successful trace from a PC to a destination FQDN of pearsonitcertification.com. Even though the trace was successful, the output still helps identify any slow links interconnecting routers along the path from the source to the destination.

Example 10-18 Sample Output from a Successful Windows **tracert** Command

```
C:\> tracert pearsonitcertification.com
Tracing route to pearsonitcertification.com [64.28.85.25]
over a maximum of 30 hops:
  1  <1 ms  <1 ms  <1 ms  THE-WALLACES-TI [192.168.1.1]
  2  12 ms  18 ms  9 ms  CPE-76-177-16-1.natcky.res.rr.com [76.177.16.1]
  3   8 ms  13 ms  11 ms  gig2-0-0.rcmdky-mx41.natcky.rr.com
[65.28.199.205]
  4  32 ms  35 ms  34 ms  tge0-2-0.chcgileq-rtr1.kc.rr.com [65.28.199.97]
```

```
  5   30 ms   28 ms   35 ms   ae-4-0.cr0.chi10.tbone.rr.com [66.109.6.100]
  6   28 ms   36 ms   51 ms   ae-0-0.pr0.chi10.tbone.rr.com [66.109.6.153]
  7   32 ms   37 ms   32 ms   if-4-0-0.core1.CT8-Chicago.as6453.net
[66.110.14.21]
  8   32 ms   31 ms   33 ms   if-1-0-0-1878.core2.CT8-Chicago.as6453.net
[66.110.27.78]
  9   58 ms   60 ms   56 ms   63.243.186.25
 10   95 ms   64 ms   73 ms   cr2-pos-0-8-0-3.nyr.savvis.net [208.173.129.29]
 11   66 ms   61 ms   72 ms   hr1-tengig-13-0-0.waltham2bo2.savvis.net
[204.70.198.182]
 12   62 ms   67 ms   62 ms   das3-v3038.bo2.savvis.net[209.202.187.182]
 13   62 ms   63 ms   66 ms   blhosting.bridgelinesw.com [64.14.81.46]
 14   63 ms   62 ms   76 ms   www1.webdialogs.com [64.28.85.25]
Trace complete.
```

Example 10-19 shows an unsuccessful trace. The first-hop router (192.168.1.1) responded; however, the router beyond that did not respond. So, in a troubleshooting situation, you might focus your attention to the interconnection between those two routers.

Example 10-19 Sample Output from an Unsuccessful Windows **tracert** Command

```
C:\> tracert 172.16.1.1
Tracing route to 172.16.1.1 over a maximum of 30 hops
  1     <1 ms       <1 ms     <1 ms      THE-WALLACES-TI [192.168.1.1]
  2       *           *         *        Request timed out.
  3       *           *         *        Request timed out.
  4       *           *         *        Request timed out.
  5       *           *         *        Request timed out.
  6       *           *         *        Request timed out.
  7       *           *         *        Request timed out.
  8       *           *         *        Request timed out.
  9       *           *         *        Request timed out.
OUTPUT OMITTED...
```

NOTE In other operating systems you will often see this command as **traceroute** instead of **tracert**. This is covered under the section "UNIX Commands."

tracert with IPv6

Similar to the **tracert** options for IPv4, the IPv6 path through a network can be verified with **tracert** for IPv6. Depending on the version of Windows being used, this may be done by using **tracert** *destination-IPv6-address*, **tracert6** *destination-IPv6-address*, or **tracert -6** *destination-IPv6-address*.

PathPing

The PathPing Windows tool combines features of ping and tracert over a period of time. It can be used with IPv4 and IPv6. PathPing shows the amount of packet loss at any given router so you can identify the routers that might be causing in the path. Options with PathPing include those outlined in Table 10-7.

Table 10-7 Parameters for the Windows PathPing Tool

Parameter	Purpose
-g *host-list*	Loose source route along *host-list*. Loose source routing permits you to specify a set of destinations the packet must visit in transit.
-h *maximum_hops*	Maximum number of hops to search for target.
-i *address*	Use the specified source address.
-n	Do not resolve addresses to hostnames.
-p *period*	Wait period milliseconds between pings.
-q *num_queries*	Number of queries per hop.
-w *timeout*	Wait timeout milliseconds for each reply.
-4	Force using IPv4.
-6	Force using IPv6.

UNIX Commands

This discussion of UNIX OS commands is more generic than Windows, in that there are many variations of UNIX implementations: some open-standard implementations and some vendor-specific implementations. This chapter describes UNIX commands as they exist in Apple'smacOS, which runs a variant of UNIX at its core.

Although some of the following UNIX commands can be used for the same purposes as some of the Windows commands, the syntax might vary slightly. Again, this chapter is not an exhaustive syntax reference, but a quick reference for common use cases and common options for the selected commands.

One of the benefits of UNIX is its extensive syntax reference in the form of manual pages (man pages). These man pages can be invoked with the following syntax:

```
HOST# man command
```

For example, if you want detailed information about the **arp** command, you can enter **man arp** to produce the output shown in Example 10-20. To leave the man pages, use the Q key.

Example 10-20 Sample Output from a Sample UNIX **man** Command

```
HOST# man arp

ARP(8)                    BSD System Manager's Manual ARP(8)

NAME
     arp -- address resolution display and control

SYNOPSIS
     arp [-n] [-i interface] hostname
     arp [-n] [-i interface] -a
     arp -d hostname [pub] [ifscope interface]
     arp -d [-i interface] -a
     arp -s hostname ether_addr [temp] [reject] [blackhole] [pub [only]]
         [ifscope interface]
     arp -S hostname ether_addr [temp] [reject] [blackhole] [pub [only]]
         [ifscope interface]
     arp -f filename

DESCRIPTION
     The arp utility displays and modifies the Internet-to-Ethernet
address
     translation tables used by the address resolution protocol (arp(4)).
     With no flags, the program displays the current ARP entry for
hostname.
     The host may be specified by name or by number, using Internet dot
notation.

:
OUTPUT OMITTED...
```

Other than the **man** command, all the UNIX commands listed in this section are commands listed in the Network+ exam (N10-007) blueprint.

arp

Similar to the Windows **arp** command, the UNIX **arp** command can be used to display MAC-address-to-IP-address mappings. The syntax of the **arp** command is as follows:

```
arp [-a]
   arp [-n] [-i interface] -a
   arp -s hostname ether_addr [temp] [reject] [blackhole] [ifscope
interface]
   arp -d hostname [ifscope interface]
   arp -d [-i interface] -a
   arp -f filename
```

Table 10-8 explains the usage of the previously listed command options.

Table 10-8 Parameters for the UNIX **arp** Command

Parameter	Purpose
-a	This option displays current ARP entries in a UNIX host's ARP table.
-n	This option displays network addresses as numbers instead of symbols.
-i *interface*	This option specifies that the **arp** command should be limited to a specified interface.
-d	An ARP entry for a host can be deleted with this option, in combination with the *inet_addr* parameter. A wildcard character of * can delete all host entries.
-s	This option, used in conjunction with the *hostname* and *eth_addr* parameters, statically adds a host entry in the ARP table.
ifscope *interface*	This option indicates that the **arp** command should be limited to a specified interface.
hostname	This option is the IP address of the host to be associated with a specified MAC address.
eth_addr	This parameter specifies a 48-bit MAC address.
temp	Used in conjunction with the **-s** option, the **temp** option says that the static ARP entry is only temporary, as opposed to the default of being permanent.
reject	Used in conjunction with the **-s** option, this option says that traffic to the destination specified in the static ARP entry will be rejected, and the sender will be notified that the host is unreachable.
blackhole	Similar to the **reject** option, the **blackhole** option says that traffic to the destination specified in the static ARP entry will be rejected. However, the sender is not notified.
-f *filename*	This option allows an external file to be used to import a collection of ARP entries. The entries in the external file should be in the following format: **hostname** *ether_addr* **[temp] [ifscope** *interface***]**

To illustrate a few uses of the **arp** command, first imagine that you want to add an entry in your UNIX host's ARP cache for an IP address of 192.168.1.32. You know the MAC address of that device is 11:22:33:44:55:66, and you know that the device is available off of interface en0. You can enter the **arp** command with the **-s** option, as demonstrated in Example 10-21, to add a static ARP entry. The example then confirms the entry has been made by issuing the **arp -a** command.

Example 10-21 Adding and Confirming a Static ARP Entry with the UNIX **arp** Command

```
HOST# arp -s 192.168.1.32 11:22:33:44:55:66 ifscope en0
HOST# arp -a
? (172.16.53.255) at (incomplete) on vmnet1 ifscope [ethernet]
? (172.16.202.255) at (incomplete) on vmnet8 ifscope [ethernet]
? (192.168.1.1) at 0:1f:f3:c9:39:fe on en0 ifscope [ethernet]
? (192.168.1.2) at 0:18:f8:50:ad:35 on en0 ifscope [ethernet]
? (192.168.1.32) at 11:22:33:44:55:66 on en0 ifscope [ethernet]
? (192.168.1.50) at 0:24:81:ee:4c:e on en0 ifscope [ethernet]
? (192.168.1.235) at 0:21:5a:b8:13:9 on en0 ifscope [ethernet]
? (192.168.1.240) at 0:23:12:18:a1:bd on en0 ifscope [ethernet]
? (192.168.1.248) at 0:21:47:3:6:94 on en0 ifscope [ethernet]
?  (192.168.1.255) at (incomplete) on en0 ifscope [ethernet
```

Next, imagine that you want to delete the entry you just added. Example 10-22 shows how the **-d** option of the **arp** command can remove an entry from a host's ARP cache. The output then confirms that the entry was removed.

Example 10-22 Deleting and Confirming the Deletion of a Static ARP Entry with the UNIX **arp** Command

```
HOST# arp -d 192.168.1.32 ifscope en0
192.168.1.32 (192.168.1.32) deleted
HOST# arp -a
? (172.16.53.255) at (incomplete) on vmnet1 ifscope [ethernet]
? (172.16.202.255) at (incomplete) on vmnet8 ifscope [ethernet]
? (192.168.1.1) at 0:1f:f3:c9:39:fe on en0 ifscope [ethernet]
? (192.168.1.2) at 0:18:f8:50:ad:35 on en0 ifscope [ethernet]
? (192.168.1.50) at 0:24:81:ee:4c:e on en0 ifscope [ethernet]
? (192.168.1.235) at 0:21:5a:b8:13:9 on en0 ifscope [ethernet]
? (192.168.1.240) at 0:23:12:18:a1:bd on en0 ifscope [ethernet]
? (192.168.1.248) at 0:21:47:3:6:94 on en0 ifscope [ethernet]
? (192.168.1.255) at (incomplete) on en0 ifscope [ethernet]
```

dig and nslookup

The Windows **nslookup** command was used to resolve a given FQDN to its IP address. UNIX has a similar **nslookup** command, which you can also use for FQDN-to-IP-address resolution.

The **dig** command can similarly be used to resolve FQDNs to IP addresses. Unlike the **nslookup** command, however, the **dig** command is entirely a command-line command. (**dig** lacks the interactive mode of the **nslookup** command.)

Example 10-23 compares the output of the **nslookup** and **dig** commands. Notice that the **dig** command offers more information than the **nslookup** command. For example, the *A* in the QUESTION SECTION output of the **dig** command identifies the DNS record type (an A record, which is an alias record). If you peruse the output, you can find a few other pieces of information present in the **dig** command output, not found in the **nslookup** command output; however, the **dig** command is rarely used to glean these more subtle pieces of information. Rather, the **dig** command is used by many UNIX administrators as simply an alternate way of resolving FQDNs to IP addresses. Notice that both commands indicate that the IP address corresponding to the FQDN of www.pearsonitcertification is 64.28.85.25.

Example 10-23 Comparing Output from the Windows **nslookup and** UNIX **dig** Commands

```
C:\> nslookup www.pearsonitcertification.com
Server: 192.168.1.1
Address: 192.168.1.1#53

Non-authoritative answer:
Name: www.pearsonitcertification.com
Address: 64.28.85.25

HOST# dig www.pearsonitcertification.com

; <<>> DiG 9.6.0-APPLE-P2 <<>> www.pearsonitcertification.com
;; global options: +cmd
;; Got answer:
;; ->>HEADER<<- opcode: QUERY, status: NOERROR, id: 10821
;; flags: qr rd ra; QUERY: 1, ANSWER: 1, AUTHORITY: 0, ADDITIONAL: 0

;; QUESTION SECTION:
;www.pearsonitcertification.com. IN A

;; ANSWER SECTION:
```

```
www.pearsonitcertification.com. 10791 IN A 64.28.85.25

;; Query time: 5 msec
;; SERVER: 192.168.1.1#53(192.168.1.1)
;; WHEN: Mon May 30 13:36:11 2011
;; MSG SIZE rcvd: 64
```

host

Yet another approach to resolving FQDNs to IP addresses is to use the **host** command. The **host** command offers a variety of options, and you can read more about them by issuing the **man host** command from a UNIX prompt. However, this discussion focuses on the most common use of the **host** command, which is FQDN-to-IP-address resolution.

Example 10-24 shows output from **host www.pearsonitcertification.com**. Notice that the resolved IP address of 64.28.85.25 matches the IP address resolved by both the **dig** and **nslookup** commands. This command can return mail server information for the resolved domain as well.

Example 10-24 Sample Output from the UNIX **host** Command

```
HOST# host www.pearsonitcertification.com
www.pearsonitcertification.com has address 64.28.85.25
```

ifconfig

The UNIX **ifconfig** command is most similar to the Windows **ipconfig** command, although the output is noticeably different. Issued by itself, the **ifconfig** command displays a UNIX host's interfaces along with configuration information about those interfaces, including MAC address, maximum transmission unit (MTU), IPv4 address, and IPv6 address information.

Beyond just displaying interface information, the **ifconfig** command can also configure interface parameters. For example, an interface's IP address can be configured with the **ifconfig** command.

Although many options are available (see the UNIX man pages for more details), the following syntax shows how to use the previously described **ifconfig** command functions:

```
ifconfig [interface [inet ip_addr netmask netmask]]
```

For example, if you want to configure interface en0 with an IP address of 192.168.1.26 and a subnet mask of 255.255.255.0, you could issue the command **ifconfig en0 inet 192.168.1.26 netmask 255.255.255.0**. Example 10-25 shows this command being issued, followed by the display generated from the **ifconfig** command to confirm that the change took effect.

Example 10-25 Configuring and Verifying the Configuration of an Interface's IP Address with the UNIX **ifconfig** Command

```
HOST# ifconfig en0 inet 192.168.1.26 netmask 255.255.255.0
HOST# ifconfig
lo0: flags=8049<UP,LOOPBACK,RUNNING,MULTICAST> mtu 16384
        inet 127.0.0.1 netmask 0xff000000
        inet6 ::1 prefixlen 128
        inet6 fe80::1%lo0 prefixlen 64 scopeid 0x1
        inet6 fdb9:537c:6f1c:705f:5a55:caff:fefa:1551 prefixlen 128
gif0: flags=8010<POINTOPOINT,MULTICAST> mtu 1280
stf0: flags=0<> mtu 1280
en0: flags=8863<UP,BROADCAST,SMART,RUNNING,SIMPLEX,MULTICAST> mtu 1500
        ether 58:55:ca:fa:15:51
        inet6 fe80::5a55:caff:fefa:1551%en0 prefixlen 64 scopeid 0x4
        inet 192.168.1.26 netmask 0xffffff00 broadcast 192.168.1.255
        media: autoselect
        status: active
OUTPUT OMITTED...
```

iptables

You use the **iptables** UNIX command to put rules in place for packet filtering. Typical criteria you specify would include the following:

- **Packet type**: Specifies the type of packets the command filters
- **Packet source/destination**: Specifies which packets the command filters based on the source or destination of the packet
- **Target**: Specifies what action is taken on packets matching the preceding criteria

Although there are many variations of this command, the following is a commonly used syntax:

```
iptables [-t <table-name>] <command> <chain-name> <parameter-1> \
  <option-1> <parameter-n> <option-n>
```

nmap

The **nmap** command (short for Network Mapper) is an open-source and very versatile tool for UNIX network admins. You use **nmap** to explore networks, perform security scans, create network audits, and find open ports on remote machine. The tool can scan for live hosts, operating systems, packet filters, and open ports. Here is an example of the syntax for this command:

```
nmap [Scan Type(s)] [Options] {target specification}
```

tcpdump

You can use the **tcpdump** command to print out the headers of packets on a network interface that match a Boolean expression. You can also run the command with the **-w** flag, which causes it to save the packet data to a file for later analysis, and/or with the **-r** flag, which causes it to read from a saved packet file rather than to read packets from a network interface. The most common format and options for the command are shown here:

```
tcpdump [ -adeflnNOpqRStuvxX ] [ -c count ] [ -C file_size ]
  [ -F file ] [ -i interface ] [ -m module ] [ -r file ]
  [ -s snaplen ] [ -T type ] [ -U user ] [ -w file ]
  [ -E algo:secret ] [ expression ]
```

traceroute

The **traceroute** UNIX command can be used for the same purpose as the **tracert** Windows command. Specifically, you can help isolate which router hop along the path from a source device to a destination device is having issues. Also, based on the round-trip response time information reported for each hop, you can better determine which network segment might be causing excessive delay because of congestion. Example 10-26 offers sample output from the **traceroute** command, which is identifying the 13 router hops a UNIX host must transit to reach pearsonitcertification.com.

Example 10-26 Sample Output from the UNIX **traceroute** Command

```
HOST# traceroute pearsonitcertification.com
traceroute to pearsonitcertification.com (64.28.85.25), 64 hops max, 52
byte packets
 1  192.168.1.1 (192.168.1.1) 3.480 ms 2.548 ms 2.404 ms
 2  cpe-76-177-16-1.natcky.res.rr.com (76.177.16.1) 22.150 ms 11.300 ms
9.719 ms
 3  gig2-0-0.rcmdky-mx41.natcky.rr.com (65.28.199.205) 9.242 ms 19.940
ms 11.735 ms
```

```
 4  tge0-2-0.chcgileq-rtr1.kc.rr.com (65.28.199.97) 38.459 ms 38.821 ms
36.157 ms
 5  ae-4-0.cr0.chi10.tbone.rr.com (66.109.6.100) 41.903 ms 37.388 ms
31.966 ms
 6  ae-0-0.pr0.chi10.tbone.rr.com (66.109.6.153) 75.757 ms 46.287 ms
35.031 ms
 7  if-4-0-0.core1.ct8-chicago.as6453.net (66.110.14.21) 48.020 ms
37.248 ms 45.446 ms
 8  if-1-0-0-1878.core2.ct8-chicago.as6453.net (66.110.27.78) 108.466
ms 55.465 ms 87.590 ms
 9  63.243.186.25 (63.243.186.25) 64.045 ms 63.582 ms 69.200 ms
10  cr2-pos-0-8-0-3.nyr.savvis.net (208.173.129.29) 64.933 ms 65.113 ms
61.759 ms
11  hr1-tengig-13-0-0.waltham2bo2.savvis.net (204.70.198.182) 71.964 ms
65.430 ms 74.397 ms
12  das3-v3038.bo2.savvis.net (209.202.187.182) 65.777 ms 64.483 ms
82.383 ms
13  blhosting.bridgelinesw.com (64.14.81.46) 63.448 ms !X * 68.879 ms
!X
```

traceroute for IPv6

Similar to the **traceroute** options for IPv4, the IPv6 path through a network can be verified with **traceroute** for IPv6. Depending on the vendor and platform, this may be done by using **traceroute** *destination-IPv6-address*, **traceroute6** *destination-IPv6-address*, **traceroute -6** *destination-IPv6-address*, or some variant specific to the vendor and product being used.

netstat

The UNIX **netstat** command serves the same basic purpose of the Windows **netstat** command, which is to display various information about current connections. This information includes source and destination IP addresses and port numbers. You can also display protocol statistics with the **netstat** command.

The following is the syntax for the **netstat** command, with some of its commonly used options:

```
netstat [-a] [-b] [-r] [-s]
```

Table 10-9 explains the usage of the previously listed command options.

Table 10-9 Parameters for the Windows **netstat** Command

Parameter	Purpose
-a	This option displays all of a UNIX host's active IP-based sessions, along with the TCP and UDP ports of each session.
-b	This option shows you the names of the program that opened up a session.
-r	This option displays a UNIX host's IP routing table.
-s	This option displays statistical information for protocols such as **udp**, **ip**, **icmp**, **igmp**, **ipsec**, **ip6**, **icmp6**, **ipsec6**, **rip6**, and **pfkey**. (Note that these protocols vary depending on your UNIX platform.)

As with Windows, the UNIX **netstat** command issued by itself produces output that details each current session, as shown in Example 10-27.

Example 10-27 Sample Output from the UNIX **netstat** Command

```
HOST# netstat
Active Internet connections
Proto Recv-Q Send-Q  Local Address          Foreign Address            (state)
tcp4      37      0  192.168.1.245.49499    172.20.202.51-st.https     CLOSE_WAIT
tcp4      37      0  192.168.1.245.49495    192.168.202.51-st.https    CLOSE_WAIT
tcp4       0      0  192.168.1.26.49472     192.168.1.50.17500         ESTABLISHED
tcp4       0      0  192.168.1.26.49471     192.168.1.240.17501        ESTABLISHED
tcp4       0      0  192.168.1.245.49436    172.16.30.42-sta.http      ESTABLISHED
tcp4       0      0  192.168.1.245.17500    192.168.1.50.2583          ESTABLISHED
tcp4       0      0  192.168.1.245.17500    192.168.1.240.60687        ESTABLISHED
tcp4       0      0  192.168.1.245.49423    10.243.202.51-st.https     CLOSE_WAIT
tcp4       0      0  192.168.1.245.49321    172.16.62.121.https        ESTABLISHED
tcp4       0      0  localhost.26164        localhost.49184            ESTABLISHED
tcp4       0      0  192.168.1.26.49505     192.168.1.240.netbios-      TIME_WAIT
OUTPUT OMITTED...
```

The **netstat** command with the **-r** option can also be used to view the IP routing table of a UNIX host, as shown in Example 10-28. On a Mac, you can use the keystroke Control+C to break out of the **netstat** output (and other commands as well, such as **ping**).

Example 10-28 Sample Output from the UNIX **netstat -r** Command

```
HOST# netstat -r
Routing tables

Internet:
Destination      Gateway            Flags    Refs      Use       Netif Expire
Default          192.168.1.1        UGSc     45        40        en0
127              localhost          UCS      0         0         lo0
Localhost        localhost          UH       2         14        lo0
169.254          link#4             UCS      0         0         en0
172.16.53/24     link#6             UC       3         0         vmnet1
172.16.53.1      0:50:56:c0:0:1     UHLWI    0         107       lo0
172.16.53.255    link#6             UHLWbI   2         184       vmnet1
172.16.202/24    link#5             UC       2         0         vmnet8
172.16.202.255   link#5             UHLWbI   2         184       vmnet8
192.168.1        link#4             UC       10        0         en0
192.168.1.1      0:1f:f3:c9:39:fe   UHLWI    67        257       en0
1183
192.168.1.2      0:18:f8:50:ad:35   UHLWI    0         0         en0
1032
192.168.1.50     0:24:81:ee:4c:e    UHLWI    2         481       en0
```

ping

The UNIX **ping** command is most typically used to test network reachability to a specified destination, like the Windows version of the **ping** command. However, unlike the Windows **ping** command, the UNIX **ping** command sends continuous pings, as opposed to the Windows default of only four pings.

Syntax for the UNIX **ping** command, along with some of its commonly used parameters, is as follows:

```
ping [-c count] [-D] [-S srcaddr] target_name
```

Table 10-10 explains the usage of the previously listed command options.

Table 10-10 Parameters for the UNIX **ping** Command

Parameter	Purpose
-c *count*	This option specifies the number of pings to send.
-D	This option sets the "don't fragment" bit in a packet's header. If the packet tries to cross a router that attempts to fragment the packet, the packet is dropped and an ICMP error message is returned.

Parameter	Purpose
-S *srcaddr*	If the UNIX host from which you are issuing the **ping** command has more than one interface, this option allows you to specify the source IP address from which the ICMP echo messages should be sent.
target_name	This option specifies the name or the IP address of the device to which you are sending ICMP echo messages.

Example 10-29 shows output from a **ping** command limited to sending only five ICMP echo packets.

Example 10-29 Sample Output from the UNIX **ping -c** Command

```
HOST# ping -c 5 192.168.1.1
PING 192.168.1.1 (192.168.1.1): 56 data bytes
64 bytes from 192.168.1.1: icmp_seq=0 ttl=255 time=7.386 ms
64 bytes from 192.168.1.1: icmp_seq=1 ttl=255 time=7.490 ms
64 bytes from 192.168.1.1: icmp_seq=2 ttl=255 time=7.485 ms
64 bytes from 192.168.1.1: icmp_seq=3 ttl=255 time=2.575 ms
64 bytes from 192.168.1.1: icmp_seq=4 ttl=255 time=7.584 ms

--- 192.168.1.1 ping statistics ---
5 packets transmitted, 5 packets received, 0.0% packet loss
round-trip min/avg/max/stddev = 2.575/6.504/7.584/1.965 ms
 route
```

Although the UNIX **route** command is not used to display a host's IP routing table, which is a use of the Windows **route** command, it can be used to modify a UNIX host's IP routing table. The **route** command has multiple options; however, this discussion focuses on using the **route** command to add or delete a route from a UNIX host's routing table.

A partial syntax description for the UNIX **route** command, which focuses on adding and deleting routes from a UNIX host's routing table, is as follows:

```
route [-qv] [[add | delete] net network/mask gateway]
```

Table 10-11 explains the usage of the previously listed command options.

Table 10-11 Parameters for the UNIX **route** Command Used to Add and Delete Routes

Parameter	Purpose
-q	This option, where the *q* stands for *quiet*, suppresses any output from appearing onscreen after the **route** command is entered.
-v	This option, where the *v* stands for *verbose*, causes additional details about the **route** command's execution to be shown onscreen.
add	This option adds a route to a UNIX host's routing table.
delete	This option deletes a route from a UNIX host's routing table.
net	This option specifies that the next parameter is a network address.
network	This option specifies the network to add or remove from a UNIX host's routing table.
mask	This option is the number of bits in a specified network's subnet mask.
gateway	This option is the IP address of the gateway, which is the next hop toward the specified network.

Example 10-30 illustrates use of the UNIX **route** command to add a static route to a UNIX host's routing table. Specifically, a route to 10.1.2.0/24 with a next-hop gateway of 192.168.1.1 is being added. Also, notice the **netstat -r** command issued after the **route** command to confirm the insertion of the 10.1.2.0/24 route into the UNIX host's routing table.

Example 10-30 Adding a Static Route with the UNIX **route** Command

```
HOST# route add 10.1.2.0/24 192.168.1.1
add net 10.1.2.0: gateway 192.168.1.1
HOST# netstat -r
Routing tables

Internet:
Destination        Gateway    Flags      Refs      Use      Netif Expire
Default        192.168.1.1     UGSc        15        0      en0
10.1.2/24      192.168.1.1     UGSc         0        0      en0
127              localhost      UCS         0        0      lo0
Localhost        localhost       UH         2        8      lo0
169.254            link#4       UCS         0        0      en0
OUTPUT OMITTED...
```

Real-World Case Study

Acme, Inc. has most of its network infrastructure in place, including connectivity to the Internet. An administrator was attempting to visit a web server on the Internet but was not able to successfully connect.

From the Windows computer that he was using, he opened up a command prompt to do some troubleshooting. He verified that the local computer had an IP address and a default gateway by using the command **ipconfig /all**. Next he used the command **arp -a** to verify that his local computer had already resolved the default gateway's Layer 2 MAC address. A **ping** command was used to verify connectivity between the local computer and the default gateway. The command **nslookup** was used to verify that the name of the website that was attempting to be visited was being correctly resolved to an IP address by DNS. The command **tracert** was used to verify the path to the server, but the **tracert** output stopped before reaching the web server's final IP address. Browser-based access to other web servers on the Internet proved to be successful.

As a result of basic connectivity working to the Internet, including name resolution working correctly, it was determined that either the web server being accessed was temporarily down or that there was some type of a firewall or filter preventing access to that specific web server.

Summary

Here are the main topics covered in this chapter:

- You can use a number of Windows CLI commands to monitor and troubleshoot a network. These commands include **arp**, **ipconfig**, **nbtstat**, **netstat**, **nslookup**, **ping**, **pathping**, **route**, and **tracert**.
- UNIX CLI commands include **man**, **arp**, **dig**, **nslookup**, **host**, **ifconfig**, **traceroute**, **netstat**, **ping**, **route**, **nmap**, **iptables**, and **tcpdump**.

Exam Preparation Tasks

Review All the Key Topics

Review the most important topics from inside the chapter, noted with the Key Topic icon in the outer margin of the page. Table 10-12 lists these key topics and the page numbers where each is found.

Key Topic

Table 10-12 Key Topics for Chapter 10

Key Topic Element	Description	Page Number
Example 10-1	Sample output from the Windows **arp -a** command	339
Example 10-2	Sample output from the Windows **ipconfig /all** command	341
Example 10-6	Sample output from the Windows **nbtstat -c** command	344
Example 10-9	Sample output from the Windows **netstat** command	347
Example 10-11	Sample output from the Windows **nslookup** noninteractive command	349
Example 10-13	Sample output from the Windows **ping** command	351
Example 10-15	Sample output from the Windows **route print** command	353
Example 10-16	Sample output from a successful Windows **tracert** command	354
Example 10-21	Adding and confirming a static ARP entry with the UNIX **arp** command	361
Example 10-23	Comparing output from the UNIX **dig** and **nslookup** commands	362
Example 10-24	Sample output from the UNIX **host** command	363
Example 10-25	Configuring and verifying the configuration of an interface's IP address with the UNIX **ifconfig** command	364
Example 10-26	Sample output from the UNIX **traceroute** command	365
Example 10-27	Sample output from the UNIX **netstat** command	367
Example 10-29	Sample output from the UNIX **ping -c** command	369
Example 10-30	Adding a static route with the UNIX **route** command	370

Complete Tables and Lists from Memory

Print a copy of Appendix C, "Memory Tables," or at least the section for this chapter, and complete as many of the tables as possible from memory. Appendix D, "Memory Tables Answer Key," includes the completed tables and lists so you can check your work.

Define Key Terms

Define the following key terms from this chapter, and check your answers in the Glossary:

arp command, **ipconfig** command, **nbtstat** command, **netstat** command, **nslookup** command, **ping** command, **route** command, **tracert** command, **dig** command, **host** command, **traceroute** command, **iptables** command, **tcpdump** command, **nmap** command

Complete Chapter 10 Hands-On Lab in Network+ Simulator Lite

- Using ARP to Discover the MAC Address
- Using **ipconfig**, **ping**, **arp**, and **tracert** to Troubleshoot Connectivity

Additional Resources

Command-line Interface: https://en.wikipedia.org/wiki/Command-line_interface

Finding Your Way with Traceroute: http://www.ajsnetworking.com/trace-route

Review Questions

The answers to these review questions are in Appendix A, "Answers to Review Questions."

1. Consider the following output:

```
C:\> arp -a

Interface: 172.16.202.128 --- 0xb
  Internet Address      Physical Address      Type
  172.16.202.2          00-50-56-fd-65-2c     dynamic
  172.16.202.255        ff-ff-ff-ff-ff-ff     static
  224.0.0.22            01-00-5e-00-00-16     static
  224.0.0.252           01-00-5e-00-00-fc     static
  255.255.255.255       ff-ff-ff-ff-ff-ff     static
```

What is the MAC address corresponding to the IP address of 172.16.202.2?

a. ff-ff-ff-ff-ff-ff

b. 00-50-56-fd-65-2c

c. 01-00-5e-00-00-16

d. 01-00-5e-00-00-fc

2. What option would you specify after the **ipconfig** command to display the IP address of a Windows PC's DNS server?

a. No option is needed because the **ipconfig** displays DNS server information by default.

b. **/full**

c. **/fqdn**

d. **/all**

3. Which Windows commands could have produced the following output? (Choose two.)

```
===========================================================================
Interface List
 20...00 0c 29 3a 21 67 ......Intel(R) PRO/1000 MT Network Connection #2
 11...00 0c 29 3a 21 5d ......Intel(R) PRO/1000 MT Network Connection
  1........................... Software Loopback Interface 1
 12...00 00 00 00 00 00 00 e0 Microsoft ISATAP Adapter
 13...00 00 00 00 00 00 00 e0 Teredo Tunneling Pseudo-Interface
===========================================================================
```

```
IPv4 Route Table
===========================================================================
Active Routes:
Network Destination  Netmask          Gateway       Interface        Metric
0.0.0.0              0.0.0.0          172.16.202.2  172.16.202.128   10
0.0.0.0              0.0.0.0          172.16.202.2  172.16.202.129   10
127.0.0.0            255.0.0.0        On-link       127.0.0.1        306
127.0.0.1            255.255.255.255  On-link       127.0.0.1        306
127.255.255.255      255.255.255.255  On-link       127.0.0.1        306
172.16.202.0         255.255.255.0    On-link       172.16.202.128   266
172.16.202.0         255.255.255.0    On-link       172.16.202.129   266
172.16.202.128       255.255.255.255  On-link       172.16.202.128   266
172.16.202.129       255.255.255.255  On-link       172.16.202.129   266
172.16.202.255       255.255.255.255  On-link       172.16.202.128   266
172.16.202.255       255.255.255.255  On-link       172.16.202.129   266
224.0.0.0            240.0.0.0        On-link       127.0.0.1        306
224.0.0.0            240.0.0.0        On-link       172.16.202.129   266
224.0.0.0            240.0.0.0        On-link       172.16.202.128   266
255.255.255.255      255.255.255.255  On-link       127.0.0.1        306
255.255.255.255      255.255.255.255  On-link       172.16.202.129   266
255.255.255.255      255.255.255.255  On-link       172.16.202.128   266
```

a. **netstat -a**

b. **route print**

c. **netstat -r**

d. **nbtstat -r**

4. Which of the following Windows commands enables you to display NetBIOS over TCP/IP information?

a. **route**

b. **nbtstat**

c. **dig**

d. **netstat**

5. What protocol is used by the **ping** command?

a. IGMP

b. PIM

c. ICMP

d. RTP

6. Which of the following commands is used on a UNIX host to generate information about each router hop along the path from a source to a destination?

   a. **ping -t**

   b. **tracert**

   c. **ping -r**

   d. **traceroute**

7. Which of the following UNIX commands can be used to check FQDN-to-IP-address resolution? (Choose three.)

   a. **nslookup**

   b. **netstat**

   c. **dig**

   d. **host**

8. Which of the following commands would you issue on a UNIX host to send five ICMP echo messages to a device with an IP address of 10.1.1.1?

   a. **ping 10.1.1.1** (No options are required because five is the default number of pings.)

   b. **ping -c 5 10.1.1.1**

   c. **ping -t 5 10.1.1.1**

   d. **ping 10.1.1.1 -t 5**

9. What command produced the following snippet of output?

```
OUTPUT OMITTED...
;; global options: +cmd
;; Got answer:
;; ->>HEADER<<- opcode: QUERY, status: NOERROR, id: 62169
;; flags: qr rd ra; QUERY: 1, ANSWER: 1, AUTHORITY: 0, ADDITIONAL: 0

;; QUESTION SECTION:
;pearsonitcertification.com. IN A

;; ANSWER SECTION:
pearsonitcertification.com. 10800 IN A 64.28.85.25

;; Query time: 202 msec
;; SERVER: 192.168.1.1#53(192.168.1.1)
;; WHEN: Wed Jun 1 20:41:57 2011
;; MSG SIZE rcvd: 60
OUTPUT OMITTED...
```

a. **traceroute -d pearsonitcertification.com**

b. **dig pearsonitcertification.com**

c. **netstat -a pearsonitcertification.com**

d. **nbtstat pearsonitcertification.com**

10. What command produced the following snippet of output?

```
OUTPUT OMITTED...
lo0: flags=8049<UP,LOOPBACK,RUNNING,MULTICAST> mtu 16384
    inet 127.0.0.1 netmask 0xff000000
    inet6 ::1 prefixlen 128
    inet6 fe80::1%lo0 prefixlen 64 scopeid 0x1
    inet6 fd4e:f9d5:c34e:acd1:5a55:caff:fefa:1551 prefixlen 128
gif0: flags=8010<POINTOPOINT,MULTICAST> mtu 1280
stf0: flags=0<> mtu 1280
en0: flags=8863<UP,BROADCAST,SMART,RUNNING,SIMPLEX,MULTICAST> mtu 1500
    ether 58:55:ca:fa:15:51
    inet6 fe80::5a55:caff:fefa:1551%en0 prefixlen 64 scopeid 0x4
    inet 192.168.1.245 netmask 0xffffff00 broadcast 192.168.1.255
    media: autoselect
    status: active
OUTPUT OMITTED...
```

a. **ifconfig**

b. **ipconfig**

c. **ipconfig /all**

d. **ifconfig /all**

After completion of this chapter, you will be able to answer the following questions:

- What are some of the more common tools used to physically maintain a network?
- What are components found in effective network documentation?
- What sorts of network monitoring tools are available to network administrators, and what types of information are included in various logs?

CHAPTER 11

Network Management

Even with a network's increasing dependence on wireless technologies, physical cabling still serves as the critical backbone of a network. Therefore, network management, monitoring, and troubleshooting require a familiarity with a variety of cable maintenance tools. These tools might be used, for example, to physically terminate cabling and troubleshoot cabling issues. This chapter addresses these and other maintenance tools, providing an overview of each.

Another key network management element is documentation, which encompasses, for example, managing device configuration information. Such configuration repositories are continually evolving entities requiring ongoing attention. This chapter discusses several of the most important configuration element components.

This chapter concludes by addressing network monitoring resources and reports whose information can be gleaned from monitoring resources. For example, the primary network management protocol used by network management systems (NMSs) is Simple Network Management Protocol (SNMP), and this chapter discusses the various versions of SNMP. In addition, syslog servers and a variety of reports are considered.

Foundation Topics

Maintenance Tools

The number of troubleshooting issues occurring in a network can be reduced by proper installation and configuration. For example, improper wiring might function immediately following an installation; however, over time, the wiring might start to experience intermittent issues that cause network disruptions. In such a situation, you, as a network administrator, need to be familiar with a collection of maintenance tools to help diagnose, isolate, and resolve the wiring issue.

Therefore, this chapter presents you with a collection of popular network tools. Having this understanding can help you better perform initial installations and resolve issues with existing installations.

Bit-Error Rate Tester

Interference on a transmission medium, or faulty cabling, can cause errors in the transmission of binary data (or bits). A common measurement for bit errors is called *bit error rate* (BER), which is calculated as follows:

BER = Bit errors / Bits transmitted

For example, imagine that a network device transmitted the binary pattern of 10101010; however, the pattern received by the destination device was 10101111. Comparing these two bit patterns reveals that the sixth and eighth bits were incorrectly received. Therefore, the BER could be calculated by dividing the number of bit errors (two) by the number of transmitted bits (eight), resulting in a BER of 25% (BER = 2 / 8 = .25).

When troubleshooting a link where you suspect a high BER, you can use a piece of test equipment called a *bit-error rate tester* (BERT), shown in Figure 11-1. A BERT contains both a *pattern generator* (which can generate a variety of bit patterns) and an *error detector* (which is synchronized with the pattern generator and can determine the number of bit errors), and it can calculate a BER for the tested transmission link.

Figure 11-1 Bit-Error Rate Tester (BERT). Photo Courtesy of BBN International (http://www.bbnint.co.uk).

Butt Set

A *butt set* is a piece of test equipment typically used by telephone technicians. The clips on the butt set can connect a punch-down block (for example, a 66 block or a 110 block) connecting to a telephone. This allows the technician to check a line (for example, to determine whether a dial tone is present on the line or to determine whether a call can be placed from the line).

The name butt set (which is sometimes called a *butt in*) comes from the device's capability to butt in to (or interrupt) a conversation in progress. For example, a telephone technician might be at the top of a telephone pole and connect to the wires of a phone currently in a call. The technician would then butt in to the call, identifying himself and stating that he was testing the line.

Although a butt set is an extremely common piece of test equipment for telephone technicians, it has less usefulness to you as a network administrator. One exception, however, is if you are working on a digital subscriber line (DSL) line. You could use a butt set while working on DSL wiring to confirm dial tone is present on the line.

Cable Certifier

Chapter 3, "Network Components," introduced you to a variety of unshielded twisted-pair (UTP) wiring categories (for example, Category 3, Category 5, and Category5e). Different UTP categories support different data rates over specific distances. If you are working with existing cable and want to determine its category, or if you simply want to test the supported frequency range (and therefore data throughput) of a cable, you can use a cable certifier.

Cable Tester

A cable tester can test the conductors in an Ethernet cable. Notice the two parts that make up the cable tester. By connecting these parts of the cable tester to each end of a cable under test, you can check the wires in the cable for continuity (that is, check to make sure there are no opens, or breaks, in a conductor). In addition, you can verify an RJ-45 connector's pinouts (that wires are connected to appropriate pins on an RJ-45 connector).

Connectivity Software

When you are physically separate from the network you are maintaining or troubleshooting, you might be able to access the network through *remote connectivity software* that enables you to take control of a PC that is located on a remote network. In addition, Microsoft has its own proprietary protocol called *Remote Desktop Protocol* (RDP), which supports remotely connecting to a Microsoft Windows computer. Figure 11-2 shows Microsoft's Remote Desktop Connection application (which comes with most professional versions of Microsoft Windows). In the figure, you see a dialog box prompting a user for an IP address (or hostname) of the remote computer with which to connect.

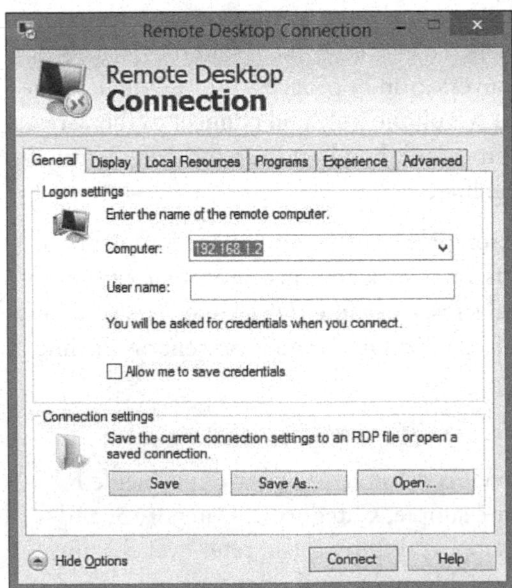

Figure 11-2 Microsoft's Remote Desktop Connection

Crimper

A crimper, as pictured in Figure 11-3, can be used to attach a connector (for example, an RJ-45 connector) to the end of a UTP cable. To accompany a crimper, you might want to purchase a spool of cable (for example, Category 6 UTP cable) and a box of RJ-45 connectors. You will then be equipped to make your own Ethernet patch cables, which might be less expensive than buying preterminated UTP cables. It's also convenient when you need a patch cable of a nonstandard length or when you need a nonstandard pinout on the RJ-45 connectors (for example, when you need a T1 crossover cable). Many crimpers have a built-in wire stripper and wire snip function as well.

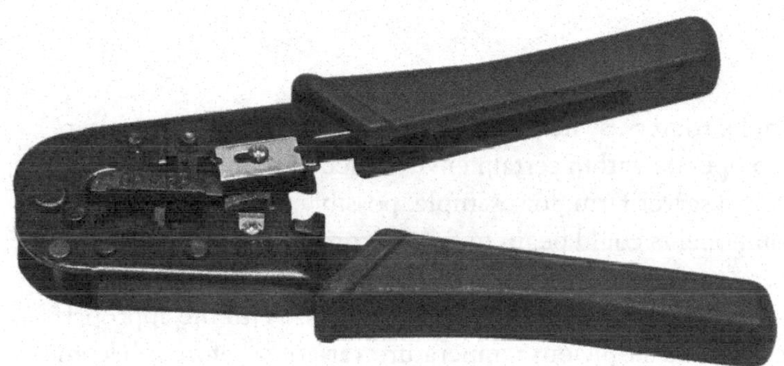

Figure 11-3 Crimper

Electrostatic Discharge Wrist Strap

Do you remember a time when you touched a metallic object and received a shock because of the static electricity you built up (for example, by walking on a carpeted floor)? That static discharge was probably a few thousand volts. Although the shock might have caused you to recoil your hand, you survived this event because the amperage of the shock was low (probably just a few milliamps). Although no damage was done to your hand or the object you touched, if the static discharge occurred when you touched a component on a circuit board, you could destroy that component.

Viewed under a microscope, the damage done to electrical components subjected to static shock is very evident, with visible craters in the components. Therefore, you must take care when handling circuit boards (for example, *blades* used in modular switches or routers) to avoid destroying potentially expensive equipment.

As a precaution, you can wear an electrostatic discharge (ESD) wrist strap. The strap is equipped with a clip that you attach to something with a ground potential (for example, a large metal desk). While wearing the wrist strap, if you have any static buildup in your body, the static flows to the object with a ground potential, to which your strap is clipped, thus avoiding damage to any electrical components you might touch.

NOTE Some ESD wrist straps contain a resistor to prevent you from being harmed if you come in contact with a voltage source capable of producing a significant current. Specifically, the formula for voltage is $V = R * I$, where V is voltage, R is resistance, and I is current. By rewriting the formula as $I = V / R$, you can see that if electricity has to flow through a greater resistance, the resulting current will be lower and, therefore, safer.

Environmental Monitor

Components (for example, routers, switches, and servers) making up a computer network are designed to operate within certain environmental limits. If the temperature rises too high in a server farm, for example, possibly because of an air-conditioner outage, components could begin to fail. To prevent such an occurrence, you can use *environmental monitors* to send an alert if the temperature in a room rises above or drops below administratively configured thresholds. With the appropriate personnel being alerted about a suspicious temperature variation before it becomes an issue, action can hopefully be taken to, for example, repair an air-conditioning unit or provide extra ventilation, thus preventing a system failure. In addition to monitoring a room's temperature, some environmental monitors check a room's humidity.

Environmental monitors, including power and temperature monitors, can alert appropriate personnel in a variety of ways. For example, some environmental monitors can send an alert to a SNMP server. This alert is known as an *SNMP trap*. Another common notification option allows an environmental monitor to send an email or SMS text message to alert appropriate personnel about the suspect environmental condition.

Having fault-tolerant power options in place, such as uninterruptible power supplies (UPSs), fault-tolerant power circuits into the building, generators, and appropriate converters or inverters for the critical network devices, can assist in preventing downtime in the event of a single power failure. Having monitoring systems in place allows you to react and restore redundancy.

Device placement in racks should be done in such a way to allow proper air flow through the systems in the racks. Racks may be two- or four-post racks organized into rows. Free-standing racks may also be used to hold the network systems and devices. A rack-mounted server has rails on the side that allow it to be inserted into a rack. Environmental monitors can trigger an alert about potential damage if the humidity or temperature goes outside of the proper values for network devices and servers.

Loopback Plug

When troubleshooting a network device, you might want to confirm that a network interface is functional (for example, that it can transmit and receive traffic). One way to perform such a test is to attach a loopback plug to a network interface and run diagnostic software designed to use the loopback plug. A loopback plug takes the transmit pins on an Ethernet connector and connects them to the receive pins, such that everything that is transmitted is received back on the interface. Similarly, a fiber-optic loopback plug, as shown in Figure 11-4, interconnects a fiber-connector's transmit fiber with a connector's receive fiber. The diagnostic software can then transmit traffic out of a network interface and confirm its successful reception on that same interface.

Figure 11-4 Fiber-Optic Loopback Plug. Photo Courtesy of Digi-Key Corporation (http://www.digikey.com).

Multimeter

When working with copper cabling (as opposed to fiber-optic cabling), you can use a multimeter to check a variety of a cable's electrical characteristics. These characteristics include resistance (in ohms), current (in amps), and voltage (in volts). Figure 11-5 shows an example of a multimeter.

Figure 11-5 Multimeter

As one example, you could use the ohmmeter function of a multimeter (the resistance feature) to check continuity of an Ethernet cable. If you connect the two leads of a multimeter to two pins of a cable, the resulting resistance is approximately 0 ohms if those two pins are connected, and the resulting resistance approaches an infinite number of ohms if the pins do not connect with one another.

Another common use of a multimeter is to use the voltmeter function (the voltage feature). As an example, you could check leads of an Ethernet cable to see whether DC voltage is being applied to a device needing to receive Power over Ethernet (PoE).

Protocol Analyzer

If you understand the characteristics of the protocols running on your network (for example, understanding the fields in a protocol's header), a protocol analyzer (also known as a *network sniffer*) can be a tremendous troubleshooting asset. A protocol analyzer can be a standalone device or software running on a laptop computer. You can use a protocol analyzer to capture traffic flowing through a network switch, using the port mirroring feature of a switch, as described in Chapter 4, "Ethernet Technology." By examining the captured packets, you can discern the details of communication flows (sessions) as they are being set up, maintained, and torn down. The examination of these captured packets is referred to as *traffic analysis*, which provides an administrator with valuable insights about the nature of traffic flowing through the veins of the network.

Protocol analyzers come in a wide range of features and costs. Wireshark is a free software program that can make your laptop act like a protocol analyzer. Protocol analyzers can assist in identifying details such as top talkers, top destinations, top protocols in use, and quantity of traffic on the network. You can download your free copy of Wireshark from http://www.wireshark.org. Figure 11-6 shows the Wireshark application.

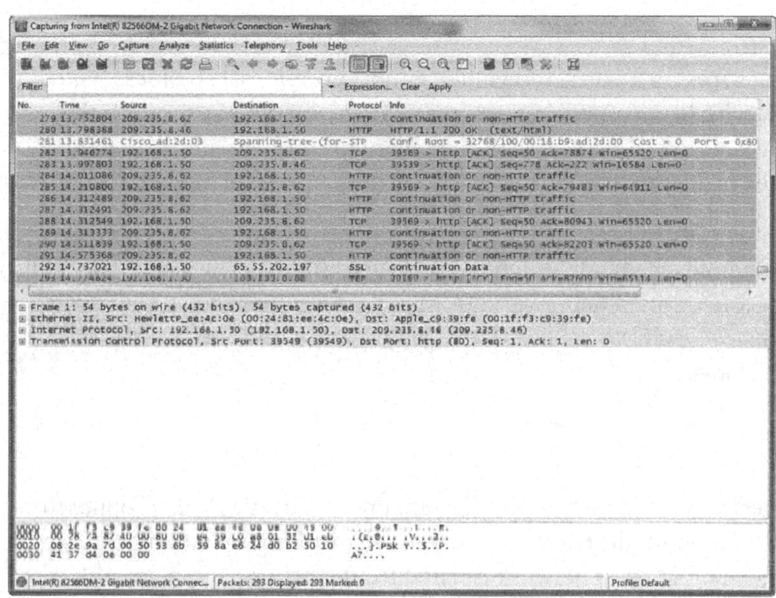

Figure 11-6 Wireshark Protocol Analyzer Software

Wi-Fi Analyzer

Software running on a general-purpose computer or on a specialized device can perform wireless analysis of Wi-Fi signals. This type of tool would be used as part of a wireless site survey after Wi-Fi has been implemented to create a heat map of the wireless airspace.

Looking-Glass Sites

A looking-glass server on the Internet allows users to connect to view the routing information from that server's perspective. These are normally related to Border Gateway Protocol (BGP) routes. There are hundreds of thousands of routes in BGP. Using a looking-glass site could assist engineers in verifying that changes they made to their local BGP router configuration are having the desired effect on the BGP routes on the Internet. To find a BGP looking-glass site, use Google to search for "BGP looking glass."

Speed Test Sites

Many speed test services are available that can assist you in verifying throughput from a local computer to an Internet site. One example is speedtest.net. Using sites such as this can assist you when determining whether the overall connection to the Internet is slow or if just a specific site or server is slow to respond.

Punch-Down Tool

When terminating wires on a punch-down block (for example, a 110 block), you insert an insulated wire between two *contact blades*. These blades cut through the insulation and make electrical contact with the inner wire. As a result, you do not have to strip off the insulation.

However, if you attempt to insert the wire between the two contact blades using a screwdriver, for example, the blades might be damaged to the point where they will not make a good connection. Therefore, you should use a punch-down tool, which is designed to properly insert an insulated wire between the two contact blades without damaging the blades.

Throughput Tester

Networks often perform differently when they are under a heavy load, as opposed to little or no load, which might be the case if you are mocking up a design in a test-bed environment (which is a test network isolated from a production network). Also, you might simply want to verify a network's maximum throughput. Either scenario could benefit from a throughput tester.

A *throughput tester* is a network appliance that typically has multiple network interfaces and can generate high volumes of pseudo-random data. You could, for example, connect a throughput tester to a proposed network that has been mocked up in a test bed to observe how the network performs under a heavy load. Also, you can attach a throughput tester to a production network to determine the actual throughput of that existing network. Figure 11-7 shows an example of a throughput tester appliance.

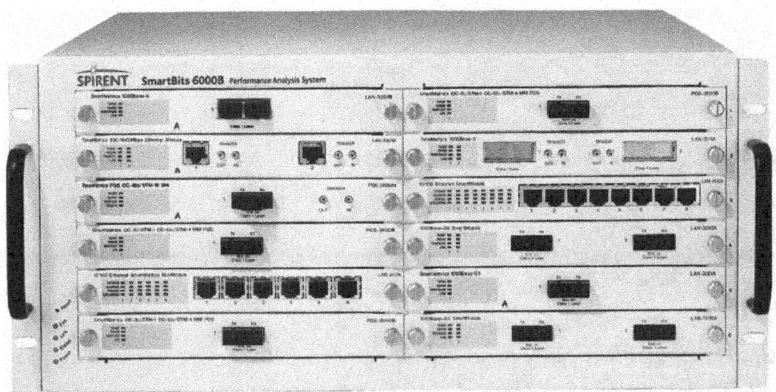

Figure 11-7 Throughput Tester. Photo Courtesy of NSS Labs (http://www.nsslabs.com).

Time Domain Reflectometer and Optical Time Domain Reflectometer

Suppose that you have been troubleshooting a network cable (either copper or fiber optic), and you determine that there is a break in (or physical damage to) the cable. However, identifying exactly where the break exists in a long length of cable can be problematic. Fortunately, you can use a time domain reflectometer (TDR) for copper cabling or an optical time domain reflectometer (OTDR) for fiber-optic cabling to locate the cable fault.

Both light and electricity travel at speeds approaching $3 * 10^8$ meters per second (approximately 186,000 miles per second), although the speeds are a bit slower and vary depending on the medium. A TDR can send an electric signal down a copper cable (or an OTDR, a light meter, which sends light down a fiber-optic cable), and when the electric signal (or light) encounters a cable fault, a portion of the electric signal (or light) reflects back to the source. Based on the speed of electricity (or light) in the medium and on the amount of time required for the reflected electric signal (or light) to be returned to the source, a TDR or an OTDR can mathematically determine where the cable fault lies. Figure 11-8 shows an example of an OTDR.

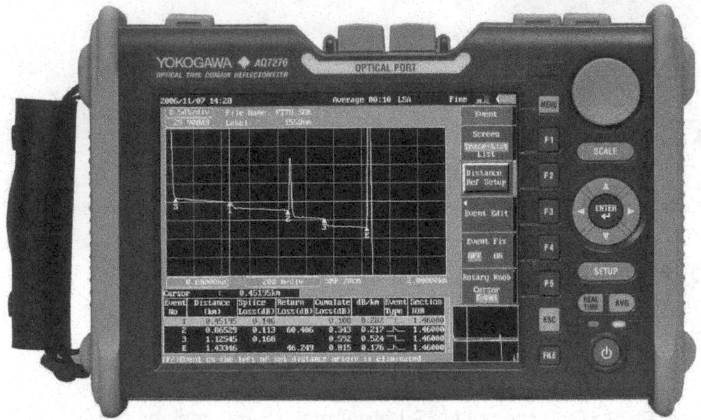

Figure 11-8 Optical Time Domain Reflectometer. Photo Courtesy of Coral-i Solutions (http://www.coral-i.com).

Toner Probe

If you are working on a punch-down block and attempting to identify which pair of wires connect back to an end-user's location (for example, someone's office), you can use a toner probe. A toner probe allows you to place a tone generator at one end of a connection (for example, someone's office) and use a probe on a punch-down block to audibly detect to which pair of wires the tone generator is connected.

A toner probe, therefore, comes in two pieces: the tone generator and the probe. Another common name for a toner probe is a *fox and hound*, where the tone generator is the fox, and the probe (which searches for the tone) is the hound. Some network devices have built-in troubleshooting tools, such as a voice-enabled Cisco router that can produce test tones.

Spectrum Analyzer

A spectrum analyzer measures the magnitude of an input signal versus frequency within the full frequency range of the instrument. The primary use of the spectrum analyzer is to measure the power of the spectrum of known and unknown signals. The input signal that a spectrum analyzer measures is electrical. However, spectral compositions of other signals (acoustic pressure waves and optical light waves) can be considered using the right transducer. Optical spectrum analyzers also exist, which use direct optical techniques, such as a monochromator, to make measurements.

By analyzing the spectra of electrical signals, you can see spectral components that you would not ordinarily be able to see. These include dominant frequency, power, distortion, harmonics, and bandwidth, and other spectral components of a signal. These parameters are useful in the characterization of electronic devices, such as wireless transmitters.

The display of a spectrum analyzer has frequency on the horizontal axis and the amplitude displayed on the vertical axis. A spectrum analyzer looks like an oscilloscope and, in fact, some lab instruments can function either as an oscilloscope or a spectrum analyzer.

Network Documentation

This text cannot stress enough the importance of up-to-date and accurate network documentation. This is not only useful for proper network management tasks, but it is also critical in troubleshooting, security, optimization, and other key areas of networking today. Consider these important aspects of network documentation:

- **Diagram symbols**: Your IT department should utilize standard templates to represent network objects in diagrams consistently; where needed, legends should clearly delineate one network device from another. The figures in this text have demonstrated many standard types of diagram symbols for the most popular network objects.
- **Standard operating procedures/work instructions**: Whenever possible, it is important to document the procedures your IT staff are to follow given certain network conditions; for example, steps for dealing with an Internet outage could aid staff members in taking quick action and minimizing disruptions.
- **Logical versus physical diagrams**: Be sure to consider the physical and logical topologies when diagramming. Remember, the logical and physical flows of data through the organization might result in very different diagrams.
- **Rack diagrams**: These days, with very small form factors in many of the network devices, we have more devices than ever coexisting in a single rack in a data center; rack diagrams become important to assist in the management of all the various devices in the rack.
- **Change management documentation**: It is critical that change controls be in place in your organization as well as careful documentation when changes actually take place; this helps ensure the accuracy of network information and can prove critical in security response and troubleshooting operations.
- **Wiring and port locations**: Another key piece of documentation is wiring and port locations. This documentation allows you to track cable runs from switches and map them to the actual wall jacks where users connect to your network; these connections might also represent trunks to additional network devices such as wireless access points.
- **IDF/MDF documentation**: Diagrams are also crucial for the independent distribution facility (IDF) and the main distribution facility (MDF). These distribution and core facilities house critical network data and devices, and proper documentation can aid in all forms of maintenance and security.
- **Labeling**: Proper labeling in diagrams as well as on physical equipment can ensure that such documentation is as useful as possible.
- **Network configuration and performance baselines**: You should document the base configurations for network devices as well as capture the data utilization and bandwidth consumption during "normal" business operations; this might also include taking SLA measurements during this time. Without this baseline information, it can be nearly impossible to gauge subtle performance problems.
- **Inventory management**: Another aspect of your documentation should be an inventory management system. This includes the tracking of spares (including hot spares) for inevitable hardware malfunctions, and inventory of software (including licenses) is just as important.

Monitoring Resources and Reports

Network administrators routinely monitor network resources and review reports to be proactive in their administration. For example, a potential network issue might be averted by spotting a trend (for example, increasing router CPU utilization or increasing bandwidth demand on a WAN link). Monitoring resources and reports come from various sources, such as a syslog server, an SNMP server, Event Viewer logs found on a Microsoft Windows server, and packet captures from a network sniffer. Remember that monitoring is also critical in the area of network security. For example, Security Information and Event Management (SIEM) software products and services combine Security Information Management (SIM) and Security Event Management (SEM).This section introduces you to many resources for monitoring network information.

SNMP

The first Request For Comments (RFC) for SNMP came out in 1988. Since then, SNMP has become the de facto standard of network management protocols. The original intent for SNMP was to manage network nodes, such as network servers, routers, and switches. SNMP Version 1 (SNMPv1) and SNMP Version 2c (SNMPv2c) specify three major components of an SNMP solution, as detailed in Table 11-1.

Table 11-1 Components of an SNMPv1 and SNMPv2c Network-Management Solution

Component	Description
SNMP manager	An SNMP manager runs a network management application. This SNMP manager is sometimes referred to as a *network management system (NMS)*.
SNMP agent	An SNMP agent is a piece of software that runs on a managed device (for example, a server, router, or switch).
Management Information Base (MIB)	Information about a managed device's resources and activity is defined by a series of objects. The structure of these management objects is defined by a managed device's MIB. Interfaces and their details, such as errors, utilization, discards, packet drops, resets, speed and duplex, system memory, utilization of bandwidth, storage, CPU, and memory, are able to be monitored and reported via SNMP.

As depicted in Figure 11-9, an SNMP manager (an NMS) can send information to, receive request information from, or receive unsolicited information from a managed device (a managed router, in this example). The managed device runs an SNMP agent and contains the MIB.

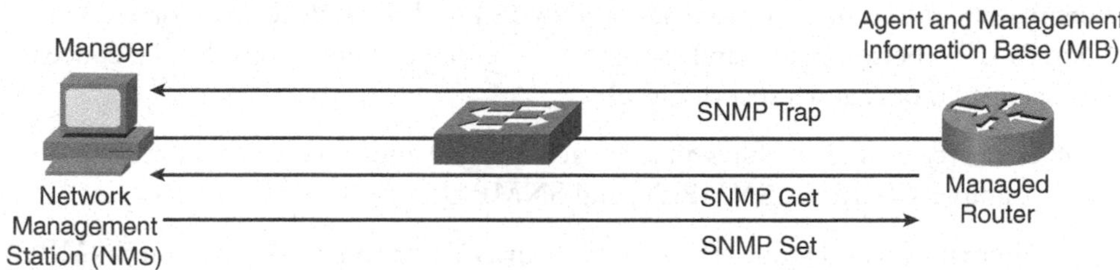

Figure 11-9 SNMPv1 and SNMPv2c Network-Management Components and Messages

Even though multiple SNMP messages might be sent between an SNMP manager and a managed device, consider the three broad categories of SNMP message types:

- **Get:** An SNMP get message retrieves information from a managed device.
- **Set:** An SNMP set message sets a variable in a managed device or triggers an action on a managed device.
- **Trap:** An SNMP trap message is an unsolicited message sent from a managed device to an SNMP manager, which can notify the SNMP manager about a significant event that occurred on the managed device.

SNMP management software can make requests for each of the MIB objects from an SNMP agent. This can be referred to as an SNMP *walk* because the management software is logically "walking" the entire MIB (also often called the *tree*) to gather information from the agent. SNMP offers security against malicious users attempting to collect information from a managed device, change the configuration of a managed device, or intercept information being sent to an NMS. However, the security integrated with SNMPv1 and SNMPv2c is considered weak. Specifically, SNMPv1 and SNMPv2c use *community strings* to gain read-only access or read-write access to a managed device. You can think of a community string like a password. Also, be aware that multiple SNMP-compliant devices on the market today have a default read-only community string of *public* and a default read-write community string of *private*. As a result, such devices, left at their default SNMP settings, could be compromised.

NOTE Notice that this section refers to SNMPv2c as opposed to SNMPv2. SNMPv2 contained security enhancements, in addition to other performance enhancements. However, few network administrators adopted SNMPv2 because of the complexity of the newly proposed security system. Instead, Community-Based Simple Network Management Protocol (SNMPv2c) gained widespread acceptance because it included the performance enhancements of SNMPv2 without using SNMPv2's complex security solution. Instead, SNMPv2c kept the SNMPv1 concept of community strings.

Fortunately, the security weaknesses of SNMPv1 and SNMPv2c are addressed in SNMPv3. To better understand these security enhancements, consider the concept of a security model and a security level:

- **Security model:** Defines an approach for user and group authentications (for example, SNMPv1, SNMPv2c, and SNMPv3).
- **Security level:** Defines the type of security algorithm performed on SNMP packets. The following are the three security levels discussed here:
  - **noAuthNoPriv:** The noAuthNoPriv (no authorization, no privacy) security level uses community strings for authorization and does not use encryption to provide privacy.
  - **authNoPriv:** The authNoPriv (authorization, no privacy) security level provides authorization using hashed message authentication code (HMAC) with Message Digest 5 (MD5) or Secure Hash Algorithm (SHA). However, no encryption is used.
  - **authPriv:** The authPriv (authorization, privacy) security level offers HMAC MD5 or SHA authentication and provides privacy through encryption. Specifically, the encryption uses the Cipher Block Chaining (CBC) Data Encryption Standard (DES) (DES-56) algorithm.

As summarized in Table 11-2, SNMPv3 supports all three security levels. Notice that SNMPv1 and SNMPv2c only support the noAuthNoPriv security level.

Table 11-2 Security Models and Security Levels Supported by Cisco IOS

Security Model	Security Level	Authentication Strategy	Encryption Type
SNMPv1	noAuthNoPriv	Community string	None
SNMPv2c	noAuthNoPriv	Community string	None
SNMPv3	noAuthNoPriv	Username	None
SNMPv3	authNoPriv	MD5 or SHA	None
SNMPv3	authPriv	MD5 or SHA	CBC-DES (DES-56)

Through the use of security algorithms, as shown in Table 11-2, SNMPv3 dramatically increases the security of network-management traffic, as compared to SNMPv1 and SNMPv2c. Specifically, SNMPv3 offers three primary security enhancements:

- **Integrity:** Using hashing algorithms, SNMPv3 ensures that an SNMP message was not modified in transit.
- **Authentication:** Hashing allows SNMPv3 to validate the source of an SNMP message.
- **Encryption:** Using the CBC-DES (DES-56) encryption algorithm, SNMPv3 provides privacy for SNMP messages, making them unreadable by an attacker who might capture an SNMP packet.

NOTE Many of the security concepts mentioned in this discussion are covered in more detail in Chapter 12, "Network Security."

In addition to its security enhancements, SNMPv3 differs architecturally from SNMPv1 and SNMPv2c. SNMPv3 defines SNMP entities, which are groupings of individual SNMP components. As shown in Figure 11-10, SNMP applications and an SNMP manager combine into an NMS SNMP entity, whereas an SNMP agent and an MIB combine into a managed node SNMP entity.

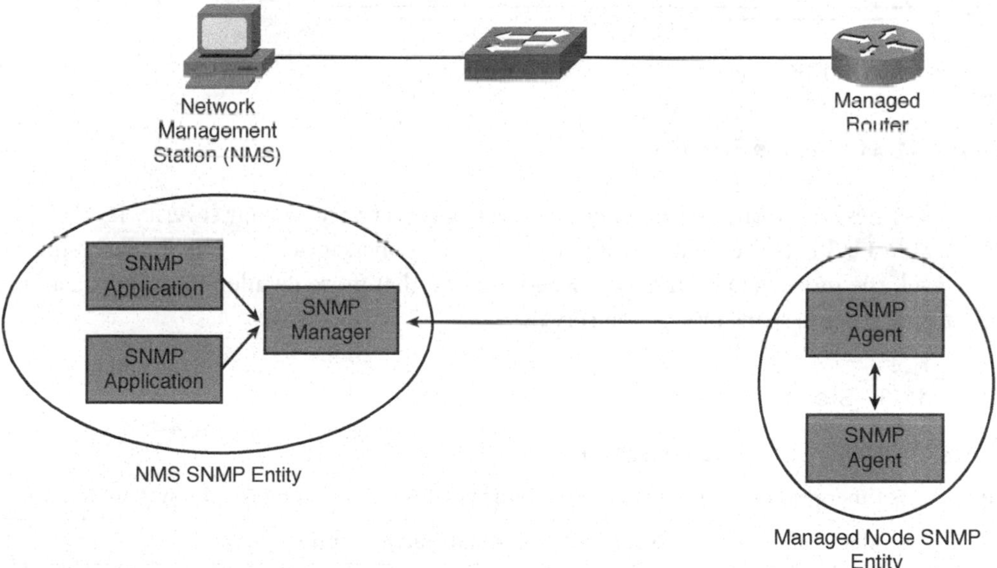

Figure 11-10 SNMPv3 Entities

Syslog

A variety of network components (for example, routers, switches, and servers) can send their log information to a common syslog server. By having information for multiple devices in a common log and examining time stamps, network administrators can better correlate events occurring on one network device with events occurring on a different network device. Syslog messages and SNMP traps can be used to trigger notification messages that may be sent via email and SMS. A syslog logging solution consists of two primary components:

- **Syslog servers:** A syslog server receives and stores log messages sent from syslog clients.
- **Syslog clients:** As shown in Figure 11-11, various types of network devices can act as syslog clients and send logging information to a syslog server.

Key Topic

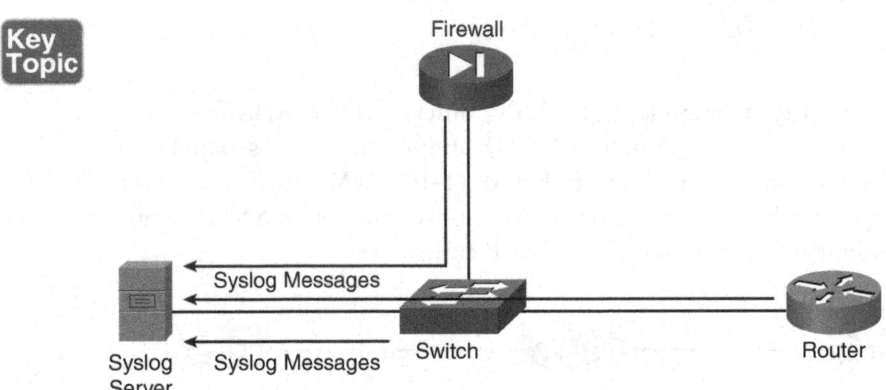

Figure 11-11 Sample Syslog Clients

Messages sent from a syslog client to a syslog server vary in their severity levels. Table 11-3 lists the eight severity levels of syslog messages. The higher the syslog level, the more detailed the logs. Keep in mind that more detailed logs require additional storage space on a syslog server.

Table 11-3 Syslog Severity Levels

Level	Name	Description
0	Emergencies	The most severe error conditions, which render the system unusable
1	Alerts	Conditions requiring immediate attention
2	Critical	A less-severe condition, as compared to alerts, that should be addressed to prevent an interruption of service
3	Errors	Notifications about error conditions within the system that do not render the system unusable
4	Warnings	Notifications that specific operations failed to complete successfully

Level	Name	Description
5	Notifications	Non-error notifications that alert an administrator about state changes within a system
6	Informational	Detailed information about the normal operation of a system
7	Debugging	Highly detailed information (for example, information about individual packets) that is typically used for troubleshooting purposes

Consider the format of a syslog message, as illustrated in Figure 11-12. The syslog log entries contain time stamps, which help you understand how one log message relates to another. The log entries also include severity level information, in addition to the text of the syslog messages.

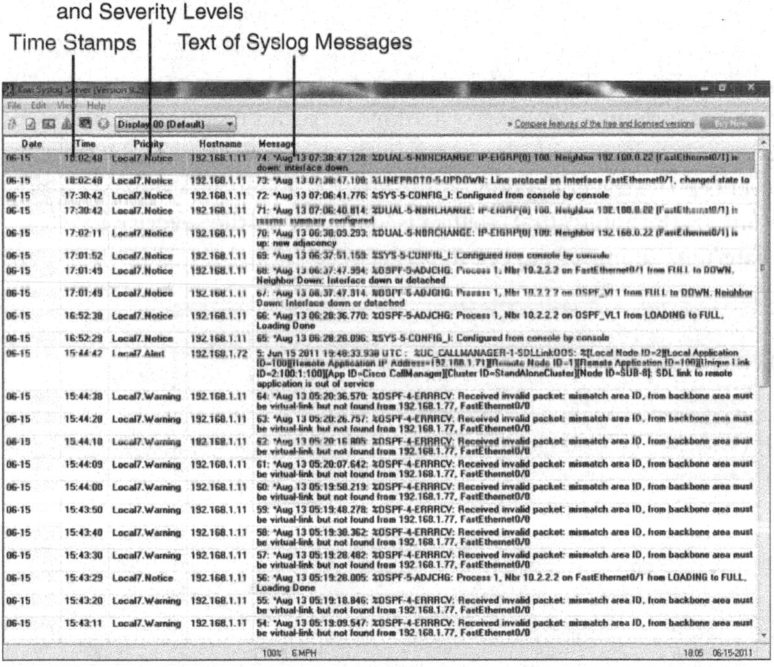

Figure 11-12 Structure of a Syslog Message

NOTE A variety of systems can act as syslog servers. You can download a free syslog utility from http://solarwinds.com/downloads.

Logs

In addition to logs generated by routers, switches, and other infrastructure gear, the operating systems powering network clients and servers generally have the capability to produce log output. Rather than containing general log information (meaning log information about all a system's tracked components), Microsoft Windows incorporates the Event Viewer application, which allows you to view various log types, including application, security, and system logs. These logs can be archived for later review. They can be used to spot network trends and serve as data for creating baselines.

> **NOTE** Logs are only beneficial in your network management endeavors if they are reviewed! Be sure to document standard operating procedures for the periodical and careful review of the many logs incorporated into your network.

Application Logs

Microsoft Windows application logs contain information about software applications running on the underlying operating system. Notice, in Figure 11-13, the three levels of severity associated with the events in the log: Information, Warning, and Error. The events provide a collection of information about the event, such as the source (for example, the application) that caused the event, the severity level of the event, and a date/time stamp of the event.

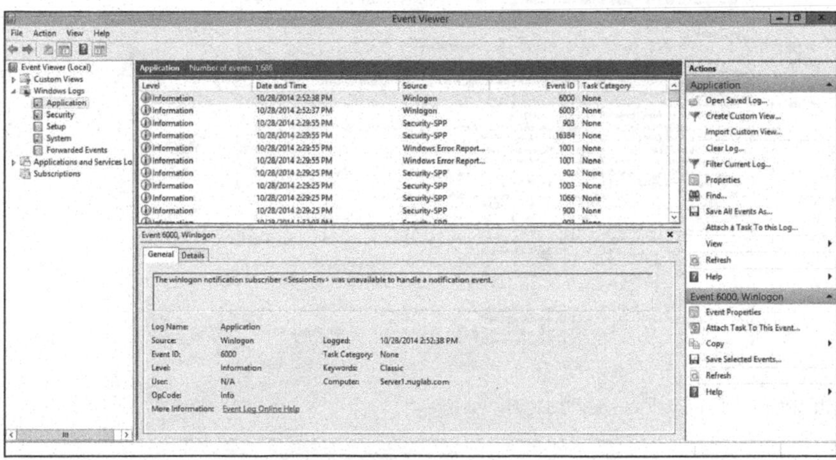

Figure 11-13 Application Log

Security Logs

Figure 11-14 shows an example of a Microsoft Windows security log. In this example, successful and failed login attempts are shown.

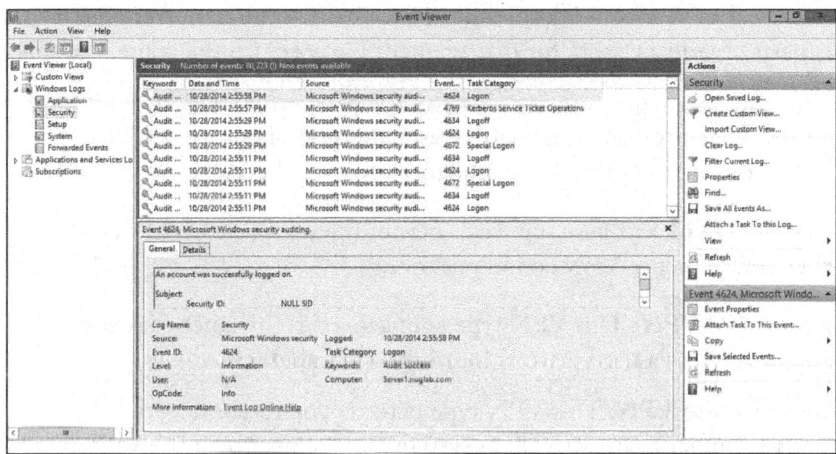

Figure 11-14 Security Log

System Logs

A Microsoft Windows system log, an example of which is shown in Figure 11-15, lists events generated by the underlying operating system.

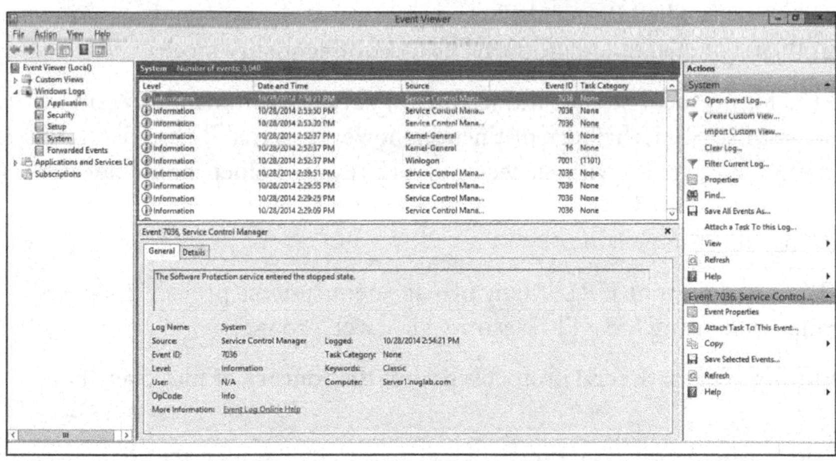

Figure 11-15 System Log

Remote Access Methods

Although remote access methods and technologies are covered elsewhere in this text, it is worth reviewing them here as a whole:

- **VPNs**: Virtual private networks permit you to make secure connections to various parts of your network for management purposes (in the context of this chapter).
    - **IPSec**: IPSec provides a standards-based method of ensuring secure authentication, integrity, and confidentiality over the VPN.
    - **SSL/TLS/DTLS**: These standards permit the use of standard web browsers for secure VPN communications.
    - **Site-to-site VPN**: This VPN type connects one entire network site to another; such as a headquarters location to a branch office.
    - **Client-to-site VPN**: This VPN type permits you to use network management software on a client system and connect over the VPN to a network site.
- **RDP**: Remote Desktop Protocol permits you to access a remote system as if you were sitting in front of it in the remote location.
- **VNC**: Virtual Network Computing is similar to RDP; it permits the access of a remote system as if you were sitting in front of it.
- **SSH**: The Secure Shell Protocol allows you to transmit commands to a remote system; these commands are protected using confidentiality mechanisms.
- **Telnet**: This protocol permits the sending of network commands to remote devices, just like SSH; the huge distinction, however, is that Telnet sends this information in clear text without security. As a result, Telnet should never be used over an unsecured connection unless security is of no concern whatsoever (like in an offline home lab).
- **HTTPS/management URL**: Many management systems provide a secured web connection using SSL/TLS security via a web browser.
- **Remote file access**: Several protocols permit the transfer of files over the network:
    - **FTP/FTPS**: Whereas FTP offers no security to speak of, FTPS works in conjunction with SSL/TLS.
    - **SFTP**: Secure FTP provides a secure alternative to FTP.

  - **TFTP**: This UDP-based version of FTP sacrifices reliability for the efficiency of the UDP protocol; it is often used to send configuration and image files through the network.
- **Out-of-band management**: You can use a modem or a console router to ensure your network management traffic does not share the same network with data. This additional separation helps to keep data secure and to preserve precious bandwidth for user data.

Real-World Case Study

Acme, Inc. realizes the importance of a solid network infrastructure. That's why it hired a cabling company that used testing tools to certify and print the results for each of the cable runs from the offices and cubes to the IDF in the wiring closets on each floor. The cabling between the IDFs and the data center (near the MDF in the basement) was also certified and guaranteed by the cable installation company. Prefabricated, certified Category 6 patch cables will be used between the computers and the RJ-45 jacks that are located in each office and cube on each floor.

To understand the traffic patterns and the most used protocols on its network, Acme is using a protocol analyzer to periodically collect information about the traffic flows on its network. This information can be used as a baseline and compared against future traffic patterns if there is a problem.

Network documentation has been created about the physical and logical topology, including the IP addressing used for the subnets. On the switches, routers, and other network devices, labeling has been implemented to clearly identify each connecter, port, and interface. The cross-connects on the patch panels have also been labeled for easy identification.

Administrative controls have been put in place on the network devices, and physical locks have been placed on the doors to the wiring closets. Environmental controls such as air conditioning have also been set up in the IDFs. Access to network devices in the IDF and MDF is being audited. Any changes made are logged to a syslog server. SNMP is also in place to report system events to a secure SNMP manager.

Change control procedures have been documented and communicated so that no changes will occur without the proper documented details about the changes that are proposed, their potential impact, the change control window, and the rollback procedure if needed. Changes must be approved by management before being implemented. Unauthorized changes are not acceptable and may be reason for the termination of an administrator. This policy has been agreed to in writing by the administrators.

Fault tolerance for power and for critical systems and network devices has been put in place, along with monitoring controls to alert an administrator in the event of a failure or degradation in performance.

Summary

Here are the main topics covered in this chapter:

- The purpose of various tools that could be used to physically maintain a network were identified. Examples include BERT, butt set, cable certifier, cable tester, connectivity software, crimper, ESD wrist strap, environmental monitor, loopback plug, multimeter, protocol analyzer, Wi-Fi analyzer, looking-glass site, speed test site, punch-down tool, throughput tester, TDR, OTDR, and toner probe.
- The operation of SNMP was discussed, as was the security enhancements available in SNMPv3.
- The operation of syslog was reviewed, as was the syslog message severity levels.
- Examples of logs collected by the Microsoft Windows Event Viewer application were provided. Specifically, examples of Microsoft Windows application, security, and system logs were presented.

Exam Preparation Tasks

Review All the Key Topics

Review the most important topics from inside the chapter, noted with the Key Topic icon in the outer margin of the page. Table 11-4 lists these key topics and the page numbers where each is found.

Table 11-4 Key Topics for Chapter 11

Key Topic Element	Description	Page Number
Figure 11-3	Crimper	383
Figure 11-5	Multimeter	386
Figure 11-6	Wireshark protocol analyzer software	387
List	Network documentation components	390

Key Topic Element	Description	Page Number
Table 11-1	Components of an SNMPv1 and SNMPv2 network management solution	392
Figure 11-9	SNMPv1 and SNMPv2c network management components and messages	393
List	Syslog logging components	395
Figure 11-11	Sample syslog clients	396
Table 11-3	Syslog severity levels	396
List	Remote access methods	400

Complete Tables and Lists from Memory

Print a copy of Appendix C, "Memory Tables," or at least the section for this chapter, and complete as many of the tables as possible from memory. Appendix D, "Memory Tables Answer Key," includes the completed tables and lists so you can check your work.

Define Key Terms

Define the following key terms from this chapter, and check your answers in the Glossary:

bit-error rate tester (BERT), butt set, cable certifier, cable tester, crimper, electrostatic discharge (ESD) wrist strap, punch-down tool, time domain reflectometer (TDR), optical time domain reflectometer (OTDR), toner probe, asset management, baseline, Simple Network Management Protocol (SNMP), syslog, logical diagrams, physical diagrams, rack diagrams, wiring and port locations, IDF/MDF documentation, baselines, inventory management, change management documentation, port scanning, SIEM, alerts, notifications, MIB, utilization, bandwidth, throughput, VPN, RDP, SSH, VNC, Telnet, HTTPS, FTP, FTPS, SFTP, TFTP, modem

Additional Resources

How Healthy Is Your Existing Network?: http://www.ajsnetworking.com/how-healthy-is-your-existing-network

SNMPv3: https://youtu.be/XoMuYWol-7s

Review Questions

The answers to these review questions are in Appendix A, "Answers to Review Questions."

1. One error occurred during the transmission of 8 bits. What is the BER?
   a. .0125
   b. .025
   c. .125
   d. .25

2. What device, traditionally used by telephone technicians, enables you to tap into a phone line to, for example, check a line for dial tone?
   a. Tester
   b. Butt set
   c. TDR
   d. Fox and hound

3. Which piece of test equipment can you use to test the throughput of a Cat 5 cable?
   a. OTDR
   b. Multimeter
   c. BERT
   d. Cable certifier

4. What is a best practice to prevent you from damaging a circuit board with static from your body?
   a. Wear an ESD wrist strap.
   b. Apply antistatic spray to the circuit board.
   c. Ground the circuit board.
   d. Stand on a carpeted floor (or a rug) when working on a circuit board to provide insulation between your body and an electric ground potential.

5. A toner probe is also known as what?
   a. TDR
   b. Fox and hound
   c. Tip and ring
   d. OTDR

6. What piece of test equipment enables you to locate a break in a fiber-optic cable?
   a. TDR
   b. Cable certifier
   c. Crimper
   d. OTDR

7. SNMP uses a series of objects to collect information about a managed device. The structure, similar to a database, containing these objects is referred to as what?
   a. RIB
   b. MIB
   c. DUAL
   d. LSA

8. A notification that a specific operation failed to complete successfully is classified as what syslog severity level?
   a. Informational (6)
   b. Critical (2)
   c. Errors (3)
   d. Warnings (4)

9. Identify the broad categories of SNMP message types. (Choose three.)
   a. Get
   b. Put
   c. Set
   d. Trap

10. What Microsoft Windows application enables you to view a variety of log types, including application, security, and system logs?
    a. Event Viewer
    b. Performance Monitor
    c. Microsoft Management Console
    d. Control Panel

11. What is a snapshot of performance on a typical usage level for the network?
    a. SLA
    b. Baseline
    c. Differential report
    d. Incremental report

12. You must send commands to a remote router and you are communicating over an unsecure channel. What protocol should you use?
    a. Telnet
    b. FTP
    c. HTTP
    d. SSH

After completion of this chapter, you will be able to answer the following questions:

- What are the goals of network security, and what sorts of attacks do you need to defend against?
- What best practices can be implemented to defend against security threats?
- What are the characteristics of various remote-access security technologies?
- How can firewalls be used to protect an organization's internal network, while allowing connectivity to an untrusted network such as the Internet?
- How can virtual private networks (VPNs) be used to secure traffic as that traffic flows over an untrusted network?
- What is the difference between intrusion prevention and intrusion detection systems, and how do they protect an organization from common security threats?

CHAPTER 12

Network Security

Today's networks are increasingly dependent on connectivity with other networks. However, connecting an organization's trusted network to untrusted networks, such as the Internet, introduces security risks. Security risks even exist within an organization.

To protect your organization's data from malicious users, you need to understand the types of threats against which you might have to defend. Then you need to know the options you have for defending your network. A key security concept to understand is that you need multiple layers of security for your network, not just a single solution, such as a firewall. Rather, you might combine user training, security policies, remote-access security protocols, firewalls, VPNs, and intrusion prevention systems. Combined, these solutions offer overlapping layers of network protection.

This chapter begins by introducing you to the fundamentals of security, which includes a discussion of common network attacks. Then the discussion turns to how to defend against those attacks. Remote-access security options are also reviewed, along with the functions and deployment considerations of dedicated security solutions, including firewalls, VPNs, and intrusion detection/prevention systems.

Foundation Topics

Security Fundamentals

Security is a vast topic, and to begin our discussion, this section introduces the goals that security can help you meet. Then, to better understand what you are defending against, this section identifies several categories of network attacks.

Network Security Goals

For most of today's corporate networks, the demands of ecommerce and customer contact require connectivity between internal corporate networks and the outside world. Here are two basic assumptions, from a security standpoint, about modern corporate networks:

- Today's corporate networks are large, interconnect with other networks, and run both standards-based and proprietary protocols.
- The devices and applications connecting to and using corporate networks are continually increasing in complexity.

Because almost all (if not all) corporate networks require network security, consider the three primary goals of network security:

- Confidentiality
- Integrity
- Availability

The following sections explain these goals in more detail.

Confidentiality

Data confidentiality implies keeping data private. This privacy could entail physically or logically restricting access to sensitive data or encrypting traffic traversing a network. A network that provides confidentiality would, as a few examples, do the following:

- Use network-security mechanisms, such as firewalls and access control lists (ACLs), to prevent unauthorized access to network resources.
- Require appropriate credentials (such as usernames and passwords) to access specific network resources.

- Encrypt traffic such that any traffic captured off of the network by an attacker could not be deciphered by the attacker.

Confidentiality can be provided by *encryption*. Encryption allows a packet to be encoded in such a way that it can be decoded by an intended party. However, if a malicious user intercepted an encrypted packet in transit, he would not be able to decrypt the packet. The way most modern encryption algorithms prevent decryption by a third party is through the use of a *key*. Because the encryption or decryption algorithm uses a key in its mathematical calculation, a third party who does not possess the key cannot interpret encrypted data that he intercepts.

Encryption has two basic forms: *symmetric encryption* and *asymmetric encryption*.

Symmetric Encryption

Symmetric encryption is fast in comparison to asymmetric encryption. The word *symmetric* in symmetric encryption implies that the same key is used by both the sender and the receiver to encrypt or decrypt a packet. Examples of symmetric encryption algorithms include the following:

- **DES:** Data Encryption Standard (DES) is an older encryption algorithm (developed in the mid-1970s) using a 56-bit key. It is considered *weak* by today's standards.
- **3DES:** Triple DES (3DES), developed in the late 1990s, uses three 56-bit DES keys (for a total of 168 bits) and is usually considered a strong encryption algorithm. However, the security of 3DES varies based on the way it is implemented. Specifically, 3DES has three keying options, where all three keys are different (keying option 1), two of the three keys are the same (keying option 2), or all three keys are the same (keying option 3) to maintain backward compatibility with DES.
- **AES:** Advanced Encryption Standard (AES), released in 2001, is typically considered the preferred symmetric encryption algorithm. AES is available in 128-bit key, 192-bit key, and 256-bit key versions.

Figure 12-1 illustrates an example of symmetric encryption, where both parties have a shared key to be used during a session (called a *session key*).

NOTE Another widely deployed encryption algorithm is Pretty Good Privacy (PGP), which is often used to encrypt email traffic. PGP uses both symmetric and asymmetric algorithms. A free variant of PGP is GNU Privacy Guard (GPG).

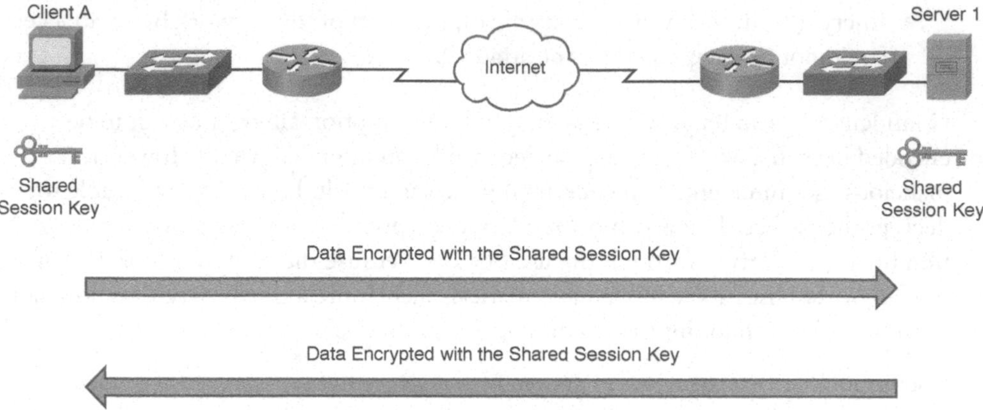

Figure 12-1 Symmetric Encryption Example

Asymmetric Encryption

Asymmetric encryption is slow in comparison to symmetric encryption but balances this slowness with higher security. As its name suggests, asymmetric encryption uses asymmetric (different) keys for the sender and the receiver of a packet. Because of its speed, asymmetric encryption algorithms are not typically used to encrypt large quantities of real-time data. Rather, asymmetric encryption might be used to encrypt a small chunk of data used, for example, to authenticate the other party in a conversation or to exchange a shared key to be used during a session (after which the parties in the conversation could start using symmetric encryption). One of the most popular asymmetric encryption algorithms in use today is RSA; its name comes from the last initials of its inventors: Ronald L. Rivest, Adi Shamir, and Leonard M. Adleman.

RSA is commonly used as part of a public key infrastructure (PKI) system. Specifically, PKI uses digital certificates and a certificate authority (CA) to authentication and encryption services.

For example, when client A wants to communicate securely with server 1, as illustrated in Figure 12-2, the following steps occur:

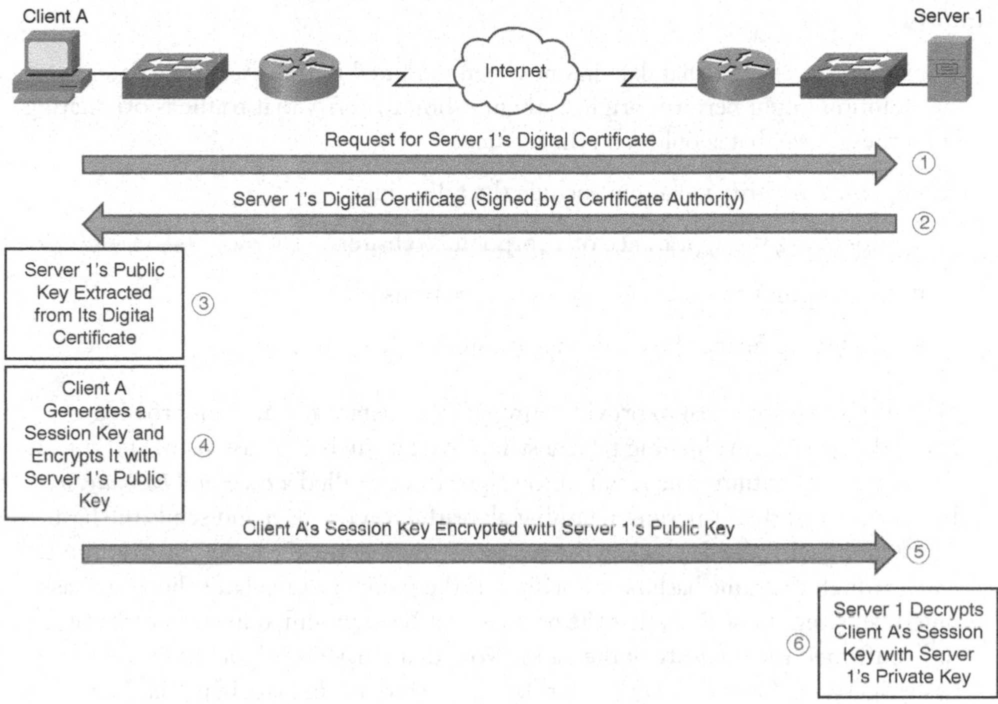

Figure 12-2 Asymmetric Encryption Example

Step 1. Client A requests server 1's digital certificate.

Step 2. Server 1 sends its digital certificate, and client A knows the received certificate is really from server 1 because the certificate has been authenticated (*signed*) by a trusted third party, called a *certificate authority*.

Step 3. Client A extracts server 1's public key from server 1's digital certificate. Data encrypted using server 1's public key can only be decrypted with server 1's private key, which only server 1 has.

Step 4. Client A generates a random string of data called a *session key*.

Step 5. The session key is then encrypted using server 1's public key and sent to server 1.

Step 6. Server 1 decrypts the session key using its private key.

At this point, both client A and server 1 know the session key, which can be used to symmetrically encrypt traffic during the session.

Integrity

Data integrity ensures that data has not been modified in transit. Also, a data integrity solution might perform origin authentication to verify that traffic is originating from the source that should send the traffic.

Examples of integrity violations include the following:

- Modifying the appearance of a corporate website
- Intercepting and altering an ecommerce transaction
- Modifying financial records that are stored electronically

Hashing is one approach to providing integrity to data transmissions crossing a network. Specifically, hashing takes a string of data (such as a password) and runs it through an algorithm. The result of the algorithm is called a *hash* or a *hash digest*. If the sender of that data runs a hashing algorithm on the data and sends the hash digest along with the data, when the recipient receives the data, she can also run the data through the same hashing algorithm. If the recipient calculates the same hash digest, she might conclude that the data has not been modified in transit (that is, she has confirmed the integrity of the data). Note that a hashing algorithm produces hash digests of the same length regardless of the size of the data being hashed.

Two of the most common hashing algorithms are the following:

- **Message digest 5 (MD5):** Creates 128-bit hash digests
- **Secure Hash Algorithm 1 (SHA-1):** Creates 160-bit hash digests

Hashing by itself, however, does not guarantee data integrity because an attacker could intercept a string of data, manipulate it, and recalculate the hash value based on the manipulated data. The victim would then determine that the hash was valid based on the data.

To overcome this limitation of pure hashing, hash-based message authentication code (HMAC) uses an additional secret key in the calculation of a hash value. So an attacker would not be able to create a valid hash value because he would not know the secret key. Other variants of hashing algorithms exist that involve longer digests, such as SHA-256. In cryptography, bigger implies better security.

NOTE Challenge-Response Authentication Mechanism Message Digest 5 (CRAM-MD5) is a common variant of HMAC frequently used in email systems.

Availability

The availability of data is a measure of the data's accessibility. For example, if a server was down only 5 minutes per year, the server would have an availability of 99.999% (that is, the *five nines of availability*).

Here are a couple of examples of how an attacker could attempt to compromise the availability of a network:

- Send improperly formatted data to a networked device, resulting in an unhandled exception error.
- Flood a network system with an excessive amount of traffic or requests, which would consume a system's processing resources and prevent the system from responding to many legitimate requests. This type of attack is referred to as a denial-of-service (DoS) attack.

The topic of availability was elaborated on in Chapter 9, "Network Optimization."

Categories of Network Attacks

The previous discussion identified confidentiality, integrity, and availability as the three primary goals of network security. Therefore, we need to better understand the types of attacks that attempt to compromise these areas.

Confidentiality Attacks

A *confidentiality attack* attempts to make confidential data (for example, personnel records, usernames, passwords, credit card numbers, or emails) viewable by an attacker. Because an attacker often makes a copy of the data, rather than trying to manipulate the data or crash a system, confidentiality attacks often go undetected. Even if auditing software to track file access were in place, if no one suspected an issue, the audit logs might never be examined.

Figure 12-3 illustrates a confidentiality attack.

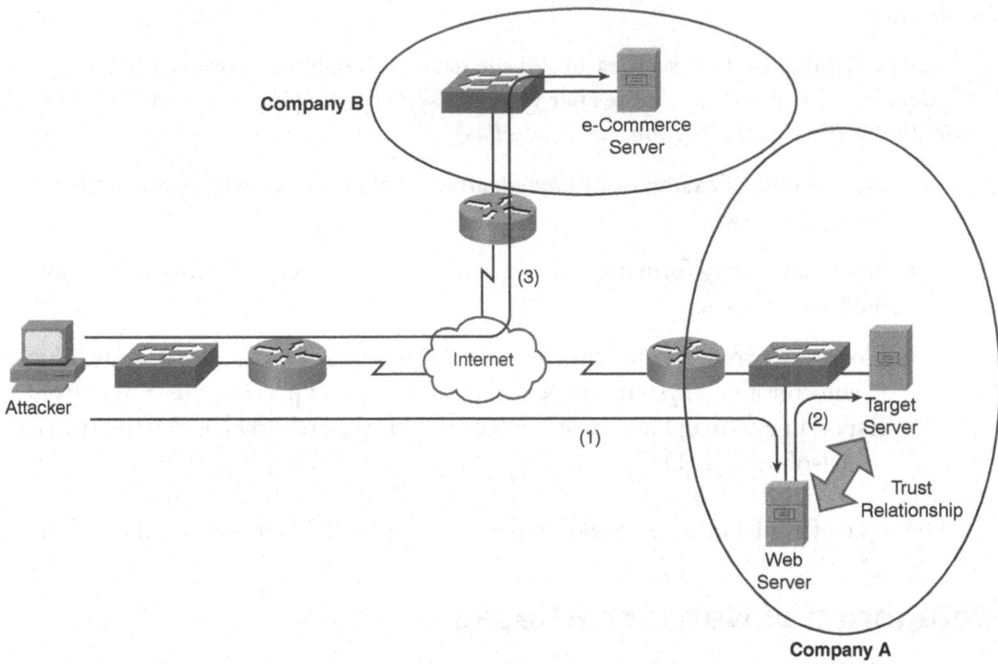

Figure 12-3 Confidentiality Attack Example

In Figure 12-3, a web server and a database server have a mutual trust relationship. The database server houses confidential customer information, such as customer credit card information. As a result, company A decided to protect the database server (for example, patching known software vulnerabilities) better than the web server. However, the attacker leverages the trust relationship between the two servers to obtain customer credit card information and then make a purchase from company B using the stolen credit card information. The procedure is as follows:

Step 1. The attacker exploits a vulnerability in company A's web server and gains control of that server.

Step 2. The attacker uses the trust relationship between the web server and the database server to obtain customer credit card information from the database server.

Step 3. The attacker uses the stolen credit card information to make a purchase from company B.

Table 12-1 identifies several methods that attackers might use in a confidentiality attack.

Table 12-1 Confidentiality Attack Tactics

Tactic	Description
Packet capture	A packet-capture (also known as *packet sniffing*) utility such as Wireshark (http://wireshark.org) can capture packets using a PC's network interface card (NIC) by placing the NIC in promiscuous mode. Some protocols, such as Telnet and HTTP, are sent in plain text. Therefore, these types of captured packets can be read by an attacker, perhaps allowing the attacker to see confidential information.
Ping sweep and port scan	A confidentiality attack might begin with a scan of network resources to identify attack targets on a network. A ping sweep could be used to ping a series of IP addresses. Ping replies might indicate to an attacker that network resources were reachable at those IP addresses. After a collection of IP addresses is identified, the attacker might scan a range of UDP or TCP ports to see what services are available on the hosts at the specified IP addresses. Also, port scans often help attackers identify the operating system running on a target system. These attacks are also commonly referred to as *reconnaissance attacks*.
Dumpster diving	Because many companies throw away confidential information, without proper shredding, some attackers rummage through company dumpsters in hopes of discovering information that could be used to compromise network resources.
Electromagnetic interference (EMI) interception	Because data is often transmitted over wire (for example, unshielded twisted pair), attackers can sometimes copy information traveling over the wire by intercepting the EMI being emitted by the transmission medium. These EMI emissions are sometimes called *emanations*. Tempest was the name of a government project to study the ability to understand the data over a network by listening to the emanations. Tempest rooms are designed to keep emanations contained within that room to increase security of data communications happening there.
Wiretapping	If an attacker gains physical access to a wiring closet, he might physically tap into telephone cabling to eavesdrop on telephone conversations, or he might insert a shared media hub inline with a network cable, allowing an attacker to connect to the hub and receive copies of packets flowing through the network cable.
Man-in-the-middle (MitM)	If an attacker can get in the direct path between a client and a server, the attacker can then eavesdrop on their conversation. If cryptography is being used and the attacker fools the client and server both into building VPNs to the attacker instead of to each other, the attacker can see all the data in clear text. On a local Ethernet network, methods such as Address Resolution Protocol (ARP) spoofing, ARP cache poisoning, Dynamic Host Configuration Protocol (DHCP) spoofing, and Domain Name System (DNS) spoofing are all mechanisms that may be used to redirect a client's traffic through the attacker, instead of directly to the server.

Tactic	Description
Social engineering	Attackers sometimes use social techniques (which often leverage people's desire to be helpful) to obtain confidential information. For example, an attacker might pose as a member of an organization's IT department and ask a company employee for his login credentials for the "IT staff to test the connection."
Sending information over overt channels	An attacker might send or receive confidential information over a network using an *overt channel*. An example of using an overt channel is tunneling one protocol inside another (for example, sending instant-messaging traffic via HTTP). Steganography is another example of sending information over an overt channel. An example of steganography is sending a digital image made up of millions of pixels with "secret" information encoded in specific pixels, where only the sender and the receiver know which pixels represent the encoded information.
Sending information over covert channels	An attacker might send or receive confidential information over a network using a covert channel, which can communicate information as a series of codes/events. For example, binary data could be represented by sending a series of pings to a destination. A single ping within a certain period of time could represent a binary 0, and two pings within that same time period could represent a binary 1.
Malware	After a single machine in a company is compromised and is running malicious software, the attacker can then use that single computer to proceed further into the internal network using the compromised host as a pivot point. The malware may have been implemented by an outside attacker or by an inside disgruntled employee. Antivirus and antimalware should be run on all systems, and users should be given very limited rights related to installation of any software on the computers they use.
FTP bounce	FTP supports a variety of commands for setting up a session and managing file transfers. One of these commands is the **port** command, and it can, in some cases, be used by an attacker to access a system that would otherwise deny the attacker. Specifically, an attacker connects to an FTP server using the standard port of 21. However, FTP uses a secondary connection to send data. The client issues a **port** command to specify the destination port and destination IP address for the data transmission. Normally, the client would send its own IP address and an ephemeral port number. The FTP server would then use a source port of 20 and a destination port specified by the client when sending data to the client. However, an attacker might issue a **port** command specifying the IP address of a device they want to access, along with an open port number on that device. As a result, the targeted device might allow an incoming connection from the FTP server's IP address, while a connection coming in from the attacker's IP address would be rejected. Fortunately, most modern FTP servers do not accept the **port** command coming from a device that specifies a different IP address than the client's IP address.

Tactic	Description
Phishing	This variation of a social engineering attack sends an email to the user that appears to be legitimate in an attempt to have that user input authentication information that is then captured. For example, the email may provide a website link for Federal Express in order to claim a package. The attacker constructs a website (at the false address) that looks just like the actual Federal Express website.

NOTE Attack types listed in this book are a partial list. New attacks and even new categories of attacks are being created all the time. For example, a newer attack type is called *ransomware*. This attack attempts to lock a system or steal or corrupt data until a ransom is paid to the attacker. Many ransomware attacks pretend to come from a legitimate organization such as Microsoft or the FBI. Also, keep in mind that many attacks are actually from employees of the organization itself. These are called *insider attacks*.

Integrity Attacks

Integrity attacks attempt to alter data (compromise the integrity of the data). Figure 12-4 shows an example of an integrity attack.

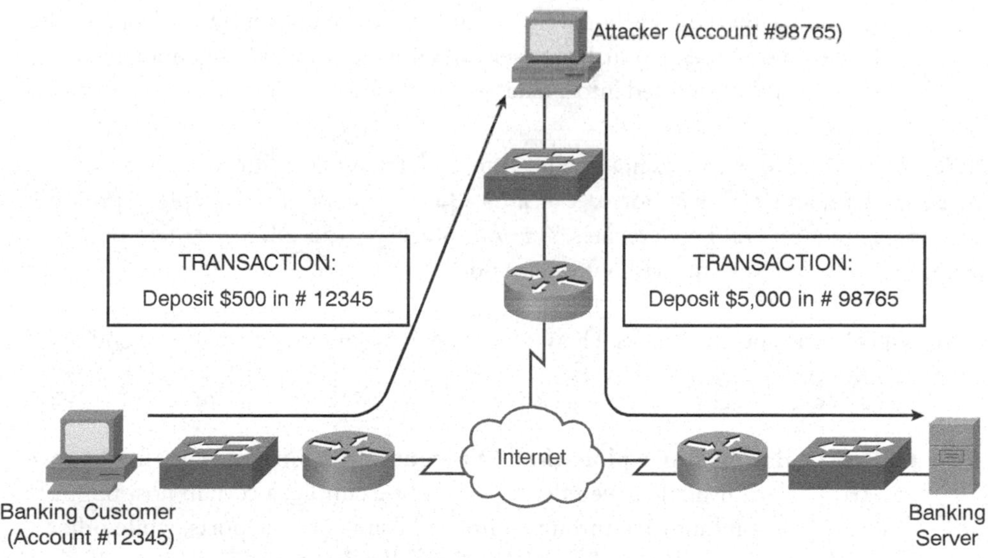

Figure 12-4 Integrity Attack

In Figure 12-4, a man-in-the-middle (MitM) attack has been launched by an attacker. This attack causes data flowing between the banking customer and the banking server to be sent via the attacker's computer. The attacker can then not only intercept but also manipulate the data. In the figure, notice that the banking customer attempts to deposit $500 into her account. However, the attacker intercepts and changes the details of the transaction, such that the instruction to the banking server is to deposit $5000 into the attacker's account. The MitM attack can compromise both confidentiality and data integrity, and that is why it is covered twice here, once in each section.

The following list identifies multiple methods attackers might use to conduct an integrity attack:

- **Salami attack:** A salami attack is a collection of small attacks that result in a larger attack when combined. For example, if an attacker has a collection of stolen credit card numbers, the attacker could withdraw small amounts of money from each credit card (possibly unnoticed by the credit card holders). Although each withdrawal is small, the combination of the multiple withdrawals results in a significant sum for the attacker.
- **Data diddling:** The process of data diddling changes data before it is stored in a computing system. Malicious code in an input application or a virus could perform data diddling. For example, a virus, Trojan horse, or worm could be written to intercept keyboard input, and while the appropriate characters are displayed onscreen (so that the user does not see an issue), manipulated characters could be entered into a database application or sent over a network.

NOTE For the Network+ exam, you need to understand the difference between a virus, a worm, and a Trojan horse. A *virus* is a piece of code (for example, a program or a script) that an end user executes. A *worm*, however, can infect a system or propagate to other systems without intervention from the end user. Finally, a *Trojan horse* is a program that appears to be for one purpose (for example, a game) but secretly performs another task (such as collecting a list of contacts from an end user's email program).

- **Trust relationship exploitation:** Different devices in a network might have a trust relationship between themselves. For example, a certain host might be trusted to communicate through a firewall using specific ports, while other hosts are denied passage through the firewall using those same ports. If an attacker were able to compromise the host that had a trust relationship with the firewall, the attacker could use the compromised host to pass normally denied data through a firewall. Another example of a trust relationship is a web server and a database server mutually trusting one another. In that case, if an attacker gained control of the web server, he might be able to leverage that trust relationship to compromise the database server.

- **Password attack:** A password attack, as its name suggests, attempts to determine the password of a user. Once the attacker gains the username and password credentials, he can attempt to log in to a system as that user and inherit that user's set of permissions. Various approaches are available to determine passwords, including the following:
  - **Trojan horse:** A Trojan horse is a program that appears to be a useful application but might capture a user's password and then make it available to the attacker.
  - **Packet capture:** A packet-capture utility can capture packets seen on a PC's NIC. Therefore, if the PC can see a copy of a plain-text password being sent over a link, the packet-capture utility can be used to glean the password.
  - **Keylogger:** A program that runs in a computer's background and logs keystrokes that a user makes. After a user enters a password, the password is stored in the log created by the keylogger. An attacker can then retrieve the log of keystrokes to determine the user's password.
  - **Brute force:** This attack tries all possible password combinations until a match is made. For example, the brute-force attack might start with the letter *a* and go through the letter *z*. Then the letters *aa* through *zz* are attempted, until the password is determined. Therefore, using a mixture of upper- and lowercase, in addition to special characters and numbers, can help mitigate a brute-force attack.
  - **Dictionary attack:** Similar to a brute-force attack, in that multiple password guesses are attempted. However, the dictionary attack is based on a dictionary of commonly used words, rather than the brute-force method of trying all possible combinations. Picking a password that is not a common word helps mitigate a dictionary attack.
  - **Botnet:** A software robot is typically thought of as an application on a machine that can be controlled remotely (for example, a Trojan horse or a backdoor in a system). If a collection of computers is infected with such software robots, called *bots*, this collection of computers (each of which is known as a *zombie*) is called a *botnet*. Because of the potentially large size of a botnet, it might compromise the integrity of a large amount of data.

- **Hijacking a session:** An attacker could hijack a TCP session, for example, by completing the third step in the three-way TCP handshake process between an authorized client and a protected server. If an attacker successfully hijacked a session of an authorized device, he might be able to maliciously manipulate data on the protected server.

Availability Attacks

Availability attacks attempt to limit the accessibility and usability of a system. For example, if an attacker were able to consume the processor or memory resources on a target system, that system might be unavailable to legitimate users.

Availability attacks vary widely, from consuming the resources of a target system to doing physical damage to that system. The following sections describe various availability attacks that might be employed by attackers.

Logic Bomb

In this type of attack, malicious code is hidden in a system and can be triggered by the author or by another attacker. An example would be a programmer who hides malicious code that starts deleting files should the programmer be terminated.

Wireless Attacks

Sadly, the popularity of wireless LANs opens us to a wide variety of availability attacks regardless this technology. Here are some examples:

- **Rogue access point**: An unauthorized AP that prevents legitimate network access thanks to intentional misconfiguration
- **Evil twin**: A special type of rogue access point designed to capture authentication information from the unsuspecting network user
- **War driving**: The surveillance of an area for open or easily compromised Wi-Fi networks.
- **Deauthentication**: The attacker sends a deauthentication frame to the victim in order to disconnect them from the wireless LAN

Denial of Service

An attacker can launch a denial-of-service (DoS) attack on a system by sending the target system a flood of data or requests that consume the target system's resources. Alternatively, some operating systems and applications crash when they receive specific strings of improperly formatted data, and the attacker can leverage such OS/

application vulnerabilities to render a system or application inoperable. The attacker often uses IP spoofing to conceal his identity when launching a DoS attack, as illustrated in Figure 12-5.

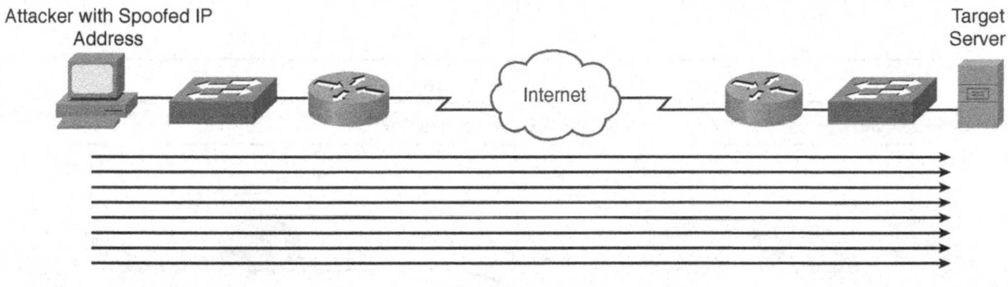

Figure 12-5 DoS Attack

DoS attacks are often categorized as follows:

- **Reflective**: With this attack, a third-party system is used to help carry out the attack; oftentimes this third party is not compromised, making this attack very difficult to track down.
- **Amplified**: A DNS server is often used in an amplification attack, but other services could be used in the exploit as well. With these attacks, legitimate servers are tricked into flooding responses at a target system; the forged request tends to be small but results in large responses hitting the target. Note that these can be tough to mitigate against because the "reflector" server is a legitimate device.

Distributed Denial of Service

Distributed denial-of-service (DDoS) attacks can increase the amount of traffic flooded to a target system. This is a coordinated attack. Specifically, an attacker compromises multiple systems, and those compromised systems, called *zombies or botnets*, can be instructed by the attacker to simultaneously launch a DDoS attack against a target system. A significant traffic spike (as compared to the baseline) could provide an early indication that an attack is in place. An intrusion prevention system (IPS) is designed to recognize and alert when attacks or malicious traffic is present on the network.

TCP SYN Flood

One variant of a DoS attack is for an attacker to initiate multiple TCP sessions by sending SYN segments but then never complete the three-way TCP handshake. As illustrated in Figure 12-6, the attack can send multiple SYN segments to a target system with false source IP addresses in the header of the SYN segments. Because many servers limit the number of TCP sessions they can have open simultaneously, a SYN flood can render a target system incapable of opening a TCP session with a legitimate user.

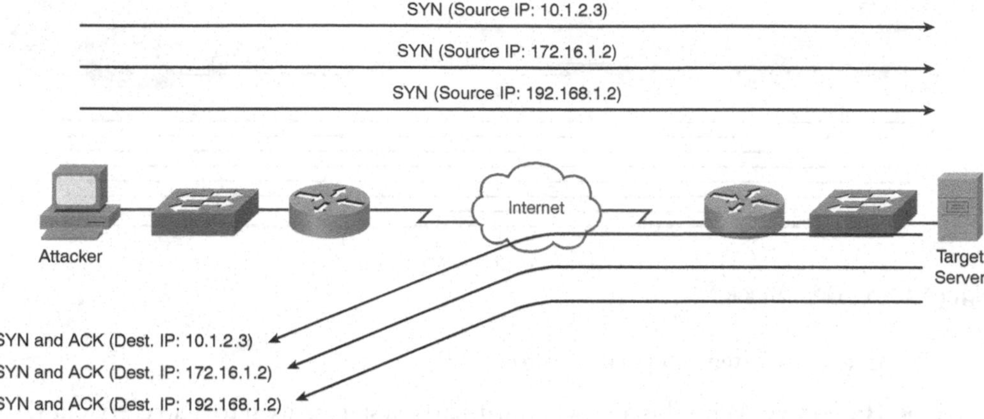

Figure 12-6 TCP SYN Flood Attack Example

Buffer Overflow

Consider a computer program that has been given a dedicated area of memory to which it can write. This area of memory is called a *buffer*. However, if the program attempts to write more information than the buffer can accommodate, a buffer overflow can occur. If permitted to do so, the program can fill up its buffer and then have its output spill over into the memory area being used for a different program. This can potentially cause the other program to crash. Some programs are known to have this vulnerability (that is, the characteristic of overrunning their memory buffers) and can be exploited by attackers.

ICMP Attacks

Many networks permit the use of Internet Control Message Protocol (ICMP) traffic (for example, ping traffic) because pings can be useful for network troubleshooting. However, attackers can use ICMP for DoS attacks. One ICMP DoS attack variant is called the *ping of death*, which uses ICMP packets that are too big. Another variant sends ICMP traffic as a series of fragments in an attempt to overflow the fragment reassembly buffers on the target device. Also, a *Smurf attack* can use ICMP traffic directed to a subnet to flood a target system with ping replies, as illustrated in Figure 12-7. Notice in the figure that the attacker sends a ping to the subnet broadcast address of 172.16.0.0/16. This collection of pings instructs devices on that subnet to send their ping replies to the target system at IP address 10.2.2.2, thus flooding the target system's bandwidth and processing resources.

NOTE For illustrative purposes, Figure 12-7 only shows three systems in the subnet being used for the Smurf attack. However, realize that thousands of systems could potentially be involved and send ping replies to the target system. This is an example of an amplification attack, which begins small and then is increased as additional devices (often unaware) contribute to the attack. Common protocols such as Domain Name Service (DNS) and Network Time Protocol (NTP) can also be used as part of an amplification attack.

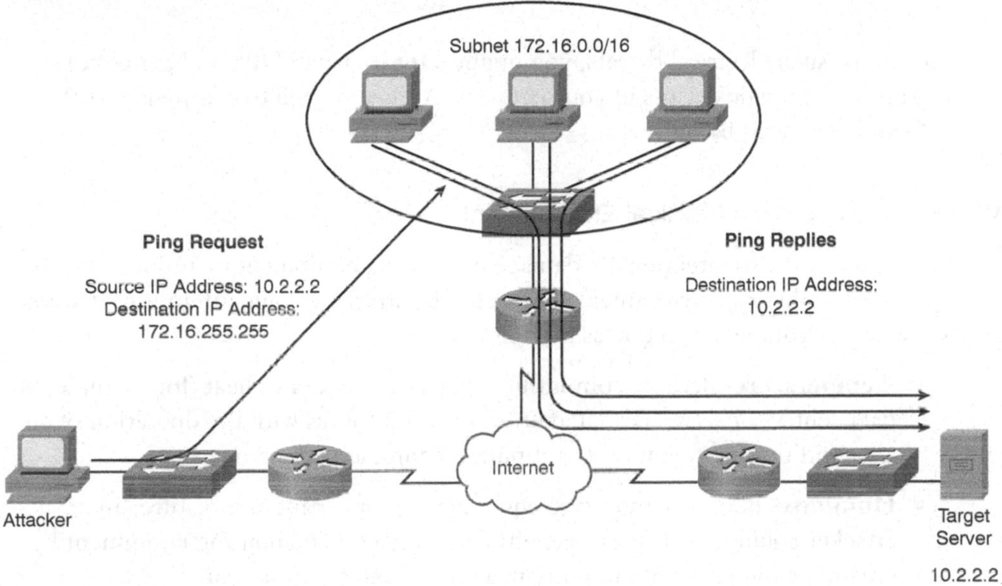

Figure 12-7 Smurf Attack Example

Electrical Disturbances

At a physical level, an attacker could launch an availability attack by interrupting or interfering with the electrical service available to a system. For example, if an attacker gained physical access to a data center's electrical system, he might be able to cause a variety of electrical disturbances, such as the following:

- **Power spikes:** Excess power for a brief period of time
- **Electrical surges:** Excess power for an extended period of time
- **Power fault:** A brief electrical outage
- **Blackout:** An extended electrical outage

- **Power sag:** A brief reduction in power
- **Brownout:** An extended reduction in power

NOTE A standby power supply (SPS) is a lower-end version of an uninterruptible power supply (UPS). Although it is less expensive than a traditional UPS, an SPS's battery is not in line with the electricity coming from a wall outlet. Instead, an SPS's battery operates in parallel with the wall power, standing by in the event that the wall power is lost. Because of this configuration, a brief period of time lapses between a power outage and the SPS taking over, which could result in the attached equipment shutting down.

To combat such electrical threats, you might want to install UPS and generator backups for strategic devices in your network. Also, you need to routinely test the UPS and generator backups.

Attacks on a System's Physical Environment

Attackers could also intentionally damage computing equipment by influencing the equipment's physical environment. For example, attackers could attempt to manipulate such environmental factors as the following:

- **Temperature:** Because computing equipment generates heat (for example, in data centers or server farms), if an attacker interferes with the operation of an air-conditioning system, the computing equipment could overheat.
- **Humidity:** Because computing equipment is intolerant of moisture, an attacker could, over time, cause physical damage to computing equipment by creating a high level of humidity in a computing environment.
- **Gas:** Because gas is often flammable, if an attacker injects gas into a computing environment, small sparks in that environment could cause a fire.

Consider the following recommendations to mitigate such environmental threats:

- Computing facilities should be locked (and not accessible via a drop ceiling, a raised floor, or any other way other than a monitored point of access).
- Access should require access credentials (for example, via a card swipe or a biometric scan).
- Access points should be visually monitored (for example, via local security personnel or remotely via a camera system).

- Climate control systems should maintain temperature and humidity and send alerts if specified temperature or humidity thresholds are exceeded.
- The fire detection and suppression systems should be designed not to damage electronic equipment.

A business should have a disaster recovery (DR) and business continuity (BC) plan in place so that, in the event of any type of downtime (due to an attack or natural disaster), the company can be back up and running to maintain its business. DR focuses on getting critical applications back online, and BC focuses on the tasks carried out by an organization to ensure that critical business functions continue to operate during and after a disaster. These plans should include training, identification, and roles of the first responders as well as practice drills to confirm the plans are functional. A company without these plans in place could be victims of a permanent denial of service, which could ultimately destroy their business if an attacker has damaged the hardware (by reflashing firmware) with corrupt or defective images to such a point that it is no longer usable.

Now that you have an understanding of the three primary targets of an attack (that is, confidentiality, integrity, and availability) and have seen examples of common attacks, the next section presents you with strategies for defending against such attacks.

Defending Against Attacks

Upcoming sections in this chapter address how to defend against security threats using network devices (that is, switches, routers, firewalls, VPN concentrators, and IDS/IPS sensors). However, this section presents a collection of best practices for defending a network against attacks.

User Training

Many attacks require user intervention to be carried out. For example, a user needs to execute an application containing a virus before the virus takes any action. Similarly, social engineering requires a user to give sensitive information (such as username and password credentials) to an attacker in order for the attacker to access the user's account. As a result, several potential attacks can be thwarted through effective user training. For instance, users could be trained on using policies such as the following:

- Never give out your password to anyone, even if that person claims to be from IT.
- Do not open email attachments from unknown sources.

- Select strong passwords, consisting of at least eight characters and containing a mixture of alphabetic (upper- and lowercase), numeric, and special characters.
- Do not visit unauthorized websites.
- Report suspicious activity.
- Do not run or install any applications not provided directly by the company.
- Change your passwords monthly.

This list is only an example, and you should develop a collection of best practices for your users based on your network's specific circumstances. Users should also know whom to contact in the event of a suspected data breach or compromise of the computers and systems the users are responsible for. The users should also know never to run penetration testing tools or other network discovery tools that may cause an unintentional DoS or other harm to the network and its devices. Technical controls such as web/content filtering, port filtering, IP filtering, and access control lists (ACLs) that deny specific traffic can be used to assist in the enforcement of the policies agreed to by the users.

As part of user training and for the safety of human life, emergency procedures should also be communicated and verified with each user, including the building layout, fire-escape plan, safety and emergency exits, doors that automatically fail closed or fail open based on their purpose to contain or allow access, emergency alert systems, fire suppression systems, and HVAC operations and emergency shutoff procedures.

In the data center, procedures for safety related to electrostatic discharge (ESD), grounding, rack installation, lifting, tool safety, and the correct placement of devices should also be planned, communicated, and verified. If there are dangerous substances in or near the work area, a material safety data sheet (MSDS) should be created to identify procedures for handling and working with those substances.

Patching

Some attacks are directed at vulnerabilities known to exist in various operating systems and applications. As these vulnerabilities are discovered, the vendors of the operating systems or applications often respond by releasing a *patch*. A patch is designed to correct a known bug or fix a known vulnerability in a piece of software. Therefore, network administrators should have a plan for implementing patches as they become available. Network and host-based vulnerability scanning should be done, with proper management authorization, to verify that well-known vulnerabilities are not present on the network. Penetration testing can be done as well to verify that the security measures in place are working as expected.

NOTE A *patch* differs from an *update*, which, in addition to fixing a known bug or vulnerability, adds one or more features to the software being updated.

Security Policies

One of the main reasons security breaches occur within an organization is the lack of a security policy or, if a security policy is in place, the lack of effectively communicating/enforcing that security policy to all concerned. A security policy is a continually changing document that dictates a set of guidelines for network use. These guidelines complement organizational objectives by specifying rules for how a network is used.

The main purpose of a security policy is to protect the assets of an organization. An organization's assets include more than just tangible items. Assets also entail things such as intellectual property, processes and procedures, sensitive customer data, and specific server functions (for example, email or web functions).

Aside from protecting an organization's assets, a security policy serves other purposes, such as the following:

- Making employees aware of their obligations in regard to security practices
- Identifying specific security solutions required to meet the goals of a security policy
- Acting as a baseline for ongoing security monitoring

One of the more well-known components of a security policy is an acceptable use policy (AUP), also known as an *appropriate use policy*. An AUP identifies what users of a network are and are not allowed to do on a network. For example, retrieving sports scores during working hours via an organization's Internet connection might be deemed inappropriate by an AUP.

Because an organization's security policy applies to various categories of employees (such as management, technical staff, and end users), a single document might not be sufficient. For example, managerial personnel might not be concerned with the technical intricacies of a security policy, whereas the technical personnel might be less concerned with why a policy is in place. Also, end users might be more likely to comply with the policy if they understand the reasoning behind the rules. Therefore, a security policy might be a collection of congruent yet separate documents. Figure 12-8 offers a high-level overview of these complementary documents.

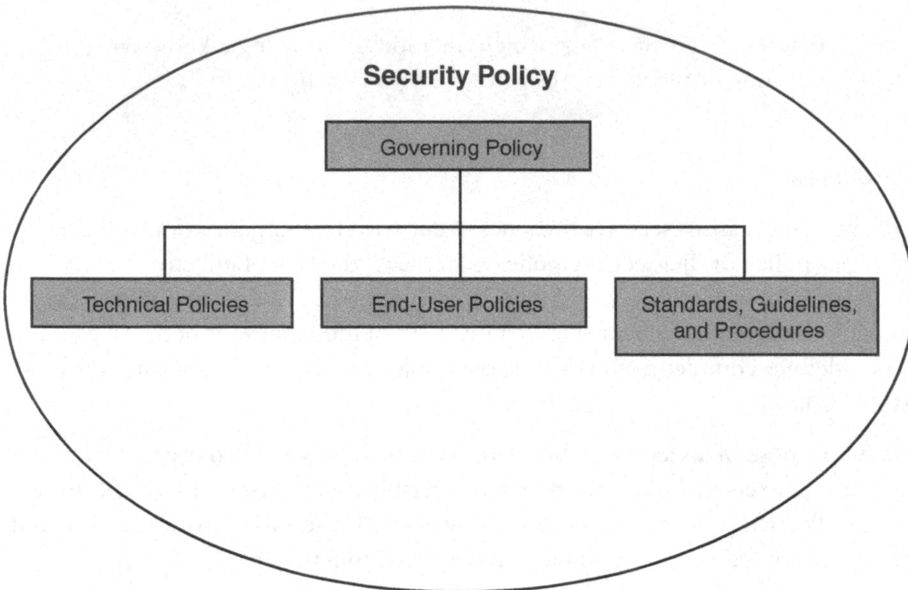

Figure 12-8 Components of a Security Policy

Governing Policy

At a very high level, a governing policy addresses security concepts deemed important to an organization. The governing policy is primarily targeted toward managerial and technical employees. The following are typical elements of a governing policy:

- Identification of the issue addressed by the policy
- Discussion of the organization's view of the issue
- Examination of the relevance of the policy to the work environment
- Explanation of how employees are to comply with the policy
- Enumeration of appropriate activities, actions, and processes
- Explanation of the consequences of noncompliance

You might want to consult with your company's legal counsel when formulating a governing policy.

Technical Policies

Technical policies provide a more detailed treatment of an organization's security policy, as opposed to the governing policy. Typical components of technical policies include specific duties of the security and IT staff in areas such as the following:

- Email
- Wireless networks
- Bring your own device (BYOD)
- Remote access

Security and IT personnel are the intended target of these technical policies, and these personnel use these policies in performing their day-to-day tasks.

BYOD also allows users to bring their own device's vulnerabilities if allowed on the network. Devices with Bluetooth capability have the vulnerability of the following attacks:

- **Bluejacking:** The sending of unauthorized messages over a Bluetooth connection to a device
- **Bluesnarfing:** Provides unauthorized access from a wireless device through a Bluetooth connection
- **Bluebugging:** Creates unauthorized backdoor access to connect a Bluetooth device back to the attacker

End-User Policies

End-user policies address security issues and procedures relevant to end users. For example, an end user might be asked to sign an AUP for Internet access. That AUP might state that Internet access is only for business purposes. Then, if an end user is found using the Internet for personal reasons, she could face the consequences outlined in the governing policy. The AUP should include the consent to have monitored the user's system, email, and digital communications from company devices.

More Detailed Documents

Because the governing policy, technical policies, and end-user policies each target a relatively large population of personnel, these policies tend to be general in nature. However, a comprehensive security policy requires a highly granular treatment of an organization's procedures. Therefore, more detailed documents, such as the following, are often contained in a security policy:

- **Standards:** Standards support consistency within a network. For example, a standard might specify a limited number of operating systems to be supported in the organization because it would be impractical for the IT staff to support any OS that a user happened to select. Also, standards could apply to configuring devices, such as routers (for example, having a standardized routing protocol).
- **Guidelines:** Standards tend to be mandatory practices, but guidelines tend to be suggestions. For example, a series of best practices might constitute a security policy's guidelines.
- **Procedures:** To support consistency in a network, and as dictated by the previously mentioned standards, a security policy might include a collection of procedures. These procedures are detailed documents that provide step-by-step instructions for completing specific tasks (for example, steps for configuring port security on an Ethernet switch that include manual assignments of access ports to avoid VLAN hopping by malicious hosts connected to a port, port security to limit the number of MAC addresses learned on a port, DHCP snooping to deny a device that is attempting a DHCP-based attack by acting as a DHCP server, MAC address filtering to only allow specific MAC addresses on the port, and dynamic ARP inspection to prevent MAC spoofing from the device connected to the switch port).

Keep in mind that this list is not comprehensive and that you need to create a set of documents to match the security needs of your company.

Incident Response

How an organization reacts to a security violation is called its *incident response*. Many deterrent controls display warnings such as, "Violators will be prosecuted to the fullest extent of the law." However, to successfully prosecute an attacker, litigators typically require the following elements to present an effective argument:

- **Motive:** A motive describes why the attacker committed the act. For example, was the attacker a disgruntled employee? Also, potential motives can be valuable to define during an investigation. Specifically, an investigation might begin with those that had a motive to carry out the attack.
- **Means:** With all the security controls in place to protect data or computer systems, you need to determine whether the accused had the means (for example, the technical skills) to carry out the attack.

- **Opportunity:** The question of whether the accused had the opportunity to commit an attack asks whether the accused was available to commit the attack. For example, if the accused claims to have been at a ball game at the time of the attack, and if there are witnesses to verify her assertion, it is less likely that the accused indeed committed the attack.

Computer forensics is about legal evidence found in computers and digital storage devices. Another challenge with prosecuting computer-based crime stems from the fragility of data. A time stamp can easily be changed on a file without detection. To prevent such evidence tampering, strict policies and procedures for data handling must be followed. For example, before any investigative work is done on a computer system, a policy might require that multiple copies of a hard drive be made. One or more master copies could be locked up, and copies could be given to the defense and prosecution for their investigation.

Also, to verify the integrity of data since a security incident occurred, you need to be able to show a chain of custody. A chain of custody documents who has been in possession of the data (evidence) since a security breach occurred. A well-prepared organization will have process and procedures that are used when an incident occurs. A plan should include first responders securing the area and then escalating to senior management and authorities when required by policy or law. The chain of custody also includes documentation of the scene, the collection and maintenance of evidence, e-discovery (which is the electronic aspect of identifying, collecting, and producing electronically stored information), transportation of data, forensics reporting, and a process to preserve all forms of evidence and data when litigation is expected. The preservation of the evidence, data, and details is referred to as *legal hold*.

Vulnerability Scanners

After you deploy your network security solution, components of that solution might not behave as expected. In addition, you might not be aware of some of the vulnerabilities in your network devices. Therefore, you should periodically test your network for weaknesses. Such a test can be performed using applications designed to check for a variety of known weaknesses. These applications are known as *vulnerability scanners*. These can assist in identifying unnecessary running services, open ports, and unpatched or legacy systems. Examples of these vulnerability scanners include Nessus and Nmap (network mapper).

Nessus

Tenable Network Security has a vulnerability scanning product called Nessus, which is available from https://www.tenable.com/products/nessus-vulnerability-scanner. Here are a few of the product features:

- Performing audits on systems without requiring an agent to be installed on the systems
- Checking system configurations for compliance with an organization's policy
- Auditing systems for specific content (for example, credit card information or adult content)
- Performing continuous scanning, thus reducing the time required to identify a network vulnerability
- Scheduling scans to run once, daily, weekly, or monthly

Tenable Network Security offers a variety of products for home and business use. Figure 12-9 shows an example of a Nessus scan result.

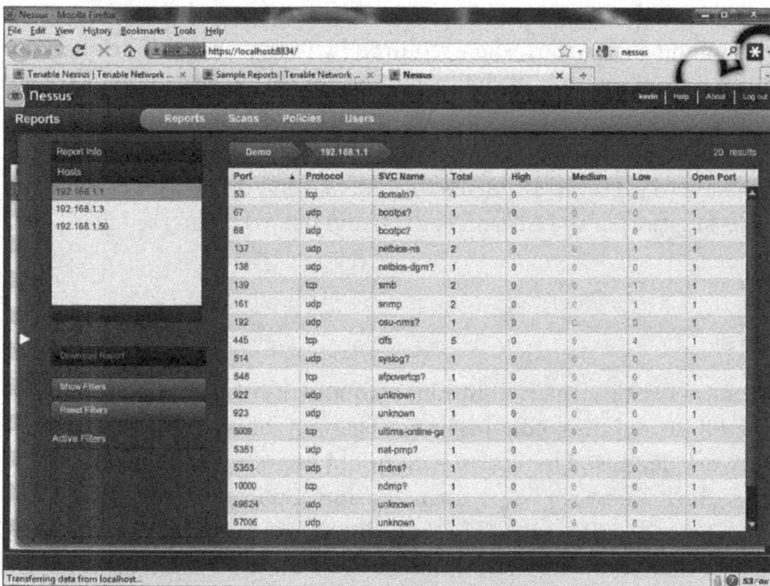

Figure 12-9 Nessus

Nmap

As another example of a vulnerability scanner, consider the Nmap utility. Nmap is a publicly available scanner that can be downloaded from http://nmap.org. Nmap offers features such as the following:

- Scanning and sweeping features that identify services running on systems in a specified range of IP addresses
- Using a stealth approach to scanning and sweeping, making the scanning and sweeping less detectible by hosts and IPS technology
- Using OS fingerprinting technology to identify an OS running on a target system (including a percentage of confidence that the OS was correctly detected)

Figure 12-10 illustrates a GUI version of Nmap, where a collection of host IP addresses are scanned for open ports, in addition to a variety of other fingerprinting operations.

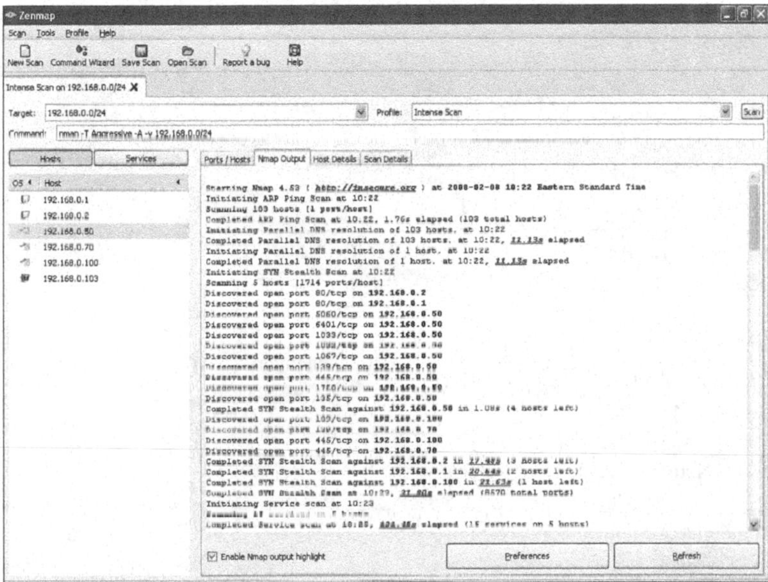

Figure 12-10 Nmap

Honey Pots and Honey Nets

A honey pot acts as a distracter. Specifically, a system designated as a honey pot appears to be an attractive attack target. One school of thought on the use of a honey pot is to place one or more honey pot systems in a network to entice attackers into thinking a system is real. The attackers then use their resources attacking the honey pot, the end result of which is that the attackers leave the real servers alone.

Another use of a honey pot is as a system that is extensively monitored to learn what an attacker is attempting to do on the system. A honey pot could, as an example, be a UNIX system configured with a weak password. After an attacker logs in, surveillance software could log what the attacker does on the system. This knowledge could then be used to protect real servers in the network.

> **NOTE** For larger networks, a network administrator might deploy multiple honey pots, forming a honey net.

Access Control Lists

Access control lists (ACLs) are rules usually applied to router interfaces that specify permitted and denied traffic. Although ACL features can vary by router vendor, examples of filtering criteria include IP addresses (source or destination), port number (source or destination), and MAC addresses (source or destination).

Consider Figure 12-11, for example, which shows an ACL being applied to an interface on a Cisco IOS router.

```
access-list 100 permit tcp any 10.1.1.0 0.0.0.255 eq www
access-list 100 permit tcp any 10.1.1.0 0.0.0.255 eq telnet
!
interface Serial1/0/1
   ip access-group 100 in
```

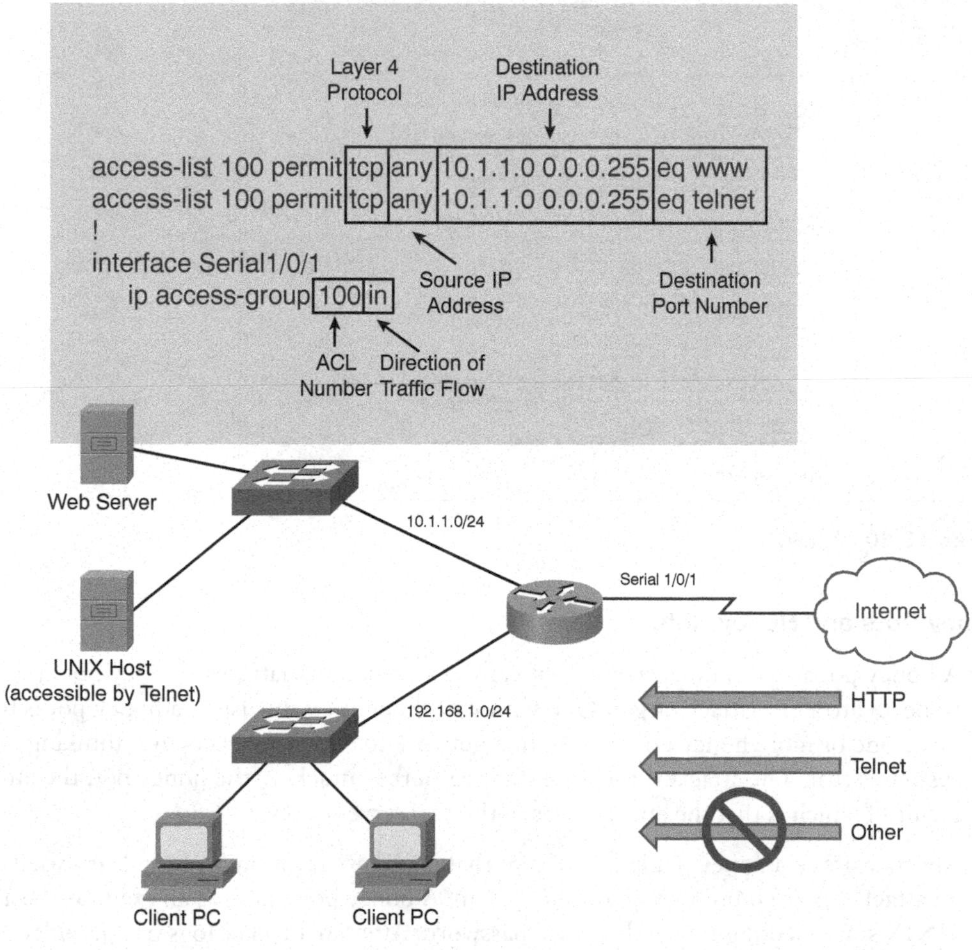

Figure 12-11 ACL Example

This syntax tells the router interface of Serial 1/0/1 to permit incoming Telnet and HTTP traffic from any source and destined for a network of 10.1.1.0/24. However, you might be curious about all the other traffic that attempts to enter interface Serial 1/0/1. Because there is no *deny* instruction in the syntax, is that traffic permitted? Actually, in the case of Cisco IOS routers, ACLs have an implicit (and invisible) *deny all* instruction. Therefore, any traffic not explicitly permitted is rejected.

Physical Security Devices

You should not overlook the importance of physical security controls and devices. Many network devices have reset capabilities once physical access is obtained—not to mention the power of something like a sledgehammer!

You can break this area down into two main categories: detection and prevention. Be familiar with the following physical security techniques and devices:

- **Detection**
  - **Motion detection**: Through either mechanical or electronic methods, you can install motion detection devices that alert you when objects change position in a physical network location.
  - **Video surveillance**: Permits the viewing of key network areas through video cameras.
  - **Asset tracking tags**: You can use various wireless technologies to track the physical location of network objects and personnel by using tag technologies attached to the entities.
  - **Tamper detection**: You can take steps to ensure network equipment is not tampered with; for example, you might place key network cable runs in clearly viewed conduits and make appliances readily viewable through glass enclosures.
- **Prevention**
  - **Badges**: Identification badges assist with physical security regarding employees. Whereas identification might be limited to name and photo, more sophisticated approaches can include electronic swipes and asset tags.
  - **Biometrics**: Although at one time biometrics was reserved for the most sophisticated of environments, now using a thumbprint reader, facial recognition, or a retina scan is a reality for such common devices as our cell phones.

- **Smart cards**: A smart card appears to be just a "normal" credit card–size component, yet the card possesses circuitry that allows it to authenticate a user against network systems; this aids security because the user must possess something (the smart card) and know something (the password). This approach has worked well for ATMs in the banking system for decades.
- **Key fobs**: A key fob is an electronic attachment for a key ring; this device might provide access to a network system, or it might simply lock or unlock a secure door.
- **Locks**: Sometimes the simplest of security mechanisms are the most effective; this is often the case with locks on all network areas and equipment.

Network Device Hardening

Another important area of defense is the hardening of network devices. This is hardly ever a single step, but a comprehensive set of steps, that when applied will help ensure that a network device is not compromised by an attacker.

Steps in network device hardening can include the following:

- **Changing default credentials**. At a minimum you should do this, because the first thing an attacker typically tries is default username and password credentials on network devices.
- **Avoiding common passwords**.
- **Upgrading firmware**.
- **Patching and updating**.
- **File hashing**.
- **Disabling unnecessary services**.
- **Using secure protocols**.
- **Generating new keys**.
- **Disabling unused ports**. This includes both ports running IP and physical ports themselves.
- **Changing the native VLAN**.

Layer 2 Protections

Remember, many protections exist at Layer 2. These include the following:

- **Spanning tree protections:** These protections include root guard, BPDU guard, and flood guard. Root guard prevents another switch in the topology from taking over the STP root role, while BPDU guard helps identify rogue or misplaced switches in the topology. Flood guard helps to prevent against Denial of Service (DoS) attacks that seek to disrupt communications through a massive flooding of frames.
- **DHCP snooping**: This involves preventing rogue DHCP servers and DHCP pool exhaustion attacks by restricting ports from accepting certain DHCP messages.
- **VLAN segmentation**: This inherently protects systems from accidental or malicious "attacks" from systems in other broadcast domains. VLAN segmentation also forces inter-VLAN communications to pass through a router, which can easily enforce security policy and security checks on the traffic.

Remote-Access Security

Although ACLs can be used to permit or deny specific connections flowing *through* a router (or switch), you also need to control connections *to* network devices (for example, routers, switches, or servers). Many of these remote-access security methods have been introduced in preceding chapters. However, as a review, Table 12-2 provides a summary of these protocols and procedures.

Table 12-2 Remote-Access Security Methods

Method	Description
RAS	Microsoft Remote Access Server (RAS) is the predecessor to Microsoft Routing and Remote Access Server (RRAS). RRAS is a Microsoft Windows Server feature that allows Microsoft Windows clients to remotely access a Microsoft Windows network.
RDP	Remote Desktop Protocol (RDP) is a Microsoft protocol that allows a user to view and control the desktop of a remote computer.
PPPoE	Point-to-Point Protocol over Ethernet (PPPoE) is a commonly used protocol between a DSL modem in a home (or business) and a service provider. Specifically, PPPoE encapsulates PPP frames within Ethernet frames. This approach allows an Ethernet connection to leverage the features of PPP, such as authentication.
PPP	Point-to-Point Protocol (PPP) is a common Layer 2 protocol that offers features such as multilink interface, looped link detection, error detection, and authentication.

Method	Description
ICA	Independent Computing Architecture (ICA) is a Citrix Systems proprietary protocol that allows an application running on one platform (for example, Microsoft Windows) to be seen and controlled from a remote client, independent of the client platform (for example, UNIX).
SSH	Secure Shell is a protocol used to securely connect to a remote host (typically via a terminal emulator).
Kerberos	Kerberos is a client/server authentication protocol that supports mutual authentication between a client and a server. Kerberos uses the concept of a trusted third party (a key distribution center) that hands out tickets that are used instead of a username and password combination.
AAA	Authentication, authorization, and accounting (AAA) allows a network to have a single repository of user credentials. A network administrator can then, for example, supply the same credentials to log in to various network devices (for example, routers and switches). RADIUS and TACACS+ are protocols commonly used to communicate with a AAA server.
RADIUS	Remote Authentication Dial-In User Service (RADIUS) is a UDP-based protocol used to communicate with a AAA server. Unlike TACACS+, RADIUS does not encrypt an entire authentication packet, but only the password. However, RADIUS does offer more robust accounting features than TACACS+. Also, RADIUS is a standards-based protocol, whereas TACACS+ is a Cisco proprietary protocol.
TACACS+	Terminal Access Controller Access-Control System Plus (TACACS+) is a Cisco proprietary TCP-based AAA protocol. TACACS+ has three separate and distinct sessions or functions for authentication, authorization, and accounting.
NAC	Network Admission Control (NAC) can permit or deny access to a network based on characteristics of the device seeking admission, rather than just checking user credentials. For example, a client's OS and version of antivirus software could be checked against a set of requirements before allowing the client to access a network. This process of checking a client's characteristics is called *posture assessment*.
IEEE 802.1X	IEEE 802.1X is a type of NAC that can permit or deny a wireless or wired LAN client access to a network. If IEEE 802.1X is used to permit access to a LAN via a switch port, then IEEE 802.1X is being used for port security. The device seeking admission to the network is called the *supplicant*. The device to which the supplication connects (either wirelessly or through a wired connection) is called the *authenticator*. The device that checks the supplicant's credentials and permits or denies the supplicant to access the network is called an *authentication server*. Usually, an authentication server is a RADIUS server.

Method	Description
CHAP	Challenge-Handshake Authentication Protocol (CHAP) performs a one-way authentication for a remote-access connection. However, authentication is performed through a three-way handshake (challenge, response, and acceptance messages) between a server and a client. The three-way handshake allows a client to be authenticated without sending credential information across a network. Password Authentication Protocol (PAP) is an unencrypted plain-text method for password exchange that should be avoided.
MS-CHAP	Microsoft Challenge-Handshake Authentication Protocol (MS-CHAP) is a Microsoft-enhanced version of CHAP, offering a collection of additional features not present with CHAP, including two-way authentication.
EAP	An Extensible Authentication Protocol (EAP) specifies how authentication is performed by IEEE 802.1X. A variety of EAP types exist: Extensible Authentication Protocol-Flexible Authentication via Secure Tunneling (EAP-FAST), Extensible Authentication Protocol-Message Digest 5 (EAP-MD5), and Extensible Authentication Protocol-Transport Layer Security (EAP-TLS).
Two-factor authentication	Two-factor authentication (TFA) requires two types of authentication from a user seeking admission to a network. For example, a user might have to *know* something (for example, a password) and *have* something (such as a specific fingerprint, which can be checked with a biometric authentication device).
Multifactor authentication	Similar to two-factor authentication, multifactor authentication requires two or more types of successful authentication before granting access to a network.
Single sign-on	Single sign-on (SSO) allows a user to authenticate only once to gain access to multiple systems, without requiring the user to independently authenticate with each system.
Local authentication	Local authentication refers to the network device authenticating the user with a database of user account information stored on the device itself; this is often an important fall back method of authentication should another external method fail.
LDAP	Lightweight Directory Access Protocol (LDAP) permits a set of standards for the storage and access of user account information. Many proprietary user stores support LDAP for ease of access. This includes Microsoft's Active Directory.
Captive portal	A captive portal is a web page that appears before the user is able to access the network resource; this web page accepts the credentials of the user for authentication and presents them to the authentication server.

While many of the technologies in this table are popular, multifactor authentication is currently surging in popularity due to its ability to help secure networks and their data. Options for components of this authentication scheme include the following:

- Something you know
- Something you have
- Something you are
- Somewhere you are
- Something you do

Firewalls

At this point, this chapter has introduced you to various security threats, along with best practices to protect your network from those threats. In addition, it reviewed a collection of remote-access security methods. In the remainder of this chapter, you are introduced to three additional layers of security that can be applied to a network, often in the form of a dedicated security appliance. These additional layers consist of firewalls, virtual private networks, and intrusion detection and prevention systems. This section focuses on firewalls.

Firewall Types

A firewall defines a set of rules to dictate which types of traffic are permitted or denied as that traffic enters or exits a firewall interface. The actual firewall devices can be either a software firewall or a hardware firewall:

- **Software firewall:** A computer running firewall software that can protect the computer itself (for example, preventing incoming connections to the computer). This is referred to as a *host-based* firewall. Alternatively, a software firewall could be a computer with more than one network interface card (NIC) running firewall software. This type of software firewall can filter traffic attempting to pass through the computer (that is, coming in one of the NICs and leaving via a different NIC). A firewall that is filtering traffic that is being routed through the firewall is known as a *network-based* firewall.

- **Hardware firewall:** A network appliance that acts as a firewall. This appliance can have multiple interfaces for connecting to areas of a network that require varying levels of security. Hardware-based firewalls usually have higher capacity than software-based firewalls. However, for a small office or home office firewall, the price and performance requirement may be better met with a software-based firewall.

As traffic flows in to or out of a firewall, the firewall checks the traffic against a set of firewall rules, which might permit or deny the traffic. In addition, many firewalls perform Network Address Translation (NAT) or Port Address Translation (PAT), described in Chapter 6, "Routing IP Packets." Some firewalls may include a content-filtering service that can deny packets through the firewall based on the type of content being requested. An example is a company policy restricting access to gaming websites, with the firewall checking before allowing traffic to a site identified as a gaming website.

Firewall Inspection Types

Some firewalls inspect traffic based solely on a packet's header. This type of firewall is called a *packet-filtering* firewall. Other firewalls, however, can recognize that a packet is part of a session that might have originated inside the local network or outside the local network. This type of firewall is called a *stateful* firewall.

Packet-Filtering Firewall

Earlier, this chapter described the function of ACLs. An ACL can decide whether a packet should be permitted or denied based on the contents of its header (for example, based on source and destination IP address information or source and destination port number information).

A device that filters traffic based on ACL-like rules is a packet-filtering firewall. However, a packet-filtering firewall lacks flexibility. For example, in Figure 12-12, a router is acting as a firewall. The ACL applied to interface Serial 1/0/1 permits all traffic from the inside network to go out to the Internet. However, all traffic coming from the Internet is blocked as it attempts to enter the router. Although this might seem like a reasonable ACL, it can prevent a session from being set up between a client on the inside network with a host on the Internet, even if the session originated from the inside client.

Key Topic

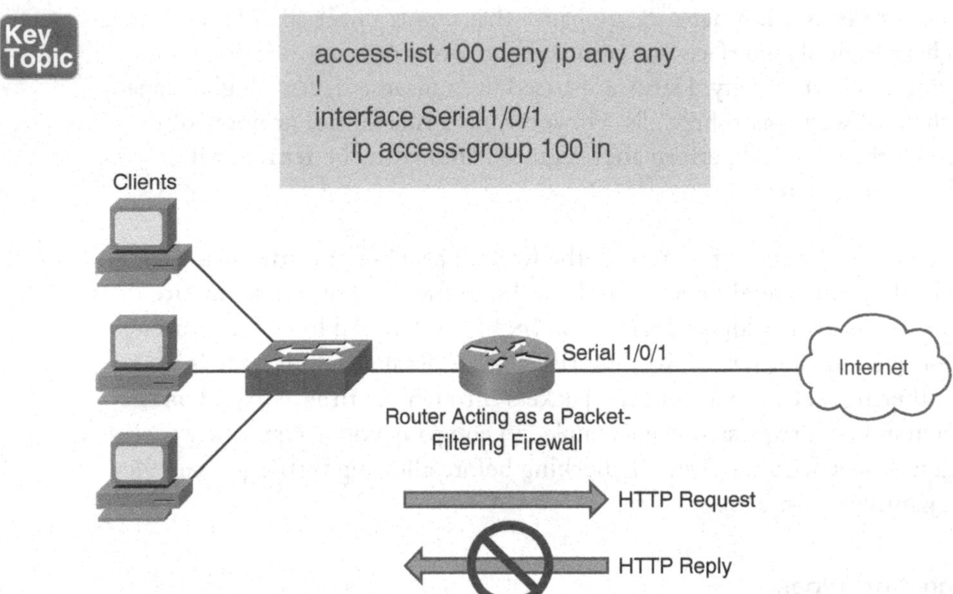

Figure 12-12 Packet-Filtering Firewall

For example, imagine that an inside client running a web browser attempts to contact a web server on the Internet. Although the outgoing HTTP request is permitted, the returning HTTP reply is blocked by the incoming ACL applied to interface Serial 1/0/1. As a result, the HTTP session cannot be established.

Stateful Firewall

Unlike a packet-filtering firewall, a stateful firewall inspects traffic leaving the inside network as it goes out to the Internet. Then, when returning traffic from the same session (as identified by source and destination IP addresses and port numbers) attempts to enter the inside network, the stateful firewall permits that traffic. The process of inspecting traffic to identify unique sessions is called *stateful inspection*.

As an example, consider Figure 12-13, where a stateful firewall allows return traffic from the Internet for a Telnet session initiated from the inside network (session A). However, Telnet traffic coming from the Internet is blocked if the Telnet session is initiated from a device on the Internet (session B).

Key Topic

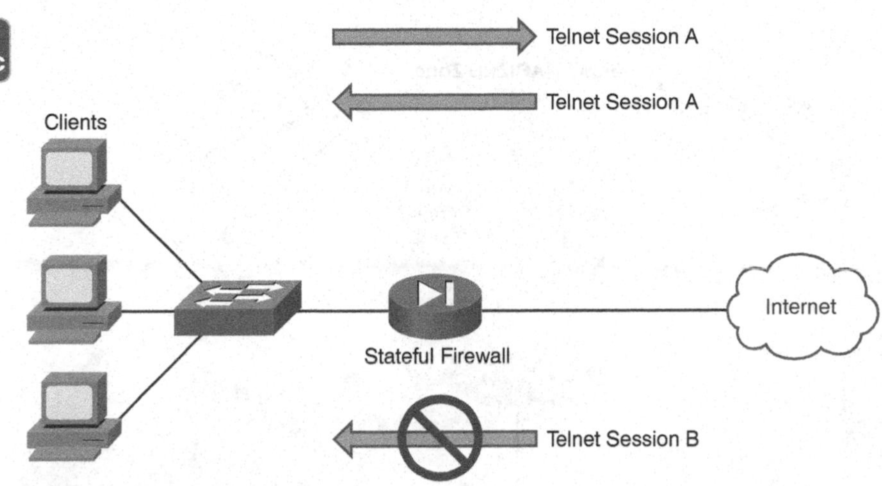

Figure 12-13 Stateful Firewall

Firewall Zones

A firewall's interfaces can be defined as belonging to different firewall zones. After you define which interfaces belong to which zones, you can set up rules saying what types of traffic are permitted to flow between zones. Consider Figure 12-14, for example. The firewall interface connecting to the inside network (trusted network) is configured as belonging to the INSIDE zone. The firewall interface connecting to the Internet (an untrusted network) is configured as belonging to the OUTSIDE zone. In this example, a rule has been applied to the firewall stating that the traffic source from the INSIDE zone is allowed to go to the OUTSIDE zone. Return traffic from sessions originating in the INSIDE zone is also permitted to come back into the INSIDE zone from the OUTSIDE zone thanks to stateful inspection. However, traffic from sessions originating in the OUTSIDE zone is not permitted to come into the INSIDE zone.

Key Topic

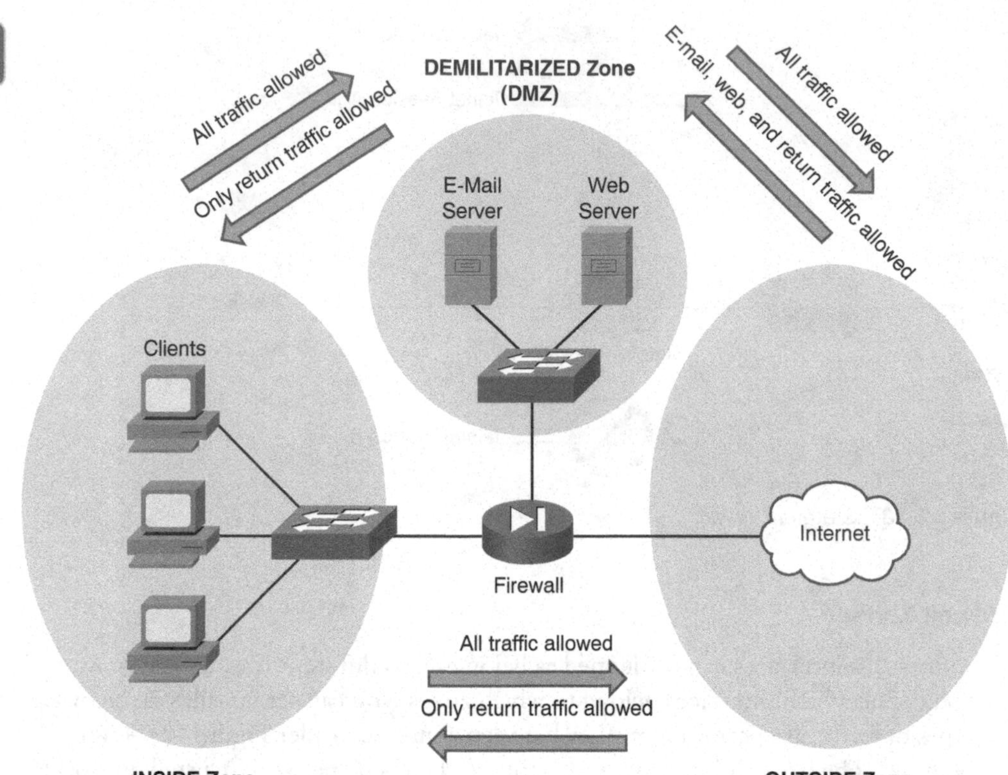

Figure 12-14 Firewall Zone Example

Notice the DEMILITARIZED zone (DMZ). A DMZ often contains servers that should be accessible from the public Internet. This approach would, in this example, allow users on the Internet to initiate an email or web session coming into an organization's email or web server. However, other protocols would be blocked.

Unified Threat Management Firewalls

A unified threat management (UTM) firewall or gateway is a device that attempts to bundle multiple security functions into a single physical or logical device. Features of an ideal UTM could include a network intrusion prevention system (IPS), network-based antivirus/antimalware, URL and content filtering, antispam, data loss prevention (DLP), regulatory compliance checking, stateful filtering, VPN services, multiple interfaces for DMZs, load balancing, user-based access control and filtering, Network Address Translation (NAT), transparent or routed implementation, Secure Sockets Layer (SSL) interception, application layer content analysis, posture assessment for a connecting computer, and more.

A device that is performing posture assessment against a client system usually involves an agent running on the client computer or mobile device, which can be queried from the UTM during the posture assessment to verify that required elements such as security updates or antimalware packages are installed before allowing the client to connect through a VPN to the UTM device. If a client does not meet the requirements, it can be given limited access to a remediation or quarantine area of the network so that the required components can be updated on the client computer before it tries to obtain full access from the UTM system. A UTM could also provide guest network access based on the authentication of the user. An agent running on the client computer could be a persistent agent that is running all the time or a temporary one that is installed/run only during an attempt by the client computer to connect to the UTM.

Depending on the vendor, these may be referred to as UTM, next-generation firewalls (NGFs), or some other marketing term to imply an all-inclusive network security device. As an alternative to purchasing their own UTM device to provide these services, many companies are turning to cloud-based services, where the service provider implements and maintains the system at the service provider location, and the customer purchases these cloud-based services from the provider.

A misconfigured firewall of any type could allow vulnerabilities to be exposed that allow attackers to exploit the firewall itself or the internal and DMZ devices the firewall was intended to protect. Leaving a default password on a firewall and permitting all traffic through the firewall from the outside untrusted network are two examples of a misconfigured firewall.

Virtual Private Networks

Much of today's workforce (approximately 40%, according to Cisco Systems) is located outside of a corporate headquarters location. Some employees work in remote offices, and others telecommute. These remote employees can connect to their main corporate network by using a variety of WAN technologies, such as leased lines and private virtual circuits (PVCs), found in Frame Relay/ATM networks. However, these WAN technologies typically cost more than widely available broadband technologies, such as digital subscriber line (DSL) and cable, which might also offer faster speeds.

Fortunately, virtual private networks (VPNs) support secure communication between two sites over an untrusted network (for example, the Internet). The two primary categories of VPNs are site-to-site and client-to-site VPNs:

- **Site-to-site VPN:** A site-to-site VPN interconnects two sites, as an alternative to a leased line, at a reduced cost. Figure 12-15 shows an example of a site-to-site VPN.

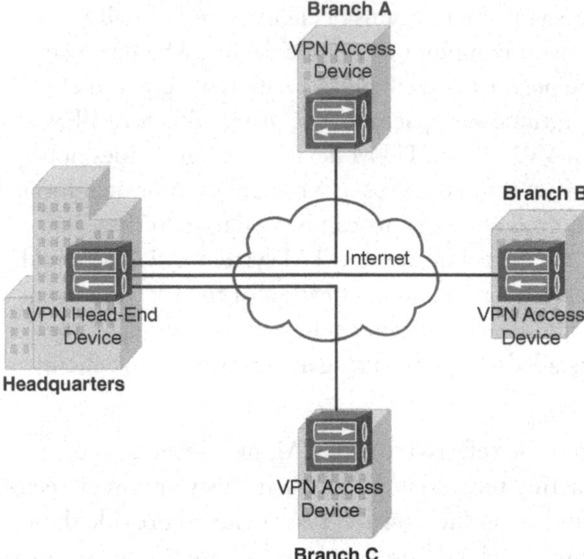

Figure 12-15 Site-to-Site VPN

- **Client-to-site VPN:** A client-to-site VPN (also known as a *remote-access VPN*) interconnects a remote user with a site, as an alternative to dial-up or ISDN connectivity, at a reduced cost. Figure 12-16 shows an example of a client-to-site VPN.

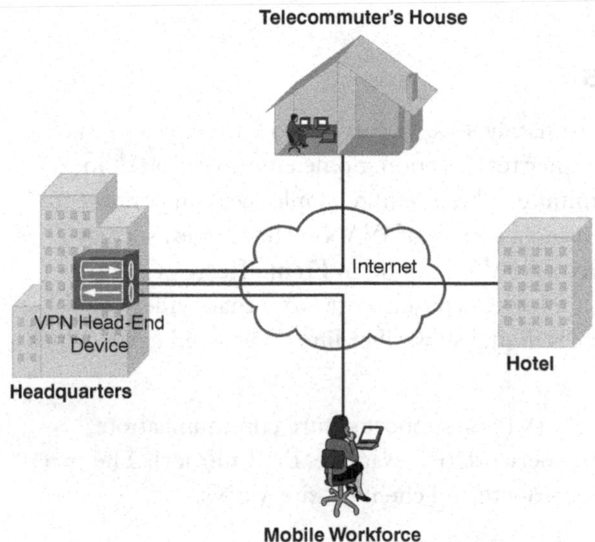

Figure 12-16 Client-to-Site VPN

Although a VPN tunnel might physically pass through multiple service provider routers, the tunnel appears to be a single router hop from the perspective of the routers at each end of the tunnel.

A client-to-site VPN allows a user with software on his client computer to connect to a centralized VPN termination device, and a site-to-site VPN interconnects two sites without requiring the computers at those sites to have any specialized VPN software installed. Client-to-site VPNs could be implemented using a VPN-compatible device, such as a router, firewall, or special-purpose device called a *VPN concentrator* that is purpose-built for handling remote-access client-to-site VPN connections. It is also possible (using the correct software) for two computers to connect to each other directly using a host-to-host IPSec VPN connection.

Overview of IPSec with IKEv1

Broadband technologies, such as cable and DSL, in addition to other VPN transport mechanisms, often traverse an untrusted network, such as the Internet. Therefore, a primary concern with using a broadband technology as a VPN transport is security.

VPN technologies such as IP Security (IPSec), generic routing encapsulation (GRE), Layer 2 Transport Protocol (L2TP), and Layer 2 Forwarding (L2F) offer a variety of features, but IPSec VPNs offer strong security features. Specifically, IPSec offers the following protections for VPN traffic:

- **Confidentiality:** Data confidentiality is provided by encrypting data. If a third party intercepts the encrypted data, he would not be able to interpret it.
- **Integrity:** Data integrity ensures that data is not modified in transit. For example, routers at each end of a tunnel can calculate a checksum value or a hash value for the data, and if both routers calculate the same value, the data has most likely not been modified in transit.
- **Authentication:** Data authentication allows parties involved in a conversation to verify that the other party is the party they claim to be.

IPSec also scales to a wide range of networks. IPSec operates at Layer 3 of the OSI model (the network layer). As a result, IPSec is transparent to applications, which means that applications do not require any sort of integrated IPSec support.

IKE Modes and Phases

IPSec uses a collection of protocols to provide its features. One of the primary protocols that IPSec uses is Internet Key Exchange (IKE). Specifically, IPSec can provide encryption between authenticated peers using encryption keys, which are periodically changed. IKE, however, allows an administrator to manually configure keys.

IKE can use the three modes of operation to set up a secure communicate path between IPSec peers. These modes are explained in Table 12-3.

Table 12-3 IKEv1 Modes

Mode	Description
Main mode	Main mode involves three exchanges of information between the IPSec peers. One peer, called the *initiator*, sends one or more proposals to the other peer, called the *responder*. The proposals include supported encryption and authentication protocols and key lifetimes. In addition, the proposals indicate whether or not perfect forward secrecy (PFS) should be used. PFS makes sure that a session key remains secure, even if one of the private keys used to derive the session key becomes compromised. The three main mode exchanges are summarized as follows: **Exchange 1**: The responder selects a proposal it received from the initiator. **Exchange 2**: Diffie-Hellman (DH) securely establishes a shared secret key over the unsecured medium. **Exchange 3**: An Internet Security Association and Key Management Protocol (ISAKMP) session is established. This secure session is then used to negotiate an IPSec session.
Aggressive mode	Aggressive mode more quickly achieves the same results as main mode, using only three packets. The initiator sends the first packet, which contains all the information necessary to establish a security association (SA), which is an agreement between the two IPSec peers about the cryptographic parameters to be used in the ISAKMP session. The responder sends the second packet, which contains the security parameters selected by the responder (the proposal, keying material, and its ID). This second packet is used by the responder to authenticate the session. The third and final packet, which is sent by the initiator, finalizes the authentication of the ISAKMP session.
Quick mode	Quick mode negotiates the parameters (the SA) for the IPSec session. This negotiation occurs within the protection of an ISAKMP session.

The IKEv1 modes reflect the two primary phases of establishing an IPSec tunnel. For example, during IKE Phase 1, a secure ISAKMP session is established using either main mode or aggressive mode. During IKE Phase 1, the IPSec endpoints establish transform sets (which are collections of encryption and authentication protocols), hash methods, and other parameters needed to establish a secure ISAKMP session (sometimes called an ISAKMP tunnel or an IKE Phase 1 tunnel). As a reminder, this collection of parameters is called a *security association* (SA). With IKE

Phase 1, the SA is bidirectional, which means that the same key exchange is used for data flowing across the tunnel in either direction.

IKE Phase 2 occurs within the protection of an IKE Phase 1 tunnel, using the previously described *quick mode* of parameter negotiation. A session formed during IKE Phase 2 is sometimes called an *IKE Phase 2 tunnel* or simply an *IPSec tunnel*. However, unlike IKE Phase 1, IKE Phase 2 performs unidirectional SA negotiations, which means that each data flow uses a separate key exchange.

Although an IPSec tunnel can be established using just IKE Phase 1 and IKE Phase 2, an optional IKE Phase 1.5 can be used. IKE Phase 1.5 uses the Extended Authentication (XAUTH) protocol to perform user authentication of IPSec tunnels. Like IKE Phase 2, IKE Phase 1.5 is performed within the protection of an IKE Phase 1 tunnel. The user authentication provided by this phase adds a layer of authentication for VPN clients. Also, parameters such as IP, WINS, and DNS server information can be provided to a VPN client during this optional phase. A newer version called IKEv2 combines many of the same functions of IKEv1 and uses an initial IKEv2 tunnel (instead of IKEv1 phase 1) and children security associations (SAs/tunnels) for the IPSec tunnels instead of calling them IKE Phase 2 tunnels.

Authentication Header and Encapsulating Security Payload

In addition to IKE, which establishes the IPSec tunnel, IPSec relies on either the Authentication Header (AH) protocol (IP protocol number 51) or the Encapsulating Security Payload (ESP) protocol (IP protocol number 50). Both AH and ESP offer origin authentication and integrity services, which ensure that IPSec peers are who they claim to be and that the data was not modified in transit.

However, the main distinction between AH and ESP is encryption support. ESP encrypts the original packet, while AH does not offer encryption. As a result, ESP is much more popular on today's networks.

Both AH and ESP can operate in one of two modes: transport mode or tunnel mode. Figure 12-17 illustrates the structure of an ESP transport mode packet versus an ESP tunnel mode packet.

NOTE You might be concerned that transport mode allows the IP address of the IPSec peers to remain visible during transit, because the original packet's IP header is used to route a packet. However, IPSec is often used in conjunction with the *generic routing encapsulation* (GRE) tunneling protocol. In such a scenario, the original IP packet is encapsulated inside of a GRE tunnel packet, which adds a new GRE tunnel header. The GRE packet is then sent over an IPSec tunnel. Even if the IPSec tunnel were running in transport mode, the original packet's IP header would still not be visible. Instead, the GRE packet's header would be visible.

Transport Mode

ESP Auth	ESP Trailer	Payload	ESP Header	Original IP Header

Tunnel Mode

ESP Auth	ESP Trailer	Payload	Original IP Header	ESP Header	New IP Header

Figure 12-17 Transport Mode Versus Tunnel Mode

Following is a detailed description of these two modes:

- **Transport mode:** Uses a packet's original IP header, as opposed to adding an additional tunnel header. This approach works well in networks where increasing a packet's size might cause an issue. Also, transport mode is often used for client-to-site VPNs, where a PC running VPN client software connects back to a VPN termination device at a headquarters location.
- **Tunnel mode:** Unlike transport mode, tunnel mode encapsulates an entire packet. As a result, the encapsulated packet has a new header (an IPSec header). This new header has source and destination IP address information that reflects the two VPN termination devices at different sites. Therefore, tunnel mode is often used in an IPSec site-to-site VPN.

One reason a GRE tunnel might be used with an IPSec tunnel is as a limitation on the part of IPSec. Specifically, an IPSec tunnel can only transmit unicast IP packets. The challenge is that large enterprise networks might have a significant amount of broadcast or multicast traffic (for example, routing protocol traffic). GRE can take any traffic type and encapsulate the traffic in a GRE tunnel packet, which is a unicast IP packet that can then be sent over an IPSec tunnel. Take, for example, a multicast packet used by a routing protocol. Although IPSec cannot directly transport the multicast packet, if the packet is first encapsulated by GRE, the GRE packet can then be sent over an IPSec tunnel, thereby securing the transmission of the multicast packet.

The Five Steps in Setting Up and Tearing Down an IPSec Site-to-Site VPN Using IKEv1

The process of establishing, maintaining, and tearing down an IPSec site-to-site VPN consists of five primary steps. These steps are illustrated in Figure 12-18 and described in detail in the following list:

Key Topic

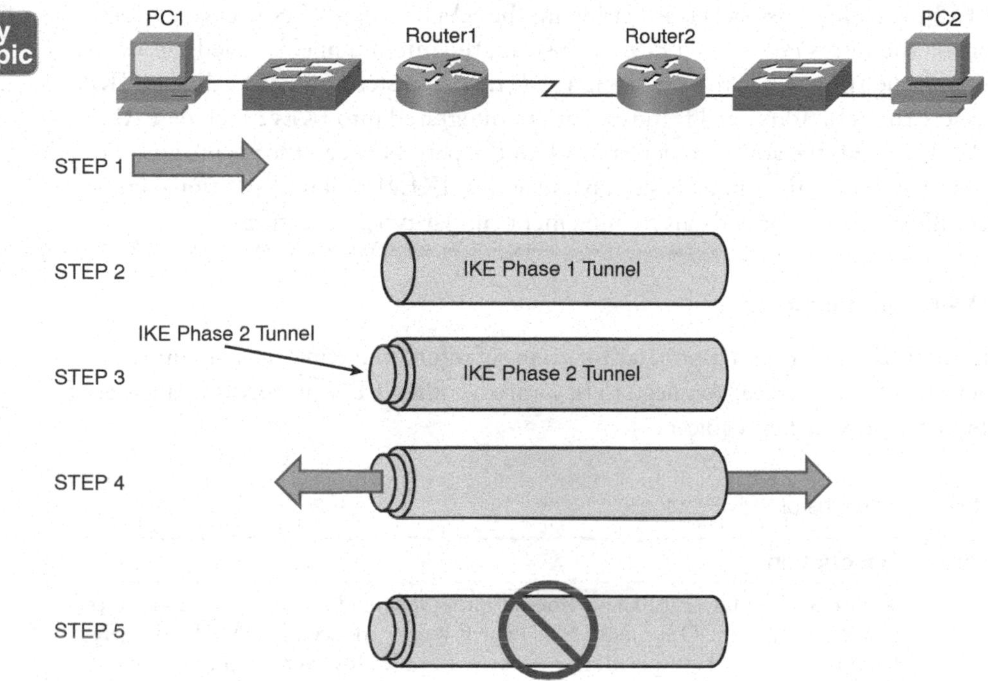

Figure 12-18 IPSec VPN Steps

Step 1. PC1 sends traffic destined for PC2. Router1 classifies the traffic as "interesting" traffic, which initiates the creation of an IPSec tunnel.

Step 2. Router1 and Router2 negotiate a security association (SA) used to form an IKE Phase 1 tunnel, which is also known as an ISAKMP tunnel.

Step 3. Within the protection of the IKE Phase 1 tunnel, an IKE Phase 2 tunnel is negotiated and set up. An IKE Phase 2 tunnel is also known as an IPSec tunnel.

Step 4. After the IPSec tunnel is established, interesting traffic (for example, traffic classified by an ACL) flows through the protected IPSec tunnel. Note that traffic not deemed interesting can still be sent between PC1 and PC2. However, the non-interesting traffic is transmitted outside of the protection of the IPSec tunnel.

Step 5. After no interesting traffic is seen for a specified amount of time, the IPSec tunnel is torn down and the IPSec SA is deleted.

The previous example described an IPSec site-to-site VPN, but the procedure is similar for a client-to-site VPN. IPSec is typically deployed using IKEv1, with its two phases (Phase 1 and Phase 2). There is another IKE version called *IKEv2*.

IKEv2 uses a few less packets in setting up the SAs between VPN peers and does not use the terms *Phase 1* and *Phase 2*. Instead, the initial tunnel is called the *IKEv2 SA*, and the IPSec SA is referred to as a *child tunnel* (instead of being called an IKE Phase 2 tunnel). Additional features that are integrated into IKEv2 include EAP, NAT traversal (the ability to detect NAT in the path between the peers), and the ability to validate the tunnel is still up and active. IKEv1 required additional configuration and vendor add-ons to implement similar types of features.

Other VPN Technologies

Although IPSec VPNs are popular for securely interconnecting sites or connecting a remote client to a site, you need to be aware of other VPN protocols, examples of which are provided in Table 12-4.

Table 12-4 Examples of VPN Protocols

Protocol	Description
SSL	Secure Sockets Layer (SSL) provides cryptography and reliability for upper layers (Layers 5–7) of the OSI model. SSL, which was introduced in 1995, has largely been replaced by Transport Layer Security (TLS). However, recent versions of SSL (for example, SSL 3.3) have been enhanced to be more comparable with TLS. Both SSL and TLS provide secure web browsing via Hypertext Transfer Protocol Secure (HTTPS).
L2TP	Layer 2 Tunneling Protocol (L2TP) is a VPN protocol that lacks security features, such as encryption. However, L2TP can still be used for a secure VPN connection if it is combined with another protocol that does provide encryption.
L2F	Layer 2 Forwarding (L2F) is a VPN protocol designed (by Cisco Systems) with the intent of providing a tunneling protocol for PPP. Like L2TP, L2F lacks native security features.
PPTP	Point-to-Point Tunneling Protocol (PPTP) is an older VPN protocol (which supported the dial-up networking feature in older versions of Microsoft Windows). Like L2TP and L2F, PPTP lacks native security features. However, Microsoft's versions of PPTP bundled with various versions of Microsoft Windows were enhanced to offer security features.
TLS	Transport Layer Security (TLS) has largely replaced SSL as the VPN protocol of choice for providing cryptography and reliability to upper layers of the OSI model. For example, when you securely connect to a website using HTTPS, you are probably using TLS.

Intrusion Detection and Prevention

When an attacker launches an attack against a network, intrusion detection system (IDS) and intrusion prevention system (IPS) technologies are often able to recognize the attack and respond appropriately. Attacks might be recognizable by comparing incoming data streams against a database of well-known attack signatures. Other mechanisms for detecting attacks include policy-based and anomaly-based approaches. In addition to dedicated network-based intrusion prevention system (NIPS) sensors, IPS software can be installed on a host to provide a host-based intrusion prevention system (HIPS) or host-based intrusion detection system (HIDS) solution.

IDS Versus IPS

Both IDS and IPS devices can recognize network attacks; they differ primarily in their network placement. Specifically, whereas an IDS device receives a copy of traffic to be analyzed, an IPS device resides inline with the traffic, as illustrated in Figure 12-19.

Key Topic

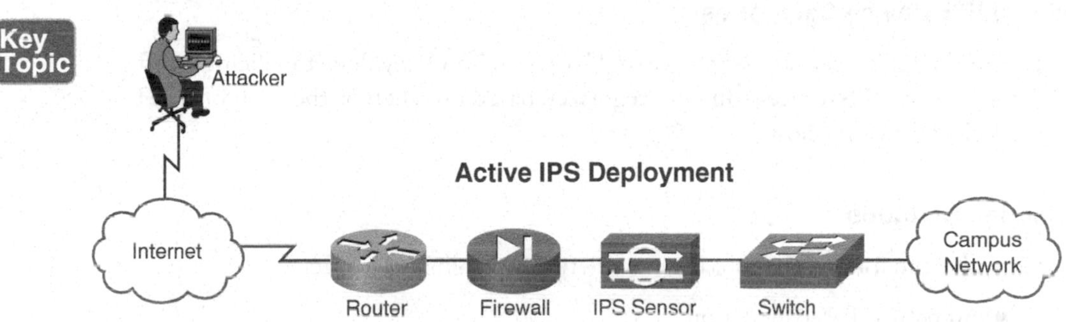

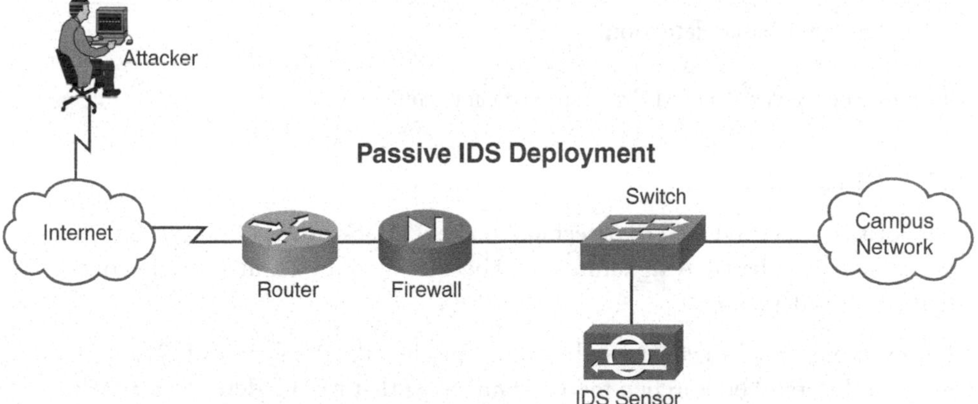

Figure 12-19 IDS and IPS Network Placement

Because the analyzed traffic does not flow through the IDS device, the IDS device is considered to be *passive*, and the IPS device is considered to be *active*. Both the IDS and the IPS devices can send alerts to, for example, a management station. Although an IDS device can also communicate with a security appliance or a router to prevent subsequent attack packets, the initially offending traffic reaches its destination. Conversely, an IPS device can drop the traffic inline, thus preventing even the first malicious packet from reaching its intended target.

The previous discussion of IDS versus IPS devices might seem to suggest that IPS devices should always be used instead of IDS devices. However, in some network environments, these two solutions complement one another. For example, an IDS device can add value to a network that already employs an IPS device by verifying that the IPS device is still operational. The IDS device might also identify suspicious traffic and send alerts about that traffic without having the IPS device drop the traffic.

IDS and IPS Device Categories

IDS and IPS devices can be categorized based on how they detect malicious traffic. Alternatively, IPS devices can be categorized based on whether they run on a network device or on a host.

Detection Methods

Consider the following approaches for detecting malicious traffic:

- Signature-based detection
- Policy-based detection
- Anomaly-based detection

The following is a detailed discussion of each method.

Signature-Based Detection

The primary method used to detect and prevent attacks using IDS or IPS technologies is signature based. A signature could be a string of bytes, in a certain context, that triggers detection.

For example, attacks against a web server typically take the form of URLs. Therefore, URLs could be searched for a certain string that would identify an attack against a web server.

As another example, the IDS or IPS device could search for a pattern in the MIME header of an email message. However, because signature-based IDS/IPS is, as its name suggests, based on signatures, the administrator needs to routinely update those signature files.

Policy-Based Detection

Another approach to IDS/IPS detection is policy based. With a policy-based approach, the IDS/IPS device needs a specific declaration of the security policy. For example, you could write a network access policy that identified which networks could communicate with other networks. The IDS/IPS device could then recognize out-of-profile traffic that does not conform to the policy, and then report that activity. A policy-based detection could also identify unencrypted channels and clear-text credentials and unsecure protocols such as Telnet, SNMPv1, HTTP, FTP, SLIP, and TFTP. Secure protocols such as SSH, SNMPv3, TLS/SSL, HTTPS, SFTP, and IPSec should be used when possible to protect the confidentiality of the data flows on the network.

Anomaly-Based Detection

A third approach to detecting or preventing malicious traffic is anomaly based. This approach is prone to false positives because a *normal* condition is difficult to measurably define. However, there are a couple of options for detecting anomalies:

- **Statistical anomaly detection:** This approach watches network-traffic patterns over a period of time and dynamically builds a baseline. Then, if traffic patterns significantly vary from the baseline, an alarm can be triggered.
- **Nonstatistical anomaly detection:** This approach allows an administrator to define what traffic patterns are supposed to look like. However, imagine that Microsoft released a large service pack for its Windows 7 OS, and your company has hundreds of computers that are configured to automatically download that service pack. If multiple employees turn on their computers at approximately the same time tomorrow morning, and multiple copies of the service pack simultaneously start to download from http://www.microsoft.com, the IDS/IPS device might consider that traffic pattern to be significantly outside of the baseline. As a result, the nonstatistical anomaly detection approach could lead to a false positive (an alarm being triggered in the absence of malicious traffic). A zero-day attack is one that exploits a previously unknown vulnerability. An anomaly-based IPS may be able to indicate abnormal behavior, compared to the baseline of normal activity, which could assist you in discovering a new type of attack that is being used against your network.

NOTE Anomaly-based detection is also known as *behavior-based detection*.

Deploying Network-Based and Host-Based Solutions

NIPS and HIPS solutions can work in tandem. For example, although a NIPS solution can inspect traffic flowing through the network, what if a host had an SSL connection to a server, and the malicious traffic traveled over the SSL connection? In that instance, the NIPS hardware would be unable to analyze the malicious traffic because it would be encrypted inside of the SSL connection. However, an HIPS software solution could analyze the malicious traffic after the traffic was decrypted on the host. Similarly, an NIPS device might be able to prevent a DoS attack or recognize network reconnaissance patterns, and an HIPS solution could focus on the protection of applications and host resources.

Figure 12-20 illustrates the deployment of network-based IDS (NIDS), NIPS, and HIPS technologies in the same network. Notice the sensors are strategically deployed at network boundaries (that is, coming into the network from the Internet and going into the DMZ). As previously discussed, both NIDS and NIPS devices complement the functions of one another. In addition, HIPS software is deployed on strategic hosts, which are the HTTP, DNS, and email hosts in this example. The NIDS, NIPS, and HIPS devices can send any alarms triggered on their respective devices to a management console. Using input from these diverse sources, the management console software might be able to perform event correlation to recognize broader network attack patterns, rather than just examining a single attack against a single device.

Key Topic

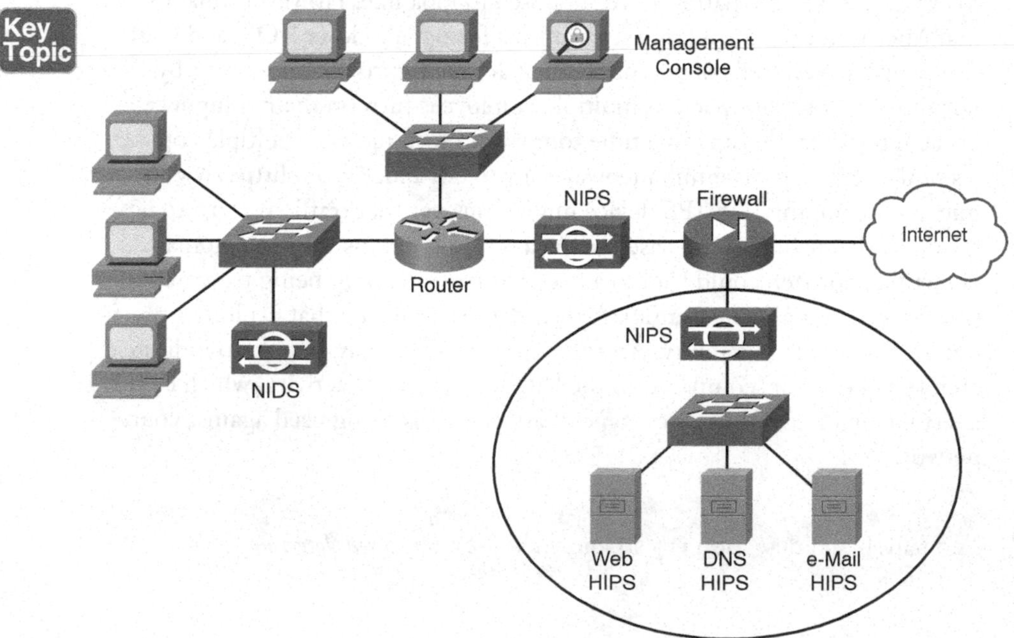

Figure 12-20 NIDS, NIPS, and HIPS Deployment Example

Real-World Case Study

Acme, Inc. has decided to use a centralized RADIUS server for the authentication authorization and accounting on its network. This server will interact with Microsoft Active Directory (AD) to verify existing usernames and passwords that are already in AD. When users log in to their local computers, Active Directory using Kerberos will authenticate those users. For wireless network access, 802.11i/WPA2 enterprise is being used, leveraging the same RADIUS server.

When users access the Internet, the firewall will implement controls based on user. By implementing a unified threat management (UTM) system such as Check Point, Acme can use the UTM to integrate with both the RADIUS server and Active Directory. Features such as intrusion prevention, stateful firewall, antimalware, VPN, application layer inspection, and URL filtering can all be integrated as part of Acme's network-based UTM solution. The interaction between the UTM system, wireless security, and Microsoft AD assists in not having to re-create the same user account in multiple different places.

In addition to the network protection provided by the UTM system, critical servers will run a host-based intrusion prevention system as an extra precaution.

Traffic sent between the headquarters location and any of the branch offices over the WAN will have confidentiality and data integrity through the implementation of a site-to-site VPN using IPSec. AES encryption will provide confidentiality, and SHA or HMAC hashing will provide data integrity. The VPN also provides the ability to authenticate the peer on the other side of the VPN to avoid a man-in-the-middle attack.

For remote users who need to connect over the Internet to either the branch or the headquarters office, remote-access VPNs will be used for the authentication, confidentiality, and data integrity that the VPNs can provide.

Acme's public-facing web servers will enroll with a certificate authority and request identity certificates. Using server-side identity certificates, Acme can implement SSL/TLS/HTTPS and provide secure connectivity for customers who are connecting to these web servers. The servers will be running as virtualized systems in VMware's vSphere.

Policies have been created and communicated to all employees, including user awareness training, about the responsibilities of users on the network. Limited rights have been given to users on their local computers. This will help reduce malicious software being installed on those computers. Each of the computers is also running host-based antivirus and antimalware software.

The company has authorized a third-party vendor to perform periodic vulnerability scans in addition to specifically controlled penetration testing on Acme's network.

Acme has decided to internally manage its updates and patch management for its local systems, including virtualized servers and workstations that are on premises.

Acme is working on a bring your own device (BYOD) policy that would allow users to have access to corporate data on their personal devices. However, until they determine a safe and best practice for BYOD, the current policy is that no company data may be accessed or stored on any device that is not company issued.

On the switch ports, the features of DHCP snooping, port security, dynamic ARP inspection, 802.1X, and MAC address filtering have been configured to reduce the risk of attack coming in on one of the switch ports.

Accounting logs and user account activity are periodically reviewed, which can assist in identifying malicious or unauthorized activity on the network.

Summary

Here are the main topics covered in this chapter:

- Security fundamentals were discussed. Specifically, you were introduced to the security goals of confidentiality, integrity, and availability. Then you were presented with several examples of common network threats.
- You reviewed best-practice recommendations for defending against threats to network security. These recommendations included such things as user training, patching, having a security policy, having an incident response policy, testing your own network with vulnerability scanners, distracting attackers with honey pots, and blocking unwanted traffic with access control lists.
- A collection of remote-access security technologies was presented (for example, SSH, AAA, and NAC).
- Firewalls were discussed, along with firewall types, inspection types, and firewall zones.
- Virtual private networks were introduced, along with various VPN protocols. However, the primary focus was on IPSec, and you saw a detailed explanation of how an IPSec tunnel is established.
- You saw how to defend your network against well-known attacks using IDS and IPS sensors.

Exam Preparation Tasks

Review All the Key Topics

Review the most important topics from inside the chapter, noted with the Key Topic icon in the outer margin of the page. Table 12-5 lists these key topics and the page numbers where each is found.

Table 12-5 Key Topics for Chapter 12

Key Topic Element	Description	Page Number
List	Network security goals	410
List	Symmetric encryption algorithms	411
Figure 12-2	Asymmetric encryption example	412
List	Types of integrity attacks	414
Table 12-1	Confidentiality attack tactics	417
Figure 12-11	ACL example	436
List	Physical security devices	437
List	Network device hardening	438
Table 12-2	Remote-access security methods	439
List	Firewall types	442
Figure 12-12	Packet-filtering firewall	444
Figure 12-13	Stateful firewall	445
Figure 12-14	Firewall zone example	446
List	VPN categories	447
Figure 12-17	Transparent mode versus tunnel mode	452
Figure 12-18	IPSec VPN steps	453
Table 12-4	Examples of VPN protocols	454
Figure 12-19	IDS and IPS network placement	455
List	IDS/IPS detection methods	456
Figure 12-20	NIDS, NIPS, and HIPS deployment example	458

Complete Tables and Lists from Memory

Print a copy of Appendix C, "Memory Tables," or at least the section for this chapter, and complete as many of the tables as possible from memory. Appendix D, "Memory Tables Answer Key," includes the completed tables and lists so you can check your work.

Define Key Terms

Define the following key terms from this chapter, and check your answers in the Glossary:

symmetric encryption, asymmetric encryption, Advanced Encryption Standard (AES), RSA, pretty good privacy (PGP), GNU Privacy Guard (GPC), public key infrastructure (PKI), Challenge-Response Authentication Mechanism Message Digest 5 (CRAM-MD5), denial of service (DoS), social engineering, FTP bounce, distributed denial of service (DDoS), buffer overflow, security policy, acceptable use policy (AUP), Nessus, Nmap, honey pot, honey net, access control list (ACL), Kerberos, Remote Authentication Dial-In User Service (RADIUS), Terminal Access Controller Access-Control System Plus (TACACS+), two-factor authentication, multifactor authentication, single sign-on (SSO), software firewall, hardware firewall, stateful firewall, unified threat management (UTM), demilitarized zone (DMZ), virtual private network (VPN), site-to-site VPN, client-to-site VPN, remote-access VPN, IP security (IPSec), Internet Key Exchange (IKE), Internet Security Association and Key Management Protocol (ISAKMP), security association (SA), Authentication Header (AH), Encapsulating Security Payload (ESP), Secure Sockets Layer (SSL), Layer 2 Tunneling Protocol (L2TP), Layer 2 Forwarding (L2F), Point-to-Point Tunneling Protocol (PPTP), intrusion detection system (IDS), intrusion prevention system (IDS), network-based IDS (NIDS), network-based IPS (NIPS), host-based IPS (HIPS), badges, biometrics, smart cards, key fobs, locks, asset tracking tags, motion detection, video surveillance, tamper detection, Lightweight Directory Access Protocol (LDAP), captive portal, insider threat, logic bomb, rogue access point, evil twin, war driving, phishing, Flood Guard, BPDU Guard, Root Guard, DHCP snooping

Complete Chapter 12 Hands-On Lab in Network+ Simulator Lite

- Configuring a Small Office/Home Office Router - Network User Security Settings
- Network Security Appliance Terminology and Methods

Additional Resources

Cloud Security and Privacy: http://www.ajsnetworking.com/ccie-evolving-technologies-2

Port Security Basics: http://www.ajsnetworking.com/port-security-basics

Review Questions

The answers to these review questions are in Appendix A, "Answers to Review Questions."

1. Which of the following is a symmetric encryption algorithm available in 128-bit, 192-bit, and 256-bit key versions?
   a. RSA
   b. 3DES
   c. AES
   d. TKIP

2. In what type of attack does the attacker compromise multiple systems and then instruct those compromised systems, called *zombies*, to simultaneously flood a target system with traffic?
   a. DoS
   b. TCP SYN flood
   c. Buffer overflow
   d. DDoS

3. Which of the following is a continually changing document that dictates a set of guidelines for network use?
   a. Security policy
   b. Post-mortem report
   c. Syslog report
   d. QoS policy

4. What type of software application should network administrators routinely use to verify the security of their network and check for any weaknesses?
   a. Honey pot
   b. Posture monitor
   c. Profile scanner
   d. Vulnerability scanner

5. Which of the following are characteristics of RADIUS? (Choose two.)
   a. TCP based
   b. UDP based
   c. Encrypts an entire authentication packet
   d. Only encrypts the password in an authentication packet

6. What feature allows a firewall to permit traffic to flow from a trusted network (for example, a corporate intranet) to an untrusted network (for example, the Internet) and then allow return traffic for that session, while blocking sessions initiated on the untrusted network?
   a. Packet filtering
   b. Stateful inspection
   c. Demilitarized zone
   d. Implicit deny all instruction

7. Which of the following is an IPSec protocol that provides authentication and integrity services but does not support encryption?

   a. IKE Phase I

   b. IKE Phase II

   c. AH

   d. ESP

8. Which of the following protocols are most commonly used to provide security for an HTTPS connection? (Choose two.)

   a. L2TP

   b. SSL

   c. PPTP

   d. TLS

9. Which of the following security solutions consists of software running on a host to protect that host against a collection of well-known attacks?

   a. HIPS

   b. NIDS

   c. L2F

   d. NIPS

10. From the following list, identify the detection methods commonly used by IPS sensors. (Choose three.)

    a. Signature based

    b. Distribution based

    c. Policy based

    d. Behavior based

After completion of this chapter, you will be able to answer the following questions:

- What are the common policies used in the modern network?
- What are the common best practices?

CHAPTER 13

Network Policies and Best Practices

If you are reading this text start to finish, you might have a newfound appreciation for how complex networking is today. Fortunately, there are many established policies and best practices you can use to help take much of the guesswork out of implementing and maintaining your network. This is especially beneficial in the complex and challenging area of network security.

This chapter begins by describing (in detail) policies you can consider for your own network. Keep in mind that some of these may not apply to your organization at all, but you should still take time to study them if you are preparing for the Network+ exam. For example, your company may not have BYOD (bring-your-own-device) policies in place because your company forbids BYOD completely, yet this topic may show up on the exam. Do not make the mistake of assuming this material is not on your exam.

The chapter also covers many best practices you can implement, such as nondisclosure agreements (NDAs) and system life cycle approaches. Again, perhaps not all best practices are applicable to you, but there is much to be gained by studying them.

Foundation Topics

Policies

Many important policies have become fairly commonplace in networks today that you should consider for your own organization. This section of the chapter lists some of the most critical for your review.

Password Policy

Because more and more sensitive data is finding its way into storage on our networks, more security measures are required than ever before. As part of this, your organization needs to possess a well-crafted security policy, and this security policy should include a comprehensive password policy. As you'll learn in this section, you should also provide detailed training on this part of the security policy.

Keep in mind that in addition to "simple" username and password combinations, many other powerful technologies found in the modern network are available for user authentication. Chapter 12, "Network Security," detailed these technologies, which include the following:

- One-time passwords (OTPs)
- Client certificates
- Smart cards
- Biometrics
- Multifactor authentication

Despite these additional security options, the "classic" password still plays a pivotal role in most networks. It is obvious by glancing at recent news headlines that user credentials represent a major area of attack.

Your password policy should include the following:

- Education for end users
- Strong password requirements, such as the following:
  - Minimum password lengths
  - Restrictions on the use of proper names
  - Password expiration
  - No previously used passwords allowed

- No words spelled out completely within the password
- The use of characters from the following groups:
  - Uppercase letters
  - Lowercase letters
  - Numbers
  - Special characters

Your password policy might also detail the use of password management software. This software stores passwords for different resources and can even help users generate complex passwords across these resources. Of course, the software itself must be protected with a strong password that the user should memorize.

Data Loss Prevention

A comprehensive data loss prevention (DLP) policy seeks to focus on accidental or malicious data losses. DLP policies consider internal and external users as well as define practices to guard against sensitive data. The best DLP policies can also cover wide network integration, not just limiting themselves to certain areas of networking such as email.

Most DLP policies focus on the use of content-level scanning and deep content inspection (DCI) to identify sensitive data and protect it. DLP policies target activities at three levels:

- Client level (data in operation)
- Network level (data in transit)
- Storage level (data at rest)

You should take the following actions when designing a DLP policy for your organization:

- Consider any risk assessments your company has performed.
- Incorporate key members of management from the various departments of your organization.
- Identify the most sensitive data of the organization.
- Outline a phased implementation of DLP and incorporate guidelines for tracking success of the initiative.
- Attempt to minimize any negative impacts on the business caused by the policy implementation.

- Periodically review the DLP policy.
- Include the appropriate event-monitoring specifics as they apply to the policy.

Remote-Access Policies

Remote access to corporate network resources presents unique challenges for organizations today. Of primary concern is the fact that the remote network might lack appropriate security controls, or may even be currently compromised.

Here are important considerations for your remote access policy:

- The scope of the policy should be clear and may include applicable targets, such as employees, contractors, vendors, and agents with company-owned or personally owned computers or workstations used to connect to the corporate network. This remote access policy typically applies to remote connections to the company itself, including reading or sending email and viewing intranet web resources. The policy also tends to cover every remote access option, including dial-up, VPN, and web portal access.
- Clearly detail the requirements of the policy itself, which might include encryption and security standards as well as the acceptable areas of network access.
- Consider a section regarding compliance, which could include exceptions to the policy, the measurements for compliance, and the consequences of noncompliance.
- You might also add a section to the policy that indicates what other security policies for the network closely relate to this policy.

Incident Response Policies

Because security issues are inevitable for your network, it is critical to prepare a comprehensive incident response policy. Such a policy might outline various phases of an incident response plan, including the following:

- **Prepare**: This often involves being able to identify the start of an incident, preparing a recovery plan, how to get everything back to normal, and creating established security policies.
- **Identify**: The focus here is on the precise identification of the actual security incident.
- **Contain**: Here, the main concern is often twofold: first, protecting and keeping available critical computing resources; second, determining the operational

status of the infected computer, system, or network. The goal is to limit the security incident from spreading.

- **Eradicate**: This phase deals specifically with the removal of the attack or infection.
- **Recover**: This phase often includes service restoration as well as a recertification of network devices and systems.
- **Review**: All phases should be analyzed in this review phase to gauge their effectiveness and modify the incident response policy as needed for the future.

Bring Your Own Device (BYOD)

Closely related to a remote access policy is the bring-your-own-device (BYOD) policy. At the very least this important policy should incorporate the following:

- An explicit and detailed list of what devices are actually permitted
- An explicit security policy for each device or device category
- The appropriate corporate support policy for each device or device category
- A clear delineation of what applications and data are owned by the corporation versus that owned by the user and/or employee
- An explicit list of applications permitted in the BYOD environment
- An integration of the BYOD policy with the acceptable use policy (AUP, covered next)
- A detailed presentation of the exit policies for employees as they relate to BYOD

Acceptable Use Policy (AUP)

This policy is sometimes referred to as a *fair use policy*. It seeks to provide restrictions and overall guidelines on how the network should be used. This policy can have tremendous legal implications for an organization should there be problems with employee actions on the network. An organization might protect itself in such legal situations if its employees have signed a detailed AUP.

An AUP should be the following:

- Clear
- Concise
- Detailed regarding acceptable and unacceptable use of the network

- Congruent with the associated overall security policies of the organization
- Concrete regarding consequences of AUP violations

Like many of the policies in this section, the AUP should be reviewed and updated as required.

Safety Procedures

I am hesitant to install a light bulb in my own home, so I have great respect for the complexity of installing large, complex, and heavy network equipment and components within an organization. Sure enough, you should consider safety policies and procedures for the networking equipment in your organization. Here are some commonalities found in such policies:

- Following the installation and maintenance guides for the equipment as closely as possible
- Keeping all work areas as clean and organized as possible
- Wearing appropriate safety equipment
- Assistance when lifting heavy network objects
- Caution when interacting with electricity
- Avoiding other risks of electric shock

Best Practices

Just as there are excellent policy ideas to assist us in our networks, there are many best practice items you should consider as well. This section of the chapter presents several of these items.

Privileged User Agreement (PUA)

Because network administrators often require "God-like" power and access over the network and the data that flows through it, it is important to consider a privileged user agreement (PUA) as part of the best practices in your IT department. A PUA agreement might stipulate the following:

- Privileged access should be granted only to authorized individuals who read and sign the agreement.
- Privileged access may be used only to perform assigned job duties.

- If methods other than using privileged access will accomplish an action, those other methods must be used unless the burden of time or other resources required clearly justifies using privileged access.
- Privileged access may be used to perform standard system-related duties only on machines and networks whose responsibility is part of the assigned job duties.
- Privileged access may be used to grant, change, or deny resources, access, or privilege to another individual only for authorized account management activities or under exceptional circumstances.

On-boarding/Off-boarding Procedures

Another excellent best practice is to have detailed on-boarding and off-boarding procedures in place for the hiring and terminating of employees as it relates to IT and the network.

Examples of typical on-boarding steps might include the following:

- ID number and pin assignment
- Username and password assignment
- ID card and access assignments
- Email mailbox setup
- Email client setup
- Workstation setup
- Workstation network access verification
- IT security and best practices training
- Phone and BYOD setup
- Time management and other HR software training

Licensing Restrictions

You may also need to provide training in the proper licensing and use of corporate hardware and software. As networks have become more complex (for example, incorporating public cloud technologies), so have licensing agreements. It is important that your users remain in compliance with all existing licensing agreements and restrictions.

International Export Controls

Another important best practice is to educate IT staff and end users on the international export rules your organization must observe. Using the U.S. government as an example, specific agencies regulate the transfer of information, commodities, technology, and software considered to be strategically important to the U.S. in the interest of national security, economic, and/or foreign policy concerns.

Your management must understand that noncompliance with export controls can result in severe monetary and criminal penalties against both an individual in your company as well as the organization itself.

> **NOTE** An important area of export regulations is in the area of cryptography. The "Additional Resources" section of this chapter provides a link for more information about this important area.

Non-Disclosure Agreement (NDA)

Another common best practice is to use a non-disclosure agreement in your organization. An NDA is a legal contract with the following common traits:

- It is between at least two parties.
- It outlines confidential material, knowledge, or information that the parties want to share with one another but want to restrict others from accessing.
- It creates a confidential relationship between the parties to protect any type of confidential and proprietary information or trade secret.
- It protects non-public business information.

NDAs have become quite common for all employees to sign.

System Life Cycle

Your IT networking personnel should also consider adhering to a well-planned system life cycle for the equipment and software in use. The system life cycle should provide valuable guidance on best practices throughout the organization concerning the network components.

Here are some examples of phases in a system life cycle:

- Conceptual design
- Preliminary system design
- Detail design and development

- Production and construction
- Utilization and support
- Phase-out
- Disposal

Real-World Case Study

Acme, Inc. wants to ensure it incorporates as many well-thought-through policies and best practices as possible in designing, operating, and maintaining its network. As such, the company has assembled a team of legal counsel and key department heads in order to draft important policy documents and best practices.

Acme now has a comprehensive network security policy that includes the following:

- A password policy.
- A data loss prevention policy.
- An incident response policy.
- An acceptable use policy.
- On-boarding and off-boarding procedures.
- A mandatory NDA for all employees.
- A detailed system life cycle for networking hardware and software.
- Also, administrators for Acme, having higher privileges over the network than standard users, are now required to sign a PUA before they are granted access to the administrative environment.

Acme has also planned for a consistent review of the documents and best practices as well as a procedure for their alteration.

Summary

Here are the main topics covered in this chapter:

- This chapter provided details on several common policies found in networks today, including password policies, data loss prevention, remote access policies, incident response policies, BYOD policies, acceptable use policies, and safety policies.
- This chapter also provided many best practice items, including privileged user agreements, on-boarding and off-boarding procedures, licensing restrictions, international export controls, non-disclosure agreements, and system life cycles.

Exam Preparation Tasks

Review All the Key Topics

Review the most important topics from inside the chapter, noted with the Key Topic icon in the outer margin of the page. Table 7-1 lists these key topics and the page numbers where each is found.

Table 13-1 Key Topics for Chapter 13

Key Topic Element	Description	Page Number
List	Typical elements of a password policy	468
List	Key elements of a data loss prevention policy	469
List	Important elements for a remote access policy	470
List	Typical phases of an incident response plan	470
List	Important elements for a BYOD policy	471
List	Sample phases of a system life cycle	474

Complete Tables and Lists from Memory

Print a copy of Appendix C, "Memory Tables," or at least the section for this chapter, and complete as many of the tables as possible from memory. Appendix D, "Memory Tables Answer Key," includes the completed tables and lists so you can check your work.

Define Key Terms

Define the following key terms from this chapter, and check your answers in the Glossary:

Password policy, data loss prevention, remote access policies, incident response policies, BYOD policies, acceptable use policy (AUP), safety procedures, privileged user agreement (PUA), on-boarding/off-boarding procedures, licensing restrictions, international export controls, non-disclosure agreement (NDA), system life cycle

Additional Resources

Information Security Policy Templates: https://www.sans.org/security-resources/policies

Export of Cryptography from the United States: https://en.wikipedia.org/wiki/Export_of_cryptography_from_the_United_States

Review Questions

The answers to these review questions are in Appendix A, "Answers to Review Questions."

1. Which is not a typical best practice found in a password policy?
   - a. Password expiration
   - b. Use of uppercase and lowercase letters only
   - c. Password uniqueness
   - d. No usage of proper names
2. Which is not an area typically targeted by a data loss prevention policy?
   - a. Cloud level
   - b. Network level
   - c. Client level
   - d. Storage level
3. An incident response policy often ends with which phase?
   - a. Prepare
   - b. Contain
   - c. Review

d. Eradicate

4. What should you follow closely when installing new network equipment?
   a. YouTube videos
   b. Certified training courses
   c. The installation and maintenance guides
   d. IETF guidelines

5. Which agreement would need to be read carefully and signed by a network administrator (not an end user in the Sales department)?
   a. AUP
   b. NDA
   c. PUA
   d. Vacation policy

6. What is often the last stage of a system life cycle used in the network?
   a. Phase-out
   b. Disposal
   c. Support
   d. Development

After completion of this chapter, you will be able to answer the following questions:

- What are the elements in a structured troubleshooting model?
- What common physical layer troubleshooting issues might you encounter?
- What potential Layer 2 issues are you most likely to face when troubleshooting a network containing Ethernet switches?
- Aside from routing protocol troubleshooting, what Layer 3 troubleshooting issues are common in a routed network?
- How do characteristics unique to wireless networks impact your troubleshooting of a network containing wireless access points?

CHAPTER 14

Network Troubleshooting

As you perform your day-to-day tasks of administering a network, a significant percentage of your time will be dedicated to resolving network issues. Whether the issues that you are troubleshooting were reported by an end user or were issues you discovered, you need an effective plan to respond to them. Specifically, you need a systematic approach to clearly articulate the issue, gather information about the issue, hypothesize the underlying cause of the issue, validate your hypothesis, create an action plan, implement that action plan, observe results, and document your resolution. Without a plan, your efforts might be inefficient, as you try one thing after another, possibly causing other issues in the process.

Although your troubleshooting efforts can most definitely benefit from a structured approach, realize that troubleshooting is part art and part science. Specifically, your intuition and instincts play a huge role in isolating an issue. Of course, those skills are developed over time and come with experience and exposure to more and more scenarios.

To help you start developing, or continue honing, your troubleshooting skills, this chapter begins by presenting you with a formalized troubleshooting methodology, which can act as a guide for addressing most any network issue. Then the remainder of this chapter presents you with a collection of common network issues to consider in your real-world troubleshooting efforts (and issues to consider on the Network+ exam).

These common network issues are broken down into the following categories: physical layer issues, data link layer issues, network layer issues, and wireless network issues.

Foundation Topics

Troubleshooting Basics

Troubleshooting network issues is implicit in the responsibilities of a network administrator. Such issues could arise as a result of human error (for example, a misconfiguration), equipment failure, software bugs, or traffic patterns (for example, high utilization or a network being under attack by malicious traffic).

Many network issues can be successfully resolved using a variety of approaches. This section begins by introducing you to troubleshooting fundamentals. Then you are presented with a structured troubleshooting methodology you should know for the Network+ exam.

Troubleshooting Fundamentals

The process of troubleshooting, at its essence, is the process of responding to a problem report (sometimes in the form of a *trouble ticket*), diagnosing the underlying cause of the problem, and resolving the problem. Although you normally think of the troubleshooting process beginning when a user reports an issue, realize that through effective network monitoring, you might detect a situation that could become a troubleshooting issue and resolve that situation before it impacts users.

After an issue is reported, the first step toward resolution is clearly defining the issue. After you have a clearly defined troubleshooting target, you can begin gathering information related to that issue. Based on the information collected, you might be able to better define the issue. Then you hypothesize the likely causes of the issue. Evaluation of these likely causes leads to the identification of the suspected underlying root cause of an issue.

After a suspected underlying cause is identified, you define approaches to resolve an issue and select what you consider to be the best approach. Sometimes the best approach to resolving an issue cannot be implemented immediately. For example, a piece of equipment might need replacing. However, implementing such an approach during working hours might disrupt a business's workflow. In such situations, a troubleshooter might use a temporary fix until a permanent fix can be put in place.

As a personal example, when helping troubleshoot a connectivity issue for a resort hotel at a major theme park, my coworkers and I discovered that a modular Ethernet switch had an issue causing Spanning Tree Protocol (STP) to fail, resulting in a Layer 2 loop. This loop flooded the network with traffic, preventing the hotel from issuing keycards for guest rooms. The underlying cause was clear. Specifically, the

Ethernet switch had a bad module. However, the time was about 4:00 p.m., a peak time for guest registration. So, instead of immediately replacing the faulty module, we disconnected one of the redundant links, thus breaking the Layer 2 loop. The logic was that it was better to have the network function at this time without STP than for the network to experience an even longer outage while the bad module was replaced. Late that night, someone came back to the switch and swapped out the module, resolving the underlying cause while minimizing user impact.

Consider Figure 14-1, which depicts a simplified model of the troubleshooting steps previously described. This simplified model consists of three steps:

Step 1 Problem report

Step 2 Problem diagnosis

Step 3 Problem resolution

Figure 14-1 Simplified Troubleshooting Flow

Of these three steps, the majority of a troubleshooter's efforts are spent in the *problem diagnosis* step. Table 14-1 describes key components of this diagnosis step.

Table 14-1 Steps to Diagnose a Problem

Step	Description
Gather information.	Because a typical problem report lacks sufficient information to give a troubleshooter insight into a problem's underlying cause, the troubleshooter should collect additional information, perhaps using network maintenance tools or interviewing impacted users.
Duplicate the problem, if possible.	Testing to see if you can duplicate the problem is often a key step in problem diagnosis.
Question users.	Although it can be difficult to gather information from your end users, this is often critical in correctly pinpointing the exact problem. Oftentimes, finding out user actions prior to the problem is critical.
Identify symptoms.	What are the actual symptoms the problem has created.
Determine if anything has changed.	Perhaps your end users will provide valuable clues if they accurately indicate what changes they might have made to systems.
Approach multiple problems individually.	Unfortunately, you might discover there are multiple issues. Be sure to approach each one individually.

Structured Troubleshooting Methodology

Troubleshooting skills vary from administrator to administrator. Therefore, although most troubleshooting approaches include the collection and analysis of information, elimination of potential causes, hypothesis of likely causes, and testing of the suspected cause, different troubleshooters might spend different amounts of time performing these tasks.

If a troubleshooter does not follow a structured approach, the temptation is to move between the previously listed troubleshooting tasks in a fairly random way, often based on instinct. Although such an approach might well lead to a problem resolution, it can become confusing to remember what you have tried and what you have not tried. Also, if another administrator comes to assist you, communicating to that other administrator the steps you have already gone through could be a challenge. Therefore, following a structured troubleshooting approach not only helps prevent you from trying the same thing more than once and inadvertently skipping a task but also aids in communicating to someone else the possibilities you already eliminated.

You might encounter a variety of structured troubleshooting methodologies in networking literature. However, for the Network+ exam, the methodology shown in Figure 14-2 is what you should memorize.

Key Topic

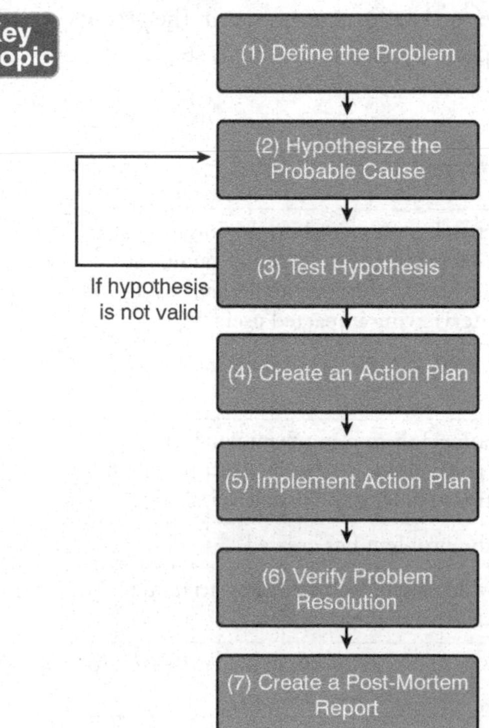

Figure 14-2 Structured Troubleshooting Approach

The following is an elaboration on this seven-step methodology:

Step 1 **Identify the problem.** Effective troubleshooting begins with a clear problem definition. This definition might include specific symptoms. Here's an example: "User A's computer is unable to communicate with server 1 (as verified by a ping test). However, user A can communicate with all other servers. Also, no other user seems to have an issue connecting to server 1." This problem definition might come from questioning the impacted user(s) and doing your own testing (for example, seeing if you can ping from user A's computer to server 1). If possible, determine whether anything has changed in the network (or in the computer) configuration. Also, find out whether this is a new installation that has never worked in the past.

Step 2 **Establish a theory of probable cause.** This is the point in the troubleshooting process where your experience and intuition can be extremely helpful because you are now going to brainstorm a list of possible causes. As you brainstorm, be sure to question the obvious. Also, think in terms of moving top-to-bottom within the OSI model, or bottom-to-top. Alternatively, you could use a divide-and-conquer approach. When examining your collected data (for example, output from the **ipconfig /all** command), question everything. For example, you might think that the issue described in step 1 could result from causes such as an ACL blocking traffic to or from the PC, a connectivity issue with the PC or server, or an incorrect IP address configuration on the PC. From your list of possible causes, select the one you consider the most likely. From the previous list, you might believe that an incorrect IP address configuration on the PC is the most likely cause of the problem. Specifically, you conclude that the issue is not related to connectivity because other PCs can get to the server, and user A's PC can get to other servers. Also, you conclude that it is more likely that user A's PC has a bad IP-address configuration than for an ACL to have been administratively added to the router to only block traffic between user A's PC and server 1.

Step 3 **Test the theory to determine the cause.** Before taking action on what you consider to be the most likely cause of a problem, do a *sanity check* on your theory. Would your hypothesized cause lead to the observed symptoms? In the example presented in the preceding steps, you might examine the subnet mask assigned to user A's computer and determine that it is incorrect. Specifically, the subnet mask makes user A's computer think that server 1 is on the same subnet as user A's computer. As a result, user A's computer does not forward traffic to its default gateway when attempting to reach server 1. If your hypothesis is technically sound, you can proceed to step 4. However, if you notice a flaw in your logic, you need to formulate an alternate hypothesis. The formation of an alternate hypothesis might involve escalating the problem to someone more familiar with the device(s) in question.

Step 4 **Establish a plan of action to resolve the problem and identify potential effects**. Now that you have confirmed that your theory makes sense technically, the time has come to develop an action plan. If time permits, you should document your action plan. The documentation of your action plan can be used as a *back-out plan* if your hypothesis is incorrect. In the example we have been building on throughout these steps, an action plan might be to change the subnet mask on user A's computer from 255.255.0.0 to 255.255.255.0.

Step 5 **Implement the solution or escalate as necessary**. Based on your documented plan of action, you should schedule an appropriate time to implement your action plan. The selection of an appropriate time is a balance between the severity of a problem and the impact your action plan will have on other users. Sometimes, when attempting to implement your action plan, you realize that you do not have sufficient administrative privileges to perform a task in your action plan. In such cases, you should escalate the issue to someone with appropriate administrative rights. In this example, changing the subnet mask on one computer should not impact any other devices. So, you might immediately make the configuration change on user A's computer.

Step 6 **Verify full system functionality and, if applicable, implement preventative measures**. After implementing your action plan, you need to verify that the symptoms listed in your original problem definition are gone. Also, attempt to determine whether your action plan has caused any other issues on the network. A mistake many troubleshooters make at this point is believing that the issue has been resolved because the specific symptom (or symptoms) they were looking for is gone. However, the user who originally reported the issue might still be having a problem. Therefore, troubleshooters should live by this mantra: "A problem isn't fixed until the user believes it's fixed." So, you should always get confirmation from the person reporting an issue that, from her perspective, the reported issue has indeed been resolved. In this example, you could attempt to ping server 1 from user A. If the ping is successful, check with user A to see whether she agrees that the problem is resolved.

Step 7 **Document findings, actions, and outcomes**. A *post-mortem* report is a document that describes the reported issue, its underlying causes, and what was done to resolve the issue. This report might be useful when troubleshooting similar issues in the future.

Keep in mind when working your way through the previous steps that you might encounter an issue that you do not have sufficient information to solve. When that happens, you might need to further research the issue yourself. However, if time is of the essence, you might need to immediately escalate the issue to someone else within your organization, to an equipment vendor, or to an outside consultant.

Physical Layer Troubleshooting

Layer 1 (the physical layer) of the OSI model is foundational to all the other layers. As a result, if Layer 1 isn't functioning, none of the upper layers will function properly. Table 14-2 presents a collection of common Layer 1 issues.

> **NOTE** Many of these issues have been discussed in previous chapters.

Table 14-2 Common Layer 1 Troubleshooting Issues

Issue	Description
Bad cables or connectors	Faulty cables (with electrical characteristics preventing a successful transmission) or faulty connectors (which do not properly make a connection) can prevent successful data transmission at Layer 1. A *bad cable* could simply be an incorrect category of cable being used for a specific purpose. For example, perhaps you interconnected two 1000BASE-TX devices using a Cat 5 cable (instead of a Cat 6 or higher cable), resulting in corrupted data. See Chapter 4, "Ethernet Technology," for a listing of Ethernet types and their corresponding supported cable types. Bent pins in a connector or incorrect pinouts could also be the issue.
Bad port	A port may be bad on your network device. Oftentimes, you can easily confirm this using the network connection LED and status indicators.
Opens and shorts	An *open* is a broken strand of copper, preventing current from flowing through a circuit. However, a *short* occurs when two copper connectors touch each other, resulting in current flowing through that short rather than the attached electrical circuit because the short has lower resistance.
Splitting pairs in a cable	An unshielded twisted-pair (UTP) cable consists of eight separate copper leads. However, only four of those eight leads are used for data (two transmit leads and two receive leads). This results in four unused leads. Some installers use those four extra leads to support a second Ethernet connection on a single UTP cable. Although such an approach can function, nonstandard wires are being used for connecting the second Ethernet connection. Therefore, you should be aware of any nonstandard pinouts used in the network that you are troubleshooting.

Issue	Description
dB loss	The signal power of a data transmission might be degraded to the point where the transmission is not correctly interpreted by a receiving device. This loss of signal power, called a *decibel loss* (dB loss), could result from exceeding the distance limitation of a copper or fiber cable.
Transposed Tx/Rx leads	Some Ethernet switches support medium dependent interface crossover (MDIX), which allows a switch port to properly configure its leads as transmit (Tx) or receive (Rx) leads. You can interconnect such switches with a straight-through cable (as opposed to a crossover cable). However, if a network device does not support MDIX, it needs an appropriate cable (that is, a crossover cable) to allow its Tx leads to connect to the Rx leads on a connected device, and vice versa. Therefore, care must be taken when selecting cable types interconnecting network components. More information on crossover cables and MDIX can be found in Chapter 3, "Network Components."
Cable placement	Because copper cables are subject to electromagnetic interference (EMI), you should arrange cables to minimize interference. Ideally, Ethernet cables should not be placed in close proximity with high-voltage cables, generators, motors, or radio transmitters. For example, when running cables between buildings via underground conduit, you should ideally place network cabling in a conduit separate from the electrical cables.
Distance limitations exceeded	If Ethernet devices are interconnected using a cable that exceeds the Ethernet distance limitations for the cable type, a digital transmission between those devices can be degraded to the point where the receiving equipment is unable to correctly interpret the transmission. Attenuation is the technical category for this problem. Therefore, network designs should consider distances between devices.
Crosstalk	Crosstalk can occur when an analog connection creates an electromagnetic field around its conductors, inducing its waveforms on a nearby analog connection. This phenomenon is most commonly experienced in an analog phone call. Crosstalk can be minimized by using a higher category of cabling because higher categories of cables better limit the radiation of electromagnetic waves.
Speed/duplex mismatch	Speed and duplex mismatches can be tricky to troubleshoot in the network, especially considering that connectivity is often maintained, just at unacceptable levels.
Transceiver mismatch	Transceivers must be selected carefully to ensure compatibility with the cable type and wavelengths in use.

Physical Layer Troubleshooting: Scenario

To practice your physical layer troubleshooting skills, consider the network diagram presented in Figure 14-3.

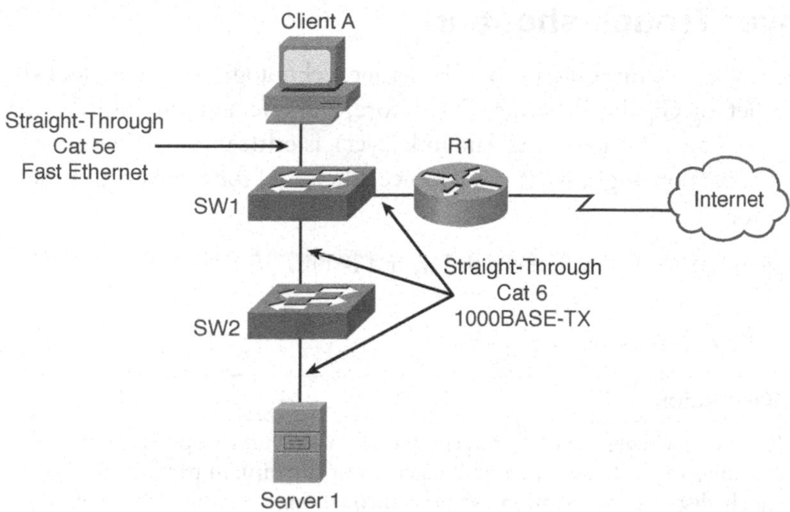

Figure 14-3 Physical Layer Troubleshooting: Sample Topology

Assume that both switches in Figure 14-3 are capable of auto-negotiating Ethernet speeds of 10, 100, or 1000Mbps. Also, assume the switches do not support MDIX. Based on the provided information, take a moment (before reading on) and identify what you believe to be a Layer 1 issue in the topology.

Physical Layer Troubleshooting: Solution

In the topology shown in Figure 14-3, notice that switches SW1 and SW2 are interconnected with a straight-through cable. Also, recall that neither switch supports MDIX. As a result, the ports interconnecting the two switches have their Tx leads interconnected and their Rx leads interconnected. As a result, no communication is possible. The resolution to such a scenario is to replace the straight-through Cat 6 cable between SW1 and SW2 with a crossover Cat 6 cable.

Physical copper cable issues could include shorts, opens, incorrect cabling, EMI/RFI, attenuation, crosstalk, bad connector, bad cable, or using too long of a run.

Physical fiber cable issues could include attenuation, connector mismatch, wavelength mismatch, fiber-type mismatch, dirty connector, extreme bends in fiber, or trying to use too long of a fiber cable based on the specifications for that fiber.

You can use the testing tools discussed in Chapter 11, "Network Management," to troubleshoot cable-related problems for copper and fiber.

Data Link Layer Troubleshooting

Most enterprise LANs rely on some form of Ethernet technology (for example, Ethernet, Fast Ethernet, or Gigabit Ethernet). Therefore, an understanding of Ethernet switch operation, at Layer 2 (that is, the data link layer), is critical to troubleshooting many LAN issues. You might want to reference Chapter 4 for a review of Ethernet switch operation.

Table 14-3 presents a collection of common Layer 2 issues.

Table 14-3 Common Layer 2 Troubleshooting Issues

Issue	Description
Power failure	Ethernet switches are often not connected to a redundant power source (for example, an electrical outlet with a generator backup), in part due to the widely dispersed installation locations throughout a building (for example, in wiring closets or in a mechanical room). As a result, you might want to equip your Ethernet switches with an uninterruptable power supply (UPS). See Chapter 12, "Network Security," for a comparison of a UPS and a standby power supply (SPS).
Bad module	A modular switch gives you the flexibility to connect a variety of media types and speeds to the switch through the use of different modules. Examples of these modules include gigabit interface converter (GBIC) and small form-factor pluggable (SFP) modules. These modular interfaces can be swapped out during your troubleshooting, as opposed to swapping out an entire switch.
Layer 2 loop	Chapter 4 discussed issues resulting from Layer 2 loops, including MAC address table corruption and broadcast storms. You also read about how to mitigate these issues with Spanning Tree Protocol (STP). However, STP can fail (as illustrated by my personal example, which you read about at the beginning of this chapter). Or, STP might be functioning suboptimally, because a root bridge was automatically selected rather than being specified, resulting in a suboptimal path. So, you should be able to examine your Ethernet switches, when troubleshooting, and determine the STP roles of your network's switches and switch ports.
Port configuration	Common settings for Ethernet switch ports include speed, duplex, and MDIX. Mismatched parameters between devices could result in slow communication (in the case of a duplex mismatch) or in no communication (in the case of a speed mismatch or incorrect MDIX settings).
VLAN configuration	In Chapter 4, you read about virtual LANs (VLANs) that are broadcast domains and represent a single subnet. Several troubleshooting issues could result from a VLAN misconfiguration on an Ethernet switch. Keep in mind that all devices belonging to the same VLAN should be assigned IP addresses in the same subnet. Also, if you want traffic to flow between VLANs, that traffic has to be routed.

Data Link Layer Troubleshooting: Scenario

Based on your knowledge of an Ethernet switch (a common example of a data link layer device), consider the following troubleshooting scenario. The network depicted in Figure 14-4 is having an issue. Specifically, client A is not able to communicate with server 1. Based on the diagram, what do you consider to be the most likely cause?

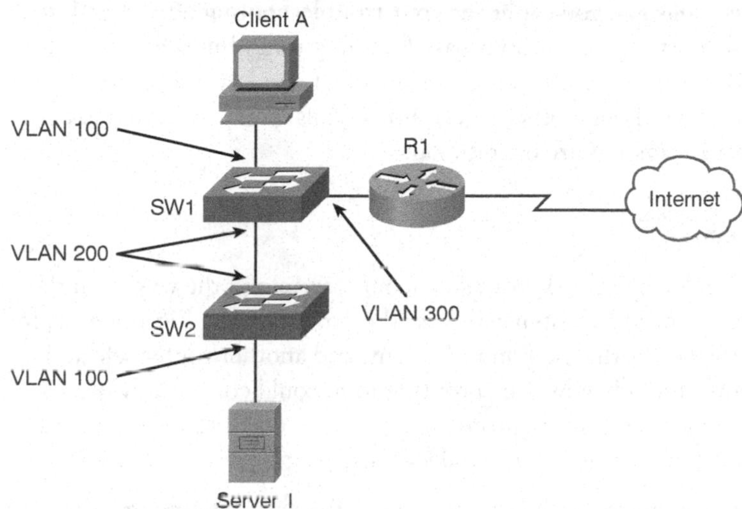

Figure 14-4 Data Link Layer Troubleshooting: Sample Topology

After determining what you believe to be the underlying cause, check your answer with the following solution.

Data Link Layer Troubleshooting: Solution

Even though client A and server 1, as shown in Figure 14-4, are on the same VLAN (VLAN 100), there is no VLAN 100 traffic flowing between switches SW1 and SW2. Specifically, the connection linking SW1 and SW2 only carries traffic for VLAN 200. A couple of solutions exist.

One solution is to change the ports on switches SW1 and SW2 to both belong to VLAN 100. Another solution is to configure an IEEE 802.1Q trunk to interconnect SW1 and SW2, because a trunk can simultaneously carry traffic for multiple VLANs.

Network Layer Troubleshooting

When you're troubleshooting connectivity issues for an IP-based network, the network layer (Layer 3) is often an appropriate place to begin your troubleshooting efforts. For example, if you are experiencing connectivity issues between two hosts on a network, you could check Layer 3 by pinging from one host to another. If the pings are successful, you can conclude that the issue resides above Layer 3 (Layers 4–7). However, if the pings fail, you can focus your troubleshooting efforts on Layers 1–3. The rationale for this conclusion is based on ping using Internet Control Message Protocol (ICMP), which is a Layer 4 protocol. If one Layer 4 protocol is functioning correctly (even though other Layer 4 protocols might be having issues), you can conclude that Layers 1–3 are operational.

Layer 3 Data Structures

As traffic is routed through a network, routers encountered along the way from the source to the destination need consistency in how they route traffic. For example, if one router selected the best path based on hop count, and another router selected the best path based on a link's bandwidth, a routing loop could conceivably occur. Fortunately, having a common routing protocol configured on all routers within a topology helps ensure consistency in routing decisions.

That is not to say that a topology could not have more than one routing protocol. You could strategically redistribute routes between different routing protocols. Also, static routes could be used in conjunction with dynamic routing protocols. However, care must be taken in environments with redundant links and multiple routing protocols to avoid potential routing loops.

To better troubleshoot specific dynamic routing protocols, let's first generically consider how dynamic routing protocols' data structures interact with a router's IP routing table.

Figure 14-5 shows the interaction between the data structures of an IP routing protocol and a router's IP routing table. Realize, however, that not all routing protocols maintain their own data structures. For example, RIP is a routing protocol that works directly with an IP routing table in a router, rather than maintaining a separate data structure.

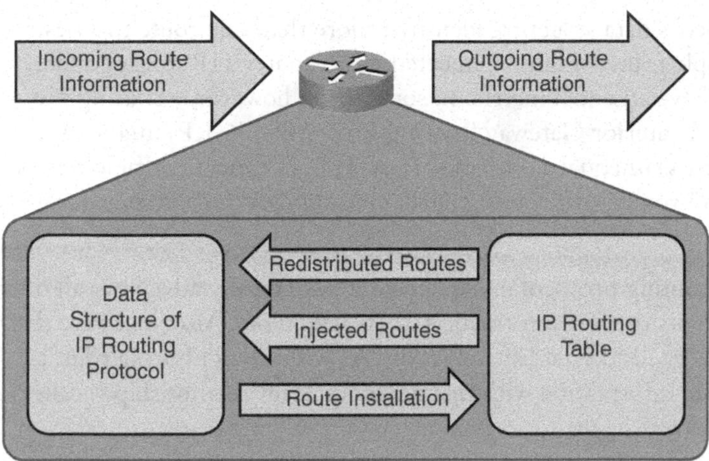

Figure 14-5 Interaction Between IP Routing Protocol Data Structures and IP Routing Tables

As a router receives route information from a neighboring router, that information is stored in the data structures of the IP routing protocol (if the IP routing protocol uses data structures). A data structure might also be populated by the local router. For example, a router might be configured for route redistribution where route information is redistributed by a routing information source (for example, a dynamic routing protocol, a static route, or a connected route). Also, the router might be configured to have specific interfaces participate in an IP routing protocol.

The data structure analyzes all the information it receives to select the best route to a certain network. This best route is determined by looking for the route with the best metric. The data structure of an IP routing protocol then injects that best route into the router's IP routing table if that same route information has not already been learned by a more believable routing source. Specifically, different routing protocols have different administrative distances (AD). An administrative distance of a routing protocol can be thought of as the believability of that routing protocol. As an example, Routing Information Protocol (RIP) has an AD of 120, and Open Shortest Path First (OSPF) has an AD of 110. Therefore, if both RIP and OSPF had knowledge of a route to a specific network, the OSPF route would be injected into the router's IP routing table because OSPF has a more believable AD (lower value). Therefore, the best route selected by an IP routing protocol's data structure is only a candidate to be injected into a router's IP routing table.

NOTE Chapter 6, "Routing IP Packets," provides additional information about the ADs of various routing protocols.

If an IP routing protocol's data structure identifies more than one route to a destination network, multiple routes might be injected into a router's IP routing table if those multiple routes have an equal metric. In some cases, however, a routing protocol such as Enhanced Interior Gateway Routing Protocol (EIGRP) might support load balancing across unequal-cost paths. In such an instance, multiple routes might be injected into a router's IP routing table, even though those routes have different metrics.

Depending on the IP routing protocol in use, a router periodically advertises all of its routes, or updates to its routing information, to its neighbors. Also, be aware that some routing protocols need to establish a relationship with a neighboring router before exchanging route information with that neighbor. This relationship is called an *adjacency* or a *neighborship*.

Common Layer 3 Troubleshooting Issues

Effectively troubleshooting Layer 3 issues, as suggested by the previous discussion, largely relies on your understanding of various routing protocols. Therefore, for the real world, you must familiarize yourself with the subtle details of the routing protocols running in your network.

However, the Network+ exam deemphasizes the intricacies of specific routing protocols, instead focusing on more generic Layer 3 troubleshooting issues. Table 14-4 describes examples of those issues.

Table 14-4 Common Layer 3 Troubleshooting Issues

Issue	Description
Mismatched MTU	Router interfaces have a parameter called the maximum transmission unit (MTU) that defines the largest packet size the interface will forward. For example, a 1500-byte packet could not be forwarded via a router interface with an MTU of 1470 bytes. A router attempts to fragment a packet that is too big unless the packet has its "don't fragment" (DF) bit set. If a packet exceeds an interface's MTU and has its DF bit set, the router drops the packet. Normally, the router responds to the sender with an ICMP message indicating why the packet was dropped. However, if a router is configured to not respond to such a condition by sending an Internet Control Message Protocol (ICMP) message, the packet is dropped without the sender being notified. Such a router is called a *black-hole router*. You can use the traceroute utility (as described in Chapter 10, "Command-Line Tools") to help locate a black-hole router.

Issue	Description
Incorrect subnet mask	When one host attempts to communicate with another host on the same subnet, the sending host sends an ARP request in an attempt to determine the MAC address of the destination host, rather than forwarding traffic to the sending host's default gateway. Therefore, if a host has an incorrect subnet mask, it could incorrectly conclude that another host is on its local subnet, when in reality the other host is on a remote subnet. As a result, the remote host is unreachable from the perspective of the sending host.
Incorrect default gateway	If a host has an incorrect default gateway configuration, traffic from that host is not forwarded off that host's local subnet.
Duplicate IP address	Hosts on a subnet should have unique IP addresses. If two hosts are configured with the same IP address, unpredictable traffic patterns for those hosts can occur.
Incorrect DNS configuration	Because hosts often use Domain Name System (DNS) to resolve domain names to IP addresses, if a host has an incorrect DNS configuration, that host will be unable to, for example, browse the Internet using domain names (as opposed to IP addresses).
Duplicate MAC address	Although it's rarer than a duplicate IP address on the network, you could experience a duplicate MAC address. This is typically caused by a software configuration of MAC addresses.
Expired IP address	Perhaps a leased DHCP address has expired for a workstation.
Exhausted DHCP scope	Although it's rare, you may have a DHCP scope that has run out of addresses to lease; this could be the result of a DHCP exhaustion type of attack.
Rogue DHCP server	This security concern could certainly cause troubleshooting headaches on the network due to the incorrect IP configurations that could result. This is often the result of users bringing in their own devices, either maliciously or accidentally.
Untrusted SSL certificate	If using certificates for authentication, you might have an issue with the SSL certificate that is preventing such authentication.
Incorrect time	Because many network configurations rely on the correct time, you might have problems in the network due to a workstation, server, or network appliance with the wrong time set.
Blocked TCP/UDP ports	Perhaps your trouble ticket is the result of blocked TCP or UDP ports. This is often the result of a misconfigured security device in the network path.
Incorrect host-based firewall settings	Another security area that could cause problems is host-based firewalls.
Incorrect ACL settings	Access control lists can have a direct effect on network traffic and could be the cause of one or many trouble tickets.
Unresponsive service	A service that has failed in the network is another common source of problems.

Network Layer Troubleshooting: Scenario

A common network layer troubleshooting issue, as described in Chapter 5, "IPv4 and IPv6 Addresses," is a host with an IP address that is not valid for the subnet to which the host is physically connected. Using your subnetting skills, determine which host (client A or server 1) in Figure 14-6 is assigned an incorrect IP address, assuming the router interface's IP address is correct.

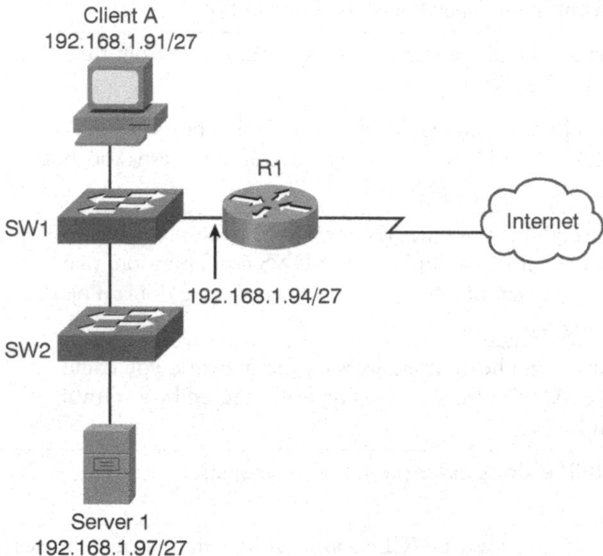

Figure 14-6 Data Link Layer Troubleshooting: Sample Topology

Network Layer Troubleshooting: Solution

The network shown in Figure 14-6 has subnetted the 192.168.1.0/24 network using a 27-bit subnet mask (255.255.255.224). To determine which client PC is assigned an IP address outside of its local VLAN, you need to determine the subnets created by the 27-bit subnet mask applied to the 192.168.1.0/24 network:

Step 1 The interesting octet for a 27-bit subnet mask is the fourth one because it is the last octet to contain a 1 in the 27-bit subnet mask (11111111.11111111.11111111.11100000, which could alternately be written as 255.255.255.224).

Step 2 The decimal value of the third octet in the subnet mask is 224. Therefore, the block size is 32 (that is, 256 – 224 = 32).

Step 3 The first subnet is 192.168.1.0/27 (192.168.1.0/27 with the three borrowed bits in the third octet set to 0).

Step 4 Beginning with the first subnet of 192.168.1.0/27 and counting by the block size of 32 in the interesting octet yields the following subnets:

192.168.1.0/27

192.168.1.32/27

192.168.1.64/27

192.168.1.96/27

192.168.1.128/27

192.168.1.160/27

192.168.1.192/27

192.168.1.224/27

Based on the IP address of the router interface (192.168.1.94/27) and the previous list of subnets, you can determine that the router's interface is in the 192.168.1.64/27 subnet. Similarly, you can determine the subnet of client A to be 192.168.1.64/27, and the subnet of server 1 to be 192.168.1.96/27. As a result, you can conclude that the host with an incorrect IP address is server 1 because its IP address is in a different subnet than the router interface's subnet.

Network layer–related issues could also include duplicate IPs, speed and duplex mismatch, routing loops, incorrect IP, incorrect default gateway, network interface card (NIC) hardware failure, misconfigured Dynamic Host Configuration Protocol (DHCP), misconfigured DNS, incorrect cable or port, incomplete routing tables, NIC misconfiguration, or malware running on the computer that's preventing normal network behavior by the computer. Many of these issues can be verified using the tools and commands previously discussed in this book. In a production network, you would isolate the fault by testing individual components and then correct the problem once it is identified.

If performance or access is limited, it may also be due to a technical control that is in place on the network. Be sure to consider filters, traffic shaping, and firewalls that are in your control as part of the troubleshooting that is being done.

Wireless Troubleshooting

Troubleshooting wireless networks can require a variety of skill sets. For example, some troubleshooting scenarios might require an understanding of antenna theory and the radio frequency spectrum. However, the Network+ exam focuses on more common wireless issues, as presented in Table 14-5.

NOTE Chapter 8, "Wireless Technologies," discusses wireless networks in detail.

Table 14-5 Common Wireless Troubleshooting Issues

Issue	Description
RFI	Wireless communication can be interrupted because of radio frequency interference (RFI). Common RFI sources that impact wireless networks include 2.4GHz cordless phones, microwave ovens, baby monitors, and game consoles.
Signal strength	The received signal strength indicator (RSSI) value measures the power of a wireless signal. An RSSI value varies based on distance from a wireless antenna and physical objects interfering with line-of-sight communication with a wireless antenna (for example, drywall, metal file cabinets, and elevator shafts). Some wireless networks automatically drop their wireless transmission rate when an RSSI value drops below a certain value.
Misconfiguration of wireless parameters	A variety of wireless parameters must match between a wireless client and a wireless access point (AP) for communication to occur. For example, the client needs to be using a wireless standard supported by the wireless AP (for example, IEEE 802.11a/b/g/n). Wireless channels must also match. However, wireless clients usually automatically set their channel based on the wireless AP's channel. Encryption standards must match, or you have a security type mismatch. For example, a wireless client using WPA would not successfully communicate with a wireless AP using WPA2. In addition, the service set identifier (SSID) of a wireless AP must be selected by the wireless client. In many cases, a wireless AP broadcasts its SSID, and a wireless client can select that SSID from a listing of visible SSIDs. In other cases, a wireless AP does not broadcast its SSID, thus requiring a wireless client to have a matching SSID manually configured. Finally, and the most common, is that the wrong passphrase is being used by the client.
Latency	Wireless networks can experience more delay than their wired counterparts. One reason for the increased delay is the use of carrier-sense multiple access/collision avoidance (CSMA/CA) in WLANs, which introduces a random delay before transmitting data, in an attempt to avoid collisions. Another, yet similar, reason for the increased delay is the fact that all wireless devices associated with a single wireless AP are in the same collision domain, introducing the possibility of collisions (retransmissions), which can increase delay.
Multiple paths of propagation	An electromagnetic waveform cannot pass through a perfect conductor. Admittedly, perfect conductors do not exist in most office environments. However, very good conductors, such as metal file cabinets, are commonplace in offices. As a result, if the waveform of a wireless transmission encounters one of these conductive objects, most of the signal bounces off the object, creating multiple paths (modes) of propagation. These multiple modes of propagation can cause data (specifically, bits) to arrive at uneven intervals, possibly corrupting data. This problem is similar to multimode delay distortion, which is seen in multimode fiber-optic cabling.

Issue	Description
Incorrect AP placement	Wireless APs should be strategically located in a building to provide sufficient coverage to all desired coverage areas. However, the coverage areas of wireless APs using overlapping channels should not overlap. To maintain coverage between coverage areas, you should have overlapping coverage areas among wireless APs using nonoverlapping channels (for example, channels 1, 6, and 11 for wireless networks using the 2.4GHz band of frequencies). A common design recommendation is that overlapping coverage areas (using nonoverlapping channels) should have an overlap of approximately 10%–15%. Also, keep in mind the use of the 5GHz band, which offers many more nonoverlapping channels.
Refraction	Refraction is the bending of a wave when it enters a medium where the speed is different as covered in Chapter 3, "Network Components." It is important to track possible refraction when designing your wireless network because if a signal changes direction in traveling from sender to receiver, it can cause lower data rates and high retries. This can lead to an overall lessening of capacity.
Absorption	This occurs when a material is converting the signal's energy into heat. Varied materials have different absorption rates. Wood and concrete, for example, can make a significant impact on signal strength because of how much they absorb the radio waves.

Wireless Network Troubleshooting: Scenario

As a practice troubleshooting scenario for wireless networks, consider Figure 14-7. Based on the topology provided, can you spot a design issue with the wireless network?

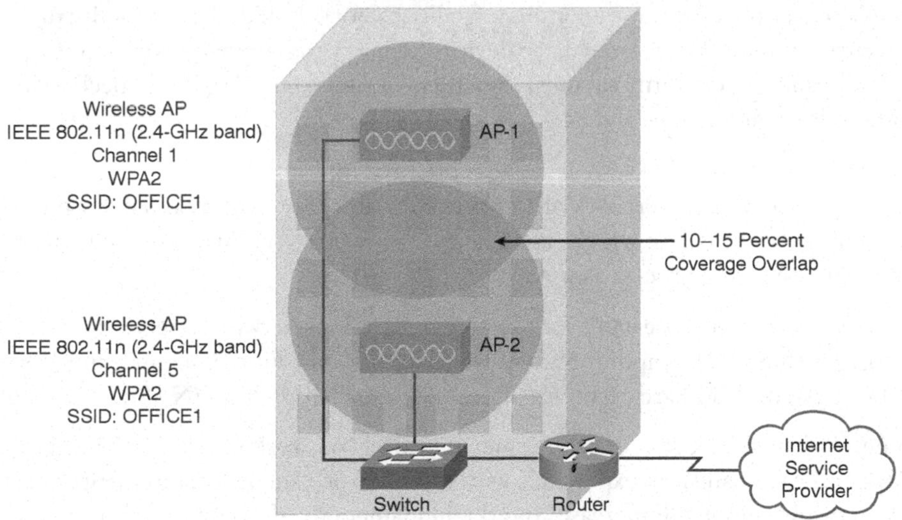

Figure 14-7 Wireless Network Troubleshooting: Sample Topology

Wireless Network Troubleshooting: Solution

The wireless network presented in Figure 14-7 has two wireless APs. Although these wireless APs have a matching wireless standard, encryption type, and SSID, the channels being used (channels 1 and 5) interfere with one another. Recall from Chapter 8 that channels in the 2.4GHz band need at least five channels of separation (for overlapping coverage areas), whereas the channels used in this example only have four channels of separation. A fix for this issue is to assign AP-2 to channel 6, thus providing five channels of separation between AP-1 and AP-2.

A wireless analyzer may be needed to identify problems such as signal loss, overlapping or mismatched channels, unacceptable signal-to-noise ratios, rogue APs, and power levels. Breaking down a problem into smaller pieces allows you to identify the fault domain or the area that is causing the problem. For example, if a user cannot access the wireless network, the pieces involved may be the user connecting to an incorrect SSID or problems existing with the AP, the switch, the WLC (Wireless LAN Controller), the RADIUS server, the AD server, or the user account and password itself. By testing the individual components where possible, you can isolate and then correct the problem.

Specialized Networks

In special-purpose networks, it may take some time to become familiar with the devices on that network. For example, a supervisory control and data acquisition (SCADA) network is used for the control of remote equipment and to monitor that equipment. This may be part of an industrial control system (ICS) that is used to manage a power plant or water treatment facility. Networks like these with distributed control systems (DCSs) may have devices such as programmable logic controllers (PLCs) and remote terminal units that are proprietary and may take specialized training to learn and troubleshoot.

In other specialized networks, such as those built for multimedia, video teleconference (VTC), and Voice over IP (VoIP), issues such as latency, jitter, and delay may cause applications to fail, in which case quality of service (QoS) may need to be part of the troubleshooting process as well.

Some networks are purpose-built for the communications between a server and its disk storage. IP Small Computer System Interface (iSCSI), Fibre Channel, and Network File System (NFS) are examples of network-attached storage (NAS).

Each network may have special requirements, and as you work with a specialized network and have hands-on experience with that network and its requirements, your ability to troubleshoot will increase, and the fundamentals of troubleshooting can be applied to these specialized networks.

Real-World Case Study

Bob is an employee at Acme, Inc. He is on a company-issued laptop that is connected wirelessly to the corporate HQ network. He is having a problem accessing a server that is located at one of the remote branch offices.

Because Bob is able to access the Internet and other local servers at the headquarters site, we can rule out issues with the local wireless or authentication because he is currently logged in.

Upon further investigation, it is discovered that Bob cannot ping the IP address of the remote server he is trying to reach. With additional testing, it is also determined that Bob cannot ping the IP address of the router at the remote branch office.

The routing table on the local HQ router is looked at, and the route to the remote site is in the routing table, but the local router cannot ping the remote router's IP address. After contacting the primary service provider for the WAN connectivity, Acme learned that the provider had an outage that was causing the problem with the connectivity over the provider's MPLS network.

Acme's fault-tolerant scenario should have triggered a VPN to be created using the Internet over the alternate service provider because of MPLS WAN connectivity failing.

Acme is going to change its router configuration to actively monitor the remote branch office routers so that in the future if there is a failure on the primary network, the VPN over the Internet to those branch offices will kick in to provide the fault-tolerant connectivity they are supposed to have.

Troubleshooting Scenarios

When working with networks and systems, you must often use both your knowledge and skills regarding several technologies, as well as apply critical thinking, to solve a problem or implement a solution. The following scenarios will help reinforce many of the topics you read about in this book, and will provide additional insights about how you can integrate the technology and troubleshooting techniques.

Scenario 1

The user at PC2 has called the help desk. Internet access is slow intermittently throughout the day. IP phone voice quality is also unacceptable during those same times periods. A technician has been asked to respond. The following are the steps taken by the technician, along with the reasoning for his actions.

From PC2, the command **ipconfig /all** was issued. Here is a partial output of the results:

```
FastEthernet adapter 1:

    Description . . . . . . . . . . . : Intel(R) Network Adapter
    Physical Address. . . . . . . . . : 68-17-29-C8-75-62
    DHCP Enabled. . . . . . . . . . . : Yes
    IPv4 Address. . . . . . . . . . . : 192.168.1.74
    Subnet Mask . . . . . . . . . . . : 255.255.255.0
    Lease Obtained. . . . . . . . . . : Monday, March 9, 6:16:33 PM
    Lease Expires . . . . . . . . . . : Tuesday, March 10, 6:16:36
PM
    Default Gateway . . . . . . . . . : 192.168.1.1
    DHCP Server . . . . . . . . . . . : 192.168.1.1
    DNS Servers . . . . . . . . . . . : 8.8.8.8
```

R1's IP address on its Ethernet interface connected to SW1 port 7 is 192.168.1.1, and the output confirms that the customer has an valid IP address for the current network, as well as default gateway that is reachable on that same network. If *Dynamic Host Control Protocol* (DHCP) services were not working, the PC might have assigned itself an *Automatic Private IP Addressing* (APIPA) address (169.x.x.x).

The technician issued the following command from PC2:

```
PC2:\ >ping 192.168.1.1

Pinging 192.168.1.1 with 32 bytes of data:
Reply from 192.168.1.1: bytes=32 time=3ms TTL=64
Reply from 192.168.1.1: bytes=32 time=2ms TTL=64
Reply from 192.168.1.1: bytes=32 time=1ms TTL=64
Reply from 192.168.1.1: bytes=32 time=2ms TTL=64

Ping statistics for 192.168.1.1:
    Packets: Sent = 4, Received = 4, Lost = 0 (0% loss),
Approximate round trip times in milli-seconds:
    Minimum = 1ms, Maximum = 3ms, Average = 2ms
```

PC2 could ping the local default gateway. This confirms that switch port number 2 on SW1 is assigned to the same (and likely correct) VLAN as the default gateway. VLAN assignment is controlled at the switch port level. The fact that the user at PC2 has Internet connectivity at all is also an indicator that IP addressing and default gateway information are correct for PC2.

The technician used the **ping** command to test reachability to an Internet server and a loopback interface address on the R2, which is across the WAN. An IPv4 loopback interface with an IP address on a router can be used for reachability testing, in addition to assisting some protocols such as *Border Gateway Protocol* (BGP) to be fault tolerant by using this internal loopback interface for establishing neighbor relationships when multiple physical paths exist between neighbors. Because the pings were successful to the Internet and R2, that indicates that routing between site 1 and the Internet, and between site 1 and site 2, is in place and working. The routing was likely implemented through statically configured routes or an interior dynamic routing protocol such as *Routing Information Protocol version 2* (RIPv2), *Open Shortest Path First* (OSPF), or an external routing protocol such as BGP. The proprietary Cisco protocol *Enhanced Interior Gateway Routing Protocol* (EIGRP) and the open-standard BGP routing protocols both use an autonomous system number as an identifier. If the routers were using incorrect autonomous system numbers, that also could break routing due to the misconfiguration of the routing protocol on the router. Some older routing protocols such as RIPv2 (which is a distance-vector routing protocol) are slow to converge and might take several minutes before the rest of the network is aware of changes in the network, such as a new network that has been added or networks that have been removed. Upon closer inspection of port 2 on SW1 (which is being used to connect PC2 to the network), the output of a **show** command on that interface revealed the following (partial output shown):

```
FastEthernet0/2 is up, line protocol is up (connected)
   Hardware is Fast Ethernet, address is 000e.8300.c400
   (bia 000e.8300.c400)
   MTU 1500 bytes, BW 100000 Kbit, DLY 100 usec,
   reliability 255/255, txload 1/255, rxload 1/255
   Encapsulation ARPA, loopback not set
   Keepalive set (10 sec)
   Half-duplex, 100Mb/s, media type is 10/100BaseTX
   input flow-control is off, output flow-control is unsupported
   ARP type: ARPA, ARP Timeout 04:00:00
   Last input 00:00:00, output 00:00:00, output hang never
```

Based on this output, the duplex setting on SW1 port 2 is currently set to half duplex. On a switch, all the access ports should be set to full duplex if the devices connected to those ports also support full duplex, which allows the device to send and receive frames simultaneously, using one pair of wires for sending and another pair of wires for receiving. This indeed could cause a slowdown for the user at PC2 when the network is busy. The technician should use proper change control procedures to schedule and modify the configuration for SW1, change port 2 to full duplex, and ensure that PC2 is also configured for auto-negotiation of the speed and duplex (or is set to full duplex to match the switch port it is connected to). Part of the change control process involves documenting the proposed changes, including the reasons why they're being done and including a full backup of the configuration before changes are made. If the changes cause a negative impact to the whole switch, a rollback procedure should be planned for and used if necessary.

After the changes are implemented, testing and follow-up should occur. A baseline for the performance of PC2 could be created before the change, and then the testing could be done again after the change and compared against the baseline. If the user has a *Voice over IP* (VoIP) solution using the same connection to the switch, it is likely that some *quality of service* (QoS) is being implemented at Layer 2 specifically for the voice traffic. Both voice and video traffic are sensitive to time delays. QoS is often done at Layer 2 using *class of service* (CoS), which gives preferential treatment to the voice traffic so that, in the event of congestion on the network, applications like VoIP and video or other applications that use codecs or are sensitive to delays on the network can still perform well, while other protocols that are not as sensitive to delays are given less throughput on the network.

Scenario 2

The manager who is using PC6 at site 3 is accessing a SQL Server application and database that is running in site 1. Every Friday, he uses the server to generate reports. Occasionally, perhaps as often as once a month, the report times out, and the manager contacts a user at site 1 who can locally run that report for him and email him the results. The manager has escalated this as a problem that has been occurring for several months. A trouble ticket has been opened, and a technician has been asked to investigate the problem.

The technician discovered that the SQL Server database application was running on a virtualized computer at site 1, and that the virtualized computer was leveraging multiple types of *network-attached storage* (NAS), including an iSCSI target. iSCSI storage devices use an iSCSI *target* (which is providing the storage), and the customer or device that is using the iSCSI target uses an iSCSI *initiator*, which is usually a specialized adapter that can understand and send and receive iSCSI packets between itself and the iSCSI target over an IP network. Another type of network storage that the virtualized SQL server was using is Fibre Channel. Fibre Channel and iSCSI can both use Ethernet networks, and, if so, they often use frames larger than the default *maximum transmission unit* (MTU) of standard Ethernet. When this occurs, the switches supporting the communication need to be configured to support these oversized (jumbo) layer frames. The technician verified that the switches being used for the NAS had been configured to support jumbo frames. Because the SQL server reports always worked if a local user (at site 1) ran them, the WAN connection became a possible cause of the problem, as it was in use by the manager in site 1 when trying to run the same reports remotely.

Then the technician (using change control procedures) implemented software on the routers and switches that collected statistical information on how much traffic and what types of traffic are going through the ports and interfaces of the routers and switches, including the interfaces connecting the routers to the WAN. The software used to do this is Cisco's NetFlow. A NetFlow collector was used to aggregate all this information into one server for analysis. The NetFlow collector was used to identify utilization of the network and to produce graphs and charts to indicate the top talkers on the network, top protocols in use, and the bandwidth that was being used over the period of a month. With this information, a baseline was created, and from that baseline, the technician was able to identify that near the end of the month, full-image backups being done over the *wide area network* (WAN) were causing significant bottlenecks and congestion on the WAN during that time, which was causing the manager's report to timeout when connecting to the SQL Server database over the WAN.

To correct this, a procedure was put in place for the archives and backups that were causing the congestion to be scheduled only for early morning hours before regular business begins. Traffic shaping and QoS were also applied on the routers for their WAN connections to provide QoS. If congestion did happen in the future, priority would then be given to those applications such as real-time traffic and other critical applications (such as the manager's SQL Server application); less-critical traffic would receive less priority for bandwidth if congestion exists and there is not enough bandwidth for all applications simultaneously.

Scenario 3

Site 3 was just acquired by the company and attached via WAN connectivity to the headquarters (site 1) and a branch office (site 2). Before the acquisition, site 3 had multiple outages on the local area network due to the following:

- Untested/improper updates to servers, routers, switches, and other network devices
- Personally owned user devices interrupting the network services

Now that site 3 is part of the company, a technician has been asked to reduce the risk of downtime due to those issues at site 3.

The technician begins by taking inventory of all the devices and systems at site 3. He discovers that in addition to the user network, management connections to a *supervisory control and data acquisition* (SCADA) system in place are being used to monitor and control a water treatment plant for a local community. This type of industrial control system needs to be up nearly all the time, and as a result, security measures, including the isolation of this network, should be implemented. By isolating the SCADA system from other generic network devices and traffic, there will be less negative impact to that system from the generic day-to-day user network traffic. This isolation can be done using separate VLANs and separate wireless networks for the SCADA network, with either no routing between the user networks and the SCADA network or very limited access by using *access control lists* (ACLs) on the router interfaces to limit the traffic that can go between the VLANs. Legacy systems can be especially vulnerable to modern attacks because they might have protocols and services running that are unsecure, such as Telnet and *File Transfer Protocol* (FTP), which do not include encryption for confidentiality—and that is yet another reason to have network isolation for these systems (to protect them against attacks). When possible, unused/unsecure protocols and services should be disabled/removed from both legacy and current systems and networks. Removing unneeded and unsecure protocols is a method of hardening a system.

In addition, the technician is recommending that a separate network be created for guest wireless access. This separate network can assist in isolating the company resources at site 3 from the unauthorized users. This isolation could once again be done through VLANs and ACLs on router interfaces.

A testing lab and test network should be set up so that any major or minor changes or updates that are proposed can be properly and fully tested before being implemented as part of the production system. This would include firmware updates to computers, switches, routers and servers, in addition to driver updates for hosts, servers, and routers. In a test environment, a minor update, such as a patch or driver update, could be tested and verified before being rolled out into production. If an issue or problem occurs with the update, a rollback can be done to the initial state. Sometimes major updates do not have a simple rollback procedure, which is an even better reason why they should be tested and practiced with in a test environment before being rolled out into production. When testing the upgrading process of the software or system, there should also be a defined downgrading process that can be used to revert to a previous version of the software or system. This might be needed if a rollout occurred and it was later discovered that there is a security or performance issue with the upgraded software. A backup of the configuration for network devices should always be created and available in case the system needs to be restored to its original state.

If a *bring-your-own-device* (BYOD) policy allows users to bring their own devices, a proper on-boarding process needs to be established that confirms that every device meets the minimum security requirements for the network, has proper protection for any company and sensitive information it will hold or have access to, and has been properly set up for access to the network. An example is having the MAC address of a mobile device included on ACLs on the wireless *access point* (AP) or *wireless LAN controller* (WLC) that allows the device to access to the network. Other requirements might include a scan of the system before the device gains access to the network. This can be done on demand, using a software agent that runs on the device, each time a device accesses the network. This agent can scan the device to determine which prerequisites (such as a personal firewall or an updated virus definition) are currently present before allowing access to the network. This agent could be persistent software that is installed on and continually resides on the device, or it could be a nonpersistent agent that is loaded and run only at the time of network access. Performing scans and requiring authentication (before allowing access to the network) at either a port on a switch or through a wireless AP are both examples of network access control at the edge of our network. Technologies such as 802.1X can provide the authentication at the edge, and third-party vendors such as Cisco, Citrix, and CheckPoint can provide the scans in conjunction with an agent to verify prerequisites of the device that wants the network access. Once the user gets access to the network, access control can be implemented between various portions of the network by using ACLs on the router interfaces. A well-defined off-boarding process should also be set up that does a cleanup process and removes access from these devices after they are no longer supposed to have access to the network. Care should also be given to the company content that might be resident on a mobile or personal device, so that sensitive company information is not left on the device after it is no longer welcome on the corporate network.

Scenario 4

A growing company is having wireless networking issues. An AP was recently added near the window of one of the floors of building 1, in the hopes that the users in building 2 would also be able to access the network. Unfortunately, the AP not only failed to provide access for the second building but also caused many users in the first building to have degraded wireless service. The technician has been called in to evaluate the problem and make recommendations.

As part of the troubleshooting methodology, the technician gathers information, verifies the problem by questioning users and having them duplicate the issues, identifies symptoms, and determines what (if anything) has changed (and whether there are multiple issues to approach them individually). With that information, the technician establishes a theory about the probable cause.

Approaches that can be used to establish a theory of probable cause include top-to-bottom and bottom-to-top troubleshooting using the OSI reference model. For example, if an application layer function such as printing works over the wireless network, that implies the lower layers are all functioning correctly. This is an example of a top-to-bottom approach. An example of a bottom-to-top approach is verifying lower layers such as basic IP connectivity using tools such as the **ping** command, and then working up until a failure or problem is found. An example of the bottom-to-top approach is to check the link status of an interface and then use the **ping** command. If those are both successful, this implies that Layer 2 and Layer 3 are working, but an application service, such as web services, might still fail. That would imply that there is a failure of the web server, or that something between the client and the web server is preventing the connection. The technician decided to divide and conquer by working on each problem individually. He began by powering off the new AP that was recently added, and as a result, functionality returned for the users in the building 1. As a result of this, it can be deduced that the new AP was causing the problem.

The technician went to the wiring closet to identify which port on the patch panel was being used to connect the AP to the network. Fortunately, it was correctly labeled, which made it easy to find. The technician then identified the switch port on the switch that connected to that patch panel connector and tried to connect to the switch on one of its vty (*Virtual Teletype*, also referred to as a *Virtual Terminal*, and used for remote management access) lines using a *Secure Shell* (SSH) application from his laptop. He was unable to connect, so he called another administrator on the phone to troubleshoot the lack of SSH access to the switch. It was determined that another administrator was already connected to the single logical vty line on the switch, and that is why a second administrator could not connect. The currently logged-in administrator increased the number of the logical vty lines, and as a result, the second technician was then able to log in to the switch. After logging in to the switch, the technician used commands on the switch that showed the following:

```
Hardware is Fast Ethernet, address is 001c.b148.3e61
MTU 1504 bytes, BW 100000 Kbit/sec, DLY 100 usec,
    reliability 255/255, txload 1/255, rxload 1/255
Encapsulation ARPA, loopback not set
Keepalive set (10 sec)
Full-duplex, 100Mb/s, media type is 10/100BaseTX
input flow-control is off, output flow-control is unsupported
ARP type: ARPA, ARP Timeout 04:00:00
Last input 00:00:00, output 00:00:00, output hang never
Last clearing of "show interface" counters never
```

Based on this output, the technician could verify that the Ethernet port on the switch was set to full duplex and 100Mbps. While in the wiring closet, he also noticed that the fiber connections used to link the wiring closet switch to the main distribution frame in the basement of the building were using older FC connectors, which twist on to connect to the switch, and that there were several yards of fiber cable stuffed behind the rack before it went through the conduit and down to the basement. The technician recommended in his notes to move the fiber to the cable trays in the closet, to keep them up and out of the way of foot traffic in the closet.

This would also help prevent accidental pulls or bending of the fiber cable, which if too extreme could damage the cables and cause them to fail.

The technician also noted that the management access to this switch was going through the same network that the users were using for common network services, such as printing and file services. This is referred to as *in-band management*, where the user traffic and management traffic both go over the same network. At this company, there is a second and isolated network just for management of network devices, such as routers and switches. If used, this separate isolated network would be for out-of-band management, which means that it would have to be a separate network, not using the same network as the users do for common network services.

The technician recommended that change control procedures be arranged to place the switch administrative interfaces for management (the vty lines) on that out-of-band network. Using an out-of-band network for management is more secure than in-band because of the isolation and separation of the networks. Additional out-of-band management might include using analog modems on the older *public switched telephone network* (PSTN) as a backup method to reach and manage remote devices in the event the primary network path is no longer available. Modems would be using analog signals as they cross over the older PSTN. Modems convert digital signals from computing devices to analog signals before sending them over the PSTN. Regardless of in-band or out-of-band management, clear-text management protocols such as *Simple Network Management Protocol version 1* (SNMPv1) and *version 2* (SNMPv2), Telnet, *Hypertext Transfer Protocol* (HTTP), *File Transfer Protocol* (FTP), and *Trivial File Transfer Protocol* (TFTP) should be avoided when possible or used inside a *virtual private network* (VPN) tunnel (which can provide authentication and confidentiality through encryption). Secure alternatives to clear-text protocols include SNMPv3, SSH, HTTPS, and SFTP. These can be used for improved confidentiality and security. Unneeded network services, especially ones that do not require authentication or are clear text, should be disabled on every router, switch, server, and host that is connected to any network. Disabling unneeded network services and unsecure protocols is an example of network hardening. Creating and using standard settings that are geared for security on each device that is added to the network is also an example of network and device hardening.

Later that night, during a maintenance window that was scheduled and communicated through proper change control procedures (when users were not using the network), the technician used that authorized downtime and powered on the AP that had been causing the problem to look at its settings. He discovered that the AP Ethernet connection that connected to the switch port was configured on the AP for half duplex. This alone might not cause problems for other users, but could definitely affect performance if the network is busy, because the AP would not be able to send and receive frames simultaneously. The technician looked up the AP information and verified that it had an omnidirectional antenna, which was appropriate for the area in building 1 that it was supposed to cover. The next thing the technician checked was the 802.11 protocol being used by that AP, and which channel or channels it was using. All the other APs on the floor were configured for 802.11g, and the new AP was also configured for 802.11g, so that was not a problem. However, the new AP was configured to use channel 11, and that was overlapping with an existing AP that was physically close to the new AP, which was also using channel 11; the antennas on these APs are omnidirectional (signals go out in all directions), as opposed to unidirectional (where the signals only go in one direction), and the APs were competing with each other for the same frequencies. The technician changed the channel to 6, which would then not overlap with the other existing AP using channel 11. The nonoverlapping channels in the 2.4GHz range in the United States are channels 1, 6, 11. A quick wireless site survey, using a smartphone application, confirmed that the APs were not using overlapping channels and, as a result, were no longer competing for the same frequency ranges.

Now with the local wireless issue addressed, the technician began looking at the issue for the users in the second (adjacent building) who also wanted wireless access. The new AP in building 1 was near the window facing the second building, but due to the distance and the windows and walls between the AP and the users in building 2, the signal would not be strong enough to be used by those users. Because the two buildings were less than 100 feet apart, it was decided that small antennas could be placed on the outside of each building to act as a repeater to extend wireless access from building 1 to building 2. In building 2, a small Layer 2 switch would be used to connect the antenna on the side of the building to a new small AP in building 2.

For the two external antennas, one for the side of each building, they decided to use the Yagi-Uda style, because it is a directional antenna and is fairly inexpensive and is not difficult to line up, which might be the case with a small dish or parabolic antenna. The technician also recommended that if the users need increased throughput, they might want to consider budgeting for and replacing their APs with 802.11n or 802.11ac. The IEEE 802.11 groups often develop *high throughput* (ht) standards for existing technologies, such as 802.11a-ht and 802.11g-ht. Newer technologies such as 802.11n support multiple antennas and *multiple-input, multiple-output* (MIMO), and 802.11ac supports *multi-user MIMO* (MUMIMO), where it can use multiple 80MHz channels and a single spatial stream to support 433Mbps. An 802.11ac AP can use multiple active streams simultaneously. High throughput enhancements are also applicable to the newer technologies of 802.11n-ht and 802.11ac-ht. The technician also recommended that implementing a WLC would allow central management and control of the APs. When APs are managed by a centralized WLC, they are said to be *thin* APs, and the WLC performs tasks such as authentication of the users. With the WLC, the APs are just being used for their radios and antenna, and the WLC handles tasks such as user authentication and ACLs.

One of the benefits of using a WLC is that an unauthorized AP (also referred to as a *rogue* AP) that is brought into the company by an employee who has *malicious intent* (referred to as a *trusted malicious user*) can be identified by the authorized APs and the WLC working together, and the authorized APs could perform jamming of the rogue AP's signals so that no users can connect to it. Jamming is a technique that a malicious person, perhaps even an untrusted user from outside the building, might use to implement a *denial-of-service* (DoS) attack against a legitimate wireless network. In the case of the WLC coordinating the effort against the nonauthorized AP, this would be done to mitigate the effectiveness of the rogue AP. This could also help to protect against a friendly or unintentional DoS attack by users who did not realize the impact of bringing their own wireless APs (that might be integrated into a small home router) into the physical office. The WLC implementation could also help to identify open networks (networks that do not require authentication) that are not authorized to be present in the building, and it could assist in bringing those APs and networks down. In the current standalone configuration of each AP, also referred to as a *fat* or *thick* configuration, each AP performs the authentication on its own, and each AP must be configured individually.

Scenario 5

A review of the log files for SW1 revealed thousands of failed login attempts to the vty lines on SW1 over the past 7 days, and two successful logins. A technician has been assigned to look into the matter and to make recommendations to improve the security.

The technician goes to the wiring closet where the switch is located and then connects directly to the console port to gain *command-line interface* (CLI) access to SW1. A partial output of the command **show running-config** revealed the following about the configuration of SW1:

```
hostname SW1
username admin privilege 15 secret 4 NNPC.a45nsE7N0.uzqy5V2pUfg
aaa new-model
aaa authentication login USE-AAA group radius local
aaa authentication login default local
!
interface GigabitEthernet0/1
 switchport mode access
 switchport access vlan 10
!
interface GigabitEthernet0/2
 switchport mode access
 switchport access vlan 10
```

```
!
interface GigabitEthernet0/7
 switchport mode access
 switchport access vlan 10
!
ip access-list standard LIMIT-VTY
 deny 10.1.5.0 0.0.0.255
!
radius server RAD-1
 address ipv4 10.1.2.3 auth-port 1645 acct-port 1646
 key Nugget!23
!
!
line con 0
 exec-timeout 30 0
 login authentication USE-AAA
 transport input all
line vty 0 4
 exec-timeout 30 0

...
```

The technician noted the following issues:

- The ACL called LIMIT-VTY is not applied to the logical vty line configuration on the switch, so it is not restricting who can attempt to log on via the vty lines. Even if the ACL were applied to the vty lines to restrict access, it would be too restrictive, because the ACL has only deny statements in it. If applied, it would block all incoming vty requests. This would be an example of a misconfigured ACL.
- The method list created for login authentication (USE-AAA) is not applied to the vty lines, so the vty access, which is used by both SSH and Telnet, is using the default method, which is not using the RADIUS server for authentication, but instead using user accounts configured on the local switch for authentication.
- The password configured for the RADIUS server (RAD-1 is the server, and Nugget!23 is the configured password) is different from the password on the RADIUS server itself. So, even if the switch tried to use a RADIUS server for authentication, due to the mismatched passwords, the RADIUS AAA-based authentication would not work because the RADIUS server would not accept requests from SW1 due to the wrong password. This is an example of a password mismatch. By correctly implementing the RADIUS password and

method list, or implementing a TACACS AAA server (similar to what would be done with a RADIUS server) with a correct method list, the authentication issues currently misconfigured on this switch would be corrected.

- SNMP is not configured on this switch, which could be done to allow reporting and management from an SNMP server. If SNMP is used, unsecure versions such as SNMPv1 and SNMPv2 should be avoided because they are unsecure protocols. Instead, SNMPv3, which supports authentication and encryption, should be used.
- The allowed input on the vty lines is "all." This implies that Telnet and SSH are allowed. This also implies that TCP port 22 for SSH and TCP port 23 for Telnet are both open for business (referred to as *open* ports). Unsecure/unneeded protocols and services, such as Telnet, should be disabled on the switch. If Telnet access is disabled, TCP port 23 would be a closed port, meaning it would not be standing by listening for incoming connections on TCP port 23.

The technician looked for unfamiliar user accounts on the local switch that might have been placed there by an unauthorized user who had gained access to the switch and created a separate account for future access to the switch. This is an example of creating backdoor access, which is a form of improper access that an attacker could use in the future for access to the switch. The individual or individuals who attempted to log in thousands of times were very likely using an automated tool that tries different username and password combinations in an attempt to access the switch. This is an example of a brute-force attack, and if implemented by an employee who already has general access to the network, this person would be considered a *malicious trusted user*. The user would be considered *trusted* because he or she has a user account on the system, but *malicious* because he or she is not authorized to access the switch as an administrator. The attack could also be launched by an unknown individual, someone who does not already have access to the network with a user account, and this type of user could be referred to as an *untrusted user*. The concept of an untrusted user could also extend to a guest account or an account that has not been authenticated by the network.

One technique that could be used to help identify when unauthorized login attempts are happening is to put a device on the network that has unsecure protocols and ports open and available and then implement logging of the login attempts on this device. This device would have nothing of value in either the data or configuration and would be implemented for the sole purpose of seeing who is trying to attack and what types of attacks are being attempted. This type of the device is referred to as a *honey pot*. A group of systems used for this purpose of inviting attacks to learn more about these attacks is called a *honey net*. With a honey pot or honey net, the intention is to learn about the attacker's methods before the attacker uses them on critical nodes and other critical assets in the network. For critical devices, you would want to implement *high availability* (HA) and fault tolerance, as well as use device hardening techniques and possibly an *intrusion detection/prevention system* (IDS/IPS) to prevent an attack or unauthorized access from being successful. You could also use AAA for the authentication authorization and accounting on these critical systems, which could not only notify you of events that are occurring on those devices but also limit the number of login attempts the attacker could make for those devices.

Scenario 6

A company just replaced most of its senior management team and would like to hire outside consultants to come in and provide a thorough technical and security audit of the existing network infrastructure and the servers and devices that are connected to it.

Before beginning the work, the consultants created a *statement of work* (SOW) that defined the activities, deliverables, and timeframes expected from the consultants. This SOW was then approved by the new senior management team before work began. Because the senior management team wanted the consultants to come back semiannually (and more often if required), a *master service agreement* (MSA) was also created that spelled out many of the terms between the consulting firm and this company. The MSA can assist in future contracts, because many of the discussion points have already been agreed to and are documented in the MSA.

The consultant team came in and made the following observations and recommendations:

- There were no dedicated firewalls between the company's routers and the Internet/WAN service provider. The recommendation to correct this is to implement at least three firewalls, one at each of the sites. If the company does not want to renumber its IP addressing scheme to accommodate a Layer 3 routed firewall between each of the sites and the service provider, it could use a transparent firewall, which from a network perspective looks and acts like a Layer 2 switch that can be inserted between the routers and the Internet service provider (ISP) without having to renumber the IP addressing scheme. Another term for this transparent firewall is a *virtual wire* firewall, based on the fact that it's not using Layer 3 interfaces and not connecting to two or more different IP networks. A firewall that is implemented at Layer 3 could be referred to as a *routed* firewall. In either case, the virtual wire or routed firewall could enforce the policies and the security on behalf of each of the sites. In addition, firewalls can be placed internally, inside the company, to provide additional isolation and protection between internal networks at any of the sites. Most modern firewalls today are stateful in nature. A stateful firewall can dynamically allow traffic from the internal users at the site to go out to the Internet, and it remembers the state of that outgoing connection (thus the term *stateful*). The benefit of a stateful firewall is that when the reply traffic comes back in from the Internet, the firewall remembers the initial state of the connection and allows the correct returning traffic to go back to the user. Using a stateful firewall can save a lot of time because you do not have to administratively configure all of the dynamic ports and IP addresses that otherwise are required to be configured (as ACLs) to allow return traffic from the Internet to come back to the internal users. This process is often referred to as stateful inspection or *stateful filtering*. A device such as a firewall that does not do stateful inspection is limited to stateless inspection or stateless filtering, which is usually done by the implementation of ACLs that specifically identify what traffic is allowed to go through the firewall. Another benefit that many firewalls offer is application inspection. This is often referred to as being *context aware*. An example of this is filtering traffic that is attempting to go through the firewall based on the type or content that is being carried at the application layer. Limitations can be put in place based on the type of website the user is trying to go to or the type of content the user is trying to retrieve while going through the firewall. Current firewalls that integrate many of these features (such as stateful filtering, application awareness, and IDS) are referred to as *unified threat management* (UTM) firewalls. Implementing a firewall could also assist in preventing an intruder from *banner grabbing*, which is a method an attacker can potentially use to determine which devices (including servers) are running specific versions of software and/or operating systems that might have known vulnerabilities or weaknesses. In addition to software, an attacker might also be able to discover information by analyzing the *organizationally unique identifier* (OUI), which is an IEEE-assigned unique number assigned to vendors and manufacturers that can assist attackers in identifying the vendor by looking up the OUI in use on a system. Loss of information from banner grabbing and OUI can be prevented by having the firewall perform filtering of specific content and/or types of requests, as systems are accessed through the firewall.

- The consultants scheduled authorized downtime, using proper change control, to use a Ethernet cable tester to verify the cabling between mission-critical systems and the switches and routers that connect those devices to the network. They used a line tester to verify the circuit being used between the routers and the ISP. For the Ethernet connections, although the cables being used were functional, nonstandard pairs for the termination of these cables were being used on both ends at the UTP cables as they connected to the RJ-45 connectors. The consultants recommend recrimping (through a certified third party) using EIA/TIA 568A standards for the UTP-to-RJ-45 connector. The incorrect crimping, though functional, was resulting in crosstalk, which is an unwanted condition where signals that are going through adjacent pairs of wire in twisted-pair cabling interfere with each other. *Near-end crosstalk* (NEXT) is crosstalk that occurs at the near end of the cable; *far-end crosstalk* is interference at the far end of the cable or circuit. The consultants also noticed that most of the crossover cables between the switches in the same wiring closets were also incorrectly crimped. These were functional, however, because pin 1 on one end of the cable went to pin 3 on the far side, and pin 2 on one end of the cable connected to pin 6 on the other side. The proper crimping would have the same pinouts for a crossover cable, but should use EIA/TIA 568A on one end and EIA/TIA 568B on the other end. If the company intends to deploy Gigabit Ethernet (1000BASE-T, Gigabit Ethernet), it will want to use Category 6 cabling and connectors.

- The interconnection of the switches between floors was being done with fiber, but the cable management of the unshielded twisted pair (UTP) that went out to the cubes on the same floor, as well as the fiber that went up and down between floors, was a mess, and reminded the consultants of cooked spaghetti. The consultants recommended cable trays to be used to organize and protect the cables from being excessively pulled or bent or stepped on. They also recommended better security for the wiring closet access, because they were able to enter the wiring closet on each floor without any type of a key or passcode.

- The consultants also interviewed (with permission from management) several employees and discovered that several outages had happened over the previous 6 months, including Wi-Fi access. It was further documented that the disruption to service was due to updates that had been applied to the APs. These updates had a bug and caused the APs to not work correctly. The downtime associated with the bug could have been circumvented by having a test environment, by avoiding untested updates, and by using proper change control procedures, including verification and a rollback procedure when needed. The consultants are recommending a structured and clearly laid out change control plan that includes documentation about the reason for change, change requests that contain configuration procedures, rollback processes, potential impact analysis, and notification. The change control should also include a formal approval process, in addition to a communicated maintenance window and authorized downtime, as well as notification and documentation about the changes that took place.

- The consultants identified plans the company had to connect to a third-party network, because they anticipated working on a joint project with that third-party. The consultants recommended implementing a *memorandum of understanding* (MOU) between the two companies to identify and confirm in writing the intentions and agreements between the companies. It is also recommended by the consultants that minimum security requirements for both companies must be in place for any systems or networks that will be connected between the two companies, because a security flaw or weakness in one of the companies could impact the security of the other.

- The contractors discovered that WAN connectivity between the sites (and Internet connectivity) has had several outages over the past 6 months, causing downtime and loss of revenue. The consultants recommended that the company get a written service level agreement (SLA) from the Internet/WAN provider regarding service levels that are guaranteed from that provider. If an SLA cannot be provided, the company is encouraged to investigate other providers (and secondary providers that can provide SLAs). It is also recommended that the company acquire a backup provider to have fault tolerance for their Internet and WAN connectivity. Regarding Internet and WAN access, the consultants recommended implementing the throttling of traffic if it is above the level needed for general business. That way, if an attack is launched from one of the company's sites, a limited amount of volume can be sent (because of throttling). Filtering and blocking of certain types of traffic should also be implemented across the WAN and out to the Internet to help mitigate the risk of content such as company-sensitive information being leaked out or sent over the Internet. The consultants also recommended getting a written fair access policy regarding Internet and WAN access from the service provider. This way, with a periodic audit, the company can verify that it is within acceptable utilization limits regarding its use of the Internet and WAN.
- The consultants identified that no IDS or IPS was in place. They recommended a network-based intrusion prevention system (NIPS) that could identify many types of attacks. An example of an attack is sending multiple TCP synchronization requests to a server but using a bogus source IP address in an attempt to implement a DoS SYN flood attack against the server. This is an example of protocol abuse. An IDS/IPS could identify this behavior and issue warnings to the administrator that this attack is underway, and potentially prevent the attack from making it all the way to the victim. Another example of an attack that can be identified with an IDS/IPS is flooding, where an attacker (or multiple attackers) sends an inordinate number of packets to consume either all the network bandwidth or resources on a given device. This packet flooding would also be considered an abuse of the system by the attacker, and an IDS/IPS would be able to identify that this type attack is happening.
- The consultants also documented that switch port security was not enabled on each of the access switches in the network. By using the features of Dynamic Host Configuration Protocol (DHCP) snooping and Address Resolution Protocol (ARP) inspection, along with the switch port security, issues such as ARP

poisoning, where an attacker attempts to redirect traffic intended for a server or router so that the attacker can see it, can be prevented from happening. It was also recommended that in addition to port security, more user VLANs should be created that are separate from the VLANs where the servers and other critical resources are kept. By setting up isolation, the company can use ACLs on router interfaces to limit and protect against traffic that should not go between these server networks and the user networks. This is an example of network segmentation and isolation.

Scenario 7

A user at PC3 (in site 2) has called the help desk, stating that PC6 (in site 3) cannot be accessed over the WAN. The technician has been called in to identify the problem, establish a theory of probable cause, test the theory, establish a plan of action to resolve the problem, and then implement the solution or escalate as necessary. The technician has also been asked to verify full system functionality and to document his findings, actions, and outcomes.

The technician used SSH to securely connect to a vty line on SW2 and then issued some **show** commands to see the configuration details regarding port number 3 on SW2, which is being used to connect PC3 to the network. A partial output is shown here:

```
interface GigabitEthernet0/3
 switchport mode access
 switchport access vlan 20
```

PC3 is supposed to be in VLAN 20, and based on the configuration of the switch, the correct VLAN assignment is currently configured. If the PC could not ping its default gateway, or failed get an IP address from DHCP, it would be possible that there was an incorrect VLAN assignment on the switch for the sport.

Next, the technician issued a **show** command on SW2 to see the status of port 3. A partial output is shown here:

```
FastEthernet0/3 is up, line protocol is up (connected)
  Hardware is Fast Ethernet, address is 001c.b1a8.6783
  MTU 1504 bytes, BW 100000 Kbit/sec, DLY 100 usec,
     reliability 255/255, txload 1/255, rxload 1/255
  Encapsulation ARPA, loopback not set
  Keepalive set (10 sec)
  Full-duplex, 100Mb/s, media type is 10/100BaseTX
  input flow-control is off, output flow-control is unsupported
  ARP type: ARPA, ARP Timeout 04:00:00
```

```
Last input 00:00:00, output 00:00:00, output hang never
Last clearing of "show interface" counters never
Input queue: 0/75/0 (size/max/drops); Total output drops: 0
Queueing strategy: fifo
Output queue: 0/40 (size/max)
5 minute input rate 1000 bits/sec, 2 packets/sec
5 minute output rate 3000 bits/sec, 2 packets/sec
   69 packets input, 4496 bytes, 0 no buffer
   Received 0 broadcasts (0 IP multicasts)
   0 runts, 0 giants, 0 throttles
   0 input errors, 0 CRC, 0 frame, 0 overrun, 0 ignored
   72 packets output, 10710 bytes, 0 underruns
   0 output errors, 0 collisions, 0 interface resets
   0 output buffer failures, 0 output buffers swapped out
```

Based on this output, there do not appear to be any interface errors on this port of the switch, and it is also up and shows as connected.

Then the technician went to PC3 and issued the command **ipconfig /all**, which revealed the following:

```
FastEthernet adapter 1:

   Description . . . . . . . . . . . : Intel(R) Network Adapter
   Physical Address. . . . . . . . . : 68-17-29-17-75-85
   DHCP Enabled. . . . . . . . . . . : Yes
   IPv4 Address. . . . . . . . . . . : 10.35.1.99
   Subnet Mask . . . . . . . . . . . : 255.255.255.0
   Lease Obtained. . . . . . . . . . : Monday, March 11, 6:16:33 PM
   Lease Expires . . . . . . . . . . : Tuesday, March 12, 6:16:36 PM
   Default Gateway . . . . . . . . . : 10.35.1.1
   DHCP Server . . . . . . . . . . . : 10.35.1.254
 DNS Servers . . . . . . . . . . . : 10.35.1.254
```

If in the output of the **ipconfig** command the computer did not show a default gateway or if the default gateway was on a different network (which would mean that the default gateway was not reachable and as a result would not be functional for the client to use), it could be a configuration issue on the local PC3. This is an example of an unreachable default gateway. The technician then proceeded to verify that the computer could ping its default gateway at 10.35.1.1, and the results were successful. It was also noticed in the output that there is only one *Domain Name System* (DNS) server being handed out as an option in DHCP, and that is an internal DNS server's address. If the internal DNS server fails, that could cause a lack of connectivity, due to the lack of name resolution, so the technician is going to recommend that a second DNS server be added as an option to the DHCP scope, pointing to an Internet DNS server, such as the service provider or a public DNS server.

If the client supported *Link Layer Discovery Protocol* (LLDP), the technician could verify based on those Layer 2 messages that are sent by LLDP whether this PC is really connected to port number 3 on SW2. In the absence of LLDP, one way to verify that PC3 really is connected to switch port 3 is to look at the MAC address table on the switch to see whether the Layer 2 address of PC3 has been associated (learned) by the switch. This is a method of discovering neighboring devices or nodes on the network. The successful ping to PC3's default gateway implies that the PC is in the correct VLAN and is very likely connected to port 3.

Next, the technician opened an SSH session to router R2 to verify that router R2 was correctly configured and had a route in its routing table to reach the networks at site 3. The technician confirmed that R2 had a default route that was using the service provider for Internet access, as well as a specific route to reach the networks at site 3. While connected to router R2, the technician issued **show** commands to look at the interface status for router R2's WAN interface, and this did not show any errors. The technician also did a ping to the IP address of PC 6 from router R2, which was successful, indicating that routing is working between site 2 and site 3.

The technician went back to PC3 to test DNS and verify that PC6 was resolvable to an IP address. The command **nslookup PC6** was used, and the partial output is shown here:

```
PC3:\nslookup PC6

Name: PC6
Addresses: 10.35.2.45
```

PC6 does have the IP address of 10.35.2.45, so the name resolution from the company's internal DNS server is working. The technician attempts a ping to PC6 by name, which is successful. This implies that full IP connectivity and DNS resolution are both working. This also means that the WAN components, which might include *channel service units/data service units* (CSU/DSUs), copper line drivers or repeaters, and any other components associated with the WAN connectivity between site 2 and site 3, are working.

The technician asked about the details regarding what application or service was being requested by the user on PC3 when connecting to PC6. The user stated that it was a *Remote Desktop Protocol* (RDP) application that uses TCP port 3389. The technician then called an assistant who was at site 3 to check the configuration of the RDP application on PC6 to see whether it was misconfigured. It was confirmed that the configuration was correct, at which point the original technician at site

2 attempted a remote desktop session from PC3 to PC6 and was successful. The technician then logged out and asked the user to attempt a connection. When the user attempted the same type of remote desktop connection to PC6, the connection failed. The technician then connected to a domain controller that was part of Microsoft's *Active Directory* (AD) to check permissions there. The domain group account that had remote desktop permissions did not include the user who had called the help desk, and the local group accounts at PC6 also did not provide that user remote desktop access to PC6. Thus, the group configurations and security restrictions were preventing the user from accessing PC6 using RDP. If a router or firewall had been blocking this port, the technician, using his own account, would also have failed to establish an RDP session to the remote PC.

Scenario 8

A department manager is being asked to contribute part of his budget toward the WAN costs, including Internet access for a new *Software as a Service* (SaaS) application that his staff needs to use. Before committing the money, the manager has asked about a separate connection for Internet access, along with options for that. The technician from the networking department has met with the manager and shared the following information:

- Different technologies can be used to access the Internet and WAN services, including digital subscriber line (DSL), cable modem, leased digital lines, packet switched networks (such as Frame Relay), Ethernet, wireless, and even legacy analog connections using modems, which convert digital signals from the computer or router into analog signals that the old telephone system has made available for many years (and is the slowest option).
- The rate at which bits are encoded on the line can be referred to as the *bit rate* (for example 1000 bps). On older modem technology, another term called *baud rate* represents the number of symbols or characters being sent per second. The baud rate will be less than the bit rate because a symbol can take multiple bits to represent a single symbol.
- The process of taking data and formatting it with the correct addressing and headers at Layers 4, 3, and 2 is called *encapsulation*, as data is being prepared to be sent over the network. The process of taking the data that received over the network and extracting the information at Layers 2, 3, 4 and higher (in that order) is referred to as *decapsulation* (or *de-encapsulation*).
- *Multiplexing* is the concept of taking multiple sets of data (such as voice traffic and email traffic) and sending them simultaneously (or almost simultaneously) over a link on a network, such as a T1 leased line between two sites. At the receiving side, the process of separating out the data streams (separating the voice traffic from the email traffic) is referred to as *demultiplexing*.

- The data that is being sent and received at its lowest level is using a binary (base 2) numbering system, which means that the data uses the numbers 1 and 0 (to represent on or off, like a light switch). Many times, we represent these binary numbers using other numbering systems, such as decimal or hexadecimal, to make them more manageable to write down and work with. Binary is base 2, decimal is base 10, and hexadecimal is base 16. There are other numbering systems, as well, including octal, which is a base 8 numbering system. When working with IP addressing, we use decimal to represent IPv4 addresses and hexadecimal to represent IPv6 addresses.
- If using wireless for Internet access, you have several options to choose from, but the reliability might be less than when using a wired connection. Higher wavelengths (which correspond to higher frequencies) tend to not travel as far (distance-wise) as lower wavelengths.
- A baseline should be created that can assist in determining the amount of bandwidth needed, along with acceptable latency values. A sampling size for this baseline should be big enough so that it accurately represents (or estimates) the amount of traffic that will be needed over a period of time, such as a week or month.
- It might be less expensive to use the existing company connection to the Internet and pay for a portion of that service instead of putting in a separate Internet connection.

Summary

The main topics covered in this chapter are the following:

- Troubleshooting concepts were discussed. In addition, you were presented with a structured troubleshooting methodology.
- Common physical layer troubleshooting issues were identified, and you tested your troubleshooting skills with a Layer 1 troubleshooting exercise.
- Data link layer troubleshooting was discussed, along with a collection of common issues (for example, VLANs, port configuration, and Layer 2 loops). Again, you were challenged with another troubleshooting scenario.
- Without dealing with the unique details of individual routing protocols, this chapter overviewed network layer troubleshooting, along with a list of the common Layer 3 issues. Then, based on the subnetting skills you learned in Chapter 6, you determined the host in a given topology that had an incorrect IP address assignment.

- You reviewed common troubleshooting issues with wireless networks, including the need for wireless clients and wireless APs to have matching parameters, such as channel, encryption type, SSID, and wireless standard. Then you examined a wireless network design and identified a design flaw.

Exam Preparation Tasks

Review All the Key Topics

Review the most important topics from inside the chapter, noted with the Key Topic icon in the outer margin of the page. Table 14-6 lists these key topics and the page numbers where each is found.

Table 14-6 Key Topics for Chapter 14

Key Topic Element	Description	Page Number
Figure 14-1	Simplified troubleshooting flow	483
Table 14-1	Steps to diagnose a problem	483
Figure 14-2	Structured troubleshooting approach	484
Step list	Steps in the Network+ structured troubleshooting approach	485
Table 14-2	Common Layer 1 troubleshooting issues	487
Table 14-3	Common Layer 2 troubleshooting issues	490
Table 14-4	Common Layer 3 troubleshooting issues	494
Step list	Determining the subnet for a host	496
Table 14-5	Common wireless troubleshooting issues	498

Complete Tables and Lists from Memory

Print a copy of Appendix C, "Memory Tables," or at least the section for this chapter, and complete as many of the tables as possible from memory. Appendix D, "Memory Tables Answer Key," includes the completed tables and lists so you can check your work.

Define Key Terms

Define the following key terms from this chapter, and check your answers in the Glossary:

trouble ticket, open, short, decibel loss, maximum transmission unit (MTU), black-hole router

Complete Chapter 14 Hands-On Lab in Network+ Simulator Lite

- Troubleshooting Practice

Additional Resources

A Sample Trouble Ticket: http://www.ajsnetworking.com/micronugget-ccie-rs-troubleshooting-sample-ticket

Sysinternals Utilities: https://www.youtube.com/watch?v=wPsYF2ncrpo

Review Questions

The answers to these review questions are in Appendix A, "Answers to Review Questions."

1. Which of the following is most likely the first step in a structured troubleshooting methodology?
   a. Hypothesize the probable cause.
   b. Create an action plan.
   c. Create a post-mortem report.
   d. Define the problem.

2. Which of the following comprise a simplified troubleshooting flow? (Choose three.)
   a. Problem resolution
   b. Problem monitoring
   c. Problem diagnosis
   d. Problem report

3. A broken copper strand in a circuit is known as which of the following?
   a. Short
   b. Impedance
   c. Open
   d. Split pair

4. What Ethernet switch feature allows a port to automatically determine which of its leads are used for transmitting data and which of its leads are used for receiving data?
   a. MDIX
   b. STP
   c. LAPD
   d. UTP

5. In the absence of STP, what issues might result from a Layer 2 loop in a network? (Choose two.)
   a. A router interface's MTU decrementing
   b. MAC address table corruption
   c. Broadcast storms
   d. Packet fragmentation

6. If you successfully ping from host A to host B, what can you conclude about host A?
   a. Its OSI Layers 1–4 are functional.
   b. Its OSI Layers 1–3 are functional.
   c. Its OSI Layers 1–7 are functional.
   d. You can only conclude that ICMP traffic can reach host B.

7. A router that drops a packet exceeding a router interface's MTU size, when that packet has its "don't fragment" bit set, is called which of the following?
   a. Route reflector
   b. Null hop
   c. Zero-point router
   d. Black-hole router

8. To what subnet does a host with an IP address of 172.16.155.10/18 belong?
   a. 172.16.0.0 /18
   b. 172.16.96.0 /18
   c. 172.16.128.0 /18
   d. 172.16.154.0 /18

9. Which of the following is a value measuring the power of a wireless signal?
   a. RSSI
   b. SSID
   c. RFI
   d. CSMA/CA

10. Which of the following are common sources of wireless network radio frequency interference (RFI)? (Choose three.)
    a. Game consoles
    b. Fax machines
    c. Microwave ovens
    d. Baby monitors

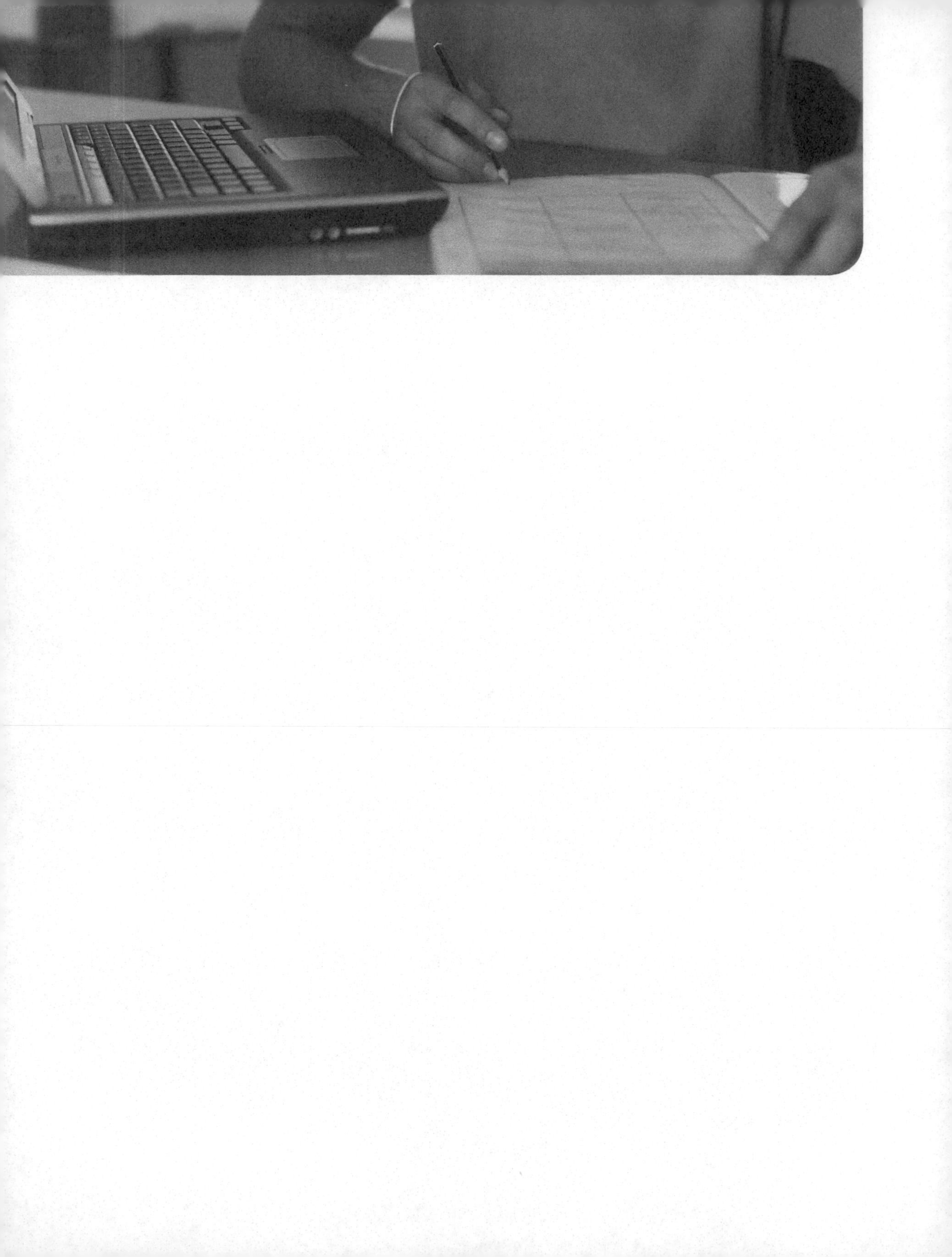

Final Preparation

The first 14 chapters of this book covered the technologies, protocols, design concepts, and considerations regarding the CompTIA Network+ N10-007 exam. This chapter details a set of tools and a study plan to help you complete your preparation for the CompTIA Network+ N10-007 exam.

This short chapter has two main sections. The first section lists the exam-preparation tools. The second section lists a suggested study plan, now that you have completed all the earlier chapters in this book.

Tools for Final Preparation

This section lists some information about available study tools and how to access them.

The digital resources associated with the book are available on the book's companion website. To access the companion website, follow these steps:

Step 1. Go to http://www.pearsonitcertification.com/register.

Step 2. Either log in to your account (if you have an existing account) or create a new account.

Step 3. Enter the ISBN of your book (9780789759818) and click Submit.

Step 4. Answer the challenge questions to validate your purchase.

Step 5. In your account page, click the **Registered Products** tab and then click the **Access Bonus Content** link.

Resources available on the companion website include the following:

- Interactive glossary flash card application
- Interactive exam essentials appendix
- Performance-based exercises
- CompTIA Network+ Hands-on Lab Simulator Software
- The Pearson Test Prep practice test software

- Video training on key exam topics
- Memory Table review exercises and answer keys
- A study planner tool
- Your Network+ certification exam voucher, which provides a 10% discount on the exam

Video Training

The companion website for this book contains ten training videos that address a couple of the most misunderstood concepts in the CompTIA Network+ curriculum—specifically the OSI model and IP addressing. The videos, which you can access from the companion website, cover the following topics:

- **Video 1:** Introduction to the OSI Model
- **Video 2:** Layer 1—The Physical Layer
- **Video 3:** Layer 2—The Data Link Layer
- **Video 4:** Layer 3—The Network Layer
- **Video 5:** Layer 4—The Transport Layer
- **Video 6:** Layers 5–7—The Upper Layers
- **Video 7:** IP Addressing—Part 1 (Binary Numbering Review)
- **Video 8:** IP Addressing—Part 2 (Basic Subnetting)
- **Video 9:** IP Addressing—Part 3 (Advanced Subnetting)
- **Video 10:** IP Addressing—Part 4 (Introduction to IPv6)

These training videos are presented by Kevin Wallace.

Memory Tables

Like most *Cert Guides* from Pearson IT Certification, this book purposefully organizes information into tables and lists for easier study and review. Rereading these tables can prove very useful before the exam. However, it is easy to skim over the tables without paying attention to every detail, especially when you remember having seen the table's contents when reading the chapter.

Instead of simply reading the tables in the various chapters, this book's Appendixes C and D, available on the companion website, give you another review tool. Appendix C, "Memory Tables," lists partially completed versions of many of the tables in this book. You can open Appendix C and print the appendix. For review, you can attempt to complete the tables.

Appendix D, "Memory Tables Answer Key," which is also a PDF, lists the completed tables so that you can check your answers. You can also just refer to the tables as printed in the book.

Simulations and Performance-Based Exercises

The CompTIA Network+ exam contains more than just multiple choice questions. It also contains performance-based questions (PBQs) that test your understanding of exam topics and hands-on skills in interactive ways. CompTIA makes some sample PBQs available on its website, so you might want to check them out prior to taking your exam. You can find these sample PBQs at https://certification.comptia.org/testing/about-testing/performance-based-questions-explained.

This book comes with a set of hands-on practice labs to help you practice and develop your hands-on skills in the CompTIA Network+ N10-007 Hands-on Lab Simulator software. This software is available for you to download on the companion website. The book also comes complete with a set of 40 performance-based exercises that mimic the performance-based questions on the actual exam.

You should practice *all* the simulations, performance-based exercises, and hands-on activities included as part of this book as you work through each chapter—and it may be useful for you to repeat the labs again when you have finished the book to make sure you have a firm grasp of these hands-on concepts. The hands-on practice with these simulations will assist you in preparing for any simulations you may encounter in the certification exam and will help you learn skills that you can apply in a live environment.

End-of-Chapter Review Tools

Chapters 1–14 all have several features in the "Exam Preparation Tasks" and "Review Questions" sections at the end of the chapter. You might have already worked through these tools in each chapter. However, it can help to use them again as you make your final preparations for the exam.

Suggested Plan for Final Review and Study

This section lists a suggested study plan from the point at which you finish reading Chapter 14 until you take the CompTIA Network+ exam. Certainly, you can ignore this plan, use it as is, or modify it to better meet your needs.

The plan uses five steps:

1. **Review key topics**. You can use the table at the end of each chapter that lists the key topics of the chapter, or you can just flip through the pages looking for key topics.
2. **Complete memory tables**. Open Appendix C on the companion website, print the entire appendix, and then complete the tables.
3. **Study "Review Questions" sections**. Go through the "Review Questions" section at the end of each chapter to identify areas in which you need more study. All of these questions are available to you in the Pearson Test Prep software. Simply select the Book Questions exam bank to run a practice exam using just these questions from the book.
4. **Use the Pearson Test Prep Practice Test engine to practice**. You can use the Pearson Test Prep Practice Test engine to study using a bank of unique exam-realistic questions available only with this book. Run through the questions the first time in study mode and assess your areas of weakness. Then run through the questions again in practice exam mode to assess your exam readiness. Run through the questions a final time in flash card mode to really challenge yourself to answer the questions without being able to see the multiple-choice answers.
5. **Use the simulations and performance-based exercises to practice**. These exercises can help confirm your knowledge and how to apply that knowledge.

The database of questions used by the Pearson Test Prep software was created specifically for this book. You can use the Pearson Test Prep practice test engine either in study mode, practice exam mode, or flash card mode, as follows:

- **Study mode:** Study mode is most useful when you want to use the questions for learning and practicing. In study mode, you can select options such as randomizing the order of the questions and answers, automatically viewing answers to the questions as you go, testing on specific topics, and many others.
- **Practice exam mode:** Practice exam mode presents questions in a timed environment, providing you with an exam-realistic experience. It also restricts your ability to see your score as you progress through the exam and view answers to questions as you are taking the exam. These timed exams not only allow you to study for the actual CompTIA Network+ exam, but also help you simulate the time pressure that can occur during an actual exam.
- **Flash card mode:** Flash card mode simply removes the multiple-choice answers, challenging you to answer the question in your head without the benefit of seeing the possible answers. This is a great way to drill on those

topics of particular weakness for you. Note that in this mode, you will not be able to record questions as right or wrong; you will have to assess that on your own when you view the correct answers, so a grade report isn't available in this mode.

When doing your final preparation, you can use study mode, practice exam mode, and flash card mode. However, after you have seen each question a few times, you tend to remember the questions, and the usefulness of the exam database might go down. Therefore, consider the following options when using the exam engine:

- Use the exam bank 1 question database for review. Use study mode to study the questions by chapter, just as with the other final review steps listed in this chapter. When you are ready to do final review, use the other exam bank you have not seen before.
- Save the question database by not using it during your review of each part of this book. Instead, save it until the end so that you will not have seen the questions before. Then, use practice exam mode to simulate the exam.

Picking the correct mode from the exam engine's user interface is straightforward. The following steps show you how to move to the screen where you can select study or practice exam mode:

1. Click the **My Products** tab if you are not already in that screen.
2. Select the product you want to use from the list of available products.
3. Click the **Exams** button.

By taking these actions, you cause the engine to display a window from which you can choose study mode, practice exam mode, or flash card mode. When in study mode or flash card mode, you can further choose the book chapters, thus limiting the questions to those explained in the specified chapters of this book.

The Pearson Test Prep software also allows you to mark questions, thus creating a custom database of questions for topics on which you might need extra review. It also allows you to enter notes on questions and review those notes, which is another handy review tool.

Strategies for Taking the Exam

Are you ready for some strategy tips for your Network+ exam attempt? This section provides several. Of course, you can apply many of these to other certification exams as well.

1. You can use one of two overall strategies for scheduling your exam. One approach is to schedule for an exam slot when you are fully ready (this is my favorite approach). You might have to wait as much as a week if all of the exam slots at your desired time are full, but typically if you are near a large city, you can find a slot for the very next day. The other approach is to schedule for several months out and then study, study, study to be ready for the exam slot you booked. Some people need this strategy to help avoid the procrastination they might face regarding their prep. If you adopt this strategy, be sure to check into the cancelation or rescheduling policy just in case your life gets in the way of your studies!

2. Schedule the exam for a time that works great for you. If you are not a morning person, do not schedule the exam for early morning! Wait an extra day or two if you have to schedule the exam for a time slot that works for you.

3. Plan for and get a good night of rest before the exam. Also be sure to eat a good meal (breakfast or lunch) before the exam. Drink plenty of water to stay hydrated. Your mind will perform better when your body has what it needs. With that said, be sure not to experiment the day of the exam. I have talked to students who decided to suddenly try consuming a bunch of caffeine before the exam. They had a terrible exam experience because they were doing something their bodies were not used to.

4. Map out where the testing center is, and confirm that you know how to get there and how long it takes to get there.

5. Bring the proper identification required for the exam.

6. Plan to arrive 30 minutes before your exam time, anticipate the traffic, and adjust your plan accordingly. Take a few moments before signing in at the testing center to relax and take several healthy breaths to increase your ability to do well on the exam. You might want to use the restroom before the exam so that your focus can be in the correct place during the exam.

7. Manage your time in the exam. It is hard to answer a question correctly if you have run out of time and never see that question! If you have questions that you are unsure about, or if there is a simulation or lengthy question that may take several minutes, consider marking that question for review and come back to it after you have had an opportunity to answer the other questions. Often, other questions will refresh your memory and provide insight into questions that you have previously marked for review.

8. Get ready for the performance-based questions to be grouped together and to be near the front of the exam. CompTIA has stuck to this formula pretty consistently. Doing this gives the students a little better chance at proper time management because these performance-based questions tend to take a bit more time than the multiple choice.

9. Smile at questions that are puzzling to you. The exam may be an opportunity to learn a couple new things, and smiling when you see a tricky question can assist you in staying positive while you continue to answer the other questions that you know. It is likely that you will want to mark the "puzzling" questions for review and come back to them.

10. Use your scratch paper in the exam to note the topics of questions that you are forced to take a best guess at. Memorize this list of topics should you not pass the exam. These are areas you should spend extra time on in your preparation for your second (and final!) attempt. Go back to step 1 of these preparation steps and repeat the process!

11. Have fun with this process. If you are enjoying the journey, everything regarding this certification process will go much more smoothly.

Summary

The tools and suggestions listed in this chapter are designed with one goal in mind: to help you develop the skills required to pass the CompTIA Network+ exam. This book has been developed from the beginning to not just present you with a collection of facts, but to also help you learn how to apply those facts. Regardless of your experience level before reading this book, it is our hope that the broad range of preparation tools, and even the structure of the book, will help you pass the exam with ease. We wish you success with your exam and hope that our paths will cross again as you continue to grow in your networking career.

APPENDIX A

Answers to Review Questions

Chapter 1

1. **b.** The local area network (LAN) consists of many different components. One critical aspect is the media (wired or wireless) that can transmit the data from node to node.
2. **c.** Switches forward traffic based on the destination MAC (hardware) address contained in the data frame. Contrast this to a router, which makes forwarding decisions based on the destination IP address.
3. **d.** The metropolitan area network is superb for connecting various buildings in a citywide area. Metro Ethernet is one example of connectivity technology for this design.
4. **c.** The personal area network features fewer nodes than typically found in a LAN. This design also features a small geographic area, such as a car or a single room office.
5. **c.** The star topology is common today in switched LANs. However, it does feature quite a bit of cabling, as the switches require media to each and every node (wired) that needs to communicate. There are also typically trunk connections between the switches for an extended star topology, which requires even more cabling.
6. **a.** The full-mesh topology might be complex and expensive to implement, but it does provide excellent levels of redundancy. Should one or more links fail, it is often possible to reroute traffic around the failures.
7. **b.** Remember, the formula for the number of connections required for the full-mesh topology is $n(n-1)/2$, where n is the number of nodes. So, in this case, $5(5-1)/2$ is 10.
8. **a, c.** The hub and spoke is actually a form of a partial-mesh topology. This topology has the advantage of being less complex, less costly, and overall more scalable than a full-mesh design.
9. **c.** The peer-to-peer (P2P) network features clients sharing information directly with each other.

10. **b.** The P2P network is often celebrated due to its simplicity and low cost. Unfortunately, it is not scalable and can actually cause administrative nightmares when attempting to scale it.
11. **c.** The infrastructure type of topology features specialized nodes (access points) that permit communications between other nodes.
12. **d.** The storage area network (SAN) assists when large amounts of data must be stored in the network and transferred efficiently from various nodes to other nodes.

Chapter 2

1. **d.** The data link layer of the OSI model is the only layer of the famous model that we typically divide into sublayers (the MAC and LLC sublayers).
2. **b.** Baseband technology uses the entire medium to transmit. You should contrast this to broadband technology, which can divide the medium up into different channels. A great example of broadband is the use of the coaxial cable you might have in your home, which carries cable television signaling as well as high-speed Internet.
3. **c.** The transport layer offers TCP and UDP. With TCP, a connection-oriented protocol, windowing can be used to dictate how much data is sent at one time.
4. **a.** An IP address is a typical ingredient at the network layer (Layer 3) of the OSI model. Routers use these addresses to route traffic through an internetwork.
5. **c.** User Datagram Protocol (UDP) sacrifices reliability for speed and efficiency in the transport of data.
6. **b, c, f, g.** The DoD TCP/IP model features just four layers. From the bottom up they are network interface, Internet, transport, and application.
7. **b.** The well-known port numbers are all below 1024. An example would be HTTP (WWW) at port 80.
8. **b.** Secure Shell (SSH) provides a secure alternative to Telnet when it comes to remotely accessing a network device for management of that device.
9. **c.** The Network Time Protocol (NTP) relies on port 123.
10. **b, c, d.** SMTP, POP3, and IMAP4 are all examples of email protocols. Note that it is very easy to confuse SMTP with SNMP. Simple Network Management Protocol aids in the robust management of network devices.

Chapter 3

1. **c.** SIP is a control protocol for VoIP and is responsible for call maintenance tasks.
2. **b, c.** Cat 5e and Cat 6 are often used for Fast Ethernet networks.
3. **b.** Plenum cable is of a special construction for use in the plenum spaces.
4. **b.** The best answer here is switch because, unlike a multilayer switch, this device must use MAC addressing for frame forwarding.
5. **d.** Routers make their forwarding decisions using IP addresses at Layer 3 of the OSI model. Specifically, the destination IP address is the key piece of information used by default.
6. **a, c.** Bridges are slower than switches (typically) and they tend to lack the port density of switches.
7. **d.** A router creates a broadcast domain on each of the router (Layer 3) ports.
8. **d.** A switch creates a collision domain on each port by default.
9. **c.** The DHCPDISCOVER message is sent by a client in order to try and locate a DHCP server and IP address information.
10. **a.** A content switch is one form of network load balancer. These devices distribute client requests across servers hosting content.
11. **b.** Ant+ is found in IoT and is specialized wireless for monitoring sensor data. Garmin helped create this technology.
12. **c.** SDN is becoming more and more popular today. This permits the centralized control and management of devices throughout the network from a single point. Usually, a graphical user interface provides the administrator interface.

Chapter 4

1. **a.** A 1000BASE-T Ethernet network features a distance limitation of 100 m.
2. **d.** A random back-off timer is used in the CSMA/CD network once a collision is detected.
3. **b.** 100GBASE-SR10 Ethernet uses multimode fiber.
4. **a, b.** VLANs are also IP subnets. A router must route between these subnets. The VLAN is also a broadcast domain.
5. **a.** The 802.1Q native VLAN is the only VLAN in the Layer 2 domain that is not tagged.
6. **b.** The designated port is forwarding, and there must be one on every network segment. Remember, all root ports are designated by default.

7. **b.** 802.3ad is the open standard version of link aggregation.
8. **b.** IEEE 802.3af standard specifies 15.4W as the maximum amount of power a switch is allowed to provide per port.
9. **c.** Port mirroring permits frame analysis in a switched network.
10. **b.** 802.1X features a supplicant, an authentication server, and an authenticator. The authentication server is responsible for actually checking the credentials.

Chapter 5

1. **b.** The binary representation of 117 is 01110101. Notice that this has values of 64 + 32 + 16 + 4 + 1.
2. **d.** 10110100 is the equivalent of 180 because we have 128 + 32 + 16 + 4.
3. **a.** Because the decimal value 10 appears in the first octet, we know that this is a Class A address.
4. **d.** 239.1.2.3 is an example of a multicast IP address. We use multicast to send a single packet to groups of systems that have "subscribed" to this address.
5. **a, d.** Notice that a key to this question is "routable IP addresses." Only BOOTP and DHCP are valid options in this case.
6. **a.** There are 5 bits left here for host address assignment, and 2 raised to the fifth power is 32. You then subtract 2 for the network ID and broadcast address.
7. **c.** /28 is the prefix notation for 255.255.255.240. Notice the mask consists of 8 bits + 8 bits + 8 bits + 4 bits.
8. **c.** Using a /27 mask gives you 3 bits for subnetting. This permits the creation of eight subnets and satisfies your requirement of seven and gives you the most possible host addresses per subnet.
9. **a.** This host address and subnet mask combination references the following subnet of usable addresses: 172.16.0.1 to 172.16.63.254.
10. **c.** Remember, you can drop the leading zeros in any field, and once within an address you can represent continuous sections of zeros with the shorthand symbol of ::.
11. **b.** EUI64 in IPv6 permits the automatic generation of host portions of addresses.

Chapter 6

1. **b.** Note that the destination IP address does not change in the packet. However, as the router sends the frame out the exit interface heading toward the destination, it will update the destination MAC address to the next hop/device.
2. **d.** ARP is one of the many name resolution protocols we deal with. In this case, the names are Layer 2 and Layer 3 addresses.
3. **d.** The default route is 0.0.0.0/0.
4. **c.** The better the administrative distance, the more believable the protocol. Lower is better for the AD score.
5. **b, c.** Split horizon and poison reverse are critical loop preventions for early routing protocols.
6. **c.** RIP cannot be used in large networks due to a maximum hop count of 15.
7. **a.** BGP is the protocol that makes the Internet a reality.
8. **b.** The inside global address permits devices on the outside to reach devices on the inside.
9. **b.** Dynamic NAT permits dynamic mappings.
10. **a.** The client-to-router protocol in multicast is IGMP.

Chapter 7

1. **b.** ISDN uses the existing telephone network to function and is circuit switched. Note that cell switched and packet switched are used interchangeably.
2. **c.** The OC-3 operates at roughly 155Mbps.
3. **b, c, d.** Cable technology uses coaxial cable, not twisted pair.
4. **c.** Thirty channels are available for carrying the various traffic forms.
5. **c.** PAP is rarely seen in use today because it is a clear-text protocol.
6. **b.** ADSL has the distance limitation provided in this question. Remember, ADSL features different upload speeds compared to download speeds.
7. **d.** The HFC typically features multiple media types.
8. **b.** The Data link Connection Identifier signifies the local node.
9. **b.** An ATM cell features a 48-byte data area.
10. **d.** The MPLS header is 32 bits in length. Inside this header is the label itself.
11. **d.** The DMVPN is a powerful options for hub-and-spoke WAN environments.

Chapter 8

1. **d.** The key to this question is the fact that power is being used in all directions in a relative equal amount.
2. **b, d, f.** The nonoverlapping channels in the U.S. are 1, 6, and 11.
3. **b.** The older carrier-sense multiple access/collision avoidance is used.
4. **c.** This scenario describes 802.11g.
5. **a.** Multiple input, multiple output is the technology described here.
6. **b.** An independent BSS or IBSS is formed directly between wireless clients.
7. **b.** The recommended amount of overlap is 10% to 15%.
8. **c.** Open authentication permits the use of the wireless LAN with no credentials. This is useful in a public, free Wi-Fi spot, or even a guest area in an enterprise.
9. **a.** The string of characters is an initialization vector.
10. **d.** The IEEE 802.11i requirements are found in WPA2.
11. **d.** Geofencing permits the creation of a boundary for administrative alerts and actions.

Chapter 9

1. **b.** Five minutes seems like little time per year, but for some this is not acceptable.
2. **c.** The active-standby approach only uses one of the available NICs.
3. **a.** A content engine is typically a network appliance, which can receive a copy of content stored elsewhere (for example, a video presentation located on a server at a corporate headquarters) and serves that content to local clients, thus reducing the bandwidth burden on an IP WAN.
4. **c.** A snapshot is a point-in-time, read-only copy of data. It is often used with virtual machines and in some file systems.
5. **c.** A hot site is one that is up and running almost instantaneously and provides nearly an identical level of service.
6. **a, b, d.** Delay, jitter, and packet drops can all occur when QoS is not finely tuned.
7. **d.** A delay of 150 ms is often considered the worst acceptable one-way delay for voice.
8. **b.** RSVP is an Integrated Services (IntServ) type of protocol.

9. **c.** Random early detection seeks to avoid congestion before it becomes a major issue on the network.

Chapter 10

1. **b.** The **arp** command permits you to see the IP-address-to-MAC-address mappings. You can read them from left to right.
2. **d.** Use the **/all** switch to learn many additional details about the IP configuration. This includes the DNS details.
3. **b, c.** Both **route** and **netstat** can provide the route information in Windows.
4. **b.** The **nbtstat** command provides NetBIOS over TCP/IP information in Windows.
5. **c.** The **ping** command uses ICMP.
6. **d.** Use **traceroute** in UNIX in order to follow the hop-by-hop path a packet takes.
7. **a, c, d.** You can use the **nslookup**, **dig**, and **host** commands in UNIX to verify DNS operations.
8. **b.** Use **ping** with the **–c** option.
9. **b.** This output is an example of the **dig** command.
10. **a.** This output is from the UNIX **ifconfig** command.

Chapter 11

1. **c.** A common measurement for bit errors is called *bit error rate* (BER), which is calculated as follows: BER = Bit errors / Bits transmitted
2. **b.** The name *butt set* (which is sometimes called a *butt in*) comes from the device's capability to butt in to (or interrupt) a conversation in progress.
3. **d.** Different UTP categories support different data rates over specific distances. If you are working with existing cable and want to determine its category, or if you simply want to test the supported frequency range (and therefore data throughput) of a cable, you can use a cable certifier.
4. **a.** An ESD strap is critical to prevent damage to network and computer components when you are handling them.
5. **b.** A toner probe comes in two pieces: the tone generator and the probe. Another common name for a toner probe is a *fox and hound*, where the tone generator is the fox, and the probe (which searches for the tone) is the hound.

6. **d.** Identifying exactly where the break exists in a long length of cable can be problematic. Fortunately, you can use a time domain reflectometer (TDR) for copper cabling or an optical time domain reflectometer (OTDR) for fiber-optic cabling to locate the cable fault.
7. **b.** The Management Information Base (MIB) stores the variables and their values for the applicable managed device in SNMP.
8. **d.** Warnings are level 4 syslog alerts. They indicate a specific operation failed to complete successfully.
9. **a, c, d.** SNMP messages include gets, sets, and traps.
10. **a.** The Microsoft Event Viewer exists on client and server operating systems and is one of the key monitoring tools.
11. **b.** A baseline is a look at typical network configuration or performance.
12. **d.** Secure Shell (SSH) is the secure protocol to use in this situation.

Chapter 12

1. **c.** Symmetric encryption algorithms include AES, which provides options of varying strength.
2. **d.** A distributed denial-of-service attack involves many systems to compromise the availability of a system.
3. **a.** A comprehensive security policy can assist dramatically in protecting the network and the equipment against attacks.
4. **d.** A vulnerability scanner permits you to find potential vulnerabilities in your network, hopefully, before they are exploited.
5. **b, d.** RADIUS uses UDP and does not encrypt the entire packet.
6. **b**. Stateful inspection means that the return traffic is dynamically permitted thanks to the scrutiny of the outbound traffic.
7. **c.** Authentication Header is part of the IPSec standard. Note that it does not provide encryption.
8. **b, d.** HTTPS relies on SSL and/or TLS to offer security in a web browser.
9. **a.** A host intrusion prevention system adds a valuable layer of security at the host level.
10. **a, c, d.** From this list, there is no typical category of distribution-based IPS.

Chapter 13

1. **b.** A strong password should use characters from uppercase letters, lowercase letters, numbers, and special characters.
2. **a.** Data loss prevention policies typically categorize activities at the client, network, and storage levels.
3. **c.** Typical phases of incident response include prepare, identify, contain, eradicate, recover, and review.
4. **c.** For the highest degree of safety, you should always follow the vendor instructions.
5. **c.** The privileged user agreement targets administrators and others who have elevated levels of access on the network.
6. **b.** Typical life cycle phases are conceptual design, preliminary system design, detailed design and development, production and construction, utilization and support, phase-out, and disposal.

Chapter 14

1. **d.** Isolating or defining the problem is often the first step in a troubleshooting methodology.
2. **a, c, d.** Identifying, fixing, and reporting the problem are often the three steps in a simplified troubleshooting flow.
3. **c.** A broken copper strand creates an open.
4. **a.** MDIX technology makes it so that wrong cable types create fewer problems.
5. **b, c.** Two problems that could result in a Layer 2 loop are MAC table corruption and broadcast storms.
6. **b.** The ability to ping successfully is often the verification of healthy layers 1 through 3.
7. **d.** A black-hole router is one that drops traffic due to its configuration.
8. **c.** The subnet for 172.16.155.10/18 is 172.16.128.0 /18.
9. **a.** RSSI is a measure of wireless signal strength.
10. **a, c, d.** RFI can be caused by microwave ovens, baby monitors, and game consoles.

CompTIA Network+ N10-07 Cert Guide Exam Updates

Over time, reader feedback allows Pearson to gauge which topics give our readers the most problems when taking the exams. To assist readers with those topics, the authors create new materials clarifying and expanding on those troublesome exam topics. As mentioned in the Introduction, the additional content about the exam is contained in a PDF on this book's companion website, at http://www.ciscopress.com/title/9780789759818.

This appendix is intended to provide you with updated information if CompTIA makes minor modifications to the exam upon which this book is based. When CompTIA releases an entirely new exam, the changes are usually too extensive to provide in a simple updated appendix. In those cases, you might need to consult the new edition of the book for the updated content. This appendix attempts to fill the void that occurs with any print book. In particular, this appendix does the following:

- Mentions technical items that might not have been mentioned elsewhere in the book
- Covers new topics if CompTIA adds new content to the exam over time
- Provides a way to get up-to-the-minute current information about content for the exam

Always Get the Latest at the Book's Product Page

You are reading the version of this appendix that was available when your book was printed. However, given that the main purpose of this appendix is to be a living, changing document, it is important that you look for the latest version online at the book's companion website. To do so, follow these steps:

Step 1. Browse to www.ciscopress.com/title/9780789759818.

Step 2. Click the Updates tab.

Step 3. If there is a new Appendix B document on the page, download it.

NOTE The downloaded document has a version number. When comparing the version of the print Appendix B (Version 1.0) with the latest online version of this appendix, you should do the following:

- **Same version:** Ignore the PDF that you downloaded from the companion website.
- **Website has a later version:** Ignore Appendix B in your book and read only the latest version that you downloaded from the companion website.

Technical Content

The current version (1.0) of this appendix does not contain additional technical coverage.

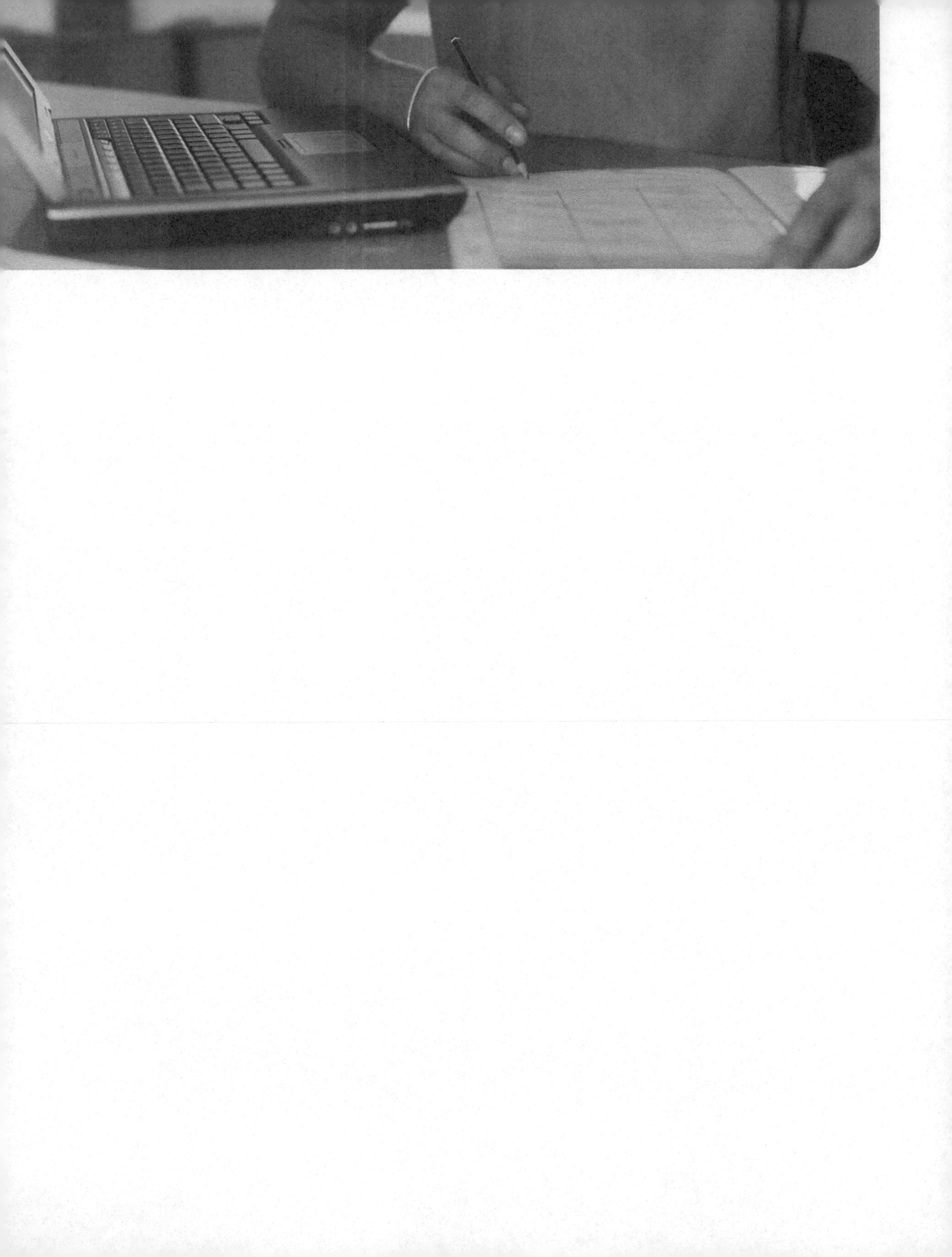

Glossary

66 block Traditionally used in corporate environments for cross-connecting phone system cabling. As 10Mbps LANs started to grow in popularity in the late 1980s and early 1990s, these termination blocks were used to cross-connect Category 3 UTP cabling. The electrical characteristics (specifically, crosstalk) of a 66 block, however, do not support higher-speed LAN technologies, such as 100Mbps Ethernet networks.

110 block Because 66 blocks are subject to too much crosstalk for higher-speed LAN connections, 110 blocks can be used to terminate a cable (such as a Category 5 cable) being used for those higher-speed LANs.

802.11a Ratified in 1999, this standard supports speeds as high as 54Mbps. Other supported data rates (which can be used if conditions are not suitable for the 54Mbps rate) include 6, 9, 12, 18, 24, 36, and 48Mbps. The 802.11a standard uses the 5GHz band and the OFDM transmission method.

802.11ac An IEEE wireless networking standard operating in the 5GHz range, with increased throughput compared to previous Wi-Fi IEEE standards.

802.11b Ratified in 1999, this standard supports speeds as high as 11Mbps. However, 5.5Mbps is another supported data rate. The 802.11b standard uses the 2.4GHz band and the DSSS transmission method.

802.11g Ratified in 2003, this standard supports speeds as high as 54Mbps. Like 802.11a, other supported data rates include 6, 9, 12, 18, 24, 36, and 48Mbps. However, like 802.11b, 802.11g operates in the 2.4GHz band, which allows it to offer backward compatibility to 802.11b devices. 802.11g can use either the OFDM or DSSS transmission method.

802.11n Ratified in 2009, this standard supports a variety of speeds, depending on its implementation. Although the speed of an 802.11n network could approach 300Mbps (through the use of channel bonding), many 802.11n devices on the market have speed ratings in the 130 Mbps–150Mbps range. Interestingly, an 802.11n WLAN can operate in the 2.4GHz band, the 5GHz band, or both simultaneously. 802.11n uses the OFDM transmission method.

acceptable use policy (AUP) Identifies what users of a network are and are not allowed to do on that network. For example, retrieving sports scores during working hours via an organization's Internet connection might be deemed inappropriate by an AUP.

access control list (ACL) Rules typically applied to router interfaces, which specify permitted and denied traffic.

Address Resolution Protocol (ARP) An ARP request is a broadcast asking for the MAC address corresponding to a known IP address. An ARP reply contains the requested MAC address.

administrative distance (AD) A routing protocol's index of believability. Routing protocols with a smaller AD are considered more believable than routing protocols with a higher AD.

Advanced Encryption Standard (AES) Released in 2001, AES is typically considered the preferred symmetric encryption algorithm. AES is available in 128-bit key, 192-bit key, and 256-bit key versions.

alerts Various monitoring devices and services can provide you with automated alerting as to network events. This is often a key element in network security to quickly learn when a potential security breach is occurring. Alerts are also popular in the area of performance monitoring.

ANT+ A wireless protocol for monitoring sensor data such as a person's heart rate or a car's tire pressure, as well as for controlling systems such as indoor lighting and television sets. ANT+ is designed and maintained by the ANT+ Alliance, which is owned by Garmin. It is based on the ANT protocol.

anycast An anycast communication flow is a one-to-nearest (from the perspective of a router's routing table) flow.

application layer (OSI model) Layer 7 of the OSI model. This layer provides application services to a network. An important yet often-misunderstood concept is that end-user applications do not reside at the application layer. Instead, the application layer supports services used by end-user applications. Another function of the application layer is advertising available services.

application layer (TCP/IP stack) Addresses concepts described by Layers 5, 6, and 7 (that is, the session, presentation, and application layers) of the OSI model.

arp command Can be used in either the Microsoft Windows or the UNIX environment to see what a Layer 2 MAC address corresponds to in a Layer 3 IP address.

asset management As related to networks, this is a formalized system of tracking network components and managing the lifecycle of those components.

asset tracking tags Tags applied to physical network assets to permit the monitoring of the location of these devices.

asymmetric encryption With asymmetric encryption, the sender and receiver of a packet use different keys.

Asynchronous Transfer Mode (ATM) A Layer 2 WAN technology that interconnects sites using virtual circuits. These virtual circuits are identified by a pair of numbers, called the *VPI/VCI pair*. A virtual path identifier (VPI) identifies a logical path, which can contain multiple virtual circuits. A virtual circuit identifier (VCI) identifies the unique logical circuit within a virtual path.

Authentication Header (AH) An IPSec protocol that provides authentication and integrity services. However, it does not provide encryption services.

authentication server In a network using 802.1X user authentication, an authentication server (typically, a RADIUS server) checks a supplicant's credentials. If the credentials are acceptable, the authentication server notifies the authenticator that the supplicant is allowed to communicate on a network. The authentication server also gives the authenticator a key that can be used to securely transmit data during the authenticator's session with the supplicant.

authenticator In a network using 802.1X user authentication, an authenticator forwards a supplicant's authentication request on to an authentication server. After the authentication server authenticates the supplicant, the authenticator receives a key that is used to communicate securely during a session with the supplicant.

Automatic Private IP Addressing (APIPA) Allows a networked device to self-assign an IP address from the 169.254.0.0/16 network. Note that this address is only usable on the device's local subnet (meaning that the IP address is not routable).

availability The measure of a network's uptime.

badges Identifiers worn by employees of an organization to assist with physical security.

bandwidth The measure of network throughput capable on a network media or path.

baseline A collection of data portraying the characteristics of a network under normal operating conditions. Data collected while troubleshooting can then be contrasted against baseline data.

Basic Rate Interface (BRI) A BRI circuit contains two 64Kbps B channels and one 16Kbps D channel. Although such a circuit can carry two simultaneous voice conversations, the two B channels can be logically bonded together into a single virtual circuit (by using PPP's multilink interface feature) to offer a 128Kbps data path.

basic service set (BSS) WLANs that have just one AP are called BSS WLANs. BSS WLANs are said to run in infrastructure mode because wireless clients connect to an AP, which is typically connected to a wired network infrastructure. A BSS network is often used in residential and SOHO locations, where the signal strength provided by a single AP is sufficient to service all of the WLAN's wireless clients.

biometrics The use of unique characteristics of the body to provide access credentials and security. For example, a thumbprint can be used to access a mobile device.

bit-error rate tester (BERT) When troubleshooting a link where you suspect a high bit-error rate (BER), you can use a piece of test equipment called a bit-error rate tester (BERT), which contains both a pattern generator (which can generate a variety of bit patterns) and an error detector (which is synchronized with the pattern generator and can determine the number of bit errors) and can calculate a BER for the tested transmission link.

black-hole router A router that drops packets that cannot be fragmented and are exceeding the MTU size of an interface without notifying the sender.

block size The number of IP addresses in a subnet, including the subnet's address and the subnet's directed broadcast address.

Bluetooth A wireless protocol for creating a personal area network, where a device such as a mobile phone can send data to a headset, for example.

Bootstrap Protocol (BOOTP) A legacy broadcast-based protocol used by networked devices to obtain IP address information.

Border Gateway Protocol (BGP) The only EGP in widespread use today. In fact, BGP is considered to be the routing protocol that runs the Internet, which is an interconnection of multiple autonomous systems. BGP is a path-vector routing protocol, meaning that it can use as its metric the number of autonomous system hops that must be transited to reach a destination network, as opposed to the number of required router hops.

borrowed bits Bits added to a classful subnet mask.

BPDU Guard The ability of a switch to block a port where unexpected BPDUs are arriving from another switch or attacker.

buffer overflow This attack occurs when an attacker leverages a vulnerability in an application, causing data to be written to a memory area (that is, a buffer) that's being used by a different application.

bus topology Typically, this topology uses a cable running through the area requiring connectivity, and devices to be networked can tap into that cable.

butt set A piece of test equipment typically used by telephone technicians. The clips on a butt set can connect to the tip and ring wires on a punch-down block (for example, a 66 block or a 110 block) connecting to a telephone. This allows the technician to check the line (for example, to determine whether a dial tone is present on the line and determine whether a call can be placed from the line).

cable certifier If you are working with existing cable and want to determine its category, or if you simply want to test the supported frequency range (and therefore data throughput) of the cable, you can use a cable certifier.

cable modem Attaches to the same coaxial cable (typically in a residence) that provides television programming. A cable modem can use predetermined frequency ranges to transmit and receive data over that coaxial cable.

cable tester A cable tester can check the conductors in an Ethernet cable. It contains two parts. By connecting these parts of the cable tester to each end of a cable under test, you can check the wires in the cable for continuity (that is, check to make sure that there are no opens, or breaks, in a conductor). In addition, you can verify an RJ-45 connector's pin-outs (which are wires connected to the appropriate pins on an RJ-45 connector).

campus area network (CAN) An interconnection of networks located in nearby buildings (for example, buildings on a college campus).

captive portal Typically a web page designed to collect the username and password of a user trying to gain access to a network or application.

carrier-sense multiple access/collision avoidance (CSMA/CA) Just as CSMA/CD is needed for half-duplex Ethernet connections, CSMA/CA is needed for WLAN connections because of their half-duplex operation. Similar to how an Ethernet device listens to an Ethernet segment to determine whether a frame exists on the segment, a WLAN device listens for a transmission on a wireless channel to determine whether it is safe to transmit. In addition, the collision-avoidance part of the CSMA/CA algorithm causes wireless devices to wait for a random back-off time before transmitting.

carrier-sense multiple access/collision detect (CSMA/CD) Used on an Ethernet network to help prevent a collision from occurring and to recover if a collision does occur. CSMA/CD is only needed on half-duplex connections.

central office (CO) A building containing a telephone company's telephone-switching equipment. COs are categorized into five hierarchical classes. A Class 1 CO is a long-distance office serving a regional area. A Class 2 CO is a second-level long-distance office; that is, it is subordinate to a Class 1 office. A Class 3 CO is a third-level long-distance office. A Class 4 CO is a fourth-level long-distance office, which provides telephone subscribers access to a live operator. A Class 5 CO is at the bottom of the five-layer hierarchy and physically connects to customer devices in a local area.

Challenge Handshake Authentication Protocol (CHAP) Like PAP, CHAP performs one-way authentication. However, authentication is performed through a three-way handshake (challenge, response, and acceptance messages) between a server and a client. The three-way handshake allows a client to be authenticated without sending credential information across a network.

Challenge-Response Authentication Mechanism Message Digest 5 (CRAM-MD5) A common variant of HMAC frequently used in email systems. Like CHAP, CRAM-MD5 only performs one-way authentication (the server authenticates the client).

change management documentation This important documentation explains the process whereby changes are permitted in the network. This often consists of a series of approvals and testing steps.

channel bonding With channel bonding, two wireless bands can be logically bonded together, forming a band with twice the bandwidth of an individual band. Some literature calls channel bonding *40MHz mode*, which refers to the bonding of two adjacent 20MHz bands into a 40MHz band.

channel service unit/data service unit (CSU/DSU) Acts as a digital modem that terminates a digital circuit (for example, a T1 or an E1 circuit).

circuit-switched connection A connection that is brought up on an as-needed basis. A circuit-switched connection is analogous to a phone call, where you pick up a phone and dial a number, and a connection is established based on the number you dial.

classful mask A classful mask is the default subnet mask applied to Class A, B, and C IPv4 networks. Specifically, Class A networks have a classful mask of 255.0.0.0. Class B networks have a classful mask of 255.255.0.0, and Class C networks have a classful mask of 255.255.255.0.

classification Classification is the process of placing traffic into different categories.

classless interdomain routing (CIDR) Shortens a classful subnet mask by removing right-justified 1s from a classful mask. As a result, CIDR allows contiguous classful networks to be aggregated. This process is sometimes called *route aggregation*.

client Defines the device an end user uses to access a network. This device might be a workstation, laptop, smartphone with wireless capabilities, tablet, or variety of other end-user terminal devices.

client/server network In a client/server network, a dedicated server (for example, a file server or a print server) provides shared access to a resource (for example, files or a printer). Clients (for example, PCs) on the network with appropriate privilege levels can gain access to those shared resources.

client-to-site VPN Also known as a *remote-access VPN*, a client-to-site VPN interconnects a remote user with a site, as an alternative to dial-up or ISDN connectivity, at a reduced cost.

clustering Connecting systems together with the intent of delivering network services from the cluster to increase responsiveness and capacity. This solution also increases availability and redundancy.

coaxial cable Also known as *coax*, a coaxial cable is composed of two conductors. One of the conductors is an inner insulated conductor. This inner conductor is surrounded by another conductor. This second conductor is sometimes made of a metallic foil or woven wire.

code-division multiple access(CDMA) An example of multiple access, where several transmitters can send information simultaneously over a single communication channel. This allows several users to share a band of frequencies. CDMA is used as the access method in many mobile phone standards.

cold sites These are redundant sites for a network, and they require time and effort to bring online.

collision A collision occurs when two devices on an Ethernet network simultaneously transmit a frame. Because an Ethernet segment cannot handle more than one frame at a time, both frames become corrupted.

committed information rate (CIR) The CIR of an interface is the average traffic rate over the period of a second.

Common Address Redundancy Protocol (CARP) An open standard variant of HSRP (Hot Standby Router Protocol), which provides first-hop router redundancy.

congestion avoidance If an interface's output queue fills to capacity, newly arriving packets are discarded (or *tail dropped*). Congestion avoidance can prevent this behavior. RED (Random Early Detection) is an example of a congestion-avoidance mechanism.

congestion management When a device, such as a switch or a router, receives traffic faster than it can be transmitted, the device attempts to buffer (or store) the extra traffic until bandwidth becomes available. This buffering process is called *queuing* or *congestion management*.

content engine A dedicated appliance whose role is to locally cache content received from a remote network (for example, a destination on the Internet). Subsequent requests for that content can be serviced locally, from the content engine, thus reducing bandwidth demand on a WAN.

content switch Can be used to load-balance requests for content across a group of servers containing that content. If one of the servers in the group needs to have maintenance performed, that server could be administratively removed from the group, as defined on the content switch. As a result, the content switch can help maximize uptime when performing server maintenance. It minimizes the load on individual servers by distributing its load across multiple identical servers. A content switch also allows a network to scale because one or more additional servers could be added to the server group defined on the content switch if the load on existing servers increases.

crimper Used to attach a connector (for example, an RJ-45 connector) to the end of an unshielded twisted-pair (UTP) cable.

current state modulation One way to electrically or optically represent a binary 1 or 0 is to use current state modulation, which represents a binary 1 with the presence of voltage (on a copper cable) or the presence of light (on a fiber-optic cable). Similarly, the absence of light or voltage represents a binary 0.

customer premise equipment (CPE) This device resides at a customer site. A router, as an example, can be a CPE that connects a customer with an MPLS service provider.

cyclic redundancy check (CRC) A mathematical algorithm that is executed on a data string by both the sender and the receiver of the data string. If the calculated CRC values match, the receiver can conclude that the data string was not corrupted during transmission.

data link layer As Layer 2 of the OSI model, this layer is concerned with the packaging of data into frames and transmitting those frames on a network, performing error detection/correction, uniquely identifying network devices with an address, and handling flow control.

decibel (dB) A ratio of radiated power to a reference value. In the case of dBi, the reference value is the signal strength (that is, the power) radiated from an isotropic antenna, which represents a theoretical antenna that radiates an equal amount of power in all directions (in a spherical pattern). An isotropic antenna is considered to have gain of 0 dBi.

decibel (dB) loss A loss of signal power. If a transmission's dB loss is too great, the transmission cannot be properly interpreted by the intended recipient.

dedicated leased line A logical connection interconnecting two sites. This logical connection might physically connect through a service provider's facility or a telephone company's central office. The expense of a dedicated leased line is typically higher than other WAN technologies offering similar data rates, because with a dedicated leased line, a customer does not have to share bandwidth with other customers.

default gateway The IP address of a router (or multilayer switch) to which a networked device sends traffic destined for a subnet other than the device's local subnet.

default static route A default static route is an administratively configured entry in a router's routing table that specifies where traffic for all unknown networks should be sent.

demarc Also known as a *demarcation point* or a *demarc extension*, this is the point in a telephone network where the maintenance responsibility passes from a telephone company to a subscriber (unless the subscriber purchased an inside wiring plan). This demarc is typically a box mounted to the outside of a customer's building (for example, a residence).

demilitarized zone (DMZ) Often contains servers that should be accessible from the Internet. This approach would, for example, allow users on the Internet to initiate an email or a web session coming into an organization's email or web server. However, other protocols would be blocked.

denial of service (DoS) A DoS attack floods a system with an excessive amount of traffic or requests, which consumes the system's processing resources and prevents the system from responding to many legitimate requests.

designated port In an STP topology, every network segment has a single designated port, which is the port on that segment that is closest to the root bridge, in terms of cost. Therefore, all ports on a root bridge are designated ports.

differential backup A type of partial backup of a data set. All data that has changed since the last full backup is targeted by the backup job.

differentiated services (DiffServ) As its name suggests, DiffServ differentiates between multiple traffic flows. Specifically, packets are marked, and routers and switches can then make decisions (for example, dropping or forwarding decisions) based on those markings.

dig command Can resolve an FQDN to an IP address on UNIX hosts.

digital subscriber line (DSL) A group of technologies that provide high-speed data transmission over existing telephone wiring. DSL has several variants, which vary in data rates and distance limitations. Three of the more popular DSL variants include asymmetric DSL (ADSL), symmetric DSL (DSL), and very high bit-rate DSL (VDSL).

direct-sequence spread spectrum (DSSS) Modulates data over an entire range of frequencies using a series of symbols called *chips*. A chip is shorter in duration than a bit, meaning that chips are transmitted at a higher rate than the actual data. These chips not only represent encoded data to be transmitted, but also what appears to be random data. Because both parties involved in a DSSS communication know which chips represent actual data and which chips do not, if a third-party intercepted a DSSS transmission, it would be difficult for that party to eavesdrop on the data because he would not easily know which chips represented valid bits. DSSS is more subject to environmental factors, as opposed to FHSS and OFDM, because it uses an entire frequency spectrum.

distance vector A category of routing protocol that sends a full copy of its routing table to its directly attached neighbors.

distributed denial of service (DDoS) These attacks can increase the amount of traffic flooded to a target system. Specifically, an attacker compromises multiple systems, and those compromised systems, called *zombies*, can be instructed by the attacker to simultaneously launch a DDoS attack against a target system.

Domain Name System (DNS) server Performs the task of taking a domain name (for example, www.ciscopress.com) and resolving that name into a corresponding IP address (for example, 10.1.2.3).

dotted-decimal notation A method of writing an IPv4 address or subnet mask, where groups of 8 bits (called *octets*) are separated by periods.

dual stack The ability of a network interface to run multiple protocols, such as IP and IPv6.

Dynamic Host Configuration Protocol (DHCP) Dynamically assigns IP address information (for example, IP address, subnet mask, DNS server's IP address, and default gateway's IP address) to network devices.

Dynamic Host Configuration Protocol (DHCP) snooping The process of securing the network against a rogue DHCP server attack or other types of DHCP security attacks.

Dynamic Host Configuration Protocol (DHCP) Version 6 The IPv6 version of DHCP.

Dynamic Multipoint VPN (DMVPN) An overlay VPN approach where VPN connections are dynamically established and secured.

Dynamic NAT (DNAT) A variant of NAT in which inside local addresses are automatically assigned an inside global address from a pool of available addresses.

E1 An E1 circuit contains 32 channels, in contrast to the 24 channels on a T1 circuit. Only 30 of those 32 channels, however, can transmit data (or voice or video). Specifically, the first of those 32 channels is reserved for framing and synchronization, and the seventeenth channel is reserved for signaling (that is, to set up, maintain, and tear down a session).

E3 A digital circuit in the same E-carrier family of standards as an E1. An E3 circuit's available bandwidth is 34.4Mbps.

edge label switch router (ELSR) Resides at the edge of an MPLS service provider's cloud and interconnects a service provider to one or more customers.

electromagnetic interference (EMI) An electromagnetic waveform that can be received by network cable (possibly corrupting data traveling on the cable) or radiated from a network cable (possibly interfering with data traveling on another cable).

electrostatic discharge (ESD) wrist strap To prevent static electricity in your body from damaging electrical components on a circuit board, you can wear an ESD wrist strap. The strap is equipped with a clip that you can attach to something with a ground potential (for example, a large metal desk). While wearing the wrist strap, if you have any static buildup in your body, the static flows to the object with a ground potential to which your strap is clipped, thus avoiding damage to any electrical components that you might touch.

Encapsulating Security Payload (ESP) An IPSec protocol that provides authentication, integrity, and encryption services.

Enhanced Interior Gateway Routing Protocol (EIGRP) A Cisco proprietary protocol. Although EIGRP is popular in Cisco-only networks, it is less popular in mixed-vendor networks. Like OSPF, EIGRP is an IGP with very fast convergence and high scalability. EIGRP is considered to be an advanced distance vector or a hybrid routing protocol.

Enterprise mode In the context of wireless networking, this refers to using a centralized authentication server such as RADIUS for authentication, instead of a preshared key (PSK).

Ethernet Ethernet is a Layer 1 technology developed by Xerox and encompasses a variety of standards that specify various media types, speeds, and distance limitations.

evil twin A device that is postured to appear like a legitimate access point on the network to carry out a wireless attack.

extended service set (ESS) WLANs containing more than one AP are called ESS WLANs. Like BSS WLANs, ESS WLANs operate in infrastructure mode. When you have more than one AP, take care to prevent one AP from interfering with another. Specifically, nonoverlapping channels (that is, channels 1, 6, and 11 for the 2.4GHz band) should be selected for adjacent wireless coverage areas.

Extended Unique Identifier-64 (EUI-64) A method in IPv6 to calculate a unique host address portion for a node.

Exterior Gateway Protocol (EGP) A routing protocol that operates between autonomous systems, which are networks under different administrative control. Border Gateway Protocol (BGP) is the only EGP in widespread use today.

Fibre Channel over Ethernet (FCoE) Technology that permits SAN traffic of FC over the Ethernet media.

File Transfer Protocol (FTP) A protocol capable of transferring files over a network.

File Transfer Protocol SSL (FTPS) Uses SSL technology to secure the FTP file transfer.

firewall Primarily a network security appliance, a firewall can protect a trusted network (for example, a corporate LAN) from an untrusted network (for example, the Internet) by allowing the trusted network to send traffic into the untrusted network and receive the return traffic from the untrusted network, while blocking traffic for sessions that were initiated on the untrusted network.

Flood Guard Serves as a preventive control against denial of service (DoS) or distributed denial of service (DDoS) attacks. A Flood Guard is available either as a standalone device or as a firewall component. It is capable of monitoring network traffic to identify DoS attacks in progress generated through packet flooding.

fox and hound See *toner probe.*

Frame Relay A Layer 2 WAN technology that interconnects sites using virtual circuits. These virtual circuits are identified by locally significant data-link connection identifiers (DLCIs).

frequency-hopping spread spectrum (FHSS) Allows the participants in a communication to hop between predetermined frequencies. Security is enhanced because the participants can predict the next frequency to be used but a third party cannot easily predict the next frequency. FHSS can also provision extra bandwidth by simultaneously using more than one frequency.

FTP bounce An FTP bounce attack uses the FTP **PORT** command to covertly open a connection with a remote system. Specifically, an attacker connects to an FTP server and uses the **PORT** command to cause the FTP server to open a communications channel with the intended victim, which might allow a connection from the FTP server, while a connection directly from the attacker might be denied.

full backup A backup job that ensures all data is backed up, regardless of when this data may have been backed up previously.

full duplex This connection allows a device to simultaneously transmit and receive data.

full-mesh topology Directly connects every site to every other site.

geofencing A virtual perimeter of a geographic area. You might create a wireless geofence boundary around a data center to start an alarm if equipment leaves the perimeter.

Global System for Mobile Communications (GSM) A standard developed by the European Telecommunications Standards Institute (ETSI) to describe the protocols for second-generation digital cellular networks used by mobile devices such as tablets. GSM was first deployed in Finland in December 1991. As of 2014, it has become the global standard for mobile communications, with over 90% market share, operating in over 219 countries and territories.

GNU Privacy Guard (GPG) A free variant of pretty good privacy (PGP), which is an asymmetric encryption algorithm.

half duplex A half-duplex connection allows a device to either receive or transmit data at any one time. However, a half-duplex device cannot simultaneously transmit and receive.

hardware firewall A network appliance dedicated to the purpose of acting as a firewall. This appliance can have multiple interfaces for connecting to areas of a network requiring varying levels of security.

hold-down timers Can speed the convergence process of a routing protocol. After a router makes a change to a route entry, the hold-down timer prevents subsequent updates for a specified period of time. This approach can help stop *flapping routes* (which are routes that oscillate between being available and unavailable) from preventing convergence.

honey net A network containing more than one honey pot.

honey pot Acts as a distracter. Specifically, a system designated as a honey pot appears to be an attractive attack target. One school of thought on the use of a honey pot is to place one or more honey-pot systems in a network to entice attackers into thinking the system is real. The attackers then use their resources attacking the honey pot, resulting in their leaving the real servers alone.

host-based IPS (HIPS) An HIPS system is a computer running intrusion prevention software for the purpose of protecting the computer from attacks.

host command Can resolve an FQDN to an IP address on hosts.

hot sites Redundant data center locations that are ready to replace a failed data center with little to no time or effort.

hub An Ethernet hub is an older technology used to interconnect network components, such as clients and servers. Hubs vary in their number of available ports. A hub does not perform an inspection of the traffic it passes. Rather, a hub simply receives traffic in a port and repeats that traffic out all of its other ports.

hub-and-spoke topology When interconnecting multiple sites (for example, multiple corporate locations) via WAN links, a hub-and-spoke topology has a WAN link from each remote site (a spoke site) to the main site (the hub site).

Hypertext Transfer Protocol over SSL (HTTPS) A method of securing web traffic over the Internet using Secure Socket Layer and Transport Layer Security technology.

incremental backup A backup job that only backs up the changed data since the last incremental backup.

independent basic service set (IBSS) A WLAN can be created without the use of an AP. Such a configuration, called an IBSS, is said to work in an *ad hoc* fashion. An ad hoc WLAN is useful for temporary connections between wireless devices. For example, you might temporarily interconnect two laptop computers to transfer a few files.

infrared (IR) A wireless line-of-sight technology that might be found in an Internet of Things deployment.

infrastructure as a service (IaaS) Providing network infrastructure as a service using cloud technologies.

insider threat In network security, this refers to an attacker who resides inside the network. Often, this might be an employee of the company.

integrated services (IntServ) Often referred to as *hard QoS* because IntServ can make strict bandwidth reservations. IntServ uses signaling among network devices to provide bandwidth reservations. Resource Reservation Protocol (RSVP) is an example of an IntServ approach to QoS. Because IntServ must be configured on every router along a packet's path, a primary drawback of IntServ is its lack of scalability.

Integrated Services Digital Network (ISDN) A digital telephony technology that supports multiple 64Kbps channels (known as *bearer channels* or *B channels*) on a single connection. ISDN was popular back in the 1980s for connecting PBXs, which are telephone switches owned and operated by a company, to a telephone company's central office. ISDN has the ability to carry voice, video, or data over its B channels. ISDN also offers a robust set of signaling protocols: Q.921 for Layer 2 signaling and Q.931 for Layer 3 signaling. These signaling protocols run on a separate channel in an ISDN circuit (known as the *delta channel*, *data channel*, or *D channel*).

Interior Gateway Protocol (IGP) A routing protocol that operates within an autonomous system, which is a network under a single administrative control. OSPF and EIGRP are popular examples of IGPs.

Intermediate Distribution Frame (IDF) documentation The documentation related to a distribution frame in a central office or customer premises, which cross-connects the user cable media to individual user line circuits and may serve as a distribution point for multipair cables from the main distribution frame (MDF) or combined distribution frame (CDF) to individual cables connected to equipment in areas remote from these frames.

Intermediate System-to-Intermediate System (IS-IS) A link-state routing protocol similar in its operation to OSPF. IS-IS uses a configurable-yet-dimensionless metric associated with an interface and runs Dijkstra's shortest path first algorithm. Although using IS-IS as an IGP offers the scalability, fast convergence, and vendor-interoperability benefits of OSPF, it has not been deployed as widely as OSPF.

Internet Group Management Protocol (IGMP) A multicast protocol used between clients and routers to let routers know which of their interfaces has a multicast receiver attached.

Internet Key Exchange (IKE) A protocol used to set up an IPSec session.

Internet layer This layer of the TCP/IP stack maps to Layer 3 (network layer) of the OSI model. Although multiple routed protocols (for example, IPv4 and IPv6) may reside at the OSI model's network layer, the Internet layer of the TCP/IP stack focuses on IP as the protocol to be routed through a network.

Internet Security Association and Key Management Protocol (ISAKMP) Negotiates parameters for an IPSec session.

intrusion detection system (IDS) IDS devices can recognize the signature of a well-known attack and respond to stop the attack. However, an IDS sensor does not reside inline with the traffic flow. Therefore, one or more malicious packets might reach an intended victim before the traffic flow is stopped by an IDS sensor.

intrusion prevention system (IPS) IPS devices can recognize the signature of a well-known attack and respond to stop the attack. An IPS device resides inline with the traffic flow, unlike an IDS sensor.

inventory management The discipline of managing network device inventory.

IP Address Management The software and processes for managing the IP addresses used in an organization.

IP Security (IPSec) A type of VPN that provides confidentiality, integrity, and authentication.

ipconfig command A Microsoft Windows command that can be used to display IP address configuration parameters on a PC. In addition, if DHCP is used by the PC, the **ipconfig** command can be used to release and renew a DHCP lease, which is often useful during troubleshooting.

iptables The software firewall that is included with most Linux distributions.

jitter The uneven arrival of packets.

Kerberos A client/server authentication protocol that supports mutual authentication between a client and a server. Kerberos uses the concept of a trusted third party (a *key distribution center*) that hands out tickets to be used instead of a username and password combination.

key fob A device on a key ring that can provide security functions in the network.

label switch router (LSR) Resides inside a service provider's MPLS cloud and makes frame-forwarding decisions based on labels applied to frames.

latency The measure of delay in a network.

Layer 2 Forwarding (L2F) A VPN protocol designed (by Cisco Systems) with the intent of providing a tunneling protocol for PPP. Like L2TP, L2F lacks native security features.

Layer 2 Tunneling Protocol (L2TP) A VPN protocol that lacks security features, such as encryption. However, L2TP can still be used for a secure VPN connection if it is combined with another protocol that provides encryption.

Lightweight Directory Access Protocol (LDAP) An open standard for storing directory information for the network such as usernames and passwords and other user and computer parameters.

link aggregation As defined by the IEEE 802.3ad standard, link aggregation allows multiple physical connections to be logically bundled into a single logical connection.

link efficiency To make the most of the limited bandwidth available on slower speed links, you might choose to implement *compression* or link fragmentation and interleaving (LFI). These QoS mechanisms are examples of link efficiency mechanisms.

link-local IP address A link-local IP address is a nonroutable IP address usable only on a local subnet.

link state A category of routing protocol that maintains a topology of a network and uses an algorithm to determine the shortest path to a destination network.

link-state advertisement (LSA) Sent by routers in a network to advertise the networks the routers know how to reach. Routers use those LSAs to construct a topological map of a network. The algorithm run against this topological map is Dijkstra's shortest path first algorithm.

load balancing Distributing client requests among different network resources that can provide the same service or data.

local area network (LAN) Interconnects network components within a local region (for example, within a building).

local loop A connection between a customer's premises and a local telephone company's central office.

locks Various types of locks are a key element in physical security for the networks. Locks can also exist on the network devices themselves.

logic bomb This is an attacker's malicious code that resides in a software system and will be triggered when certain conditions are met.

logical diagrams A logical network diagram details the network path from a logical perspective as opposed to a physical one.

logical topology The actual traffic flow of a network determines the network's logical topology.

loopback A loopback interface on a network device is a logical (virtual) interface that is often used for testing purposes.

Management Information Base (MIB) This is the database of variables that exist on an SNMP-managed device.

marking Alters bits within a frame, cell, or packet to indicate how a network should treat that traffic. Marking alone does not change how a network treats a packet. Other tools (such as queuing tools) can, however, reference markings and make decisions (for example, forwarding decisions or dropping decisions) based on those markings.

maximum transmission unit (MTU) The largest packet size supported on an interface.

mean time between failures (MTBF) The predicted elapsed time between inherent failures in a mechanical system.

mean time to repair (MTTR) The predicted time it takes to repair a network or network object.

media Devices need to be interconnected via some sort of media. This media could be copper cabling. Alternatively, it could be a fiber-optic cable. Media might not even be a cable, as is the case with wireless networks, where radio waves travel through the media of *air*.

metric A value assigned to a route. Lower metrics are preferred over higher metrics.

metropolitan area network (MAN) Interconnects locations scattered throughout a metropolitan area.

Microsoft Challenge Handshake Authentication Protocol (MS-CHAP) A Microsoft-enhanced version of CHAP, offering a collection of additional features not present with PAP or CHAP, including two-way authentication.

Microsoft Routing and Remote Access Server (RRAS) A Microsoft Windows server feature that allows Microsoft Windows clients to remotely access a Microsoft Windows network.

modem A device that permits a remote connection to the Internet or other remote networks. This device might be dial-up or newer technologies such as cable.

motion detection This physical security approach uses sensors to detect motion in a secured area.

multicast A multicast communication flow is a one-to-many flow.

multifactor authentication Similar to two-factor authentication, multifactor authentication requires two or more types of successful authentication before granting access to a network.

multilayer switch Like a router, a multilayer switch can make traffic forwarding decisions based on Layer 3 information. Although multilayer switches more closely approach wire-speed throughput than most routers, routers tend to have a greater feature set and are capable of supporting more interface types than a multilayer switch.

multimode fiber (MMF) Multimode fiber-optic cabling has a core with a diameter large enough to permit the injection of light at multiple angles. The different paths (that is, *modes*) that light travels can lead to multimode delay distortion, which causes bits to be received out of order because the pulses of light representing the bits traveled different paths (and therefore different distances).

multiple-input multiple-output (MIMO) MIMO uses multiple antennas for transmission and reception. These antennas do not interfere with one another, thanks to MIMO's use of spatial multiplexing, which encodes data based on the antenna from which the data will be transmitted. Both reliability and throughput can be increased with MIMO's simultaneous use of multiple antennas.

Multiprotocol Label Switching (MPLS) A WAN technology popular among service providers. MPLS performs label switching to forward traffic within an MPLS cloud by inserting a 32-bit header (which contains a 20-bit label) between a frame's Layer 2 and Layer 3 headers and making forwarding decisions based on the label within an MPLS header.

nbtstat command Displays NetBIOS information for IP-based networks. The *nbt* prefix of the **nbtstat** command refers to NetBIOS over TCP/IP, which is called *NBT* (or *NetBT*). This command can, for example, display a listing of NetBIOS device names learned by a Microsoft Windows–based PC.

Near Field Communication (NFC) A wireless communications technology that might be seen in the Internet of Things. This technology is often used in payment systems.

neighbor discovery Any process whereby network elements can discover each other on the network. In the case of EIGRP, hello packets are used, for example.

Nessus A network-vulnerability scanner available from Tenable Network Security.

netstat command Can display a variety of information about IP-based connections on a Windows or UNIX host.

Network Access Server (NAS) A network device specialized in controlling access to the network. NAS might also stand for network-attached storage.

network address translation (NAT) Allows private IP addresses (as defined in RFC 1918) to be translated into Internet-routable IP addresses (public IP addresses).

network as a service (NaaS) A service provider offering where clients can purchase data services (for example, email, LDAP, and DNS services) traditionally hosted in a corporate data center.

network interface card (NIC) teaming This technology permits multiple network interface cards to function as a single interface to the network. NIC teaming provides excellent redundancy.

network interface layer The network interface layer of the TCP/IP stack (also known as the *network access layer*) encompasses the technologies addressed by Layers 1 and 2 (that is, the physical and data link layers) of the OSI model.

network layer Layer 3 of the OSI model. This layer is primarily concerned with forwarding data based on logical addresses.

network-based IDS (NIDS) An NIDS device is a network appliance dedicated to acting as an IDS sensor.

network-based IPS (NIPS) An NIPS device is a network appliance dedicated to acting as an IPS sensor.

next-generation firewall (NGF) More modern firewalls that can perform tasks such as deep packet inspection.

next hop An IP address on the next router to which traffic should be forwarded.

nmap This management tool permits the scanning of the network for hosts and services.

nondesignated port In STP terms, nondesignated ports block traffic to create a loop-free topology.

notifications Many network devices and technologies support notifications for key events. These are often used in the area of security.

nslookup command Can resolve an FQDN to an IP address on Microsoft Windows and UNIX hosts.

octet A grouping of 8 bits. An IPv4 address consists of four octets (that is, a total of 32 bits).

offsite The term *offsite* in the context of virtualization technologies refers to hosting virtual devices on hardware physically located in a service provider's data center.

omnidirectional antenna Radiates power at relatively equal power levels in all directions (somewhat similar to the theoretical isotropic antenna). Omnidirectional antennas are popular in residential WLANs and SOHO locations.

onsite The term *onsite* in the context of virtualization technologies refers to hosting virtual devices on hardware physically located in a corporate data center.

open A broken strand of copper that prevents current from flowing through a circuit.

Open Shortest Path First (OSPF) A link-state routing protocol that uses a metric of *cost*, which is based on the link speed between two routers. OSPF is a popular IGP because of its scalability, fast convergence, and vendor interoperability.

Open Systems Interconnection (OSI) reference model Commonly referred to as the *OSI model* or the *OSI stack*. This seven-layer model categorizes various network technologies.

optical carrier (OC) Optical networks often use OC levels to indicate bandwidth. As a base reference point, the speed of an OC-1 link is 51.84Mbps. Other OC levels are multiples of an OC-1. For example, an OC-3 link has three times the bandwidth of an OC-1 link (that is, 3 * 51.84Mbps = 155.52Mbps).

optical time domain reflectometer (OTDR) Detects the location of a fault in a fiber cable by sending light down the fiber-optic cable and measuring the time required for the light to bounce back from the cable fault. The OTDR can then mathematically calculate the location of the fault.

orthogonal frequency-division multiplexing (OFDM) Whereas DSSS uses a high modulation rate for the symbols it sends, OFDM uses a relatively slow modulation rate for symbols. This slower modulation rate, combined with the simultaneous transmission of data over 52 data streams, helps OFDM support high data rates while resisting crosstalk between the various data streams.

packet-switched connection Similar to a dedicated leased line, because most packet-switched networks are always on. However, unlike a dedicated leased line, packet-switched connections allow multiple customers to share a service provider's bandwidth.

partial-mesh topology A hybrid of a hub-and-spoke topology and a full-mesh topology. A partial-mesh topology can be designed to provide an optimal route between selected sites, while avoiding the expense of interconnecting every site to every other site.

Password Authentication Protocol (PAP) Performs one-way authentication (that is, a client authenticates with a server). However, a significant drawback to PAP, other than its unidirectional authentication, is its clear-text transmission of credentials, which could permit an eavesdropper to learn authentication credentials.

peer-to-peer network Allows interconnected devices (for example, PCs) to share their resources with one another. These resources could be, for example, files or printers.

personal area network (PAN) A network whose scale is smaller than a LAN. As an example, a connection between a PC and a digital camera via a USB cable is considered to be a PAN.

personal mode In the context of wireless networking, this refers to using a preshared key (PSK) instead of a centralized server, such as RADIUS, for authentication.

phishing This network attack uses email or other messages to attempt to capture the authentication information (or other information) from an end user.

physical diagrams These diagrams provide a map of the physical layout of the network.

physical layer Layer 1 of the OSI model. This layer is concerned with the transmission of bits on a network.

physical topology The way a network's components are physically interconnected determines the network's physical topology.

ping command One of the most commonly used command-line commands, **ping** can check IP connectivity between two network devices. Multiple platforms (for example, routers, switches, and hosts) support the **ping** command.

plain old telephone service (POTS) A POTS connection links a customer device (such as a telephone) to the public switched telephone network (PSTN).

platform as a service (PaaS) This category of cloud permits the delivery of operating systems and libraries needed by developers.

plenum Plenum cabling is fire retardant and minimizes toxic fumes released by network cabling if that cable were to catch on fire. As a result, plenum cabling is often a requirement of local fire codes for cable in raised flooring or in other open-air return ducts.

Point-to-Point Protocol (PPP) A common Layer 2 protocol offering features such as multilink interface, looped link detection, error detection, and authentication.

Point-to-Point Protocol over Ethernet (PPPoE) Commonly used between a DSL modem in a home (or business) and a service provider. Specifically, PPPoE encapsulates PPP frames within Ethernet frames. PPP is used to leverage its features, such as authentication.

Point-to-Point Tunneling Protocol (PPTP) An older VPN protocol that supported the *dial-up networking* feature in older versions of Microsoft Windows. Like L2TP and L2F, PPTP lacks native security features. However, Microsoft's versions of PPTP bundled with various versions of Microsoft Windows were enhanced to offer security features.

poison reverse This feature of a distance-vector routing protocol causes a route received on one interface to be advertised back out of that same interface with a metric considered to be infinite.

policing Instead of making a minimum amount of bandwidth available for specific traffic types, you might want to limit available bandwidth. Both policing and traffic-shaping tools can accomplish this objective. Collectively, these tools are called *traffic conditioners*. Policing can drop exceeding traffic, as opposed to buffering it.

port address translation (PAT) A variant of NAT in which multiple inside local IP addresses share a single inside global IP address. PAT can distinguish between different flows based on port numbers.

port aggregation Joining multiple network device ports together for increased bandwidth and redundancy.

port scanning The process of scanning for open TCP or UDP ports on the network.

Power over Ethernet (PoE) Defined by the IEEE 802.3af and 802.3at standards, PoE allows an Ethernet switch to provide power to an attached device (for example, a wireless access point, security camera, or IP phone) by applying power to the same wires in a UTP cable that are used to transmit and receive data.

prefix notation A method of indicating how many bits are in a subnet mask. For example, */24* is prefix notation for a 24-bit subnet mask. Prefix notation is also known as *slash notation*.

presentation layer Layer 6 of the OSI model. This layer is responsible for the formatting of data being exchanged and securing the data with encryption.

pretty good privacy (PGP) PGP is a widely deployed asymmetric encryption algorithm and is often used to encrypt email traffic.

primary rate interface (PRI) A PRI circuit is an ISDN circuit built on a T1 or E1 circuit. Recall that a T1 circuit has 24 channels. Therefore, if a PRI circuit is built on a T1 circuit, the ISDN circuit has 23 B channels and one 64Kbps D channel. The twenty-fourth channel in the T1 circuit serves as the ISDN D channel (that is, the channel used to carry the Q.921 and Q.931 signaling protocols, which set up, maintain, and tear down connections).

private IP addresses Specific Class A, B, and C networks have been designed for private use. Although these networks are routable (with the exception of the 169.254.0.0–169.254.255.255 address range), within the organization, service providers do not route these private networks over the public Internet.

protocol data unit (PDU) The name given to data at different layers of the OSI model. Specifically, the PDU for Layer 4 is *segment*. The Layer 3 PDU is *packet*, the Layer 2 PDU is *frame*, and the Layer 1 PDU is *bit*.

Protocol Independent Multicast (PIM) A multicast protocol used between multicast-enabled routers to construct a multicast distribution tree.

proxy server Intercepts requests being sent from a client and forwards those requests on to their intended destination. The proxy server then sends any return traffic to the client that initiated the session. This provides address hiding for the client. Also, some proxy servers conserve WAN bandwidth by offering a content-caching function. In addition, some proxy servers offer URL filtering to, for example, block users from accessing social networking sites during working hours.

public key infrastructure (PKI) A PKI system uses digital certificates and a certificate authority to allow secure communication across a public network.

public switched telephone network (PSTN) The worldwide telephony network consisting of multiple telephone carriers.

punch-down tool When terminating wires on a punch-down block (for example, a 110 block), you should use a punch-down tool, which is designed to properly insert an insulated wire between two contact blades in a punch-down block, without damaging the blades.

rack diagrams A diagram of the network devices mounted in a physical or virtual rack of equipment.

radio-frequency identification (RFID) Radio-frequency identification (RFID) uses electromagnetic fields to automatically identify and track tags attached to objects. The tags contain electronically stored information.

Real-time Transport Protocol (RTP) A Layer 4 protocol that carries voice (and interactive video).

Remote Desktop Protocol (RDP) A solution that permits the access of an OS desktop remotely from another device on the network. As an example, this is the default solution for accessing a Windows system hosted in the cloud via Amazon Web Services (AWS).

reliability The measure of how error-free a network transmits packets.

remote-access VPN See *client-to-site VPN*.

Remote Authentication Dial-In User Service (RADIUS) A UDP-based protocol used to communicate with an AAA server. Unlike TACACS+, RADIUS does not encrypt an entire authentication packet, but only the password. However, RADIUS offers more robust accounting features than TACACS+. Also, RADIUS is a standards-based protocol, whereas TACACS+ is a Cisco proprietary protocol.

ring topology In a ring topology, traffic flows in a circular fashion around a closed network loop (that is, a ring). Typically, a ring topology sends data, in a single direction, to each connected device in turn, until the intended destination receives the data.

rogue access point An access point that is not permitted on the network.

Root Guard A switch protection mechanism for STP. The switch ensures that superior BPDU messages are ignored.

root port In an STP topology, every nonroot bridge has a single root port, which is the port on that switch that is closest to the root bridge, in terms of cost.

route command Can add, modify, or delete routes in the IP routing table of Microsoft Windows and UNIX hosts. In addition, the **route** command can be used to view the IP routing table of Microsoft Windows hosts.

route redistribution Allows routes learned by one routing protocol to be injected into the routing process of another routing protocol.

routed protocol A protocol with an addressing scheme (for example, IP) that defines different network addresses.

router A router is considered a Layer 3 device, meaning that it makes its forwarding decisions based on logical network addresses. Most modern networks use IP addressing.

Routing Information Protocol (RIP) A distance-vector routing protocol that uses a metric of *hop count*. The maximum number of hops between two routers in an RIP-based network is 15. Therefore, a hop count of 16 is considered to be infinite. RIP is considered to be an IGP.

routing protocol A routing protocol (for example, RIP, OSPF, or EIGRP) that advertises route information between routers, which describes how to reach specified destination networks.

RSA A popular and widely deployed asymmetric encryption algorithm.

satellite (WAN technology) Provides WAN access to sites where terrestrial WAN solutions are unavailable. Satellite WAN connections can suffer from long round-trip delay (which can be unacceptable for latency-sensitive applications) and are susceptible to poor weather conditions.

Secure Shell (SSH) A cryptographic network protocol for operating network services securely over an unsecured network. The best known sample application is for remote login to computer systems by users.

Secure Sockets Layer (SSL) Provides cryptography and reliability for upper layers (Layers 5–7) of the OSI model. SSL, which was introduced in 1995, has largely been replaced by Transport Layer Security (TLS). However, recent versions of SSL (for example, SSL 3.3) have been enhanced to be more comparable with TLS. Both SSL and TLS are able to provide secure web browsing via HTTPS.

security association (SA) An agreement between the two IPSec peers about the cryptographic parameters to be used in an ISAKMP session.

security information and event management (SIEM) These products seek to monitor the network for security issues and notify personnel should issues arise.

security policy A continually changing document that dictates a set of guidelines for network use. These guidelines complement organizational objectives by specifying rules for how a network is used.

server As its name suggests, a server serves up resources to a network. These resources might include email access as provided by an email server, web pages as provided by a web server, or files available on a file server.

service-level agreement (SLA) A contract between a provider and the client regarding what services and service levels are to be provided. This also could reference monitoring software on a switch or router.

service set identifier (SSID) A string of characters that identifies a WLAN. APs participating in the same WLAN can be configured with identical SSIDs. An SSID shared among multiple APs is called an extended service set identifier (ESSID).

Session Initiation Protocol (SIP) A VoIP signaling protocol used to set up, maintain, and tear down VoIP phone calls.

session layer As Layer 5 of the OSI model, it's responsible for setting up, maintaining, and tearing down sessions.

shielded twisted-pair (STP) cable STP cabling prevents wires in a cable from acting as an antenna, which might receive or transmit EMI. STP cable might have a metallic shielding, similar to the braided wire that acts as an outer conductor in a coaxial cable.

short A short occurs when two copper connectors touch each other, resulting in current flowing through that short rather than the attached electrical circuit, because the short has lower resistance.

Simple Network Management Protocol (SNMP) A protocol used to monitor and manage network devices, such as routers, switches, and servers.

single-mode fiber (SMF) SMF cabling has a core with a diameter large enough to permit only a single path for light pulses (that is, only one mode of propagation). By having a single path for light to travel, SMF eliminates the concern of multimode delay distortion.

single sign-on (SSO) Allows a user to authenticate once to gain access to multiple systems, without requiring the user to independently authenticate with each system.

site-to-site VPN Interconnects two sites, as an alternative to a leased line, at a reduced cost.

slash notation See *prefix notation*.

smart cards Any pocket-sized card with embedded integrated circuits. Often, smart cards are used for network security, specifically authentication.

snapshots A backup method where a point-in-time capture of the data is performed.

social engineering Attackers sometimes use social techniques (which often leverage people's desire to be helpful) to obtain confidential information. For example, an attacker might pose as a member of an IT department and ask a company employee for her login credentials in order for the "IT staff to test the connection." This type of attack is called social engineering.

software as a service (SaaS) Providing applications or application services via the cloud.

software-defined networking (SDN) An approach to computer networking that allows network administrators to programmatically initialize, control, change, and manage network behavior dynamically via open interfaces and provide abstraction of lower-level functionality.

software-defined networking (SDN) controller Often referred to as the "brains" of the SDN network, this device sends commands to the network devices to have configurations made.

software firewall A computer running firewall software. For example, the software firewall could protect the computer itself (for instance, preventing incoming connections to the computer). Alternatively, a software firewall could be a computer with more than one network interface card that runs firewall software to filter traffic flowing through the computer.

Spanning Tree Protocol (STP) Defined by the IEEE 802.1D standard, STP allows a network to have redundant Layer 2 connections while logically preventing a loop, which could lead to symptoms such as broadcast storms and MAC address table corruption.

split horizon This feature of a distance-vector routing protocol prevents a route learned on one interface from being advertised back out of that same interface.

SSH File Transfer Protocol (SFTP) A network protocol that provides file access, file transfer, and file management over any reliable data stream. It was designed by the Internet Engineering Task Force (IETF) as an extension of version 2.0 of the Secure Shell protocol (SSH) to provide secure file-transfer capabilities.

star topology In a star topology, a network has a central point (for example, a switch) from which all attached devices radiate.

state transition modulation One way to electrically or optically represent a binary 1 or 0 is to use the transition between a voltage level (for example, going from a state of no voltage to a state of voltage, or vice versa, on a copper cable) or the transition of having light or no light on a fiber-optic cable to represent a binary 1. Similarly, a binary 0 is represented by having no transition in a voltage level or light level from one time period to the next. This approach of representing binary digits is called state transition modulation.

stateful firewall Inspects traffic leaving the inside network as it goes out to the Internet. Then, when returning traffic from the same session (as identified by source and destination IP addresses and port numbers) attempts to enter the inside network, the stateful firewall permits that traffic. The process of inspecting traffic to identify unique sessions is called *stateful inspection*.

static NAT (SNAT) A variant of NAT in which an inside local IP address is statically mapped to an inside global IP address. SNAT is useful for servers inside a network that need to be accessible from an outside network.

storage area network (SAN) A specialized network for the storage of data.

subnet mask A 32-bit value (in IPv4) that indicates what portion of the IP address is the network ID versus what portion is the host ID.

supervisory control and data acquisition (SCADA) network Specialized network that provides monitoring and control of remote equipment. A power plant or gas refinery would have a SCADA network.

supplicant In a network using 802.1X user authentication, a supplicant is the device that wants to gain access to a network.

switch Like an Ethernet hub, an Ethernet switch interconnects network components. Like a hub, switches are available with a variety of port densities. However, unlike a hub, a switch doesn't simply take traffic in on one port and forward copies of that traffic out all other ports. Rather, a switch learns which devices reside off of which ports. As a result, when traffic comes in a switch port, the switch interrogates the traffic to see where it's destined. Then, based on what the switch has learned, it forwards the traffic out of the appropriate port and not out all of the other ports.

symmetric encryption With symmetric encryption, both the sender and the receiver of a packet use the same key (a *shared key*) for encryption and decryption.

Synchronous Optical Network (SONET) A Layer 1 technology that uses fiber-optic cabling as its media. Because SONET is a Layer 1 technology, it can be used to transport various Layer 2 encapsulation types, such as ATM. Also, because SONET uses fiber-optic cabling, it offers high data rates, typically in the 155Mbps–10Gbps range, and long-distance limitations, typically in the 20 km–250 km range.

syslog A syslog-logging solution consists of two primary components: syslog servers (which receive and store log messages sent from syslog clients) and syslog clients (which can be a variety of network devices that send logging information to a syslog server).

T1 T1 circuits were originally used in telephony networks, with the intent of one voice conversation being carried in a single channel (that is, a single DS0). A T1 circuit consists of 24 DS0s, and the bandwidth of a T1 circuit is 1.544Mbps.

T3 In the same T-carrier family of standards as a T1, a T3 circuit offers an increased bandwidth capacity. Whereas a T1 circuit combines 24 DS0s into a single physical connection to offer 1.544Mbps of bandwidth, a T3 circuit combines 672 DS0s into a single physical connection, with a resulting bandwidth capacity of 44.7Mbps.

tcpdump A common packet analyzer that runs under the command line. It allows the user to display TCP/IP and other packets being transmitted or received over a network to which the computer is attached.

TCP/IP stack Also known as the *DoD model*, this four-layer model (as opposed to the seven-layer OSI model) targets the suite of TCP/IP protocols.

telco A telephone company. Some countries have government-maintained telcos, and other countries have multiple telcos that compete with one another.

Telnet A method of remote access for network devices that does not provide any security mechanisms.

Terminal Access Controller Access-Control System Plus (TACACS+) A TCP-based protocol used to communicate with an AAA server. Unlike RADIUS, TACACS+ encrypts an entire authentication packet rather than just the password. TACACS+ offers authentication features, but they are not as robust as the accounting features found in RADIUS. Also, unlike RADIUS, TACACS+ is a Cisco-proprietary protocol.

time-division multiple access (TDMA) A channel access method for shared-medium networks. It allows several users to share the same frequency channel by dividing the signal into different time slots.

time-division multiplexing (TDM) Supports different communication sessions (for example, different telephone conversations in a telephony network) on the same physical medium by allowing sessions to take turns. For a brief period of time, defined as a time slot, data from the first session is sent, followed by data from the second session. This continues until all sessions have had a turn, and the process repeats itself.

time domain reflectometer (TDR) Detects the location of a fault in a copper cable by sending an electric signal down the copper cable and measuring the time required for the signal to bounce back from the cable fault. A TDM can then mathematically calculate the location of the fault.

Time To Live (TTL) The TTL field in an IP header is decremented once for each router hop. Therefore, if the value in a TTL field is reduced to 0, a router discards the frame and sends a *time exceeded* Internet Control Message Protocol (ICMP) message back to the source.

tip and ring The red and green wires found in RJ-11 wall jacks, which carry voice, ringing voltage, and signaling information between an analog device (for example, a phone or a modem) and an RJ-11 wall jack.

toner probe Sometimes called a *fox and hound*, a toner probe allows you to place a tone generator at one end of the connection (for example, in someone's office) and use a probe on the punch-down block to audibly detect to which pair of wires the tone generator is connected.

traceroute command A UNIX command that displays every router hop along the path from a source host to a destination host on an IP network. Information about the router hop can include the IP address of the router hop and the round-trip delay of that router hop.

tracert command A Microsoft Windows–based command that displays every router hop along the path from a source host to a destination host on an IP network. Information about a router hop can include such information as the IP address of the router hop and the round-trip delay of that router hop.

traffic shaping Instead of making a minimum amount of bandwidth available for specific traffic types, you might want to limit available bandwidth. Both policing and shaping tools can accomplish this objective. Collectively, these tools are called *traffic conditioners*. Traffic shaping delays excess traffic by buffering it as opposed to dropping the excess traffic.

Transmission Control Protocol (TCP) A connection-oriented transport protocol. Connection-oriented transport protocols provide reliable transport, in that if a segment is dropped, the sender can detect that drop and retransmit that dropped segment. Specifically, a receiver acknowledges segments that it receives. Based on those acknowledgments, a sender can determine which segments were successfully received.

transport layer (OSI model) As Layer 4 of the OSI model, it acts as a dividing line between the upper layers and the lower layers. Specifically, messages are taken from the upper layers (Layers 5–7) and encapsulated into segments for transmission to the lower layers (Layers 1–3). Similarly, data streams coming from lower layers are decapsulated and sent to Layer 5 (the session layer) or some other upper layer, depending on the protocol.

transport layer (TCP/IP stack) The transport layer of the TCP/IP stack maps to Layer 4 (transport layer) of the OSI model. The two primary protocols found at the TCP/IP stack's transport layer are TCP and UDP.

Trivial File Transfer Protocol (TFTP) A UDP version of File Transfer Protocol that allows a client to get a file from or put a file onto a remote host. One of its primary uses is in the early stages of nodes booting from a local area network. TFTP has been used for this application because it is very simple to implement.

trouble ticket A problem report explaining the details of an issue being experienced in a network.

trunk In the context of an Ethernet network, this is a single physical or logical connection that simultaneously carries traffic for multiple VLANs. However, a trunk also refers to an interconnection between telephone switches, in the context of telephony.

tunneling Transmitting traffic with additional encapsulation.

twisted-pair cable Today's most popular media type is twisted-pair cable, where individually insulated copper strands are intertwined into a twisted-pair cable. Two categories of twisted-pair cable include shielded twisted pair (STP) and unshielded twisted pair (UTP).

two-factor authentication (TFA) Requires two types of authentication from a user seeking admission to a network. For example, a user might need to know something (for example, a password) and have something (for example, a specific fingerprint that can be checked with a biometric authentication device).

unicast A unicast communication flow is a one-to-one flow.

unidirectional antenna Unidirectional antennas can focus their power in a specific direction, thus avoiding potential interference with other wireless devices and perhaps reaching greater distances than those possible with omnidirectional antennas. One application for unidirectional antennas is interconnecting two nearby buildings.

unified threat management (UTM) A firewall or gateway that attempts to bundle multiple security functions into a single physical or logical device.

uninterruptible power supply (UPS) An appliance that provides power to networking equipment in the event of a power outage.

unshielded twisted-pair (UTP) cable Blocks EMI from the copper strands making up a twisted-pair cable by having more tightly twisted strands (that is, more twists per centimeter). Because these strands are wrapped around each other, the wires insulate each other from EMI.

User Datagram Protocol (UDP) A connectionless transport protocol. Connectionless transport protocols provide unreliable transport, in that if a segment is dropped, the sender is unaware of the drop, and no retransmission occurs.

variable-length subnet masking (VLSM) The process of assigning various subnetwork IDs in the network to issue the appropriate number of IP addresses.

video surveillance A form of physical security where cameras monitor a network area.

virtual desktop A virtual desktop solution allows a user to store data in a centralized data center, as opposed to the hard drive of his local computer. Then, with appropriate authentication credentials, that user can access his data from various remote devices (for example, his smartphone or another computer).

virtual LAN (VLAN) A single broadcast domain, representing a single subnet. Typically, a group of ports on a switch is assigned to a single VLAN. For traffic to travel between two VLANs, that traffic needs to be routed.

Virtual Network Computing (VNC) An alternative to RDP, VNC allows the access of a desktop from another system on the network.

virtual PBX Usually a VoIP telephony solution hosted by a service provider, which interconnects with a company's existing telephone system.

virtual private network (VPN) Extends a private network across a public network and enables users to send and receive data across shared or public networks as if their computing devices were directly connected to the private network.

virtual server Allows a single physical server to host multiple virtual instances of various operating systems. This allows, for example, a single physical server to simultaneously host multiple Microsoft Windows servers and multiple Linux servers.

virtual switch Performs Layer 2 functions (for example, VLAN separation and filtering) between various server instances running on a single physical server.

war chalking If an open WLAN (or a WLAN whose SSID and authentication credentials are known) is found in a public place, a user might write a symbol on a wall (or some other nearby structure) to let others know the characteristics of the discovered network. This practice, which is a variant of the decades-old practice of hobos leaving symbols as messages to fellow hobos, is called war chalking.

war driving Searching for Wi-Fi wireless networks by a person in a moving vehicle, using a laptop or smartphone. Software for war driving is freely available on the Internet.

warm sites A redundant site that can be brought online with minimal time and effort.

wide area network (WAN) Interconnects network components that are geographically separated.

wide area network (WAN) link An interconnection between two devices in a WAN.

Wi-Fi Protected Access (WPA) The Wi-Fi Alliance (a nonprofit organization formed to certify interoperability of wireless devices) developed its own security standard to address the weaknesses of Wired Equivalent Privacy (WEP). This new security standard was called Wi-Fi Protected Access (WPA) Version 1.

Wi-Fi Protected Access Version 2 (WPA2) Uses Counter Mode with Cipher Block Chaining Message Authentication Code Protocol (CCMP) for integrity checking and Advanced Encryption Standard (AES) for encryption. These algorithms enhance the security offered by WPA.

Wired Equivalent Privacy (WEP) A security standard for WLANs. With WEP, an AP is configured with a static WEP key. Wireless clients needing to associate with an AP are configured with an identical key (making this a preshared-key approach to security). The IEEE 802.11 standard specifies a 40-bit WEP key, which is considered to be a relatively weak security measure.

wireless access point (AP) A device that connects to a wired network and provides access to that wired network for clients that wirelessly attach to the AP.

wireless router Attaches to a wired network and provides access to that wired network for wirelessly attached clients, like a wireless AP. However, a wireless router is configured such that the wired interface that connects to the rest of the network (or to the Internet) is on a different IP network than the wireless clients. Typically, a wireless router performs NATing between these two IP address spaces.

Z-Wave A wireless communications protocol used primarily for home automation. It is a mesh network using low-energy radio waves to communicate from appliance to appliance, allowing for wireless control of residential appliances and other devices, such as lighting control, security systems, thermostats, windows, locks, swimming pools, and garage door openers.

Zeroconf A technology that performs three basic functions: assigning link-local IP addresses, resolving computer names to IP addresses, and locating network services.

Index

Symbols

2.4GHz band channel frequencies, 281-282
3DES (Triple DES) algorithm, 411
4 parameter (PathPing command), 358
5GHz band channel frequencies, 281-283
6 parameter (PathPing command), 358
8-bit subnet masks, 162
9-pin D-subminiature (DB-9) connectors, 69
10BASE2 Ethernet standard, 118, 125
10BASE5 Ethernet standard, 118, 125
10BASE-T Ethernet standard, 119, 125
10GBASE-ER Ethernet standard, 125
10GBASE-EW Ethernet standard, 125
10GBASE-LR Ethernet standard, 125
10GBASE-LW Ethernet standard, 125
10GBASE-SR Ethernet standard, 125
10GBASE-SW Ethernet standard, 125
10GBASE-T Ethernet standard, 125
10-Gigabit Ethernet, 124
40MHz mode, 286
66 blocks, 76
80-20 rule, 239
100BASE-FX Ethernet standard, 125
100BASE-T Ethernet standard, 125
100BASE-TX Ethernet standard, 125
100GBASE-ER4 Ethernet standard, 125
100GBASE-LR4 Ethernet standard, 125
100GBASE-SR10 Ethernet standard, 125
100-gigabit Ethernet, 124
110 blocks, 76
802.1aq protocol, 131
802.1D. *See* STP
802.1w protocol, 131
802.11 wireless signals, 79
802.11a WLAN standard, 285
802.11ac WLAN standard, 286
802.11b WLAN standard, 285
802.11g WLAN standard, 285
802.11n WLAN standard, 285-286
1000BASE-LH Ethernet standard, 125
1000BASE-LX Ethernet standard, 125
1000BASE-T Ethernet standard, 125
1000BASE-TX Ethernet standard, 125
1000BASE-ZX Ethernet standard, 125

A

A (address) records, 95
a parameter
  arp command, 338, 360-361
  nbtstat command, 344
  netstat command, 346, 367
A parameter (nbtstat command), 344
AAA (authentication, authorization, and accounting), 440
AAAA records, 95
acceptable use policies (AUPs), 429, 471
access
  ACLs
    attacks, preventing, 436-437
    packet-filtering firewalls, 443
  CLI, 511
  control lists (ACLs), 436-437
  Ethernet devices, 122
  Internet, 521-522
  points (APs), 77
  ports, switch configuration, 128
  remote, 400-401, 439-442
  slow Internet, troubleshooting, 501-504
  WAN services technologies, 521-522
acknowledgment messages, 40
ACLs (access control lists)
  attacks, preventing, 436-437
  packet-filtering firewalls, 443
active-active mode (NICs), 308
active hubs, 80
active IPS devices, 455
active routers, 144, 310
active-standby mode (NICs), 308
AD (administrative distance), 214
ad hoc wireless networks, 20, 276
add parameter (route command), 355, 370
address (A) records, 95
Address Resolution Protocol. *See* ARP

addresses
APIPA, 502
dotted-decimal notation, 161
IP
assignable in subnets, 176
configuration parameters, displaying, 340
DHCP server, 97
DNS records pointing to, 95
duplicate, 495
expired, 495
FQDNs, resolving, 362-363
host, 180-181
interfaces, configuring, 364
leases, 98
listing, 347
loopback, 163
management (IPAM), 96
NAT classifications, 221
NAT names, 221
next-hop, 211
parameters, displaying, 340
ranges, calculating, 183-186
scopes, 98
target, specifying, 356
IPv4, 161
APIPA, 174-176
assignment, 164
available hosts, number of, 180-181
bits, 154
BOOTP protocol, 173
borrowed bits, 179
broadcast, 165
CIDR, 190-191
classes, 163
classful masks, extending, 179
components, 167-168
DHCP, 173-174
dotted-decimal notation, 161
dynamic configuration, 172
FQDN translation, 167
multicast, 166
network address calculation, 162
network/host address divisions, 162
private addressing, 164
ranges, calculating, 183-186
static configuration, 168-172
structure, 161-163
subnet masks, 161
subnet notation, 177-178
subnet octet values, 178
subnets created, number of, 180
transitioning to IPv6, 192
unicast, 165
IPv6, 191
anycast, 195-196
bits, 154
features, 192
IPv4 transitions, 192
multicast, 195
NDP, 193
ping command, 352
records, 95
structure, 192-193
traceroute command, 366
tracert command, 358
types, 193
unicast, 194
link-local IP, assigning, 175
logical, 42
MAC
duplicate, 495
filtering, 145, 294
table corruption, 131-132
network, 126
physical, 39
prefix notation, 162
private, 222
public, 222
translation
NAT, 220-222
PAT, 222-224
adjacencies, 494
administrative distance (AD), 214
ADSL (Asymmetric DSL), 252-254
advanced distance-vector routing protocols, 219
Advanced Encryption Standard (AES), 297, 411
advertisements
link-state (LSAs), 218
neighbor, 194
routing, 194, 216-218
services, 49
AES (Advanced Encryption Standard), 297, 411
agents
call, 108
relay, 98
SNMP, 392
aggressive mode (IKE), 450
AHs (Authentication Headers), 451-452
AirDrop, 20
algorithms
3DES, 411
AES, 411
DES, 411
Dijkstra's shortest path first, 218
DUAL, 219
GPG, 411
hashing, 414
MD5, 414
PGP, 411
queuing, 319
RSA, 412
SHA-1, 414
symmetric encryption, 411
all parameter (ipconfig command), 340-341
AM (amplitude modulation), 36
Amazon Web Services (AWS), 106
American Registry for Internet Numbers (ARIN), 164
American Standard Code for Information Interchange (ASCII), 48
amplified DoS attacks, 423
amplitude modulation (AM), 36
analog phones, 108
analysis (traffic), 386
analyzers
protocols, 386
Wi-Fi, 387
anomaly-based detection, 457
Ant+, 78
antennas (WLANs), 278-281
gain, 279
omnidirectional, 279
orientation, 281
selecting, 279
throughput, increasing, 510
unidirectional, 280

anycast IPv6 addresses, 195-196
APIPA (Automatic Private IP Addressing), 174-176, 502
Apple AirDrop, 20
application layer
OSI model, 48-49
TCP/IP stack, 53-56
application-specific integrated circuits (ASICs), 82
applications
logs, 398
open connections, 347
services, 49
appropriate use policies, 429, 471
APs (access points), 77
evil twins, 422
fat configurations, 511
incorrect placement, 499
rogue, 293, 422
updates, troubleshooting, 516
wireless, 277-278, 291
arc four, 296
arguments. *See* parameters
ARIN (American Registry for Internet Numbers), 164
ARP (Address Resolution Protocol), 361
cache, 338
replies, 85-86
requests, 83-84
arp command
UNIX, 360-361
Windows, 338-340
ASCII (American Standard Code for Information Interchange), 48
ASICs (application-specific integrated circuits), 82
asset tracking tags, 437
assigning
IP addresses, 164, 176
IPv4 addresses
APIPA, 174-176
BOOTP protocol, 173
components, 167-168
DHCP, 173-174
dynamic configuration, 172
FQDN translation, 167
static configuration, 168-172
associations, 277
Asymmetric DSL (ADSL), 252-254
asymmetric encryption, 412-413
asynchronous bit synchronization, 37
asynchronous transmissions, 40
ATM (Asynchronous Transfer Mode), 8, 242, 264-265
attacks
availability, 422
buffer overflow, 424
DDoS, 423
DoS, 422-423
electrical disturbances, 425-426
ICMP, 424
logic bombs, 422
physical environment, 426-427
TCP SYN floods, 423
wireless attacks, 422
banner-grabbing, 515
Bluetooth, 431
confidentiality, 415-419
covert channels, 418
dumpster diving, 417
EMI interceptions, 417
FTP bounce, 418
insider, 419
malware, 418
MitM, 417
overt channels, 418
packet captures, 417
phishing, 419
ping sweeps, 417
port scans, 417
social engineering, 418
wiretapping, 417
integrity, 419-422
botnets, 421
brute force, 421
data diddling, 420
dictionary attacks, 421
hijacking sessions, 422
keyloggers, 421
MitM, 420
packet captures, 421
password, 421
salami, 420
Trojan horses, 421
trust relationship exploitation, 420
means, 432
motives, 432
opportunities, 433
preventing
ACLs, 436-437
detailed documentation, 431-432
end-user policies, 431
governing policies, 430
honey pots, 435
incident response, 432-433
Layer 2 protections, 439
network device hardening, 438
patching, 428
physical devices, 437-438
security policies, 429
technical policies, 431
user training, 427-428
vulnerability scanners, 433-435
auditing infrastructure, 514-518
AUPs (acceptable use policies), 429, 471
authentication
certificates, 413
CHAP, 250
headers, 451-452
HMACs, 414
LCP, 249
local, 441
multifactor, 441
passwords, 249
servers, 142, 440
SNMP messages, 395
SSO, 441
switches, 142-143
two-factor, 441
users, 141-142
VPN traffic, 449
WLANs, 294
authentication, authorization, and accounting (AAA), 440
authenticators, 141, 440
authNoPriv security level, 394
authPriv security level, 394
Automatic Private IP Addressing (APIPA), 174-176, 502
availability, 415
attacks, 422
buffer overflow, 424
DDoS, 423

DoS, 422-423
electrical disturbances, 425-426
ICMP, 424
logic bombs, 422
physical environment, 426-427
TCP SYN floods, 423
wireless attacks, 422
five nines, 130, 415
high, 514
best practices, 311
designing, 310-311
measuring, 306
host IP addresses, calculating, 180-181
network faults, 306
reliability, compared, 306
avoiding congestion, 319
AWS (Amazon Web Services), 106

B

B channels, 260
b parameter (netstat command), 346-347, 367
back-off timers, 121
back-out plans, 486
backups, 311
backward explicit congestion notification (BECN), 263
bad cables, 487
bad modules, 490
bad ports, 487
badges, 437
bands (frequency), 281
bandwidth
CIR, 320
Ethernet, 124
Frame Relay, 263
measuring, 123
QoS issues, 314-315
usage, 37
WANs, 243
banking bits/bytes, 321
banner-grabbing, 515
baseband technologies, 38
basic rate interface circuits (BRI), 261
basic routing process, 206-208
basic service set (BSS) WLANs, 288
bayonet connectors, 73
BC (business continuity) plans, 427
Bc (committed burst), 321
Be (excess burst) parameter, 321
bearer channels, 260
BECN (backward explicit congestion notification), 263
behavior-based detection, 457
believability (routes), 214
benefits
bus topology, 12
client/server networks, 21
content switches, 101
full-mesh topology, 17
hub-and-spoke topology, 16
partial-mesh topology, 19
peer-to-peer networks, 23
proxy servers, 99
ring topology, 14
star topology, 15
UNXI, 359
BER (bit error rate), 380
BERT (bit-error rate tester), 380
best-effort treatment, 316
best practices
international export controls, 474
licensing restrictions, 473
non-disclosure agreements, 474
on-boarding/off-boarding, 473
privileged user agreements (PUAs), 472-473
system life cycle, 474
BGP (Border Gateway Protocol), 219, 387, 503
bidirectional Telnet sessions, 88
binary data, displaying, 36
binary numbering, 154
converting to decimal numbers, 155-158
decimal to binary conversions, 155-160
biometrics, 437
bit error rate (BER), 380
bit-error rate tester (BERT), 380
bits
banking, 321
Bc, 321
borrowed, 179
DE, 263
defined, 123
error detectors, 380
errors, 380
goodput, 290
IPv4/IPv6 addresses, 154
marking, 318
octets, 161
parity, 41
pattern generators, 380
rates, 521
splitters, 80
synchronization, 37
blackhole parameter (arp command), 360
black-hole routers, 494
blackouts, 425
block sizes, 184
blocked TCP/UDP ports, 495
blocking state, 135
bluebugging, 431
bluejacking, 431
bluesnarfing, 431
Bluetooth, 79, 431
bonding
channels, 286
NICs, 308
ports, 137
BOOTP protocol, 173
BOOTPS (BOOTP server), 173
Border Gateway Protocol (BGP), 219, 387, 503
borrowed bits, 179
botnets, 421
bots, 421
BPDUs (bridge protocol data units), 135
BRI (basic rate interface) circuits, 261
bridges, 81-82
bring-your-own-device (BYOD) policies, 471, 506
broadband technologies, 37
broadcasts
domains
network addresses, 126
switches, 88

IPv4 addresses, 165
SSID, disabling, 294
storms, 132-133
brownouts, 426
brute force attacks, 421, 513
BSS (basic service set) WLANs, 288
buffer overflow attacks, 424
buffering, 45
bus topology, 11-12
business continuity (BC) plans, 427
butt sets, 381
BYOD (bring-your-own-device) policies, 471, 506
bytes, 321

C

c parameter
nbtstat command, 344
ping command, 368
cable modems, 254-255
cables
10BASE2, 118
10BASE-T, 119
bad, 487
breaks, identifying, 389
certifiers, 381
coaxial, 64-65, 244
crossover, 68
distance limitations exceeded, 488
distribution, 75-77
fiber-optic, 70
MMF, 70-72
mode of propagation, 71
polishing styles, 74
SMF, 72-74
WANs, 244
locations, documenting, 391
multimeters, 385-386
placement, 488
plenum/nonplenum, 70
recrimping, 515
rollover, 68
splitting pairs, 487
testers, 382
tip and ring, 260
troubleshooting, 515
twisted-pair, 66-69
UTP, 15, 243
wires connecting back to end-user location, 390
caching, 99, 312
calculating
IP address ranges, 183-186
network addresses, 162
number of host IP addresses available, 180-181
number of subnets created, 180
call agents, 108
canonical name (CNAME) records, 95
CANs (campus area networks), 9
captive portals, 441
capturing packets
network sniffers, 139
port mirroring, 140
CARP (Common Address Redundancy Protocol), 310
carrier sense, 121
carrier-sense multiple access/collision avoidance. *See* **CSMA/CA**
carrier-sense multiple access/collision detection. *See* **CSMA/CD**
Cat 3 cables, 67
Cat 5 cables, 68
Cat 5e cables, 68
Cat 6 cables, 68
Cat 6a cables, 68
CCMP (Counter Mode with Cipher Block Chaining Message Authentication Code Protocol), 297
CDMA (Code Division Multiple Access), 244
CE (customer edge) routers, 267
cells (WLANs), 291
cellular phones, 244
cellular technologies, 287
center frequencies, 284
central offices (COs), 260
certificates
authentication, 413
authorities, 413
untrusted SSL, 495
chain of custody, 433
challenge-handshake authentication protocol (CHAP), 250, 441
Challenge-Response Authentication Mechanism Message Digest 5 (CRAM-MD5), 414
change management documentation, 391
channel service unit/data service unit (CSU/DSU), 246
channels
2.4GHz band frequencies, 282
5GHz band frequencies, 283
bonding, 286
center frequencies, 284
covert, 418
nonoverlapping, 282-283
overt, 418
sources of interference, 289-291
transmission methods, 284
WLANs, 281
CHAP (challenge-handshake authentication protocol), 250, 441
characteristics
802.11x standards, 286
bus topology, 12
client/server networks, 21
full-mesh topology, 17
hub-and-spoke topology, 16
infrastructure devices, 91
partial-mesh topology, 19
peer-to-peer networks, 23
ring topology, 14
routing protocols
believability, 214
distance-vector, 216-218
interior versus exterior, 215
link-state, 218
metrics, 214
star topology, 15
cheapernet, 118
child tunnels, 454
CIDR (classless interdomain routing), 190-191
CIR (committed information rate), 263, 320
circuit-switched connections, 241
circuits
CSU/DSU, 248
E1, 247

E3, 247
ISDN, 261
switching, 42
T1, 246-247
T3, 247
virtual. *See* VCs
CIRs (committed information rates), 263
Class A addresses, 163
Class B addresses, 163
Class C addresses, 163
Class D addresses, 163
Class E addresses, 163
class of service (CoS), 504
classes
addresses, 163-164
traffic, 316
classful masks, 163, 179
classifying
NAT IP addresses, 221
networks
geographic dispersion7-9
resource location, 21-23
QoS, 318
STP switches, 133
classless interdomain routing (CIDR), 190-191
CLI (command-line interface), 511
clients
defined, 5
syslog, 396
client/server networks, 21-22
client-to-site VPNs, 400, 448
cloud computing, 105-106
clustering computers, 309
CNAME (canonical name) records, 95
coarse wavelength-division multiplexing (CWDM), 256
coaxial cables, 64-65
common, 64
connectors, 65
WANs, 243
Code Division Multiple Access (CDMA), 244
cold sites, 313
collisions
bus, 12
detection, 122
domains, 80, 122
Ethernet, 120-121
command-line interface (CLI), 511
command parameter (route command), 352
Command Prompt (Windows), accessing, 338
commands
UNIX, 358
arp, 360-361
dig, 362
host, 363
ifconfig, 363-364
iptables, 364
man, 359
netstat, 366
nmap, 365
nslookup, 362
ping, 368-369
route, 369-370
tcpdump, 365
traceroute, 365-366
Windows, 338
arp, 338-340
ipconfig, 340-343
nbtstat, 343-345
netstat, 346-347
nslookup, 348-349
PathPing, 358
ping, 350-352
route, 352-355
tracert, 356-358
committed burst (Bc), 321
committed information rate (CIR), 263, 320
Common Address Redundancy Protocol (CARP), 310
community cloud, 106
community strings, 393
companion website, 529, 530-531
components. *See also* devices
environmental monitors, 384
IPv4 addresses, 167-168
media, 64
cable distribution, 75-77
coaxial cables, 64-65
converters, 75
fiber-optic cables, 70-74
plenum/nonplenum cables, 70
twisted-pair cables, 66-69
wireless, 77
networks, 5-7
QoS, 316-317
SNMP, 392
compressing headers, 322
computers
clustering, 309
forensics, 433
names, resolving, 175
concentrators (VPN), 449
confidentiality, 410-411
attacks, 415-419
covert channels, 418
dumpster diving, 417
EMI interceptions, 417
FTP bounce, 418
insider, 419
malware, 418
MitM, 417
overt channels, 418
packet captures, 417
phishing, 419
ping sweeps, 417
port scans, 417
social engineering, 418
wiretapping, 417
encryption
asymmetric, 412-413
defined, 411
keys, 411
PKI, 412
session keys, 411
symmetric, 411
VPN traffic, 449
configuring
APs, 511
baselines, documenting, 391
DNS, 495
interface IP addresses, 364
IPv4 addresses, 168-172
LACP, 137
ports, 141, 490
QoS, 315-316
sessions, 46
switch access ports, 128
time, 495
trunk ports, 130
VLANs, 490

conforming traffic, 321

congestion

avoidance, 319

backward explicit congestion notification, 263

flow control, 40, 43

management, 319

uplink, 136

connections

application open, 347

bad, 487

cable modems, 254-255

CSU/DSU, 248

dedicated leased line, 246

DSL, 252-254

E1, 247

E3, 247

Internet access technologies, 521-522

LLC sublayer, 40

networks, 4

outages, troubleshooting, 505-507

point-to-point, 246

POTS, 258-260

remote desktop, 382

satellite, 257-258

services, 43

T1, 246-247

T3, 247

testing with ping command, 350

third-party networks, troubleshooting, 516

trunks, 129-130

WANs

circuit-switched, 241

dedicated leased line, 240

packet-switched, 241

RDP applications, troubleshooting, 518-521

services, 521-522

troubleshooting, 517

connectivity software, 382

connectors

coaxial cables, 65

crimpers, 383

Ethernet, 124

fiber-optic cables, 74

SMF cables, 73-74

UTP cables, 69

consultant infrastructure audits, 514-518

contact blades, 388

content engines, 99, 312

content switches, 100-101, 312

control protocols (CPs), 249

convergence, 4, 213, 216

converters (media), 75

converting

binary numbers to decimal numbers, 155-158

decimal numbers to binary numbers, 155-160

cordless phone interference, 290

corruption, MAC address tables, 131-132

COs (central offices), 260

CoS (class of service), 504

Counter Mode with Cipher Block Chaining Message Authentication Code Protocol (CCMP), 297

counter-rotating rings, 14

covert channels, 418

CPE (customer premises equipment) devices, 267

CPs (control protocols), 249

cracking WLANs, 293

CRAM-MD5 (Challenge-Response Authentication Mechanism Message Digest 5), 414

CRC (cyclic redundancy check), 41

credentials, changing, 438

cross-connect blocks, 76

crossover cables, 68

crosstalk, 488

cRTP (RTP header compression), 322

CSMA/CA (carrier-sense multiple access/collision avoidance)

Ethernet, 122

WLANs, 283

CSMA/CD (carrier-sense multiple access/collision detection), 121-123

CSU/DSU (channel service unit/data service unit), 246-248

current state modulation, 36

customer edge (CE) routers, 267

customer premises equipment (CPE) devices, 267

CWDM (coarse wavelength-division multiplexing), 256

cyclic redundancy check (CRC), 41

D

D channels, 260

d parameter (arp command), 338, 360-361

D parameter (ping command), 368

data

authentication, 449

availability

attacks, 422-427

five nines, 415

binary, 36

confidentiality, 410

attacks, 415-419

encryption, 411-413

VPN traffic, 449

diddling, 420

encapsulation/decapsulation, 521

formatting, 48

fragility, 433

integrity, 414

attacks, 419-422

hash digests, 414

hashing, 414

hashing algorithms, 414

violations, 414

VPN traffic, 449

loss prevention (DLP), 469-470

rates, 242-243

service units, 34

Data Encryption Standard (DES) algorithm, 411

data link layer (OSI model), 38-41

sublayers

LLC, 40-41

MAC, 39

troubleshooting, 490

bad modules, 490

example, 491

loops, 490

port configuration, 490

power failure, 490

VLAN configuration, 490

data-link connection identifiers (DLCIs), 263
Data-Over-Cable Service Interface Specification (DOCSIS), 255
Datagram Transport Layer Security (DTLS), 400
dB (decibels), 279, 488
DB-9 (9-pin D-subminiature) connectors, 69
DCSs (distributed control systems), troubleshooting, 500
DDNS (dynamic DNS), 95
DDoS (distributed denial-of-service) attacks, 423
DE (discard eligible) bits, 263
deauthentication attacks, 422
decapsulation, 521
decibels (dB), 279, 488
decimals
- binary number conversions, 155-158
- converting to binary, 155-160

decryption keys, 411
dedicated leased lines, 240, 246
default gateways, 144, 167
default static routes, 210
default subnet masks, 176
delay, 314
- satellite transmissions, 257
- serialization, 322

delete parameter (route command), 354, 370
deleting routing table entries, 354
delta channels, 260
demarcs, 260
DEMILITARIZED (DMZ) zone (firewalls), 446
demultiplexing, 521
denial-of-service (DoS attacks), 422-423
dense wavelength-division multiplexing (DWDM), 256
deploying
- NIPS/HIPS, 458
- WLANs
  - *BSS, 288*
  - *ESS, 288*
  - *IBSS, 287*
  - *mesh topology, 289*

DES (Data Encryption Standard) algorithm, 411
design
- fault-tolerant, 307-308
- high-availability networks, 310-311

designated ports, 134
desktops (virtual), 104
destination parameter
- route command, 352
- tracert command, 356

detailed documentation, preventing attacks, 431-432
detection devices, 437
devices. *See also* components
- CPE, 267
- credentials, changing, 438
- full-duplex/half-duplex mode, 123
- hardening, 438
- IDS/IPS
  - *active, 455*
  - *anomaly-based, 457*
  - *passive, 455*
  - *policy-based, 457*
  - *signature-based, 456*
- infrastructure, 79
  - *bridges, 81-82*
  - *characteristics, 91*
  - *hubs, 80*
  - *multilayer switches, 89-90*
  - *routers, 90*
  - *switches, 85-89*
  - *switches.* See *switches*
- ISDNs, 262
- NAS storage, 22
- physical security, 437-438
- placement, 384
- sources of WLAN interference, 289
- specialized, 91
  - *content engines, 99*
  - *content switches, 100-101*
  - *DHCP servers, 96-98*
  - *DNS servers, 93-96*
  - *firewalls, 92-93*
  - *next-generation firewall, 101*
  - *proxy servers, 98-99*
  - *software-defined networking, 101*
  - *VPN concentrators, 91-92*
  - *wireless range extenders, 101*
- switches
  - *forwarding Telnet segments, 87*
  - *Layer 3, 89*
- virtual, 101
  - *cloud computing, 105-106*
  - *desktops, 104*
  - *firewalls, 103*
  - *off-site, 105*
  - *routers, 103*
  - *SDN, 107*
  - *servers, 101-103*
  - *switches, 103*
- VoIP networks, 107

DHCP (Dynamic Host Configuration Protocol), 54, 96
- exhaustion, 495
- IPv4 address assignment, 173-174
- leases, releasing/renewing, 342
- servers, 96-98
  - *IP addressing, 97*
  - *relay agents, 98*
  - *reservations, 98*
  - *rogue, 495*
- snooping, 439

DHCPv6 (DHCP for IPv6), 193
diagnosing problems, 482-483
diagraming, 390-391
dictionary attacks, 421
differential backups, 311
differentiated service code point (DSCP), 318
DiffServ (differentiated services), 317
diffusing update algorithm (DUAL), 219
dig command, 362
Digital Signal 1 (DS1), 246
Digital Signal 3 (DS3), 247
digital subscriber line (DSL), 250
Dijkstra's shortest path first algorithm, 218
directly connected routes, 209-210
direct-sequence spread spectrum (DSSS), 284
disabling SSID broadcasts, 294
disaster recovery (DR) plans, 427
discard eligible (DE) bits, 263
discovery (routes), 43

displaying binary data, 36

distance-vector routing protocols, 216-218

distributed control systems (DCSs), troubleshooting, 500

distributed denial-of-service (DDoS) attacks, 423

distribution, cables, 75-77

distribution trees

multicast, 226

shared, 229

source, 227

SPT switchover, 230

DLCIs (data-link connection identifiers), 263

DLP (data loss prevention), 469-470

DMVPN (Dynamic Multipoint VPN), 268

DMZ (DEMILITARIZED) zone (firewalls), 446

DNAT (dynamic NAT), 222

DNS (Domain Name System), 54

advanced TCP/IP settings, 171

FQDN translation, 167

incorrect configuration, 495

servers, 93-96

dynamic, 95

extension mechanisms, 96

FQDNs, 94

hierarchy, 94

IP addresses, 95-96

record types, 94-95

DNS-SD (DNS-based Service Discovery), 175

DNS DOCSIS (Data-Over-Cable Service Interface Specification), 255

documentation, 390, 391

chain of custody, 433

preventing attacks, 431-432

DoD model. ***See*** **TCP/IP stack**

Domain Name System. ***See*** **DNS**

DoS (denial-of-service) attacks, 422-423

dotted-decimal notation, 161, 177-178

downstream data frequencies, 255

DR (disaster recovery) plans, 427

drawbacks

bus topology, 12

client/server networks, 21

distance-vector protocols, 216

full-mesh topology, 17

hub-and-spoke topology, 16

hubs, 80

partial-mesh topology, 19

peer-to-peer networks, 23

ring topology, 14

star topology, 15

drops, 314

DS1 (Digital Signal 1), 246

DS3 (Digital Signal 3), 247

DSCP (differentiated service code point), 318

DSL (digital subscriber line), 250-254

asymmetric, 252-254

dial tone, confirming, 381

symmetric, 254

very high bit-rate, 254

DSSS (direct-sequence spread spectrum), 284

DTLS (Datagram Transport Layer Security), 400

DUAL (diffusing update algorithm), 219

dual stack (IPv6 addresses), 192

duplex mismatches, troubleshooting, 488

duplicate IP addresses, 495

duplicate MAC addresses, 495

duplicating problems, 483

DWDM (dense wavelength-division multiplexing), 256

dynamic configuration (IPv4 addresses), 172

dynamic DNS (DDNS), 95

Dynamic Host Configuration Protocol ***See*** **DHCP**

Dynamic Multipoint VPN (DMVPN), 268

dynamic NAT (DNAT), 222

dynamic routes, 211-213

dynamic routing protocols, 503

E

e parameter (netstat command), 346

E1 circuits WANs, 247

E3 circuits WANs, 247

EAP (Extensible Authentication Protocol)

IEEE 802.1X security, 295

remote-access security, 441

EAP-FAST (EAP-Flexible Authentication via Secure Tunneling), 295

EAP-TLS (EAP-Transport Layer Security), 295

EAP-TTLS (EAP-Tunneled Transport Layer Security), 295

EBCDIC (Extended Binary Coded Decimal Interchange Code), 48

edge label switch routers (ELSRs), 267

EDNS (Extension Mechanisms for DNS), 96

EGPs (Exterior Gateway Protocols), 215

EIGRP (Enhanced Interior Gateway Routing Protocol), 219, 503

electric power lines, 244

electrical disturbance attacks, 425-426

electrical surges, 425

electromagnetic interference (EMI) interceptions, 417

electrostatic discharge (ESD) wrist straps, 383-384

ELSRs (edge label switch routers), 267

emanations, 417

EMI (electromagnetic interference), 417

coaxial cables, 64

fiber-optic cables, 70

Encapsulating Security Payload (ESP), 451-452

encapsulation, 521

encryption

AH versus ESP, 451

asymmetric, 412-413

defined, 411

keys, 411-412

presentation layer, 48

SNMP messages, 395
symmetric, 411
VPN concentrators, 92
end-of-chapter reviews, 531
end-user policies, preventing attacks, 431
endpoints, sending Telnet segments, 86
Enhanced Interior Gateway Routing Protocol (EIGRP), 219, 503
enterprise-class WLANs, 276
Enterprise mode (WLANs), 297
environmental monitors, 384-385
ephemeral ports, 54
errors
bits, 380
collisions, 12
controlling, 40
detection, 249, 380
ESD (electrostatic discharge) wrist straps, 383-384
ESF (extended super frame), 247
ESP (Encapsulating Security Payload), 451-452
ESS (extended service set) WLANs, 288
ESSID (extended service set identifier), 293
eth_addr parameter (arp command), 339, 360
EtherChannel, 137
Ethernet
10BASE2, 118
10BASE5, 118
10BASE-T, 119
bandwidth, 124
collisions, 120-122
connectors, 124
CSMA/CA, 122
CSMA/CD, 121-123
development, 118
frames, 118
hubs, 80
origins, 118-119
shared bus topology, 120
standards, 124-125
switches, 126
access port configuration, 128
broadcast storms, 132-133
diagnostics, 145
first-hop redundancy, 144
LACP configuration, 137
link aggregation, 136-137
MAC address filtering, 145
MAC address table corruption, 131-132
management access, 142-143
PoE, 138-139
port mirroring, 141
port monitoring, 139-140
ports on same subnet, 126
QoS, 145
STP, 130-135
trunking, 129-130
trunk port configuration, 130
user authentication, 141-142
VLANs, 127
VLANs, 127-128
WANs, 248
EUI-64 (Extended Unique Identifier), 193
Euro-DOCSIS, 255
evil twins, 422
exam preparation tools
companion website, 529-530
end-of-chapter reviews, 531
exam taking strategies, 533-535
memory tables, 530
performance-based questions, 531
suggested study plan, 531-533
training videos, 530
exam taking strategies, 533-535
exceeding traffic, 321
excess burst (Be) parameter, 321
exhausted DHCP scope, 495
expired IP addresses, 495
export controls, 474
Extended Authentication (XAUTH) protocol, 451
Extended Binary Coded Decimal Interchange Code (EBCDIC), 48
extended service set (ESS) WLANs, 288
extended service set identifier (ESSID), 293
extended super frame (ESF), 247
Extended Unique Identifier (EUI-64), 193
extending classful masks, 179
Extension Mechanisms for DNS (EDNS), 96
Extensive Authentication Protocol. ***See*** **EAP**
Exterior Gateway Protocols (EGPs), 215
external routing protocols, 503

F

f parameter
arp command, 360
netstat command, 346
ping command, 350
route command, 352
failures
fault-tolerant design, 307-308
logins on vyt lines, troubleshooting, 511-514
MTBF, 306
single points, 307
fair use policies, 471
fast Ethernet, 124
fat configurations (APs), 511
fault-tolerant design, 306-308
FCC (Federal Communications Commission), 245
FCoE (Fibre Channel over Ethernet), 103
FDDI (Fiber Distributed Data Interface), 14
FDM (frequency-division multiplexing), 38
FEP (fluorinated ethylene polymer), 70
FHSS (frequency-hopping spread spectrum), 284
fiber-optic cables, 70
MMF, 70-72
mode of propagation, 71
polishing styles, 74
SMF, 72-74
WANs, 244
Fibre channel, 103, 500
Fibre Channel over Ethernet (FCoE), 103
files, remote access, 400
File Transfer Protocol. ***See*** **FTP**

filtering
MAC addresses, 145, 294
packets, 364
stateful, 515
firewalls, 92-93, 442
hardware, 443
incorrect host-based settings, 495
packet-filtering, 443-444
software, 442
stateful, 93, 444, 515
troubleshooting, 514
UTM, 446-447, 515
virtual, 103
virtual wire, 514
zones, 445-446
firing employees, 473
first-hop redundancy, 144
five nines of availability, 130, 415
flash card mode (Pearson Test Prep Practice Test engine), 532
flooding
ARP requests, 84
PIM-DM, 227
flow control, 40, 43
fluorinated ethylene polymer (FEP), 70
FM (frequency modulation), 36
forensics (computer), 433
formatting
data, 48
IPv4 addresses, 161-163
IPv6 addresses, 193
TCP segments, 51
forwarding
ARP replies, 85-86
ports, 220
Telnet segments, 86-87
forwarding state, 135
fox and hound, 390
FQDNs (fully qualified domain names), 93-94
DNS translation, 167
resolving to IP addresses, 362-363
fragility (data), 433
Frame Relay, 262-263
Frame Relay Traffic Shaping (FRTS), 263
frames
Ethernet, 118
extended super, 247
jumbo, 103
MPLS labels, 268
super, 247
frequencies
2.4GHz band, 282
5GHz band, 283
bands, 281
cable modems, 255
center, 284
channels, 281
DOCSIS, 255
modulation (FM), 36
sources of interference, 289-291
transmission methods, 284
WLANs, 281
frequency-division multiplexing (FDM), 38
frequency-hopping spread spectrum (FHSS), 284
FRTS (Frame Relay Traffic Shaping), 263
FTP (File Transfer Protocol), 55
bounce attacks, 418
remote file access, 400
FTPS (FTP over SSL), 400
full backups, 311
full-duplex mode, 123
full-mesh topology, 17
fully qualified domain names. ***See*** **FQDNs**

G

g parameter
arp command, 338
PathPing command, 358
gain, 279
gas attacks, 426
Gateway Load Balancing Protocol (GLBP), 310
gateway parameter (route command), 352, 370
gateways
default, 144, 167
incorrect default, 495
VoIP networks, 108
gathering information (troubleshooting), 483
GBICs (gigabit interface converters), 124
Generic Flow Control (GFC), 264
generic routing encapsulation (GRE), 451
geofencing, 297
geographic dispersion of networks, 7-9
get messages, 393
GFC (Generic Flow Control), 264
gigabit Ethernet, 124
gigabit interface converters (GBICs), 124
GLBP (Gateway Load Balancing Protocol), 310
global positioning system (GPS), 297
Global System for Mobiles (GSM), 244
GNU Privacy Guard (GPG), 411
goodput, 290
governing policies, preventing attacks, 430
GPG (GNU Privacy Guard), 411
GPS (global positioning system), 297
GRE (generic routing encapsulation), 451
GSM (Global System for Mobiles), 244
guidelines, preventing attacks, 432

H

h parameter (PathPing command), 358
H.323 protocol, 55
HA (high availability), 514
half-duplex mode, 123
hardening devices, 438
hardware
firewalls, 443
redundancy, 308-309, 313
hash-based message authentication codes (HMACs), 414
hashing, 395, 414
HDLC (High-Level Data Link Control), 246

Header Error Control (HEC), 264
headers
- ATM, 264-265
- authentication, 451-452
- compressing, 322
- IEEE 802.1Q, 129
- MPLS, 266
- TCP segments, 52
- UDP segments, 52

heat maps, 281
HEC (Header Error Control), 264
HFC (hybrid fiber-coax), 254
HIDS (host-based intrusion detection system), 455
high availability (HA), 514
- best practices, 311
- designing, 310-311
- measuring, 306

High-Level Data Link Control (HDLC), 246
High-Speed Packet Access (HSPA+), 245
high throuput (ht), 510
hijacking sessions, 422
HIPS (host-based intrusion prevention system), 455, 458
hiring employees, 473
HMACs (hash-based message authentication codes), 414
hold-down timers, 216
honeynets, 513
honeypots, 435, 513
hop counts, 212, 216
host addresses, 162, 180-181
host command, 363
host routing tables, viewing, 367
host-based firewalls, 442
host-based intrusion detection system (HIDS), 455
host-based intrusion prevention system (HIPS), 455, 458
hostname parameter (arp command), 360
hotspots, 276
HSPA+ (High-Speed Packet Access), 245
HSRP (Hot Standby Router Protocol), 144, 309
ht (high throughput), 510
HTTP (Hypertext Transfer Protocol), 53-55
HTTPS (Hypertext Transfer Protocol Secure), 55, 400
hub-and-spoke topology, 16
hubs,6, 80
humidity attacks, 426
hybrid cloud services, 105
hybrid fiber-coax (HFC), 254
hybrid networks, 24
hybrid routing protocols, 219
Hypertext Transfer Protocol (HTTP), 53-55
Hypertext Transfer Protocol Secure (HTTPS), 55, 400
hypervisors, 102

I

i (isotropic), 279
i parameter
- arp command, 360
- PathPing command, 358
- ping command, 350

IaaS (infrastructure as a service), 105
IANA (Internet Assigned Numbers Authority), 164
IB (InfiniBand), 103
IBSS (independent basic service set) WLANs, 287
ICA (Independent Computing Architecture), 252, 440
ICANN (Internet Corporation for Assigned Names and Numbers), 164
ICMP (Internet Control Message Protocol), 46
- attacks, 424
- echo messages, 350-351

ICS (Internet connection sharing), 245
ICSs (industrial control systems), troubleshooting, 500
identifying problems, 485
IDF (independent distribution facility), 391
IDFs (intermediate distribution frames), 75-76
IDS (intrusion detection system), 454
- detection methods, 456-457
- devices, 455
- host-based, 458
- implementing, 517
- IPS, compared, 455-456
- network-based, 458

IEEE (Institute of Electrical and Electronics Engineers), 7
IEEE 802.1Q standard, 129
IEEE 802.1X standard, 141-142, 294, 440
IEEE 802.3. *See* Ethernet
IEEE 802.3af standard, 138
IEEE Registration Authority, 39
if parameter (route command), 352
if_addr parameter (arp command), 339
ifconfig command, 363-364
ifscope parameter (arp command), 360
IGMP (Internet Group Management Protocol), 224-226
IGMPv1, 224
IGMPv2, 224
IGMPv3, 225
IGPs (Interior Gateway Protocols), 215
IKE (Internet Key Exchange), 449-451
IKEv1, 450
IMAP (Internet Message Access Protocol), 55
IMAP4 (Internet Message Access Protocol Version 4), 55
implementing troubleshooting solutions, 486
in-band management, 509
incident response
- policies, 470-471
- preventing attacks, 432-433

incorrect AP placement, troubleshooting, 499
incorrect default gateways, 495
incorrect DNS configuration, 495
incorrect host-based firewall settings, 495

incorrect subnet masks, 495
incorrect time, 495
incremental backups, 311
independent basic service set (IBSS) WLANs, 287
Independent Computing Architecture (ICA), 252, 440
independent distribution facility (IDF), 391
industrial control systems (ICSs), troubleshooting, 500
inet_addr parameter (arp command), 338
InfiniBand (IB), 103
infrared (IR), 79
infrastructure as a service (IaaS), 105
infrastructure audits by consultants, troubleshooting, 514-518
infrastructure devices, 79
- bridges, 81-82
- characteristics, 91
- hubs, 80
- routers, 90
- switches, 82-89
  - *ARP replies sent from servers, 85*
  - *bidirectional Telnet sessions, 88*
  - *broadcast domains, 88*
  - *endpoints sending ARP requests, 83*
  - *endpoints sending Telnet segments, 86*
  - *flooding ARP requests, 84*
  - *forwarding ARP replies, 85-86*
  - *forwarding Telnet segments, 86*
  - *multilayer, 89-90*

initiators
- IPSec peers, 450
- iSCSI, 103

inside global addresses, 221
inside local addresses, 221
INSIDE zone (firewalls), 445
insider attacks, 419
inspecting traffic, 443-444
Institute of Electrical and Electronics Engineers (IEEE), 7
Integrated Services Digital Networks (ISDNs), 260
integrated services (IntServ), 316
integrity, 414
- attacks, 419-422
  - *botnets, 421*
  - *brute force, 421*
  - *data diddling, 420*
  - *dictionary attacks, 421*
  - *hijacking sessions, 422*
  - *keyloggers, 421*
  - *MitM, 420*
  - *packet captures, 421*
  - *password, 421*
  - *salami, 420*
  - *Trojan horses, 421*
  - *trust relationship exploitation, 420*
- hashing, 414
- SNMP messages, 395
- violations, 414
- VPN traffic, 449

interesting octets, 184, 325
interfaces
- functionality, confirming, 385
- IP addresses, configuring, 364

interference (WLANs), 289-291
interior dynamic routing protocols, 503
Interior Gateway Protocols (IGPs), 215
intermediate distribution frames (IDFs), 75-76
Intermediate System-to-Intermediate System (IS-IS), 219
international export controls, 474
International Organization for Standardization (ISO), 31
Internet access technologies, 521-522
Internet Assigned Numbers Authority (IANA), 164
Internet Connection Sharing (ICS), 245
Internet Control Message Protocol. *See* ICMP
Internet Corporation for Assigned Names and Numbers (ICANN), 164
Internet Group Management Protocol (IGMP), 224-226
Internet Key Exchange (IKE), 449-451
Internet layer (TCP/IP stack), 50
Internet Message Access Protocol (IMAP), 55
Internet Message Access Protocol Version 4 (IMAP4), 55
Internet of Things (IoT), 78-79
Internet Protocol. *See* IP
intranets, 167
intrusion detection system. *See* IDS
intrusion prevention system. *See* IPS
IntServ (integrated services), 316
inventory management, documenting, 391
IoT (Internet of Things), 78-79
IP (Internet Protocol)
- helpers, 174
- phones, 108
- phone voice quality, troubleshooting, 501-504
- precedence, 318
- routing tables, 209

IP addresses
- assignable in subnets, 176
- configuration parameters, displaying, 340
- DHCP server, 97
- DNS records pointing to, 95
- duplicate, 495
- expired, 495
- FQDNs, resolving, 362-363
- host, 180-181
- interfaces, configuring, 364
- leases, 98
- listing, 347
- loopback, 163
- management (IPAM), 96
- NAT classifications, 221
- NAT names, 221
- next-hop, 211
- parameters, displaying, 340
- ranges, calculating, 183-186
- scopes, 98
- target, specifying, 356
- translation
  - *NAT, 220-222*
  - *PAT, 222-224*

IP Address Manager subnet calculator, 189

IP small computer system interface (iSCSI), 103, 500, 504
IPAM (IP address management), 96
ipconfig command, 340-343
IPCP (IP control protocol), 249
IPS (intrusion prevention system), 454
detection methods, 456-457
devices, 455
host-based, 458
IDS, compared, 455-456
implementing, 517
network-based, 458
IPSec (IP Security), 268
IKE modes/phases, 451
overlay networks, 268
remote access, 400
tunnels, 451
VPNs, 449
AH, 451-452
ESP, 451-452
IKE modes/phases, 449-451
site-to-site example, 452-454
iptables command, 364
IPv4 (IP Version 4), 153, 161
APIPA, 174-176
assignment, 164
available hosts, number of, 180-181
bits, 154
BOOTP protocol, 173
borrowed bits, 179
broadcast, 165
CIDR, 190-191
classes, 163
classful masks, extending, 179
components, 167-168
DHCP, 173-174
dotted-decimal notation, 161
dynamic configuration, 172
FQDN translation, 167
multicast, 166
network address calculation, 162
network/host address divisions, 162
private addressing, 164
ranges, calculating, 183-186
static configuration, 168-172
structure, 161-163
subnet masks, 161
subnet notation, 177-178
subnet octet values, 178
subnets created, number of, 180
transitioning to IPv6, 192
unicast, 165
IPv6 (IP Version 6), 153, 191
anycast, 195-196
bits, 154
features, 192
IPv4 transitions, 192
multicast, 195
NDP, 193
ping command, 352
records, 95
structure, 192-193
traceroute command, 366
tracert command, 358
types, 193
unicast, 194
IP Version 4. *See* IPv4
IP Version 6. *See* IPv6
IR (infrared), 79
iSCSI (IP small computer system interface), 103, 500, 504
ISDNs (Integrated Services Digital Networks), 260-262
IS-IS (Intermediate System-to-Intermediate System), 219
ISM bands, 281
isochronous transmissions, 40
ISO (International Organization for Standardization), 31
isotropic (i), 279

J-K

jitter, 314
jumbo frames, 103

Kerberos, 440
key fobs, 438
keyloggers, 421
keys
encryption/decryption, 411
HMACs, 414
IKE, 449-451
PKI, 412
session, 411

L

L2F (Layer 2 Forwarding) protocol, 454
L2TP (Layer 2 Tunneling Protocol), 454
labels, 391
MPLS frames, 268
switching, 266
label switch router (LSR), 267
LACP (Link Aggregation Control Protocol), 137
LAGs (link aggregation groups), 137
LANs (local area networks), 7
virtual, 127-128
configuration, troubleshooting, 490
native, 129
segmentation, 439
trunking, 129-130
wireless, 8, 275
ad hoc, 276
antennas, 278-281
APs, 277-278
attacks, 422
BSS, 288
cells, 291
cellular technologies, 287
channels, 281-283
CSMA/CA, 283
enterprise-class, 276
ESS, 288
frequencies, 281
geofencing, 297
hotspots, 276
IBSS, 287
mesh topology, 289
networking issues, troubleshooting, 507-511
personal mode, 294
routers, 276-277
security, 292-297
sources of interference, 289-291
standards, 285-286
transmission methods, 284
wireless AP placement, 291
latency, 313, 498
Layer 1, troubleshooting, 487-489
bad cables/connections, 487
bad ports, 487

cable placement, 488
crosstalk, 488
dB loss, 488
distance limitations exceeded, 488
example, 488-489
opens/shorts, 487
speed/duplex mismatches, 488
splitting pairs in cables, 487
transposed Tx/Rx leads, 488

Layer 2
- Forwarding (L2F) protocol, 454
- security protections, 439
- troubleshooting, 490-491
- Tunneling Protocol (L2TP), 454

Layer 3
- Layer 2 mapping, 209
- redundancy, 309-310
- switches, 89
- troubleshooting, 492-495
  - *blocked TCP/UDP ports, 495*
  - *data structures, 492-494*
  - *duplicate IP address, 495*
  - *duplicate MAC addresses, 495*
  - *example, 496-497*
  - *exhausted DHCP scope, 495*
  - *expired IP addresses, 495*
  - *incorrect ACL settings, 495*
  - *incorrect default gateways, 495*
  - *incorrect DNS configuration, 495*
  - *incorrect host-based firewall settings, 495*
  - *incorrect subnet masks, 495*
  - *incorrect time, 495*
  - *mismatched MTU, 494*
  - *rogue DHCP servers, 495*
  - *unresponsive services, 495*
  - *untrusted SSL certificates, 495*

layers
- OSI model, 32-33
  - *application, 48, 49*
  - *data link, 38-41*
  - *listing of, 33*
  - *network, 41-43*
  - *order, 34*
  - *physical, 35-38*
  - *presentation, 47-48*
  - *session, 46-47*
  - *transport, 44-46*
- TCP/IP stack, 49-53
  - *application, 53*
  - *Internet, 50*
  - *network interface, 50*
  - *transport, 51*

LC (Lucent connectors), 73
LCP (Link Control Protocol), 249-250
LDAP (Lightweight Directory Access Protocol), 55, 441
LDAPS (Lightweight Directory Access Protocol over SSH), 55
LEAP (Lightweight Extensible Authentication Protocol), 295
learning state, 135
leases, 98, 342
LED (light emitting diodes), 70
legal holds, 433
LFI (link fragmentation and interleaving), 322
licensing restrictions, 473
light propagation, 72
Lightweight Directory Access Protocol (LDAP), 55, 441
Lightweight Directory Access Protocol over SSH (LDAPS), 55
Lightweight Extensive Authentication Protocol (LEAP), 295
Link Aggregation Control Protocol (LACP), 137
link aggregation groups (LAGs), 137
Link Control Protocol (LCP), 249-250
link fragmentation and interleaving (LFI), 322
Link Layer Discovery Protocol (LLDP), 520
link-local IP addresses, assigning, 175
link-state advertisements (LSAs), 218
link-state routing protocols, 218
links
- aggregation, 136-137
- efficiency, 322
- high BER, 380
- looped detection, 249
- uplink congestion, 136
- WANs, 7

listening state, 135
LLC (Logical Link Control) sublayer, 40-41
LLDP (Link Layer Discovery Protocol), 520
LLQ (low-latency queuing), 319
load balancing, 100, 312
Local Area Connection properties, 170
Local Area Connection Status window, 170
local area networks. *See* LANs
local authentication, 441
local loops, 260
locating network services, 175
locks, 438
logic bombs, 422
logical addressing, 42
logical diagrams, 391
Logical Link Control (LLC sublayer), 40-41
logical topologies
- MAC, 39
- physical topology, compared, 10-11

logins, failed attempts on vty lines, 511-514
logs, 398-399
long STP, 135
Long-Term Evolution (LTE), 244
looking-glass sites, 387
loopback IP addresses, 163
loopback plugs, 385
looped link detection, 249
loops
- Layer 2, 490
- local, 260
- routing, 217-218

Low Delay, 316
low-latency queuing (LLQ), 319
Low Priority, 316
LSAs (link-state advertisements), 218
LSR (label switch router), 267
LTE (Long-Term Evolution), 244
Lucent connectors (LC), 73

M

MAC (Media Access Control) addresses
- duplicate, 495
- filtering, 145, 294
- table corruption, 131-132

MAC (Media Access Control) sublayer, 39

mail exchange (MX) records, 95

main distribution facility (MDF), 391

main distribution frames (MDFs), 77

main mode (IKE), 450

maintenance tools, 380
- BERT, 380
- butt sets, 381
- cable certifiers, 381
- cable testers, 382
- connectivity software, 382
- crimpers, 383
- electrostatic discharge wrist straps, 383-384
- environmental monitors, 384-385
- looking-glass sites, 387
- loopback plugs, 385
- multimeters, 385-386
- protocol analyzers, 386
- punch-down tool, 388
- speed testing, 388
- TDR, 389
- throughput tester, 388
- toner probes, 390
- Wi-Fi analyzer, 387

malicious intent, 511

malware, 418

management
- change, 391
- congestion, 319
- in-band, 509
- inventory, documenting, 391
- switches, 142-143

Management Information Base (MIB), 392

man command, 359

man-in-the-middle (MitM) attacks, 417, 420

MANs (metropolitan area networks), 9

marking (QoS), 318

mask netmask parameter (route command), 352

mask parameter (route command), 370

masks
- classful, 163
- subnet, 495

master service agreements (MSAs), 514

maximum transmission unit (MTU), 494

MD5 (message digest 5) algorithm, 414

MDF (main distribution facility) documentation, 391

MDFs (main distribution frames), 77

MDI (media-dependent interface) ports, 69

MDIX (media-dependent interface crossover) ports, 69

mDNS (Multicast Domain Name Service), 175

means (attackers), 432

mean time between failures (MTBF), 306

measuring
- bandwidth, 123
- bit errors, 380
- gain, 279
- high-availability, 306

media, 64
- cables
  - *coaxial, 64-65*
  - *distribution, 75-77*
  - *plenum/nonplenum, 70*
  - *twisted-pair, 66-69*
- converters, 75
- defined, 6
- fiber-optic cables, 70
  - *MMF, 70-72*
  - *mode of propagation, 71*
  - *polishing styles, 74*
  - *SMF, 72-74*
- WANs, 243
  - *physical, 243-244*
  - *wireless, 244-245*
- wireless, 77

Media Access Control (MAC) sublayer, 39

media converters, 77

media-dependent interface (MDI) ports, 69

media-dependent interface crossover (MDIX) ports, 69

Media Gateway Control Protocol (MGCP), 55

media termination recommended jacks (MTRJs), 73

memorandum of understanding (MOU), 516

memory
- buffer overflow attacks, 424
- tables, 530

mesh cloud, 289

mesh topology, 289

mesh wireless topology, 20

message digest 5 (MD5) algorithm, 414

Message Integrity Check (MIC), 297

messages
- acknowledgment, 40
- ICMP echo, sending to target, 351
- PIM-DM pruning, 228
- SNMP, 393-394
- switching, 43
- syslog, 395-397

metric parameter (route command), 352

metro Ethernet, 248

metropolitan area networks (MANs), 9

MGCP (Media Gateway Control Protocol), 55

mGRE (multiple GRE) tunnels, 268

MIB (Management Information Base), 392

MIC (Message Integrity Check), 297

Microsoft Challenge-Handshake Authentication Protocol (MS-CHAP), 250, 441

Microsoft RRAS (Routing and Remote Access Server), 251-252

microwave oven interference, 290

MIMO (multiple input, multiple output), 286, 510

Miredo, 192

mirroring ports, 140-141

misconfiguration of wireless parameters, 498
mismatched MTU, 494
MitM (man-in-the-middle) attacks, 417, 420
MMF (multimode fiber) cables, 70-72
mode of propagation, 71-72
mode selection (Pearson Test Prep Practice Test engine), 533
modulation, 36
modules, 490
monitoring
- environmental monitors, 384-385
- ports, 139-140
- switches, 145
- tools, 392
  - *application logs, 398*
  - *logs, 398*
  - *security logs, 399*
  - *SNMP, 392-395*
  - *syslog, 395-397*
  - *system logs, 399*

motion detection devices, 437
motives (attackers), 432
MOU (memorandum of understanding), 516
MPLS (Multiprotocol Label Switching), 8, 266-268
- elements, 266-267
- frame labels, 268
- headers, 266
- label switching, 266

MSAs (master service agreements), 514
MS-CHAP (Microsoft Challenge-Handshake Authentication Protocol), 250, 441
MTBF (mean time between failures), 306
MTRJs (media-termination recommended jacks), 73
MTU (maximum transmission unit), mismatched, 494
multicast distribution trees, 226
Multicast Domain Name Service (mDNS), 175
multicast groups, 166, 224
multicast IPv4 addresses, 166
multicast IPv6 addresses, 195
multicast routing
- distribution trees, 226
- IGMP, 224-226
- PIM, 226
- PIM-DM, 227-229
- PIM-SM, 229-230

multifactor authentication, 441
multiframes, 247
multilayer switches, 89-90
multilink interfaces, 249
multimedia networks, troubleshooting, 500
multimeters, 385-386
multimode delay distortion, 72
multimode fiber cables (MMF cables), 70-72
multipath issues, 290
Multiprotocol label switching. *See* MPLS
multiple GRE (mGRE) tunnels, 268
multiple input, multiple output (MIMO), 286, 510
multiple paths of propagation, troubleshooting, 498
multiplexing, 38, 521
MUMIMO (multi-user MIMO), 510
MX (mail exchange) records, 95

N

n parameter
- arp command, 360
- nbtstat command, 344
- PathPing command, 358
- ping command, 350

N parameter (arp command), 338
NaaS (network as a service), 105
NAC (Network Admission Control), 142, 440
names
- NAT IP addresses, 221
- NetBIOS
  - *resolving, 345*
  - *viewing, 344*
- PDUs, 34
- universal naming convention (UNC), 167

narrowband transmission, 284
NAS (network-attached storage) devices, 22, 500
NAT (Network Address Translation), 220-222
native VLANs, 129
nbtstat command, 343-345
NCP (Network Control Protocol), 49
NDAs (non-disclosure agreements), 474
NDP (Neighbor Discovery Protocol), 193
near-end crosstalk (NEXT), 516
near field communication (NFC), 79
neighbor advertisements, 194
neighbor solicitations, 194
neighborships, 494
Nessus, 434
net parameter (route command), 370
NetBEUI (NetBIOS Extended User Interface), 47
NetBIOS (Network Basic Input/Output System), 47, 55
- Extended User Interface (NetBEUI), 47
- information, displaying, 343
- names
  - *cache, viewing, 344*
  - *resolving, 345*
- tables, viewing, 345

netstat command
- output, 347
- UNIX, 366-367
- Windows, 346-347

network addresses
- broadcast domains, 126
- calculating, 162
- IPv4 addresses, 162

Network Address Translation. *See* NAT
Network Admission Control (NAC), 142, 440
Network and Internet control panel, 168
Network as a Service (NaaS), 105
network-attached storage (NAS) devices, 22, 500

network-based firewalls, 442
network-based intrusion prevention system (NIPS), 455, 458
Network Basic Input/Output System. *See* NetBIOS
Network Connections window, 170
Network Control Protocol (NCP), 49
Network File System (NFS), 22, 500
Network Interface Cards (NICs), 308
network interface devices (NIDs), 260
network interface layer (TCP/IP stack), 50
network layer, 41-43, 492-495
blocked TCP/UDP ports, 495
data structures, 492-494
duplicate IP address, 495
duplicate MAC addresses, 495
example, 496-497
exhausted DHCP scope, 495
expired IP addresses, 495
incorrect ACL settings, 495
incorrect default gateways, 495
incorrect DNS configuration, 495
incorrect host-based firewall settings, 495
incorrect subnet masks, 495
incorrect time, 495
mismatched MTU, 494
rogue DHCP servers, 495
unresponsive services, 495
untrusted SSL certificates, 495
network management system (NMS), 392
Network News Transport Protocol (NNTP), 55
network-node interfaces (NNIs), 265
network operating system (NOS), 22
network parameter (route command), 370
network termination 1s (NT1s), 262
Network Time Protocol (NTP), 55
networks, 7
CANs, 9
client/server, 21-22
components, 5-7
connections, 4
converged, 4
defined, 4
hybrid, 24
faults, 306
LANs. *See* LANs
MANs, 9
PANs, 9
peer-to-peer, 22-23
purpose, 4
resource locations, 21
SANs, 9
services, locating, 175
sniffers, 139, 386
topologies, 10
bus, 11
characteristics/benefits/drawbacks, 12
full-mesh, 17
hub-and-spoke, 16
partial-mesh, 18-19
physical versus logical, 10-11
ring, 11-14
star, 15
wireless, 20
WANs, 8
WLANs, 8
next-generation firewalls (NGFs), 447
next-hop IP addresses, 211
NEXT (near-end crosstalk), 516
NFC (near field communication), 79
NFS (Network File System), 22, 500
NGFs (next-generation firewalls), 447
NGFW (next-generation firewall), 101
NHRP (Next-Hop Resolution Protocol), 268
NICs (Network Interface Cards), 308
NIDs (network interface devices), 260
NIPS (network-based intrusion prevention system), 455, 458
Nmap utility, 365, 434
NMS (network management system), 392
NNIs (network-node interfaces), 265
NNTP (Network News Transport Protocol), 55
noAuthNo Priv security level, 394
nondesignated ports, 134-135
non-disclosure agreements (NDAs), 474
nonoverlapping channels, 282-283
nonplenum cables, 70
nonroot bridge switches, 133
nonstatistical anomaly detection, 457
no single points of failure, 307
NOS (network operating system), 22
notation
dotted-decimal, 161
prefix, 162
subnet masks, 177-178
notifications
backward explicit congestion, 263
SNMP traps, 384
NS records, 95
nslookup command
UNIX, 362
Windows, 348-349
NT1s (network termination 1s), 262
NTP (Network Time Protocol), 55
numbering
binary, 154
converting
binary to decimal, 155-158
decimal to binary, 155-160
dotted-decimal notation, 161
prefix notation, 162
Nyquist theorem, 246

O

octets, 161
interesting, 184, 325
subnet mask values, 178
OFDM (orthogonal frequency-division multiplexing), 284
off-boarding best practices, 473
off-site virtual devices, 105
omnidirectional antennas, 279
on-boarding best practices, 473
on demand WANs, 240
OOB (out-of-band) management, 142, 401

open authentication, 294
Open Shortest Path First (OSPF), 212, 219, 503
Open Systems Interconnection. *See* **OSI model**
opens, troubleshooting, 487
opportunities (attackers), 433
optical time domain reflectometer (OTDR), 389
optimization
- content caching, 312
- fault-tolerant design, 307-308
- hardware redundancy, 308-313
- high-availability
  - *best practices, 311*
  - *design, 310-311*
  - *measuring, 306*
- Layer 3 redundancy, 309-310
- load balancing, 312
- QoS, 313
  - *classification, 318*
  - *components, 316-317*
  - *configuration, 315-316*
  - *congestion, 319*
  - *lack of bandwidth, 314-315*
  - *link efficiency, 322*
  - *marking, 318*
  - *mechanisms, 317*
  - *policing, 320*
  - *shaping, 320-322*

ordering OSI model layers, 34
organizationally unique identifiers (OUIs), 515
orthogonal frequency-division multiplexing (OFDM), 284
OSI (Open Systems Interconnection) model, 31
- layers, 32-33
  - *application, 48-49*
  - *data link, 38-41*
  - *listing of, 33*
  - *network, 41-43*
  - *order, 34*
  - *physical, 35-38*
  - *presentation, 47-48*
  - *session, 46-47*
  - *transport, 44-46*
- TCP/IP stack, 49
  - *application layer protocols, 53-56*
  - *layers, 49-53*

OSPF (Open Shortest Path First), 212, 219, 503
ot sites, 313
OTDR (optical time domain reflectometer), 389
OUIs (organizationally unique identifiers), 515
outages (WANs), 505-507
out-of-band management (OOB), 142, 401
outside global addresses, 221
outside local addresses, 221
OUTSIDE zone (firewalls), 445
overlay networks, 268
overt channels, 418

P

P (provider) routers, 267
p parameter
- netstat command, 346
- PathPing command, 358
- route command, 352

PaaS (platform as service), 106
packets
- capturing
  - *attacks, 417, 421*
  - *network sniffers, 139*
  - *port mirroring, 140*
- delay, 314
- drops, 314
- filtering
  - *firewalls, 443-444*
  - *rules, 364*
- GRE, 451
- ICMP echo, sending, 369
- jitter, 314
- LFI, 322
- loss, 358
- marking, 318
- reordering, 43
- shapers, 263
- sniffing, 417
- switched connections, 241
- switching. *See* routing
- tail dropped, 319
- transport mode, 452
- tunnel mode, 452

PANs (personal area networks), 9
PAP (Password Authentication Protocol), 249, 441
parameters
- arp command, 338, 360
- IP addresses, displaying, 340
- ipconfig command, 340
- nbtstat command, 344
- netstat command, 346, 366
- PathPing command, 358
- ping command, 350, 368
- route command, 352, 369

Pareto principal, 239
parity bits, 41
partial-mesh topology, 18-19
passive hubs, 80
passive IDS devices, 455
passive optical networks (PONs), 257
Password Authentication Protocol (PAP), 249, 441
passwords
- attacks, 421
- policies, 468-469

patches
- panels, 75
- preventing attacks, 428
- updates, compared, 429

path-vector routing protocols, 219
PathPing command, 358
PAT (Port Address Translation), 220-224
pattern generators, 380
Payload Type Indicator (PTI), 264
PBQs (performance-based questions), 531
PBX (private branch exchange), 106
- five nines of availability, 130
- VoIP networks, 108

PDUs (protocol data units), 34
PE (provider edge) routers, 267
PEAP-GTC (Protected EAP–Generic Token Card), 295
PEAP-MSCHAPv2 (Protected EAP–Microsoft Challenge Handshake Authentication Protocol version 2), 295

Pearson Test Prep Practice Test engine, 532
flash card mode, 532
mode selection, 533
practice exam mode, 532
study mode, 532
peer-to-peer networks, 22-23
performance-based questions (PBQs), 531
performance baselines, documenting, 391
permanent virtual circuits (PVCs), 263
personal area networks (PANs), 9
personal mode (WLANs), 294
PGP (Pretty Good Privacy) algorithm, 411
phishing, 419
physical addressing, 39
physical diagrams, 391
physical environment attacks, 426-427
physical layer, 35-38, 487-489
physical media (WANs), 243-244
physical obstacles (WLANs), 290
physical security devices, 437-438
physical topology, 10-11
PIM (Protocol Independent Multicast), 226
PIM-DM (PIM dense mode), 227-229
PIM-SM (PIM sparse mode), 229-230
ping command
UNIX, 368-369
ICMP echo packets, sending, 369
parameters, 368
syntax, 368
Windows, 350-351
ICMP echo messages, sending to target, 351
IPv6, 352
parameters, 350
syntax, 350
unreachable destinations, 351
ping of death, 424
ping sweep attacks, 417
PKI (public key infrastructure), 412
placement
APs, 499
cables, 488
devices, 384
wireless APs, 291
plain old telephone service (POTS), 258-260
plan of action (troubleshooting), 486
plans
back-out, 486
incident response, 432-433
platform as a service (PaaS), 106
PLCs (programmable logic controllers), troubleshooting, 500
plenum cables, 70
PoE (Power over Ethernet), 138-139
pointer (PTR) records, 95
point-to-point connections, 246
Point-to-Point Protocol (PPP), 246, 249, 439
Point-to-Point Protocol over Ethernet (PPPoE), 250, 439
Point-to-Point Tunneling Protocol (PPTP), 454
poison reverse feature, 218
policies, 468
acceptable use, 471
AUPs, 429
BYOD, 471, 506
DLP, 469-470
end-user, 431
governing, 430
incident-response, 470-471
passwords, 468-469
remote-access, 470
safety procedures, 472
security, 429
technical, 431
policing traffic, 320
policy-based detection, 457
polishing styles, 74
polyvinyl chloride (PVC), 70
PONs (passive optical networks), 257
POP3 (Post Office Protocol Version 3), 55
Port Address Translation (PAT), 220-224
portals, 441
ports
access, 128
bad, 487
blocked TCP/UDP, 495
bonding, 137
configuration, 490
defined, 6
ephemeral, 54
forwarding, 220
locations, documenting, 391
MDI, 69
MDIX, 69
mirroring, 140-141
monitoring, 139-140
on switches on same subnet, 126
scans, 417
STP
costs, 134-135
states, 135
types, 133-134
switch port security, 517
trunk configuration, 130
well-known, 54
post-mortem reports, 486
Post Office Protocol Version 3 (POP3), 55
posture assessment, 440
POTS (plain old telephone service) connections, 258-260
power failures, 490
power faults, 425
Power over Ethernet (PoE), 138-139
power sags, 426
power spikes, 425
PPP (Point-to-Point Protocol), 246, 249, 439
LCP, 249-250
Microsoft RRAS, 251
PPPoE (Point-to-Point Protocol over Ethernet), 250, 439
PPTP (Point-to-Point Tunneling Protocol), 454
practice exam mode (Pearson Test Prep Practice Test engine), 532
prefix notation, 162, 177-178
preparing for exam
companion website, 529-530
end-of-chapter reviews, 531

exam taking strategies, 533-535
memory tables, 530
performance-based questions, 531
suggested study plan, 531-533
training videos, 530
presentation layer (OSI model), 47-48
preshared keys (PSKs), 293
Pretty Good Privacy (PGP) algorithm, 411
preventing
attacks
ACLs, 436-437
detailed documentation, 431-432
end-user policies, 431
governing policies, 430
honey pots, 435
incident response, 432-433
Layer 2 protections, 439
network device hardening, 438
patching, 428
physical devices, 437-438
security policies, 429
technical policies, 431
user training, 427-428
vulnerability scanners, 433-435
data loss (DLP), 469-470
prevention security devices, 437
print parameter (route command), 353
priority treatment, 316
PRI (primary rate interface) circuits, 261
private addresses, 222
private branch exchange (PBX), 106
private IP addressing, 164, 174
privileged user agreements (PUAs), 472-473
probable cause theory, 485
procedures, preventing attacks, 432
programmable logic controllers (PLCs), troubleshooting, 500
Protected EAP-Generic Token Card (PEAP-GTC), 295
Protected EAP-Microsoft Challenge Handshake Authentication Protocol version 2 (PEAP-MSCHAPv2), 295
protocol data units (PDUs), 34
Protocol Independent Multicast (PIM), 226
protocols
AH, 451-452
analyzers, 386
Ant+, 78
application layer, 53-56
ARP, 83
BGP, 503
BOOTP, 173
CARP, 310
CCMP, 297
CHAP, 250, 441
DHCP, 54, 173-174
DHCPv6, 193
DNS, 54
dynamic routing, 503
EAP
IEEE 802.1X security, 295
remote-access security, 441
EGPs, 215
EIGRP, 503
ESP, 451-452
FTP, 55, 400
FTPS, 400
GLBP, 310
H.323, 55
HSRP, 144, 309
HTTP, 53-55
HTTPS, 55
ICMP, 46, 350, 424
IGMP, 224-226
IGPs, 215
IMAP, 55
IMAP4, 55
IPSec
AH, 451-452
ESP, 451-452
IKE modes/phases, 449-451
site-to-site VPN example, 452-454
VPNs, 449
Kerberos, 440
L2F, 454
L2TP, 454
LACP, 137
LCP, 249-250
LDAP, 55, 441
LDAPS, 55
LLDP, 520
MGCP, 55
MS-CHAP, 441
NCP, 49
NDP, 193
NHRP, 268
NNTP, 55
NTP, 55
OSPF, 503
PAP, 249, 441
PIM, 226
PIM-DM, 227-229
PIM-SM, 229-230
POP3, 55
PPP, 249, 439
LCP, 249-250
Microsoft RRAS, 251
PPPoE, 250, 439
PPTP, 454
RADIUS, 440
Rapid Spanning Tree, 131
RARP, 174
RDP, 55, 382, 439
RIPv2, 503
routing
believability, 214
BGP, 219
distance-vector, 216-218
EIGRP, 219
interior versus exterior, 215
IS-IS, 219
link-state, 218
metrics, 214
OSPF, 219
RIP, 218
routed protocols, compared, 213
route redistribution, 220
RTP, 55, 108
RTSP, 56
SCP, 56
SFTP, 400
SIP, 56, 108
SLP, 175
SMB, 56
SMTP, 56
SNMP, 56, 392-395
agents, 392
components, 392
managers, 392
message types, 393

MIB, 392
security enhancements, 394
trap, 56
walk, 393
SPB, 131
SSDP, 175
SSH, 400
SSL, 454
statistics, displaying, 366
STP, 130-131
port costs, 134-135
port states, 135
port types, 133-134
switches, classifying, 133
TACACS+, 440
TCP, 44
Telnet, 400
TFTP, 56, 401
TKIP, 296
TLS, 454
transport layer, 44
UDP, 44
VNC, 400
VoIP networks, 107
VPNs, 454
VRRP, 310
VTP, 128
XAUTH, 451
Z-Wave, 78
provider (P) routers, 267
provider edge (PE) routers, 267
proxy servers, 98-99
pruning PIM-DM, 228
PSKs (preshared keys), 293-294
PSTN (Public Switched Telephone Network), 105, 258, 509
PTI (Payload Type Indicator), 265
PTR (pointer records), 95
PUAs (privileged user agreements), 472-473
public addresses, 222
public key infrastructure (PKI), 412
Public Switched Telephone Network (PSTN), 105, 258, 509
punch down tools, 388
PVC (polyvinyl chloride), 70
PVCs (permanent virtual circuits), 263

Q

q parameter
PathPing command, 358
route command, 370
QoS (quality of service), 145, 313
components, 316-317
configuration, 315-316
lack of bandwidth, 314-315
mechanisms, 317
classification, 318
congestion avoidance, 319
congestion management, 319
link efficiency, 322
marking, 318
policing, 320
shaping, 320-322
switches, 145
troubleshooting, 500
questioning users, 483
queue depth, 319
queuing, 319
quick mode (IKE), 450

R

r parameter
nbtstat command, 344
netstat command, 347, 367
R parameter (nbtstat command), 344
R reference points, 262
rack diagrams, 391
radio, 245
radio frequency identification (RFID), 79, 297
radio frequency interference. *See* RFI
RADIUS (Remote Authentication Dial-In User Service), 440
random early detection (RED), 319
ranges
IP addresses, calculating, 183-186
wireless extenders, 101
Rapid Spanning Tree, 131
RARP (Reverse Address Resolution Protocol), 174
RAS (Remote Access Server), 439
RC4 (Ron's Code), 296
RDP (Remote Desktop Protocol), 55, 382, 439
access, troubleshooting, 518-521
remote access, 400
Real-time Streaming Protocol (RTSP), 56
Real-time Transport Protocol (RTP), 55, 108
real transfer time, 45
receive (Rx) leads, 488
reconnaissance attacks, 417
records, 94-95
recrimping cables, 515
redirecting routers, 194
redistributing routes, 220
RED (random early detection), 319
redundancy
hardware, 308-309, 313
Layer 3, 309-310
NICs, 308
reference points, 262
reflective DoS attacks, 423
refraction, 71
registries (IP addresses), 164
reject parameter (arp command), 360
relay agents, 98
release parameter (ipconfig command), 340-342
release6 parameter (ipconfig command), 340
releasing DHCP leases, 342
reliability
availability, compared, 306
hardware redundancy, 308-309
remote access, 400-401
policies, 470
RDP applications, troubleshooting, 518-521
security, 439-442
SQL Server database, troubleshooting, 504-505
VPNs, 400, 448
Remote Access Server (RAS), 439
Remote Authentication Dial-In User Service (RADIUS), 440
remote desktop
connections, 382
control, 252

Remote Desktop Protocol (RDP), 55, 382, 439
remote shell (rsh), 55
rendezvous points (RPs), 229
renew6 parameter (ipconfig command), 340
renewing DHCP leases, 342
renew parameter (ipconfig command), 340, 343
reordering packets, 43
reporting problems, 482
reporting tools, 392
logging, 398-399
SNMP, 392-395
agents, 392
components, 392
managers, 392
message types, 393
MIB, 392
security enhancements, 394
walk, 393
syslog, 395-397
reservations (DHCP), 98
resolving problems, 482
resource locations, 21
client/server, 21-22
peer-to-peer, 22-23
Resource Reservation Protocol (RSVP), 316
resources (exam)
companion website, 529-530
end-of-chapter reviews, 531
memory tables, 530
performance-based questions, 531
suggested study plan, 531-533
training videos, 530
responders (IPSec peers), 450
responding to incidents
policies, 470-471
preventing attacks, 432-433
restricting licensing, 473
Reverse Address Resolution Protocol (RARP), 174
RFI (radio frequency interference), 64, 70
troubleshooting, 498
WLANs, 289-291
RFID (radio frequency identification), 79, 297
RG-6 cables, 65
RG-58 cables, 65
RG-59 cables, 64
ring topology, 11-14
RIP (Routing Information Protocol), 218
RIPv2 (Routing Information Protocol version 2), 503
Rivest Cipher, 296
Rivest, Shamir, Adleman (RSA) algorithm, 412
RJ-11 (type 11 registered jack) connectors, 69
RJ-45 (type 45 registered jack) connectors, 69
rogue APs, 293, 422
rogue DHCP servers, 495
rollover cables, 68
Ron's Code (RC4), 296
root bridge switches, 133
root ports, 134
round-trip time (RTT), 45
route aggregation, 190-191
route command, 352-355
add parameter, 355
delete parameter, 354
parameters, 352
print parameter, 353
syntax, 352
UNIX, 369-370
routed protocols, 213
routers, 90
active, 144, 310
advertisements, 194
black-hole, 494
CE, 267
defined, 6
ELSRs, 267
LSR, 267
P, 267
packet loss, 358
PE, 267
redirecting, 194
solicitations, 193
standby, 144, 310
virtual, 103, 310
wireless, 276-277
routing, 42
address translation
NAT, 220-222
PAT, 222-224
advertisements, 216-218
basic process, 206-208
convergence, 213
directly connected routes, 209-210
discovery, 43
distribution trees, 226
shared, 229
source, 227
SPT switchover, 230
dynamic routes, 211-213
IP routing tables, 209
loops, 217-218
multicast
IGMP, 224-226
PIM, 226
PIM-DM, 227-229
PIM-SM, 229, 230
protocols
believability, 214
BGP, 219
distance-vector, 216-218
EIGRP, 219
interior versus exterior gateway, 215
IS-IS, 219
link state, 218
metrics, 214
OSPF, 219
RIP, 218
routed protocols, compared, 213
route redistribution, 220
route redistribution, 220
selection, 43
static routes, 210-211
tables
contents, displaying, 353
directly connected routes, 209-210
dynamic routes, 211-213
entries, deleting, 354
routes, adding, 355
static routes, 210-211
UNIX host, viewing, 367

Routing and Remote Access Server (RRAS), 439
Routing Information Protocol (RIP), 218
Routing Information Protocol version 2 (RIPv2), 503
RPs (rendezvous points), 229
RRAS (Routing and Remote Access Server), 251-252, 439
RSA (Rivest, Shamir, Adleman) algorithm, 412
rsh (remote shell), 55
RSVP (Resource Reservation Protocol), 316
RTP (Real-time Transport Protocol), 55, 108
RTP header compression (cRTP), 322
RTSP (Real-time Streaming Protocol), 56
RTT (round-trip time), 45
Rx (receive) leads, 488

S

s parameter
arp command, 339, 360
netstat command, 347, 367
S parameter
nbtstat command, 344
ping command, 351, 369
SaaS (software as s service), 105, 521-522
safety procedures policies, 472
salami attacks, 420
sanity checks (troubleshooting), 485
SANs (storage area networks), 9
SAs (security associations), 450
satellite connections, 257-258
satellites, 245, 258
SC (subscriber connector), 73
SCADA (supervisory control and data acquisition) networks, troubleshooting, 500, 505
scanner vulnerability, 433-435
scanning ports, 417
scope (DHCP), 173, 495
SCP (Secure Copy Protocol), 56
SDH (Synchronous Digital Hierarchy), 256
SDN (software-defined networking), 101, 107
SDSL (Symmetric DSL), 254
Secure Copy Protocol (SCP), 56
Secure Hash Algorithm 1 (SHA-1), 414
Secure Shell (SSH), 56, 400, 440
Secure Sockets Layer (SSL), 454
security
associations (SAs), 450
attacks
availability, 422-427
Bluetooth, 431
confidentiality, 415-419
integrity, 419-422
means, 432
motives, 432
opportunities, 433
availability
attacks, 422-427
five nines, 415
BC plans, 427
confidentiality, 410-411
attacks, 415-419
encryption, 411-413
DR plans, 427
encryption, 451
firewalls, 442
hardware, 443
packet-filtering, 443-444
software, 442
stateful, 444
UTM, 446-447
zones, 445-446
goals, 410
IDS/IPS
anomaly-based detection, 457
comparison, 455-456
host-based, 458
implementing, 517
network-based, 458
policy-based detection, 457
signature-based detection, 456
integrity, 414
attacks, 419-422
hash digests, 414
hashing, 414
hashing algorithms, 414
violations, 414
logs, 399
overlay networks, 268
policies, preventing attacks, 429
prevention
ACLs, 436-437
detailed documentation, 431-432
end-user policies, 431
governing policies, 430
honey pots, 435
incident response, 432-433
Layer 2 protections, 439
network device hardening, 438
patching, 428
physical devices, 437-438
security policies, 429
technical policies, 431
user training, 427-428
vulnerability scanners, 433-435
remote-access, 439-442
SNMP enhancements, 394
switch ports, 517
Trojan horses, 420
viruses, 420
VPNs, 447
authentication headers, 451-452
client-to-site, 448
concentrators, 449
encapsulating security payload, 451-452
IKE modes/phases, 449-451
IPSec, 449
IPSec site-to-site, 452-454
protocols, 454
site-to-site, 447
wiring closets, 516
WLANs, 292
MAC address filtering, 294
open authentication, 294
standards, 295
threats, 292-293
WEP, 296
WPA, 296-297
WPA2, 297
worms, 420
Security Event Management (SEM) software, 392

Security Information and Event Management (SIEM) software, 392
Security Information Management (SIM) software, 392
segments
Ethernet, 122
TCP, 51-52
Telnet, 86-87
UDP, 52
VLANs, 439
Seifert, Rich, 33
SEM (Security Event Management) software, 392
sending
ARP
replies from servers, 85
requests, 83
Telnet segments, 86
sensitivity to weather conditions (satellites), 258
sequencing packets, 43
serialization delay, 322
Serial Line Internet Protocol (SLIP), 252
Server Message Block (SMB), 56
servers
authentication, 142, 440
BOOTPS, 173
defined, 5
DHCP, 96-98
IP address assignment, 97, 173-174
relay agents, 98
reservations, 98
rogue, 495
DNS, 93-96
advanced TCP/IP settings, 171
dynamic, 95
extension mechanisms, 96
FQDNs, 94
hierarchy, 94
IP addresses, pointing to, 95
IP address management, 96
record types, 94, 95
looking-glass sites, 387
proxy, 98-99
RAS, 439
RRAS, 251-252, 439
sending ARP replies, 85
syslog, 396
virtual, 101-103
WINS, 167
service-level agreements (SLAs), 306
Service Location Protocol (SLP), 175
service location (SRV) records, 95
service set identifier (SSID), 293
services
advertisements, 49
Amazon Web Services (AWS), 106
applications, 49
cloud computing, 105-106
connection, 43
disruptions, troubleshooting, 516
hybrid cloud, 105
network, 175
unresponsive, 495
WAN, 521-522
Session Initiation Protocol (SIP), 56, 108
session layer (OSI model), 46-47
sessions
bidirectional Telnet, 88
hijacking, 422
keys, 411
maintenance, 46
setting up, 46
stateful inspection, 444
TCP SYN floods, 423
tearing down, 47
set messages, 393
severity levels, 396
SF (super frame), 247
SFTP (SSH File Transfer Protocol), 400
SHA-1 (Secure Hash Algorithm 1), 414
shaping traffic, 320-322
shared bus topology, 120
shared distribution trees, 229
shielded twisted pair. *See* STP cables
shim headers, 266
Shortest Path Bridging (SPB) protocols, 131
shortest path tree (SPT) switchover, 230
shorts, troubleshooting, 487
SIEM (Security Information and Event Management) software, 392
signal strength
troubleshooting, 498
WLANs, 290
signature-based detection, 456
Simple Mail Transfer Protocol (SMTP), 56
Simple Network Management Protocol. *See* SNMP
Simple Network Management Protocol Trap (SNMP Trap), 56
Simple Network Time Protocol (SNTP), 56
Simple Service Discovery Protocol (SSDP), 175
SIM (Security Information Management) software, 392
single-mode fiber (SMF) cables, 72-74
single sign-on (SSO), 441
SIP (Session Initiation Protocol), 56, 108
site-to-site VPNs, 400, 447
slash notation, 162, 177-178
SLAs (service-level agreements), 306
SLIP (Serial Line Internet Protocol), 252
slow Internet access, troubleshooting, 501-504
SLP (Service Location Protocol), 175
small office/home office (SOHO), 252
smart cards, 438
smart hubs, 80
smart jacks, 260
smartphones, tethering, 244
SMB (Server Message Block), 56
SMF (single-mode fiber) cables, 72-74
SMTP (Simple Mail Transfer Protocol), 56
Smurf attacks, 424
snapshots, 311
SNAT (static NAT), 222
SNMP (Simple Network Management Protocol), 56, 392-395

agents, 392
components, 392
managers, 392
message types, 393
MIB, 392
security enhancements, 394
traps, 56, 384
walk, 393
SNMP Trap (Simple Network Management Protocol Trap), 56
snooping, 225
SNTP (Simple Network Time Protocol), 56
SOA (start of authority) records, 95
social engineering attacks, 418
software
connectivity, 382
firewalls, 442
software as a service (SaaS), 105
software-defined networking (SDN), 101, 107
SOHO (small office/home office), 252
SOHO network design case study, 323
cost savings versus performance, 329
design, 324
environmental factors, 329
IP addressing, 325-326
Layer 1 media, 326
Layer 2 devices, 327
Layer 3 devices, 327-328
scenario, 323
suggested solution, 325
topology, 323, 329
wireless design, 328
soliciting
neighbors, 194
routers, 193
SONETs (Synchronous Optical Network), 255-257
source distribution trees, 227
source-specific multicast (SSM), 225
SOW (statement of work), 514
spanning tree protection, 439
Spanning Tree Protocol (STP), 130-131
spatial multiplexing, 286
SPB (Shortest Path Bridging) protocol, 131
special-purpose networks, troubleshooting, 500
specialized devices, 91
content engines, 99
content switches, 100-101
DHCP servers, 96-98
IP addressing, 97
relay agents, 98
reservations, 98
DNS servers, 93-96
dynamic, 95
extension mechanisms, 96
FQDNs, 94
hierarchy, 94
IP addresses, pointing to, 95
IP address management, 96
record types, 94-95
firewalls, 92-93
next-generation firewall, 101
proxy servers, 98-99
software-defined networking, 101
VPN concentrators, 91-92
wireless range extenders, 101
speed mismatches, troubleshooting, 488
speed testing, 388
split-horizon feature, 218
spread spectrum, 284
SPSs (standby power supplies), 426
SPT (shortest path tree) switchover, 230
SQL Server database remote-access, troubleshooting, 504-505
SRV (service location) records, 95
SSDP (Simple Service Discovery Protocol), 175
SSH File Transfer Protocol (SFTP), 400
SSH (Secure Shell), 56, 400, 440
SSIDs (service set identifiers), 293-294, 498
SSL (Secure Sockets Layer), 454
remote access, 400
untrusted certificates, 495
SSM (source-specific multicast), 225
SSO (single sign-on), 441
standard Ethernet, 124
standards
Ethernet, 124-125
operating procedures, documenting, 391
preventing attacks, 432
WLANs, 285-286
WLAN security, 295-297
ST (straight tip) connectors, 73
standby power supplies (SPSs), 426
standby routers, 144, 310
star topology, 15
start of authority (SOA) records, 95
stateful filtering, 515
stateful firewalls, 93, 444, 515
stateful inspection, 444
statement of work (SOW), 514
states
modulation, 36
ports, transitioning through, 135
transition modulation, 36
static ARP entries, 361
static IPv4 addresses, 168-172
static NAT (SNAT), 222
static routes, 210-211, 370
statistical anomaly detection, 457
StatTDM (statistical time-division multiplexing), 38
steganography, 418
storage
NAS, 22
virtual servers, 102
storage area networks (SANs), 9
store-and-forward networks, 43
STP (shielded twisted pair) cables, 66
ports
costs, 134-135
states, 135
types, 133-134
switches, classifying, 133
STP (Spanning Tree Protocol), 130-131
straight-through UTP cables, 68
straight tip (ST) connectors, 73
strategies for taking the exam, 533-535

S/T reference points, 262
structure
IPv4 addresses, 161-163
IPv6 addresses, 192-193
syslog messages, 397
structured troubleshooting approach, 484-486
identifying the problem, 485
plan of action, 486
post-mortem reports, 486
probable cause theory, 485
solution, implementing, 486
testing theories, 485
verifying system functionality, 486
study mode (Pearson Test Prep Practice Test engine), 532
study plan, 531-533
sublayers (data link layer), 39-41
subnets, 126
assignable IP addresses, 176
calculators, 189
masks
available hosts, number of, 180-181
borrowed bits, 179
CIDR, 190-191
classful, 179
default, 176
incorrect, 495
IP address ranges, calculating, 183-186
IPv4 addresses, 161
notation, 177-178
octet values, 178
subnets created, number of, 180
VLSM, 176
number created, calculating, 180
subscriber connectors (SC), 73
suggested study plan, 531-533
super frame (SF), 247
supervisory control and data acquisition (SCADA) networks, troubleshooting, 500
supplicants, 141, 440
SVCs (switched virtual circuits), 263
The Switch Book (Seifert), 33
switched virtual circuits (SVCs), 263
switches, 82-89
ARP replies sent from servers, 85
bidirectional Telnet sessions, 88
broadcast domains, 88
broadcast storms, 132-133
content, 100-101
defined, 6
diagnostics, 145
endpoints sending ARP requests, 83
endpoints sending Telnet segments, 86
Ethernet, 126, 132
first-hop redundancy, 144
flooding ARP requests, 84
forwarding ARP replies, 85-86
forwarding Telnet segments, 86-87
LACP configuration, 137
Layer 3, 89
link aggregation, 136-137
MAC address
filtering, 145
table corruption, 131
management access, 142-143
multilayer, 89-90
PoE, 138-139
ports
access port configuration, 128
mirroring, 141
monitoring, 139-140
same subnet, 126
security, 517
trunk configuration, 130
QoS, 145
STP, 130-131
classifying, 133
port costs, 134-135
port states, 135
port types, 133-134
switches, classifying, 133
troubleshooting, 516
trunking, 129-130
user authentication, 141-142
virtual, 103
VLANs, 127
switching
circuits, 42
messages, 43
network layer, 42
packets. *See* routing
switchovers, 230
symbols (diagrams), 390
Symmetric DSL (SDSL), 254
symmetric encryption, 411
symptoms (problems), 483
synchronizing
bits, 37
transmissions, 40
synchronous bit synchronization, 37
Synchronous Digital Hierarchy (SDH), 256
Synchronous Optical Networks (SONETs), 255-257
synchronous transmissions, 41
syntax
arp command, 338, 360
ipconfig command, 340
nbtstat command, 343
netstat command, 346, 366
nmap command, 365
ping command, 350, 368
route command, 352, 369
syslog, 395-397
clients, 396
message structure, 397
servers, 396
severity levels, 396
system
functionality, verifying, 486
life cycle best practices, 474
logs, 399

T

t parameter (ping command), 350
T1 circuits WANs, 246-247
T3 circuits WANs, 247
TACACS+ (Terminal Access Controller Access-Control System Plus), 440
tail dropped, 319
taking the exam strategies, 533-535
tamper detection devices, 437
target IP addresses, specifying, 356
target_name parameter (ping command), 351, 369
TAs (Terminal adapters), 262
Tc (timing interval), 321

tcpdump command, 365
TCP (Transmission Control Protocol), 44
ports, blocked, 495
segments, 51-52
SYN floods, 423
TCP/IP stack, 49
application layer protocols, 53-56
layers, 49-53
application, 53
Internet, 50
network interface, 50
transport, 51
TDM (time-division multiplexing), 38, 256
TDMA (Time Division Multiple Access), 244
TDR (time domain reflectometer), 389
TE1s (Terminal endpoint 1s), 262
TE2s (Terminal endpoint 2s), 262
teaming (NICs), 308
tearing down sessions, 47
technical policies, preventing attacks, 431
telcos, 260
Telecommunications Industry Association/Electronic Industries Alliance (TIA/EIA), 66
Telnet, 56
remote access, 400
segments, 86-87
sessions, bidirectional, 88
temperature attacks, 426
Tempest rooms, 417
Temporal Key Integrity Protocol (TKIP), 296
temp parameter (arp command), 360
Tenable Network Security, 434
Terminal Access Controller Access-Control System Plus (TACACS+), 440
Terminal adapters (TAs), 262
Terminal endpoint 1s (TE1s), 262
Terminal endpoint 2s (TE2s), 262
Test Prep Practice Test engine, 532
flash card mode, 532
mode selection, 533
practice exam mode, 532
study mode, 532
testing
DSL dial tone, 381
IP connectivity, 350
tethering smartphones, 244
text DNS records, 95
TFA (two-factor authentication), 441
TFTP (Trivial File Transfer Protocol), 56, 401
thick configurations (APs), 511
thinnet, 118
third-party network connections, troubleshooting, 516
threats (WLANs), 292-293
throughput, increasing, 510
throughput testers, 388
TIA/EIA (Telecommunications Industry Association/Electronic Industries Alliance), 66
TIA/EIA-568-A standard, 66
TIA/EIA-568-B standard, 66
time, incorrect configuration, 495
Time Division Multiple Access (TDMA), 244
time-division multiplexing (TDM), 38, 256
time domain reflectometer (TDR), 389
Time-to-Live (TTL) fields, 131
timers, hold-down, 216
timing interval (Tc), 321
tip and ring wires, 260
TKIP (Temporal Key Integrity Protocol), 296
TLS (Transport Layer Security), 400, 454
token ring networks, 120
toner probes, 390
tools, 380
BERT, 380
butt sets, 381
cable certifiers, 381
cable testers, 382
connectivity software, 382
crimpers, 383
environmental monitors, 384-385
ESD wrist straps, 383-384
looking-glass sites, 387
loopback plugs, 385
monitoring, 392
application logs, 398
logs, 398
security logs, 399
SNMP, 392-395
syslog, 395-397
system logs, 399
multimeters, 385-386
protocol analyzers, 386
punch down, 388
speed testing, 388
TDR, 389
toner probes, 390
troughput tester, 388
Wi-Fi analyzers, 387
topologies, 10
ATM, 265
basic routing, 206-208
bus, 11-12
Ethernet shared bus, 120
Frame Relay, 262
full-mesh, 17
HSRP, 144
hub-and-spoke, 16
IGMP, 225
ISDNs, 261
logical, 39
MPLS, 266
NAT, 220
partial-mesh, 18-19
PAT, 223
physical versus logical, 10-11
PPPoE, 250
ring, 11-14
star, 15
VoIP networks, 107
wireless, 20
WLANs, 276
ToS (type of service) bytes, 318
traceroute command, 365-366
tracert command, 356-358
destination parameter, 356
IPv6, 358
successful trace, 356
unsuccessful trace, 357
traffic
analysis, 386

classes, 316
conditioners, 320-322
conforming, 321
congestion avoidance/management, 319
exceeding, 321
firewall inspection, 443-444
flow control, 43
in-band management, 509
multicast
distribution trees, 226
IGMP, 224-226
PIM, 226
PIM-DM, 227-229
PIM-SM, 229-230
policing, 320
QoS issues, 314-315
shaping, 320-322
uplink congestion, 136
VPN, 449

training videos, 530

translation addresses
NAT, 220-222
PAT, 222-224

Transmission Control Protocol. *See* TCP

transmissions
delay, 257
sensitivity to weather conditions, 258
synchronizing, 40
WLANs
methods, 284
sources of interference, 289-291

transmit (Tx) leads, 488

transport layer
OSI model), 44-46
TCP/IP stack, 51

Transport Layer Security (TLS), 454

transport mode (AH/ESP), 452

transposed Tx/Rx leads, 488

trap messages, 393

Triple DES (3DES) algorithm, 411

Trivial File Transfer Protocol (TFTP), 56, 401

Trojan horses, 420-421

trouble tickets, 482

troubleshooting
brute-force attacks, 513
cables, 515
data link layer, 490-491
diagnosing problems, 482, 483
firewalls, 514
honeypots/honeynets, 513
Internet access technologies, 521-522
network layer, 492-495
blocked TCP/UDP ports, 495
data structures, 492-494
duplicate IP address, 495
duplicate MAC addresses, 495
example, 496-497
exhausted DHCP scope, 495
expired IP addresses, 495
incorrect ACL settings, 495
incorrect default gateways, 495
incorrect DNS configuration, 495
incorrect host-based firewall settings, 495
incorrect subnet masks, 495
incorrect time, 495
mismatched MTU, 494
rogue DHCP servers, 495
unresponsive services, 495
untrusted SSL certificates, 495
physical layer, 487-488
bad cables/connections, 487
bad ports, 487
cable placement, 488
crosstalk, 488
dB loss, 488
distance limitations exceeded, 488
example, 488-489
opens/shorts, 487
speed/duplex mismatches, 488
splitting pairs in cables, 487
transposed Tx/Rx leads, 488
questioning users, 483
reporting problems, 482
resolving problems, 482
scenarios
failed logins on vty lines, 511-514
infrastructure audit by consultants, 514-518
slow Internet access, 501-504
SQL Server database remote-access, 504-505
unacceptable IP phone voice quality, 501-504
WAN connectivity outages, 505-507
wireless networking issues, 507-511
service disruptions, 516
special-purpose networks, 500
structured approach, 484-486
identifying the problem, 485
plan of action, 486
post-mortem reports, 486
probably cause theory, 485
solution, implementing, 486
testing theories, 485
verifying system functionality, 486
switches, 145, 516
third-party network connections, 516
tools
BERT, 380
butt sets, 381
cable certifiers, 381
cable testers, 382
connectivity software, 382
crimpers, 383
environmental monitors, 384-385
ESD wrist straps, 383-384
looking glass sites, 387
loopback plugs, 385
multimeters, 385-386
protocol analyzers, 386
punch down, 388
speed testing, 388
TDR, 389
throughput tester, 388
toner probes, 390
Wi-Fi analyzers, 387
trouble tickets, 482
WANs
access technologies, 521-522
connectivity, 517
RDP application access, 518-521
wireless, 497-499
example, 499-500
incorrect AP placement, 499
latency, 498
misconfiguration of wireless parameters, 498
multiple paths of propagation, 499
RFI, 498
signal strength, 498

trunking, 129-130
trusted malicious users, 511
trust relationship exploitation, 420
TTL (Time-to-Live) fields, 131
tunneling
IPv6/IPv4, 192
mGRE, 268
tunnel mode (AH/ESP), 452
twisted-pair cables, 66
shielded, 66
TIA/EIA-568-A standard, 66
TIA/EIA-568-B standard, 66
unshielded, 67-69
two-factor authentication (TFA), 441
Tx (transmit) leads, 488
TXT records, 95
type 11 registered jack (RJ-11) connectors, 69
type 45 registered jack (RJ-45) connectors, 69
type of service (ToS) bytes, 318

U

U reference points, 262
UC (unified communications), 107
UDP (User Datagram Protocol), 44
ports, blocked, 495
segments, 52
UNC (universal naming convention), 167
unicast IPv4 addresses, 165
unicast IPv6 addresses, 194
unidirectional antennas, 280
unified communications (UC), 107
unified threat management (UTM) firewalls, 446-447, 515
uninterruptible power supplies (UPSs), 426
UNIs (user-network interfaces), 265
universal naming convention (UNC), 167
UNIX
benefits, 359
commands, 358
arp, 360-361
dig, 362
host, 363
ifconfig, 363-364
iptables, 364
man, 359
netstat, 366
nmap, 365
nslookup, 362
ping, 368-369
route, 369-370
tcpdump, 365
traceroute, 365-366
unreachable destinations, ping command, 351
unresponsive services, 495
unshielded twisted pair. *See* UTP cables
untrusted SSL certificates, 495
updates
APs, 516
patches, compared, 429
uplink congestion, 136
UPSs (uninterruptible power supplies), 426
upstream data frequencies, 255
uptime, 306
User Datagram Protocol. *See* UDP
users
authentication, 141-142
network interfaces (UNIs), 265
questioning, 483
training, preventing attacks, 427-428
trusted malicious, 511
utilities. *See* commands
UTM (unified threat management) firewalls, 446-447, 515
UTP (unshielded twisted pair) cables, 15, 66-69
categories, 67
connectors, 69
star topology, 15
straight-through, 68
WANs, 243

V

v parameter
arp command, 338
route command, 370
Variable-Length Subnet Masking (VLSM), 176
VCI (Virtual Circuit Identifier), 264
VCs (virtual circuits), 262
ATM, 265
Frame Relay, 262
permanent virtual (PVCs), 263
VDSL (Very High Bit-Rate DSL), 254
vendor codes, 39
verifying system functionality, 486
video surveillance devices, 437
video teleconference (VTC), troubleshooting, 500
Virtual Circuit Identifier (VCI), 264
virtual circuits. *See* VCs
virtual desktops, 104
virtual devices, 101
cloud computing, 105-106
desktops, 104
firewalls, 103
off-site, 105
routers, 103
SDN, 107
servers, 101-103
switches, 103
virtual firewalls, 103
virtual LANs. *See* VLANs
virtual network computing (VNC), 252
Virtual Path Identifier (VPI), 264
virtual PBX, 106
virtual private networks. *See* VPNs
Virtual Router Redundancy Protocol (VRRP), 310
virtual routers, 103, 310
virtual servers, 101-103
virtual switches, 103
Virtual Teletype (vty), 508
virtual wire firewalls, 514
viruses, 420
VLAN Trunking Protocol (VTP), 128
VLANs (virtual LANs), 127-128
configuration, troubleshooting, 490
native, 129
segmentation, 439
trunking, 129-130
VLSM (Variable-Length Subnet Masking), 176

VNC (virtual network computing), 252, 400

VoIP (Voice over IP), 106
- devices/protocols, 107
- topology, 107
- troubleshooting, 500

VPI/VCI pairs, 265

VPI (Virtual Path Identifier), 264

VPNs (virtual private networks), 91, 268, 447
- authentication headers, 451-452
- client-to-site, 448
- concentrators, 91-92, 449
- encapsulating security payload, 451-452
- IKE modes/phases, 449-451
- IPSec site-to-site, 452-454
- overlay networks, 268
- protocols, 454
- remote access, 400
- security, 449
- site-to-site, 447

VRRP (Virtual Router Redundancy Protocol), 310

VTC (video teleconference), troubleshooting, 500

VTP (VLAN Trunking Protocol), 128

vty (Virtual Teletype), 508, 511-514

vulnerability scanners, 433-435

W

Wallace, Kevin, 530

WANs (wide area networks), 7-8
- access technologies, 521-522
- ATM, 264-265
- cable modems, 254-255
- connections, 240-242
  - *circuit-switched, 241*
  - *dedicated leased line, 240*
  - *outages, troubleshooting, 505-507*
  - *packet-switched, 241*
  - *troubleshooting, 517*
- CSU/DSU, 248
- data rates, 242-243
- dedicated leased line, 246
- DSL, 252-254
- E1 circuits, 247
- E3 circuits, 247
- Frame Relay, 262-263
- full-mesh topology, 17
- hub-and-spoke topology, 16
- ISDNs, 260-262
- links, 7
- media, 243
  - *physical, 243-244*
  - *wireless, 244-245*
- metro Ethernet, 248
- MPLS, 266-268
  - *elements, 266-267*
  - *frame labels, 268*
  - *headers, 266*
  - *label switching, 266*
- on demand, 240
- overlay networks, 268
- partial-mesh topology, 18-19
- POTS, 258-260
- PPP, 249-250
- PPPoE, 250
- RDP application access, troubleshooting, 518-521
- RRAS, 251-252
- satellites, 257-258
- SONETs, 255-257
- T1 circuits, 246-247
- T3 circuits, 247

WAPs (wireless access points), 20, 277-278

war chalking, 292

war driving, 422

warm sites, 313

websites
- companion, 529
  - *accessing, 530*
  - *memory tables, 530*
  - *performance-based questions, 531*
  - *training videos, 530*
- IEEE Registration Authority vendor codes, 39
- IP Address Manager, 189
- Nessus, 434
- Nmap utility, 434
- Wireshark, 139, 387, 417

weighted fair queuing (WFQ), 319

weighted round-robin (WRR), 319

well-known ports, 54

WEP (Wired Equivalent Privacy), 293, 296

WFQ (weighted fair queuing), 319

wide area networks. ***See* WANs**

Wi-Fi analyzers, 387-388

Wi-Fi Protected Access (WPA), 293

WiMAX (Worldwide Interoperability for Microwave Access), 245

Windows
- Command Prompt, accessing, 338
- commands, 338
  - *arp, 338-340*
  - *ipconfig, 340-343*
  - *nbtstat, 343-345*
  - *netstat, 346-347*
  - *nslookup, 348-349*
  - *PathPing, 358*
  - *ping, 350-352*
  - *route, 352-355*
  - *tracert, 356-358*
- control panel, 168
- Internet Name Service (WINS) servers, 167

WINS (Windows Internet Name Service) servers, 167

Wired Equivalent Privacy (WEP), 293, 296

wireless
- access points (WAPs), 20, 277-278, 291
- attacks, 422
- IoT technologies, 78-79
- LAN controllers (WLCs), 506
- local area networks. *See* WLANs
- media, 244-245
- PAN networks (WPANs), 9
- range extenders, 101
- routers, 276-277
- security system devices interference, 290
- service disruptions, troubleshooting, 516
- technologies, 77
- topologies, 20
- troubleshooting, 497-499
  - *example, 499-500*
  - *incorrect AP placement, 499*
  - *latency, 498*

misconfiguration of wireless parameters, 498
multiple paths of propagation, 499
networking issues, 507-511
RFI, 498
service disruptions, 516
signal strength, 498
Wireshark, 139, 387, 417
wiretapping, 417
wiring closets, 75, 516
wiring locations, documenting, 391
WLANs (wireless LANs), 8, 275
ad hoc, 276
antennas, 278-281
gain, 279
omnidirectional, 279
orientation, 281
selecting, 279
unidirectional, 280
APs, 277-278
attacks, 422
BSS, 288
cells, 291
cellular technologies, 287
channels, 281-283
CSMA/CA, 283
enterprise-class, 276
ESS, 288
frequencies, 281
geofencing, 297
hotspots, 276
IBSS, 287
mesh topology, 289
networking issues, troubleshooting, 507-511
personal mode, 294
routers, 276-277
security, 292
MAC address filtering, 294
open authentication, 294
standards, 295
threats, 292-293
WEP, 296
WPA, 296-297
WPA2, 297
sources of interference, 289-291
standards, 285-286
transmission methods, 284
wireless AP placement, 291
WLCs (wireless LAN controllers), 506
work instructions, documenting, 391
Worldwide Interoperability for Microwave Access (WiMAX), 245
worms, 420
WPA (Wi-Fi Protected Access), 293, 296-297
WPA2 (WPA Version 2), 297
WPAN (wireless PAN networks), 9
w parameter (PathPing command), 358
WRR (weighted round-robin), 319

X-Z

XAUTH (Extended Authentication) protocol, 451

Z-Wave protocol, 78
Zero Configuration (Zeroconf), 175
zombies, 421
zones (firewalls), 445-446

To receive your 10% off Exam Voucher, register your product at:

www.pearsonitcertification.com/register

and follow the instructions.